Wow! 1001 Homemade Sandwich Recipes

(Wow! 1001 Homemade Sandwich Recipes - Volume 1)

Mary Thompson

Content

CHAPTER 3: CHICKEN SALAD SANDWICH RECIPES...............85

CHAPTER 4: SALAD SANDWICH RECIPES.....................133

CHAPTER 5: GRILLED CHEESE SANDWICH RECIPES 201

Chapter 1: Cheese Sandwich Recipes

***

1. Apple And Cheddar French Toast Sandwich

Serving: 2 | Prep: 15mins | Cook: 10mins |Ready in:

Ingredients

- 2 eggs
- 1 1/2 tablespoons milk
- 1 teaspoon herbes de Provence, or to taste
- 4 slices day-old artisan-style bread
- 2 tablespoons butter
- 1 cup fresh spinach, or to taste
- 1/2 Granny Smith apple, cored and thinly sliced
- 4 slices Cheddar cheese, or to taste

Direction

- In a bowl, whisk the herbes de Provence, milk, and eggs until smooth. Soak a slice of bread evenly by dipping it into the egg mixture.
- In a skillet, melt the butter over medium heat. Cook the dipped bread for 1-2 minutes until slightly browned. Place the cooked bread into a paper towel-lined plate. Repeat dipping the remaining slices of bread into the egg mixture and cook each into the skillet.
- In the same skillet, cook and stir spinach over medium heat for 2-3 minutes until wilted. Arrange the spinach on top of the 2 slices of French toast. Top the spinach with Cheddar cheese and apple slices. Form it a sandwich by arranging a piece of French toast on top of the Cheddar cheese layer.

Nutrition Information

- Calories: 559 calories;
- Total Fat: 37.2
- Sodium: 861
- Total Carbohydrate: 31.8
- Cholesterol: 277
- Protein: 25.3

2. Avocado And Bacon Grilled Cheese

Serving: 1 | Prep: 10mins | Cook: 4mins |Ready in:

Ingredients

- 1/4 avocado
- 1 tablespoon lemon juice
- 1 tablespoon BelGioioso Mascarpone cheese or butter
- 2 slices sourdough bread
- 2 slices BelGioioso Fontina cheese
- 2 slices cooked bacon

Direction

- Heat a skillet or griddle over medium heat.
- Chop the avocado quarter into 3 pieces, put them in a bowl and then use lemon juice to coat.
- Onto one side of every slice of bread, spread Mascarpone.
- Onto a slice of bread, spread bacon, slices of avocado, one slice of Fontina, and the Fontina remaining. Lay another slice of bread on top.
- In the skillet, put the sandwich and let to cook for about 2 to 4 minutes on each side until the cheese has melted and the bread turns golden brown.

Nutrition Information

- Calories: 374 calories;

- Total Fat: 21
- Sodium: 807
- Total Carbohydrate: 29.7
- Cholesterol: 58
- Protein: 18.4

- Calories: 482 calories;
- Total Fat: 21.9
- Sodium: 1166
- Total Carbohydrate: 27
- Cholesterol: 118
- Protein: 41.7

3. Bacon Jack Chicken Sandwich

Serving: 4 | Prep: 5mins | Cook: 20mins | Ready in:

Ingredients

- 8 slices bacon
- 4 skinless, boneless chicken breast halves
- 2 teaspoons poultry seasoning
- 4 slices pepperjack cheese
- 4 hamburger buns, split
- 4 leaves of lettuce
- 4 slices tomato
- 1/2 cup thinly sliced onions
- 12 slices dill pickle

Direction

- Set the grill over medium heat.
- In the meantime, set the large skillet over medium-high heat. Add the bacon and cook both sides until browned. Remove the bacon from the pan and place it on paper towels, drain.
- Rub the chicken pieces with the poultry seasoning. Place the chicken onto the grill and cook each side for 6 minutes until the center is no longer pink. Place 2 bacon slices and 1 pepper jack cheese slice on top of each chicken. Grill them for 2-3 more minutes until the cheese has melted.
- Set each chicken piece on a bun. Place the tomato, lettuce, pickle slices, and onion on top. Serve it together with your favorite condiments.

Nutrition Information

4. Bacon, Asparagus, And Cheese Sandwiches

Serving: 4 | Prep: 5mins | Cook: 5mins | Ready in:

Ingredients

- 8 slices bacon
- 1 (10 ounce) can asparagus tips, drained
- 4 thick slices sourdough bread, lightly toasted
- 4 slices sharp Cheddar cheese

Direction

- Set oven to broil after adjusting the oven rack to upper position. In case you don't want to use the oven, you may use a toaster oven to cook the sandwiches.
- Cook bacon in a big, deep pan on medium heat until it is brown on all sides and crisp. Remove and place on paper towels to drain.
- Arrange a small quantity of asparagus on a bread slice. Add 2 slices of crisp bacon and a slice of cheese to top.
- Let it toast under broiler until the cheese melts and starts to bubbles.

Nutrition Information

- Calories: 327 calories;
- Total Carbohydrate: 22.1
- Cholesterol: 50
- Protein: 19.4
- Total Fat: 18.1
- Sodium: 1026

5. Baguette With Caramelized Onions, Fresh Figs, Arugula, And Goat Cheese

Serving: 24 | Prep: 30mins | Cook: 43mins | Ready in:

Ingredients

- 2 tablespoons butter
- 6 onions, thinly sliced
- 2 tablespoons extra-virgin olive oil
- 1 pinch salt
- 16 figs, halved
- 3 tablespoons superfine sugar
- 1/2 cup chevre (soft goat cheese)
- 1/2 cup herbed goat cheese
- 1 tablespoon milk, or more as needed
- 1 bunch arugula
- sea salt and ground black pepper to taste
- 2 baguettes

Direction

- Put butter in a large skillet and melt over medium-low heat. Mix olive oil and onion then put them into the skillet. Cook slowly for about 40 minutes till onions get caramelized but the color has not changed to brown. Stir once in a while. Use salt to season and let cool for half an hour.
- Move the oven rack about 6 inches from the heat source then preheat the broiler of the oven.
- Spread figs onto a baking sheet, put the cut side up and use sugar to sprinkle. Grill figs under the broiler for 3-5 minutes till sugar has melted. Let cool.
- Put milk, herbed goat cheese and chevre together in a small bowl and mix till creamy.
- Slice baguettes in half lengthwise and spread over lower haves of baguettes with evenly the goat cheese mixture. Put caramelized onions over the goat cheese in a layer then add arugula on top. Chop figs into slices or quarters according to size and put a layer of figs on arugula. Put the remaining baguette halves on top and use plastic wrap to cover baguettes. Put baguettes in a fridge for 2-3 hours so that flavours can blend together. Cut into slices and serve.

Nutrition Information

- Calories: 183 calories;
- Sodium: 253
- Total Carbohydrate: 29.8
- Cholesterol: 8
- Protein: 6
- Total Fat: 5

6. Basil Pesto Sunshine Sandwich

Serving: 1 | Prep: 10mins | Cook: | Ready in:

Ingredients

- 1 slice focaccia bread, cut in half horizontally
- 1 tablespoon mayonnaise
- 2 teaspoons basil pesto
- 2 tablespoons sun-dried tomato pesto
- 1/4 cup roasted red peppers
- 1/2 cup crumbled feta cheese
- 1/2 cup fresh basil leaves

Direction

- Combine basil pesto and mayonnaise in a small bowl; use it to spread on one half of the bread. Use sun-dried tomato pesto to spread the rest half. Top the bottom piece with roasted red pepper. Add feta cheese, then fresh basil to cover. Arrange the second slice of bread on top.

Nutrition Information

- Calories: 720 calories;
- Total Fat: 50.2
- Sodium: 2127

- Total Carbohydrate: 40.6
- Cholesterol: 121
- Protein: 27

7. Basil, Tomato And Mozzarella Sandwich

Serving: 4 | Prep: 15mins | Cook: | Ready in:

Ingredients

- 1 (1 pound) loaf Italian bread
- 6 fresh basil leaves, chopped
- 2 tomatoes, sliced
- 4 ounces fresh mozzarella cheese, sliced
- 1/8 teaspoon red pepper flakes
- 1/2 cup balsamic vinegar

Direction

- Cut the loaf of bread in half lengthwise. Layer between the 2 halves of the bread with basil, tomato slices and mozzarella cheese. Slice into 4 sandwiches.
- Combine red pepper flakes and balsamic vinegar in a small dish to make a dipping sauce.

Nutrition Information

- Calories: 421 calories;
- Cholesterol: 22
- Protein: 16
- Total Fat: 10.3
- Sodium: 714
- Total Carbohydrate: 64.7

8. Best Bacon Caprese Sandwich

Serving: 2 | Prep: 10mins | Cook: 15mins | Ready in:

Ingredients

- Basil Garlic Aioli:
- 1/4 cup mayonnaise
- 2 tablespoons chopped fresh basil
- 1 tablespoon fresh lemon juice
- 1 teaspoon minced garlic
- 1/2 teaspoon garlic powder
- 1/2 teaspoon freshly grated lemon zest
- 1 pinch salt and ground black pepper to taste
- Sandwich:
- 7 slices bacon, halved
- 2 ciabatta rolls, split and toasted
- 1 (4 ounce) ball fresh mozzarella, sliced
- 1 heirloom tomato, sliced

Direction

- In a bowl, combine lemon zest, garlic powder, garlic, lemon juice, basil and mayonnaise together. Add pepper and salt to season. Seal with plastic wrap and keep aioli refrigerated until ready for usage.
- Set oven to 190 deg C (375 deg F) to preheat. Position a wire rack in a cookie sheet to catch the grease.
- Arrange 3 bacon halves beside each other on wire rack. Twist another 3-4 bacon halves under and over the halves on rack making a square lattice. Repeat with the bacon halves left.
- Allow to bake for 15-20 minutes until brown and crisp. Transfer bacon lattices with a spatula to paper towels.
- Scatter basil garlic aioli on every ciabatta roll; top with mozzarella slices, tomato and bacon lattices.

Nutrition Information

- Calories: 692 calories;
- Total Fat: 46.5
- Sodium: 1677
- Total Carbohydrate: 36.4
- Cholesterol: 82
- Protein: 31.9

9. Brie, Cranberry, And Turkey Paninis For 2

Serving: 2 | Prep: 10mins | Cook: 5mins | Ready in:

Ingredients

- 1 tablespoon butter
- 1 tablespoon Dijon mustard
- 2 ciabatta rolls, sliced in half
- 1/2 pound cooked turkey, sliced
- 4 ounces Brie cheese, sliced
- 3 tablespoons cranberry sauce

Direction

- Set a panini press to medium-high heat and start preheating, then coat the surface lightly with butter.
- Place the Dijon mustard over the ciabatta rolls. Arrange turkey slices, Brie cheese, and cranberry sauce in layers onto the bottom halves. Put the other halves on top.
- In the preheated panini press, grill the sandwiches for 5 minutes until the rolls turn golden brown and the cheese melts.

Nutrition Information

- Calories: 1710 calories;
- Total Fat: 43
- Sodium: 3324
- Total Carbohydrate: 238.8
- Cholesterol: 158
- Protein: 85.1

10. Caprese Salad Sandwiches

Serving: 4 | Prep: 15mins | Cook: | Ready in:

Ingredients

- 8 slices artisan-style whole wheat bread

- 2 tablespoons white truffle oil, or to taste
- 1/2 pound buffalo mozzarella, thinly sliced
- 1/2 cup fresh basil leaves, or to taste
- 1 large heirloom tomato, thinly sliced
- coarse sea salt and ground black pepper to taste

Direction

- Sprinkle truffle oil evenly over each slice of bread and cover 4 slices of bread with tomato slices, basil leaves, and slices of buffalo mozzarella cheese. Flavor with black pepper and sea salt to taste. Place a remaining bread slice on top of each sandwich.

Nutrition Information

- Calories: 375 calories;
- Sodium: 432
- Total Carbohydrate: 26.6
- Cholesterol: 45
- Protein: 18.1
- Total Fat: 21.2

11. Cheddar, Baby Leek And Tomato Sandwich

Serving: 2 | Prep: 15mins | Cook: 5mins | Ready in:

Ingredients

- 4 slices sourdough bread
- 3 tablespoons butter, room temperature
- 3 small leeks, white part only, julienned
- 2/3 cup shredded white Cheddar cheese
- 4 slices firm tomatoes
- 2 tablespoons mayonnaise

Direction

- Heat pan on medium heat. Evenly slather butter on one part of every bread slices. Arrange two slices in the pan with their buttered side down. Add tomato slices, 1/2 of the cheese, leeks, and remaining cheese on top. Slather mayonnaise on the other side of remaining slices; arrange on top of the sandwich with their mayonnaise-side down. Toast each side in the pan until golden.

Nutrition Information

- Calories: 614 calories;
- Sodium: 822
- Total Carbohydrate: 36.7
- Cholesterol: 99
- Protein: 18.7
- Total Fat: 44.6

12. Chicken Parmesan Burgers

Serving: 2 | Prep: 30mins | Cook: 35mins | Ready in:

Ingredients

- 4 small skinless, boneless chicken breasts, cubed
- 1 teaspoon dried parsley
- 1 teaspoon dried oregano
- 1 teaspoon dried basil
- 1/2 teaspoon salt
- 1/4 teaspoon ground black pepper
- 1 cup bread crumbs
- 1 cup grated Parmesan cheese
- 1/4 cup butter, divided
- 4 slices bread
- 1/3 cup chopped onion
- 1 clove garlic, minced
- 4 mushrooms, thinly sliced
- 2 tablespoons all-purpose flour
- 1 (8 ounce) can spaghetti sauce

Direction

- Heat oven to 200°C (400°F) beforehand.
- In a food processor, mix pepper, salt, basil, oregano, parsley, and chicken breasts; let process till a smooth paste forms. Form chicken mixture into two patties with round shape.
- In a shallow bowl, mix Parmesan cheese and breadcrumbs together. Sprinkle patties to coat both sides. On an ungreased baking sheet, lay patties.
- Use one and a half teaspoon of butter to spread over every slice of bread; use remaining breadcrumb-Parmesan mixture to dredge over top. On the baking sheet, lay bread slices near the chicken patties.
- In the preheated oven, allow to bake for 10-15 minutes till bread turns browned. Remove bread to a serving plate. Keep baking chicken for 10-15 more minutes till an instant-read thermometer reads 74°C (165°F) when being pricked into the center.
- In a saucepan, melt remaining 2 tablespoons of butter. Cook and stir garlic and onion in melted butter for approximately 5 minutes till onion becomes translucent. Put in flour and mushrooms; keep cooking and stirring for about 5 minutes till beginning to brown. Mix spaghetti sauce in; allow to simmer for 5-10 minutes till thickened.
- Pour sauce over two bread slices. In the center, lay one chicken patty; use remaining bread slices to cover.

Nutrition Information

- Calories: 1063 calories;
- Sodium: 2646
- Total Carbohydrate: 92.9
- Cholesterol: 195
- Protein: 66.5
- Total Fat: 46.4

13. Chicken And Brie Sandwiches With Roasted Cherry Tomatoes

Serving: 4 | Prep: 30mins | Cook: 36mins | Ready in:

Ingredients

- 1 pound skinless, boneless chicken breasts
- 1/2 cup Italian-style salad dressing, or to taste
- 3 ounces Brie cheese, sliced
- 1 tablespoon olive oil, divided
- 2 cups cherry tomatoes, halved
- 1/4 teaspoon kosher salt, divided
- 3 tablespoons balsamic vinegar, divided
- 1 tablespoon chopped fresh basil
- 2 cups fresh spinach leaves
- 1/4 cup mayonnaise
- 1 tablespoon Dijon mustard
- 2 cloves garlic, minced
- 1/8 teaspoon ground black pepper
- 1 loaf French bread, halved lengthwise

Direction

- Arrange chicken breasts in a shallow baking dish. Coat chicken with Italian dressing. Use plastic wrap to cover; allow to marinate for 8 hours to overnight in the fridge.
- Prepare a grill pan over medium-high heat. Take chicken breasts out of the marinade and put into the skillet. Cook chicken, about 6 minutes on each side, until center is no longer pink and chicken juices run clear.
- Cut chicken breasts into slices; top with Brie cheese and allow cheese to melt.
- Turn oven to 300°F (150°C) to preheat.
- Heat 1 teaspoon olive oil over medium heat in an ovenproof skillet. Stir in 1/8 teaspoon salt and tomatoes; cook for about 4 minutes or until tomatoes release their juices, stirring once. Turn off the heat; add basil and 2 tablespoons balsamic vinegar; stir to combine.
- Remove the skillet to the preheated oven; bake tomatoes for approximately 15 minutes or until tender.
- In a mixing bowl, mix 1/8 teaspoon salt, 1 tablespoon balsamic vinegar, and the remaining 2 teaspoons olive oil. Toss in spinach until well coated.
- In another mixing bowl, combine pepper, garlic, Dijon mustard, and mayonnaise.

- Lay the bottom half of the loaf on a baking sheet. Spread top of the loaf with mayonnaise mixture. Arrange tomatoes and spinach atop mayonnaise layer. Top with chicken and Brie cheese. Place the top half of the loaf atop cheese to close the sandwich.
- Bake sandwich for 5 to 10 minutes in the preheated oven until heated through. Slice sandwich into 4 portions to serve.

Nutrition Information

- Calories: 771 calories;
- Total Fat: 33.6
- Sodium: 1727
- Total Carbohydrate: 74.7
- Cholesterol: 91
- Protein: 42.8

---

14. Cinnamon Apple And Havarti Tea Sandwiches

Serving: 8 | Prep: 15mins | Cook: | Ready in:

Ingredients

- 1 (8 ounce) package cream cheese, softened
- 8 slices cinnamon raisin bread
- 4 slices Havarti cheese
- 1 large Granny Smith apple, cored and thinly sliced

Direction

- Spread four bread slices with a thin layer of the cream cheese. Add one Havarti cheese slice on top of cream cheese, followed by 1 thin apple slices layer. Top with remaining bread slices to make four sandwiches.
- Cut every sandwich with 2 diagonal cuts into four triangles.

Nutrition Information

- Calories: 250 calories;
- Sodium: 310
- Total Carbohydrate: 18
- Cholesterol: 49
- Protein: 8.2
- Total Fat: 16.8

15. Creamy Jack Grilled Cheese With Fruit Glazed Avocado

Serving: 2 | Prep: 15mins | Cook: 5mins | Ready in:

Ingredients

- 1 ripe avocado from Mexico, peeled, pitted and cubed
- 2 tablespoons mango jam
- 1 teaspoon fresh lemon juice
- 1 tablespoon minced red onion
- Salt and black pepper to taste
- 2 tablespoons butter with canola oil
- 2 teaspoons Dijon mustard
- 4 slices country white bread
- 4 thin slices Monterey Jack cheese

Direction

- Cut avocado in half and then remove the pit. Score the avocado flesh on each half in a crisscross pattern. Use a spoon to carefully transfer the cubes into a bowl.
- In a small bowl, add mango jam and then heat for about 20 seconds in microwave on high until warm and thinned.
- Carefully mix the jam into avocado and then add in lemon juice, pepper, salt, and red onion.
- In another bowl, combine the Dijon mustard and butter-canola blend together. Mix well until smooth. Pour the mixture evenly onto one side of bread. Flip over the slices onto a cutting board.
- Arrange cheese over the unbuttered sides of bread. Subdivide avocado mixture atop the

cheese and then spread evenly. Carefully top with slice of bread with butter side up.
- Over medium-high heat, heat a non-stick skillet. Transfer the sandwiches into the pan and let to cook on each side for about 2 to 3 minutes until crispy and golden brown. Chop in half diagonally before serving.

Nutrition Information

- Calories: 563 calories;
- Total Fat: 36
- Sodium: 794
- Total Carbohydrate: 49.5
- Cholesterol: 40
- Protein: 12.9

16. Herbed Grilled Cheese And Pork Sandwiches

Serving: 4 | Prep: 10mins | Cook: 35mins | Ready in:

Ingredients

- 1 Smithfield® Rosemary & Olive Oil Seasoned Pork Tenderloin
- 8 slices sandwich bread
- 2 tablespoons olive oil
- 1/4 cup mayonnaise
- 4 teaspoons capers
- 1/2 teaspoon lemon pepper
- 2 cups baby arugula
- 4 slices Havarti cheese with dill

Direction

- Roast pork according to instructions printed on package (takes about half an hour). Cut meat into thin slices.
- Heat skillet, waffle iron or panini sandwich press, depend the gadget you use to cook your sandwiches.
- Put lemon pepper, capers and mayonnaise together in a small bowl then stir.

- Use olive oil to lightly brush one side of each bread slice. Spread the mayonnaise mixture on the opposite side of four bread slices.
- For each sandwich, put Havarti, arugula, sliced pork and arugula leaves on top of the mayonnaise mixture. Cover with another slice of bread. The side without mayo is outside. (Olive oil should be facing out.)
- Put each sandwich in hot skillet or sandwich press. Cook until cheese is melted and bread is toasted, flipping if needed. Cut the sandwich into 2 equal parts and serve right away.

Nutrition Information

- Calories: 543 calories;
- Total Carbohydrate: 30.9
- Cholesterol: 104
- Protein: 32.2
- Total Fat: 32.9
- Sodium: 1187

17. Jeremy's Philly Steak And Cheese Sandwich

Serving: 4 | Prep: 15mins | Cook: 15mins | Ready in:

Ingredients

- 1 teaspoon butter
- 1/2 white onion, sliced
- 1/2 red onion, sliced
- 8 fresh mushrooms, sliced
- 1 clove garlic, minced
- 6 ounces beef sirloin, thinly sliced
- 3/4 cup cream cheese, softened
- 1 teaspoon Worcestershire sauce
- salt and pepper to taste
- 1 French baguette, cut in half lengthwise
- 1/2 cup shredded Swiss cheese

Direction

- In a big pan, melt the butter on medium-high heat. Sauté the garlic, mushrooms and red and white onions until it becomes soft. Take it out of the pan then put aside.
- In the pan, put the sliced beef and fry it for about 5 minutes until not pink. Lower the heat to low, then stir in the Worcestershire sauce and cream cheese, mixing and cooking until the beef is coated well. Sprinkle pepper and salt to taste.
- In the meantime, preheat the oven's broiler.
- On the bottom half of the baguette, put the beef mixture, then cover with the onion mixture. Put Swiss cheese on top. Lay the sandwich open under the hot broiler until the cheese melts. Put the top piece of baguette on top of the toppings; serve.

Nutrition Information

- Calories: 654 calories;
- Cholesterol: 91
- Protein: 29.9
- Total Fat: 28.6
- Sodium: 939
- Total Carbohydrate: 70.2

18. Killer Bacon Cheese Dogs

Serving: 8 | Prep: 10mins | Cook: 20mins | Ready in:

Ingredients

- 8 slices bacon
- 8 all-beef hot dogs
- 8 hot dog buns
- 8 slices Swiss cheese
- 1/2 cup barbeque sauce, or amount to taste
- 1 small red onion, diced

Direction

- Preheat outdoor grill to medium high heat; oil grate lightly then put it 4-in. away from heat.

- Cook bacon in big deep skillet on medium high heat till browned evenly; on paper towels, drain.
- Cook hot dogs on grill for 5-8 minutes till done to preference, turning once. Grill hotdog buns lightly.
- Assemble sandwiches: Put 1 slice of bacon and cheese on every roll; add hot dog. Put 1 tbsp. or desired amount of barbecue sauce and red onion over each.

Nutrition Information

- Calories: 493 calories;
- Total Fat: 30.5
- Sodium: 1299
- Total Carbohydrate: 31.7
- Cholesterol: 66
- Protein: 21.6

19. Marination's Korean Philly Cheese Steak

Serving: 4 | Prep: 20mins | Cook: 20mins | Ready in:

Ingredients

- 3/4 pound top round beef, thinly sliced
- 1/2 cup Kalbi-style steak marinade, or as needed
- 2 tablespoons oil, divided
- 2 cups chopped onions
- 1 cup diced jalapeno peppers
- 1/2 cup chopped kimchi
- 1 cup shredded American cheese
- 1/4 cup mayonnaise
- 4 sandwich rolls, split and toasted

Direction

- In a bowl, combine marinade and beef; put aside to marinate.

- In a skillet, bring 1 Tbsp. of oil to medium-high heat; sauté onions for 5-10 minutes until firm and lightly goldened.
- In another skillet, bring 1 Tbsp. of oil to medium-high heat; sauté jalapeno peppers for about 5 minutes until it turns light golden. Blend onions with jalapeno peppers. Put in kimchi and cook for 2-3 minutes until cooked through. Take skillet off the heat.
- Bring a different skillet to medium-high heat; cook and stir steak constantly for about 5 minutes until heated through and browned.
- Bring three-fourths cup of kimchi mixture to medium heat in the skillet; add in a quarter cup of American cheese. Heat, covered, for 2-3 minutes until cheese has melted.
- Onto the bottom half of 1 roll, spread 1 tablespoon mayonnaise and add 1/4 of the beef on top. Layer on top of beef with kimchi-cheese mixture and put roll on top. Do the same layers with the rest of ingredients to make 3 more sandwiches.

Nutrition Information

- Calories: 824 calories;
- Total Carbohydrate: 88.4
- Cholesterol: 74
- Protein: 35.3
- Total Fat: 36.2
- Sodium: 1873

20. Open Face Toasted Caprese

Serving: 6 | Prep: 10mins | Cook: 10mins | Ready in:

Ingredients

- Balsamic Drizzle:
- 1/2 cup balsamic vinegar
- 1 teaspoon brown sugar (optional)
- Toast:
- 1 loaf crusty sourdough or ciabatta bread, sliced

- Olive oil, to drizzle over bread slices and avocados
- 1 clove garlic
- salt and pepper to taste
- 2 avocados - peeled, pitted and sliced
- 1 (8 ounce) package Stella® fresh mozzarella, sliced
- Fresh basil leaves
- 4 heirloom tomatoes, sliced

Direction

- Put vinegar and brown sugar (if using), into a small saucepan and make it boil.
- Minimize to very low simmer and cook 10-15 minutes, until liquid was lessened by about half and is slightly syrupy. Separate from heat, then put vinegar in a glass or bowl for later use, and reserve to cool and thicken.
- Prepare the oven by preheating to 450°F (230°C) or grill to high heat.
- On a baking sheet, put the bread slices and trickle with olive oil on both sides. Massage each side of bread with the halved garlic clove. Dust with pepper and salt to taste.
- Sprinkle avocado with pepper, salt and olive oil to season.
- Put avocado and bread slices in the preheated oven or grill until both are lightly charred, for about 2 to 3 minutes on each side. Take out from the oven or grill.
- Then cut Stella fresh mozzarella and split evenly among the sandwiches. Put on top of toast, then put fresh basil to taste. Put tomato slices and grilled avocado slices. Sprinkle everything with balsamic drizzle, olive oil and add pepper and salt to taste.

Nutrition Information

- Calories: 630 calories;
- Total Fat: 26
- Sodium: 1046
- Total Carbohydrate: 79.1
- Cholesterol: 27
- Protein: 23.7

21. Pancetta Fresh Mozzarella Panini

Serving: 2 | Prep: 5mins | Cook: 8mins | Ready in:

Ingredients

- 8 slices thinly sliced pancetta
- 2 ciabatta rolls
- 8 ounces apricot preserves
- 8 slices Galban®i Fresh Mozzarella cheese

Direction

- Cook pancetta for about 1 minute in a frying pan, flipping once.
- Split ciabatta rolls and spread inside with a thick layer of apricot preserves.
- Put pancetta and 4 slices of fresh mozzarella into each roll and close the sandwich.
- Cook sandwiches on both sides in a cast iron skillet or panini grill pan until bread is crisp and cheese is melted.

Nutrition Information

- Calories: 955 calories;
- Total Fat: 41.9
- Sodium: 1400
- Total Carbohydrate: 105.2
- Cholesterol: 129
- Protein: 39.8

22. Philly Cheese Steak

Serving: 4 | Prep: 15mins | Cook: 15mins | Ready in:

Ingredients

- 1 pound fresh steak (rib-eye, round, or sirloin)*
- 1 large yellow onion, sliced thin

- 3 tablespoons Kikkoman Teriyaki Marinade & Sauce
- 4 soft sandwich rolls
- 1 (8 fl oz) jar cheese spread

Direction

- Pour oil into a large non-stick skillet and then add 2 tablespoons of teriyaki sauce and onions. Sauté until onions become soft. Place in the chopped meat and then cook until the meat turns brown a bit. Mix in the remaining one tablespoon of teriyaki sauce and mix. Add cheese on top of meat and mix until melted. Combine the meat, cheese and onions together. Spoon the meat mixture onto the sandwich rolls.

Nutrition Information

- Calories: 520 calories;
- Total Carbohydrate: 42
- Cholesterol: 83
- Protein: 27.6
- Total Fat: 26.4
- Sodium: 1763

23. Philly Cheese Steak Sliders

Serving: 12 | Prep: 20mins | Cook: 30mins | Ready in:

Ingredients

- 1 (12 ounce) beef skirt steak, thinly sliced
- 1 (12 count) package Hawaiian bread rolls
- 1/2 large green bell pepper, chopped
- 1/2 large onion, chopped
- 1/4 cup mayonnaise
- 8 slices pepper Jack cheese
- 2 tablespoons butter, melted

Direction

- Heat a pan on medium-high heat. Put onion, bell pepper and steak, then cook for 7-10

minutes until the preferred color is achieved and the steak is hot.
- Set an oven to preheat at 190°C (375°F). Use aluminum foil to line an 8x8-inch baking pan.
- Halve the connected rolls widthwise so it resembles 2 giant bread slices. In the bottom of the prepped baking pan, place the bottom half of the rolls. Put mayonnaise on top and spread it evenly.
- On top of the mayonnaise, put 4 slices of pepper Jack cheese. Layer the steak mixture and the leftover cheese on top. Use the top half of the bread to cover. Put the melted butter on top, then spread.
- Bake in the oven for about 20 minutes, until the bread turns brown and the cheese melts. Cut into individual portions.

Nutrition Information

- Calories: 386 calories;
- Sodium: 315
- Total Carbohydrate: 43.4
- Cholesterol: 63
- Protein: 19.6
- Total Fat: 9.8

24. Philly Cheesesteak Sandwich With Garlic Mayo

Serving: 4 | Prep: 10mins | Cook: 20mins | Ready in

Ingredients

- 1 cup mayonnaise
- 2 cloves garlic, minced
- 1 tablespoon olive oil
- 1 pound beef round steak, cut into thin
- 2 green bell peppers, cut into 1/4 inch
- 2 onions, sliced into rings
- salt and pepper to taste
- 4 hoagie rolls, split lengthwise and
- 1 (8 ounce) package shredded mo cheese

- 1 teaspoon dried oregano

Direction

- Mix the minced garlic and mayonnaise in a small bowl. Put cover and let it chill in the fridge. Set an oven to preheat at 260°C (500°F).
- In a big pan, heat the oil on medium heat. Sauté the beef until it browns lightly. Stir in the onion and green pepper, then sprinkle with pepper and salt to season. Sauté until the veggies become soft, then take it off from heat.
- Spread garlic mayonnaise liberally on each bun. Distribute the beef mixture in the buns. Put shredded cheese on top and sprinkle with oregano. Lay sandwiches on a baking pan.
- Heat the sandwiches in the preheated oven until it turns slightly brown, or cheese has melted.

Nutrition Information

- Calories: 935 calories;
- Total Fat: 66.4
- Sodium: 1405
- Total Carbohydrate: 49.6
- Cholesterol: 96
- Protein: 35.3

Philly Steak And Cheese Sliders

| Prep: 20mins | Cook: 11mins | Ready in:

loin steak, cut into 1/8-inch strips
tenderizer
il
strips   iced
strips   ll pepper
                soning, or to taste
toasted   taste
zarella   shrooms

- 1 (12 count) package Hawaiian-style dinner rolls, sliced in half
- 8 slices provolone cheese

Direction

- Place the oven rack approximately 6-inches away from heat source and prepare the oven's broiler by preheating. In a bowl, combine meat tenderizer and steak.
- In a skillet set on medium heat, add olive oil. Add bell pepper and onion; stir and cook for approximately 3 minutes until slightly tender. Mix in steak mixture; stir and cook for approximately 3 minutes until flavors blend. Stir in pepper and Italian seasoning; mix in mushrooms. Stir and cook for approximately 3 minutes until steak is mostly browned.
- Transfer steak mixture on lower half of dinner rolls until they are covered; put provolone cheese on top. Put on a baking sheet.
- Then broil in preheated oven for 1-3 minutes until cheese is dissolved; take from the broiler. Put the dinner rolls onto dissolved provolone cheese; then broil for 1-2 minutes until tops become toasted.

Nutrition Information

- Calories: 403 calories;
- Total Fat: 7.7
- Sodium: 512
- Total Carbohydrate: 45.9
- Cholesterol: 69
- Protein: 26.2

26. Prosciutto And Provolone Panini Sandwiches

Serving: 4 | Prep: 15mins | Cook: | Ready in:

Ingredients

- 1/2 cup CARAPELLI® Extra Virgin Olive Oil

- 1 teaspoon dried oregano

Direction

- Mix the minced garlic and mayonnaise in a small bowl. Put cover and let it chill in the fridge. Set an oven to preheat at 260°C (500°F).
- In a big pan, heat the oil on medium heat. Sauté the beef until it browns lightly. Stir in the onion and green pepper, then sprinkle with pepper and salt to season. Sauté until the veggies become soft, then take it off from heat.
- Spread garlic mayonnaise liberally on each bun. Distribute the beef mixture in the buns. Put shredded cheese on top and sprinkle with oregano. Lay sandwiches on a baking pan.
- Heat the sandwiches in the preheated oven until it turns slightly brown, or cheese has melted.

Nutrition Information

- Calories: 935 calories;
- Total Fat: 66.4
- Sodium: 1405
- Total Carbohydrate: 49.6
- Cholesterol: 96
- Protein: 35.3

25. Philly Steak And Cheese Sliders

Serving: 12 | Prep: 20mins | Cook: 11mins | Ready in:

Ingredients

- 1 pound sirloin steak, cut into 1/8-inch strips
- 1 pinch meat tenderizer
- 1 splash olive oil
- 1 onion, thinly sliced
- 1/2 cup minced bell pepper
- 1 teaspoon Italian seasoning, or to taste
- ground black pepper to taste
- 2 cups canned sliced mushrooms

- 1 (12 count) package Hawaiian-style dinner rolls, sliced in half
- 8 slices provolone cheese

Direction

- Place the oven rack approximately 6-inches away from heat source and prepare the oven's broiler by preheating. In a bowl, combine meat tenderizer and steak.
- In a skillet set on medium heat, add olive oil. Add bell pepper and onion; stir and cook for approximately 3 minutes until slightly tender. Mix in steak mixture; stir and cook for approximately 3 minutes until flavors blend. Stir in pepper and Italian seasoning; mix in mushrooms. Stir and cook for approximately 3 minutes until steak is mostly browned.
- Transfer steak mixture on lower half of dinner rolls until they are covered; put provolone cheese on top. Put on a baking sheet.
- Then broil in preheated oven for 1-3 minutes until cheese is dissolved; take from the broiler. Put the dinner rolls onto dissolved provolone cheese; then broil for 1-2 minutes until tops become toasted.

Nutrition Information

- Calories: 403 calories;
- Total Fat: 7.7
- Sodium: 512
- Total Carbohydrate: 45.9
- Cholesterol: 69
- Protein: 26.2

26. Prosciutto And Provolone Panini Sandwiches

Serving: 4 | Prep: 15mins | Cook: | Ready in:

Ingredients

- 1/2 cup CARAPELLI® Extra Virgin Olive Oil

- 3 tablespoons Kikkoman Teriyaki Marinade & Sauce
- 4 soft sandwich rolls
- 1 (8 fl oz) jar cheese spread

Direction

- Pour oil into a large non-stick skillet and then add 2 tablespoons of teriyaki sauce and onions. Sauté until onions become soft. Place in the chopped meat and then cook until the meat turns brown a bit. Mix in the remaining one tablespoon of teriyaki sauce and mix. Add cheese on top of meat and mix until melted. Combine the meat, cheese and onions together. Spoon the meat mixture onto the sandwich rolls.

Nutrition Information

- Calories: 520 calories;
- Total Carbohydrate: 42
- Cholesterol: 83
- Protein: 27.6
- Total Fat: 26.4
- Sodium: 1763

23. Philly Cheese Steak Sliders

Serving: 12 | Prep: 20mins | Cook: 30mins | Ready in:

Ingredients

- 1 (12 ounce) beef skirt steak, thinly sliced
- 1 (12 count) package Hawaiian bread rolls
- 1/2 large green bell pepper, chopped
- 1/2 large onion, chopped
- 1/4 cup mayonnaise
- 8 slices pepper Jack cheese
- 2 tablespoons butter, melted

Direction

- Heat a pan on medium-high heat. Put onion, bell pepper and steak, then cook for 7-10

minutes until the preferred color is achieved and the steak is hot.
- Set an oven to preheat at 190°C (375°F). Use aluminum foil to line an 8x8-inch baking pan.
- Halve the connected rolls widthwise so it resembles 2 giant bread slices. In the bottom of the prepped baking pan, place the bottom half of the rolls. Put mayonnaise on top and spread it evenly.
- On top of the mayonnaise, put 4 slices of pepper Jack cheese. Layer the steak mixture and the leftover cheese on top. Use the top half of the bread to cover. Put the melted butter on top, then spread.
- Bake in the oven for about 20 minutes, until the bread turns brown and the cheese melts. Cut into individual portions.

Nutrition Information

- Calories: 386 calories;
- Sodium: 315
- Total Carbohydrate: 43.4
- Cholesterol: 63
- Protein: 19.6
- Total Fat: 9.8

24. Philly Cheesesteak Sandwich With Garlic Mayo

Serving: 4 | Prep: 10mins | Cook: 20mins | Ready in:

Ingredients

- 1 cup mayonnaise
- 2 cloves garlic, minced
- 1 tablespoon olive oil
- 1 pound beef round steak, cut into thin strips
- 2 green bell peppers, cut into 1/4 inch strips
- 2 onions, sliced into rings
- salt and pepper to taste
- 4 hoagie rolls, split lengthwise and toasted
- 1 (8 ounce) package shredded mozzarella cheese

- 8 slices rustic Italian or sourdough bread
- 1/4 cup prepared basil pesto
- 16 thin slices Provolone cheese
- 12 thin slices prosciutto
- 4 whole, well-drained bottled roasted red peppers, cut into strips

Direction

- Heat a waffle iron/panini grill. Brush bread slices with oil; flip 4 slices over. Evenly spread pesto on bread. Top with 1/2 of the cheese, tearing if needed, leftover cheese and all pepper strips and prosciutto. Use leftover bread, oil sides up, to close sandwiches.
- In batches, cook in a panina maker/waffle iron till cheese melts and turns golden brown for 3-4 minutes.

Nutrition Information

- Calories: 798 calories;
- Cholesterol: 76
- Protein: 31
- Total Fat: 63.9
- Sodium: 1754
- Total Carbohydrate: 27.4

27. Quick N' Easy Chicken Cheese Steak

Serving: 1 | Prep: 5mins | Cook: 4mins | Ready in:

Ingredients

- 1 (5 ounce) can chicken chunks, drained
- 1 tablespoon hot pepper sauce
- 1 slice Cheddar cheese
- 1 hot dog bun, split

Direction

- In a nonstick skillet, cook chicken with hot sauce over medium heat, turning to coat

evenly with hot sauce, for about 3 minutes, until evenly heated.

- Gather chicken into the pan's center into a mold that looks like a hot dog bun. Divide Cheddar cheese slice into 2 equal pieces and lay atop chicken; heat for 1 to 2 minutes until cheddar cheese is melted. Lay the bottom half of hot dog bun atop chicken and cheese mixture, slide a spatula underneath, and turn upside down onto a plate. Lay the top half of hot dog bun atop Cheddar cheese.

Nutrition Information

- Calories: 470 calories;
- Total Fat: 22.6
- Sodium: 1466
- Total Carbohydrate: 21.9
- Cholesterol: 118
- Protein: 42.1

28. Roasted Red Pepper And Cheese Sandwich

Serving: 1 | Prep: 10mins | Cook: | Ready in:

Ingredients

- 2 teaspoons mayonnaise
- 1/2 teaspoon Ranch dressing
- 2 (1 inch thick) slices French bread
- 1 slice smoked fontina cheese
- 1 slice Havarti cheese
- 1/4 cup jarred roasted red pepper, drained and chopped
- 1 pepperoncini, sliced
- 3 slices dill pickle (optional)
- 1 leaf leaf lettuce

Direction

- Stir the Ranch dressing together with mayonnaise, then smear over 1 slice of bread. On the bread, arrange Havarti and fontina cheese slices, then put lettuce, pickle, pepperoncini, and roasted red pepper on top. Put the other slice of bread on top.

Nutrition Information

- Calories: 512 calories;
- Total Fat: 30.2
- Sodium: 1993
- Total Carbohydrate: 39.6
- Cholesterol: 73
- Protein: 21.7

29. Seattle Cream Cheese Dogs

Serving: 4 | Prep: 10mins | Cook: 20mins | Ready in:

Ingredients

- 1/4 cup butter
- 1 Walla Walla or other sweet onion, thinly sliced
- 1 (4 ounce) package cream cheese
- 4 hot dogs, or your favorite sausages
- 4 hot dog buns
- brown mustard
- sauerkraut (optional)

Direction

- Preheat grill pan or grill on medium high heat.
- Toss some onions on melted butter in a skillet place over medium high flame. Cook it for 15 minutes to allow the onions to deeply brown and become tender. In separate small skillet on low heat, place the cream cheese and allow to heat through until it becomes very soft.
- Brown the hotdogs on a grill along with the buns on both sides.
- Put together the cheese dogs by smearing the bun with the heated cream cheese and placing on top the sausage or hotdog. Garnish with onions, and add some sauerkraut and mustard if you wish.

Nutrition Information

- Calories: 533 calories;
- Protein: 13.8
- Total Fat: 40.6
- Sodium: 1354
- Total Carbohydrate: 28.8
- Cholesterol: 92

30. Smoked Mozzarella And Pesto Sandwich

Serving: 1 | Prep: 10mins | Cook: | Ready in:

Ingredients

- 2 tablespoons prepared basil pesto sauce
- 2 slices sourdough bread, lightly toasted
- 1 tablespoon mayonnaise
- 1 tablespoon freshly grated Parmesan cheese
- 1 slice provolone cheese
- 1/4 cup shredded smoked mozzarella cheese
- 1 lettuce leaf
- 2 slices tomato

Direction

- On one side of one bread slice, add pesto sauce and spread out to form a thin layer. On one side of the other bread slice, add mayonnaise and spread out to form a thin layer. Use Parmesan cheese to sprinkle over mayonnaise and pesto. On one slice of bread, add a layer of provolone and a layer of mozzarella cheese; then add tomato and lettuce on top; finish with the other bread slice.

Nutrition Information

- Calories: 603 calories;
- Sodium: 1145
- Total Carbohydrate: 34.8
- Cholesterol: 57

- Protein: 28.2
- Total Fat: 39.7

31. Tangy Turkey And Swiss Sandwiches

Serving: 4 | Prep: 15mins | Cook: 10mins | Ready in:

Ingredients

- 3/4 cup chopped red onion
- 1 tablespoon dried thyme
- 1/2 cup mayonnaise
- 1/4 cup coarse-grain brown mustard
- 8 slices country style French Bread
- 6 tablespoons butter, softened
- 1 pound thinly sliced roast turkey
- 8 slices tomato
- 8 slices Swiss cheese

Direction

- Mix mustard, red onion, mayonnaise, and thyme together in a small bowl. Spread one side of each bread slice with some of the mixtures. On the other side of each bread slice, spread butter over.
- Set a large skillet over medium heat. Arrange 4 bread slices into the skillet, butter-side down. Layer each slice of the bread with 1/4 of the turkey slices, and then 2 tomato slices. Top them with 2 Swiss cheese slices. Arrange the remaining bread slices on top, butter-side up. Once the bottoms of the sandwiches turn golden brown, flip them over and cook the other side until golden.

Nutrition Information

- Calories: 856 calories;
- Cholesterol: 154
- Protein: 41.9
- Total Fat: 58.9
- Sodium: 2243

- Total Carbohydrate: 42.6

32. Toasted Apple Pecan Brie Sandwiches

Serving: 4 | Prep: 10mins | Cook: 12mins | Ready in:

Ingredients

- 3 tablespoons butter
- 4 Granny Smith apple - peeled, cored and sliced
- 1/2 cup packed brown sugar
- 1 teaspoon ground cinnamon
- 1/4 cup chopped pecans
- 4 slices sourdough bread
- 2 tablespoons butter
- 6 ounces Brie cheese, cut into long, even slices
- 1 pinch ground cinnamon, for dusting

Direction

- In a large skillet, melt 3 tablespoons butter over medium heat. Put in the apples and cook for 7 to 8 minutes, stirring constantly until they are tender. Add pecans, 1 teaspoon of cinnamon and the brown sugar while continue mixing and cooking for 1 to 2 more minutes. Take the skillet off the heat and put it aside.
- Preheat the broiler of the oven.
- If the bread slices are too large, cut them in half and toast lightly. Spread the rest of the butter on one side of each toasted bread slice. On the unbuttered side of each toast, add two slices of brie cheese. Add a big scoop of spiced apple on top. Place the open face toasts onto a baking sheet.
- Broil for about 1 minute, until the cheese is melted. Sprinkle more cinnamon on top to your liking.

Nutrition Information

- Calories: 560 calories;

- Sodium: 541
- Total Carbohydrate: 60.1
- Cholesterol: 81
- Protein: 13.1
- Total Fat: 32

33. Toasted Caprese Sandwich

Serving: 4 | Prep: 25mins | Cook: 50mins |Ready in:

Ingredients

- 1 head garlic
- 1 tablespoon olive oil
- 2 tablespoons butter
- 1 (1 pound) loaf ciabatta bread, split in half horizontally
- 1 tablespoon dried rosemary
- 10 leaves fresh basil leaves, chopped
- 3 tomatoes, sliced
- 2 teaspoons balsamic vinegar (optional)
- 8 ounces fresh mozzarella cheese, sliced

Direction

- Set the oven to 200°C or 400°F to preheat.
- Cut the top of the head of garlic off to expose the cloves, trimming off approximately 1/4 inch of the top of each clove. Use olive oil to drizzle the cut cloves, then nestle into piece of aluminum foil with the head. Put in the preheated oven and bake for 35 minutes, until cloves are soft. Take garlic out of the oven without turning off the oven. Squeeze garlic from cloves into a small dish and mash them into a paste.
- Spread on the cut sides of bread with butter and sprinkle rosemary over, then put in a baking sheet. In the preheated oven, toast bread for about 5 minutes. Take out of the oven and spread over the bread with garlic paste, then put basil and tomatoes on top of one half of loaf. Drizzle balsamic vinegar over tomato slices, then put sliced mozzarella on

top of leftover half of loaf. Bring the sandwich halves back to baking sheet.
- Put in hot oven and cook for 10 minutes, until cheese is melted. Let the sandwich cool a bit prior to assembling, then cut into four pieces to serve.

Nutrition Information

- Calories: 596 calories;
- Total Fat: 25.7
- Sodium: 794
- Total Carbohydrate: 67.9
- Cholesterol: 60
- Protein: 22.1

34. Turkey And Provolone Sandwiches

Serving: 6 | Prep: 15mins | Cook: 5mins |Ready in:

Ingredients

- 1 tablespoon butter
- 6 large mushrooms, sliced
- 1 small onion, chopped
- 6 hoagie rolls, split lengthwise
- 1 pound sliced deli turkey meat
- 1 pound sliced provolone cheese
- 1/4 cup sliced black olives
- 6 slices tomato
- 6 leaves iceberg lettuce

Direction

- Preheat an oven to 200°C/400°F.
- Melt butter in a small skillet on medium heat. Sauté onion and mushrooms till tender; put aside. Put bottom bread halves on a lined cookie sheet; put 1-2 cheese slices, mushroom/onion mixture and 1-2 turkey slices on each.
- In the preheated oven, bake till cheese melts for 5 minutes. Take out of oven; top each with

lettuce, tomato and olives. Put top bread half on every sandwich; serve.

Nutrition Information

- Calories: 576 calories;
- Total Fat: 29.2
- Sodium: 1939
- Total Carbohydrate: 40.9
- Cholesterol: 88
- Protein: 39.7

35. Vegetarian Brie And Cranberry Paninis For 2

Serving: 2 | Prep: 10mins | Cook: 5mins | Ready in:

Ingredients

- 1 tablespoon butter
- 1 tablespoon Dijon mustard
- 2 ciabatta rolls, sliced in half
- 4 ounces Brie cheese, sliced
- 3 tablespoons cranberry sauce
- 2 cups baby spinach leaves

Direction

- Preheat a panini press to medium-high heat and lightly butter the surface.
- Spread over ciabatta rolls with Dijon mustard. Layer the bottom halves with Brie cheese, cranberry sauce, and spinach leaves. Place the top halves over spinach to finish sandwiches.
- Place sandwiches in the preheated panini press and grill for about 5 minutes until rolls turn golden brown and cheese is melted.

Nutrition Information

- Calories: 455 calories;
- Sodium: 965
- Total Carbohydrate: 42.7
- Cholesterol: 72

- Protein: 18
- Total Fat: 23.7

36. Vegetarian Mushroom Philly Cheese Steak Sandwiches

Serving: 2 | Prep: 10mins | Cook: 17mins | Ready in:

Ingredients

- 1 tablespoon butter, divided
- 1 tablespoon olive oil, divided
- 1 (8 ounce) package baby bella (cremini) mushrooms, sliced
- 1/2 teaspoon fresh thyme leaves
- salt and freshly ground black pepper to taste
- 1 tablespoon soy sauce
- 1 bell pepper, sliced into strips
- 1 onion, sliced
- 2 slices provolone cheese, cut in half
- 2 hoagie rolls, split lengthwise
- 2 teaspoons Dijon mustard, or more to taste

Direction

- Preheat the toaster oven to 150°C or 300°F.
- On medium-high heat, heat 1 1/2 tsp. each of oil and butter in a big non-stick pan for 2 mins until hot yet not smoking. Stir in slices of mushroom; sprinkle pepper, salt, and thyme leaves to season. Cook for 5 mins while continuously stirring until tender and brown. Pour in soy sauce; toss to cover. Move to a bowl.
- Wipe the pan. On medium-high heat, heat remaining oil and butter for 2 mins until hot yet not smoking. Mix in onions and peppers; sprinkle pepper and salt to season. Sauté for 5 mins until the onions and peppers are soft. Move to a bowl and toss with cooked mushrooms.
- Arrange rolls on a baking tray of the toaster oven; slather mustard and put a piece of provolone on top of two halves. While open-faced, toast for 3 mins until the cheese melts.

- Transfer toasted rolls on platters; add mushroom mixture on top.

Nutrition Information

- Calories: 664 calories;
- Sodium: 1708
- Total Carbohydrate: 81.8
- Cholesterol: 35
- Protein: 23.9
- Total Fat: 27.5

37. Waffle Sandwich With Cheese, Spinach And Spicy Mustard

Serving: 2 | Prep: 15mins | Cook: 5mins | Ready in:

Ingredients

- 1 roma (plum) tomato, thinly sliced
- salt and ground black pepper to taste
- 2 teaspoons butter, softened
- 4 thickly-sliced pieces multigrain bread
- 1 teaspoon spicy brown mustard
- 1 cup fresh spinach, or to taste
- 4 slices part-skim mozzarella cheese
- 2 teaspoons chopped sweet onion

Direction

- Start preheating waffle iron following the manufacturer's directions.
- On work surface, place tomato slices, pouring all the excess juice off. Add pepper and salt to season the tomato slices.
- Spread on one side each bread slice with half teaspoon of butter. In hot waffle iron, lay one bread slice, the butter-side facing down. Spread the bread slice in waffle iron with half teaspoon of mustard. Respectively, add a quarter cup of spinach, 2 mozzarella cheese slices, 1 teaspoon onion, half the tomato slices, and 1/4 cup spinach over top. Lay one slice

bread on top spinach layer, the butter-side facing up.
- Close the waffle iron; toast the sandwich for 2 minutes until browned lightly. Do the same with the remaining ingredients.

Nutrition Information

- Calories: 284 calories;
- Sodium: 656
- Total Carbohydrate: 24.2
- Cholesterol: 51
- Protein: 18.6
- Total Fat: 14.3

Chapter 2: Cold Sandwich Recipes

***

38. "ABC" Sandwiches

Serving: 6 servings. | Prep: 15mins | Cook: 0mins | Ready in:

Ingredients

- 12 slices bread, toasted
- 1/4 cup butter, softened
- 2 cups shredded cheddar cheese
- 1 medium apple, finely chopped
- 3/4 cup Miracle Whip
- 1/2 cup finely chopped walnuts
- 12 bacon strips, cooked
- 6 hard-boiled large eggs, sliced
- 6 tomato slices, optional

Direction

- Spread 1 teaspoon butter on each toast slice. Combine walnuts, salad dressing, apple, and cheese in a bowl. Put over 6 toast slices evenly; arrange 2 bacon slices on each. Cover egg slices atop. Arrange the rest of toast slices over top together with tomatoes if wanted.

Nutrition Information

- Calories:
- Sodium:
- Fiber:
- Total Carbohydrate:
- Cholesterol:
- Protein:
- Total Fat:

39. Angel Sandwiches

Serving: 8 sandwiches. | Prep: 25mins | Cook: 0mins | Ready in:

Ingredients

- 6 ounces cream cheese, softened
- 1/4 cup orange marmalade
- 16 slices white bread

Direction

- Beat the marmalade and cream cheese in a small bowl until combined. Cut out 16 angels from the bread using a 2-inch angel-shaped cookie cutter. Spread the cream cheese mixture on half of bread, then put the leftover bread on top.

Nutrition Information

- Calories:
- Fiber:
- Total Carbohydrate:
- Cholesterol:
- Protein:

- Total Fat:
- Sodium:

40. Apricot Turkey Sandwiches

Serving: 2 servings. | Prep: 15mins | Cook: 0mins | Ready in:

Ingredients

- 2 turkey bacon strips
- 4 pieces multigrain bread, toasted
- 2 tablespoons apricot jam
- 3 ounces thinly sliced deli peppered turkey
- 2 slices tomato
- 2 slices red onion
- 2 pieces leaf lettuce
- 2 slices reduced-fat Swiss cheese
- 4 teaspoons Dijon mustard

Direction

- Cook the bacon in a small frying pan on medium heat until it becomes crisp. Transfer it to paper towels to drain.
- Spread jam on two slices of toast, then layer it with turkey, bacon, tomato, onion, lettuce and cheese. Spread mustard on the leftover toast, then put it on top.

Nutrition Information

- Calories: 338 calories
- Sodium: 1109mg sodium
- Fiber: 4g fiber)
- Total Carbohydrate: 43g carbohydrate (14g sugars
- Cholesterol: 40mg cholesterol
- Protein: 23g protein.
- Total Fat: 10g fat (3g saturated fat)

41. Artichoke Lamb Sandwich Loaves

Serving: 24 servings. | Prep: 50mins | Cook: 01hours20mins | Ready in:

Ingredients

- 1/2 cup lemon juice
- 1/2 cup olive oil
- 6 garlic cloves, minced
- 2 tablespoons minced fresh rosemary
- 1 teaspoon salt
- 1/4 teaspoon cayenne pepper
- 1 boneless leg of lamb (2-1/2 pounds)
- 2 cans (14 ounces each) water-packed artichoke hearts, rinsed and drained
- 2/3 cup plus 6 tablespoons reduced-fat balsamic vinaigrette, divided
- 2 sourdough baguettes (1 pound each)
- 1 medium cucumber, thinly sliced
- 2 medium tomatoes, thinly sliced
- 1 package (5.3 ounces) fresh goat cheese, sliced

Direction

- Mix together the initial 6 ingredients in a big resealable plastic bag, then add the lamb. Seal the bag and turn to coat, then let it chill in the fridge for 8 hours or overnight.
- Drain and get rid of the marinade. Put the lamb in a shallow roasting pan on a rack and let it bake for 80 to 90 minutes at 325 degrees without a cover, or until the meat achieves your preferred doneness; a thermometer should read 170 degrees for well done, 160 degrees for medium, 145 degrees for medium-rare. Allow it to cool to room temperature. Put cover and let it chill in the fridge for a minimum of two hours.
- In a resealable plastic bag, put the artichokes then add 2/3 cup of vinaigrette. Seal the bag and turn to coat and allow it to stand for 10 minutes. Drain and get rid of the marinade.
- Slice the lamb into thin slices, then halve the baguette horizontally. Hollow out the bottom and top gently, leaving a 3/4-inch shell. Use 2

tbsp. of vinaigrette to brush the bottom half of each loaf, then layer it with cucumber, tomatoes, lamb and artichokes. Drizzle it with the leftover vinaigrette, then put goat cheese on top.

- Place back the bread tops and firmly press down; tightly wrap in a plastic wrap and let it chill in the fridge for a minimum of two hours, then cut into slices.

Nutrition Information

- Calories: 239 calories
- Total Carbohydrate: 26g carbohydrate (2g sugars
- Cholesterol: 33mg cholesterol
- Protein: 15g protein.
- Total Fat: 8g fat (2g saturated fat)
- Sodium: 511mg sodium
- Fiber: 1g fiber)

42. Avocado Tomato Wraps

Serving: 2 servings. | Prep: 10mins | Cook: 0mins | Ready in:

Ingredients

- 1 medium ripe avocado, peeled and thinly sliced
- 2 flavored tortillas of your choice (10 inches), room temperature
- 2 lettuce leaves
- 1 medium tomato, thinly sliced
- 2 tablespoons shredded Parmesan cheese
- 1/4 teaspoon garlic powder
- 1/8 teaspoon salt
- 1/8 teaspoon pepper

Direction

- Use a fork to mash a fourth of the avocado in a small bowl, then spread it on top of the tortillas. Layer with lettuce, tomato and leftover avocado, then sprinkle pepper, salt, garlic powder and cheese on top; roll it up. Serve right away.

Nutrition Information

- Calories: 352 calories
- Protein: 9g protein.
- Total Fat: 17g fat (3g saturated fat)
- Sodium: 456mg sodium
- Fiber: 8g fiber)
- Total Carbohydrate: 45g carbohydrate (3g sugars
- Cholesterol: 4mg cholesterol

43. B Is For Book Sandwich

Serving: 6 servings. | Prep: 10mins | Cook: 0mins | Ready in:

Ingredients

- 12 slices bread
- 1/4 cup butter, softened
- 1/2 teaspoon minced chives
- 1/8 teaspoon onion salt
- 6 slices fully cooked ham
- 6 slices American cheese

Direction

- Cut each bread slice into a 3 1/4x3 1/2-in. rectangle, leaving the crust on one side. Cut letters in 1/2 of the bread slices with a 1-1/2-in. letter cookie cutter.
- Stir the onion salt, chives and butter until blended in a small bowl. Spread the mixture on one side of each bread slice. Put cheese and ham on top of whole bread slices; top with cutout bread.

Nutrition Information

- Calories:
- Cholesterol:

- Protein:
- Total Fat:
- Sodium:
- Fiber:
- Total Carbohydrate:

44. BLT Wraps

Serving: 4 | Prep: 15mins | Cook: 10mins | Ready in:

Ingredients

- 1 pound thick sliced bacon, cut into 1 inch pieces
- 4 (12 inch) flour tortillas
- 1 cup shredded Cheddar cheese
- 1/2 head iceberg lettuce, shredded
- 1 tomato, diced

Direction

- Cook bacon till evenly brown in a big, deep skillet on medium high heat. Drain; put aside.
- On microwave-safe plate, put 1 tortilla; sprinkle 1/4 cup cheese on tortilla. Cook for 1-2 minutes till cheese melts in microwave. Put tomato, lettuce and 1/4 bacon over immediately. Fold tortilla sides over; roll up. Repeat using leftover ingredients; before serving, halve each wrap.

Nutrition Information

- Calories: 695 calories;
- Cholesterol: 71
- Protein: 31.4
- Total Fat: 34.1
- Sodium: 1788
- Total Carbohydrate: 64.2

45. Bacon Avocado Wraps

Serving: 4 servings. | Prep: 15mins | Cook: 0mins | Ready in:

Ingredients

- 1/3 cup mayonnaise
- 2 tablespoons chipotle sauce
- 1 tablespoon sour cream
- 1 package (2.1 ounces) ready-to-serve fully cooked bacon
- 4 flour tortillas (8 inches)
- 4 large lettuce leaves
- 1 large tomato, sliced
- 2 medium ripe avocados, peeled and sliced

Direction

- Mix together sour cream, chipotle sauce and mayonnaise in a small bowl until smooth. Following package directions, heat bacon.
- Spread over tortillas with chipotle mayonnaise, then put in layer of lettuce, tomato, bacon and avocados. Roll tortilla up tightly.

Nutrition Information

- Calories: 527 calories
- Cholesterol: 9mg cholesterol
- Protein: 12g protein.
- Total Fat: 39g fat (7g saturated fat)
- Sodium: 584mg sodium
- Fiber: 5g fiber)
- Total Carbohydrate: 35g carbohydrate (3g sugars

46. Bagel With A Veggie Schmear

Serving: 4 servings. | Prep: 0mins | Cook: 20mins | Ready in:

Ingredients

- 4 ounces fat-free cream cheese
- 4 ounces fresh goat cheese
- 1/2 teaspoon grated lime zest
- 1 tablespoon lime juice
- 2/3 cup finely chopped cucumber
- 1/4 cup finely chopped celery
- 3 tablespoons finely chopped carrot
- 1 radish, finely chopped
- 2 tablespoons finely chopped red onion
- 2 tablespoons thinly sliced fresh basil
- 4 whole wheat bagels, split and toasted
- 8 slices tomato
- Coarsely ground pepper, optional

Direction

- Beat the lime juice, lime zest and cheeses in a bowl until combined. Fold in the basil and chopped vegetables. Serve with tomato slices on bagels, then sprinkle pepper on top if preferred.

Nutrition Information

- Calories: 341 calories
- Sodium: 756mg sodium
- Fiber: 10g fiber)
- Total Carbohydrate: 56g carbohydrate (15g sugars
- Cholesterol: 22mg cholesterol
- Protein: 20g protein.
- Total Fat: 6g fat (3g saturated fat)

47. Beef N Olive Sandwiches

Serving: 4 servings. | Prep: 20mins | Cook: 0mins | Ready in:

Ingredients

- 1 package (8 ounces) cream cheese, softened
- 2 tablespoons heavy whipping cream
- 1/2 teaspoon white pepper
- 1/4 cup chopped dried beef

- 3 tablespoons sliced pimiento-stuffed olives
- 3 tablespoons chopped walnuts
- 8 slices bread

Direction

- Beat pepper, cream and cream cheese in a big bowl until smooth. Stir in walnuts, olives and beef.
- Spread the mixture on each of 4 bread slices, then put leftover bread on top. Place on a cover and freeze for a maximum of 2 months.
- Take out of the freezer for a minimum of 4 hours prior to serving. You can freeze for a maximum of 3 months.

Nutrition Information

- Calories:
- Total Carbohydrate:
- Cholesterol:
- Protein:
- Total Fat:
- Sodium:
- Fiber:

48. Berry Turkey Sandwich

Serving: 2 servings. | Prep: 10mins | Cook: 0mins | Ready in:

Ingredients

- 2 tablespoons reduced-fat spreadable cream cheese
- 2 teaspoons finely chopped pecans
- 4 slices whole wheat bread
- 2 lettuce leaves
- 2 slices reduced-fat Swiss cheese
- 1/4 pound thinly sliced deli turkey breast
- 4 fresh strawberries, sliced

Direction

- Mix pecans and cream cheese in a small bowl, then spread it on top of the 2 bread slices. Top with lettuce, cheese, turkey, strawberries and remaining bread.

Nutrition Information

- Calories: 319 calories
- Total Carbohydrate: 32g carbohydrate (5g sugars
- Cholesterol: 45mg cholesterol
- Protein: 26g protein. Diabetic Exchanges: 3 lean meat
- Total Fat: 12g fat (5g saturated fat)
- Sodium: 847mg sodium
- Fiber: 4g fiber)

49. Bistro Turkey Sandwiches

Serving: 6 servings. | Prep: 20mins | Cook: 10mins | Ready in:

Ingredients

- 1 small red onion, thinly sliced
- 4 teaspoons brown sugar, divided
- 1 tablespoon olive oil
- 1/4 teaspoon salt
- 1/8 teaspoon cayenne pepper
- 1/4 cup Dijon mustard
- 1 tablespoon apple cider or unsweetened apple juice
- 6 wheat sandwich buns, split
- 6 Bibb or Boston lettuce leaves
- 1 medium pear, peeled and thinly sliced
- 1 pound cooked turkey breast, thinly sli
- 1/4 cup loosely packed basil leaves
- 6 tablespoons crumbled Gorgonzola ch

Direction

- Cook 1 tsp of brown sugar and onio a small frying pan on medium heat, minutes or until it turns golden brown, stirring often. Mix in the cayenne and salt.

- Mix together the leftover brown sugar, apple cider and mustard, then spread it on top of the bun bottoms. Layer it with lettuce, pear, turkey, basil and cheese, then put caramelized onion on top. Place back the tops.

Nutrition Information

- Calories: 346 calories
- Protein: 31g protein. Diabetic Exchanges: 3 lean meat
- Total Fat: 8g fat (3g saturated fat)
- Sodium: 708mg sodium
- Fiber: 4g fiber)
- Total Carbohydrate: 35g carbohydrate (11g sugars
- Cholesterol: 71mg cholesterol

50. California Clubs

Serving: 4 servings. | Prep: 10mins | Cook: 0mins | Ready in:

Ingredients

- 1/2 cup ranch salad dressing
- 1/4 cup Dijon mustard
- slices sourdough bread, toasted
- oneless skinless chicken breast halves, ked and sliced
- e tomato, sliced
- um ripe avocado, peeled and sliced
- strips, cooked and drained

ed

eese

mustard and salad dressing in a n spread on each bread slice. slices with chicken, tomato, n, then place leftover bread

in oil in for 8 to 10

Nutrition Information

- Calories: 837 calories
- Total Fat: 41g fat (9g saturated fat)
- Sodium: 1765mg sodium
- Fiber: 7g fiber)
- Total Carbohydrate: 74g carbohydrate (4g sugars
- Cholesterol: 84mg cholesterol
- Protein: 42g protein.

51. Champion Roast Beef Sandwiches

Serving: 4 servings. | Prep: 15mins | Cook: 0mins | Ready in:

Ingredients

- 1/2 cup sour cream
- 1 tablespoon onion soup mix
- 1 tablespoon prepared horseradish, drained
- 1/8 teaspoon pepper
- 8 slices rye or pumpernickel bread
- 1/2 pound sliced roast beef
- Lettuce leaves

Direction

- Mix the first 4 ingredients together in a small bowl, then spread on each bread slice with 1 tbsp. of mixture. Put lettuce and roast beef on top of 4 bread slices, then use leftover bread to cover.

Nutrition Information

- Calories: 318 calories
- Total Carbohydrate: 34g carbohydrate (4g sugars
- Cholesterol: 60mg cholesterol
- Protein: 18g protein.
- Total Fat: 11g fat (6g saturated fat)
- Sodium: 1401mg sodium

- Fiber: 4g fiber)

52. Christmas Tree Sandwiches

Serving: 6 servings. | Prep: 10mins | Cook: 0mins | Ready in:

Ingredients

- 12 slices white and/or wheat bread, frozen
- Christmas tree cookie cutter (about 3-1/2 inches)
- Plastic drinking straw
- 1/4 cup creamy peanut butter
- 1/2 cup red or green jelly or jam
- Pastry bag or small heavy-duty resealable plastic bag

Direction

- Use cookie cutter to cut the bread into trees. Punch holes into 6 trees using a straw, then put aside. Spread jelly and peanut butter on the leftover trees. Put the trees that have holes on top, then use pastry bag to fill the holes with extra jelly.

Nutrition Information

- Calories:
- Total Carbohydrate:
- Cholesterol:
- Protein:
- Total Fat:
- Sodium:
- Fiber:

53. Club Roll Ups

Serving: 8 servings. | Prep: 25mins | Cook: 0mins | Ready in:

Ingredients

- 3 ounces cream cheese, softened
- 1/2 cup ranch salad dressing
- 2 tablespoons ranch salad dressing mix
- 8 bacon strips, cooked and crumbled
- 1/2 cup finely chopped onion
- 1 can (2-1/4 ounces) sliced ripe olives, drained
- 1 jar (2 ounces) diced pimientos, drained
- 1/4 cup diced canned jalapeno peppers
- 8 flour tortillas (10 inches), room temperature
- 8 thin slices deli ham
- 8 thin slices deli turkey
- 8 thin slices deli roast beef
- 2 cups shredded cheddar cheese

Direction

- Beat together dressing mix, ranch dressing and cream cheese in a small bowl until well combined. Mix together jalapenos, pimientos, olives, onion and bacon in a separate bowl.
- Spread over tortillas with cream cheese mixture, then place in layer of ham, turkey and roast beef. Use bacon mixture as well as cheddar cheese to sprinkle on top, then roll up.

Nutrition Information

- Calories: 554 calories
- Fiber: 7g fiber)
- Total Carbohydrate: 39g carbohydrate (2g sugars
- Cholesterol: 80mg cholesterol
- Protein: 27g protein.
- Total Fat: 29g fat (12g saturated fat)
- Sodium: 1802mg sodium

54. Club Sandwiches

Serving: 4 servings. | Prep: 25mins | Cook: 0mins | Ready in:

Ingredients

- 1/2 cup mayonnaise
- 4 French rolls, split
- 1 cup shredded lettuce
- 8 slices tomato
- 1 medium ripe avocado, peeled and sliced
- 1/4 cup prepared Italian salad dressing
- 1/2 teaspoon coarsely ground pepper
- 12 cooked bacon strips
- 1/2 pound sliced deli turkey
- 1/2 pound sliced deli ham
- 4 slices Swiss cheese

Direction

- Over cut side of rolls, spread mayonnaise. Layer lettuce, tomato and avocado on roll bottoms, then drizzle with dressing and use pepper to sprinkle over top. Layer bacon, turkey, ham and cheese on top, then replace tops.

Nutrition Information

- Calories: 815 calories
- Cholesterol: 101mg cholesterol
- Protein: 41g protein.
- Total Fat: 54g fat (13g saturated fat)
- Sodium: 2242mg sodium
- Fiber: 5g fiber)
- Total Carbohydrate: 40g carbohydrate (4g sugars

55. Cool Cucumber Sandwich

Serving: 1 serving. | Prep: 10mins | Cook: 0mins | Ready in:

Ingredients

- 1 tablespoon prepared ranch salad dressing
- 2 slices bread, toasted
- 12 to 15 thin cucumber slices
- 2 bacon strips, cooked
- 1 slice tomato

Direction

- Spread on 1 side of each slice of toast with salad dressing, then put on one slice of bread with layer of cucumber, bacon and tomato. Place another slice of bread on top.

Nutrition Information

- Calories:
- Protein:
- Total Fat:
- Sodium:
- Fiber:
- Total Carbohydrate:
- Cholesterol:

56. Corned Beef And Cabbage Sandwiches

Serving: 4 servings. | Prep: 10mins | Cook: 0mins | Ready in:

Ingredients

- 1/3 cup mayonnaise
- 1 tablespoon white vinegar
- 1/4 teaspoon ground mustard
- 1/4 teaspoon celery seed
- 1/4 teaspoon pepper
- 1-1/2 cups thinly shredded raw cabbage
- 4 kaiser or hard rolls, split
- 3/4 to 1 pound cooked corned beef, sliced

Direction

- Mix together pepper, celery seed, mustard, vinegar and mayonnaise in a small bowl until combined, then stir in cabbage. Pour the mixture on bottom halves of rolls. Put in corned beef to cover and replace tops.

Nutrition Information

- Calories: 522 calories
- Fiber: 2g fiber)
- Total Carbohydrate: 32g carbohydrate (4g sugars
- Cholesterol: 90mg cholesterol
- Protein: 22g protein.
- Total Fat: 33g fat (8g saturated fat)
- Sodium: 1379mg sodium

57. Crab Sandwiches

Serving: 4 servings. | Prep: 25mins | Cook: 0mins | Ready in:

Ingredients

- 2 large sweet red peppers
- 1 small red onion
- 2 hard-boiled large eggs
- 4 pitted ripe olives, halved
- 4 croissants, split
- Fresh parsley sprigs
- 1 package (8 ounces) flake-style imitation crabmeat
- 1/4 cup mayonnaise
- 1 teaspoon lemon juice

Direction

- Chop 2 tbsp. of onion and 1/2 cup of pepper, then put aside to make filling. Cut 4 sets of claws and legs from leftover peppers. From leftover onion, cut 4 slices thinly to make mouths.
- Cut 8 slices of egg white thinly. Attach egg slices and olive halves to croissants' tops to make eyes, using toothpicks. Tuck in parsley to make eyelashes.
- Mix together onion, reserved red pepper, lemon juice, mayonnaise and crabmeat in a small bowl, then scoop onto bottoms of croissant and replace their tops. Put in mouths, legs and claws.

Nutrition Information

- Calories:
- Protein:
- Total Fat:
- Sodium:
- Fiber:
- Total Carbohydrate:
- Cholesterol:

58. Crisp Finger Sandwich

Serving: 1 serving. | Prep: 10mins | Cook: 0mins | Ready in:

Ingredients

- 1 slice whole wheat bread, toasted
- 2 tablespoons reduced-fat spreadable garden vegetable cream cheese
- 1/3 cup thinly sliced English cucumber
- 3 tablespoons alfalfa sprouts
- Dash coarsely ground pepper

Direction

- Spread cream cheese on the toast, then put pepper, sprouts and cucumber on top.

Nutrition Information

- Calories: 136 calories
- Total Carbohydrate: 13g carbohydrate (4g sugars
- Cholesterol: 15mg cholesterol
- Protein: 7g protein. Diabetic Exchanges: 1 starch
- Total Fat: 6g fat (3g saturated fat)
- Sodium: 323mg sodium
- Fiber: 2g fiber)

59. Crowd Pleasin' Muffuletta

Serving: 12-14 servings. | Prep: 60mins | Cook: 0mins | Ready in:

Ingredients

- 1 cup pimiento-stuffed olives, finely chopped
- 1 cup pitted ripe olives, finely chopped
- 2/3 cup olive oil
- 1/2 cup chopped roasted sweet red peppers
- 3 tablespoons minced fresh parsley
- 2 tablespoons red wine vinegar
- 3 garlic cloves, minced
- 1 round loaf (2 pounds) unsliced Italian bread
- 1 pound thinly sliced deli turkey
- 12 ounces thinly sliced part-skim mozzarella cheese (about 16 slices)
- 1 pound thinly sliced hard salami
- 1 pound thinly sliced deli ham

Direction

- Mix the first 7 ingredients together in a big bowl then put aside. Halve bread horizontally. Hollow out the bottom and top carefully to leave a 1 inch shell. Reserve removed bread for another use.
- On bottom bread shell, spread 1 1/2 cups of olive mixture, then spread leftover olive mixture over cut side of top bread shell. Layer turkey, 1/2 of the cheese, salami, leftover cheese and ham in the bottom bread, then replace the bread top. Use plastic wrap to wrap bread tightly and chill about 4 hours to overnight. Slice into wedges and serve.

Nutrition Information

- Calories: 573 calories
- Cholesterol: 77mg cholesterol
- Protein: 32g protein.
- Total Fat: 33g fat (10g saturated fat)
- Sodium: 2291mg sodium
- Fiber: 2g fiber)
- Total Carbohydrate: 37g carbohydrate (1g sugars

60. Curried Beef Sandwiches

Serving: 6 sandwiches. | Prep: 10mins | Cook: 0mins | Ready in:

Ingredients

- 1/3 cup mayonnaise
- 1/4 cup chutney
- 1/4 teaspoon curry powder
- 12 slices whole wheat bread
- 1-1/4 pounds thinly sliced deli roast beef
- 6 lettuce leaves
- 6 tomato slices

Direction

- Mix together curry, chutney and mayonnaise in a small bowl, then spread 1 tbsp. of mayonnaise mixture over 6 bread slices. Layer beef, lettuce and tomato on top, then place leftover bread on top.

Nutrition Information

- Calories: 420 calories
- Total Carbohydrate: 38g carbohydrate (13g sugars
- Cholesterol: 43mg cholesterol
- Protein: 33g protein.
- Total Fat: 16g fat (3g saturated fat)
- Sodium: 1730mg sodium
- Fiber: 5g fiber)

61. Deli Club Sandwich

Serving: 2 servings. | Prep: 15mins | Cook: 0mins | Ready in:

Ingredients

- 2 tablespoons Dijon mustard
- Dash dried basil
- Dash dill weed
- 2 sandwich buns, split or 4 slices sourdough bread
- 4 slices smoked turkey
- 10 slices pepperoni
- 4 to 6 slices tomato
- 4 slices Swiss cheese

Direction

- Mix together dill, basil and mustard, then spread the mixture over buns or 2 bread pieces. Put in layer of turkey, pepperoni, tomato and cheese, then use bun tops or leftover bread to cover.

Nutrition Information

- Calories: 510 calories
- Protein: 32g protein.
- Total Fat: 25g fat (14g saturated fat)
- Sodium: 1311mg sodium
- Fiber: 2g fiber)
- Total Carbohydrate: 39g carbohydrate (7g sugars
- Cholesterol: 73mg cholesterol

62. Deli Sandwich Party Platter

Serving: 24 servings. | Prep: 30mins | Cook: 0mins | Ready in:

Ingredients

- 1 bunch green leaf lettuce
- 2 pounds sliced deli turkey
- 2 pounds sliced deli roast beef
- 1 pound sliced deli ham
- 1 pound thinly sliced hard salami
- 2 cartons (7 ounces each) roasted red pepper hummus

- 2 cartons (6-1/2 ounces each) garden vegetable cheese spread
- Assorted breads and mini bagels

Direction

- On serving platter, put lettuce leaves; top using deli meats; if desired, rolled up. Serve with bagels, breads, cheese spread and hummus.

Nutrition Information

- Calories: 205 calories
- Cholesterol: 75mg cholesterol
- Protein: 25g protein.
- Total Fat: 10g fat (4g saturated fat)
- Sodium: 1235mg sodium
- Fiber: 1g fiber)
- Total Carbohydrate: 4g carbohydrate (1g sugars

63. Dill Spiral Bites

Serving: 2 servings. | Prep: 15mins | Cook: 0mins | Ready in:

Ingredients

- 3 ounces cream cheese, softened
- 1 tablespoon minced chives
- 1 tablespoon snipped fresh dill
- 2 flour tortillas (8 inches)
- 6 thin slices tomato
- 6 large spinach leaves

Direction

- Beat dill, chives and cream cheese till blended in a small bowl. On one side of every tortilla, spread 1 tablespoonful. Layer with spinach and tomato. Spread with leftover cream cheese mixture.
- Tightly roll up; wrap in plastic. Refrigerate for 1 hour more. Unwrap. Slice each to 4 slices.

Nutrition Information

- Calories: 271 calories
- Protein: 10g protein.
- Total Fat: 12g fat (6g saturated fat)
- Sodium: 458mg sodium
- Fiber: 2g fiber)
- Total Carbohydrate: 31g carbohydrate (3g sugars
- Cholesterol: 30mg cholesterol

64. Dilly Roast Beef Sandwich

Serving: 1 serving. | Prep: 5mins | Cook: 0mins | Ready in:

Ingredients

- 3 tablespoons cream cheese, softened
- Pinch each dill weed, garlic powder and pepper
- 2 slices bread
- 2 slices cooked roast beef
- 3 tomato slices

Direction

- Mix pepper, garlic powder, dill and cream cheese together, then spread on 1 bread slice. Put tomato, beef and leftover bread on top.

Nutrition Information

- Calories: 346 calories
- Fiber: 2g fiber)
- Total Carbohydrate: 29g carbohydrate (4g sugars
- Cholesterol: 72mg cholesterol
- Protein: 16g protein.
- Total Fat: 19g fat (10g saturated fat)
- Sodium: 639mg sodium

65. Easy Cucumber Party Sandwiches

Serving: 15 | Prep: 20mins | Cook: | Ready in:

Ingredients

- 1 (8 ounce) package whipped cream cheese with chives
- 1/2 cup sour cream
- 1/2 cup mayonnaise
- 1 (1 ounce) package ranch dressing mix (such as Hidden Valley Ranch®)
- 1 1/2 teaspoons dried dill weed
- 1 (1 pound) loaf thinly sliced white bread
- 1 cucumber, thinly sliced
- 1/4 cup snipped fresh dill leaves, or as needed

Direction

- In a bowl, mix dried dill, ranch dressing mix, mayonnaise, sour cream and cream cheese until smooth and creamy.
- Cut crusts from the bread slices. Cut the sliced bread to decorative shapes like flowers or rounds using cookie cutters. Spread every bread piece with cream cheese mixture. Put a cucumber slice on top. Top every canape with several fresh dill leaves.

Nutrition Information

- Calories: 205 calories;
- Total Fat: 13.2
- Sodium: 454
- Total Carbohydrate: 18.1
- Cholesterol: 19
- Protein: 3.8

66. Easy Southwestern Veggie Wraps

Serving: 6 servings. | Prep: 30mins | Cook: 0mins | Ready in:

Ingredients

- 1 can (15 ounces) black beans, rinsed and drained
- 2 large tomatoes, seeded and diced
- 1 cup frozen corn, thawed
- 1 cup cooked brown rice, cooled
- 1/3 cup fat-free sour cream
- 1/4 cup minced fresh cilantro
- 2 shallots, chopped
- 1 jalapeno pepper, seeded and chopped
- 2 tablespoons lime juice
- 1/2 teaspoon ground cumin
- 1/2 teaspoon chili powder
- 1/2 teaspoon salt
- 6 romaine leaves
- 6 whole wheat tortillas (8 inches), at room temperature

Direction

- In a big bowl, put all the ingredients except for the tortillas and romaine, then toss to blend. Put the romaine on tortillas, then put the beam mixture on top and roll it up. Use toothpicks to secure if preferred, then serve.

Nutrition Information

- Calories: 0

67. Fast Italian Subs

Serving: 10 servings. | Prep: 15mins | Cook: 0mins | Ready in:

Ingredients

- 1/3 cup olive oil

- 4-1/2 teaspoons white wine vinegar
- 1 tablespoon dried parsley flakes
- 2 to 3 garlic cloves, minced
- 1 can (2-1/4 ounces) sliced ripe olives, drained
- 1/2 cup chopped pimiento-stuffed olives
- 1 loaf (1 pound, 20 inches) French bread, unsliced
- 24 thin slices hard salami
- 24 slices provolone or mozzarella cheese
- 24 slices fully cooked ham
- Lettuce leaves, optional

Direction

- Mix together garlic, parsley, vinegar and oil in a small bowl. Mix in olives, then place on a cover and chill about 8 hours to overnight.
- Halve bread lengthways and spread bottom of bread with olive mixture. Put ham, cheese and salami on top, then put in lettuce if you want. Replace bread top and cut into 2-inch slices. Insert one toothpick into each slice.

Nutrition Information

- Calories: 600 calories
- Sodium: 2075mg sodium
- Fiber: 2g fiber)
- Total Carbohydrate: 29g carbohydrate (2g sugars
- Cholesterol: 92mg cholesterol
- Protein: 39g protein.
- Total Fat: 37g fat (17g saturated fat)

68. Fiesta Loaf

Serving: 6 servings. | Prep: 15mins | Cook: 0mins | Ready in:

Ingredients

- 1 round loaf (1 pound) sourdough bread
- 1/2 cup refried beans
- 4 ounces sliced Colby cheese

- 1 small sweet red pepper, sliced
- 4 ounces sliced Monterey Jack cheese
- 1 can (4 ounces) chopped green chilies
- 1 can (2-1/4 ounces) sliced ripe olives, drained
- 1 small tomato, seeded and diced
- 1 cup shredded Mexican cheese blend
- 2 tablespoons ranch salad dressing
- 1 avocado, peeled and sliced
- 4 ounces sliced cheddar cheese

Direction

- Slice the top fourth off the bread loaf. Hollow out the bottom and top of the loaf gently, then leave a 1/2-inch shell; get rid of the removed bread or reserve for later use. Put the top aside.
- Scatter refried beans inside the shell's bottom and layer it with Colby cheese, red pepper, Monterey jack cheese, chilies, olives and tomato. Press the layers together gently to flatten as necessary.
- Mix together the ranch dressing and cheese blend then scoop it on top of the tomato. Put avocado and cheddar cheese on top. Place back the bread top and use plastic wrap to wrap it tightly, then chill.

Nutrition Information

- Calories: 609 calories
- Protein: 26g protein.
- Total Fat: 34g fat (17g saturated fat)
- Sodium: 1210mg sodium
- Fiber: 6g fiber)
- Total Carbohydrate: 49g carbohydrate (3g sugars
- Cholesterol: 73mg cholesterol

69. Focaccia Sandwich

Serving: 10-12 servings. | Prep: 10mins | Cook: 0mins | Ready in:

Ingredients

- 1 loaf (1 pound) Focaccia bread
- 1/2 cup spinach dip or chive and onion cream cheese spread
- 2 tablespoons Dijon mustard
- 8 ounces thinly sliced deli smoked turkey
- 4 slices Swiss cheese (1 ounce each)
- 1 medium tomato, thinly sliced

Direction

- Horizontally cut the bread in 1/2. Spread over each half with a quarter cup of the spinach dip, then spread with the mustard. On bottom half, layer turkey, the cheese, and the tomato; place the top half back. Slice into wedges

Nutrition Information

- Calories: 210 calories
- Fiber: 1g fiber)
- Total Carbohydrate: 21g carbohydrate (1g sugars
- Cholesterol: 21mg cholesterol
- Protein: 9g protein.
- Total Fat: 9g fat (3g saturated fat)
- Sodium: 546mg sodium

70. Fresh Mozzarella Basil Sandwiches

Serving: 4 servings. | Prep: 15mins | Cook: 0mins | Ready in:

Ingredients

- 8 slices sourdough bread, toasted
- 1/4 cup wasabi mayonnaise
- 1/2 pound fresh mozzarella cheese, sliced
- 2 medium tomatoes, sliced
- 4 thin slices sweet onion
- 8 fresh basil leaves

Direction

- Spread mayonnaise on toast. Layer the cheese, tomatoes, onion and basil on 4 slices, then put the leftover toast on top.

Nutrition Information

- Calories: 466 calories
- Sodium: 576mg sodium
- Fiber: 3g fiber)
- Total Carbohydrate: 42g carbohydrate (5g sugars
- Cholesterol: 50mg cholesterol
- Protein: 18g protein.
- Total Fat: 24g fat (10g saturated fat)

71. Fresh Mozzarella Sandwiches For 2

Serving: 2 servings. | Prep: 15mins | Cook: 0mins | Ready in:

Ingredients

- 4 slices sourdough bread, toasted
- 2 tablespoons wasabi mayonnaise
- 1/4 pound fresh mozzarella cheese, sliced
- 1 medium tomato, sliced
- 2 thin slices sweet onion
- 4 fresh basil leaves

Direction

- Spread mayonnaise on toast. Layer cheese, tomatoes, onion, and basil on 2 slices, then put the leftover toast on top.

Nutrition Information

- Calories: 466 calories
- Sodium: 576mg sodium
- Fiber: 3g fiber)
- Total Carbohydrate: 42g carbohydrate (5g sugars
- Cholesterol: 50mg cholesterol

- Protein: 18g protein.
- Total Fat: 24g fat (10g saturated fat)

72. Garbanzo Bean Pitas

Serving: 4 servings. | Prep: 20mins | Cook: 0mins | Ready in:

Ingredients

- 1 can (15 ounces) garbanzo beans or chickpeas, rinsed and drained
- 1/2 cup fat-free mayonnaise
- 1 tablespoon water
- 2 tablespoons minced fresh parsley
- 2 tablespoons chopped walnuts
- 1 tablespoon chopped onion
- 1 garlic clove, minced
- 1/8 teaspoon pepper
- 4 whole wheat pita pocket halves
- 4 lettuce leaves
- 1/2 small cucumber, thinly sliced
- 1 small tomato, seeded and chopped
- 1/4 cup fat-free ranch salad dressing, optional

Direction

- Mix together the initial 8 ingredients in a blender. Put on a cover and process until combined. On each pita half, place 1/3 cup of the bean mixture, then put lettuce, cucumber and tomato on top. If preferred, serve with ranch dressing.

Nutrition Information

- Calories: 241 calories
- Protein: 9g protein. Diabetic Exchanges: 3 starch
- Total Fat: 6g fat (0 saturated fat)
- Sodium: 552mg sodium
- Fiber: 8g fiber)
- Total Carbohydrate: 41g carbohydrate (6g sugars

- Cholesterol: 3mg cholesterol

73. Giant Focaccia Sandwich

Serving: 12 servings. | Prep: 25mins | Cook: 30mins | Ready in:

Ingredients

- 5-1/2 cups all-purpose flour
- 1 cup quick-cooking oats
- 2 packages (1/4 ounce each) active dry yeast
- 2 teaspoons salt
- 2-1/4 cups water
- 1/2 cup molasses
- 1 tablespoon butter
- 1 egg, lightly beaten
- 1 tablespoon dried minced onion
- 1 tablespoon sesame seeds
- 1 teaspoon garlic salt
- SANDWICH FILLING:
- 6 tablespoons mayonnaise
- 2 tablespoons prepared mustard
- 6 to 8 lettuce leaves
- 12 to 16 thin slices fully cooked ham
- 6 to 8 thin slices Swiss or cheddar cheese
- 4 slices red onion, separated into rings
- 1 medium green pepper, sliced
- 2 medium tomatoes, thinly sliced

Direction

- Combine salt, yeast, oats and flour in large bowl. Heat butter, molasses and water in a saucepan to about 120° to 130°. Put into the dry ingredients, then beat until they are just moistened. Put into a greased bowl; grease the top by flipping once. Allow to rise in warm place with a cover for 45 mins or until doubled.
- Press the dough on a greased pizza pan (about 14 inches). Allow to rise with a cover for half an hour, until doubled.
- Brush egg over. Sprinkle garlic salt, sesame seeds and onion over. Bake for 30 to 35 mins at

350°, until it turns golden brown. Transfer to a wire rack to cool.
- Split focaccia horizontally in 1/2. Then spread on the cut sides with mustard and mayonnaise. Layer lettuce, the ham, the cheese, the onion, the green pepper, and the tomatoes on bottom half. Place the bread half back. Let chill till serving. Slice into wedges.

Nutrition Information

- Calories: 428 calories
- Protein: 16g protein.
- Total Fat: 13g fat (5g saturated fat)
- Sodium: 898mg sodium
- Fiber: 3g fiber)
- Total Carbohydrate: 62g carbohydrate (11g sugars
- Cholesterol: 45mg cholesterol

74. Giant Picnic Sandwich

Serving: 6-8 servings. | Prep: 15mins | Cook: 20mins | Ready in:

Ingredients

- 1 package (16 ounces) hot roll mix
- 1 teaspoon milk
- 2 teaspoons sesame seeds
- 1/2 cup creamy Italian salad dressing
- 6 to 8 lettuce leaves
- 6 ounces thinly sliced fully cooked ham
- 6 ounces thinly sliced Genoa salami
- 1 medium cucumber, sliced
- 4 slices red onion, separated into rings
- 6 ounces sliced Swiss cheese
- 1 medium green pepper, sliced
- 2 medium tomatoes, thinly sliced

Direction

- Prepare the hot roll mix following the package directions. Roll or pat into a circle (about 12-

inch). Put into an oiled 12" pizza pan. Allow to rise with a cover in warm place for half an hour or until doubled.

- Brush milk over and sprinkle sesame seeds over. Bake at 375° until golden brown, about 20-25 mins. Place on wire rack to cool.
- Cut horizontally in 1/2, then spread onto the cut sides with salad dressing. Layer lettuce, the ham, the salami, followed by the cucumber, the onion, the cheese, then the green pepper and tomatoes on bottom half. Replace the top half. Place in the refrigerator until ready to enjoy. Slice into wedges.

Nutrition Information

- Calories: 471 calories
- Protein: 22g protein.
- Total Fat: 21g fat (8g saturated fat)
- Sodium: 1147mg sodium
- Fiber: 3g fiber)
- Total Carbohydrate: 46g carbohydrate (7g sugars
- Cholesterol: 51mg cholesterol

75. Gourmet Deli Turkey Wraps

Serving: 6 servings. | Prep: 15mins | Cook: 0mins | Ready in:

Ingredients

- 2 tablespoons water
- 2 tablespoons red wine vinegar
- 1 tablespoon olive oil
- 1/8 teaspoon pepper
- 3/4 pound sliced deli turkey
- 6 flour tortillas (8 inches), room temperature
- 4 cups spring mix salad greens
- 2 medium pears, peeled and sliced
- 6 tablespoons crumbled blue cheese
- 6 tablespoons dried cranberries
- 1/4 cup chopped walnuts

Direction

- Whisk the pepper, oil, vinegar and water in a small bowl.
- Among the tortillas, distribute the turkey, then top with salad greens, pears, cheese, cranberries and walnuts. Drizzle it with dressing and roll it up tightly. Use toothpicks to secure.

Nutrition Information

- Calories: 330 calories
- Fiber: 3g fiber)
- Total Carbohydrate: 44g carbohydrate (10g sugars
- Cholesterol: 25mg cholesterol
- Protein: 17g protein.
- Total Fat: 11g fat (2g saturated fat)
- Sodium: 819mg sodium

76. Greek Hero

Serving: 4 servings. | Prep: 15mins | Cook: 0mins | Ready in:

Ingredients

- HUMMUS:
- 2 tablespoons lemon juice
- 1 tablespoon olive oil
- 1 can (15 ounces) garbanzo beans or chickpeas, rinsed and drained
- 2 garlic cloves, minced
- 1 teaspoon dried oregano
- 1/4 teaspoon salt
- 1/8 teaspoon pepper
- SANDWICH:
- 1 loaf (8 ounces) unsliced French bread
- 2 medium sweet red peppers, cut into thin strips
- 1/2 medium cucumber, sliced
- 2 small tomatoes, sliced
- 1/4 cup thinly sliced red onion

- 1/4 cup chopped ripe olives
- 1/4 cup chopped pimiento-stuffed olives
- 1/2 cup crumbled feta cheese
- 4 lettuce leaves

Direction

- To make hummus: Mix the beans, oil and lemon juice in a food processor, put on a cover and process until smooth. Mix in the pepper, salt, oregano and garlic.
- Halve the bread horizontally. Hollow out the bottom half gently and leave a 1/2-inch shell. Fill the shell with hummus. Layer it with red peppers, cucumber, tomatoes, onion, olives, cheese and lettuce, then place back the bread top. Slice it into quarters.

Nutrition Information

- Calories: 350 calories
- Protein: 12g protein.
- Total Fat: 12g fat (4g saturated fat)
- Sodium: 1219mg sodium
- Fiber: 9g fiber)
- Total Carbohydrate: 50g carbohydrate (0 sugars
- Cholesterol: 17mg cholesterol

77. Ham And Double Cheese Sandwiches

Serving: 4 servings. | Prep: 15mins | Cook: 0mins | Ready in:

Ingredients

- 3 ounces cream cheese, softened
- 2 tablespoons chopped green chilies
- 1 tablespoon onion soup mix
- 1 cup shredded cheddar cheese
- 1/4 cup chopped hazelnuts, toasted, optional
- 8 slices whole wheat bread
- 16 slices fully cooked ham

- 4 lettuce leaves

Direction

- Whisk soup mix, chilies, and cream cheese in a bowl until smooth. Stir in nuts and cheese if wished. Mix well. Place on flour slices of bread then equally spread; then layer each with four ham slices and one lettuce leaf. Put remaining bread on top.

Nutrition Information

- Calories: 444 calories
- Total Fat: 22g fat (13g saturated fat)
- Sodium: 1815mg sodium
- Fiber: 4g fiber)
- Total Carbohydrate: 34g carbohydrate (3g sugars
- Cholesterol: 93mg cholesterol
- Protein: 33g protein.

78. Ham And Spinach Loaf

Serving: 6 servings. | Prep: 25mins | Cook: 0mins | Ready in:

Ingredients

- 1 pound fully cooked ham
- 1/3 cup mayonnaise
- 1 tablespoon Dijon mustard
- 1/4 cup chopped pistachios, toasted
- 2 cups packed fresh spinach
- 3 ounces cream cheese, softened
- 1 tablespoon milk
- 2 teaspoons dill weed
- 1 loaf (1 pound) French bread

Direction

- Process ham till ground/minced in a food processor. Put into medium bowl; add pistachios, mustard and mayonnaise. Mix well; put aside. In cold water, rinse spinach;

cook with only the water clinging to leaves till limp in big skillet. Drain.

- Process dill, milk, cream cheese and spinach till smooth in a food processor; put aside. Lengthwise halve bread; hollow out bottom and top. Leave 1/2-in. shell. Save/discard removed bread. Inside bottom and top halves of bread, spread spinach mixture. Pack ham mixture, slightly mounding, into bottom half. Replace bread top; tightly wrap with foil and chill for 2 hours.

Nutrition Information

- Calories: 506 calories
- Total Carbohydrate: 44g carbohydrate (2g sugars
- Cholesterol: 60mg cholesterol
- Protein: 23g protein.
- Total Fat: 26g fat (7g saturated fat)
- Sodium: 1630mg sodium
- Fiber: 3g fiber)

79. Hassleback Tomato Clubs

Serving: 2 servings | Prep: 15mins | Cook: 0mins |Ready in:

Ingredients

- 4 plum tomatoes
- 2 slices slices Swiss cheese, quartered
- 4 slices cooked bacon strips, halved
- 4 slices deli turkey
- 1/2 medium ripe avocado, peeled and cut into 8 slices
- Cracked pepper

Direction

- Cut in each tomato with 4 crosswise slices and leave them intact at bottom. Fill avocado, turkey, bacon and cheese into each slice, then use pepper to sprinkle over top.

Nutrition Information

- Calories: 272 calories
- Sodium: 803mg sodium
- Fiber: 4g fiber)
- Total Carbohydrate: 9g carbohydrate (3g sugars
- Cholesterol: 48mg cholesterol
- Protein: 21g protein.
- Total Fat: 17g fat (5g saturated fat)

80. Havarti Turkey Hero

Serving: 8 servings. | Prep: 15mins | Cook: 0mins | Ready in:

Ingredients

- 1/3 cup mango chutney
- 2 tablespoons reduced-fat mayonnaise
- 2 tablespoons chopped unsalted peanuts
- Dash cayenne pepper
- 1 loaf (1 pound) French bread, halved lengthwise
- 3/4 pound thinly sliced deli turkey
- 6 lettuce leaves
- 2 ounces thinly sliced Havarti cheese
- 1 medium Red Delicious apple, cored and cut into thin rings

Direction

- Mix together the cayenne, peanuts, mayonnaise and chutney in a small bowl, then spread it evenly on top of the cut side of the bread bottom. Layer it with turkey, lettuce, cheese and apple, then place back the bread top. Slice it into 8 pieces.

Nutrition Information

- Calories: 302 calories
- Protein: 16g protein. Diabetic Exchanges: 3 starch
- Total Fat: 7g fat (2g saturated fat)

- Sodium: 973mg sodium
- Fiber: 2g fiber)
- Total Carbohydrate: 45g carbohydrate (9g sugars
- Cholesterol: 27mg cholesterol

81. Hearty Ham Sandwiches

Serving: 4 servings. | Prep: 5mins | Cook: 0mins | Ready in:

Ingredients

- 2 tablespoons mayonnaise
- 1 tablespoon prepared horseradish
- 1 tablespoon prepared mustard
- 1 tablespoon chopped onion
- 8 slices rye or sourdough bread
- 8 thin slices fully cooked ham
- 4 slices Swiss cheese

Direction

- Mix together onion, mustard, horseradish and mayonnaise in a small bowl, then spread on 4 bread slices. Layer with ham and cheese, then put leftover bread on top.

Nutrition Information

- Calories: 371 calories
- Total Carbohydrate: 34g carbohydrate (5g sugars
- Cholesterol: 48mg cholesterol
- Protein: 22g protein.
- Total Fat: 17g fat (7g saturated fat)
- Sodium: 1034mg sodium
- Fiber: 4g fiber)

82. Hearty Muffuletta Loaf

Serving: 8 servings. | Prep: 15mins | Cook: 0mins | Ready in:

Ingredients

- 1 loaf (1 pound) French bread
- 1/2 cup olive oil
- 1/3 cup red wine vinegar
- 1 teaspoon dried oregano
- 2 garlic cloves, minced
- 1 cup shredded mozzarella cheese
- 1 jar (6-1/2 ounces) marinated quartered artichoke hearts, drained and chopped
- 1/2 cup sliced pimiento-stuffed olives
- 1 can (2-1/4 ounces) sliced ripe olives, drained
- 1/2 cup sliced fresh banana peppers
- 1/4 cup chopped red onion
- 1/4 pound sliced Genoa salami
- 1/4 pound sliced Cotto salami
- 1/4 pound sliced pepperoni
- 1/4 pound sliced provolone cheese

Direction

- Slice bread in 1/2 lengthwise, then hollow out bottom and top, leaving a one-inch shell. (Reserve the removed bread for another use or discard it). Mix the garlic, oregano, vinegar and oil; brush 1/2 on inside of the shell. Put onion, peppers, olives, artichoke hearts and mozzarella cheese into remaining oil mixture. Spoon the mixture into the bottom of the bread shell. Layer with meats then cheese. Replace the bread top. Tightly cover in plastic wrap. Place in the refrigerator until ready to enjoy.

Nutrition Information

- Calories: 606 calories
- Fiber: 2g fiber)
- Total Carbohydrate: 35g carbohydrate (2g sugars
- Cholesterol: 60mg cholesterol
- Protein: 22g protein.
- Total Fat: 43g fat (13g saturated fat)

- Sodium: 1673mg sodium

83. Hearty Veggie Sandwiches

Serving: 2 servings. | Prep: 20mins | Cook: 0mins | Ready in:

Ingredients

- 2 teaspoons mayonnaise
- 2 teaspoons prepared mustard
- 4 slices whole wheat bread
- 4 slices cheddar cheese (3/4 ounce each)
- 2 slices red onion
- 1/4 cup sliced ripe olives, drained
- 1 small tomato, sliced
- 1 medium ripe avocado, peeled and sliced
- 1/8 teaspoon pepper
- 4 tablespoons Italian salad dressing
- 2 lettuce leaves

Direction

- Spread the 2 bread slices with mayonnaise and mustard and layer each with cheese, onion, olives, tomato and avocado. Sprinkle pepper on top.
- Drizzle 1 tbsp. of dressing on each sandwich, then put lettuce on top. Drizzle the leftover bread with leftover dressing, then put them on top of the sandwiches.

Nutrition Information

- Calories: 479 calories
- Total Carbohydrate: 42g carbohydrate (8g sugars
- Cholesterol: 27mg cholesterol
- Protein: 22g protein.
- Total Fat: 29g fat (8g saturated fat)
- Sodium: 1259mg sodium
- Fiber: 10g fiber)

84. Home Run Hoagies

Serving: 12 servings. | Prep: 20mins | Cook: 0mins | Ready in:

Ingredients

- 3/4 cup mayonnaise
- 1/2 cup Italian salad dressing
- 12 hoagie buns, split
- 24 slices thinly sliced deli chicken (about 2-1/2 pounds)
- 12 slices cheddar cheese, halved
- 12 lettuce leaves
- 8 medium tomatoes, sliced

Direction

- Mix together salad dressing and mayonnaise in a small bowl. Spread on cut side of buns. Layer chicken, cheese, lettuce, and tomatoes on bun bottoms, then replace tops of bun.

Nutrition Information

- Calories: 458 calories
- Sodium: 974mg sodium
- Fiber: 3g fiber)
- Total Carbohydrate: 39g carbohydrate (6g sugars
- Cholesterol: 41mg cholesterol
- Protein: 18g protein.
- Total Fat: 26g fat (8g saturated fat)

85. Home Run Slugger Sub

Serving: 8 servings. | Prep: 15mins | Cook: 0mins | Ready in:

Ingredients

- 1 French bread baguette (1 pound and 20 inches long)

- 1/4 pound thinly sliced fully cooked ham
- 1/4 pound thinly sliced bologna
- 1/4 pound thinly sliced hard salami
- 4 romaine leaves
- 6 slices Swiss cheese
- 6 slices Colby cheese
- 1 medium tomato, sliced

Direction

- Slice one end of baguette in the shape of a baseball bat handle using a sharp knife. Halve the loaf lengthwise.
- Place on the bottom half with layer of ham, bologna, salami, romaine, cheeses and tomato, then replace top. Use toothpicks to secure if needed, then cut into slices.

Nutrition Information

- Calories: 511 calories
- Sodium: 1068mg sodium
- Fiber: 4g fiber)
- Total Carbohydrate: 45g carbohydrate (1g sugars
- Cholesterol: 67mg cholesterol
- Protein: 23g protein.
- Total Fat: 27g fat (13g saturated fat)

86. Hot Dog Sandwiches

Serving: 6 servings. | Prep: 10mins | Cook: 0mins | Ready in:

Ingredients

- 6 hot dogs, minced
- 1/2 cup dill pickle relish
- 1/4 cup chili sauce
- 2 tablespoons prepared mustard
- 12 slices bread

Direction

- Mix mustard, chili sauce, relish and hot dogs in a small bowl until well combined. Spread on 6 bread slices; top with the rest of bread. Keep frozen for a maximum of 2 months. Before serving, remove from the freezer for a minimum of 4 hours.

Nutrition Information

- Calories:
- Protein:
- Total Fat:
- Sodium:
- Fiber:
- Total Carbohydrate:
- Cholesterol:

87. Hummus & Veggie Wrap Up

Serving: 1 serving. | Prep: 15mins | Cook: 0mins | Ready in:

Ingredients

- 2 tablespoons hummus
- 1 whole wheat tortilla (8 inches)
- 1/4 cup torn mixed salad greens
- 2 tablespoons finely chopped sweet onion
- 2 tablespoons thinly sliced cucumber
- 2 tablespoons alfalfa sprouts
- 2 tablespoons shredded carrot
- 1 tablespoon balsamic vinaigrette

Direction

- Spread hummus on top of the tortilla and layer it with salad greens, onion, cucumber, sprouts and carrot, then drizzle vinaigrette on top and roll it up tightly.

Nutrition Information

- Calories: 235 calories
- Sodium: 415mg sodium

- Fiber: 5g fiber)
- Total Carbohydrate: 32g carbohydrate (4g sugars
- Cholesterol: 0 cholesterol
- Protein: 7g protein. Diabetic Exchanges: 2 starch
- Total Fat: 8g fat (1g saturated fat)

- Total Carbohydrate: 29g carbohydrate (3g sugars
- Cholesterol: 24mg cholesterol
- Protein: 18g protein. Diabetic Exchanges: 2 medium-fat meat
- Total Fat: 8g fat (3g saturated fat)

88. Italian Turkey Roll Ups

Serving: 6 servings. | Prep: 20mins | Cook: 0mins | Ready in:

Ingredients

- 1 package (8 ounces) fat-free cream cheese
- 1 tablespoon Italian seasoning
- 1/2 teaspoon onion powder
- 1/4 teaspoon garlic powder
- 6 whole wheat tortillas (8 inches), room temperature
- 6 slices deli turkey
- 3 ounces Havarti cheese, cut into six slices
- 1-1/2 cups shredded lettuce
- 3 plum tomatoes, thinly sliced
- 1 medium carrot, shredded
- 1 small cucumber, thinly sliced
- 3 thin slices red onion, separated into rings

Direction

- Beat the garlic powder, onion powder, Italian seasoning and cream cheese in a small bowl until smooth. Over each tortilla, spread 1 heaping tbsp. and layer each with 1 slice of turkey and cheese. Put leftover ingredients on top and roll it up tightly, then use toothpicks to secure.

Nutrition Information

- Calories: 271 calories
- Sodium: 662mg sodium
- Fiber: 3g fiber)

89. Jack O' Lantern Sandwiches

Serving: 8 servings. | Prep: 15mins | Cook: 0mins | Ready in:

Ingredients

- 1/2 cup mayonnaise
- 2 teaspoons Italian salad dressing mix
- 16 slices whole wheat or white bread
- 8 slices American cheese
- 1 pound shaved deli chicken or turkey
- 8 lettuce leaves

Direction

- Combine salad dressing mix and mayonnaise in a bowl, arrange over one side of each bread slice. Arrange lettuce, chicken and cheese atop half of the slices. Place the rest of bread on top of each.
- Use a 4-inch pumpkin-shaped cutter to cut sandwiches. Take out the top slice; with a knife and a small triangular cutter, decorate as wanted. Replace slice.

Nutrition Information

- Calories:
- Protein:
- Total Fat:
- Sodium:
- Fiber:
- Total Carbohydrate:
- Cholesterol:

90. Layered Deli Loaf

Serving: 8 servings. | Prep: 15mins | Cook: 0mins | Ready in:

Ingredients

- 1/4 cup mayonnaise
- 2 tablespoons prepared horseradish, drained
- 1 tablespoon Dijon mustard
- 1 round loaf (1 pound) unsliced bread
- 2 tablespoons butter, softened
- 1/3 pound thinly sliced deli ham
- 1/3 pound sliced Monterey Jack cheese
- 1/3 pound thinly sliced deli turkey
- 1/3 pound sliced cheddar cheese
- 1/3 pound thinly sliced deli roast beef
- 1 medium tomato, sliced
- 1 large dill pickle, sliced lengthwise
- 1 small red onion, thinly sliced
- Lettuce leaves

Direction

- Mix together mustard, horseradish and mayonnaise in a small bowl. Halve bread and hollow out top and bottom of loaf carefully to leave a shell, 3/4 inch in size. Get rid of removed bread or reserve for another use. Spread on cut sides of bread with butter.
- Layer in the shell with ham, 1/3 mayonnaise mixture, Monterey Jack cheese, turkey, another 1/3 of the mayonnaise mixture, cheddar cheese, roast beef, leftover mayonnaise mixture, tomato, pickle, onion and lettuce.
- Replace bread top and use plastic wrap to wrap bread tightly. Place on a cover and chill for a minimum of an hour.

Nutrition Information

- Calories: 474 calories
- Total Carbohydrate: 33g carbohydrate (3g sugars
- Cholesterol: 75mg cholesterol
- Protein: 27g protein.

- Total Fat: 25g fat (12g saturated fat)
- Sodium: 1541mg sodium
- Fiber: 2g fiber)

91. Layered Picnic Loaves

Serving: 2 loaves (12 servings each). | Prep: 15mins | Cook: 0mins | Ready in:

Ingredients

- 2 unsliced loaves (1 pound each) Italian bread
- 1/4 cup olive oil
- 3 garlic cloves, minced
- 2 teaspoons Italian seasoning, divided
- 1/2 pound deli roast beef
- 12 slices part-skim mozzarella cheese (1 ounce each)
- 16 fresh basil leaves
- 3 medium tomatoes, thinly sliced
- 1/4 pound thinly sliced salami
- 1 jar (6-1/2 ounces) marinated artichoke hearts, drained and sliced
- 1 package (10 ounces) ready-to-serve salad greens
- 8 ounces thinly sliced deli chicken
- 1 medium onion, thinly sliced
- 1/4 teaspoon salt
- 1/8 teaspoon pepper

Direction

- Horizontally slice loaves in half; hollow out bottoms and tops, keeping 1/2-inch shells (get rid of the removed bread or keep for other purposes).
- Mix garlic and oil together then brush the inner part of bread shells. Sprinkle a teaspoon Italian seasoning over the brushed surface. Layer onion, chicken, salad greens, artichokes, salami, tomatoes, basil, mozzarella and 1/4 the roast beef onto the bottom of each loaf. Repeat layers. Put in remaining Italian seasoning, pepper, and salt to season.

- If wished, drizzle with the rest of oil mixture. Replace bread tops then use plastic wrap to wrap around tightly. Keep in the fridge for a minimum of 1 hour; slice.

Nutrition Information

- Calories: 341 calories
- Protein: 19g protein.
- Total Fat: 18g fat (7g saturated fat)
- Sodium: 991mg sodium
- Fiber: 2g fiber)
- Total Carbohydrate: 26g carbohydrate (3g sugars
- Cholesterol: 47mg cholesterol

92. Liverwurst Deluxe

Serving: 4 servings. | Prep: 10mins | Cook: 0mins | Ready in:

Ingredients

- 4 onion rolls, split
- 4 teaspoons prepared mustard
- 1/3 to 1/2 pound liverwurst, cut into 1/4-inch slices
- 1/2 pound cooked turkey breast, sliced
- 8 bacon strips, cooked and drained
- 2 slices onion, separated into rings
- Dill pickle slices
- 4 slices cheddar cheese

Direction

- Spread mustard over rolls. Layer the liverwurst, the turkey and the bacon, followed by the onion, then the pickles and the cheese on the bottoms of the rolls. Replace the tops.

Nutrition Information

- Calories:
- Cholesterol:

- Protein:
- Total Fat:
- Sodium:
- Fiber:
- Total Carbohydrate:

93. Lunch Box Special

Serving: 4 servings. | Prep: 10mins | Cook: 0mins | Ready in:

Ingredients

- 1/2 cup peanut butter
- 1/4 cup orange juice
- 1/2 cup finely chopped apples
- 1/2 cup finely chopped dates, optional
- 1/2 cup chopped walnuts, optional
- 8 slices bread

Direction

- Mix orange juice and peanut butter together in a small bowl until blended. Put in walnuts (if wanted), dates, and apples. Spread over 4 bread slices; place the rest of bread atop.

Nutrition Information

- Calories: 401 calories
- Sodium: 419mg sodium
- Fiber: 5g fiber)
- Total Carbohydrate: 51g carbohydrate (22g sugars
- Cholesterol: 1mg cholesterol
- Protein: 13g protein.
- Total Fat: 18g fat (4g saturated fat)

94. Mediterranean Turkey Wraps

Serving: 4 servings. | Prep: 15mins | Cook: 0mins | Ready in:

Ingredients

- 1/3 cup mayonnaise
- 1/4 cup pitted Greek olives
- 2-1/2 teaspoons capers, drained
- 1 teaspoon lemon juice
- 1 small garlic clove
- 4 flour tortillas (10 inches), room temperature
- 4 lettuce leaves
- 3/4 pound thinly sliced cooked turkey
- 2 medium tomatoes, sliced
- 1/2 cup crumbled feta cheese

Direction

- In a food processor, add the first 5 ingredients together and process the mixture, covered, until mixed. Spread mixture over tortillas, then put in layer of lettuce, turkey, tomatoes and cheese. Roll up tortilla and use toothpicks to secure.

Nutrition Information

- Calories: 566 calories
- Protein: 34g protein.
- Total Fat: 28g fat (6g saturated fat)
- Sodium: 886mg sodium
- Fiber: 8g fiber)
- Total Carbohydrate: 36g carbohydrate (2g sugars
- Cholesterol: 79mg cholesterol

- 1/2 teaspoon garlic powder
- 1/2 teaspoon pepper
- 1/8 teaspoon cayenne pepper, optional
- 1 large tomato, chopped
- 1 cup chopped seeded cucumber
- 1/2 cup chopped red onion
- 1 can (2-1/4 ounces) sliced ripe olives, drained
- 2 cups torn romaine
- 8 whole wheat pita pocket halves
- 1/2 cup crumbled feta cheese

Direction

- Whisk the initial 6 ingredients in a big bowl until combined; mix in cayenne if preferred. Add olives, onion, cucumber and tomato, then toss until coated. Let it chill in the fridge until ready to serve.
- Add the lettuce to the vegetables and toss to blend. Spoon into pita halves and sprinkle cheese on top, then serve.

Nutrition Information

- Calories: 354 calories
- Cholesterol: 8mg cholesterol
- Protein: 9g protein.
- Total Fat: 19g fat (4g saturated fat)
- Sodium: 580mg sodium
- Fiber: 7g fiber)
- Total Carbohydrate: 39g carbohydrate (5g sugars

95. Mediterranean Vegetable Pitas

Serving: 4 servings. | Prep: 20mins | Cook: 0mins | Ready in:

Ingredients

- 1/4 cup olive oil
- 2 tablespoons balsamic vinegar
- 2 teaspoons grated lemon peel
- 2 teaspoons minced fresh oregano or 1/2 teaspoon dried oregano

96. Mini Subs

Serving: 4 servings. | Prep: 10mins | Cook: 0mins | Ready in:

Ingredients

- 3 tablespoons mayonnaise
- 4 hot dog buns, split
- 4 slices process American cheese
- 1/4 pound sliced deli ham

- 1/4 pound sliced deli turkey
- 4 slices tomato, halved
- 1 cup shredded lettuce

Direction

- Spread over cut side of bun bottoms with mayonnaise. Put in layer of cheese, ham, turkey, tomato and lettuce, then replace tops.

Nutrition Information

- Calories: 321 calories
- Cholesterol: 43mg cholesterol
- Protein: 19g protein.
- Total Fat: 16g fat (5g saturated fat)
- Sodium: 1082mg sodium
- Fiber: 1g fiber)
- Total Carbohydrate: 26g carbohydrate (5g sugars

97. Mini Tomato Sandwiches

Serving: 4 servings. | Prep: 20mins | Cook: 0mins | Ready in:

Ingredients

- 3 ounces cream cheese, softened
- 1/4 cup mayonnaise
- 2 teaspoons minced fresh basil
- 1/4 teaspoon salt, divided
- 1/4 teaspoon pepper, divided
- 1 French bread baguette (10-1/2 ounces)
- 8 ounces Brie cheese, thinly sliced
- 4 plum tomatoes, sliced

Direction

- Mix together the 1/8 tsp pepper, 1/8 tsp salt, basil, mayonnaise and cream cheese in a small bowl. Put on a cover and chill in the fridge for a minimum of 4 hours.
- Halve the baguette horizontally. Spread the cream cheese mixture on top of the baguette

bottom and layer it with Brie cheese and slices of tomato. Sprinkle leftover pepper and salt. Place back the top and slice it into 4 pieces.

Nutrition Information

- Calories: 562 calories
- Protein: 20g protein.
- Total Fat: 34g fat (16g saturated fat)
- Sodium: 1120mg sodium
- Fiber: 2g fiber)
- Total Carbohydrate: 43g carbohydrate (3g sugars
- Cholesterol: 85mg cholesterol

98. Mint Cucumber Sandwiches

Serving: 16 tea sandwiches. | Prep: 25mins | Cook: 0mins | Ready in:

Ingredients

- 16 slices white bread, crusts removed
- 1/2 cup mint jelly
- 1 large cucumber, peeled and thinly sliced
- 3 medium tomatoes, sliced
- 1/4 teaspoon salt
- 1/4 teaspoon pepper
- 1/3 cup butter, softened

Direction

- Use jelly to spread over 8 bread slices, then put tomatoes and cucumber on top. Use pepper and salt to sprinkle over top. Coat leftover bread with butter and put on top. Slice each sandwich into 2 triangles.

Nutrition Information

- Calories: 132 calories
- Sodium: 236mg sodium
- Fiber: 1g fiber)

- Total Carbohydrate: 21g carbohydrate (8g sugars
- Cholesterol: 10mg cholesterol
- Protein: 2g protein. Diabetic Exchanges: 1 starch
- Total Fat: 5g fat (3g saturated fat)

99. Orange Turkey Croissants

Serving: 6 servings. | Prep: 10mins | Cook: 0mins | Ready in:

Ingredients

- 6 tablespoons spreadable cream cheese
- 6 tablespoons orange marmalade
- 6 croissants, split
- 1/2 cup chopped pecans
- 1 pound thinly sliced deli turkey

Direction

- Smear marmalade and cream cheese onto the bottom half of croissants. Scatter with pecans. Place turkey atop pecans. Place top half over turkey to finish.

Nutrition Information

- Calories: 479 calories
- Cholesterol: 80mg cholesterol
- Protein: 21g protein.
- Total Fat: 25g fat (11g saturated fat)
- Sodium: 1165mg sodium
- Fiber: 3g fiber)
- Total Carbohydrate: 43g carbohydrate (19g sugars

100.   Patriotic Picnic Club

Serving: 3-6 servings. | Prep: 15mins | Cook: 0mins | Ready in:

Ingredients

- 1/2 cup mayonnaise
- 1 to 2 tablespoons chili sauce
- 1 tablespoon sweet pickle relish
- 9 slices bread, toasted
- 3 thin slices deli ham
- 3 slices Swiss cheese
- 3 thin slices deli turkey
- 6 thin slices tomato
- 3 lettuce leaves

Direction

- Mix together pickle relish, chili sauce and mayonnaise in a bowl, then spread 1 tablespoonful on top of each bread slice. Put a slice of ham and Swiss cheese on top of 3 bread slices. Put another bread slice on top of each, then layer turkey, tomato, and lettuce on top and then place leftover bread on top. Use toothpicks to secure if needed, then slice into quarters.

Nutrition Information

- Calories: 349 calories
- Protein: 14g protein.
- Total Fat: 23g fat (6g saturated fat)
- Sodium: 924mg sodium
- Fiber: 1g fiber)
- Total Carbohydrate: 21g carbohydrate (3g sugars
- Cholesterol: 41mg cholesterol

101.   Peanut Butter And Banana Teddy Bear Sandwiches

Serving: 4 sandwiches. | Prep: 20mins | Cook: 0mins | Ready in:

Ingredients

- 4 slices bread
- 2/3 cup creamy peanut butter

- 2 tablespoons honey
- 1 medium banana, thinly sliced or 1/4 cup seedless strawberry jam
- 6 raisins, halved

Direction

- From each bread slice, cut out 2 bear shapes using a 3 1/2-inch teddy bear cookie cutter.
- Mix together the honey and peanut butter in a small bowl. Spread it on top of the 4 teddy bear cutouts. Spread jam or put banana slices and leftover bear cutouts on top. Place 3 raisins on each for the nose and eyes.

Nutrition Information

- Calories: 393 calories
- Cholesterol: 0 cholesterol
- Protein: 13g protein.
- Total Fat: 23g fat (5g saturated fat)
- Sodium: 335mg sodium
- Fiber: 4g fiber)
- Total Carbohydrate: 40g carbohydrate (21g sugars

102. Pear Tea Sandwiches

Serving: 8 tea sandwiches. | Prep: 20mins | Cook: 10mins | Ready in:

Ingredients

- 1 cup dried pears
- 1/4 cup spreadable cream cheese
- 2 tablespoons maple syrup
- 2/3 cup chopped walnuts, toasted
- 8 slices cinnamon-raisin bread, toasted and crusts removed

Direction

- In a small bowl, put the pears. Pour boiling water to cover and allow it to stand for 5

minutes, then drain. Let it cool a bit then chop the pears.
- Mix together the syrup and cream cheese in a small bowl, then mix in the nuts and pears.
- Spread on top of the 4 toast slices, then put leftover toast on top. Slice each sandwich into 2 triangles.

Nutrition Information

- Calories: 230 calories
- Cholesterol: 8mg cholesterol
- Protein: 6g protein.
- Total Fat: 9g fat (2g saturated fat)
- Sodium: 97mg sodium
- Fiber: 4g fiber)
- Total Carbohydrate: 36g carbohydrate (18g sugars

103. Pepper Lover's BLT

Serving: 4 servings. | Prep: 15mins | Cook: 0mins | Ready in:

Ingredients

- 1/4 cup mayonnaise
- 1 tablespoon diced pimientos
- 1/8 teaspoon coarsely ground pepper
- 1/4 teaspoon hot pepper sauce
- 8 slices sourdough bread, toasted
- 4 teaspoons Dijon-mayonnaise blend
- 6 tablespoons shredded sharp cheddar cheese
- 4 pickled jalapeno peppers or green chilies, thinly sliced
- 12 bacon strips, cooked and drained
- 8 tomato slices
- 4 lettuce leaves
- 8 thin slices cooked turkey

Direction

- Mix together pepper sauce, pepper, pimientos and mayonnaise in a small bowl, then refrigerate for a minimum of an hour.
- Spread Dijon-mayonnaise blend on 4 toast slices, then use cheese to sprinkle over. Put turkey, lettuce, tomato, bacon and jalapenos on top. Spread on leftover toast with mayonnaise mixture and put over turkey.

Nutrition Information

- Calories: 485 calories
- Fiber: 3g fiber)
- Total Carbohydrate: 39g carbohydrate (3g sugars
- Cholesterol: 51mg cholesterol
- Protein: 23g protein.
- Total Fat: 26g fat (7g saturated fat)
- Sodium: 1469mg sodium

104.   Pigskin Sandwiches

Serving: 18 servings. | Prep: 40mins | Cook: 20mins | Ready in:

Ingredients

- 1 package (1/4 ounce) active dry yeast
- 1/2 cup sugar, divided
- 2 cups warm water (110° to 115°), divided
- 1/2 cup plus 2 tablespoons butter, softened, divided
- 1-1/2 teaspoons salt
- 1 egg, lightly beaten
- 6-1/2 to 7 cups all-purpose flour
- Mayonnaise or mustard, optional
- Lettuce leaves and sliced tomatoes
- 18 slices process American cheese
- 2-1/2 pounds sliced deli ham
- 4 ounces cream cheese, softened

Direction

- Dissolve in a big bowl with 1/4 cup of warm water with yeast and 2 tsp. of sugar. Allow to stand about 5 minutes. Put in 4 cups of flour, water, leftover sugar, egg, salt and 1/2 cup of butter, then beat the mixture until smooth. Stir in enough amount of leftover flour to make a soft dough.
- Turn dough out on a surface coated with flour and knead for 6 to 8 minutes, until elastic and smooth. Put kneaded dough in a bowl coated with grease and turn one time to grease the top. Place on a cover and allow to rise in a warm area for an hour, until doubled in volume.
- Punch dough down. Turn out dough on a surface coated lightly with flour and split into 18 portions. Shape each into oval and arrange on baking sheets coated with grease, spaced 2 inches apart. Place on a cover and allow to rise for half an hour, until doubled.
- Bake at 350 degrees until turning golden, about 18 to 23 minutes. Melt leftover butter and brush over buns' surface. Transfer from pans to wire racks to cool.
- Divide buns and use mustard or mayonnaise to spread buns if you want. Put lettuce, ham, tomato and cheese on top, then replace bun's tops. Put in a plastic bag with cream cheese, then cut in the corner of bag with a small hole. Pipe on sandwiches with football laces.

Nutrition Information

- Calories: 443 calories
- Total Carbohydrate: 42g carbohydrate (7g sugars
- Cholesterol: 73mg cholesterol
- Protein: 21g protein.
- Total Fat: 20g fat (10g saturated fat)
- Sodium: 1362mg sodium
- Fiber: 1g fiber)

105. Pizza Wraps

Serving: 4 wraps. | Prep: 15mins | Cook: 0mins | Ready in:

Ingredients

- 1 package (8 ounces) sliced pepperoni
- 4 flour tortillas (8 inches), room temperature
- 1/2 cup chopped tomatoes
- 1/4 cup each chopped sweet onion, chopped fresh mushrooms and chopped ripe olives
- 1/4 cup chopped green pepper, optional
- 1 cup shredded part-skim mozzarella cheese

Direction

- Place down off center of each tortilla with pepperoni, then put leftover ingredients on top. Fold sides and bottom tortilla over filling, then roll it up.

Nutrition Information

- Calories: 498 calories
- Sodium: 1428mg sodium
- Fiber: 1g fiber)
- Total Carbohydrate: 29g carbohydrate (2g sugars
- Cholesterol: 64mg cholesterol
- Protein: 22g protein.
- Total Fat: 33g fat (13g saturated fat)

106. Quick Taco Wraps

Serving: 4 servings. | Prep: 15mins | Cook: 0mins | Ready in:

Ingredients

- 1/2 cup cream cheese, softened
- 1/4 cup canned chopped green chilies
- 1/4 cup sour cream
- 2 tablespoons taco seasoning
- 1/2 cup bean dip

- 4 flour tortillas (10 inches)
- 1/2 cup guacamole dip
- 1 small onion, chopped
- 1 small sweet red pepper, chopped
- 1/2 cup shredded cheddar cheese
- 1 can (2-1/4 ounces) sliced ripe olives, drained

Direction

- Beat the cream cheese in a small bowl until it becomes smooth. Mix in the taco seasoning, sour cream and green chilies.
- Spread the bean dip on top of the tortillas to within one-half inch of the edges, then layer it with guacamole dip, cream cheese mixture, onion, pepper, cheese and olives and roll it up tightly, then serve.

Nutrition Information

- Calories: 533 calories
- Sodium: 1538mg sodium
- Fiber: 8g fiber)
- Total Carbohydrate: 48g carbohydrate (3g sugars
- Cholesterol: 51mg cholesterol
- Protein: 14g protein.
- Total Fat: 28g fat (13g saturated fat)

107. Raisin Bagel Stackers

Serving: 2 servings. | Prep: 10mins | Cook: 0mins | Ready in:

Ingredients

- 2 cinnamon raisin bagels (3-1/2 inches), split
- 4 teaspoons reduced-fat cream cheese
- 4 lettuce leaves
- 1/4 pound shaved deli smoked turkey
- 2 fresh dill sprigs
- 2 green onions, sliced
- 2 slices (1/2 ounce each) reduced-fat Swiss cheese

- 4 thin tomato slices
- 1/8 teaspoon salt
- 1/8 teaspoon pepper
- 2 teaspoons reduced-fat mayonnaise

Direction

- Toast the bagels lightly, then spread the bottom halves with cream cheese. Layer it with lettuce, turkey, dill, onions, cheese and tomato, then sprinkle pepper and salt on top. On top halves of the bagels, spread the mayonnaise, then put over tomato.

Nutrition Information

- Calories: 321 calories
- Fiber: 3g fiber)
- Total Carbohydrate: 46g carbohydrate (0 sugars
- Cholesterol: 32mg cholesterol
- Protein: 22g protein. Diabetic Exchanges: 3 starch
- Total Fat: 5g fat (2g saturated fat)
- Sodium: 1029mg sodium

108. Ranch Turkey Wraps

Serving: 4 servings. | Prep: 10mins | Cook: 0mins | Ready in:

Ingredients

- 1/4 cup cream cheese, softened
- 1/4 cup prepared ranch salad dressing
- 4 flour tortillas (10 inches), warmed
- 3/4 pound sliced deli turkey
- 8 slices Monterey Jack cheese
- 1 medium ripe avocado, peeled and sliced
- 1 medium tomato, sliced

Direction

- Beat salad dressing and cream cheese together in a small bowl until smooth, then spread over

tortillas. Put in layer of turkey, cheese, avocado and tomato, then roll tortilla up tightly and halve it.

Nutrition Information

- Calories: 661 calories
- Protein: 35g protein.
- Total Fat: 37g fat (14g saturated fat)
- Sodium: 1719mg sodium
- Fiber: 9g fiber)
- Total Carbohydrate: 41g carbohydrate (2g sugars
- Cholesterol: 96mg cholesterol

109. Ranch Turkey Wraps For 2

Serving: 2 servings. | Prep: 10mins | Cook: 0mins | Ready in:

Ingredients

- 2 tablespoons cream cheese, softened
- 2 tablespoons ranch salad dressing
- 2 flour tortillas (10 inches), warmed
- 6 ounces sliced deli turkey
- 4 slices Monterey Jack cheese
- 1/2 medium ripe avocado, peeled and sliced
- 1/2 medium tomato, sliced

Direction

- Beat salad dressing and cream cheese in a small bowl until they become smooth. Then spread the mixture over the tortillas. Layer with the turkey, the cheese, the avocado, and the tomato. Tightly roll up and cut in 1/2.

Nutrition Information

- Calories: 668 calories
- Protein: 35g protein.
- Total Fat: 37g fat (14g saturated fat)

- Sodium: 1596mg sodium
- Fiber: 9g fiber)
- Total Carbohydrate: 39g carbohydrate (2g sugars
- Cholesterol: 88mg cholesterol

110. Roast Beef BLT

Serving: 4 servings. | Prep: 15mins | Cook: 0mins | Ready in:

Ingredients

- 1 loaf (12 ounces) focaccia bread
- 1/2 cup mayonnaise
- 1 teaspoon prepared horseradish
- 3 lettuce leaves
- 3/4 pound sliced deli roast beef
- 6 bacon strips, cooked
- 8 slices tomato

Direction

- Halve focaccia bread horizontally. Mix horseradish and mayonnaise together, then spread the mixture over cut sides of bread. Layer over bread bottom with lettuce, roast beef, bacon and tomato, then replace top. Slice into wedges.

Nutrition Information

- Calories:
- Protein:
- Total Fat:
- Sodium:
- Fiber:
- Total Carbohydrate:
- Cholesterol:

111. Roast Beef Sandwich Supreme

Serving: 6 servings. | Prep: 15mins | Cook: 0mins | Ready in:

Ingredients

- 1/2 cup sour cream
- 1 tablespoon onion soup mix
- 2 teaspoons prepared horseradish, drained
- 1/8 teaspoon salt
- 1/8 teaspoon pepper
- 12 slices rye bread or pumpernickel bread
- 1 pound sliced deli roast beef (about 12 slices)
- 6 lettuce leaves

Direction

- Mix together pepper, salt, horseradish, soup mix and sour cream in a small bowl, then spread the mixture over 6 bread slices. Put in layer of beef, lettuce and leftover bread.

Nutrition Information

- Calories: 295 calories
- Total Fat: 8g fat (4g saturated fat)
- Sodium: 1008mg sodium
- Fiber: 4g fiber)
- Total Carbohydrate: 33g carbohydrate (3g sugars
- Cholesterol: 55mg cholesterol
- Protein: 21g protein.

112. Salami Pork Sub

Serving: 4 servings. | Prep: 15mins | Cook: 0mins | Ready in:

Ingredients

- 1 loaf (1 pound) unsliced French bread
- 12 slices salami
- 16 slices cooked pork (1/8 inch thick)

- 8 slices provolone cheese
- 24 thin dill pickle slices
- Lettuce leaves
- 1/4 cup mayonnaise
- 2 tablespoons prepared mustard

Direction

- Halve bread lengthwise. Put on the bottom half with layer of salami, pork, cheese, pickles and lettuce. Mix mustard and mayonnaise together, then spread over cut-side of top half of loaf. Replace top and quarter the sandwich.

Nutrition Information

- Calories:
- Cholesterol:
- Protein:
- Total Fat:
- Sodium:
- Fiber:
- Total Carbohydrate:

113.   Seafood Pitas

*Serving: 3 servings. | Prep: 15mins | Cook: 0mins
| Ready in:*

Ingredients

- 1 can (7-1/2 ounces) salmon, drained, bones and skin removed
- 1 can (6 ounces) crabmeat, drained, flaked and cartilage removed
- 1 can (4 ounces) small shrimp, rinsed and drained or 1 cup frozen cooked salad shrimp
- 3/4 cup mayonnaise
- 1/4 cup finely chopped celery
- 1/4 cup finely chopped onion
- 1 teaspoon dill weed
- 3 pita breads (6 inches), halved
- 3 lettuce leaves

Direction

- Mix together dill, onion, celery, mayonnaise, shrimp, crab and salmon in a bowl. Use lettuce to line each pita half, then fill seafood mixture into pita.

Nutrition Information

- Calories: 770 calories
- Cholesterol: 181mg cholesterol
- Protein: 39g protein.
- Total Fat: 51g fat (7g saturated fat)
- Sodium: 1649mg sodium
- Fiber: 2g fiber)
- Total Carbohydrate: 35g carbohydrate (2g sugars

114.   Sloppy Joe BLT's

*Serving: 6 servings. | Prep: 15mins | Cook: 0mins
| Ready in:*

Ingredients

- 4 cups hearts of romaine salad mix
- 1 large tomato, chopped
- 1 cup shredded part-skim mozzarella cheese
- 1 cup shredded cheddar cheese
- 1/2 cup real bacon bits
- 1/2 cup mayonnaise
- 4-1/2 teaspoons cider vinegar
- 1/4 teaspoon salt
- 1/8 teaspoon pepper
- 12 slices Italian bread (3/4 inch thick), toasted

Direction

- Mix together bacon, cheeses, tomato and salad mix in a big bowl. Mix together pepper, salt, vinegar and mayonnaise in a small bowl, then pour over salad mixture and toss to coat well. Pour over 6 slices of bread with 3/4 cup of the salad mixture and place leftover bread on top.

Nutrition Information

- Calories: 460 calories
- Protein: 17g protein.
- Total Fat: 28g fat (10g saturated fat)
- Sodium: 1042mg sodium
- Fiber: 3g fiber)
- Total Carbohydrate: 34g carbohydrate (5g sugars
- Cholesterol: 48mg cholesterol

---

115. Smoked Turkey Vegetable Wraps

Serving: 2 servings. | Prep: 10mins | Cook: 0mins | Ready in:

Ingredients

- 1/2 medium cucumber, peeled, seeded and cut into strips
- 1/2 medium carrot, cut into strips
- 1/2 medium green pepper, cut into strips
- 1/4 cup fat-free Italian salad dressing
- 1/4 cup reduced-fat spreadable garden vegetable cream cheese
- 2 flour tortillas (8 inches), room temperature
- 1/4 pound thinly sliced deli smoked turkey
- 1/2 cup chopped fresh spinach

Direction

- Mix together the Italian dressing, green pepper, carrot and cucumber in a small resealable plastic bag. Close the bag tightly and flip to coat. Chill in the fridge for a minimum of 2 hours.
- Over the tortillas, spread the cream cheese, then put turkey and spinach on top. Drain and get rid of the dressing, then put vegetables on top of the spinach; roll up. Put the wraps in the microwave to warm prior to serving if preferred.

Nutrition Information

- Calories: 299 calories
- Protein: 21g protein.
- Total Fat: 9g fat (3g saturated fat)
- Sodium: 1024mg sodium
- Fiber: 2g fiber)
- Total Carbohydrate: 32g carbohydrate (6g sugars
- Cholesterol: 36mg cholesterol

---

116. South Of The Border Wraps

Serving: 4 servings. | Prep: 10mins | Cook: 10mins | Ready in:

Ingredients

- 1/2 cup black beans, rinsed and drained
- 2 tablespoons salsa
- 1 tablespoon chopped green onions
- 1 tablespoon minced fresh cilantro
- 4 flour tortillas (6 inches)
- 1 medium tomato, chopped
- 1 cup shredded Monterey Jack cheese
- 2 to 4 tablespoons butter

Direction

- Slightly mash the beans in a small bowl, then add the cilantro, onions and salsa. Spread it on top of the tortillas, then sprinkle cheese and tomato on top. Roll it up tightly.
- Melt 2-4 tbsp. of butter in a big frying pan, then add tortillas, seam side facing down. Cook the tortillas on all sides until it turns golden brown in color; add butter if needed.

Nutrition Information

- Calories: 191 calories
- Cholesterol: 40mg cholesterol
- Protein: 9g protein.

- Total Fat: 14g fat (9g saturated fat)
- Sodium: 308mg sodium
- Fiber: 2g fiber)
- Total Carbohydrate: 7g carbohydrate (2g sugars

Special Eggplant Subs

Serving: 4 servings. | Prep: 15mins | Cook: 30mins | Ready in:

Ingredients

- 2 eggs
- 1 cup dry bread crumbs
- 1 medium eggplant, peeled and sliced 1/4 inch thick
- 4 submarine sandwich buns (10 inches), split
- Leaf lettuce
- 1 jar (7-1/4 ounces) roasted red peppers, drained and sliced
- 8 slices part-skim mozzarella cheese
- 2 medium tomatoes, thinly sliced
- 1 can (4-1/4 ounces) chopped ripe olives, drained
- Italian or vinaigrette salad dressing

Direction

- Beat the eggs in a shallow bowl. In a separate bowl, put the breadcrumbs. Dunk the slices of eggplant into the egg, then coat it with crumbs. Put it on a greased baking tray.
- Let it bake for 30 minutes at 350 degrees or until it becomes crispy; allow it to cool. Layer the lettuce, eggplant, red peppers, cheese, tomatoes and olives on the bottom of each bun, then drizzle the salad dressing on top and place back the bun tops.

Nutrition Information

- Calories: 770 calories

- Total Carbohydrate: 102g carbohydrate (14g sugars
- Cholesterol: 150mg cholesterol
- Protein: 31g protein.
- Total Fat: 25g fat (10g saturated fat)
- Sodium: 1569mg sodium
- Fiber: 8g fiber)

---

118. Spicy Shrimp Slaw Pitas

Serving: 6 servings. | Prep: 30mins | Cook: 5mins | Ready in:

Ingredients

- 1-1/2 pounds uncooked shrimp (31-40 per pound), peeled, deveined and coarsely chopped
- 1 tablespoon olive oil
- 1 teaspoon paprika
- SLAW:
- 1/3 cup reduced-fat plain Greek yogurt
- 1/3 cup peach salsa or salsa of your choice
- 1 tablespoon honey
- 1/2 teaspoon salt
- 1/2 teaspoon pepper
- 1 package (12 ounces) broccoli coleslaw mix
- 2 cups fresh baby spinach
- 1/4 cup shredded carrots
- 1/4 cup frozen shelled edamame, thawed
- 12 whole wheat pita pocket halves

Direction

- Preheat broiler. Toss shrimp, paprika and oil together in a small bowl, then remove to a 15"x10"x1" baking pan lined with foil. Broil 4 to 5 inches until shrimp are pink, about 3 to 4 minutes while stirring one time.
- Whisk together pepper, salt, honey, salsa and yogurt in a small bowl, then put in shrimp, edamame, carrots, spinach and coleslaw mix, toss to coat.
- Put pita pockets on a baking sheet, then broil 4 to 5 inches until browned slightly, about 1 to 2

minutes per side. Fill 1/2 cup of shrimp mixture into each pita half.

Nutrition Information

- Calories: 322 calories
- Fiber: 7g fiber)
- Total Carbohydrate: 41g carbohydrate (7g sugars
- Cholesterol: 139mg cholesterol
- Protein: 28g protein. Diabetic Exchanges: 3 lean meat
- Total Fat: 6g fat (1g saturated fat)
- Sodium: 641mg sodium

119.   Spinach Feta Croissants

Serving: 6 servings. | Prep: 20mins | Cook: 0mins | Ready in:

Ingredients

- 1/2 cup Italian salad dressing
- 6 croissants, split
- 3 cups fresh baby spinach
- 4 plum tomatoes, thinly sliced
- 1 cup (4 ounces) crumbled feta cheese

Direction

- Brush the salad dressing on top of the cut sides of the croissants. Layer the spinach, tomatoes and feta cheese on the bottom halves, then place back the tops.

Nutrition Information

- Calories: 363 calories
- Fiber: 3g fiber)
- Total Carbohydrate: 30g carbohydrate (4g sugars
- Cholesterol: 48mg cholesterol
- Protein: 9g protein.
- Total Fat: 23g fat (10g saturated fat)

- Sodium: 959mg sodium

120.   Stuffed Ham Slices

Serving: 8 servings. | Prep: 10mins | Cook: 0mins | Ready in:

Ingredients

- 1 package (8 ounces) cream cheese, softened
- 3/4 cup minced celery
- 1/2 cup shredded cheddar cheese
- 1/3 cup minced fresh parsley
- 1/4 cup mayonnaise
- 2 tablespoons finely chopped onion
- 1 loaf Italian bread (1 pound), unsliced
- 1/2 pound fully cooked ham, thinly sliced
- 3 to 4 whole dill pickles, sliced lengthwise

Direction

- Mix together the first 6 ingredients in a bowl. Halve the bread lengthwise, then spread the cheese mixture on the cut sides. Put 1/2 of the ham on the bottom half, then put the pickles and leftover ham on top. Place back the top. Wrap it in plastic wrap tightly, then let it chill in the fridge for a minimum of 2 hours prior to serving. Slice it into 8 pieces.

Nutrition Information

- Calories: 372 calories
- Protein: 15g protein.
- Total Fat: 21g fat (8g saturated fat)
- Sodium: 1070mg sodium
- Fiber: 2g fiber)
- Total Carbohydrate: 31g carbohydrate (2g sugars
- Cholesterol: 59mg cholesterol

121. Summer Tea Sandwiches

Serving: 12 servings. | Prep: 45mins | Cook: 20mins | Ready in:

Ingredients

- 1/2 teaspoon dried tarragon
- 1/2 teaspoon salt, divided
- 1/4 teaspoon pepper
- 1 pound boneless skinless chicken breasts
- 1/2 cup reduced-fat mayonnaise
- 1 tablespoon finely chopped red onion
- 1 teaspoon dill weed
- 1/2 teaspoon lemon juice
- 24 slices soft multigrain bread, crusts removed
- 1 medium cucumber, thinly sliced
- 1/4 medium cantaloupe, cut into 12 thin slices

Direction

- Mix together the pepper, 1/4 tsp salt and tarragon, then massage it over the chicken. Put it on a baking tray coated with cooking spray.
- Let it bake for 20 to 25 minutes at 350 degrees or until a thermometer registers 170 degrees. Allow it to cool to room temperature, then slice it thinly.
- Mix together the leftover salt, lemon juice, dill, onion and mayonnaise in a small bowl, then spread it on top of the 12 slices of bread. Put the cantaloupe, chicken, cucumber and leftover bread on top. Halve the sandwiches diagonally, then serve it right away.

Nutrition Information

- Calories: 212 calories
- Fiber: 4g fiber)
- Total Carbohydrate: 27g carbohydrate (5g sugars
- Cholesterol: 24mg cholesterol
- Protein: 13g protein.
- Total Fat: 6g fat (1g saturated fat)
- Sodium: 450mg sodium

122. Summer Veggie Sandwiches

Serving: 4 servings. | Prep: 15mins | Cook: 0mins | Ready in:

Ingredients

- 4 ounces cream cheese, softened
- 8 slices whole wheat bread
- 1 small cucumber, sliced
- 1/2 cup alfalfa sprouts
- 2 teaspoons olive oil
- 2 teaspoons red wine vinegar
- 1 large tomato, sliced
- 4 lettuce leaves
- 3/4 cup sliced pepperoncini
- 1 medium ripe avocado, peeled and mashed

Direction

- Spread the cream cheese on top of the 4 bread slices, then layer each with cucumber and sprouts. Mix together the vinegar and oil, then drizzle on top of the sprouts. Layer with tomato, lettuce and pepperoncini. Spread avocado on top of the leftover bread, then put over the top.

Nutrition Information

- Calories: 356 calories
- Sodium: 360mg sodium
- Fiber: 8g fiber)
- Total Carbohydrate: 32g carbohydrate (5g sugars
- Cholesterol: 32mg cholesterol
- Protein: 11g protein.
- Total Fat: 21g fat (8g saturated fat)

123.   Super Sandwich

Serving: 8 servings. | Prep: 30mins | Cook: 0mins | Ready in:

Ingredients

- 1 medium cucumber, peeled, seeded and chopped
- 1 medium tomato, seeded and chopped
- 1 small onion, chopped
- 1/2 cup pitted ripe olives, chopped
- 1/2 cup pimiento-stuffed olives, chopped
- 1/4 cup prepared Italian salad dressing
- 1 round loaf (1-1/2 pounds) unsliced sourdough, white or whole wheat bread
- 1/2 pound sliced fully cooked ham
- 1/4 pound sliced salami
- 1/4 pound sliced cooked pork
- 1/2 pound sliced Swiss cheese
- 1/2 pound sliced Muenster cheese

Direction

- Blend salad dressing, olives, onion, tomato and cucumber in a big bowl; put aside.
- Carve out 1" off the bread top and put aside. Gently remove the inside of the loaf, keeping a 1/2" shell (throw removed bread away or reserve for another purpose.) Pack 1/4 ham, salami, pork and cheeses into the shell in the exact order. Add 1/3 of vegetable mixture on top. Make more layers, finishing with meat and cheeses, then carefully press down to flatten if necessary.
- Top with bread piece carved out earlier; cover securely in plastic wrap. Leave in the fridge before serving.

Nutrition Information

- Calories: 641 calories
- Fiber: 4g fiber)
- Total Carbohydrate: 50g carbohydrate (4g sugars
- Cholesterol: 100mg cholesterol
- Protein: 35g protein.

- Total Fat: 33g fat (15g saturated fat)
- Sodium: 1767mg sodium

124.   Super Sub Sandwich

Serving: 10-15 servings. | Prep: 10mins | Cook: 0mins | Ready in:

Ingredients

- 3 ounces cream cheese, softened
- 1 loaf (20 inches) unsliced French bread, halved lengthwise
- 6 slices deli ham
- 6 slices provolone cheese
- 1 jar (4-1/2 ounces) sliced mushrooms, drained
- 2 medium tomatoes, thinly sliced, optional
- 1 small onion, thinly sliced
- 2 banana peppers, thinly sliced
- 2 cups shredded lettuce

Direction

- Lather bottom half of bread with cream cheese. Place ham, followed by the cheese, then the mushrooms, the tomatoes if preferred, then the onion, finally peppers and lettuce. Replace the top. Cut into slices (1 1/2 inches)

Nutrition Information

- Calories: 159 calories
- Fiber: 2g fiber)
- Total Carbohydrate: 18g carbohydrate (1g sugars
- Cholesterol: 18mg cholesterol
- Protein: 8g protein.
- Total Fat: 6g fat (3g saturated fat)
- Sodium: 418mg sodium

125.   Super Supper Hero

*Serving: 6 servings. | Prep: 20mins | Cook: 10mins
| Ready in:*

Ingredients

- 1/4 cup olive oil
- 2-1/2 cups cubed eggplant
- 1 each medium green, sweet yellow and red peppers, julienned
- 1 large red onion, thinly sliced
- 1 medium tomato, chopped
- 1 teaspoon dried oregano
- 1/2 teaspoon salt
- 1/4 teaspoon pepper
- 1 loaf (1 pound) unsliced Italian bread
- Lettuce leaves
- 1/2 pound sliced fully cooked ham
- 1/2 pound sliced cooked turkey breast
- 1/4 pound sliced hard salami
- 8 slices part-skim mozzarella cheese

Direction

- Heat oil in a big skillet over moderately high heat. Put in onion, peppers and eggplant, then cook and stir until vegetables are tender yet still crispy, about 4 to 6 minutes. Put in pepper, salt, oregano and tomato, then take away from the heat.
- Halve bread lengthways, then hollow out bottom of loaf to leave a shell of 3/4 inch. Reserve removed bread for another use. Layer lettuce, ham, turkey, salami, and cheese on bottom, then put vegetables on top and replace top. Use toothpicks to secure and cut bread crosswise into 6 slices.

Nutrition Information

- Calories: 606 calories
- Sodium: 1650mg sodium
- Fiber: 5g fiber)
- Total Carbohydrate: 49g carbohydrate (8g sugars
- Cholesterol: 96mg cholesterol

- Protein: 42g protein.
- Total Fat: 27g fat (8g saturated fat)

126.   Tom & Ava Sandwiches

*Serving: 4 servings. | Prep: 15mins | Cook: 0mins
| Ready in:*

Ingredients

- 1/2 cup cream cheese, softened
- 8 slices whole wheat bread
- 1 medium ripe avocado, peeled and thinly sliced
- 1 large tomato, thinly sliced
- 8 slices red onion
- 1 cup alfalfa sprouts

Direction

- Spread cream cheese on 4 bread slices, then layer it with avocado, tomato, onion and sprouts; put the leftover bread on top.

Nutrition Information

- Calories: 329 calories
- Protein: 11g protein.
- Total Fat: 19g fat (8g saturated fat)
- Sodium: 357mg sodium
- Fiber: 8g fiber)
- Total Carbohydrate: 31g carbohydrate (5g sugars
- Cholesterol: 32mg cholesterol

127.   Tomato & Avocado Sandwiches

*Serving: 2 servings. | Prep: 10mins | Cook: 0mins
| Ready in:*

Ingredients

- 1/2 medium ripe avocado, peeled and mashed
- 4 slices whole wheat bread, toasted
- 1 medium tomato, sliced
- 2 tablespoons finely chopped shallot
- 1/4 cup hummus

Direction

- Spread the avocado on top of 2 toast slices, then put shallot and tomato on top. Spread the hummus on top of the leftover toasts, then place over tops.

Nutrition Information

- Calories: 278 calories
- Sodium: 379mg sodium
- Fiber: 9g fiber)
- Total Carbohydrate: 35g carbohydrate (6g sugars
- Cholesterol: 0 cholesterol
- Protein: 11g protein. Diabetic Exchanges: 2 starch
- Total Fat: 11g fat (2g saturated fat)

128.   Tomato Sandwiches

Serving: 4 servings. | Prep: 5mins | Cook: 0mins |Ready in:

Ingredients

- 8 slices white bread, toasted if desired
- 1/2 cup mayonnaise, divided
- 2 large ripe tomatoes, sliced 1/2 inch thick
- 1/4 teaspoon salt
- 1/4 teaspoon pepper

Direction

- Spread 1/2 of the mayonnaise on 4 bread slices. Put tomatoes on top and sprinkle pepper and salt to season. Spread the leftover mayonnaise on top of the leftover bread, then close the sandwiches.

Nutrition Information

- Calories:
- Cholesterol:
- Protein:
- Total Fat:
- Sodium:
- Fiber:
- Total Carbohydrate:

129.   Triple Decker Salmon Club

Serving: 2 servings. | Prep: 15mins | Cook: 0mins | Ready in:

Ingredients

- 3/4 cup 4% cottage cheese
- 1/4 cup dill pickle relish
- 1 can (6 ounces) salmon, drained, bones and skin removed
- 1 celery rib, chopped
- 6 slices bread, toasted
- 2 lettuce leaves, optional

Direction

- Mix together pickle relish and cottage cheese in a small bowl. Mix celery and salmon in another bowl.
- To make each sandwich, put lettuce, if desired, and 1/2 of cottage cheese mixture on top of a toast piece. Place another toast piece on top, then spread with 1/2 of the salmon mixture. Put a third toast piece on top.

Nutrition Information

- Calories: 455 calories
- Cholesterol: 57mg cholesterol
- Protein: 33g protein.
- Total Fat: 13g fat (4g saturated fat)

- Sodium: 1494mg sodium
- Fiber: 3g fiber)
- Total Carbohydrate: 51g carbohydrate (15g sugars

- Sugar: 3
- Protein: 18
- Total Fat: 16
- Saturated Fat: 2
- Fiber: 5
- Cholesterol: 21
- Total Carbohydrate: 25

---

130.   Tuna Salad Pockets

Serving: 4 | Prep: 15mins | Cook: | Ready in:

Ingredients

- 1 (12 ounce) can solid white tuna (water-pack), drained
- ¼ cup finely chopped onion
- ¼ cup thinly sliced celery
- ¼ cup shredded carrot
- 1 tablespoon capers, rinsed and drained
- 2 tablespoons olive oil
- 2 tablespoons lime juice
- 1 tablespoon Dijon-style mustard
- 1 tablespoon Champagne vinegar or white wine vinegar
- 1½ cups torn mixed salad greens
- ½ cup slivered almonds, toasted
- 2 large whole wheat pita bread rounds, halved crosswise

Direction

- Mix capers, carrot, celery, onion and tuna in a medium bowl; put aside. Vinaigrette: Mix vinegar, Dijon mustard, lime juice and olive oil in small screw-top jar. Cover; shake well to mix. Put vinaigrette on tuna mixture; gently toss to mix. Add almonds and greens; gently toss to mix.
- Halve pita breads; in each of the 4 shallow salad bowls, put pita bread. Put tuna mixture over pita bread halves; creates 4 servings.

Nutrition Information

- Calories: 305 calories;
- Sodium: 447

---

131.   Tuna Salad Wraps

Serving: | Prep: 15mins | Cook: | Ready in:

Ingredients

- 1 can albacore tuna
- 2 large flour tortilla
- 3 tablespoons olive oil
- 4 ounces chopped onion
- 4 ounces chopped kalamata olives
- 1 ounces chopped chives
- 1/2 teaspoon salt
- 1 teaspoon black pepper
- 4 ounces fresh spinach
- 2 ounces salad dressing
- 2 ounces chopped dill pickels

Direction

- Preparation
- To make tuna salad, combine chives, pepper, salt, olive oil, pickles, onions and chopped olives.
- Distribute tuna salad onto tortillas.
- On top of salad, put dressing and fresh spinach, together with any other preferred embellishments.
- Fold or roll tortilla, then cut into sections as you want.

132. Turkey & Swiss With Herbed Greens

Serving: 8 servings. | Prep: 30mins | Cook: 0mins | Ready in:

Ingredients

- 2 tablespoons balsamic vinegar
- 1 tablespoon olive oil
- 1/2 teaspoon dried oregano
- 1/4 teaspoon garlic powder
- 1/4 teaspoon dried basil
- 4 cups torn mixed salad greens
- 2 tablespoons finely chopped onion
- 16 slices multigrain bread
- 3/4 pound thinly sliced deli turkey
- 8 slices Swiss cheese
- 2 large tomatoes, sliced

Direction

- Whisk together basil, garlic powder, oregano, oil and vinegar in a big bowl, then put in onion and salad greens, toss to coat well.
- Layer turkey, cheese, tomatoes and salad greens on 8 bread slices, then put leftover bread on top.

Nutrition Information

- Calories: 297 calories
- Protein: 20g protein. Diabetic Exchanges: 2 starch
- Total Fat: 12g fat (6g saturated fat)
- Sodium: 686mg sodium
- Fiber: 5g fiber)
- Total Carbohydrate: 28g carbohydrate (7g sugars
- Cholesterol: 40mg cholesterol

133. Turkey Avocado Sandwiches

Serving: 2 servings. | Prep: 10mins | Cook: 0mins | Ready in:

Ingredients

- 3 ounces fat-free cream cheese
- 2 teaspoons taco sauce
- 4 drops hot pepper sauce
- 4 slices whole wheat bread
- 4 ounces sliced cooked turkey
- 1/2 medium ripe avocado, peeled and sliced
- 1 medium tomato, sliced
- 2 to 4 tablespoons minced fresh cilantro
- 2 lettuce leaves

Direction

- Beat the cream cheese in a big bowl until it becomes smooth. Beat in pepper sauce and taco sauce, then spread it on top of the bread.
- On 2 bread slices, layer the turkey, avocado and tomato, then sprinkle cilantro on top. Put lettuce and leftover bread on top.

Nutrition Information

- Calories: 399 calories
- Total Fat: 11g fat (2g saturated fat)
- Sodium: 617mg sodium
- Fiber: 7g fiber)
- Total Carbohydrate: 40g carbohydrate (0 sugars
- Cholesterol: 52mg cholesterol
- Protein: 33g protein. Diabetic Exchanges: 3 lean meat

134. Turkey BLT

Serving: 2 servings. | Prep: 5mins | Cook: 5mins | Ready in:

Ingredients

- 2 tablespoons mayonnaise
- 1 tablespoon spicy brown mustard
- 1 tablespoon honey
- 2 large pumpernickel rolls, split
- 4 slices cooked turkey
- 4 bacon strips, cooked and drained
- 2 slices Swiss cheese
- 4 slices tomato
- Lettuce leaves

Direction

- Mix together honey, mustard and mayonnaise in a small bowl, then spread mixture on cut sides of rolls. Layer turkey, bacon and cheese on the bottom halves of rolls, then broil 4 inches away from the heat until cheese starts to melt, about 2 to 3 minutes. Put lettuce and tomato on top, then replace roll tops.

Nutrition Information

- Calories:
- Total Fat:
- Sodium:
- Fiber:
- Total Carbohydrate:
- Cholesterol:
- Protein:

135. Turkey Gouda Club

Serving: 2 servings. | Prep: 15mins | Cook: 0mins | Ready in:

Ingredients

- 1/2 cup shredded smoked Gouda cheese
- 4-1/2 teaspoons mayonnaise
- 1 tablespoon thinly sliced green onion
- 1/4 teaspoon garlic powder
- 1/4 teaspoon coarsely ground pepper

- 4 slices whole wheat bread, crusts removed and toasted
- 2 teaspoons butter, softened
- 1/4 pound shaved deli hickory smoked turkey
- 4 slices tomato
- 1/2 medium ripe avocado, peeled and mashed
- 2 romaine leaves

Direction

- Mix together pepper, garlic powder, onion, mayonnaise and cheese in a small bowl. Use butter to spread on 2 toast slices. Put in layer of cheese mixture, turkey, tomato, avocado and romaine, then place leftover toast on top. Slice each sandwich in half.

Nutrition Information

- Calories: 495 calories
- Protein: 28g protein.
- Total Fat: 30g fat (10g saturated fat)
- Sodium: 1013mg sodium
- Fiber: 8g fiber)
- Total Carbohydrate: 31g carbohydrate (5g sugars
- Cholesterol: 66mg cholesterol

136. Turkey Guacamole Wraps

Serving: 2 servings. | Prep: 15mins | Cook: 0mins | Ready in:

Ingredients

- 1 small ripe avocado, peeled
- 2 tablespoons mayonnaise
- 1-1/2 teaspoons lime juice
- 1/4 teaspoon minced garlic
- 1/8 teaspoon Louisiana-style hot sauce
- 2 flour tortillas (10 inches), room temperature
- 1/4 pound sliced deli smoked turkey
- 1/2 cup chopped red onion
- 1 cup torn romaine

Direction

- In a food processor, add the first 5 ingredients together and process the mixture until smooth. Spread mixture over tortillas, then put lettuce, onion and turkey on top. Roll up tortilla.

Nutrition Information

- Calories: 506 calories
- Total Carbohydrate: 46g carbohydrate (5g sugars
- Cholesterol: 21mg cholesterol
- Protein: 20g protein.
- Total Fat: 27g fat (5g saturated fat)
- Sodium: 1045mg sodium
- Fiber: 8g fiber)

---

137. Turkey Pitas With Creamy Slaw

Serving: 4 servings. | Prep: 10mins | Cook: 0mins | Ready in:

Ingredients

- 3 cups coleslaw mix
- 1/4 cup golden raisins
- 3 tablespoons chopped red onion
- 1/3 cup reduced-fat mayonnaise
- 3 tablespoons mango chutney
- 8 pita pocket halves
- 1/2 pound sliced deli turkey
- 8 ready-to-serve fully cooked bacon strips, warmed
- 1 medium cucumber, thinly sliced

Direction

- Mix together onion, raisins and coleslaw mix in a big bowl, then put in chutney and mayonnaise, tossing to coat well. Use turkey, cucumber and bacon to line pita halves, then fill in coleslaw mixture.

Nutrition Information

- Calories: 427 calories
- Fiber: 3g fiber)
- Total Carbohydrate: 57g carbohydrate (18g sugars
- Cholesterol: 27mg cholesterol
- Protein: 21g protein.
- Total Fat: 12g fat (2g saturated fat)
- Sodium: 1257mg sodium

---

138. Turkey Roll Ups

Serving: 10 servings. | Prep: 15mins | Cook: 0mins | Ready in:

Ingredients

- 1 package (8 ounces) fat-free cream cheese
- 1/2 cup reduced-fat mayonnaise
- 1/4 teaspoon dried basil
- 1/4 teaspoon dried oregano
- 1/4 teaspoon dill weed
- 1/4 teaspoon garlic powder
- 10 flour tortillas (6 inches), room temperature
- 1 medium onion, chopped
- 10 slices deli turkey breast (1 ounce each)
- Shredded lettuce

Direction

- Mix initial 6 ingredients in a small bowl; beat till smooth. Spread on tortillas. Sprinkle onion on. Put lettuce and turkey on top. Tightly roll up like a jellyroll. Immediately serve.

Nutrition Information

- Calories: 259 calories
- Protein: 13g protein. Diabetic Exchanges: 2 starch
- Total Fat: 9g fat (2g saturated fat)
- Sodium: 701mg sodium
- Fiber: 2g fiber)

- Total Carbohydrate: 33g carbohydrate (0 sugars
- Cholesterol: 17mg cholesterol

139. Turkey Tea Sandwiches With Basil Mayonnaise

Serving: 20 tea sandwiches. | Prep: 15mins | Cook: 0mins | Ready in:

Ingredients

- 1/2 cup mayonnaise
- 1/3 cup loosely packed basil leaves
- 10 slices white bread, crusts removed
- 10 ounces thinly sliced deli turkey
- 5 slices provolone cheese

Direction

- In food processor, process basil and mayonnaise till basil is chopped finely, scraping sides down if needed. Over each bread slice, spread mayonnaise mixture. With cheese and turkey, layer 5 bread slices. Put leftover bread on top. Cut every sandwich to 4 triangles.

Nutrition Information

- Calories:
- Cholesterol:
- Protein:
- Total Fat:
- Sodium:
- Fiber:
- Total Carbohydrate:

140. Turkey Tortilla Roll Ups

Serving: 6 servings. | Prep: 10mins | Cook: 0mins | Ready in:

Ingredients

- 3/4 cup sour cream
- 6 spinach tortillas or flour tortillas of your choice (8 inches)
- 1-1/2 cups cubed cooked turkey or ready-to-use grilled chicken breast strips
- 1 cup (4 ounces) finely shredded cheddar cheese
- 1 cup shredded lettuce
- 1/2 cup chopped ripe olives
- 1/2 cup chunky salsa

Direction

- Use 2 tbsp. of sour cream to spread over each tortilla. Put turkey, lettuce, olives, cheese and salsa on top, then roll up tortilla tightly and use plastic to wrap each. Chill until ready to serve.

Nutrition Information

- Calories: 353 calories
- Protein: 20g protein.
- Total Fat: 16g fat (9g saturated fat)
- Sodium: 577mg sodium
- Fiber: 0 fiber)
- Total Carbohydrate: 29g carbohydrate (2g sugars
- Cholesterol: 67mg cholesterol

141. Turkey Wraps With Maple Mustard Dressing

Serving: 4 servings. | Prep: 30mins | Cook: 0mins | Ready in:

Ingredients

- 8 fresh asparagus spears
- 4 teaspoons stone-ground mustard
- 1 tablespoon fat-free mayonnaise
- 1 tablespoon maple syrup
- 4 whole wheat tortilla (8 inches), warmed

- 1/2 pound sliced deli turkey
- 1/2 medium ripe avocado, peeled and sliced
- 2 turkey bacon strips, diced and cooked
- 1 cup shredded lettuce
- 1/8 teaspoon pepper

Direction

- Boil 3 cups of water in a big frying pan, then add asparagus. Put cover and let it cook for 2 to 4 minutes. Drain and put the asparagus right away in an ice water. Let it drain pat it dry.
- Mix together the syrup, mayonnaise and mustard, then spread it on top of each tortilla. Layer it with turkey, avocado, bacon, lettuce and asparagus, then sprinkle pepper on top. Roll it up and use toothpicks to secure.

Nutrition Information

- Calories: 288 calories
- Cholesterol: 28mg cholesterol
- Protein: 18g protein.
- Total Fat: 9g fat (1g saturated fat)
- Sodium: 894mg sodium
- Fiber: 5g fiber)
- Total Carbohydrate: 32g carbohydrate (5g sugars

---

142. Turkey Wraps With Maple Mustard Dressing For Two

Serving: 2 servings. | Prep: 30mins | Cook: 0mins | Ready in:

Ingredients

- 4 fresh asparagus spears
- 2 teaspoons stone-ground mustard
- 1-1/2 teaspoons fat-free mayonnaise
- 1-1/2 teaspoons maple syrup
- 2 whole wheat tortilla (8 inches), warmed

- 1/4 pound sliced deli turkey
- 1/4 medium ripe avocado, peeled and sliced
- 1 turkey bacon strip, diced and cooked
- 1/2 cup shredded lettuce
- Dash pepper

Direction

- Boil 3 cups of water in a big frying pan, then add asparagus. Put a cover and let it cook for 2 to 4 minutes. Drain and put the asparagus right away in an ice water. Drain and pat it dry.
- Mix together the syrup, mayonnaise and mustard, then spread it on top of each tortilla. Layer it with turkey, avocado, bacon, lettuce and asparagus, then sprinkle pepper on top. Roll it up and use toothpicks to secure.

Nutrition Information

- Calories: 286 calories
- Protein: 18g protein.
- Total Fat: 9g fat (1g saturated fat)
- Sodium: 917mg sodium
- Fiber: 4g fiber)
- Total Carbohydrate: 31g carbohydrate (5g sugars
- Cholesterol: 28mg cholesterol

---

143. Turkey, Gouda & Apple Tea Sandwiches

Serving: 4 dozen. | Prep: 25mins | Cook: 0mins |Ready in:

Ingredients

- 2/3 cup reduced-fat mayonnaise
- 2 tablespoons whole-berry cranberry sauce
- 24 very thin slices white bread, crusts removed
- 12 slices deli turkey
- 2 medium apples, thinly sliced
- 12 thin slices smoked Gouda cheese

- 4 cups fresh baby spinach

Direction

- In a small food processor, add cranberry sauce and mayonnaise. Place on a cover and process the mixture until well mixed. Spread mixture over each slice of bread.
- Place on each of twelve slices of bread with layer of turkey, apples, cheese, and spinach, then put leftover bread on top. Quarter each sandwich to serve.

Nutrition Information

- Calories: 258 calories
- Total Fat: 12g fat (4g saturated fat)
- Sodium: 456mg sodium
- Fiber: 1g fiber)
- Total Carbohydrate: 22g carbohydrate (5g sugars
- Cholesterol: 48mg cholesterol
- Protein: 16g protein. Diabetic Exchanges: 2 lean meat

144. Turkey Jalapeno Sandwiches

Serving: 6 servings. | Prep: 15mins | Cook: 0mins | Ready in:

Ingredients

- 6 tablespoons mayonnaise
- 6 hoagie buns, split
- 6 tablespoons jalapeno pepper jelly
- 12 lettuce leaves
- 1-1/2 pounds thinly sliced deli turkey
- Fresh cilantro leaves
- Thinly sliced seeded jalapeno pepper, optional

Direction

- Spread on bun bottoms with mayonnaise, then spread over mayonnaise with pepper jelly.

Layer with lettuce and turkey, then put cilantro and jalapeno, if wanted, on top. Replace bun tops.

Nutrition Information

- Calories: 483 calories
- Protein: 31g protein.
- Total Fat: 17g fat (3g saturated fat)
- Sodium: 1500mg sodium
- Fiber: 2g fiber)
- Total Carbohydrate: 53g carbohydrate (16g sugars
- Cholesterol: 41mg cholesterol

145. Vegetable Turkey Hoagies

Serving: 4 servings. | Prep: 20mins | Cook: 0mins | Ready in:

Ingredients

- 1 medium sweet yellow pepper, julienned
- 1 medium sweet red pepper, julienned
- 1 medium red onion, halved and thinly sliced
- 1 tablespoon olive oil
- 1/4 teaspoon salt
- 1/4 teaspoon pepper
- 2 loaves (8 ounces each) French bread, halved lengthwise
- 1/2 cup spreadable garden vegetable cream cheese
- 3/4 pound thinly sliced deli smoked turkey

Direction

- Sauté together onion and peppers in a big skillet with oil until softened, then stir in pepper and salt. Hollow out the bottom and top of loaves to leave a shell, 1/4 inch in size. Get rid of removed bread or reserve for another use. Spread over cut sides with cream cheese, then put sautéed vegetables and turkey on top. Halve the bread.

Nutrition Information

- Calories: 404 calories
- Total Carbohydrate: 38g carbohydrate (5g sugars
- Cholesterol: 63mg cholesterol
- Protein: 22g protein.
- Total Fat: 18g fat (8g saturated fat)
- Sodium: 1466mg sodium
- Fiber: 3g fiber)

---

146. Vegetarian Hummus Wraps

Serving: 2 servings. | Prep: 10mins | Cook: 0mins | Ready in:

Ingredients

- 6 tablespoons hummus
- 2 flour tortillas (8 inches), room temperature
- 1/2 cup shredded carrots
- 1 cup fresh baby spinach
- 6 slices tomato
- 2 tablespoons green goddess salad dressing

Direction

- Spread hummus on top of each tortilla, then layer it with carrots, spinach and tomato. Drizzle the dressing on top and roll it up tightly.

Nutrition Information

- Calories: 276 calories
- Total Fat: 8g fat (1g saturated fat)
- Sodium: 630mg sodium
- Fiber: 5g fiber)
- Total Carbohydrate: 43g carbohydrate (5g sugars

- Cholesterol: 0 cholesterol
- Protein: 9g protein.

---

147. Veggie Checkerboard Sandwiches

Serving: 20 sandwiches. | Prep: 45mins | Cook: 0mins | Ready in:

Ingredients

- 3 ounces cream cheese, softened
- 1 carton (7 ounces) roasted eggplant hummus
- 10 slices white bread, crusts removed
- 10 slices whole wheat bread, crusts removed
- 20 cucumber slices
- 20 spinach leaves
- 1 large sweet red pepper, cut into 2-inch strips
- 10 slices red onion, halved
- 8 pimiento-stuffed olives, drained and patted dry
- 8 pitted ripe olives, drained and patted dry

Direction

- Beat the cream cheese in a small bowl until it becomes smooth. Add hummus and beat it until blended. Halve each bread slice widthwise. Spread the hummus mixture on top of the 10 wheat bread halves and 10 white bread halves. Top each with cucumber, spinach, red pepper and red onion.
- Put leftover white bread on top of the white bread halves, then put leftover wheat bread on top of the wheat bread halves. Thread toothpicks through the olives then insert into 16 sandwiches.
- On a covered board that resembles a checkerboard or a platter, layout the sandwiches. Place the 4 plain sandwiches in the middle, the green olive-topped sandwiches on one side and the black olive-topped sandwiches on the other side.

Nutrition Information

- Calories: 112 calories
- Cholesterol: 5mg cholesterol
- Protein: 4g protein.
- Total Fat: 4g fat (1g saturated fat)
- Sodium: 280mg sodium
- Fiber: 2g fiber)
- Total Carbohydrate: 16g carbohydrate (2g sugars

---

148.   Walnut Cream Cheese Finger Sandwiches

Serving: 3 dozen. | Prep: 30mins | Cook: 0mins |Ready in:

Ingredients

- 12 ounces cream cheese, softened
- 1/2 cup finely chopped walnuts, toasted
- 2 tablespoons minced fresh parsley
- 1 tablespoon finely chopped green pepper
- 1 tablespoon finely chopped onion
- 1 teaspoon lemon juice
- 1/4 teaspoon ground nutmeg
- Dash salt and pepper
- 24 thin slices white sandwich bread, crusts removed

Direction

- Beat the pepper, salt, nutmeg, lemon juice, onion, green pepper, parsley, walnuts and cream cheese in a small bowl until combined.
- Spread approximately 2 tablespoonfuls on top of each of the 12 slices of bread, then put leftover bread on top. Slice each sandwich into three 1-inch wide strips.

Nutrition Information

- Calories: 176 calories
- Sodium: 291mg sodium

- Fiber: 1g fiber)
- Total Carbohydrate: 18g carbohydrate (2g sugars
- Cholesterol: 21mg cholesterol
- Protein: 5g protein. Diabetic Exchanges: 1 fat
- Total Fat: 10g fat (5g saturated fat)

---

149.   Zesty Bacon 'n' Ham Sandwiches

Serving: 2 servings. | Prep: 15mins | Cook: 0mins | Ready in:

Ingredients

- 1 tablespoon pickled pepper rings, chopped
- 2 teaspoons mayonnaise
- 1-1/2 teaspoons prepared mustard
- 1-1/2 teaspoons sweet pickle relish
- 2 kaiser rolls, split
- 2 bacon strips, cooked and halved
- 16 spinach leaves
- 2 slices tomato
- 4 red onion rings
- 2 slices provolone cheese
- 2 ounces sliced lean deli ham

Direction

- Mix relish, mustard, mayonnaise and pickled peppers in small bowl. Smear on every roll's cut sides. Layer ham, cheese, onion, tomato, spinach and bacon over bottom halves; put back the tops of rolls.

Nutrition Information

- Calories: 292 calories
- Total Fat: 9g fat (3g saturated fat)
- Sodium: 885mg sodium
- Fiber: 4g fiber)
- Total Carbohydrate: 39g carbohydrate (6g sugars
- Cholesterol: 20mg cholesterol

- Protein: 17g protein.

---

150. Zesty Garlic Avocado Sandwiches

Serving: 6 servings. | Prep: 30mins | Cook: 0mins | Ready in:

Ingredients

- 1 package (8 ounces) cream cheese, softened
- 2 medium ripe avocados, peeled
- 1 garlic clove, minced
- 1/8 teaspoon salt
- 6 whole grain bagels, split and toasted
- 6 slices tomato
- 1/2 cup sliced cucumber
- 6 slices red onion
- 6 sweet red pepper rings
- 6 lettuce leaves

Direction

- Beat the salt, garlic, avocados and cream cheese in a small bowl until it has a smooth consistency. Spread it on bagels then top with tomato, cucumber, onion, pepper rings and lettuce.

Nutrition Information

- Calories:
- Protein:
- Total Fat:
- Sodium:
- Fiber:
- Total Carbohydrate:
- Cholesterol:

Chapter 3: Chicken Salad Sandwich Recipes

***

151. Apricot Pistachio Chicken Salad Sandwiches

Serving: 2 servings. | Prep: 20mins | Cook: 0mins | Ready in:

Ingredients

- 1-1/2 cups shredded rotisserie chicken
- 1/3 cup chopped dried apricots
- 2 tablespoons mayonnaise
- 2 tablespoons sour cream
- 4 teaspoons coarsely chopped pistachios
- 1 teaspoon prepared horseradish
- 1 teaspoon stone-ground mustard
- 1 teaspoon honey
- Dash salt
- Dash white pepper
- Dash hot pepper sauce
- 4 slices sourdough bread
- 2 Bibb lettuce leaves
- 2 slices tomato
- 2 slices sweet onion

Direction

- Mix the initial 11 ingredients in a small bowl. On 2 bread slices, spread it on. Put onion, tomato, lettuce and leftover bread on top.

Nutrition Information

- Calories: 677 calories
- Sodium: 1254mg sodium
- Fiber: 5g fiber)

- Total Carbohydrate: 59g carbohydrate (17g sugars
- Cholesterol: 102mg cholesterol
- Protein: 42g protein.
- Total Fat: 30g fat (7g saturated fat)

- Fiber: 2g fiber)
- Total Carbohydrate: 11g carbohydrate (6g sugars
- Cholesterol: 42mg cholesterol
- Protein: 19g protein.
- Total Fat: 13g fat (3g saturated fat)

152. Asian Chicken Salad Lettuce Cups

Serving: 8 servings. | Prep: 20mins | Cook: 0mins | Ready in:

Ingredients

- 3/4 cup reduced-fat sesame ginger salad dressing
- 1/2 cup creamy peanut butter
- 1 tablespoon sesame oil
- 2 to 3 teaspoons cider vinegar
- 1 teaspoon salt
- 1/2 teaspoon crushed red pepper flakes
- 1/4 teaspoon pepper
- 3 packages (6 ounces each) ready-to-use grilled chicken breast strips
- 4 cups chopped cucumbers
- 1 cup chopped sweet red pepper
- 3/4 cup chopped green onions
- 1/4 cup grated carrot
- 8 Bibb or Boston lettuce leaves
- Chopped fresh cilantro, optional

Direction

- Combine the first 7 ingredients in a small bowl. Mix carrot, onions, pepper, cucumbers, and chicken together in a big bowl. Use the dressing to sprinkle; mix to combine. Refrigerate until eating. Enjoy on lettuce leaves. Use cilantro to garnish if you want.

Nutrition Information

- Calories: 237 calories
- Sodium: 1253mg sodium

153. Asian Chicken Salad Wraps

Serving: 6 servings. | Prep: 25mins | Cook: 0mins | Ready in:

Ingredients

- 3 cups shredded cooked chicken breasts
- 4 green onions, finely chopped
- 1 cup finely shredded cabbage
- 1/2 cup shredded carrot
- DRESSING:
- 3 tablespoons seasoned rice vinegar
- 3 tablespoons canola oil
- 2 tablespoons honey
- 1 tablespoon water
- 1 garlic clove, halved
- 3/4 teaspoon minced fresh gingerroot
- 1/4 teaspoon coarsely ground pepper
- 1 cup fresh cilantro leaves
- 6 lettuce leaves
- 6 whole wheat tortillas (8 inches), room temperature

Direction

- Mix the carrot, cabbage, green onions and chicken together in a big bowl. To make the dressing, mix the pepper, ginger, garlic, water, honey, oil and vinegar together in a small food processor. Put on a cover and process until incorporated. Add cilantro, put on a cover and process until chopped. Pour the mixture on top of the chicken mixture then toss until coated.
- On each tortilla, put a lettuce leaf. Put the chicken mixture on top and roll it up tightly.

Nutrition Information

- Calories: 370 calories
- Fiber: 3g fiber)
- Total Carbohydrate: 34g carbohydrate (11g sugars
- Cholesterol: 60mg cholesterol
- Protein: 26g protein.
- Total Fat: 13g fat (1g saturated fat)
- Sodium: 503mg sodium

---

154.   Avocado Ranch Chicken Wraps

Serving: 6 servings. | Prep: 20mins | Cook: 25mins | Ready in:

Ingredients

- 1-1/2 pounds boneless skinless chicken breast
- 1/4 cup lime juice
- 1/2 teaspoon garlic salt
- 1/3 cup plus 1/4 cup chopped fresh cilantro
- 1/2 medium onion, chopped
- 1-1/2 cups cherry tomatoes, halved
- 1 medium ripe avocado, peeled and cubed
- 3/4 cup shredded cheddar cheese
- 1 cup ranch salad dressing
- 6 flour tortillas (10 inches), warmed

Direction

- Preheat oven to 350 degrees. Add chicken to an 8-in. square baking dish. Sprinkle with lime juice. Drizzle with a third cup of cilantro and garlic salt; add onion on top. Bake, while covered till a thermometer reach 165 degrees, for 25 to 30 minutes. Let it cool for 10 minutes.
- At the same time, mix leftover cilantro, cheese, avocado and tomatoes in a big bowl. Cut the chicken; transfer into a bowl. Sprinkle with ranch dressing; coat by tossing.

- Scoop chicken mixture down in each tortilla middle. Fold bottom of tortilla over filling; fold both sides to close. Secure using toothpicks if you want.
- ,

Nutrition Information

- Calories:
- Protein:
- Total Fat:
- Sodium:
- Fiber:
- Total Carbohydrate:
- Cholesterol:

---

155.   Barbecued Chicken Salad Sandwiches

Serving: 8 servings. | Prep: 15mins | Cook: 20mins | Ready in:

Ingredients

- 1-1/2 pounds boneless skinless chicken breast
- 1/2 cup barbecue sauce
- 1 cup mayonnaise
- 1/2 cup finely chopped onion
- 1/2 cup chopped celery
- 1/4 teaspoon salt
- 1/4 teaspoon crushed red pepper flakes
- 8 kaiser rolls, split
- 8 tomato slices
- 8 lettuce leaves

Direction

- In a big plastic resealable bag, put chicken. Add barbecue sauce. Seal bag. Turn to coat. Keep in the fridge overnight.
- Grill chicken on medium-high heat, covered, for 6-8 minutes per side till a thermometer registers 170°. Refrigerate chicken, covered, till chilled.

- Slice chicken; put into big bowl. Mix pepper flakes, salt, celery, onion and mayonnaise in. Serve on tolls with lettuce and tomato.

Nutrition Information

- Calories: 481 calories
- Fiber: 2g fiber)
- Total Carbohydrate: 34g carbohydrate (6g sugars
- Cholesterol: 57mg cholesterol
- Protein: 24g protein.
- Total Fat: 27g fat (4g saturated fat)
- Sodium: 712mg sodium

---

156. Blue Cheese Chicken Pitas

Serving: 2 servings. | Prep: 10mins | Cook: 0mins | Ready in:

Ingredients

- 1 package (9 ounces) ready-to-use grilled Italian chicken strips
- 1 cup shredded carrots
- 1 cup shredded romaine
- 1 large tomato, seeded and chopped
- 1/4 cup real bacon bits
- 1/2 cup blue cheese salad dressing
- 2 whole wheat pita pocket halves

Direction

- Mix the first 5 ingredients together in a bowl. Add the dressing and mix to combine. Use 1/2 cup of chicken salad to fill each pita half.

Nutrition Information

- Calories: 734 calories
- Sodium: 1489mg sodium
- Fiber: 8g fiber)

- Total Carbohydrate: 59g carbohydrate (14g sugars
- Cholesterol: 100mg cholesterol
- Protein: 46g protein.
- Total Fat: 39g fat (8g saturated fat)

---

157. Blue Cheese Chicken Salad Sandwiches

Serving: 6 servings. | Prep: 15mins | Cook: 0mins | Ready in:

Ingredients

- 2/3 cup chunky blue cheese salad dressing
- 1 celery rib, diced
- 1/2 cup seeded and diced cucumber
- 1/3 cup diced carrot
- 2 tablespoons finely chopped onion
- 1 garlic clove, minced
- 1/4 teaspoon salt
- 1/4 teaspoon pepper
- 2 cups shredded rotisserie chicken, chilled
- 12 slices sourdough bread
- Crumbled blue cheese, optional

Direction

- Mix the initial 8 ingredients and stir chicken in. On half of the bread slices, spread it over. Sprinkle blue cheese if you want. Put remaining bread on top.

Nutrition Information

- Calories: 418 calories
- Total Carbohydrate: 40g carbohydrate (5g sugars
- Cholesterol: 50mg cholesterol
- Protein: 22g protein.
- Total Fat: 19g fat (4g saturated fat)
- Sodium: 747mg sodium
- Fiber: 2g fiber)

158. Buffalo Chicken Lettuce Wraps

Serving: 6 servings | Prep: 10mins | Cook: |Ready in:

Ingredients

- 2 cups shredded cooked chicken breasts
- 1/2 cup halved thin carrot slices
- 1 stalk celery, chopped
- 1/4 cup KRAFT Mayo with Olive Oil Reduced Fat Mayonnaise
- 1/4 cup Buffalo wing sauce
- 6 romaine lettuce leaves
- 1/3 cup ATHENOS Crumbled Reduced Fat Feta Cheese

Direction

- 1. Mix first five ingredients together.
- 2. Pour the mixture on centers of lettuce leaves.
- 3. Put cheese on top.

Nutrition Information

- Calories: 140
- Cholesterol: 55 mg
- Total Carbohydrate: 3 g
- Sugar: 0.9888 g
- Protein: 19 g
- Total Fat: 6 g
- Saturated Fat: 1 g
- Sodium: 400 mg
- Fiber: 1 g

159. Buffalo Chicken Wraps

Serving: 4 | Prep: 20mins | Cook: 10mins |Ready in:

Ingredients

- 1 tablespoon vegetable oil
- 1 tablespoon butter
- 1 pound skinless, boneless chicken breasts, cut into bite-size pieces
- 1/4 cup hot sauce
- 4 (10 inch) flour tortillas
- 2 cups shredded lettuce
- 1 celery stalk, diced
- 1/2 cup blue cheese dressing

Direction

- In a big skillet, heat butter and vegetable oil on moderately high heat. Put into pan with chicken, then cook and stir for about 10 minutes, until juices run clear and chicken is not pink in the center anymore. Take pan away from the heat and drizzle over cooked chicken with hot sauce. Toss to coat well.
- Lay out the flour tortillas and split chicken among tortillas evenly. Put lettuce, celery and blue cheese dressing on top of the chicken, then fold in sides of tortillas and roll the wrap as burrito-style.

Nutrition Information

- Calories: 588 calories;
- Cholesterol: 83
- Protein: 30.4
- Total Fat: 32.6
- Sodium: 1208
- Total Carbohydrate: 39.8

160. Butterfly Shaped Chicken Sandwiches

Serving: 9 servings. | Prep: 30mins | Cook: 15mins |Ready in:

Ingredients

- 1 pound boneless skinless chicken breasts
- 3 green onions, chopped
- 1/4 cup shredded carrot

- 1/4 cup shredded cheddar cheese
- 1 envelope (1 ounce) ranch salad dressing mix
- 3/4 cup mayonnaise
- 18 slices white bread
- 18 fresh baby carrots
- 36 fresh chive pieces (about 1-1/2 inch long)
- 36 carrot strips (about 1-1/2 inches long)
- Sliced pimiento-stuffed olives

Direction

- Add chicken into a big-sized skillet; pour in enough water to cover. Boil. Lower heat; keep it covered and simmered till softened chicken and juices run out clear for 12 to 14 minutes. Drain and let it cool down.
- Shred the chicken; add to a bowl. Put in cheese, carrot and onions. Mix mayonnaise and the salad dressing mix; pour into the chicken mixture. Spread over 1/2 of the slices of bread; add the leftover bread. Halve each sandwich diagonally, making 4 triangles.
- For shaping wings, arrange 2 triangles with points toward each other and crust facing outward. Per butterfly body, add 1 baby carrot between triangles; for making antennae, insert 2 chives into filling. Add one carrot strip in the each triangle middle. Add slices of olive over wings.

Nutrition Information

- Calories: 360 calories
- Sodium: 1060mg sodium
- Fiber: 2g fiber)
- Total Carbohydrate: 32g carbohydrate (3g sugars
- Cholesterol: 38mg cholesterol
- Protein: 15g protein.
- Total Fat: 19g fat (3g saturated fat)

161.   Caesar Chicken Wraps

Serving: 5 servings. | Prep: 30mins | Cook: 0mins | Ready in:

Ingredients

- 1/2 cup creamy Caesar salad dressing
- 1/2 cup grated Parmesan cheese, divided
- 1 teaspoon lemon juice
- 1 garlic clove, minced
- 1/4 teaspoon pepper
- 1 package (8 ounces) cream cheese, softened
- 3 cups shredded romaine
- 1/2 cup diced sweet red pepper
- 1 can (2-1/4 ounces) sliced ripe olives, drained
- 5 flour tortillas (10 inches)
- 1-3/4 cups cubed cooked chicken

Direction

- Mix together pepper, garlic, lemon juice, 1/4 cup of Parmesan cheese and salad dressing in a small bowl. Beat cream cheese in a separate small bowl until smooth, then put in 1/2 of the salad dressing mixture and blend well together. Put aside.
- Mix together olives, red pepper and romaine in a big bowl, then put in leftover salad dressing mixture and toss to coat well. Spread over each tortilla with 1/4 cup of cream cheese mixture, then put chicken and romaine mixture on top. Use leftover Parmesan cheese to sprinkle over top, then roll up and halve tortilla.

Nutrition Information

- Calories: 614 calories
- Cholesterol: 108mg cholesterol
- Protein: 29g protein.
- Total Fat: 36g fat (15g saturated fat)
- Sodium: 1065mg sodium
- Fiber: 7g fiber)
- Total Carbohydrate: 36g carbohydrate (2g sugars

162. California Chicken Wraps

Serving: 4 servings. | Prep: 15mins | Cook: 0mins | Ready in:

Ingredients

- 1/3 cup prepared hummus
- 4 whole wheat tortillas (8 inches)
- 2 cups cubed cooked chicken breast
- 1/4 cup chopped roasted sweet red peppers
- 1/4 cup crumbled feta cheese
- 1/4 cup thinly sliced fresh basil leaves

Direction

- On tortillas, spread the hummus and put chicken, peppers, cheese, and basil on top, then roll up.

Nutrition Information

- Calories: 300 calories
- Total Carbohydrate: 26g carbohydrate (2g sugars
- Cholesterol: 58mg cholesterol
- Protein: 27g protein. Diabetic Exchanges: 3 lean meat
- Total Fat: 8g fat (2g saturated fat)
- Sodium: 408mg sodium
- Fiber: 3g fiber)

163. Cashew Chicken Salad Sandwiches

Serving: 6 servings. | Prep: 15mins | Cook: 0mins | Ready in:

Ingredients

- 2 cups diced cooked chicken
- 1/2 cup chopped salted cashews
- 1/2 cup chopped red apple

- 1/2 cup chopped peeled cucumber
- 1/2 cup mayonnaise
- 1/2 teaspoon sugar
- 1/2 teaspoon salt
- Dash pepper
- 6 lettuce leaves, optional
- 6 kaiser rolls or croissants, split

Direction

- Mix together the cucumber, apple, cashews and chicken in a big bowl. Mix together the pepper, salt, sugar and mayonnaise in a small bowl. Put into chicken mixture and coat by tossing.
- If wished, put a lettuce leaf and a half cup chicken salad on every roll bottom; substitute tops.

Nutrition Information

- Calories: 463 calories
- Protein: 21g protein.
- Total Fat: 26g fat (4g saturated fat)
- Sodium: 720mg sodium
- Fiber: 2g fiber)
- Total Carbohydrate: 36g carbohydrate (3g sugars
- Cholesterol: 48mg cholesterol

164. Cherry Chicken Salad Croissants

Serving: 7 servings. | Prep: 15mins | Cook: 0mins | Ready in:

Ingredients

- 2-1/2 cups cubed cooked chicken breast
- 2/3 cup dried cherries
- 1/3 cup chopped celery
- 1/3 cup chopped tart apple
- 1/3 cup chopped pecans, toasted
- 1/2 cup mayonnaise

- 4 teaspoons buttermilk
- 1/2 teaspoon salt
- 1/8 teaspoon pepper
- 7 croissants, split

Direction

- Mix pecans, apple, celery, cherries and chicken in a large bowl. Then in another bowl, mix together salt, pepper, buttermilk, mayonnaise; put into chicken mixture and stir well. Transfer half a cup of the chicken salad onto each croissant.

Nutrition Information

- Calories: 481 calories
- Sodium: 710mg sodium
- Fiber: 3g fiber)
- Total Carbohydrate: 37g carbohydrate (15g sugars
- Cholesterol: 71mg cholesterol
- Protein: 16g protein.
- Total Fat: 30g fat (9g saturated fat)

165. Chicken Caesar Pitas

Serving: 6 | Prep: 30mins | Cook: 20mins | Ready in:

Ingredients

- 1 pound skinless, boneless chicken breast halves
- 1 teaspoon garlic powder
- 1 teaspoon dried thyme
- 1 teaspoon dried rosemary
- 3 slices bread, cut into 1/2 inch cubes
- butter flavored cooking spray
- 1 teaspoon garlic salt
- 1 teaspoon dried parsley
- 1/2 pound bacon
- 1 large head romaine lettuce leaves, torn into bite size pieces

- 1 (8 ounce) bottle bottled Caesar salad dressing
- freshly grated Parmesan cheese to taste
- salt and black pepper to taste
- 1 (10 ounce) package (6-inch) pocket pita bread, halved

Direction

- Set an oven to preheat to 175°C (350°F).
- Put the chicken in the saucepan with rosemary, thyme and garlic powder, then add water to cover. Boil over high heat, then lower the heat to medium-low, and simmer with a cover for about 15 minutes until no pink color remains and the chicken becomes tender. Take out the chicken, allow it to cool and slice into strips.
- In the meantime, on a baking tray, place the bread cubes, then spritz with butter spray. Sprinkle parsley and garlic salt on top.
- Bake the bread cubes for 5 minutes in the preheated oven. Flip the cubes and spritz with butter spray once again and sprinkle parsley and garlic salt on top. Bake for an additional 5-10 minutes until crunchy and golden brown. Take out the croutons and allow to cool.
- In a deep, big frying pan, put the bacon and cook over medium heat until it becomes crispy and browned evenly. Take the bacon out of the frying pan and drain on paper towels, then crumble.
- In a big bowl, mix together the croutons, lettuce, bacon and chicken. Toss with Parmesan cheese and Caesar salad dressing. Sprinkle pepper and salt to season, then toss again. On pita bread halves, place the salad mixture.

Nutrition Information

- Calories: 562 calories;
- Total Fat: 33.5
- Sodium: 1351
- Total Carbohydrate: 36.6
- Cholesterol: 77
- Protein: 26.4

166.   Chicken Caesar Wraps

Serving: 4 servings | Prep: 10mins | Cook: | Ready in:

Ingredients

- 3 cups loosely packed shredded romaine lettuce
- 2 cups chopped cooked chicken
- 4 slices cooked OSCAR MAYER Bacon , crumbled
- 1/4 cup KRAFT Grated Parmesan Cheese
- 1/4 cup croutons
- 1/2 cup KRAFT Classic Caesar Dressing
- 4   flour tortilla s (8 inch)

Direction

- In a big bowl, put the initial 5 ingredients, then add the dressing and toss gently.
- Spoon the mixture onto tortillas and roll up tightly.

Nutrition Information

- Calories: 480
- Protein: 31 g
- Saturated Fat: 7 g
- Sodium: 1040 mg
- Sugar: 2 g
- Total Carbohydrate: 29 g
- Total Fat: 26 g
- Fiber: 2 g
- Cholesterol: 90 mg

167.   Chicken Cheddar Wraps

Serving: 12 wraps. | Prep: 15mins | Cook: 0mins | Ready in:

Ingredients

- 1 cup sour cream
- 1 cup chunky salsa
- 2 tablespoons mayonnaise
- 4 cups cubed cooked chicken
- 2 cups shredded cheddar cheese
- 1 cup thinly sliced fresh mushrooms
- 2 cups shredded lettuce
- 1 cup guacamole, optional
- 12 flour tortillas (6 inches), room temperature
- Tomato wedges and additional guacamole, optional

Direction

- Mix mayonnaise, salsa, and sour cream together in a big bowl. Mix in mushrooms, cheese, and chicken.
- Split guacamole and lettuce among tortillas if you want. Put about 1/2 cup of chicken mixture on each tortilla. Wrap the sides over the stuffing. Use more guacamole and tomato to garnish if you want.

Nutrition Information

- Calories: 271 calories
- Protein: 18g protein. Diabetic Exchanges: 2 starch
- Total Fat: 6g fat (0 saturated fat)
- Sodium: 537mg sodium
- Fiber: 2g fiber)
- Total Carbohydrate: 35g carbohydrate (0 sugars
- Cholesterol: 34mg cholesterol

168.   Chicken Croissant Sandwiches

Serving: 4 servings. | Prep: 15mins | Cook: 0mins | Ready in:

Ingredients

- 1/3 cup mayonnaise

- 1/4 teaspoon ground ginger
- 1/4 teaspoon ground mustard
- Dash salt
- 1-1/2 cups diced cooked chicken
- 1/3 cup diced apple
- 1/3 cup sunflower kernels
- 2 green onions, finely chopped
- 1/3 cup mandarin oranges
- 4 croissants, split
- Lettuce leaves, optional

Direction

- Combine salt, mustard, ginger, and mayonnaise in a small bowl. Mix in green onions, sunflower kernels, apple, and chicken. Carefully tuck in mandarin oranges. Eat on croissants with lettuce if you want.

Nutrition Information

- Calories:
- Cholesterol:
- Protein:
- Total Fat:
- Sodium:
- Fiber:
- Total Carbohydrate:

---

169. Chicken Roll Em Ups

Serving: 4 servings. | Prep: 10mins | Cook: 0mins | Ready in:

Ingredients

- 1/2 cup spreadable chive and onion cream cheese
- 1 teaspoon Dijon mustard
- 4 whole wheat tortillas (8 inches)
- 1/2 pound sliced cooked chicken
- 2 cups shredded lettuce
- 1/2 cup crumbled cooked bacon
- 1-1/4 cups shredded Swiss cheese

- 1 medium tomato, chopped

Direction

- Mix together mustard and cream cheese in a small bowl, then spread the mixture over tortillas. Put tomato, Swiss cheese, bacon, lettuce and chicken on top, then roll up tightly.

Nutrition Information

- Calories: 545 calories
- Cholesterol: 121mg cholesterol
- Protein: 37g protein.
- Total Fat: 29g fat (15g saturated fat)
- Sodium: 929mg sodium
- Fiber: 3g fiber)
- Total Carbohydrate: 28g carbohydrate (6g sugars

---

170. Chicken Roll Em Ups For Two

Serving: 2 servings. | Prep: 10mins | Cook: 0mins | Ready in:

Ingredients

- 1/4 cup spreadable chive and onion cream cheese
- 1/2 teaspoon Dijon mustard
- 2 whole wheat tortilla (8 inches)
- 1/4 pound sliced cooked chicken
- 1 cup shredded lettuce
- 1/4 cup crumbled cooked bacon
- 2/3 cup shredded Swiss cheese
- 1/4 cup chopped tomato

Direction

- Mix together mustard and cream cheese in a small bowl, then spread the mixture over tortillas. Put tomato, Swiss cheese, bacon, lettuce and chicken on top, then roll up tightly.

Nutrition Information

- Calories: 551 calories
- Total Fat: 30g fat (16g saturated fat)
- Sodium: 934mg sodium
- Fiber: 3g fiber)
- Total Carbohydrate: 28g carbohydrate (5g sugars
- Cholesterol: 123mg cholesterol
- Protein: 38g protein.

---

171.   Chicken Salad Club

Serving: 6 servings. | Prep: 15mins | Cook: 0mins | Ready in:

Ingredients

- 3 cups shredded cooked chicken breast
- 3/4 cup chopped celery
- 1/3 cup plus 1 tablespoon fat-free mayonnaise
- 1/3 cup plus 1 tablespoon fat-free plain yogurt
- 3 tablespoons chopped green onions
- 2 tablespoons dried parsley flakes
- 1 tablespoon lemon juice
- 1/2 teaspoon salt
- 1/4 teaspoon pepper
- 12 slices white bread or 6 hard rolls, split
- 6 cooked bacon strips

Direction

- Mix onions, celery and chicken in a big bowl. Mix pepper, salt, lemon juice, parsley, yogurt and mayonnaise in a small-sized bowl. Add on top of chicken mixture and stir well. Serve over bread rolls with a bacon strip.

Nutrition Information

- Calories: 315 calories
- Protein: 29g protein. Diabetic Exchanges: 3-1/2 lean meat
- Total Fat: 9g fat (2g saturated fat)
- Sodium: 771mg sodium

- Fiber: 2g fiber)
- Total Carbohydrate: 29g carbohydrate (4g sugars
- Cholesterol: 67mg cholesterol

---

172.   Chicken Salad Clubs

Serving: 4 servings. | Prep: 10mins | Cook: 0mins | Ready in:

Ingredients

- 8 bacon strips
- 4 lettuce leaves
- 8 slices rye or pumpernickel bread
- 1 pound prepared chicken salad
- 4 slices Swiss cheese
- 8 slices tomato
- 1/3 cup honey mustard salad dressing

Direction

- Cook bacon in a big frying pan over medium heat until crunchy. Transfer to paper towels to strain. Put lettuce on 4 bread slices; put two tomato slices, one cheese slice, two bacon strips, and chicken salad on each. Spread salad dressing on one side of the rest of the bread, put on tomatoes.

Nutrition Information

- Calories: 696 calories
- Fiber: 7g fiber)
- Total Carbohydrate: 47g carbohydrate (14g sugars
- Cholesterol: 98mg cholesterol
- Protein: 27g protein.
- Total Fat: 45g fat (13g saturated fat)
- Sodium: 1489mg sodium

173. Chicken Salad Croissant Sandwiches

*Serving: 4 servings. | Prep: 25mins | Cook: 0mins
| Ready in:*

Ingredients

- 2 cups shredded cooked chicken breast
- 1 cup seedless red grapes, halved
- 1/2 cup chopped cashews
- 1 celery rib, chopped
- 1/3 cup grated Parmesan cheese
- 1 green onion, chopped
- 1/2 cup mayonnaise
- 1/3 cup buttermilk
- 2 teaspoons lemon juice
- 1 teaspoon dill weed
- 1 teaspoon dried parsley flakes
- 1/4 teaspoon salt
- 1/4 teaspoon garlic powder
- 1/4 teaspoon pepper
- 4 croissants, split

Direction

- Mix the initial 6 ingredients in a small-sized bowl. Mix seasoning, lemon juice, buttermilk and mayonnaise in a different bowl. Add on top of chicken mixture; stir well. Scoop chicken salad onto bottoms of croissant. Replace tops.

Nutrition Information

- Calories: 706 calories
- Total Fat: 46g fat (13g saturated fat)
- Sodium: 1009mg sodium
- Fiber: 3g fiber)
- Total Carbohydrate: 41g carbohydrate (15g sugars
- Cholesterol: 109mg cholesterol
- Protein: 31g protein.

174. Chicken Salad Croissants

*Serving: 6 servings. | Prep: 15mins | Cook: 0mins
| Ready in:*

Ingredients

- 2/3 cup mayonnaise
- 1/2 cup dill pickle relish
- 1 tablespoon minced fresh parsley
- 1 teaspoon lemon juice
- 1/2 teaspoon seasoned salt
- 1/8 teaspoon pepper
- 2 cups cubed cooked chicken
- 1 cup cubed Swiss cheese
- 6 croissants, split
- Lettuce leaves

Direction

- Stir in the initial 6 ingredients; mix in cheese and chicken. Serve over lettuce-lined croissants.

Nutrition Information

- Calories: 593 calories
- Sodium: 818mg sodium
- Fiber: 2g fiber)
- Total Carbohydrate: 33g carbohydrate (6g sugars
- Cholesterol: 102mg cholesterol
- Protein: 24g protein.
- Total Fat: 40g fat (14g saturated fat)

175. Chicken Salad Croissants With Fresh Dill

*Serving: 21 servings. | Prep: 20mins | Cook: 0mins
| Ready in:*

Ingredients

- 3 cups diced grilled chicken

- 1 can (11 ounces) mandarin oranges, drained and halved
- 1 cup halved seedless red grapes
- 2 celery ribs, finely chopped
- 1/2 cup mayonnaise
- 1/4 cup sunflower kernels
- 2 tablespoons minced fresh dill or 2 teaspoons dill weed
- 7 croissants or 21 miniature croissants, split

Direction

- Mix the first 7 ingredients together in a big bowl. Put on the croissants, replace tops. If using big croissants, slice into 3 parts. Eat immediately.

Nutrition Information

- Calories: 178 calories
- Cholesterol: 32mg cholesterol
- Protein: 8g protein.
- Total Fat: 11g fat (3g saturated fat)
- Sodium: 201mg sodium
- Fiber: 1g fiber)
- Total Carbohydrate: 13g carbohydrate (4g sugars

---

176.   Chicken Salad Crossiants

Serving: 1 dozen. | Prep: 55mins | Cook: 60mins | Ready in:

Ingredients

- 2-1/2 cups cubed cooked chicken
- 2 celery ribs, finely chopped
- 1/2 cup sliced almonds, toasted
- 3/4 cup mayonnaise
- 1/2 teaspoon salt
- 1/4 teaspoon coarsely ground pepper
- 1/4 cup heavy whipping cream
- 1 tablespoon sugar
- 12 miniature croissants, split

- Bibb lettuce leaves, optional

Direction

- Mix almonds, celery, and chicken together in a big bowl. Mix pepper, salt, and mayonnaise together in a small bowl. In a separate bowl, whisk the cream until it starts to thicken. Add sugar, whisk until forming firm peaks. Tuck into the mayonnaise mixture. Put on the chicken mixture; mix to combine.
- If you want, use lettuce leaves to layer the bottoms of croissant and put 1/3 cup of chicken salad on top. Replace tops.

Nutrition Information

- Calories: 305 calories
- Fiber: 1g fiber)
- Total Carbohydrate: 15g carbohydrate (2g sugars
- Cholesterol: 52mg cholesterol
- Protein: 12g protein.
- Total Fat: 22g fat (7g saturated fat)
- Sodium: 411mg sodium

---

177.   Chicken Salad Mini Croissants

Serving: 16 appetizers. | Prep: 25mins | Cook: 0mins | Ready in:

Ingredients

- 2 cups cubed cooked chicken
- 12 seedless red or green grapes, halved
- 1 medium apple, chopped
- 1/2 cup mayonnaise
- 1/3 cup chopped walnuts, toasted
- 1/4 cup plain yogurt
- 3 tablespoons cider vinegar
- 1/8 teaspoon salt
- Dash pepper
- 16 miniature croissants or rolls, split

- 4 to 6 lettuce leaves, torn
- 16 frilled toothpicks, optional

Direction

- Mix the initial 9 ingredients in a small-sized bowl. Scoop roughly a quarter cup onto the bottom of each croissant; add lettuce on top. Replace croissant tops. If you want, insert toothpicks into sandwiches.

Nutrition Information

- Calories: 225 calories
- Fiber: 1g fiber)
- Total Carbohydrate: 16g carbohydrate (3g sugars
- Cholesterol: 38mg cholesterol
- Protein: 8g protein.
- Total Fat: 14g fat (5g saturated fat)
- Sodium: 284mg sodium

---

178. Chicken Salad Party Sandwiches

Serving: 16 servings. | Prep: 25mins | Cook: 0mins | Ready in:

Ingredients

- 4 cups cubed cooked chicken breast
- 1-1/2 cups dried cranberries
- 2 celery ribs, finely chopped
- 2 green onions, thinly sliced
- 1/4 cup chopped sweet pickles
- 1 cup fat-free mayonnaise
- 1/2 teaspoon curry powder
- 1/4 teaspoon coarsely ground pepper
- 1/2 cup chopped pecans, toasted
- 16 whole wheat dinner rolls
- Leaf lettuce

Direction

- Mix together first 5 ingredients in a large bowl. Combine pepper, curry powder and mayonnaise then stir the combination into the chicken mixture. Keep in the fridge until ready to serve.
- To serve, add pecans to the mixture then stir. Line the rolls with lettuce then spoon the fillings onto the lettuce.

Nutrition Information

- Calories: 235 calories
- Fiber: 4g fiber)
- Total Carbohydrate: 33g carbohydrate (13g sugars
- Cholesterol: 30mg cholesterol
- Protein: 14g protein. Diabetic Exchanges: 2 starch
- Total Fat: 6g fat (1g saturated fat)
- Sodium: 361mg sodium

---

179. Chicken Salad Pitas

Serving: 5 servings. | Prep: 15mins | Cook: 0mins | Ready in:

Ingredients

- 1-1/2 cups cubed cooked chicken
- 1 medium carrot, julienned
- 1/2 cup julienned cucumber
- 1/4 cup sliced radishes
- 1/4 cup sliced ripe olives
- 1/4 cup cubed part-skim mozzarella cheese (1/2-inch cubes)
- 1/3 to 1/2 cup Italian salad dressing
- 5 pita breads (6 inches), halved
- Lettuce leaves

Direction

- Mix cheese, olives, radishes, cucumber, carrot, and chicken in a bowl. Pour in dressing and coat by tossing. Use lettuce leaves to line pita breads. Tuck roughly a third cup of chicken mixture into each half.

Nutrition Information

- Calories: 276 calories
- Protein: 20g protein. Diabetic Exchanges: 2-1/2 starch
- Total Fat: 4g fat (1g saturated fat)
- Sodium: 674mg sodium
- Fiber: 2g fiber)
- Total Carbohydrate: 38g carbohydrate (0 sugars
- Cholesterol: 39mg cholesterol

---

180.   Chicken Salad Pockets

Serving: 4 servings. | Prep: 15mins | Cook: 0mins | Ready in:

Ingredients

- 2 cups cubed cooked chicken breast
- 1 medium cucumber, seeded and chopped
- 1 medium tomato, seeded and chopped
- 3 green onions, thinly sliced
- 1/4 cup lemon juice
- 3 tablespoons canola oil
- 2 garlic cloves, minced
- 1 teaspoon sugar
- 1/2 to 1 teaspoon dried basil
- 2 cups shredded red leaf lettuce or romaine
- 6 pita breads (6 inches), halved

Direction

- Mix onions, tomato, cucumber, and chicken together in a big bowl. Mix basil, sugar, garlic, oil, and lemon juice together in a small bowl. Put on the chicken mixture and mix to coat. Put a cover on and chill for 2 hours.
- Right before eating, add lettuce and mix to combine. Put about 1/2 cup on each pita half.

Nutrition Information

- Calories: 406 calories
- Total Carbohydrate: 41g carbohydrate (0 sugars
- Cholesterol: 60mg cholesterol
- Protein: 29g protein. Diabetic Exchanges: 3 lean meat
- Total Fat: 14g fat (2g saturated fat)
- Sodium: 380mg sodium
- Fiber: 3g fiber)

---

181.   Chicken Salad Puffs

Serving: 6 servings. | Prep: 25mins | Cook: 30mins | Ready in:

Ingredients

- CREAM PUFFS:
- 1/2 cup water
- 1/4 cup butter, cubed
- Dash salt
- 1/2 cup all-purpose flour
- 2 large eggs
- FILLING:
- 2 cups diced cooked chicken
- 3/4 cup chopped celery
- 1 can (2-1/4 ounces) sliced ripe olives, drained
- 1/3 cup mayonnaise
- 1 tablespoon lemon juice
- 1 teaspoon grated onion
- 1/4 teaspoon Worcestershire sauce
- 1/8 teaspoon pepper
- Salt to taste

Direction

- Boil a big saucepan of salt, butter and water. Put in flour all at once and mix till forms a smooth ball. Take out of the heat; let rest for 5 minutes. Pour in eggs, one at a time, and beating well after each addition of eggs. Keep on beating till mixture turns shiny and smooth in texture.

- Onto a greased baking sheet, drop in six rounded tablespoonful 3 inches away. Bake at 400° till turns golden brown in color for 30 to 35 minutes.
- Transfer to a wire rack. Split puffs open right away; discard tops and put aside. Discard soft dough from inside. Let puffs cool.
- To make filling, mix olives, celery, and chicken in a big-sized bowl. Mix the leftover ingredients in a small-sized bowl; mix into chicken mixture. Fill puffs just prior to serving.

Nutrition Information

- Calories: 323 calories
- Cholesterol: 137mg cholesterol
- Protein: 17g protein.
- Total Fat: 24g fat (8g saturated fat)
- Sodium: 338mg sodium
- Fiber: 1g fiber)
- Total Carbohydrate: 10g carbohydrate (1g sugars

---

182. Chicken Salad Sandwiches

Serving: Makes 6 servings, one sandwich each. | Prep: 10mins | Cook: |Ready in:

Ingredients

- 1 pkg. (9 oz.) OSCAR MAYER Deli Fresh Rotisserie Seasoned Chicken Breast , cut into 1/4 inch-wide strips
- 4 stalks celery , chopped
- 1/3 cup KRAFT Light Mayo Reduced Fat Mayonnaise
- 1/4 cup sliced green onion s
- 6 kaiser roll s, split
- 6 leaf lettuce leaves

Direction

- Mix together onions, mayo, celery, and chicken.
- Stuff rolls with chicken mixture and lettuce.

Nutrition Information

- Calories: 260
- Saturated Fat: 1.5 g
- Sodium: 850 mg
- Total Carbohydrate: 34 g
- Protein: 14 g
- Total Fat: 8 g
- Fiber: 2 g
- Sugar: 1 g
- Cholesterol: 30 mg

---

183. Chicken Salad For 50

Serving: 50 servings (1 cup each). | Prep: 20mins | Cook: 20mins |Ready in:

Ingredients

- 9 cups cubed cooked chicken
- 9 cups cooked small pasta shells
- 8 cups chopped celery
- 8 cups seedless green grapes halves
- 18 hard-boiled large eggs, chopped
- 2 cans (20 ounces each) pineapple tidbits, drained
- DRESSING:
- 4 cups mayonnaise
- 2 cups sour cream
- 2 cups whipped topping
- 1/4 cup lemon juice
- 1/4 cup sugar
- 1-1/2 teaspoons salt
- 2 cups cashew halves

Direction

- Mix the first 6 ingredients in two huge bowls. Mix the first 6 dressing ingredients in a separate big bowl. Put atop the chicken mixture; coat by tossing. Cover and chill for minimum of an hour. Mix in cashews just prior serving.

Nutrition Information

- Calories: 328 calories
- Protein: 12g protein.
- Total Fat: 23g fat (5g saturated fat)
- Sodium: 274mg sodium
- Fiber: 1g fiber)
- Total Carbohydrate: 16g carbohydrate (8g sugars
- Cholesterol: 112mg cholesterol

184.   Chicken Salad On Buns

Serving: 6-8 servings. | Prep: 10mins | Cook: 20mins | Ready in:

Ingredients

- 2 cups diced leftover cooked chicken
- 1/4 pound process cheese (Velveeta), diced
- 1 to 2 tablespoons pickle relish
- 1/4 cup mayonnaise
- 2 tablespoons chopped onion
- 2 tablespoons chopped green pepper
- Kaiser rolls

Direction

- Mix the first 6 ingredients together in a bowl. Put about 1/3 cup on each roll. Fold each securely in foil. Bake at 300° until cooked through, about 20-30 minutes.

Nutrition Information

- Calories: 167 calories
- Total Fat: 12g fat (4g saturated fat)
- Sodium: 252mg sodium
- Fiber: 0 fiber)

- Total Carbohydrate: 2g carbohydrate (2g sugars
- Cholesterol: 43mg cholesterol
- Protein: 13g protein.

185.   Chicken Salad With Cranberries

Serving: 4-8 servings. | Prep: 10mins | Cook: 0mins | Ready in:

Ingredients

- 2 cups cubed cooked turkey
- 3/4 cup dried cranberries
- 1 celery rib, chopped
- 1/2 cup chopped pecans, toasted
- 3/4 cup honey-mustard salad dressing
- 8 whole wheat pita pocket halves
- Lettuce leaves, optional

Direction

- Mix pecans, celery, cranberries and turkey in a bowl. Pour in dressing and coat by tossing. Use lettuce to line pita halves if you want; use turkey mixture to fill.

Nutrition Information

- Calories: 313 calories
- Total Carbohydrate: 33g carbohydrate (11g sugars
- Cholesterol: 27mg cholesterol
- Protein: 14g protein.
- Total Fat: 15g fat (2g saturated fat)
- Sodium: 357mg sodium
- Fiber: 4g fiber)

186.   Chicken Satay Wraps

Serving: 4 servings. | Prep: 15mins | Cook: 0mins | Ready in:

Ingredients

- 2 tablespoons olive oil
- 2 tablespoons creamy peanut butter
- 2 green onions, chopped
- 1 teaspoon reduced-sodium soy sauce
- 1/4 teaspoon pepper
- 2 cups sliced cooked chicken
- 1 cup coleslaw mix
- 4 flour tortillas (8 inches), room temperature

Direction

- Whisk pepper, soy sauce, onions, peanut butter and oil in a large bowl until mixed. Place in chicken and mix to coat. Scatter 1/4 cup of coleslaw mix on top of every tortilla. Add chicken mixture on top and then roll up tightly.

Nutrition Information

- Calories: 321 calories
- Sodium: 325mg sodium
- Fiber: 3g fiber)
- Total Carbohydrate: 23g carbohydrate (1g sugars
- Cholesterol: 62mg cholesterol
- Protein: 26g protein.
- Total Fat: 16g fat (3g saturated fat)

187.   Chicken Tender Wraps

Serving: 4 servings. | Prep: 10mins | Cook: 15mins | Ready in:

Ingredients

- 16 frozen breaded chicken tenders
- 1/2 cup ranch salad dressing

- 4 sun-dried tomato tortillas (10 inches), room temperature
- 3 cups shredded lettuce
- 1 can (2-1/4 ounces) sliced ripe olives, drained
- 4 slices pepper Jack cheese
- Hot pepper sauce, optional

Direction

- Following package direction, bake chicken. In the meantime, spread over each tortilla with 2 tbsp. of salad dressing. Sprinkle down the center of each tortilla with lettuce and olives, then put chicken and cheese on top. Use hot pepper sauce to drizzle over if you want. Roll tortilla up and use toothpicks to secure.

Nutrition Information

- Calories: 760 calories
- Protein: 27g protein.
- Total Fat: 47g fat (11g saturated fat)
- Sodium: 1368mg sodium
- Fiber: 3g fiber)
- Total Carbohydrate: 59g carbohydrate (4g sugars
- Cholesterol: 81mg cholesterol

188.   Chicken Wraps

Serving: 10 | Prep: 4hours5mins | Cook: 20mins | Ready in:

Ingredients

- 1 pound skinless, boneless chicken breast halves
- 1/2 pound bacon
- 1 (20 ounce) can pineapple chunks
- 18 fluid ounces teriyaki sauce

Direction

- Slice the chicken into bite-size pieces and wrap it with approximately 1/3 slice of bacon, thread onto a toothpick and put pineapple chuck on top. Let it marinate for 4 hours or more in teriyaki sauce.

- Set an oven to preheat to 190°C (375°F).
- Put the marinated appetizers onto baking sheets lined with parchment. Let it bake for 20 minutes or until the bacon turns golden brown in color and the chicken is done. Let it drain on paper towels, then serve hot.

Nutrition Information

- Calories: 245 calories;
- Sodium: 2703
- Total Carbohydrate: 19
- Cholesterol: 42
- Protein: 17.2
- Total Fat: 10.8

189.   Chicken Apple Croissants

Serving: 6 servings. | Prep: 15mins | Cook: 0mins | Ready in:

Ingredients

- 2 cups diced cooked chicken
- 1 cup diced peeled apple
- 3/4 cup mayonnaise
- 1/2 cup halved green grapes
- 1/4 cup sliced almonds, toasted
- 1/2 teaspoon seasoned salt
- 1/4 teaspoon pepper
- 6 croissants or hard rolls, split
- 6 lettuce leaves

Direction

- Mix the initial 7 ingredients in a bowl. Scoop roughly half cup of the mixture to each croissant; add lettuce on top.

Nutrition Information

- Calories: 365 calories
- Sodium: 592mg sodium
- Fiber: 3g fiber)
- Total Carbohydrate: 32g carbohydrate (7g sugars
- Cholesterol: 80mg cholesterol
- Protein: 19g protein.
- Total Fat: 18g fat (8g saturated fat)

190.   Chickenwiches

Serving: 3 servings. | Prep: 10mins | Cook: 0mins | Ready in:

Ingredients

- 1 cup finely chopped cooked chicken
- 1/2 cup chopped celery
- 1/4 cup mayonnaise
- 2 tablespoons sliced pimiento-stuffed olives
- 2 tablespoons minced fresh parsley
- 2 teaspoons lemon juice
- 1/4 teaspoon salt
- Dash pepper
- 6 slices sandwich bread
- 6 bacon strips, cooked and crumbled

Direction

- Mix the initial 8 ingredients in a medium-sized bowl. Spread over three bread slices; drizzle with bacon. Add leftover bread on top.

Nutrition Information

- Calories:
- Total Carbohydrate:
- Cholesterol:
- Protein:
- Total Fat:
- Sodium:
- Fiber:

191.   Chutney Chicken Croissants

Serving: 2 servings. | Prep: 10mins | Cook: 0mins | Ready in:

Ingredients

- 3 tablespoons reduced-fat cream cheese
- 3 tablespoons mango chutney
- 2 croissants, split
- 2 lettuce leaves
- 2 slices red onion
- 1 cup shredded cooked chicken breast

Direction

- Spread over croissant bottoms with chutney and cream cheese, then put in layer of lettuce, onion and chicken. Replace croissant tops.

Nutrition Information

- Calories: 486 calories
- Protein: 27g protein.
- Total Fat: 19g fat (10g saturated fat)
- Sodium: 818mg sodium
- Fiber: 2g fiber)
- Total Carbohydrate: 49g carbohydrate (21g sugars
- Cholesterol: 107mg cholesterol

192.   Coleslaw Chicken Wraps

Serving: 8 servings. | Prep: 15mins | Cook: 15mins | Ready in:

Ingredients

- 1 bottle (16 ounces) reduced-fat poppy seed salad dressing, divided
- 2 pounds boneless skinless chicken breasts
- 1 can (20 ounces) unsweetened pineapple tidbits, drained
- 1 package (14 ounces) coleslaw mix
- 1 medium sweet red pepper, finely chopped
- 8 whole wheat tortillas (8 inches)
- 1/2 cup sliced almonds, toasted

Direction

- In a big resealable plastic bag, put one cup of the dressing, then add the chicken. Seal the bag and turn to coat. Let it chill in the fridge for one hour.
- Drain and get rid of the marinade, then use cooking oil to moisten a paper towel. Coat the grill rack lightly using long-handled tongs.
- Grill the chicken on medium heat with a cover or let it broil for 6-8 minutes per side, placed 4 inches from the heat source or until a thermometer registers 170 degrees. Allow it to stand for 5 minutes prior to slicing.
- In the meantime, mix together the leftover dressing, red pepper, coleslaw mix and pineapple in a big bowl, then toss until coated. Distribute among the tortillas, then put chicken on top and sprinkle it with almonds. Roll it up tightly and use toothpicks to secure.

Nutrition Information

- Calories: 407 calories
- Total Carbohydrate: 46g carbohydrate (21g sugars
- Cholesterol: 63mg cholesterol
- Protein: 29g protein. Diabetic Exchanges: 3 lean meat
- Total Fat: 11g fat (1g saturated fat)
- Sodium: 628mg sodium
- Fiber: 5g fiber)

193. Colorful Chicken Croissants

Serving: 4 servings. | Prep: 15mins | Cook: 0mins | Ready in:

Ingredients

- 1/4 cup diced celery
- 1/4 cup golden raisins
- 1/4 cup dried cranberries
- 1/4 cup sliced almonds
- 3/4 cup mayonnaise
- 2 tablespoons chopped red onion
- 1/4 teaspoon pepper
- 1/4 teaspoon salt, optional
- 2 cups cubed cooked chicken breast
- 4 croissants, split

Direction

- Mix salt if you want with the initial 7 ingredients in a big bowl. Mix in the chicken. Scoop roughly half a cup into each croissant.

Nutrition Information

- Calories: 184 calories
- Total Fat: 5g fat (0 saturated fat)
- Sodium: 331mg sodium
- Fiber: 2g fiber)
- Total Carbohydrate: 20g carbohydrate (0 sugars
- Cholesterol: 43mg cholesterol
- Protein: 13g protein. Diabetic Exchanges: 2 lean meat

194. Copycat Chicken Salad

Serving: 2 servings. | Prep: 10mins | Cook: 10mins | Ready in:

Ingredients

- 1/2 cup reduced-fat mayonnaise

- 1/3 cup sweet pickle relish
- 1/3 cup finely chopped celery
- 1/2 teaspoon sugar
- 1/4 teaspoon salt
- 1/4 teaspoon pepper
- 1 hard-boiled large egg, cooled and minced
- 2 cups chopped cooked chicken breast
- 4 slices whole wheat bread, toasted
- 2 romaine leaves

Direction

- Combine the initial 7 ingredients; mix in chicken. Use lettuce to line 2 toast slices. Add leftover toast and chicken salad on top.

Nutrition Information

- Calories: 651 calories
- Cholesterol: 222mg cholesterol
- Protein: 51g protein.
- Total Fat: 29g fat (5g saturated fat)
- Sodium: 1386mg sodium
- Fiber: 4g fiber)
- Total Carbohydrate: 45g carbohydrate (18g sugars

195. Cranberry Chicken Focaccia

Serving: 6 servings. | Prep: 25mins | Cook: 40mins | Ready in:

Ingredients

- 1-3/4 pounds bone-in chicken breast halves
- 6 fresh thyme sprigs
- 1/2 teaspoon salt
- 1/4 teaspoon pepper
- 1 cup fresh or frozen cranberries, thawed
- 1/2 cup orange segments
- 2 tablespoons sugar
- 1 loaf (12 ounces) focaccia bread, split
- 1/3 cup crumbled goat cheese

- 3 large lettuce leaves
- 1/4 cup chopped pecans, toasted

Direction

- Carefully loosen the skin from each chicken breast using your fingers, to create pocket. Under the skin, put thyme sprigs and sprinkle it with pepper and salt. Put it in a cooking spray-coated 11x7-inch baking dish. Bake for 40-45 minutes at 350 degrees without a cover, until a thermometer registers 170 degrees.
- Put the chicken aside until cool enough to be handled. Take the meat away from the bones and cut the chicken. In a small food processor, put the sugar, orange segments and cranberries, put on a cover and process until incorporated.
- Layer the cheese, lettuce, cranberry mixture, chicken and pecans over the bread bottom, then place back the top. Slice it into 6 wedges.

Nutrition Information

- Calories: 363 calories
- Total Carbohydrate: 40g carbohydrate (9g sugars
- Cholesterol: 63mg cholesterol
- Protein: 27g protein.
- Total Fat: 11g fat (4g saturated fat)
- Sodium: 628mg sodium
- Fiber: 3g fiber)

196. Cranberry Chicken Salad Sandwiches

Serving: 4 servings. | Prep: 25mins | Cook: 0mins | Ready in:

Ingredients

- 2 cups cubed cooked chicken breast
- 1/2 cup dried cranberries
- 1/4 cup finely chopped onion

- 1/4 cup chopped celery
- 1/2 teaspoon salt
- 1/4 teaspoon pepper
- 6 tablespoons Miracle Whip Light
- 8 dinner rolls
- 8 lettuce leaves

Direction

- Mix together the pepper, salt, celery, onion, cranberries and chicken in a small bowl. Mix in Miracle Whip.
- Chop tops off rolls. Hollow out each roll and leave a 1/2-inch shell. Use lettuce leaf to line each roll, then stuff it with chicken salad. Place back the tops.

Nutrition Information

- Calories: 354 calories
- Sodium: 796mg sodium
- Fiber: 3g fiber)
- Total Carbohydrate: 41g carbohydrate (13g sugars
- Cholesterol: 83mg cholesterol
- Protein: 25g protein. Diabetic Exchanges: 3 lean meat
- Total Fat: 10g fat (2g saturated fat)

197. Cranberry Chicken Wraps

Serving: 2 servings. | Prep: 20mins | Cook: 0mins | Ready in:

Ingredients

- 1 cup shredded cooked chicken breast
- 1 cup chopped apple
- 1/4 cup plus 2 teaspoons fat-free Miracle Whip, divided
- 1/4 cup dried cranberries
- 3 tablespoons crumbled feta cheese
- 1/4 teaspoon minced fresh rosemary or 1/8 teaspoon dried rosemary, crushed

- 1/8 teaspoon pepper
- 2 whole wheat tortillas (8 inches), room temperature
- 1/2 cup fresh baby spinach

Direction

- Mix together pepper, rosemary, feta cheese, cranberries, 1/4 cup Miracle Whip, apple and chicken in a small bowl. Spread remaining Miracle Whip over tortillas. Put chicken mixture and spinach on top. Roll the tortillas up and use toothpicks to secure, or leave tortillas open-faced to serve.

Nutrition Information

- Calories: 387 calories
- Sodium: 614mg sodium
- Fiber: 5g fiber)
- Total Carbohydrate: 49g carbohydrate (22g sugars
- Cholesterol: 60mg cholesterol
- Protein: 27g protein.
- Total Fat: 7g fat (2g saturated fat)

198.   Cranberry Walnut Chicken Salad Sandwiches

Serving: 8 servings. | Prep: 15mins | Cook: 0mins | Ready in:

Ingredients

- 1/2 cup mayonnaise
- 2 tablespoons honey Dijon mustard
- 1/4 teaspoon pepper
- 2 cups cubed rotisserie chicken
- 1 cup shredded Swiss cheese
- 1/2 cup chopped celery
- 1/2 cup dried cranberries
- 1/4 cup chopped walnuts
- 1/2 teaspoon dried parsley flakes
- 8 lettuce leaves

- 16 slices pumpernickel bread

Direction

- Mix pepper, mustard and mayonnaise in a big bowl. Mix in parsley, walnuts, cranberries, celery, cheese and chicken.
- Add lettuce onto eight bread slices; add leftover bread and half cup of chicken salad on each top.

Nutrition Information

- Calories: 411 calories
- Total Carbohydrate: 35g carbohydrate (7g sugars
- Cholesterol: 49mg cholesterol
- Protein: 20g protein.
- Total Fat: 22g fat (5g saturated fat)
- Sodium: 469mg sodium
- Fiber: 5g fiber)

199.   Creamy Chicken Salad

Serving: 12 | Prep: 10mins | Cook: 20mins | Ready in:

Ingredients

- 1/2 cup whipping cream
- 1/2 cup smoked almonds
- 4 grilled skinless, boneless chicken breast halves
- 1/2 cup mayonnaise
- 1 tablespoon minced fresh tarragon
- salt and pepper to taste

Direction

- Beat cream to soft peaks. In a food processor, put almonds to chop. Strip chicken or finely chop.
- Mix pepper, salt, tarragon, mayonnaise, chicken, almonds and cream together in a large bowl. Blend well then serve.

Nutrition Information

- Calories: 175 calories;
- Sodium: 78
- Total Carbohydrate: 1.8
- Cholesterol: 33
- Protein: 11.5
- Total Fat: 13.7

---

200. Creamy Chicken Spread

Serving: 5 | Prep: 8hours10mins | Cook: |Ready in:

Ingredients

- 1 (10.75 ounce) can condensed cream of chicken soup
- 1 envelope (1 tablespoon) unflavored gelatin
- 3 tablespoons water
- 3/4 cup mayonnaise
- 1 (8 ounce) package cream cheese, softened
- 1 onion, chopped
- 1 cup celery, minced
- 1 (5 ounce) can chicken chunks, drained

Direction

- Heat the chicken soup in a small pot.
- Mix water and gelatin in a small bowl and stir the mixture into the heated soup. Stir celery, onion, cream cheese, mayonnaise into the soup mixture. Then put in chicken and continue mixing. Keep in the fridge overnight.

Nutrition Information

- Calories: 512 calories;
- Protein: 12.9
- Total Fat: 47.7
- Sodium: 886
- Total Carbohydrate: 9.4
- Cholesterol: 84

---

201. Crowd Pleasing Chicken Salad

Serving: 8 servings. | Prep: 15mins | Cook: 0mins | Ready in:

Ingredients

- 3 cups cubed cooked chicken or turkey
- 1 cup mayonnaise
- 1/4 cup sour cream
- 1/4 teaspoon salt
- Dash pepper
- 2 cups cooked rice
- 1 cup chopped celery
- 1/2 cup chopped green pepper
- 1/4 cup chopped onion
- 1 can (20 ounces) pineapple tidbits, drained
- 1 can (8 ounces) sliced water chestnuts, drained
- 1 cup shredded cheddar cheese
- 1/2 cup sliced almonds, toasted, optional
- Cantaloupe, optional

Direction

- Mix the initial 5 ingredients in a big bowl. Fold in cheese, water chestnuts, pineapple, onion, green pepper, celery and rice. Put in almonds just prior to serving if you want. Serve over wedges if desired or cantaloupe halves, or use as a sandwich spread.

Nutrition Information

- Calories: 463 calories
- Protein: 20g protein.
- Total Fat: 31g fat (8g saturated fat)
- Sodium: 377mg sodium
- Fiber: 2g fiber)
- Total Carbohydrate: 24g carbohydrate (8g sugars
- Cholesterol: 77mg cholesterol

202. Crunchy Chicken Salad Pitas

Serving: 4 servings. | Prep: 20mins | Cook: 0mins | Ready in:

Ingredients

- 3 cups cubed cooked chicken
- 1/2 cup chopped cucumber
- 1/2 cup halved seedless red grapes
- 1/2 cup chopped carrots
- 1/4 cup chopped walnuts
- 1/4 cup mayonnaise
- 1/4 cup ranch salad dressing
- 4 pita breads (6 inches), halved
- 8 lettuce leaves

Direction

- Mix together walnuts, carrots, grapes, cucumber and chicken in a large bowl. Mix together ranch dressing and mayonnaise. Add on top of the chicken mixture; toss to coat.
- Use lettuce to line pita halves; place about half a cup chicken salad into each. Keep in the fridge until serving.

Nutrition Information

- Calories: 612 calories
- Protein: 38g protein.
- Total Fat: 32g fat (5g saturated fat)
- Sodium: 624mg sodium
- Fiber: 3g fiber)
- Total Carbohydrate: 41g carbohydrate (6g sugars
- Cholesterol: 101mg cholesterol

203. Crunchy Chicken Salad Sandwiches

Serving: 4 servings. | Prep: 15mins | Cook: 0mins | Ready in:

Ingredients

- 2 cups cubed cooked chicken
- 1 cup diced Monterey Jack cheese
- 1/2 cup green grapes, halved
- 1/2 cup mayonnaise
- 1/4 cup thinly sliced celery
- 1/4 cup sunflower kernels
- 1/4 teaspoon salt
- 1/4 teaspoon pepper
- Lettuce leaves
- 4 pita breads, halved or 8 slices bread

Direction

- Mix the initial 8 ingredients in a bowl. Use lettuce to line bread or pita and pour half a cup of chicken salad into each.

Nutrition Information

- Calories: 689 calories
- Total Carbohydrate: 39g carbohydrate (5g sugars
- Cholesterol: 102mg cholesterol
- Protein: 36g protein.
- Total Fat: 43g fat (11g saturated fat)
- Sodium: 914mg sodium
- Fiber: 2g fiber)

204. Cucumber Chicken Croissants

Serving: 4 servings. | Prep: 15mins | Cook: 0mins | Ready in:

Ingredients

- 2 tablespoons mayonnaise
- 1/4 to 1/2 teaspoon dill weed
- 4 croissants, split
- 4 lettuce leaves
- 4 slices provolone cheese
- 1 medium cucumber, thinly sliced

- 1/2 pound thinly sliced deli chicken

Direction

- Combine dill and mayonnaise in a small bowl, then spread over croissant bottoms. Put lettuce, cheese, cucumber and chicken on top, then replace croissant tops.

Nutrition Information

- Calories: 443 calories
- Total Carbohydrate: 29g carbohydrate (8g sugars
- Cholesterol: 91mg cholesterol
- Protein: 23g protein.
- Total Fat: 26g fat (12g saturated fat)
- Sodium: 1065mg sodium
- Fiber: 3g fiber)

205. Cucumber Chicken Salad Sandwiches

Serving: 2 servings. | Prep: 10mins | Cook: 0mins | Ready in:

Ingredients

- 1 cup cubed cooked chicken breast
- 1/3 cup chopped seeded peeled cucumber
- 1/4 cup fat-free mayonnaise
- 1/4 teaspoon salt
- 1/8 teaspoon dill weed
- 2 lettuce leaves
- 4 slices tomato
- 2 sandwich buns, split

Direction

- Mix together the initial 5 ingredients in a small bowl. Put tomato and lettuce on the bun bottoms, then put chicken salad on top. Place back the bun tops.

Nutrition Information

- Calories: 350 calories
- Sodium: 930mg sodium
- Fiber: 3g fiber)
- Total Carbohydrate: 42g carbohydrate (9g sugars
- Cholesterol: 57mg cholesterol
- Protein: 28g protein. Diabetic Exchanges: 3 lean meat
- Total Fat: 8g fat (3g saturated fat)

206. Curried Chicken Pita Pockets

Serving: 10 servings. | Prep: 15mins | Cook: 0mins | Ready in:

Ingredients

- 3/4 cup mayonnaise
- 1 teaspoon soy sauce
- 1 teaspoon lemon juice
- 1/2 teaspoon curry powder
- 1 small onion, finely chopped
- 2-1/2 cups cubed cooked chicken
- 1-1/2 cups halved seedless green grapes
- 3/4 cup chopped celery
- 1/2 cup sliced almonds
- 20 pita pocket halves

Direction

- Mix the first 5 ingredients together in a big bowl. Mix in celery, grapes, and chicken and chill. Add almonds right before serving. Fill about 1/4 cup into each pita half.

Nutrition Information

- Calories: 401 calories
- Protein: 17g protein.
- Total Fat: 19g fat (3g saturated fat)
- Sodium: 481mg sodium

- Fiber: 2g fiber)
- Total Carbohydrate: 40g carbohydrate (6g sugars
- Cholesterol: 37mg cholesterol

207. Curried Chicken Pitas

Serving: 4 | Prep: | Cook: 15mins | Ready in:

Ingredients

- 6 tablespoons nonfat plain yogurt
- ¼ cup low-fat mayonnaise
- 1 tablespoon curry powder
- 2 cups cooked, cubed chicken breast (see Tip)
- 1 ripe but firm pear, diced
- 1 stalk celery, finely diced
- ½ cup dried cranberries
- ¼ cup sliced or slivered almonds, toasted (see Tip)
- 4 4- to 5-inch whole-wheat pita breads, cut in half
- 2 cups sprouts

Direction

- In a big bowl, put together the curry powder, mayonnaise and yogurt. Put in almonds, cranberries, celery, pear and chicken; mix by tossing.
- Fill every pita half with a half cup of chicken salad and a quarter cup of sprouts.

Nutrition Information

- Calories: 352 calories;
- Sodium: 324
- Fiber: 6
- Sugar: 17
- Protein: 27
- Total Fat: 9
- Saturated Fat: 2
- Cholesterol: 61
- Total Carbohydrate: 43

208. Curried Chicken Pockets

Serving: 12 sandwiches. | Prep: 35mins | Cook: 10mins | Ready in:

Ingredients

- 1/2 cup mayonnaise
- 1/2 cup chutney
- 1 tablespoon curry powder
- 6 cups cubed cooked chicken
- PITA BREAD:
- 1 package (1/4 ounce) active dry yeast
- 1-1/3 cups warm water (110° to 115°), divided
- 3 to 3-1/2 cups all-purpose flour
- 1 tablespoon vegetable oil
- 1 teaspoon salt
- 1/4 teaspoon sugar
- 3 tablespoons cornmeal
- Lettuce leaves

Direction

- Mix chicken, curry powder, chutney, mayonnaise together in a large bowl then keep the mixture refrigerated until serving.
- Dissolve yeast in 1/3 cup warm water in a large bowl. Mix together sugar, salt, oil, one and a half cups of flour and the remaining water then beat until the mixture gets smooth. Put enough remaining flour in the mixture to form a soft dough. Transfer the dough onto a floured surface then knead for about 10 minutes until the dough gets elastic and smooth. Put the dough in a greased bowl and turn the dough once so that the top of the dough is also greased. Cover the bowl and keep it in a warm place to allow the dough to rise for about an hour until it doubles its size.
- Punch dough down and form into 6 balls. Allow to rise for half an hour. Sprinkle cornmeal on three ungreased baking sheets. Roll each ball to form into a circle of 7 inches

in diameter. Arrange 2 circles on each baking sheet. Allow to rise for half an hour.

- Bake at 500 degrees till the outside gets lightly browned, about 10 minutes. Allow to cool. Halve each of the pitas. Use lettuce to line each pita, use 1/3 cup chicken mixture to fill each pita.

Nutrition Information

- Calories: 352 calories
- Protein: 24g protein.
- Total Fat: 14g fat (3g saturated fat)
- Sodium: 310mg sodium
- Fiber: 2g fiber)
- Total Carbohydrate: 31g carbohydrate (5g sugars
- Cholesterol: 66mg cholesterol

---

209. **Curried Chicken Salad Sandwiches**

Serving: 6 servings. | Prep: 20mins | Cook: 0mins | Ready in:

Ingredients

- 2 cups cubed cooked chicken breast
- 3/4 cup chopped apple
- 3/4 cup dried cranberries
- 3/4 cup mayonnaise
- 1/2 cup chopped walnuts
- 1/2 cup chopped celery
- 2 teaspoons lemon juice
- 1 tablespoon chopped green onion
- 1 teaspoon curry powder
- 6 lettuce leaves
- 6 croissants, split

Direction

- Mix curry powder, onion, lemon juice, celery, walnuts, mayonnaise, cranberries, apple, and chicken together in a big bowl. Put lettuce on

croissants. Put the chicken salad mixture on top.

Nutrition Information

- Calories: 625 calories
- Total Carbohydrate: 43g carbohydrate (14g sugars
- Cholesterol: 84mg cholesterol
- Protein: 21g protein.
- Total Fat: 41g fat (10g saturated fat)
- Sodium: 614mg sodium
- Fiber: 4g fiber)

---

210. **Curried Chicken Tea Sandwiches**

Serving: 6 | Prep: 20mins | Cook: | Ready in:

Ingredients

- 2 cups cubed, cooked chicken
- 1 unpeeled red apple, chopped
- 3/4 cup dried cranberries
- 1/2 cup thinly sliced celery
- 1/4 cup chopped pecans
- 2 tablespoons thinly sliced green onions
- 3/4 cup mayonnaise
- 2 teaspoons lime juice
- 1/2 teaspoon curry powder
- 12 slices bread
- 12 lettuce leaves

Direction

- In a bowl, mix green onions, pecans, celery, cranberries, apple and chicken. In a small bowl, mix curry powder, lime juice and mayonnaise. Fold the mayonnaise mixture in the chicken mixture. Mix to coat. Refrigerate, covered, until serving time.
- Cut every slice of bread using a 3-in. heart-shaped cookie cutter. Put a lettuce leaf and the chicken salad on top.

Nutrition Information

- Calories: 528 calories;
- Total Fat: 32.7
- Sodium: 540
- Total Carbohydrate: 43.9
- Cholesterol: 47
- Protein: 16.5

---

211.   Curried Chicken And Avocado Salad Sandwiches

Serving: 4 servings. | Prep: 20mins | Cook: 0mins | Ready in:

Ingredients

- 1/4 cup reduced-fat mayonnaise
- 2 teaspoons McCormick® Curry Powder
- 1/4 teaspoon salt
- 2 cups cubed cooked chicken breast
- 1 medium ripe avocado, peeled and cubed
- 1/4 cup dried cranberries
- 2 tablespoons minced fresh cilantro
- 8 slices reduced-calorie wheat bread
- 4 leaf lettuce leaves, optional

Direction

- Mix together salt, curry powder, mayonnaise in a large bowl until everything blends well. Put in cilantro, cranberries, avocado and chicken; toss gently to combine.
- Place the same amount of chicken salad on four bread slices. Put lettuce leaves on the salad layer then add remaining slices of bread on top of lettuce leaves.

Nutrition Information

- Calories:
- Fiber:
- Total Carbohydrate:

- Cholesterol:
- Protein:
- Total Fat:
- Sodium:

---

212.   Curry Chicken Croissants

Serving: 4-6 servings. | Prep: 15mins | Cook: 0mins | Ready in:

Ingredients

- 2-1/2 cups cubed cooked chicken
- 1/2 cup chopped walnuts
- 1/3 cup finely chopped celery
- 2 tablespoons grated onion
- 1/2 cup mayonnaise
- 2 tablespoons sour cream
- 3/4 teaspoon curry powder
- 1/8 teaspoon Cajun seasoning
- Lettuce leaves
- 4 to 6 croissants, split

Direction

- Cover up the food processor then puree the chicken inside till chopped finely. Add into a big bowl; put in onion, celery and walnuts.
- Mix Cajun seasoning, curry powder, sour cream and mayonnaise in a small-sized bowl. Add on top of chicken mixture; coat by tossing. Keep it covered and let chill in the refrigerator for no less than 60 minutes. Over each croissant, add roughly three quarters cup of chicken mixture and lettuce.

Nutrition Information

- Calories: 475 calories
- Protein: 23g protein.
- Total Fat: 34g fat (9g saturated fat)
- Sodium: 455mg sodium
- Fiber: 2g fiber)

- Total Carbohydrate: 20g carbohydrate (2g sugars
- Cholesterol: 87mg cholesterol

---

213. Curry Chicken Salad Wraps

Serving: 6 servings. | Prep: 25mins | Cook: 0mins | Ready in:

Ingredients

- 1/2 cup mayonnaise
- 1/2 cup sour cream
- 1/4 cup finely chopped green onions
- 2 tablespoons curry powder
- 1 tablespoon mango chutney
- 1/2 teaspoon salt
- 1/2 teaspoon pepper
- 1 package (9 ounces) ready-to-serve roasted chicken breast strips
- 1 cup seedless red grapes, halved
- 1/2 cup julienned carrot
- 6 tablespoons chopped pecans, toasted
- 1/4 cup thinly sliced onion
- 6 lettuce leaves
- 6 flour tortillas (10 inches), room temperature
- 24 fresh mint leaves

Direction

- To make dressing, mix the initial 7 ingredients in a small-sized bowl. Put aside one and a half cups to make serving. Mix onion, pecans, carrot, grapes and chicken in a big-sized bowl. Mix in the leftover dressing.
- Add a lettuce leaf to each tortilla; add mint leaves and two thirds cup of chicken salad on top. Roll up. Serve alongside reserved dressing.

Nutrition Information

- Calories: 543 calories

- Total Carbohydrate: 45g carbohydrate (8g sugars
- Cholesterol: 45mg cholesterol
- Protein: 19g protein.
- Total Fat: 29g fat (6g saturated fat)
- Sodium: 963mg sodium
- Fiber: 9g fiber)

---

214. Dijon Chicken Salad

Serving: 6 | Prep: 20mins | Cook: | Ready in:

Ingredients

- 2 (10 ounce) cans chunk chicken
- 1 cup sliced celery
- 1 cup halved seedless green grapes
- 1 cup halved seedless red grapes
- 1/4 cup dried cranberries
- 2 teaspoons dried chives
- 2 tablespoons honey
- 1 tablespoon Dijon mustard
- 3/4 cup mayonnaise
- 1/2 teaspoon salt
- 1/8 teaspoon ground black pepper

Direction

- In a bowl, combine chives, cranberries, red grapes, green grapes, celery, and chicken. In another bowl, stir together pepper, salt, mayonnaise, mustard, and honey. Combine chicken mixture and mustard mixture until evenly coated.

Nutrition Information

- Calories: 432 calories;
- Cholesterol: 68
- Protein: 21.1
- Total Fat: 29.6
- Sodium: 900
- Total Carbohydrate: 21.4

215. Favorite Chicken Salad Sandwiches

Serving: 2 servings. | Prep: 20mins | Cook: 0mins | Ready in:

Ingredients

- 1 cup shredded cooked chicken
- 1/2 cup chopped celery
- 1 tablespoon chopped green onion
- 2 tablespoons chopped ripe olives
- 2 tablespoons chopped dill pickle
- 1/4 cup mayonnaise
- 1/4 teaspoon pepper
- 1/8 teaspoon salt
- 4 slices sourdough bread, toasted
- 2 lettuce leaves

Direction

- Mix the first 8 ingredients in a small bowl. Spread over 2 slices of toast; put lettuce and the rest of the toasts on top.

Nutrition Information

- Calories: 537 calories
- Sodium: 989mg sodium
- Fiber: 3g fiber)
- Total Carbohydrate: 39g carbohydrate (2g sugars
- Cholesterol: 72mg cholesterol
- Protein: 28g protein.
- Total Fat: 29g fat (5g saturated fat)

216. Flavorful Chicken Salad Sandwiches

Serving: 10 servings. | Prep: 35mins | Cook: 10mins | Ready in:

Ingredients

- 3 cups pineapple juice
- 1/3 cup soy sauce
- 3 pounds boneless skinless chicken breasts
- 2 cups water
- 1/2 cup each chopped green pepper, red onion and celery
- 1-1/2 cups mayonnaise
- 1/2 teaspoon garlic salt
- 1/2 teaspoon pepper
- 1/2 teaspoon Italian seasoning
- 1/2 teaspoon dried basil
- 1/4 teaspoon seasoned salt
- 10 lettuce leaves
- 10 sandwich rolls, split

Direction

- Mix soy sauce and pineapple juice in a small bowl. Add 1-1/2 cups to a big resalable bag; add chicken. Close the bag and massage to blend; let chill overnight. Put a cover on and chill the rest of the marinade.
- Strain and throw away the marinade from the chicken. Mix the saved marinade, water, and chicken together in a big saucepan. Boil it. Lower the heat; put a cover on and simmer until a thermometer displays 170°, about 10-15 minutes. Strain, let cool slightly. Pull apart the chicken.
- Mix celery, onion, green pepper, and chicken together in a big bowl. Mix the seasonings and mayonnaise together in a small bowl. Put on the chicken mixture; lightly toss to combine. Chill until eating. Enjoy on rolls lined with lettuce.

Nutrition Information

- Calories:
- Total Carbohydrate:
- Cholesterol:
- Protein:
- Total Fat:
- Sodium:
- Fiber:

217. Fried Chicken Pitas

Serving: 6 servings. | Prep: 10mins | Cook: 0mins | Ready in:

Ingredients

- 3 cups thinly sliced fried chicken (including crispy skin)
- 1 cup coleslaw salad dressing
- 1/3 cup crumbled cooked bacon
- 2 tablespoons chopped green onions with tops
- 1/4 teaspoon ground mustard
- 1/8 teaspoon pepper
- 6 pita bread halves

Direction

- Mix pepper, mustard, onions, bacon, dressing and the chicken in a big bowl. Scoop into pita bread.

Nutrition Information

- Calories: 478 calories
- Protein: 24g protein.
- Total Fat: 28g fat (6g saturated fat)
- Sodium: 969mg sodium
- Fiber: 1g fiber)
- Total Carbohydrate: 29g carbohydrate (10g sugars
- Cholesterol: 89mg cholesterol

218. Fruity Chicken Salad Mini Sandwiches

Serving: 12 servings. | Prep: 25mins | Cook: 0mins | Ready in:

Ingredients

- 6 cups chopped cooked chicken
- 3/4 cup sliced fresh strawberries
- 1/2 cup halved seedless red grapes
- 2 celery ribs, finely chopped
- 1/3 cup chopped pecans, toasted
- 3/4 cup sour cream
- 3/4 cup mayonnaise
- 1/3 cup chopped fresh basil
- 2 teaspoons lemon juice
- 3/4 teaspoon salt
- 1/4 teaspoon garlic powder
- 1/4 teaspoon pepper
- 24 potato dinner rolls or Hawaiian sweet rolls, split

Direction

- In a big bowl, put the first 5 ingredients. Combine seasonings, lemon juice, basil, mayonnaise, and sour cream in a small bowl; mix in the chicken mixture. Chill with a cover on until eating.
- Stuff each roll with 1/3 cup of chicken mixture to eat.

Nutrition Information

- Calories: 524 calories
- Fiber: 3g fiber)
- Total Carbohydrate: 49g carbohydrate (8g sugars
- Cholesterol: 67mg cholesterol
- Protein: 29g protein.
- Total Fat: 23g fat (5g saturated fat)
- Sodium: 669mg sodium

219. Fruity Chicken Wraps

Serving: 3 wraps. | Prep: 20mins | Cook: 0mins | Ready in:

Ingredients

- 1/2 cup cubed cooked chicken breast

- 1/2 cup chopped peeled mango
- 1/2 cup chopped peeled papaya
- 1/4 cup chopped red onion
- 2 tablespoons golden raisins
- 3 tablespoons fat-free mayonnaise
- 1/8 teaspoon curry powder
- Dash salt and pepper
- 3 flour tortillas (8 inches), room temperature

Direction

- Mix the first 5 ingredients together in a small bowl. Mix pepper, salt, curry powder, and mayonnaise together in a separate bowl; put on the chicken mixture and mix to combine.
- Put 2/3 cup of stuffing down the middle of each tortilla; roll up securely. Fold in plastic and chill or enjoy immediately.

Nutrition Information

- Calories: 243 calories
- Total Fat: 4g fat (1g saturated fat)
- Sodium: 435mg sodium
- Fiber: 2g fiber)
- Total Carbohydrate: 40g carbohydrate (11g sugars
- Cholesterol: 20mg cholesterol
- Protein: 12g protein. Diabetic Exchanges: 2 vegetable

220.   Grilled Chicken Salad Wraps

Serving: 4 servings. | Prep: 15mins | Cook: 10mins | Ready in:

Ingredients

- 3/4 pound boneless skinless chicken breasts
- 1/2 teaspoon salt
- 1/2 teaspoon pepper
- 1 small onion, sliced
- 1 teaspoon olive oil

- 1 cup seedless red grapes, halved
- 2/3 cup chopped peeled mango
- 1/2 cup chopped walnuts, toasted
- 1/2 cup mayonnaise
- 2 teaspoons minced fresh tarragon or 1/2 teaspoon dried tarragon
- 4 flour tortillas (8 inches)
- 1 cup fresh baby spinach

Direction

- Season the chicken with pepper and salt. Arrange onion in a grill wok or basket and brush it with oil. Grill onion and chicken over medium heat, covered, until the onion is tender and the chicken juices run clear, about 5-7 minutes per side. Cut the onion and chicken once it's cool enough to handle.
- Mix onion, tarragon, grapes, mayonnaise, chicken, walnuts, and mango in a huge bowl. Place a cup of the mixture down to the center of each tortilla and top each with spinach. Roll them up tightly and serve.

Nutrition Information

- Calories: 599 calories
- Protein: 26g protein.
- Total Fat: 37g fat (5g saturated fat)
- Sodium: 743mg sodium
- Fiber: 2g fiber)
- Total Carbohydrate: 41g carbohydrate (12g sugars
- Cholesterol: 57mg cholesterol

221.   Guacamole Chicken Roll Ups

Serving: 4 servings. | Prep: 15mins | Cook: 0mins | Ready in:

Ingredients

- 1/4 cup guacamole

- 4 flavored flour tortillas of your choice (10 inches)
- 4 large lettuce leaves
- 1-1/3 cups chopped fresh tomatoes
- 2 packages (6 ounces each) thinly sliced deli smoked chicken breast
- 2 cups shredded Mexican cheese blend

Direction

- Spread over each tortilla with 1 tbsp. of guacamole. Put on top with layer of lettuce, tomatoes, chicken and cheese, then roll up tortilla tightly.

Nutrition Information

- Calories: 523 calories
- Protein: 34g protein.
- Total Fat: 26g fat (13g saturated fat)
- Sodium: 1428mg sodium
- Fiber: 3g fiber)
- Total Carbohydrate: 41g carbohydrate (3g sugars
- Cholesterol: 89mg cholesterol

222.   Guacamole Chicken Wraps

Serving: 4 servings. | Prep: 10mins | Cook: 0mins | Ready in:

Ingredients

- 1/2 cup guacamole
- 4 spinach tortillas (8 inches)
- 1/2 cup salsa
- 1 cup shredded Mexican cheese blend
- 2 packages (6 ounces each) ready-to-use Southwestern chicken strips
- 4 lettuce leaves

Direction

- Spread over half of each tortilla with guacamole. Put to within 2 inches of edges with layer of salsa, cheese, chicken and lettuce, then roll up tightly.

Nutrition Information

- Calories: 381 calories
- Fiber: 3g fiber)
- Total Carbohydrate: 31g carbohydrate (2g sugars
- Cholesterol: 53mg cholesterol
- Protein: 21g protein.
- Total Fat: 19g fat (8g saturated fat)
- Sodium: 939mg sodium

223.   Guacamole Chicken Wraps For Two

Serving: 2 servings. | Prep: 10mins | Cook: 0mins | Ready in:

Ingredients

- 1/4 cup guacamole
- 2 spinach tortillas (8 inches), room temperature
- 1/4 cup salsa
- 1/2 cup shredded Mexican cheese blend
- 1 package (6 ounces) ready-to-use Southwestern chicken strips
- 2 lettuce leaves

Direction

- Spread over half of each tortilla with guacamole. Put to within 2 inches of edges with salsa, cheese, chicken and lettuce, then roll up tightly.

Nutrition Information

- Calories: 436 calories
- Protein: 31g protein.

- Total Fat: 20g fat (8g saturated fat)
- Sodium: 1124mg sodium
- Fiber: 2g fiber)
- Total Carbohydrate: 33g carbohydrate (2g sugars
- Cholesterol: 81mg cholesterol

224. Hearty Chicken Club

Serving: 2 servings. | Prep: 15mins | Cook: 0mins | Ready in:

Ingredients

- 1/4 cup mayonnaise
- 2 tablespoons salsa
- 4 slices seven-grain sandwich bread
- 2 lettuce leaves
- 4 slices tomato
- 8 ounces sliced cooked chicken or turkey
- 4 bacon strips, cooked
- 4 slices cheddar cheese
- 1 ripe avocado, sliced

Direction

- Mix together salsa and mayonnaise, then spread on 2 bread slices. Put on slice with layer of lettuce, tomato, turkey or chicken, bacon, cheese and avocado, then place leftover bread on top.

Nutrition Information

- Calories: 926 calories
- Protein: 46g protein.
- Total Fat: 67g fat (21g saturated fat)
- Sodium: 2029mg sodium
- Fiber: 9g fiber)
- Total Carbohydrate: 36g carbohydrate (7g sugars
- Cholesterol: 133mg cholesterol

225. Italian Chicken Salad Sandwiches

Serving: 2 servings. | Prep: 15mins | Cook: 0mins | Ready in:

Ingredients

- 2/3 cup shredded cooked chicken breast
- 3 tablespoons shredded carrot
- 3 tablespoons finely chopped celery
- 2 tablespoons mild giardiniera, chopped
- 2 teaspoons finely chopped onion
- 1 small garlic clove, minced
- 1/4 cup fat-free mayonnaise
- Dash pepper
- 4 slices sourdough bread
- 2 lettuce leaves

Direction

- Mix the first six ingredients in a small bowl. Then put in pepper and mayonnaise; toss to coat.
- Place half a cup of salad onto 2 bread slices; add lettuce and remaining bread on top.

Nutrition Information

- Calories: 302 calories
- Cholesterol: 43mg cholesterol
- Protein: 23g protein. Diabetic Exchanges: 3 starch
- Total Fat: 4g fat (1g saturated fat)
- Sodium: 732mg sodium
- Fiber: 3g fiber)
- Total Carbohydrate: 43g carbohydrate (5g sugars

226. Italian Chicken Wraps

Serving: 6 servings. | Prep: 10mins | Cook: 15mins | Ready in:

Ingredients

- 1 package (16 ounces) frozen stir-fry vegetable blend
- 2 packages (6 ounces each) ready-to-use grilled chicken breast strips
- 1/2 cup fat-free Italian salad dressing
- 3 tablespoons shredded Parmesan cheese
- 6 flour tortillas (8 inches), room temperature

Direction

- Cook the vegetables following the package instructions in a big saucepan; drain. Mix in the cheese, salad dressing and chicken and heat through. In the middle of each tortilla, place about 3/4 cup of the mixture and roll it up tightly.

Nutrition Information

- Calories: 290 calories
- Sodium: 1129mg sodium
- Fiber: 3g fiber)
- Total Carbohydrate: 38g carbohydrate (2g sugars
- Cholesterol: 40mg cholesterol
- Protein: 20g protein.
- Total Fat: 6g fat (2g saturated fat)

227. Lunch Box Chicken Wrap

Serving: 1 serving. | Prep: 10mins | Cook: 0mins | Ready in:

Ingredients

- 1/4 cup hummus
- 1 whole wheat tortilla (8 inches), room temperature
- 1/2 cup fresh baby spinach
- 1/3 cup shredded cooked chicken breast
- 2 carrot sticks
- 2 sweet red pepper strips

Direction

- Over the tortilla, spread the hummus, then put spinach on top. Put the red pepper, carrot and chicken in a row near the middle of tortilla, then roll it up tightly. Cut it into crosswise slices if preferred. Pack it in an airtight container or wrap securely then let it chill in the fridge until ready to serve.

Nutrition Information

- Calories: 324 calories
- Sodium: 441mg sodium
- Fiber: 7g fiber)
- Total Carbohydrate: 35g carbohydrate (3g sugars
- Cholesterol: 36mg cholesterol
- Protein: 23g protein. Diabetic Exchanges: 3 lean meat
- Total Fat: 10g fat (1g saturated fat)

228. Mango Chicken Wraps

Serving: 5 servings. | Prep: 30mins | Cook: 10mins | Ready in:

Ingredients

- 1-1/2 cups chopped peeled mangoes
- 1/4 cup chopped red onion
- 1 jalapeno pepper, seeded and chopped
- 2 tablespoons lime juice
- 1 teaspoon honey
- 1/4 cup fresh cilantro leaves
- 2 packages (6 ounces each) ready-to-use grilled chicken breast strips
- 1-1/2 teaspoons ground cumin
- 3/4 teaspoon garlic powder

- 3/4 teaspoon chili powder
- 1/8 teaspoon cayenne pepper
- Dash dried oregano
- 4 teaspoons olive oil
- 5 whole wheat tortillas (8 inches)
- 3/4 cup shredded Monterey Jack cheese
- 1 small sweet red pepper, julienned
- 3/4 cup chopped tomatoes
- 1 cup torn leaf lettuce

Direction

- Mix together honey, lime juice, jalapeno, onion and mangoes in a food processor, then put a cover on and process the mixture until pureed. Mix in cilantro, then put aside.
- Sauté together oregano, cayenne, chili powder, garlic powder, cumin and chicken in a big skillet with oil until heated through. Spread over tortillas with the mango sauce, then place in layer of chicken, cheese, red pepper, tomatoes, and lettuce. Roll up tortilla.

Nutrition Information

- Calories: 476 calories
- Sodium: 1116mg sodium
- Fiber: 5g fiber)
- Total Carbohydrate: 46g carbohydrate (15g sugars
- Cholesterol: 75mg cholesterol
- Protein: 31g protein.
- Total Fat: 18g fat (6g saturated fat)

229. Mediterranean Chicken Sandwiches

Serving: 6 servings. | Prep: 20mins | Cook: 0mins | Ready in:

Ingredients

- 1-1/4 pounds boneless skinless chicken breasts, cut into 1-inch strips

- 2 medium tomatoes, seeded and chopped
- 1/2 cup sliced quartered seeded cucumber
- 1/2 cup sliced sweet onion
- 2 tablespoons cider vinegar
- 1 tablespoon olive oil
- 1 tablespoon minced fresh oregano or 1 teaspoon dried oregano
- 1 to 2 teaspoons minced fresh mint or 1/2 teaspoon dried mint
- 1/4 teaspoon salt
- 6 whole wheat pita pocket halves, warmed
- 6 lettuce leaves

Direction

- Cook the chicken for 5 minutes in a big nonstick frying pan coated with cooking spray until pink color is no longer visible. Take it out of the frying pan and let it cool a bit.
- Mix together the onion, cucumber, tomatoes and chicken in a big bowl. Whisk together the salt, mint, oregano, oil and vinegar in a small bowl, then pour the mixture on top of the chicken mixture and gently toss.
- Put on a cover and chill in the fridge for a minimum of 1 hour. Line lettuce on the pita halves, then use a slotted spoon to fill with chicken mixture.

Nutrition Information

- Calories: 227 calories
- Total Fat: 4g fat (1g saturated fat)
- Sodium: 335mg sodium
- Fiber: 3g fiber)
- Total Carbohydrate: 22g carbohydrate (0 sugars
- Cholesterol: 55mg cholesterol
- Protein: 26g protein. Diabetic Exchanges: 3 lean meat

230. Mini Chicken Salad Croissants

Serving: 20 servings. | Prep: 25mins | Cook: 0mins | Ready in:

Ingredients

- 1/3 cup sour cream
- 1/3 cup mayonnaise
- 4 teaspoons lemon juice
- 1 teaspoon salt
- 1/4 teaspoon pepper
- 4 celery ribs, thinly sliced
- 1 cup chopped fresh mushrooms
- 1/4 cup chopped green pepper
- 1/4 cup chopped sweet red pepper
- 3 cups cubed cooked chicken
- 4 bacon strips, cooked and crumbled
- 1/2 cup chopped pecans, toasted
- 20 miniature croissants, split
- Lettuce leaves

Direction

- Combine the first 5 ingredients in a big bowl; mix in the vegetables. Add chicken; mix to coat. Chill with a cover on for a minimum of 4 hours.
- Mix in pecans and bacon. Use lettuce to line croissants; stuff each with 1/4 cup of the chicken mixture.

Nutrition Information

- Calories: 217 calories
- Protein: 10g protein.
- Total Fat: 14g fat (5g saturated fat)
- Sodium: 403mg sodium
- Fiber: 1g fiber)
- Total Carbohydrate: 14g carbohydrate (1g sugars
- Cholesterol: 41mg cholesterol

231. Nutty Chicken Pita Sandwiches

Serving: 6 servings. | Prep: 15mins | Cook: 0mins | Ready in:

Ingredients

- 1 package (8 ounces) cream cheese, softened
- 3 tablespoons whole milk
- 1 tablespoon lemon juice
- 2 cups cubed cooked chicken
- 1/2 cup chopped green pepper
- 2 tablespoons chopped green onions
- 1 teaspoon ground mustard
- 1/2 teaspoon dried thyme
- 1/2 teaspoon salt
- 1/8 teaspoon pepper
- 1/4 cup chopped walnuts
- 6 pita pocket halves

Direction

- Beat lemon juice, milk, and cream cheese together in a big bowl. Mix in pepper, salt, thyme, mustard, onions, green pepper, and chicken; chill.
- Mix in walnuts right before eating. Put about 1/2 cup of stuffing into each pita half.

Nutrition Information

- Calories:
- Fiber:
- Total Carbohydrate:
- Cholesterol:
- Protein:
- Total Fat:
- Sodium:

232. Nutty Chicken Roll Ups

Serving: 7 servings. | Prep: 25mins | Cook: 0mins | Ready in:

Ingredients

- 3 cups chopped cooked chicken breast
- 1/2 cup finely chopped pecans, toasted
- 1/4 cup finely chopped onion
- 1 celery rib, finely chopped
- 1/2 cup mayonnaise
- 1/2 teaspoon chili powder
- 1/4 teaspoon salt
- 1/4 teaspoon ground cumin
- 1/8 teaspoon pepper
- 7 lettuce leaves
- 7 flour tortillas (8 inches)

Direction

- Mix together celery, onion, pecans and chicken in a big bowl. Mix together pepper, cumin, salt, chili powder and mayonnaise, then stir into chicken mixture.
- On tortillas, put lettuce and put 1/2 cup of chicken mixture on top of each, then roll up tortillas tightly. Serve instantly or use plastic to wrap and chill until ready to serve.

Nutrition Information

- Calories: 416 calories
- Total Fat: 24g fat (3g saturated fat)
- Sodium: 465mg sodium
- Fiber: 1g fiber)
- Total Carbohydrate: 28g carbohydrate (1g sugars
- Cholesterol: 52mg cholesterol
- Protein: 23g protein.

---

233. Nutty Chicken Sandwiches

Serving: 16 tea sandwiches. | Prep: 20mins | Cook: 0mins | Ready in:

Ingredients

- 1 cup shredded cooked chicken breast
- 1 hard-boiled large egg, chopped
- 1/2 cup unsweetened crushed pineapple, drained
- 1/3 cup mayonnaise
- 1/2 teaspoon salt
- 1/8 teaspoon pepper
- 1/4 cup chopped pecans, toasted
- 1/2 cup fresh baby spinach
- 8 slices white bread, crusts removed

Direction

- Mix pepper, salt, mayonnaise, pineapple, egg, and chicken together in a small bowl. Put a cover on and put in the fridge to chill for a minimum of 1 hour.
- Mix in pecans right before eating. On 4 bread slices, put spinach; put chicken salad and the rest of the bread on top. Slice each sandwich into 4 parts.

Nutrition Information

- Calories:
- Protein:
- Total Fat:
- Sodium:
- Fiber:
- Total Carbohydrate:
- Cholesterol:

---

234. Olive Chicken Roll Ups

Serving: 8 servings. | Prep: 20mins | Cook: 0mins | Ready in:

Ingredients

- 1 package (8 ounces) cream cheese, softened
- 2 cans (4 ounces each) chopped green chilies, drained
- 1 can (4-1/4 ounces) chopped ripe olives, drained

- 1 jar (2 ounces) diced pimientos, drained
- 1/4 teaspoon garlic powder
- 1/4 teaspoon chili powder
- 1/4 teaspoon hot pepper sauce
- 8 flour tortillas (8 inches)
- 1-1/4 pounds deli smoked chicken
- Salsa or picante sauce, optional

Direction

- Beat cream cheese till smooth in a big bowl. Fold pepper sauce, chili powder, garlic powder, pimientos, olives and chilies in.
- On every tortilla, spread on one side. Put chicken on top; tightly roll up. Use plastic to wrap. Refrigerate for 1 hour minimum. If desired, serve with salsa.

Nutrition Information

- Calories: 338 calories
- Sodium: 1078mg sodium
- Fiber: 1g fiber)
- Total Carbohydrate: 29g carbohydrate (1g sugars
- Cholesterol: 64mg cholesterol
- Protein: 20g protein.
- Total Fat: 16g fat (7g saturated fat)

235. Open Faced Chicken Salad Sandwiches

Serving: 6 servings. | Prep: 20mins | Cook: 5mins | Ready in:

Ingredients

- 3 cups cubed cooked chicken breast
- 3 celery ribs, finely chopped
- 1 cup fat-free mayonnaise
- 1 small onion, finely chopped
- 1/2 cup dried cranberries
- 1/4 cup chopped pecans
- 2 tablespoons white wine vinegar

- 2 tablespoons Creole mustard
- 1 tablespoon lemon juice
- 1/4 teaspoon pepper
- 6 slices sourdough bread
- Butter-flavored cooking spray
- 3/4 cup sugar-free apricot preserves
- 6 slices Brie cheese (1/2 ounce each)

Direction

- Mix together the initial 10 ingredients gently in a big bowl. On a baking tray, put the slices of bread then spritz it with butter-flavored cooking spray. Let it broil for 2-3 minutes, placed 4 inches from the heat source or until it turns golden brown.
- On top of the untoasted sides of the slices of bread, spread the preserves, then put a slice of cheese and 2/3 cup chicken salad on top of each bread. Let it broil for 2-3 minutes more or until the cheese melts.

Nutrition Information

- Calories: 381 calories
- Total Fat: 12g fat (4g saturated fat)
- Sodium: 780mg sodium
- Fiber: 3g fiber)
- Total Carbohydrate: 46g carbohydrate (12g sugars
- Cholesterol: 72mg cholesterol
- Protein: 28g protein.

236. Orange Chicken Wraps

Serving: 8 servings. | Prep: 20mins | Cook: 0mins | Ready in:

Ingredients

- 4 cups coleslaw mix
- 2 cans (11 ounces each) mandarin oranges, drained
- 1-1/2 cups fresh broccoli florets

- 1 medium sweet yellow pepper, thinly sliced
- 1/4 cup chopped celery
- 1 tablespoon sunflower kernels
- 1 teaspoon grated orange zest
- 1/3 cup coleslaw salad dressing
- 2 packages (6 ounces each) ready-to-serve roasted chicken breast strips, chopped
- 3/4 cup honey barbecue sauce
- 8 flour tortillas (10 inches)

Direction

- Mix the first 7 ingredients together in a big bowl, then put in salad dressing and toss to coat well. Mix barbecue sauce and chicken together in a separate bowl.
- Scoop 3/4 cup of coleslaw mixture down the center of each tortilla, then put 1/4 cup of chicken mixture on top and roll up.

Nutrition Information

- Calories: 399 calories
- Sodium: 948mg sodium
- Fiber: 8g fiber)
- Total Carbohydrate: 55g carbohydrate (20g sugars
- Cholesterol: 26mg cholesterol
- Protein: 17g protein.
- Total Fat: 9g fat (2g saturated fat)

237.   Peanut Chicken Pockets

Serving: 4 servings. | Prep: 15mins | Cook: 15mins |Ready in:

Ingredients

- 2 cups cubed cooked chicken
- 2 celery ribs, chopped
- 1/4 cup chopped cucumber
- 1/4 cup bean sprouts
- 1/4 cup chopped peanuts
- 1/4 cup mayonnaise

- 2 green onions, chopped
- 1 tablespoon minced fresh parsley
- 1 tablespoon lemon juice
- 1/4 teaspoon salt
- 1/4 teaspoon pepper
- 4 pita breads (6 inches), halved
- 8 lettuce leaves
- 8 tomato slices

Direction

- Mix the first 11 ingredients together in a big bowl. Use tomato slices and lettuce leaves to line pita halves. Put the chicken mixture into the pitas.

Nutrition Information

- Calories: 474 calories
- Total Carbohydrate: 40g carbohydrate (3g sugars
- Cholesterol: 67mg cholesterol
- Protein: 29g protein.
- Total Fat: 22g fat (4g saturated fat)
- Sodium: 669mg sodium
- Fiber: 3g fiber)

238.   Pesto Chicken Salad Sandwiches

Serving: 6 servings. | Prep: 20mins | Cook: 0mins |Ready in:

Ingredients

- 2/3 cup reduced-fat mayonnaise
- 1/3 cup prepared pesto
- 2 tablespoons lemon juice
- 1/4 teaspoon garlic powder
- 1/4 teaspoon pepper
- 3 cups cubed cooked chicken
- 1 jar (7 ounces) roasted sweet red peppers, drained and chopped
- 1 celery rib, finely chopped

- 6 romaine leaves
- 6 ciabatta rolls, split

Direction

- Mix the first 5 ingredients together in a big bowl. Add celery, red peppers, and chicken, mix to combine. Enjoy on rolls lined with lettuce.

Nutrition Information

- Calories: 636 calories
- Sodium: 1047mg sodium
- Fiber: 4g fiber)
- Total Carbohydrate: 75g carbohydrate (7g sugars
- Cholesterol: 76mg cholesterol
- Protein: 33g protein.
- Total Fat: 24g fat (5g saturated fat)

---

239. Picnic Chicken Pitas

Serving: 4 servings. | Prep: 20mins | Cook: 0mins | Ready in:

Ingredients

- 1 package (16 ounces) frozen broccoli florets, cooked and drained
- 2 cups shredded cooked chicken
- 1 cup shredded cheddar cheese
- 1 medium tomato, chopped
- 1/4 cup mayonnaise
- 2 tablespoons prepared mustard
- 1/8 teaspoon pepper
- 8 pita pocket halves
- 4 bacon strips, cooked and crumbled

Direction

- Mix tomato, cheese, chicken, and broccoli in a big-sized bowl. Mix pepper, mustard, and mayonnaise in a small-sized bowl; add on top of the broccoli mixture and coat by tossing.

Scoop roughly three quarters cup into each pita half; add bacon on top.

Nutrition Information

- Calories: 587 calories
- Total Fat: 29g fat (9g saturated fat)
- Sodium: 878mg sodium
- Fiber: 5g fiber)
- Total Carbohydrate: 40g carbohydrate (4g sugars
- Cholesterol: 100mg cholesterol
- Protein: 37g protein.

---

240. Pineapple Chicken Salad Sandwiches

Serving: 6 servings. | Prep: 15mins | Cook: 0mins | Ready in:

Ingredients

- 2 cups cubed cooked chicken breast
- 1/2 cup crushed pineapple, drained
- 1/4 cup chopped pecans
- 1/4 cup chopped celery
- 2 tablespoons finely chopped onion
- 2 tablespoons sweet pickle relish
- 1/2 cup mayonnaise
- 1/4 teaspoon onion salt
- 1/4 teaspoon garlic salt
- 1/4 teaspoon paprika
- 6 lettuce leaves
- 6 sandwich rolls, split

Direction

- Mix the first 6 ingredients together in a small bowl. Mix together paprika, garlic salt, onion salt, and mayonnaise together; add to the chicken mixture and toss well. Eat on rolls lined with lettuce.

Nutrition Information

- Calories: 433 calories
- Sodium: 637mg sodium
- Fiber: 2g fiber)
- Total Carbohydrate: 38g carbohydrate (9g sugars
- Cholesterol: 43mg cholesterol
- Protein: 20g protein.
- Total Fat: 22g fat (3g saturated fat)

241. Pita Pocket Chicken Salad

Serving: 6 servings. | Prep: 15mins | Cook: 0mins | Ready in:

Ingredients

- 2 cups cubed cooked chicken
- 1-1/2 cups seedless red grapes, halved
- 1 cup chopped cucumber
- 3/4 cup sliced almonds
- 3/4 cup shredded part-skim mozzarella cheese
- 1/2 cup poppy seed salad dressing
- 6 pita pocket halves
- Leaf lettuce, optional

Direction

- Mix mozzarella cheese, almonds, cucumber, grapes and chicken in a big bowl. Sprinkle with dressing and coat by tossing. If you want, use lettuce to line pita breads; use chicken salad to fill.

Nutrition Information

- Calories: 492 calories
- Fiber: 3g fiber)
- Total Carbohydrate: 49g carbohydrate (12g sugars
- Cholesterol: 59mg cholesterol
- Protein: 25g protein.

- Total Fat: 21g fat (4g saturated fat)
- Sodium: 549mg sodium

242. Quick Cranberry Chicken Salad Sandwiches

Serving: 2 servings. | Prep: 15mins | Cook: 5mins | Ready in:

Ingredients

- 2 sandwich buns, split
- 2 teaspoons butter, softened
- 2 teaspoons cream cheese, softened
- 1 cup shredded cooked chicken
- 1/3 cup whole-berry cranberry sauce
- 3 tablespoons mayonnaise
- 2 green onions, chopped
- 1 teaspoon lemon juice
- 2 lettuce leaves

Direction

- Cut buns in half then place them cut side up on an ungreased baking sheet. Use butter to spread on bun bottoms. Broil 3-4 in. from the heat until golden brown color forms, about 1 to 2 minutes. Use cream cheese to spread on bun tops.
- Mix together lemon juice, onions, mayonnaise, cranberry sauce and chicken in a small bowl. Spread the mixture on bun bottoms. Put a lettuce leaf on top of each bun bottom, then replace the bun tops.

Nutrition Information

- Calories: 520 calories
- Fiber: 2g fiber)
- Total Carbohydrate: 56g carbohydrate (18g sugars
- Cholesterol: 79mg cholesterol
- Protein: 29g protein.
- Total Fat: 20g fat (5g saturated fat)

- Sodium: 697mg sodium

243. Ranch Chicken Salad Sandwiches

Serving: 6 servings. | Prep: 15mins | Cook: 0mins | Ready in:

Ingredients

- 1/4 cup reduced-fat mayonnaise
- 3 tablespoons fat-free ranch salad dressing
- 3 tablespoons fat-free sour cream
- 1 tablespoon lemon juice
- 1/8 teaspoon pepper
- 2 cups cubed cooked chicken breast
- 1/2 cup thinly sliced celery
- 2 tablespoons diced sweet red pepper
- 1 tablespoon chopped green onion
- 6 hamburger buns, split
- 6 lettuce leaves
- 6 slices tomato

Direction

- Mix together pepper, lemon juice, sour cream, ranch dressing, mayonnaise in a small bowl. Mix in onion, red pepper, celery and chicken until everything combines. Place 1/3 cup of the mixture onto each bun bottom, put lettuce and tomato on top of the mixture. Then replace bun tops.

Nutrition Information

- Calories: 257 calories
- Fiber: 2g fiber)
- Total Carbohydrate: 29g carbohydrate (6g sugars
- Cholesterol: 41mg cholesterol
- Protein: 18g protein. Diabetic Exchanges: 2 starch
- Total Fat: 7g fat (1g saturated fat)
- Sodium: 456mg sodium

244. Raspberry Pecan Chicken Salad

Serving: 6 servings. | Prep: 15mins | Cook: 0mins | Ready in:

Ingredients

- 1 carton (6 ounces) orange yogurt
- 1/2 cup mayonnaise
- 1/4 teaspoon Chinese five-spice powder
- 3 cups cubed cooked chicken
- 2 green onions, chopped
- 1/4 cup sliced celery
- 1/4 cup chopped pecans, toasted
- 1 cup fresh raspberries
- 12 slices multigrain bread

Direction

- Combine five-spice powder, mayonnaise, and yogurt in a big bowl. Add in pecans, celery, green onions, and chicken and mix. Toss carefully with raspberries. Serve with bread.

Nutrition Information

- Calories: 463 calories
- Sodium: 371mg sodium
- Fiber: 6g fiber)
- Total Carbohydrate: 31g carbohydrate (10g sugars
- Cholesterol: 65mg cholesterol
- Protein: 29g protein.
- Total Fat: 24g fat (4g saturated fat)

245. Sesame Chicken Veggie Wraps

Serving: 8 servings. | Prep: 20mins | Cook: 10mins | Ready in:

Ingredients

- 1 cup frozen shelled edamame
- DRESSING:
- 2 tablespoons orange juice
- 2 tablespoons olive oil
- 1 teaspoon sesame oil
- 1/2 teaspoon ground ginger
- 1/4 teaspoon salt
- 1/8 teaspoon pepper
- WRAPS:
- 2 cups fresh baby spinach
- 1 cup thinly sliced cucumber
- 1 cup fresh sugar snap peas, chopped
- 1/2 cup shredded carrots
- 1/2 cup thinly sliced sweet red pepper
- 1 cup chopped cooked chicken breast
- 8 whole wheat tortillas (8 inches), room temperature

Direction

- Follow package directions to cook edamame. Drain and rinse edamame under cold water, then drain well. Whisk dressing ingredients together.
- Mix edamame, chicken and leftover vegetables together in a big bowl, then toss along with dressing. Put on each tortilla with 1/2 cup of the mixture, then fold bottom and sides of tortilla over filling. Roll up tortilla.

Nutrition Information

- Calories: 214 calories
- Fiber: 5g fiber)
- Total Carbohydrate: 28g carbohydrate (2g sugars
- Cholesterol: 13mg cholesterol
- Protein: 12g protein. Diabetic Exchanges: 2 starch

- Total Fat: 7g fat (1g saturated fat)
- Sodium: 229mg sodium

246. Sesame Chicken Wraps

Serving: 2 servings. | Prep: 10mins | Cook: 0mins | Ready in:

Ingredients

- 1 package (6 ounces) ready-to-use grilled chicken breast strips
- 1/4 cup plus 2 tablespoons sesame ginger salad dressing, divided
- 2 whole wheat tortillas (8 inches)
- 1/2 cup bean sprouts
- 1/2 cup julienned carrot
- 1/4 cup chopped sweet red pepper
- 2 tablespoons chopped red onion

Direction

- Mix together 1/4 cup of salad dressing and chicken in a small bowl, then pour over tortillas. Put onion, pepper, carrot and bean sprouts on top, then use leftover dressing to drizzle over top. Roll tortilla up and use toothpicks to secure.

Nutrition Information

- Calories: 446 calories
- Total Carbohydrate: 40g carbohydrate (14g sugars
- Cholesterol: 56mg cholesterol
- Protein: 25g protein.
- Total Fat: 20g fat (3g saturated fat)
- Sodium: 1423mg sodium
- Fiber: 4g fiber)

247. Strawberry Chicken Salad Croissants

Serving: 9 servings. | Prep: 25mins | Cook: 0mins | Ready in:

Ingredients

- 4 cups shredded cooked chicken breasts
- 1/2 cup mayonnaise
- 2 tablespoons sweet pickle relish
- 2 tablespoons seedless strawberry jam
- 1/4 teaspoon salt
- 12 fresh strawberries, quartered
- 1/2 cup salted roasted almonds
- 9 croissants, split

Direction

- Mix salt, jam, relish, mayonnaise, and chicken in a big bowl. Mix in almonds and strawberries. Scoop half a cup of chicken salad over each bottom of croissant; replace tops.

Nutrition Information

- Calories: 494 calories
- Protein: 26g protein.
- Total Fat: 29g fat (9g saturated fat)
- Sodium: 658mg sodium
- Fiber: 3g fiber)
- Total Carbohydrate: 33g carbohydrate (11g sugars
- Cholesterol: 96mg cholesterol

248. Tarragon Chicken Salad Sandwiches

Serving: 8 servings. | Prep: 15mins | Cook: 0mins | Ready in:

Ingredients

- 1/2 cup mayonnaise
- 1 tablespoon lemon juice

- 1 teaspoon Dijon mustard
- 3 cups cubed cooked chicken
- 3/4 cup chopped celery
- 1 tablespoon minced fresh tarragon or 1 teaspoon dried tarragon
- 1/3 cup sunflower kernels
- 8 croissants or rolls, split
- Lettuce leaves

Direction

- Mix the first 3 ingredients together in a large bowl. Mix in tarragon, celery, and chicken. Add sunflower seeds right before eating. Use lettuce to line croissants and put 1/2 cup of chicken salad on top.

Nutrition Information

- Calories: 471 calories
- Cholesterol: 90mg cholesterol
- Protein: 21g protein.
- Total Fat: 30g fat (10g saturated fat)
- Sodium: 604mg sodium
- Fiber: 2g fiber)
- Total Carbohydrate: 28g carbohydrate (2g sugars

249. Tea Room Chicken Salad

Serving: 12 servings. | Prep: 10mins | Cook: 0mins | Ready in:

Ingredients

- 2 cups mayonnaise
- 3/4 cup chopped celery
- 1 tablespoon prepared mustard
- 1-1/4 teaspoons poppy seeds
- 1/2 teaspoon salt
- 10 cups cubed cooked chicken
- Chopped pecans

Direction

- Mix salt, poppy seeds, mustard, celery, and mayonnaise together in a big bowl. Tuck in chicken. Put a cover on and refrigerate for 3-4 hours. Before eating, put pecans on top.

Nutrition Information

- Calories: 492 calories
- Total Carbohydrate: 0 carbohydrate (0 sugars
- Cholesterol: 117mg cholesterol
- Protein: 34g protein.
- Total Fat: 38g fat (6g saturated fat)
- Sodium: 419mg sodium
- Fiber: 0 fiber)

---

250.   Thai Chicken Lettuce Wraps

Serving: 6 servings. | Prep: 35mins | Cook: 0mins | Ready in:

Ingredients

- 1/4 cup rice vinegar
- 2 tablespoons lime juice
- 2 tablespoons reduced-fat mayonnaise
- 2 tablespoons reduced-fat creamy peanut butter
- 1 tablespoon brown sugar
- 1 tablespoon reduced-sodium soy sauce
- 2 teaspoons minced fresh gingerroot
- 1 teaspoon sesame oil
- 1 teaspoon Thai chili sauce
- 1 garlic clove, chopped
- 3 tablespoons canola oil
- 1/2 cup minced fresh cilantro
- CHICKEN SALAD:
- 2 cups cubed cooked chicken breast
- 1 small sweet red pepper, diced
- 1/2 cup chopped green onions
- 1/2 cup shredded carrot
- 1/2 cup unsalted dry roasted peanuts, chopped, divided

- 6 Bibb or Boston lettuce leaves

Direction

- Mix the first ten ingredients together in a blender. Pour in a steady stream of oil gradually while processing, then stir in cilantro. Put aside.
- Mix together 1/4 cup peanuts, carrot, onions, red pepper and chicken in a big bowl, then put in dressing and toss coat well. Distribute mixture into lettuce leaves and sprinkle leftover peanuts over top, then fold lettuce over filling.

Nutrition Information

- Calories: 284 calories
- Sodium: 222mg sodium
- Fiber: 2g fiber)
- Total Carbohydrate: 12g carbohydrate (6g sugars
- Cholesterol: 38mg cholesterol
- Protein: 19g protein. Diabetic Exchanges: 3 fat
- Total Fat: 19g fat (2g saturated fat)

---

251.   Toasted Almond Chicken Salad Sandwiches

Serving: 12 servings. | Prep: 15mins | Cook: 0mins | Ready in:

Ingredients

- 2 cups cubed cooked chicken
- 2 celery ribs, chopped
- 1/2 cup chopped green pepper
- 1/2 cup mayonnaise
- 1/3 cup slivered almonds, toasted
- 1/4 cup sweet pickle relish
- 1/4 cup sliced pimiento-stuffed olives
- 2 tablespoons chopped onion
- 2 teaspoons prepared mustard
- 3/4 to 1-1/4 teaspoons salt

- 1/4 teaspoon pepper
- 12 English muffins, split and toasted
- 12 lettuce leaves
- 12 thin tomato slices

Direction

- Mix together the first 11 ingredients in a bowl. Put lettuce leaves on top of 12 muffin halves then spread chicken salad on lettuce leaves. Put tomato slices then the remaining muffin halves on top.

Nutrition Information

- Calories: 213 calories
- Total Carbohydrate: 31g carbohydrate (0 sugars
- Cholesterol: 21mg cholesterol
- Protein: 3g protein. Diabetic Exchanges: 2 starch
- Total Fat: 4g fat (1g saturated fat)
- Sodium: 635mg sodium
- Fiber: 3g fiber)

252. Veggie Chicken Wraps

Serving: 4 servings. | Prep: 15mins | Cook: 0mins | Ready in:

Ingredients

- 1 carton (8 ounces) spreadable garden vegetable cream cheese
- 4 flour tortillas (8 inches)
- 2 cups shredded romaine
- 2 small tomatoes, thinly sliced
- 8 slices provolone cheese
- 1 small red onion, thinly sliced
- 2 cups diced cooked chicken

Direction

- On each tortilla, spread cream cheese evenly. Arrange romaine, tomatoes, cheese, onion and chicken in layers on each tortilla. Roll up firmly. Slice the wraps into two halves then serve.

Nutrition Information

- Calories:
- Total Carbohydrate:
- Cholesterol:
- Protein:
- Total Fat:
- Sodium:
- Fiber:

253. Waldorf Chicken Salad Sandwiches

Serving: 4 servings. | Prep: 15mins | Cook: 0mins | Ready in:

Ingredients

- 3 cups cubed cooked chicken
- 1 medium tart apple, chopped
- 3/4 cup mayonnaise
- 1/4 cup raisins
- 1/4 cup chopped pecans, toasted
- 1 tablespoon apple juice
- 1/2 teaspoon salt
- 1/4 teaspoon ground nutmeg
- 8 slices pumpernickel bread
- Lettuce leaves, optional

Direction

- Mix the first 8 ingredients in a big bowl. Spread about 1 cup of chicken salad over 4 bread slices. Use the rest of the bread and lettuce if you want to put on top.

Nutrition Information

- Calories: 731 calories
- Protein: 36g protein.

- Total Fat: 48g fat (7g saturated fat)
- Sodium: 960mg sodium
- Fiber: 5g fiber)
- Total Carbohydrate: 39g carbohydrate (13g sugars
- Cholesterol: 108mg cholesterol

---

254. Zippy Chicken Wraps

Serving: 4 servings. | Prep: 30mins | Cook: 0mins | Ready in:

Ingredients

- 1/2 pound boneless skinless chicken breast, cut into thin slices
- 1 tablespoon butter
- 1 garlic clove, minced
- 1 teaspoon chili powder
- 1/2 teaspoon ground cumin
- Dash cayenne pepper
- 3 ounces cream cheese, softened
- 1/2 cup shredded cheddar cheese
- 1/4 cup sour cream
- 1 can (10 ounces) diced tomatoes and green chilies, drained
- 2 green onions, thinly sliced
- 4 flour tortillas (8 inches), room temperature
- Sliced avocado, sliced ripe olives and salsa

Direction

- Sauté chicken in a big skillet with butter until not pink anymore. Put in cayenne, cumin, chili powder and garlic, then cook and stir until the mixture is heated through. Take away from the heat and allow to cool.
- Beat together sour cream, cheddar cheese and cream cheese in a small bowl until mixed, then stir in onions, tomatoes and chicken.
- Pour down the center of each tortilla with 1/2 cup of the chicken mixture, then put avocado and olives on top. Fold over filling with sides of tortilla and use a toothpick to secure if wanted. Serve along with salsa.

Nutrition Information

- Calories: 404 calories
- Protein: 22g protein.
- Total Fat: 21g fat (12g saturated fat)
- Sodium: 753mg sodium
- Fiber: 1g fiber)
- Total Carbohydrate: 31g carbohydrate (2g sugars
- Cholesterol: 87mg cholesterol

Chapter 4: Salad Sandwich Recipes

***

---

255. Antipasto Focaccia Sandwiches

Serving: 3 sandwiches (6 servings each). | Prep: 45mins | Cook: 0mins | Ready in:

Ingredients

- 1/2 pound Genoa salami, diced
- 1/2 pound deli ham, diced
- 1/2 pound pepperoni, diced
- 1 block (8 ounces) provolone cheese, diced
- 1 cup canned garbanzo beans or chickpeas, rinsed, drained and chopped
- 1 cup canned kidney beans, rinsed, drained and chopped
- 2 medium tomatoes, chopped
- 1/2 cup finely chopped red onion
- 1/2 cup pepperoncini
- 1/2 teaspoon coarsely ground pepper
- 1 cup Italian salad dressing
- 3 loaves (1 pound each) focaccia bread

- 3 cups torn leaf lettuce

Direction

- Mix the initial ten ingredients in a big bowl; pour in salad dressing and coat by tossing. Keep it covered and let chill in the refrigerator for 8 hours or overnight.
- Horizontally halve each focaccia loaf. Hollow out bottom halves, leaving three quarters inch shells. Mix in antipasto mixture; scoop into shells. Replace bread tops. Use plastic wrap to wrap sandwiches tightly; keep chilled in the refrigerator for no less than 2 hours.
- Just prior to serving, put lettuce into sandwiches. Chop into wedges.

Nutrition Information

- Calories:
- Sodium:
- Fiber:
- Total Carbohydrate:
- Cholesterol:
- Protein:
- Total Fat:

256.	Apple Tuna Sandwiches

Serving: 3 servings. | Prep: 15mins | Cook: 0mins | Ready in:

Ingredients

- 1/3 cup fat-free mayonnaise
- 1/4 cup finely chopped celery
- 1/4 cup finely chopped walnuts
- 2 tablespoons finely chopped onion
- 1 tablespoon sweet pickle relish
- 1 teaspoon sugar
- 1 pouch (7.1 ounces) light water-packed tuna
- 1/2 cup chopped red apple
- 6 slices reduced-calorie bread, toasted
- 6 lettuce leaves

Direction

- Mix the first 6 ingredients together in a big bowl; mix in apple and tuna. On 3 bread slices, spread 1/2 cup of tuna mixture. Put lettuce and the rest of the bread on top.

Nutrition Information

- Calories: 286 calories
- Total Fat: 8g fat (1g saturated fat)
- Sodium: 704mg sodium
- Fiber: 7g fiber)
- Total Carbohydrate: 33g carbohydrate (9g sugars
- Cholesterol: 23mg cholesterol
- Protein: 24g protein. Diabetic Exchanges: 2 starch

257.	Apple Walnut Turkey Sandwiches

Serving: 4 servings. | Prep: 15mins | Cook: 0mins | Ready in:

Ingredients

- 3/4 cup mayonnaise
- 1/4 cup chopped celery
- 1/4 cup raisins
- 1/4 cup chopped walnuts, toasted
- 1 medium tart apple, chopped
- 3/4 pound sliced deli turkey
- 8 slices sourdough bread
- Lettuce leaves

Direction

- Mix together walnuts, raisins, celery and mayonnaise in a big bowl, then stir in apple and put aside. Put on 4 bread slices with turkey, then put apple mixture, lettuce and leftover bread on top.

Nutrition Information

- Calories: 663 calories
- Sodium: 1655mg sodium
- Fiber: 4g fiber)
- Total Carbohydrate: 50g carbohydrate (11g sugars
- Cholesterol: 53mg cholesterol
- Protein: 22g protein.
- Total Fat: 42g fat (6g saturated fat)

---

258.   Arkansas Travelers

Serving: 5 servings. | Prep: 15mins | Cook: 0mins | Ready in:

Ingredients

- 1 pound turkey breast
- 1 block (5 ounces) Swiss cheese
- 1 avocado, peeled and pitted
- 1 large tomato
- 10 bacon strips, cooked and crumbled
- 1/3 to 1/2 cup ranch salad dressing
- 10 slices whole wheat bread, toasted

Direction

- Cut the tomato, avocado, cheese and turkey into a quarter inch cubes; add to a big bowl. Put in dressing and bacon. Scoop half a cup of the mixture between two toast slices.

Nutrition Information

- Calories: 464 calories
- Protein: 30g protein.
- Total Fat: 27g fat (8g saturated fat)
- Sodium: 1378mg sodium
- Fiber: 5g fiber)
- Total Carbohydrate: 30g carbohydrate (4g sugars
- Cholesterol: 66mg cholesterol

---

259.   Bacon 'n' Egg Salad Sandwiches

Serving: 6-8 servings. | Prep: 10mins | Cook: 0mins | Ready in:

Ingredients

- 12 hard-boiled large eggs, chopped
- 1/2 cup mayonnaise
- 1 small onion, chopped
- 1 small sweet pickle, diced
- 1 tablespoon prepared mustard
- 2 teaspoons sweet pickle juice
- 1-1/2 teaspoons salt
- 1 teaspoon minced fresh parsley
- 1/4 teaspoon pepper
- 1/4 teaspoon Italian seasoning
- 1/4 teaspoon dried oregano
- 1/8 teaspoon garlic powder
- 1/8 teaspoon chili powder
- 1/8 teaspoon paprika
- 5 bacon strips, cooked and crumbled
- Lettuce leaves
- 6 to 8 sandwich rolls, split

Direction

- Mix the first 14 ingredients together in a large bowl. Put a lid on and keep in the fridge for at least an hour. Right before serving, add bacon and stir. Put a lettuce leaf and about half a cup egg salad on each roll.

Nutrition Information

- Calories:
- Fiber:
- Total Carbohydrate:
- Cholesterol:
- Protein:
- Total Fat:
- Sodium:

260.   Bacon Egg Salad Croissants

Serving: 4 servings. | Prep: 15mins | Cook: 0mins | Ready in:

Ingredients

- 1/3 cup diced celery
- 1/3 cup mayonnaise
- 1 teaspoon prepared mustard
- 1/4 teaspoon salt
- 1/8 teaspoon pepper
- 6 hard-boiled large eggs, chopped
- 1/3 cup crumbled cooked bacon
- 4 lettuce leaves
- 4 thin tomato slices
- 4 croissants, split

Direction

- Mix pepper, salt, mustard, mayonnaise and celery in a big-sized bowl. Mix in bacon and eggs. Over each croissant, add half cup of egg salad, a tomato slice and a lettuce leaf.

Nutrition Information

- Calories: 521 calories
- Sodium: 1088mg sodium
- Fiber: 2g fiber)
- Total Carbohydrate: 29g carbohydrate (4g sugars
- Cholesterol: 370mg cholesterol
- Protein: 18g protein.
- Total Fat: 36g fat (12g saturated fat)

261.   Bacon And Egg Salad Sandwich

Serving: 2 servings. | Prep: 10mins | Cook: 0mins | Ready in:

Ingredients

- 2 bacon strips, cooked and crumbled
- 3 tablespoons mayonnaise
- 1 tablespoon spicy brown mustard
- 1-1/2 teaspoons capers, drained
- 3 hard-boiled large eggs, chopped
- 4 slices sandwich bread
- 2 lettuce leaves

Direction

- Mix capers, mustard, mayonnaise and bacon in a small-sized bowl. Put in eggs; combine by mixing lightly. Spread on two bread slices; add leftover bread and lettuce on top. Serve right away.

Nutrition Information

- Calories: 364 calories
- Fiber: 1g fiber)
- Total Carbohydrate: 26g carbohydrate (5g sugars
- Cholesterol: 333mg cholesterol
- Protein: 16g protein.
- Total Fat: 21g fat (5g saturated fat)
- Sodium: 843mg sodium

262.   Better Than Egg Salad

Serving: 4 servings. | Prep: 20mins | Cook: 0mins | Ready in:

Ingredients

- 1/4 cup reduced-fat mayonnaise
- 1/4 cup chopped celery
- 2 green onions, chopped
- 2 tablespoons sweet pickle relish
- 1 tablespoon Dijon mustard
- 1/4 teaspoon ground turmeric
- 1/4 teaspoon salt
- 1/8 teaspoon cayenne pepper
- 1 package (12.3 ounces) silken firm tofu, cubed

- 8 slices whole wheat bread
- 4 lettuce leaves
- Coarsely ground pepper, optional

Direction

- Mix the initial eight ingredients, then stir in tofu. Line lettuce on 4 bread slices and put tofu mixture on top. Sprinkle with pepper if preferred, then close the sandwiches.

Nutrition Information

- Calories: 266 calories
- Cholesterol: 5mg cholesterol
- Protein: 14g protein. Diabetic Exchanges: 2 starch
- Total Fat: 9g fat (2g saturated fat)
- Sodium: 692mg sodium
- Fiber: 4g fiber)
- Total Carbohydrate: 31g carbohydrate (7g sugars

---

263.   Bologna Salad Sandwiches

Serving: 15 sandwiches. | Prep: 20mins | Cook: 0mins | Ready in:

Ingredients

- 1-1/2 pounds bologna or ham, ground
- 1 to 1-1/4 cups mayonnaise
- 3/4 cup sweet pickle relish, well drained
- 3 tablespoons chopped onion
- 1 tablespoon Worcestershire sauce
- 30 slices bread
- 15 slices process American cheese
- Lettuce leaves, optional

Direction

- Whisk Worcestershire sauce, onion, relish, mayonnaise and bologna in a bowl. For each sandwich, add roughly a third cup of the

---

salad, and if you want, add lettuce and a cheese slice on top.

Nutrition Information

- Calories:
- Protein:
- Total Fat:
- Sodium:
- Fiber:
- Total Carbohydrate:
- Cholesterol:

---

264.   Calla Lily Tea Sandwiches

Serving: 1-1/2 dozen. | Prep: 40mins | Cook: 0mins | Ready in:

Ingredients

- 1/4 cup mayonnaise
- 1 teaspoon grated onion
- 1/4 teaspoon dried tarragon
- 1/8 teaspoon pepper
- 1 can (4-1/2 ounces) chunk white chicken, drained
- 1 celery rib, finely chopped
- 18 slices white bread, crusts removed
- 2 tablespoons butter, softened
- 1 tablespoon minced fresh parsley
- 18 pieces (1 inch each) julienned carrot

Direction

- Mix the first 4 ingredients together in a big bowl; mix in celery and chicken; put aside. Flatten each bread slice to 1/8-in. thickness using a rolling pin; slice into 2-1/2-in. squares. Use butter to brush. Roll up to form a funnel shape, overlapping 2 adjacent sides; use a toothpick to keep in place.

- Put about 1 teaspoon of chicken stuffing into each sandwich. Use a plastic wrap to cover; chill for 1 hour.
- Take out the toothpicks. Use parsley to drizzle sandwiches. Put a carrot piece in the stuffing of each sandwich.

Nutrition Information

- Calories: 108 calories
- Total Fat: 5g fat (1g saturated fat)
- Sodium: 195mg sodium
- Fiber: 1g fiber)
- Total Carbohydrate: 13g carbohydrate (1g sugars
- Cholesterol: 8mg cholesterol
- Protein: 3g protein.

---

265. Cashew Turkey Salad Sandwiches

Serving: 4 servings. | Prep: 15mins | Cook: 0mins | Ready in:

Ingredients

- 1/4 cup reduced-fat mayonnaise
- 2 tablespoons reduced-fat plain yogurt
- 1 green onion, chopped
- 1/4 teaspoon salt
- 1/4 teaspoon pepper
- 1-1/2 cups cubed cooked turkey breast
- 1/4 cup thinly sliced celery
- 2 tablespoons chopped dried apricots
- 2 tablespoons chopped unsalted cashews
- 8 slices pumpernickel bread
- 4 lettuce leaves

Direction

- Combine the first 5 ingredients in a bowl. Mix in cashews, apricots, celery and turkey.
- With lettuce, line 1/2 of the bread slices. Put turkey mixture and leftover bread on top.

Nutrition Information

- Calories: 298 calories
- Protein: 22g protein. Diabetic Exchanges: 2 starch
- Total Fat: 9g fat (2g saturated fat)
- Sodium: 664mg sodium
- Fiber: 4g fiber)
- Total Carbohydrate: 32g carbohydrate (4g sugars
- Cholesterol: 51mg cholesterol

---

266. Chow Mein Tuna Salad

Serving: 6 servings. | Prep: 10mins | Cook: 0mins | Ready in:

Ingredients

- 3 cans (12 ounces each) white water-packed tuna, drained and flaked
- 1-1/2 cups mayonnaise
- 1-1/2 cups chopped cashews
- 3/4 cup finely chopped green onions
- 3 jars (2 ounces each) diced pimientos, drained and finely chopped
- 3 tablespoons finely chopped green pepper
- 3 tablespoons sour cream
- 1 tablespoon cider vinegar
- 3/4 teaspoon salt
- 3 cups chow mein noodles

Direction

- In a big bowl, put the tuna; reserve. Mix the salt, vinegar, sour cream, green pepper, pimientos, onions, cashews and mayonnaise in a separate big bowl.
- Put atop tuna and coat by tossing. Serve along with chow mein noodles.

Nutrition Information

- Calories: 804 calories
- Sodium: 1112mg sodium
- Fiber: 2g fiber)
- Total Carbohydrate: 26g carbohydrate (4g sugars
- Cholesterol: 42mg cholesterol
- Protein: 22g protein.
- Total Fat: 69g fat (11g saturated fat)

267. Cilantro Avocado Tuna Salad Sandwiches

Serving: 4 servings. | Prep: 15mins | Cook: 0mins | Ready in:

Ingredients

- 2 pouches (5 ounces each) albacore white tuna in water
- 1/3 cup mayonnaise
- 3 tablespoons minced fresh cilantro
- 2 tablespoons lime juice
- 2 garlic cloves, minced
- 1/4 teaspoon salt
- 1/8 teaspoon pepper
- 8 slices whole wheat bread, toasted if desired
- 4 slices Muenster or provolone cheese
- 1 medium ripe avocado, peeled and sliced

Direction

- Combine the first 7 ingredients in a small bowl. Spread on 4 bread slices with the tuna mixture; put avocado, cheese and the rest of the bread on top. Enjoy immediately.

Nutrition Information

- Calories: 506 calories
- Protein: 30g protein.
- Total Fat: 30g fat (8g saturated fat)
- Sodium: 908mg sodium
- Fiber: 6g fiber)

- Total Carbohydrate: 28g carbohydrate (3g sugars
- Cholesterol: 56mg cholesterol

268. Cobb Salad Sandwiches

Serving: 4 servings. | Prep: 20mins | Cook: 0mins | Ready in:

Ingredients

- 1/4 cup mayonnaise
- 1/2 teaspoon prepared horseradish
- 1/4 teaspoon dried basil
- 4 croissants, split
- 4 lettuce leaves
- 1 medium tomato, sliced
- 4 cooked bacon strips, halved
- 4 slices deli ham
- 3 hard-boiled large eggs, sliced

Direction

- Mix basil, horseradish, and mayonnaise together in a small bowl; spread over the cut side of croissant bottoms. Place eggs, ham, bacon, tomato, and lettuce on in a layer; put the tops on.

Nutrition Information

- Calories: 454 calories
- Protein: 16g protein.
- Total Fat: 30g fat (10g saturated fat)
- Sodium: 896mg sodium
- Fiber: 2g fiber)
- Total Carbohydrate: 29g carbohydrate (8g sugars
- Cholesterol: 219mg cholesterol

269. Cottage Cheese Crab Salad

Serving: 2 servings. | Prep: 15mins | Cook: 0mins | Ready in:

Ingredients

- 1/2 cup 4% cottage cheese
- 1/4 cup sour cream
- 1 teaspoon Dijon mustard
- 1/8 teaspoon garlic powder
- 1/8 teaspoon pepper
- 1 package (8 ounces) imitation crabmeat, chopped
- 1/4 cup chopped celery
- 1/4 cup chopped green onions
- Lettuce leaves
- 1 medium tomato, cut into wedges

Direction

- Mix pepper, garlic powder, mustard, sour cream and cottage cheese in a bowl. Mix onions, celery and crab in. On lettuce-lined plates, serve with tomato wedges.

Nutrition Information

- Calories: 253 calories
- Total Carbohydrate: 24g carbohydrate (6g sugars
- Cholesterol: 46mg cholesterol
- Protein: 19g protein.
- Total Fat: 8g fat (5g saturated fat)
- Sodium: 927mg sodium
- Fiber: 1g fiber)

270. Crab Salad Croissants

Serving: 4 servings. | Prep: 15mins | Cook: 0mins | Ready in:

Ingredients

- 1 package (8 ounces) imitation crabmeat, chopped
- 1/2 cup mayonnaise
- 1/4 cup chopped celery
- 2 tablespoons shredded cheddar cheese
- 1 tablespoon finely chopped onion
- 1 teaspoon prepared mustard
- 1/4 teaspoon dill weed
- 1/8 teaspoon salt
- 1/8 teaspoon pepper
- 4 lettuce leaves
- 4 croissants, split

Direction

- Mix the initial 9 ingredients in a small-sized bowl. Serve over croissants that are lined with lettuce.

Nutrition Information

- Calories: 502 calories
- Cholesterol: 59mg cholesterol
- Protein: 11g protein.
- Total Fat: 35g fat (10g saturated fat)
- Sodium: 1004mg sodium
- Fiber: 2g fiber)
- Total Carbohydrate: 35g carbohydrate (2g sugars

271. Crab Salad Pockets

Serving: 1 serving. | Prep: 15mins | Cook: 0mins | Ready in:

Ingredients

- 2 ounces imitation crabmeat, flaked or canned crabmeat, drained, flaked and cartilage removed
- 1/4 cup finely chopped cucumber
- 2 tablespoons chopped sweet red pepper
- 2 tablespoons chopped green pepper
- 1 tablespoon sliced green onion

- 1 tablespoon finely chopped celery
- 1/4 teaspoon seafood seasoning
- 2 tablespoons fat-free mayonnaise
- 2 whole wheat pita pocket halves

Direction

- Mix seafood seasoning and celery, onion, peppers, cucumber, and crab in a small-sized bowl. Mix in mayonnaise. Use crab mixture to fill pita halves.

Nutrition Information

- Calories: 239 calories
- Total Fat: 2g fat (0 saturated fat)
- Sodium: 829mg sodium
- Fiber: 6g fiber)
- Total Carbohydrate: 46g carbohydrate (2g sugars
- Cholesterol: 7mg cholesterol
- Protein: 12g protein.

272. Crab Salad Tea Sandwiches

Serving: 4 dozen. | Prep: 60mins | Cook: 0mins | Ready in:

Ingredients

- 4 celery ribs, finely chopped
- 2 cups reduced-fat mayonnaise
- 4 green onions, chopped
- 1/4 cup lime juice
- 1/4 cup chili sauce
- 1/2 teaspoon seasoned salt
- 8 cups cooked fresh or canned crabmeat
- 6 hard-boiled large eggs, chopped
- 48 slices whole wheat bread
- 1/2 cup butter, softened
- 48 lettuce leaves
- 1/2 teaspoon paprika
- Green onions, cut into thin strips, optional

Direction

- Mix the first 6 ingredients together in a big bowl; lightly mix in eggs and crab. Chill.
- Cut a circle from each slice of bread using a 3-in. round cookie cutter. Use 1/2 teaspoons of butter to spread on each. Put 2 rounded tablespoonfuls of crab salad and lettuce on top; use paprika to drizzle. Use onion strips to garnish if you want.

Nutrition Information

- Calories: 119 calories
- Fiber: 1g fiber)
- Total Carbohydrate: 8g carbohydrate (2g sugars
- Cholesterol: 55mg cholesterol
- Protein: 7g protein.
- Total Fat: 7g fat (2g saturated fat)
- Sodium: 265mg sodium

273. Crab Salad Wraps

Serving: 6 servings. | Prep: 10mins | Cook: 0mins | Ready in:

Ingredients

- 1/4 cup mayonnaise
- 2 tablespoons finely chopped onion
- 2 tablespoons sweet pickle relish
- 2 tablespoons prepared mustard
- 1 package (8 ounces) imitation crabmeat, flaked
- 1 cup shredded Swiss cheese
- 2 bacon strips, cooked and crumbled, optional
- 6 flour tortillas (6 inches), room temperature

Direction

- Mix mustard, relish, onion, and mayonnaise together in a small bowl. Mix in bacon, cheese, and crab if you want. Put about 1/2 cup down the middle of each tortilla, roll up securely.

Nutrition Information

- Calories:
- Cholesterol:
- Protein:
- Total Fat:
- Sodium:
- Fiber:
- Total Carbohydrate:

---

274.   Crab Salad On Croissants

Serving: | Prep: 20mins | Cook: 0mins |Ready in:

Ingredients

- 2 packages (8 ounces each) imitation crabmeat, flaked
- 2 celery ribs, chopped
- 1/4 cup chopped green onions
- 1/4 cup shredded cheddar cheese
- 3 tablespoons mayonnaise
- 3 tablespoons plain yogurt
- 8 croissants, split
- Lettuce leaves and tomato slices

Direction

- Mix together cheese, onions, celery and crab in a large bowl. Stir together yogurt and mayonnaise in a small bowl until incorporated. Pour onto the crab mixture; toss to make sure the crab mixture is coated evenly. Use lettuce to line croissants, put the crab mixture then tomato slices on top of the lettuce.

Nutrition Information

- Calories: 320 calories
- Sodium: 645mg sodium
- Fiber: 2g fiber)

- Total Carbohydrate: 32g carbohydrate (3g sugars
- Cholesterol: 48mg cholesterol
- Protein: 9g protein.
- Total Fat: 17g fat (8g saturated fat)

---

275.   Crabby Bagels

Serving: 4 servings. | Prep: 15mins | Cook: 0mins |Ready in:

Ingredients

- 1 can (6 ounces) crabmeat, drained, flaked and cartilage removed
- 1/2 cup shredded cheddar cheese
- 1/4 cup finely chopped celery
- 1/4 cup sour cream
- 3/4 teaspoon Worcestershire sauce
- 1/4 teaspoon salt
- 4 onion bagels, split
- 3 ounces cream cheese, softened
- 4 lettuce leaves

Direction

- Mix the first 6 ingredients together in a bowl. Toast bagels, use cream cheese to spread. Put 1/4 cup of the crab mixture and a lettuce leaf on each bagel bottom. Put the tops on.

Nutrition Information

- Calories: 395 calories
- Protein: 21g protein.
- Total Fat: 16g fat (10g saturated fat)
- Sodium: 842mg sodium
- Fiber: 2g fiber)
- Total Carbohydrate: 40g carbohydrate (2g sugars
- Cholesterol: 86mg cholesterol

276.   Creamy Beef Sandwiches

Serving: 6 servings. | Prep: 20mins | Cook: 0mins | Ready in:

Ingredients

- 1/2 cup mayonnaise
- 2 to 3 tablespoons prepared ranch salad dressing
- 2 packages (2-1/2 ounces each) thinly sliced dried beef, chopped
- 1 cup shredded cheddar cheese
- 12 slices white bread
- 1-1/2 cups shredded lettuce

Direction

- Mix ranch dressing and mayonnaise in a small-sized bowl. Mix in the cheese and beef. Spread roughly one third cup over six bread slices; add the leftover bread and lettuce on top.

Nutrition Information

- Calories: 381 calories
- Total Fat: 25g fat (7g saturated fat)
- Sodium: 934mg sodium
- Fiber: 1g fiber)
- Total Carbohydrate: 26g carbohydrate (3g sugars
- Cholesterol: 33mg cholesterol
- Protein: 12g protein.

277.   Creamy Egg Salad

Serving: 3 cups. | Prep: 10mins | Cook: 0mins | Ready in:

Ingredients

- 3 ounces cream cheese, softened
- 1/4 cup mayonnaise
- 1/2 teaspoon salt
- 1/8 teaspoon pepper
- 1/4 cup finely chopped green or sweet red pepper
- 1/4 cup finely chopped celery
- 1/4 cup sweet pickle relish
- 2 tablespoons minced fresh parsley
- 8 hard-boiled large eggs, chopped

Direction

- Combine pepper, salt, mayonnaise, and cream cheese in a bowl until smooth. Mix in parsley, relish, celery, and green pepper. Tuck in eggs. Chill with a cover on until eating.

Nutrition Information

- Calories: 228 calories
- Total Carbohydrate: 6g carbohydrate (4g sugars
- Cholesterol: 264mg cholesterol
- Protein: 9g protein.
- Total Fat: 19g fat (6g saturated fat)
- Sodium: 456mg sodium
- Fiber: 0 fiber)

278.   Creamy Egg Salad Sandwiches

Serving: 4 servings. | Prep: 15mins | Cook: 0mins | Ready in:

Ingredients

- 3 ounces cream cheese, softened
- 2 tablespoons butter, softened
- 1 tablespoon mayonnaise
- 1 teaspoon finely chopped onion
- 1 teaspoon sugar
- 1/2 teaspoon prepared horseradish
- 1/2 teaspoon lemon juice
- 1/4 teaspoon salt
- 1/8 teaspoon pepper
- Dash garlic powder
- 6 hard-boiled large eggs, chopped

- 8 slices rye bread

Direction

- Mix together the initial 10 ingredients in a big bowl until it turns smooth, then stir in the eggs. Let it chill for 1 hour.
- Spread 1/2 cup onto 4 bread slices, then cover it with the leftover bread.

Nutrition Information

- Calories: 437 calories
- Cholesterol: 358mg cholesterol
- Protein: 17g protein.
- Total Fat: 26g fat (11g saturated fat)
- Sodium: 804mg sodium
- Fiber: 4g fiber)
- Total Carbohydrate: 34g carbohydrate (7g sugars

279. Creamy Waldorf Sandwiches

Serving: 7-8 servings. | Prep: 15mins | Cook: 0mins | Ready in:

Ingredients

- 2 cups shredded unpeeled apple
- 1 tablespoon lemon juice
- 2 celery ribs, finely chopped
- 1 cup chopped walnuts
- 1/4 cup mayonnaise
- 14 to 16 slices cinnamon-raisin bread

Direction

- Toss apple with lemon juice in a bowl. Mix in mayonnaise, walnuts and celery, then stir well. On 7-8 slices of bread, spread the apple mixture, then put the leftover bread on top.

Nutrition Information

- Calories:
- Protein:
- Total Fat:
- Sodium:
- Fiber:
- Total Carbohydrate:
- Cholesterol:

280. Create Your Own Egg Salad

Serving: about 3 cups. | Prep: 30mins | Cook: 0mins | Ready in:

Ingredients

- 1/4 to 1/3 cup mayonnaise
- 1/4 to 1/2 teaspoon dried herbs (dill, basil, thyme or tarragon)
- 1/4 teaspoon salt, optional
- 1/8 teaspoon pepper
- 6 hard-boiled large eggs, chopped or sliced
- 1 to 1-1/2 cups cooked long grain rice or pasta
- Assorted fresh fruit or fresh vegetables, optional

Direction

- Mix together the pepper, salt if preferred, herbs and dressing in a big bowl. Stir in the vegetables or fruits if preferred, pasta or rice and eggs gently. Put a cover and let it chill until ready to serve.

Nutrition Information

- Calories: 317 calories
- Total Carbohydrate: 19g carbohydrate (3g sugars
- Cholesterol: 431mg cholesterol
- Protein: 14g protein.
- Total Fat: 20g fat (5g saturated fat)
- Sodium: 251mg sodium
- Fiber: 0 fiber)

281.　　Crunchy Tuna Sandwiches

Serving: 2 servings. | Prep: 10mins | Cook: 0mins | Ready in:

Ingredients

- 1 can (8 ounces) sliced water chestnuts, drained and chopped
- 1 can (6 ounces) tuna, drained and flaked
- 1/3 cup mayonnaise
- 1 tablespoon minced fresh parsley
- 1 teaspoon soy sauce
- 1/4 teaspoon salt
- 1/8 to 1/4 teaspoon ground ginger
- 2 sandwich rolls, split
- Lettuce leaves

Direction

- Mix the initial 7 ingredients in a bowl. Keep it covered and let chill in the refrigerator for 60 minutes. Just prior to serving, scoop onto rolls and add a lettuce leaf on top.

Nutrition Information

- Calories: 634 calories
- Total Fat: 35g fat (6g saturated fat)
- Sodium: 1292mg sodium
- Fiber: 5g fiber)
- Total Carbohydrate: 50g carbohydrate (8g sugars
- Cholesterol: 39mg cholesterol
- Protein: 30g protein.

282.　　Crunchy Tuna Wraps

Serving: 2 servings. | Prep: 10mins | Cook: 0mins | Ready in:

Ingredients

- 1 pouch (6.4 ounces) light tuna in water
- 1/4 cup finely chopped celery
- 1/4 cup chopped green onions
- 1/4 cup sliced water chestnuts, chopped
- 3 tablespoons chopped sweet red pepper
- 2 tablespoons reduced-fat mayonnaise
- 2 teaspoons prepared mustard
- 2 spinach tortillas (8 inches), room temperature
- 1 cup shredded lettuce

Direction

- Combine the first 7 ingredients in a small bowl until blended. Spread over the tortillas; use lettuce to drizzle. Roll up securely in jelly-roll style.

Nutrition Information

- Calories: 312 calories
- Protein: 23g protein. Diabetic Exchanges: 3 lean meat
- Total Fat: 10g fat (2g saturated fat)
- Sodium: 628mg sodium
- Fiber: 3g fiber)
- Total Carbohydrate: 34g carbohydrate (2g sugars
- Cholesterol: 38mg cholesterol

283.　　Crunchy Veggie Sandwiches

Serving: 6 servings. | Prep: 20mins | Cook: 0mins | Ready in:

Ingredients

- 1 cup chopped green pepper
- 1 cup chopped seeded cucumber
- 1 cup chopped celery
- 1 cup chopped seeded tomato

- 2 tablespoons chopped onion
- 2 tablespoons minced fresh parsley
- 2 tablespoons chopped dill pickles
- 1/3 cup fat-free sour cream
- 1/4 cup reduced-fat mayonnaise
- 1/4 teaspoon salt
- Lettuce leaves
- 6 sandwich rolls, split

Direction

- Mix together the initial 7 ingredients in a big bowl. Whisk the salt, mayonnaise and sour cream in a small bowl until combined, then mix it into the vegetable mixture. Put a cover and let it chill in the fridge for 1-2 hours. Serve it on rolls lined with lettuce.

Nutrition Information

- Calories: 162 calories
- Sodium: 519mg sodium
- Fiber: 0 fiber)
- Total Carbohydrate: 0 carbohydrate (0 sugars
- Cholesterol: 1mg cholesterol
- Protein: 5g protein. Diabetic Exchanges: 2 starch.
- Total Fat: 3g fat (1g saturated fat)

284. Cucumber Canoes

Serving: 4 servings. | Prep: 20mins | Cook: 0mins | Ready in:

Ingredients

- 2 medium cucumbers
- 2 cans (6 ounces each) tuna, drained
- 1/2 cup mayonnaise
- 1 celery rib, finely chopped
- 1 teaspoon finely chopped onion
- Salt and pepper to taste
- 8 cherry tomatoes
- 1 medium carrot, cut into eight sticks

Direction

- Chop cucumbers in half lengthwise. Use a spoon to remove the seeds then throw them away. Cut a thin slice from the bottom of each cucumber half if required to make the cucumbers sit flat. Mix together salt, pepper, onion, celery, mayonnaise and tuna in a bowl. Spoon the mixture into the cucumber halves. Use carrot sticks to make paddles and tomatoes to make people. Add "paddles" and "people" to the cucumber halves.

Nutrition Information

- Calories: 288 calories
- Sodium: 311mg sodium
- Fiber: 3g fiber)
- Total Carbohydrate: 8g carbohydrate (5g sugars
- Cholesterol: 23mg cholesterol
- Protein: 13g protein.
- Total Fat: 23g fat (3g saturated fat)

285. Cucumber Tea Sandwiches

Serving: 12 | Prep: 5mins | Cook: | Ready in:

Ingredients

- 24 Snack Factory® Gluten Free Original Pretzel Crisps® Minis
- 1 cucumber, sliced
- 1 (4 ounce) package cream cheese, softened, or more as needed
- Dried dill

Direction

- Split the cucumber slices into 3 or 4 pieces. Put on half of the Gluten-Free Original Pretzel Crisps(R) Minis.
- Pipe or spread cream cheese on top of the cucumbers, then use dill to drizzle. Put

another mini on top to create itty bitty gluten-free tea sandwiches.

Nutrition Information

- Calories: 51 calories;
- Total Fat: 3.7
- Sodium: 76
- Total Carbohydrate: 4.2
- Cholesterol: 10
- Protein: 0.8

286.   Cucumber Tuna Boats

Serving: 3 servings. | Prep: 15mins | Cook: 0mins | Ready in:

Ingredients

- 3 medium cucumbers
- 1 can (6 ounces) tuna, drained and flaked
- 2 hard-boiled large eggs, chopped
- 1/2 cup shredded cheddar cheese
- 1/2 cup diced celery
- 1/4 cup Miracle Whip
- 2 tablespoons sweet pickle relish
- 1 tablespoon finely chopped onion
- 1 teaspoon lemon juice
- 1/2 teaspoon salt

Direction

- Slice cucumbers in two lengthwise; take out and dispose of the seeds. From the bottom of the cucumber, slice a thin slice if needed to make them sit flat. Mix the rest of the ingredients together in a bowl. Put in the cucumbers. Eat immediately.

Nutrition Information

- Calories: 381 calories
- Total Fat: 24g fat (7g saturated fat)
- Sodium: 940mg sodium

- Fiber: 4g fiber)
- Total Carbohydrate: 15g carbohydrate (10g sugars
- Cholesterol: 185mg cholesterol
- Protein: 26g protein.

287.   Curried Egg Salad

Serving: Makes 4 servings | Prep: 15mins | Cook: 40mins | Ready in:

Ingredients

- 1/3 cup mayonnaise
- 1 tablespoon fresh lime juice
- 1 1/2 teaspoons curry powder
- 1 teaspoon Dijon mustard
- 1/4 teaspoon salt
- 1/8 teaspoon cayenne
- 6 hard-boiled large eggs, chopped
- 1 cup diced (1/4-inch) Granny Smith apple (from 1 apple)
- 1/3 cup finely chopped red onion
- 1/4 cup chopped fresh cilantro

Direction

- In a bowl, combine cayenne, salt, mustard, curry powder, lime juice, and mayonnaise until blended. Add cilantro, onion, apple, and eggs and toss to coat.

Nutrition Information

- Calories: 266
- Total Fat: 22 g(34%)
- Saturated Fat: 5 g(23%)
- Sodium: 330 mg(14%)
- Fiber: 1 g(6%)
- Total Carbohydrate: 6 g(2%)
- Cholesterol: 287 mg(96%)
- Protein: 10 g(20%)

288. Curried Olive Egg Salad

Serving: 4 servings. | Prep: 15mins | Cook: 0mins | Ready in:

Ingredients

- 6 hard-boiled large eggs, chopped
- 1/2 cup reduced-fat mayonnaise
- 1/3 cup chopped sweet onion
- 1/4 cup chopped pimiento-stuffed olives
- 1/2 teaspoon celery seed
- 1/2 teaspoon curry powder
- 1/4 teaspoon sugar
- 1/4 teaspoon pepper
- 1/8 teaspoon salt
- 8 pita pocket halves
- 8 lettuce leaves

Direction

- Mix together the initial 9 ingredients in a big bowl. Line lettuce on pita halves, then fill each with 1/4 cup of egg salad.

Nutrition Information

- Calories: 398 calories
- Fiber: 2g fiber)
- Total Carbohydrate: 38g carbohydrate (4g sugars
- Cholesterol: 329mg cholesterol
- Protein: 15g protein. Diabetic Exchanges: 2-1/2 starch
- Total Fat: 20g fat (4g saturated fat)
- Sodium: 893mg sodium

289. Curried Tuna Sandwiches

Serving: 2 servings. | Prep: 10mins | Cook: 0mins | Ready in:

Ingredients

- 1/4 cup chopped apple
- 2 tablespoons raisins
- 2 tablespoons mayonnaise
- 1/4 teaspoon onion salt
- 1/8 teaspoon curry powder
- 1 can (6 ounces) tuna, drained and flaked
- 2 sandwich rolls, split
- Additional mayonnaise, optional
- Lettuce leaves

Direction

- Mix the first 5 ingredients together in a small bowl; add tuna and toss well. Spread on the rolls with more mayonnaise if you want; put lettuce and 1/2 cup of the tuna mixture on top of each.

Nutrition Information

- Calories: 170 calories
- Sodium: 375mg sodium
- Fiber: 0 fiber)
- Total Carbohydrate: 15g carbohydrate (0 sugars
- Cholesterol: 15mg cholesterol
- Protein: 26g protein. Diabetic Exchanges: 3 lean meat
- Total Fat: 1g fat (0 saturated fat)

290. Curry & Parmesan Tuna Salad

Serving: 2 servings. | Prep: 5mins | Cook: 0mins | Ready in:

Ingredients

- 1 can (5 ounces) light water-packed tuna, drained
- 1/4 cup reduced-fat mayonnaise
- 1 tablespoon grated Parmesan cheese
- 1 tablespoon sweet pickle relish
- 1 tablespoon minced fresh parsley

- 1 teaspoon spicy brown mustard
- 1/4 teaspoon dill weed
- 1/8 teaspoon onion powder
- 1/8 teaspoon curry powder
- 1/8 teaspoon garlic powder
- 4 slices whole wheat bread

Direction

- Mix together the initial ten ingredients in a small bowl, then spread the mixture on top of the 2 bread slices. Put leftover bread on top.

Nutrition Information

- Calories: 346 calories
- Protein: 27g protein. Diabetic Exchanges: 3 lean meat
- Total Fat: 13g fat (3g saturated fat)
- Sodium: 877mg sodium
- Fiber: 4g fiber)
- Total Carbohydrate: 29g carbohydrate (6g sugars
- Cholesterol: 34mg cholesterol

---

291. Cute Caterpillar Sandwich

Serving: 6 servings. | Prep: 30mins | Cook: 0mins | Ready in:

Ingredients

- 1 loaf (1 pound) French bread
- 4 cups chicken, ham or tuna salad
- 1 package (8 ounces) cream cheese, softened
- Yellow liquid or paste food coloring
- 2 ripe olive slices
- 3 pimiento strips
- 1 medium green pepper, sliced into rings
- 2 medium carrots, shredded

Direction

- Chop the top fourth off the loaf of bread. Remove the inside of the top and bottom of

the loaf carefully, only leave a 1/2-in. shell (discard the inside or save for other use). Stuff shell with salad mixture. Replace the bread top. Mix together food coloring and cream cheese; spread the mixture over sides and top of loaf. Put olives at one end for eyes of the caterpillar. Assemble pimiento strips to get the shape of a mouth. Chop 1 pepper ring into two 3-in. pieces; put above eyes to make the antennae. Cut each remaining pepper ring in one point; arrange them a few inches apart over the bread loaf; if required, trim ends. Use carrots to sprinkle next to the rings. Serve right away.

Nutrition Information

- Calories: 687 calories
- Protein: 23g protein.
- Total Fat: 42g fat (14g saturated fat)
- Sodium: 1380mg sodium
- Fiber: 6g fiber)
- Total Carbohydrate: 56g carbohydrate (9g sugars
- Cholesterol: 115mg cholesterol

---

292. Dilled Seafood Salad Sandwiches

Serving: 4 servings. | Prep: 15mins | Cook: 0mins | Ready in:

Ingredients

- 8 ounces imitation crabmeat (flake-style)
- 2/3 cup reduced-fat mayonnaise
- 1 can (2-1/4 ounces) sliced ripe olives, drained
- 1 celery rib, chopped
- 2 green onions, chopped
- 1 tablespoon snipped fresh dill
- 1 tablespoon lemon juice
- 3/4 teaspoon salt
- 1/2 teaspoon sugar
- 1/2 teaspoon garlic powder

- 1/2 teaspoon lemon-pepper seasoning
- 4 whole wheat hamburger buns, split

Direction

- Mix the first eleven ingredients together in a small bowl, cut the crab into bite-sized chunks. Enjoy on buns.

Nutrition Information

- Calories: 328 calories
- Protein: 10g protein.
- Total Fat: 17g fat (3g saturated fat)
- Sodium: 1487mg sodium
- Fiber: 4g fiber)
- Total Carbohydrate: 36g carbohydrate (6g sugars
- Cholesterol: 21mg cholesterol

293. Dilled Tuna Sandwiches

Serving: 6 servings. | Prep: 15mins | Cook: 0mins | Ready in:

Ingredients

- 1/4 cup fat-free mayonnaise
- 1/4 cup reduced-fat sour cream
- 3/4 teaspoon dill weed
- 1/2 teaspoon sugar
- 1/8 teaspoon pepper
- 1/4 cup shredded carrot
- 1-1/2 teaspoons finely chopped onion
- 3 English muffins, split and toasted
- 6 lettuce leaves
- 6 slices reduced-fat process American cheese product
- 2 cans (6 ounces each) light water-packed tuna, drained and flaked

Direction

- Mix together the pepper, sugar, dill weed, sour cream and mayonnaise in a bowl, until it

becomes smooth. Stir in onion, carrot and tuna. Put 1/2 cup tuna mixture, cheese and lettuce leaf over each English muffin half.

Nutrition Information

- Calories: 182 calories
- Cholesterol: 31mg cholesterol
- Protein: 22g protein. Diabetic Exchanges: 3 lean meat
- Total Fat: 5g fat (3g saturated fat)
- Sodium: 636mg sodium
- Fiber: 2g fiber)
- Total Carbohydrate: 13g carbohydrate (0 sugars

294. Dilly Egg Salad

Serving: 2 servings. | Prep: 15mins | Cook: 0mins | Ready in:

Ingredients

- 3 hard-boiled large eggs, chopped
- 1/4 cup 4% cottage cheese
- 1 celery rib, chopped
- 2 tablespoons dill pickle relish
- 3 tablespoons mayonnaise
- 1 teaspoon Dijon mustard
- Salt and pepper to taste
- 4 slices bread
- Lettuce leaves

Direction

- Mix together the pepper, salt, mustard, mayonnaise, relish, celery, cottage cheese and eggs in a bowl. On 2 bread slices, spread 2/3 cup of the mixture and put the lettuce and leftover bread on top.

Nutrition Information

- Calories:

- Protein:
- Total Fat:
- Sodium:
- Fiber:
- Total Carbohydrate:
- Cholesterol:

---

295. Diploma Sandwiches

Serving: 22 sandwiches. | Prep: 30mins | Cook: 0mins | Ready in:

Ingredients

- 1 loaf (16 ounces) thin white sandwich bread, crusts removed
- 2 cups prepared ham, tuna or chicken salad
- Whole chives or green onion tops

Direction

- Using a rolling pin to flatten the slices of bread. Spread a rounded tablespoonful of ham salad to each bread slice. Roll up lightly; use a chive to tie each.

Nutrition Information

- Calories: 102 calories
- Total Fat: 4g fat (1g saturated fat)
- Sodium: 339mg sodium
- Fiber: 0 fiber)
- Total Carbohydrate: 13g carbohydrate (1g sugars
- Cholesterol: 8mg cholesterol
- Protein: 3g protein. Diabetic Exchanges: 1 starch

---

296. Edible Inner Tubes

Serving: 6 servings. | Prep: 10mins | Cook: 0mins | Ready in:

Ingredients

- 1 can (12 ounces) tuna, drained
- 1/3 cup seasoned bread crumbs
- 1/4 cup creamy Italian salad dressing
- 2 to 3 tablespoons Dijon mustard
- 2 tablespoons dill pickle relish
- 6 plain bagels
- Lettuce leaves

Direction

- Mix initial 5 ingredients in a bowl. Horizontally halve the bagels. Add lettuce over bottom halves; add tuna mixture on top. Replace top halves.

Nutrition Information

- Calories: 337 calories
- Sodium: 932mg sodium
- Fiber: 2g fiber)
- Total Carbohydrate: 46g carbohydrate (4g sugars
- Cholesterol: 17mg cholesterol
- Protein: 23g protein.
- Total Fat: 6g fat (1g saturated fat)

---

297. Egg 'n' Cress Tea Sandwiches

Serving: 8 tea sandwiches. | Prep: 30mins | Cook: 0mins | Ready in:

Ingredients

- 4 hard-boiled large eggs, finely chopped
- 1/4 cup minced watercress, chives or parsley
- 2 tablespoons chopped pimiento-stuffed olives
- 2 tablespoons mayonnaise
- 1/4 teaspoon salt
- 1/4 teaspoon white pepper
- 2 tablespoons butter, softened
- 8 slices whole wheat and/or white bread

Direction

- Mix together the pepper, salt, mayonnaise, olives, watercress and eggs in a small bowl. Spread one side of each bread slice with butter.
- Spread egg mixture on top of the buttered side of 4 slices of bread. Put the leftover slices of bread on top. Put the leftover bread on top, buttered side facing down. From each sandwich, cut out 2 tea sandwiches using a 3-inch holly-leaf-shaped cookie cutter.

Nutrition Information

- Calories:
- Total Fat:
- Sodium:
- Fiber:
- Total Carbohydrate:
- Cholesterol:
- Protein:

298. Egg Salad Burritos

Serving: 2 servings. | Prep: 15mins | Cook: 0mins | Ready in:

Ingredients

- 1/4 cup mayonnaise
- 2 teaspoons minced fresh cilantro
- 1 tablespoon lime juice
- 1/4 teaspoon cayenne pepper, optional
- 1/8 teaspoon salt
- Dash pepper
- 4 hard-boiled large eggs, chopped
- 2 whole wheat tortillas (8 inches)
- 1 medium tomato, thinly sliced
- 1 medium tomatillo, husks removed, rinsed and thinly sliced

Direction

- Mix together the pepper, salt, cayenne (if preferred), lime juice, cilantro and mayonnaise in a big bowl. Mix in the eggs.
- Layer the tomato, tomatillo and egg salad mixture on the tortillas, then fold the sides and ends atop the filling and roll it up.

Nutrition Information

- Calories: 341 calories
- Cholesterol: 427mg cholesterol
- Protein: 17g protein.
- Total Fat: 16g fat (4g saturated fat)
- Sodium: 505mg sodium
- Fiber: 3g fiber)
- Total Carbohydrate: 28g carbohydrate (5g sugars

299. Egg Salad Pitas

Serving: 3-6 servings. | Prep: 15mins | Cook: 0mins | Ready in:

Ingredients

- 2/3 cup mayonnaise
- 2 tablespoons sweet pickle relish
- 1 teaspoon prepared mustard
- 1/4 teaspoon pepper
- 1/4 teaspoon celery salt
- 1/4 teaspoon paprika
- 1/4 teaspoon dried basil
- 1/4 teaspoon salt
- 6 hard-boiled large eggs, coarsely chopped
- 1/2 cup shredded cheddar cheese
- 1 small onion, finely chopped
- 1 large carrot, grated
- 2 bacon strips, cooked and crumbled
- 3 pita breads (6 inches), halved
- Lettuce leaves and sliced tomatoes, optional

Direction

- Mix the initial 8 ingredients in a bowl. Mix in bacon, carrot, onion, cheese and eggs. Scoop roughly half a cup into each pita half. If you want, put in tomatoes and lettuce.

Nutrition Information

- Calories: 401 calories
- Total Fat: 29g fat (7g saturated fat)
- Sodium: 662mg sodium
- Fiber: 1g fiber)
- Total Carbohydrate: 22g carbohydrate (4g sugars
- Cholesterol: 233mg cholesterol
- Protein: 12g protein.

300.   Egg Salad Pockets

Serving: 3 servings. | Prep: 20mins | Cook: 0mins | Ready in:

Ingredients

- 3 ounces cream cheese, softened
- 1/4 cup Miracle Whip
- 1 celery rib, finely chopped
- 2 tablespoons finely chopped onion
- 1 tablespoon sweet pickle relish
- 3/4 teaspoon dill weed
- 1/2 teaspoon salt
- 1/2 teaspoon ground mustard
- 6 hard-boiled large eggs, chopped
- 3 pita breads (6 inches), halved
- 6 lettuce leaves

Direction

- Mix together the Miracle Whip and cream cheese in a small bowl, then add mustard, salt, dill weed, relish, onion and celery. Stir in the eggs gently. Line lettuce on pita halves, then fill each with 1/2 cup of egg salad.

Nutrition Information

- Calories: 497 calories
- Protein: 21g protein.
- Total Fat: 27g fat (10g saturated fat)
- Sodium: 1148mg sodium
- Fiber: 2g fiber)
- Total Carbohydrate: 42g carbohydrate (6g sugars
- Cholesterol: 462mg cholesterol

301.   Egg Salad Sandwiches

Serving: 4 | Prep: 10mins | Cook: 8hours | Ready in:

Ingredients

- 8 hard-cooked eggs, diced
- 1 cup mayonnaise
- 1/4 cup dried onion flakes
- 1/2 teaspoon salt
- 1 teaspoon mustard powder
- 1/4 teaspoon garlic powder
- 1/4 teaspoon black pepper
- 1 teaspoon dill weed
- 8 slices white bread

Direction

- In a bowl, slowly mix mayonnaise, eggs, salt, onion flakes, mustard powder, pepper, garlic powder and dill. Cover and let it chill in the refrigerator for 8 hours or overnight. Put evenly on 4 bread slices and cover with remaining bread slices to serve.

Nutrition Information

- Calories: 701 calories;
- Total Fat: 56.2
- Sodium: 1069
- Total Carbohydrate: 31.6
- Cholesterol: 445
- Protein: 17.5

302. Egg Salad Supreme

Serving: 6 servings. | Prep: 10mins | Cook: 0mins | Ready in:

Ingredients

- 3 ounces cream cheese, softened
- 1/4 cup Miracle Whip
- 1/2 teaspoon prepared mustard
- 1/2 teaspoon salt
- 1/2 teaspoon dill weed
- Pinch pepper
- 6 hard-boiled large eggs, chopped
- 1/2 cup chopped celery
- 1 can (2-1/4 ounces) sliced ripe olives, drained
- 2 tablespoons chopped onion
- 1 tablespoon chopped pimientos
- Bread or pita bread

Direction

- Mix together the initial 6 ingredients in a bowl, then stir well. Add pimientos, onion, olives, celery and eggs, then stir well. Put a cover and let it chill for a minimum of 1 hour. Serve it on pita bread or bread; use approximately 1/2 cup for each sandwich.

Nutrition Information

- Calories: 210 calories
- Cholesterol: 231mg cholesterol
- Protein: 8g protein.
- Total Fat: 19g fat (6g saturated fat)
- Sodium: 457mg sodium
- Fiber: 1g fiber)
- Total Carbohydrate: 2g carbohydrate (1g sugars

303. Egg Salad Tacos

Serving: 2-3 servings. | Prep: 15mins | Cook: 0mins | Ready in:

Ingredients

- 2 tablespoons mayonnaise
- 2 tablespoons salsa
- 1 tablespoon sour cream
- 1/8 teaspoon salt
- 1/8 teaspoon pepper
- 4 hard-boiled large eggs, chopped
- 1/4 cup shredded sharp cheddar cheese
- 1 tablespoon sliced green onion
- 4 to 6 taco shells or 4 to 6 slices of bread
- Shredded lettuce
- Additional salsa or taco sauce, optional

Direction

- Mix together the initial 5 ingredients in a bowl and mix in the onion, cheese and eggs. Line a slice of bread or each taco shell with lettuce, then fill it with egg salad. Put taco sauce or additional salsa on top if preferred.

Nutrition Information

- Calories: 284 calories
- Cholesterol: 299mg cholesterol
- Protein: 11g protein.
- Total Fat: 21g fat (6g saturated fat)
- Sodium: 397mg sodium
- Fiber: 1g fiber)
- Total Carbohydrate: 10g carbohydrate (1g sugars

304. Egg Salad Tuna Wraps

Serving: 6 servings. | Prep: 15mins | Cook: 0mins | Ready in:

Ingredients

- 12 hard-boiled large eggs, chopped
- 2 cans (6 ounces each) tuna, drained and flaked
- 2 celery ribs, chopped
- 1/2 cup sweet pickle relish
- 1/2 cup mayonnaise
- 3 tablespoons onion soup mix
- 1 tablespoon minced fresh parsley
- 1/2 teaspoon pepper
- Lettuce leaves, optional
- 6 flour tortillas (10 inches)

Direction

- Mix the initial 8 ingredients in a bowl. Add lettuce leaves over tortillas if you want. Add three quarters cup of egg mixture on top of each; roll up tightly. Using plastic wrap to cover then place in the fridge or serve right away.

Nutrition Information

- Calories: 573 calories
- Protein: 26g protein.
- Total Fat: 30g fat (6g saturated fat)
- Sodium: 1199mg sodium
- Fiber: 7g fiber)
- Total Carbohydrate: 42g carbohydrate (8g sugars
- Cholesterol: 439mg cholesterol

305. Egg Salad And Bacon Sandwich

Serving: 8 servings. | Prep: 25mins | Cook: 0mins | Ready in:

Ingredients

- 4 bacon strips, cooked and crumbled
- 1/2 cup shredded cheddar cheese
- 1/2 cup sour cream
- 1/3 cup mayonnaise

- 2 tablespoons minced chives
- 1/4 teaspoon salt
- 1/4 teaspoon pepper
- 10 hard-boiled large eggs, chopped
- 8 lettuce leaves
- 8 croissants, split

Direction

- Mix the initial 7 ingredients in a big bowl. Put in eggs and stir well. Keep it covered and chilled in the refrigerator for at least 2 hours. Serve over croissants that are lined with lettuce.

Nutrition Information

- Calories: 470 calories
- Protein: 16g protein.
- Total Fat: 32g fat (13g saturated fat)
- Sodium: 727mg sodium
- Fiber: 2g fiber)
- Total Carbohydrate: 28g carbohydrate (3g sugars
- Cholesterol: 327mg cholesterol

306. Egg Salad And Cucumber Sandwiches

Serving: 6 servings. | Prep: 15mins | Cook: 0mins | Ready in:

Ingredients

- 1/2 cup chopped red onion
- 1/2 cup mayonnaise
- 1/4 cup sour cream
- 2 tablespoons Dijon mustard
- 1/2 teaspoon pepper
- 1/4 teaspoon salt
- 8 hard-boiled large eggs, chopped
- 1 large cucumber, sliced
- 1 tablespoon dill weed
- 12 slices sourdough bread, toasted

Direction

- Mix together the initial 6 ingredients in a small bowl, then add eggs. Gently stir to blend. Toss the dill and cucumber in a separate bowl, then spread the egg salad on top of the 6 toast slices. Put cucumbers and leftover toast on top.

Nutrition Information

- Calories: 458 calories
- Sodium: 823mg sodium
- Fiber: 2g fiber)
- Total Carbohydrate: 41g carbohydrate (4g sugars
- Cholesterol: 296mg cholesterol
- Protein: 17g protein.
- Total Fat: 25g fat (6g saturated fat)

307.   Egg Salad For A Crowd

Serving: 50 sandwiches, 50 servings, 1 sandwich per serving. | Prep: 20mins | Cook: 0mins |Ready in:

Ingredients

- 36 hard-boiled large eggs, chopped
- 6 celery ribs, chopped
- 3 large carrots, finely shredded
- 3 small green peppers, finely chopped
- 3 small onions, finely chopped
- 3 cans (2-1/4 ounces each) sliced ripe olives, drained
- 3 cups mayonnaise
- 3/4 cup milk
- 1 tablespoon ground mustard
- Salt and pepper to taste
- Lettuce leaves, halved cherry tomatoes and sliced hard-boiled large egg, optional
- 100 bread slices (about 6 loaves)

Direction

- Mix together the initial 6 ingredients in a big bowl. Whisk the pepper, salt, mustard, milk

and mayonnaise until it becomes smooth, then mix it into the egg mixture. Put a cover and let it chill in the fridge for a minimum of 1 hour. If preferred, put a sliced egg, tomatoes and lettuce on top to garnish.
- To make the sandwiches, spread approximately 1/3 cup of the egg salad on one slice of bread, then put another bread slice on top.

Nutrition Information

- Calories:
- Sodium:
- Fiber:
- Total Carbohydrate:
- Cholesterol:
- Protein:
- Total Fat:

308.   Egg Salad/Cucumber Sandwiches

Serving: 4 servings. | Prep: 10mins | Cook: 0mins |Ready in:

Ingredients

- 3 hard-boiled large eggs, chopped
- 1/2 cup chopped green pepper
- 1/4 cup mayonnaise
- 2 tablespoons chopped red onion
- 1/2 teaspoon lemon juice
- 1/8 teaspoon salt
- 1/8 teaspoon pepper
- 8 slices whole wheat bread
- 1 small cucumber, thinly sliced
- 4 lettuce leaves

Direction

- Mix pepper, salt, lemon juice, onion, mayonnaise, green pepper, and eggs in a small-sized bowl. Spread over four bread slices. Add lettuce and cucumber on top. Add leftover bread on top.

Nutrition Information

- Calories: 310 calories
- Sodium: 493mg sodium
- Fiber: 5g fiber)
- Total Carbohydrate: 29g carbohydrate (4g sugars
- Cholesterol: 164mg cholesterol
- Protein: 11g protein.
- Total Fat: 17g fat (3g saturated fat)

309.   Eggcellent Finger Sandwiches

Serving: 16 sandwiches. | Prep: 40mins | Cook: 0mins | Ready in:

Ingredients

- 4 hard-boiled large eggs, chopped
- 5 bacon strips, cooked and crumbled
- 1/4 cup tartar sauce
- 16 slices swirled rye and pumpernickel bread
- 2 tablespoons butter, softened
- 16 slices pimiento-stuffed olives, optional

Direction

- Mix tartar sauce, bacon, and eggs together in a small bowl. Put a cover on and chill for 30 minutes.
- From each piece of bread, slice out 2 bells with a 2-1/2-in. bell-shaped cookie cutter. Use butter to gently spread on one side of each bell. Spread on half of the buttered bells with the egg mixture; put the other part of the bells on top with the buttered side turning down.
- If you want, use an olive slice to garnish each sandwich and a little egg mixture to secure it. Put a cover on and chill until eating.

Nutrition Information

- Calories: 268 calories
- Cholesterol: 119mg cholesterol
- Protein: 10g protein.
- Total Fat: 11g fat (4g saturated fat)
- Sodium: 622mg sodium
- Fiber: 4g fiber)
- Total Carbohydrate: 32g carbohydrate (3g sugars

310.   Extra Creamy Egg Salad

Serving: about 5 cups. | Prep: 15mins | Cook: 0mins | Ready in:

Ingredients

- 2 packages (8 ounces each) cream cheese, softened
- 1/2 cup mayonnaise
- 1 teaspoon ground mustard
- 1/2 teaspoon paprika
- 1/2 teaspoon salt
- 8 hard-boiled large eggs, chopped
- 1 medium onion, chopped
- Croissants or sandwich rolls, optional
- Lettuce leaves, optional

Direction

- Beat the salt, paprika, mustard, mayonnaise and cream cheese in a bowl, then mix in the onion and eggs. If preferred, serve with lettuce on croissants.

Nutrition Information

- Calories: 458 calories
- Sodium: 591mg sodium
- Fiber: 1g fiber)
- Total Carbohydrate: 5g carbohydrate (3g sugars
- Cholesterol: 397mg cholesterol
- Protein: 14g protein.

- Total Fat: 42g fat (15g saturated fat)

---

311. Festive Tea Sandwiches

Serving: 8 servings. | Prep: 20mins | Cook: 0mins | Ready in:

Ingredients

- 1/2 cup mayonnaise
- 1/3 cup chopped fresh or frozen cranberries
- 2 tablespoons chopped pecans
- 1/4 teaspoon salt
- 1/8 teaspoon pepper
- 16 slices bread, crusts removed
- 16 to 24 thin slices cooked chicken
- 8 lettuce leaves

Direction

- Mix the initial 5 ingredients; spread on 1 side of each bread slice. Layer 1/2 the slices with lettuce and chicken. Add leftover bread on top. Chop into garnishing shapes or quarters.

Nutrition Information

- Calories: 181 calories
- Sodium: 279mg sodium
- Fiber: 1g fiber)
- Total Carbohydrate: 13g carbohydrate (2g sugars
- Cholesterol: 5mg cholesterol
- Protein: 2g protein.
- Total Fat: 13g fat (2g saturated fat)

---

312. Fiesta Tuna Salad Sandwiches

Serving: 12 servings. | Prep: 20mins | Cook: 0mins | Ready in:

Ingredients

- 6 cans (5 ounces each) white water-packed tuna, drained and flaked
- 1 large red onion, chopped
- 2 medium tomatoes, chopped
- 2/3 cup reduced-fat mayonnaise
- 2 jalapeno peppers, seeded and finely chopped
- 1/4 cup lemon juice
- 2 garlic cloves, minced
- 1 teaspoon seafood seasoning
- 1 teaspoon coarsely ground pepper
- 2 loaves (14 ounces each) ciabatta bread, split
- 3/4 pound sliced pepper Jack cheese
- 12 lettuce leaves

Direction

- Mix the first 9 ingredients together in a big bowl, spread over the bottoms of the bread. Put lettuce and cheese on in a layer. Replace bread tops. Slice each loaf into 6 slices.

Nutrition Information

- Calories: 451 calories
- Total Fat: 18g fat (6g saturated fat)
- Sodium: 920mg sodium
- Fiber: 3g fiber)
- Total Carbohydrate: 46g carbohydrate (5g sugars
- Cholesterol: 64mg cholesterol
- Protein: 30g protein.

---

313. Freaky Hand Sandwiches

Serving: 6 sandwiches. | Prep: 25mins | Cook: 0mins | Ready in:

Ingredients

- 2 cups finely chopped cooked chicken
- 1 small cucumber, finely chopped
- 2 hard-boiled large eggs, finely chopped
- 1 celery rib, finely chopped

- 1/3 cup mayonnaise
- 1/4 teaspoon salt
- 1/8 teaspoon ground mustard
- 1/8 teaspoon white pepper
- 24 slices thin sandwich bread, crusts removed
- Sliced almonds
- 1 tablespoon spreadable cream cheese
- Neon green food coloring, optional

Direction

- Mix the first 8 ingredients together in a small bowl. On 12 slices of bread, spread 1/4 cup of chicken salad; put the other rest of the bread on top.
- To make fingers, slice each of 6 sandwiches into four 3/4-in. band. Cut one end of each band with a small knife, creating a point. To make fingernails, stick each band with an almond by a dab of cream cheese. If you want, pain almond nails with green food coloring with a clean paintbrush.
- Slice out one band from each of the rest of the sandwiches to make the thumb and one 2-in. oval to make the palm. Cut the band; stick almonds and paint the thumbnails. Put 1 thumb, 4 fingers, and 1 palm on each dish.

Nutrition Information

- Calories: 195 calories
- Protein: 16g protein.
- Total Fat: 13g fat (3g saturated fat)
- Sodium: 258mg sodium
- Fiber: 0 fiber)
- Total Carbohydrate: 3g carbohydrate (1g sugars
- Cholesterol: 119mg cholesterol

314.   Fruited Tuna Salad Pitas

Serving: 4 servings. | Prep: 15mins | Cook: 0mins | Ready in:

Ingredients

- 1/2 cup mayonnaise
- 1 tablespoon honey
- 1 can (12 ounces) white water-packed tuna, drained
- 1 can (11 ounces) mandarin oranges, drained
- 1 medium apple, chopped
- 1/3 cup chopped pecans
- 1 celery rib, thinly sliced
- 1/4 cup dried cranberries
- 1/8 teaspoon salt
- 4 whole wheat pita breads (6 inches)
- 2-3/4 cups alfalfa sprouts

Direction

- Mix together honey and mayonnaise in a large bowl. Mix in salt, cranberries, celery, pecans, apple, oranges and tuna. Spoon the mixture on pita breads and serve with sprouts.

Nutrition Information

- Calories: 640 calories
- Protein: 29g protein.
- Total Fat: 34g fat (5g saturated fat)
- Sodium: 899mg sodium
- Fiber: 8g fiber)
- Total Carbohydrate: 60g carbohydrate (21g sugars
- Cholesterol: 46mg cholesterol

315.   Fruited Turkey Salad Pitas

Serving: 8 servings. | Prep: 30mins | Cook: 0mins | Ready in:

Ingredients

- 1/2 cup reduced-fat plain yogurt
- 1/2 cup reduced-fat mayonnaise
- 2 tablespoons lemon juice

- 1/2 teaspoon pepper
- 4 cups cubed cooked turkey breast
- 2 celery ribs, thinly sliced
- 1 medium apple, peeled and chopped
- 1/2 cup finely chopped fresh spinach
- 1/3 cup dried cranberries
- 1/3 cup chopped pecans
- 8 pita breads (6 inches), halved
- 16 romaine leaves
- 8 slices red onion, separated into rings

Direction

- Mix together the pepper, lemon juice, mayonnaise and yogurt in a small bowl. Mix together the pecans, cranberries, spinach, apple, celery and turkey in a big bowl, then add yogurt mixture and mix until coated. Put on a cover and chill in the fridge.
- Line lettuce and onion on pita halves, then fill each with 1/2 cup of the turkey mixture.

Nutrition Information

- Calories: 393 calories
- Sodium: 501mg sodium
- Fiber: 3g fiber)
- Total Carbohydrate: 45g carbohydrate (9g sugars
- Cholesterol: 66mg cholesterol
- Protein: 29g protein. Diabetic Exchanges: 3 starch
- Total Fat: 11g fat (2g saturated fat)

316.   Fruity Ham Sandwiches

Serving: 2 servings. | Prep: 20mins | Cook: 0mins | Ready in:

Ingredients

- 3/4 cup cubed deli ham
- 1/3 cup chopped apple
- 1/3 cup drained crushed pineapple

- 1/4 cup thinly sliced celery
- 1/4 cup mayonnaise
- 4 slices cinnamon-raisin bread, toasted
- 4 thin apple slices
- 2 slices Muenster cheese (3/4 ounce each)

Direction

- Mix the initial 5 ingredients in a small-sized bowl. Layer the ham mixture, apple and cheese on 2 toast slices. Add leftover toast slices on top.

Nutrition Information

- Calories: 431 calories
- Sodium: 1087mg sodium
- Fiber: 6g fiber)
- Total Carbohydrate: 48g carbohydrate (20g sugars
- Cholesterol: 55mg cholesterol
- Protein: 20g protein.
- Total Fat: 18g fat (6g saturated fat)

317.   Garden Snake Sandwiches

Serving: 1 dozen. | Prep: 20mins | Cook: 15mins | Ready in:

Ingredients

- 12 frozen bread dough dinner rolls, thawed
- 3-1/2 cups cubed cooked chicken
- 1/2 cup mayonnaise
- 1 celery rib, chopped
- 1/4 cup raisins
- 3 tablespoons sunflower kernels
- 1/2 teaspoon salt
- 1/4 teaspoon pepper
- 1/4 teaspoon curry powder
- 12 lettuce leaves
- 12 tomato slices
- 2 ripe olive slices

- 1 green onion
- 6 cherry tomatoes, halved

Direction

- On a big greased baking tray, arrange rolls as "S-letter" shape 1/2 in. apart. Keep it covered and let rise for 30 to 35 minutes in a warm location till doubled. Bake at 350 degrees till becomes golden brown for 12 to 17 minutes. Take out to a wire rack gently.
- Mix curry powder, pepper, salt, sunflower kernels, raisins, celery, mayonnaise and chicken in a bowl. Horizontally halve the rolls avoid separating rolls. Layer with chicken mixture, lettuce and tomato slices; replace roll tops.
- Attach slices of olives to the first sandwiches to make eyes of snake by using toothpicks. Chop green portion of onion into shape of a tongue; insert into sandwich. Add cherry tomato halves to the leftover sandwiches; use toothpicks to secure.

Nutrition Information

- Calories: 260 calories
- Sodium: 388mg sodium
- Fiber: 2g fiber)
- Total Carbohydrate: 23g carbohydrate (4g sugars
- Cholesterol: 40mg cholesterol
- Protein: 16g protein.
- Total Fat: 12g fat (2g saturated fat)

318. Garden Tuna Pita Sandwiches

Serving: 3 servings. | Prep: 20mins | Cook: 0mins | Ready in:

Ingredients

- 2 pouches (one 5 ounces, one 2-1/2 ounces) light water-packed tuna
- 3/4 cup 2% cottage cheese
- 1/2 cup chopped cucumber
- 1/4 cup reduced-fat mayonnaise
- 1/4 cup shredded carrot
- 2 tablespoons minced fresh chives
- 2 tablespoons minced fresh parsley
- 1/2 teaspoon dill weed
- 1/4 teaspoon salt
- Dash pepper
- 6 whole wheat pita pocket halves
- 1 cup fresh baby spinach
- 6 slices tomato

Direction

- Mix the initial ten ingredients in a small-sized bowl. Use tomato and spinach to line pita halves; use a third cup of tuna mixture to fill each.

Nutrition Information

- Calories: 362 calories
- Total Carbohydrate: 39g carbohydrate (5g sugars
- Cholesterol: 36mg cholesterol
- Protein: 31g protein.
- Total Fat: 10g fat (2g saturated fat)
- Sodium: 1114mg sodium
- Fiber: 5g fiber)

319. Garden Tuna Sandwiches

Serving: 4 servings. | Prep: 15mins | Cook: 0mins | Ready in:

Ingredients

- 1 can (6 ounces) water-packed tuna, drained and flaked
- 2/3 cup chopped seeded peeled cucumber
- 1/2 cup shredded carrot

- 1/4 cup finely chopped green onions
- 1/4 cup fat-free mayonnaise
- 1/4 cup Dijon mustard
- 2 tablespoons fat-free sour cream
- 1 tablespoon lemon juice
- Pepper to taste
- 8 slices whole wheat bread
- 4 lettuce leaves

Direction

- Mix the initial 9 ingredients, in a big bowl. Spread over four bread slices; add leftover bread and lettuce on top.

Nutrition Information

- Calories: 237 calories
- Sodium: 936mg sodium
- Fiber: 5g fiber)
- Total Carbohydrate: 35g carbohydrate (0 sugars
- Cholesterol: 13mg cholesterol
- Protein: 18g protein. Diabetic Exchanges: 2 starch
- Total Fat: 4g fat (1g saturated fat)

---

320.   Grandma's French Tuna Salad Wraps

Serving: 2 servings. | Prep: 15mins | Cook: 0mins | Ready in:

Ingredients

- 1 can (5 ounces) light water-packed tuna, drained and flaked
- 1 celery rib, finely chopped
- 1/4 cup fat-free mayonnaise
- 1/4 teaspoon pepper
- 2 whole wheat tortillas (8 inches), room temperature
- 1/2 cup shredded lettuce
- 1 small carrot, shredded

- 4 slices tomato
- 2 slices red onion, separated into rings
- 1 hard-boiled large egg, sliced

Direction

- Mix together the pepper, mayonnaise, celery and tuna in a small bowl. In the center of each tortilla, place the tuna mixture, then put lettuce, carrot, tomato, onion and egg on top, then roll up tightly.

Nutrition Information

- Calories: 328 calories
- Total Fat: 7g fat (1g saturated fat)
- Sodium: 770mg sodium
- Fiber: 4g fiber)
- Total Carbohydrate: 32g carbohydrate (7g sugars
- Cholesterol: 135mg cholesterol
- Protein: 30g protein. Diabetic Exchanges: 3 lean meat

---

321.   Greek Salad Pitas

Serving: 2 servings. | Prep: 20mins | Cook: 0mins | Ready in:

Ingredients

- 2/3 cup chopped seeded cucumber
- 2/3 cup chopped sweet red pepper
- 2/3 cup chopped tomato
- 2/3 cup chopped zucchini
- 1/4 cup crumbled feta cheese
- 2 tablespoons chopped ripe olives
- 2 teaspoons red wine vinegar
- 2 teaspoons lemon juice
- 3/4 teaspoon dried oregano
- 1/8 teaspoon salt
- 1/8 teaspoon pepper
- 4 lettuce leaves
- 4 pita pocket halves

Direction

- Mix together the olives, feta cheese, zucchini, tomato, red pepper and cucumber in a small bowl. Whisk the pepper, salt, oregano, lemon juice and vinegar in a separate bowl, then pour it on top of the vegetables and toss until coated. Scoop into pita halves lined with lettuce.

Nutrition Information

- Calories: 255 calories
- Sodium: 688mg sodium
- Fiber: 5g fiber)
- Total Carbohydrate: 45g carbohydrate (5g sugars
- Cholesterol: 8mg cholesterol
- Protein: 10g protein. Diabetic Exchanges: 2 starch
- Total Fat: 4g fat (2g saturated fat)

---

322. Greek Salad With Bean Spread Pitas

Serving: 2 servings. | Prep: 20mins | Cook: 0mins | Ready in:

Ingredients

- 3/4 cup canned chickpeas, rinsed and drained
- 2 tablespoons lemon juice
- 1 tablespoon sliced green olives with pimientos
- 1 teaspoon olive oil
- 1 garlic clove, minced
- 1 cup fresh baby spinach
- 1/4 cup chopped seeded peeled cucumber
- 1/4 cup crumbled feta cheese
- 2 tablespoons chopped marinated quartered artichoke hearts
- 2 tablespoons sliced Greek olives
- 1/4 teaspoon dried oregano
- 2 whole wheat pita pocket halves

Direction

- In a food processor, place the initial 5 ingredients, put a cover and process until it has a smooth consistency, then put aside.
- Mix together the oregano, olives, artichokes, cheese, cucumber and spinach in a small bowl.
- On pita halves, spread the bean mixture then add the salad. Serve right away.

Nutrition Information

- Calories: 292 calories
- Sodium: 687mg sodium
- Fiber: 7g fiber)
- Total Carbohydrate: 38g carbohydrate (3g sugars
- Cholesterol: 8mg cholesterol
- Protein: 10g protein. Diabetic Exchanges: 2 starch
- Total Fat: 12g fat (3g saturated fat)

---

323. Ham & Potato Salad Sandwiches

Serving: 6 servings. | Prep: 15mins | Cook: 0mins | Ready in:

Ingredients

- 1-1/2 cups deli potato salad
- 6 diagonally cut French bread baguette slices (1/2 inch thick)
- 6 ounces fully cooked ham, thinly sliced
- 6 slices tomato
- 12 dill pickle slices
- 2 hard-boiled large eggs, sliced
- 2 slices red onion, separated into rings

Direction

- Over each slice of baguette, spread a quarter cup of potato salad. Layer with ham, tomato, pickle, eggs and onion.

Nutrition Information

- Calories: 229 calories
- Total Fat: 10g fat (2g saturated fat)
- Sodium: 821mg sodium
- Fiber: 2g fiber)
- Total Carbohydrate: 25g carbohydrate (3g sugars
- Cholesterol: 96mg cholesterol
- Protein: 12g protein.

324.   Ham Pecan Pitas

Serving: 4 servings. | Prep: 20mins | Cook: 0mins | Ready in:

Ingredients

- 1 cup diced fully cooked ham
- 1 hard-boiled large egg, chopped
- 1/2 cup shredded sharp cheddar cheese
- 1/2 cup chopped pecans
- 2/3 cup sour cream
- 2 tablespoons chopped green onions
- 8 pita pocket halves

Direction

- Mix the initial 6 ingredients in a big-sized bowl. Scoop into pita bread.

Nutrition Information

- Calories: 475 calories
- Sodium: 890mg sodium
- Fiber: 3g fiber)
- Total Carbohydrate: 38g carbohydrate (3g sugars
- Cholesterol: 113mg cholesterol
- Protein: 19g protein.
- Total Fat: 26g fat (10g saturated fat)

325.   Ham Salad Croissants

Serving: 8 servings. | Prep: 30mins | Cook: 0mins | Ready in:

Ingredients

- 3 cups ground fully cooked ham
- 2 cups shredded cheddar cheese
- 2 celery ribs, finely chopped
- 8 green onions, chopped
- 1/3 cup unsalted sunflower kernels
- 1/3 cup finely chopped green pepper
- 1/3 cup chopped dill pickle
- 1/3 cup mayonnaise
- 1/3 cup sour cream
- 1 jar (4 ounces) diced pimientos, drained
- 1 teaspoon ranch salad dressing mix
- 1 teaspoon coarsely ground pepper
- 1 teaspoon minced fresh parsley
- 8 lettuce leaves
- 8 croissants, split

Direction

- Mix together the first seven ingredients in a large bowl. Mix parsley, pepper, salad dressing mix, pimientos, sour cream and mayonnaise in a small bowl. Put the dressing on top of the ham mixture; toss to coat. Serve the salad on lettuce-lined croissants.

Nutrition Information

- Calories:
- Protein:
- Total Fat:
- Sodium:
- Fiber:
- Total Carbohydrate:
- Cholesterol:

326. Ham Salad Puffs

Serving: 4 servings. | Prep: 15mins | Cook: 0mins
| Ready in:

Ingredients

- 1-1/2 cups diced fully cooked ham
- 1/2 cup unsweetened crushed pineapple, drained and patted dry
- 1/4 cup golden raisins
- 1/4 cup chopped pecans, toasted
- 1 tablespoon diced pimientos, drained
- 3 tablespoons mayonnaise
- 1 tablespoon ranch salad dressing
- 1 tablespoon sour cream
- 1 tablespoon minced chives
- 1/8 teaspoon pepper
- 4 cream puff shells

Direction

- Mix the initial 5 ingredients in a big-sized bowl. Mix pepper, chives, sour cream, ranch dressing and the mayonnaise in a small bowl. Add on top of ham mixture and coat by lightly tossing. Keep chilled in the refrigerator till serving. Just prior to serving, scoop half cup of ham salad into each cream puff shell; replace tops.

Nutrition Information

- Calories: 524 calories
- Protein: 17g protein.
- Total Fat: 38g fat (7g saturated fat)
- Sodium: 1129mg sodium
- Fiber: 2g fiber)
- Total Carbohydrate: 30g carbohydrate (11g sugars
- Cholesterol: 164mg cholesterol

327. Ham Salad Sandwiches

Serving: 50 servings. | Prep: 30mins | Cook: 0mins
| Ready in:

Ingredients

- 4 pounds fully cooked ham or ring bologna, coarsely ground
- 3 cups chopped sweet pickles
- 2 cups Miracle Whip
- 1 jar (2 ounces) diced pimientos, drained
- 100 slices of bread
- Lettuce leaves, optional

Direction

- Mix pimientos, Miracle Whip, pickles, and ham together in a several big bowl. Put 1/4 cup on 50 bread slices; put lettuce on top if you want and the rest of the bread.

Nutrition Information

- Calories:
- Cholesterol:
- Protein:
- Total Fat:
- Sodium:
- Fiber:
- Total Carbohydrate:

328. Ham And Mango Wraps

Serving: 6 servings. | Prep: 25mins | Cook: 0mins
| Ready in:

Ingredients

- 1/3 cup sour cream
- 1/3 cup mayonnaise
- 2 tablespoons minced fresh basil
- 2 tablespoons minced chives
- 1 tablespoon lemon juice
- 1/8 teaspoon salt

- 1/8 teaspoon pepper
- 3 cups cubed fully cooked ham (about 1 pound)
- 2 to 3 medium mangoes, peeled, chopped and patted dry (about 2 cups)
- 6 flour tortillas (10 inches), room temperature

Direction

- Whisk the first 7 ingredients together in a large bowl. Mix in mangoes and ham. Drop about 2/3 cup of the mixture down the center of each tortilla then roll up firmly.

Nutrition Information

- Calories: 488 calories
- Protein: 20g protein.
- Total Fat: 22g fat (6g saturated fat)
- Sodium: 1412mg sodium
- Fiber: 7g fiber)
- Total Carbohydrate: 45g carbohydrate (11g sugars
- Cholesterol: 50mg cholesterol

329. Hamburger Salad Sandwiches

Serving: 6 servings. | Prep: 10mins | Cook: 10mins | Ready in:

Ingredients

- 1 pound ground beef
- 1 medium onion, chopped
- 1 garlic clove, minced
- 1 medium tomato, chopped
- 1/2 cup mayonnaise
- 1/3 cup chopped dill pickles
- 2 tablespoons prepared mustard
- 1/2 teaspoon salt
- 1/2 teaspoon pepper
- 6 hamburger buns, split
- Lettuce leaves

Direction

- Cook garlic, onion, and beef in a big frying pan over medium heat until the meat is no longer pink; strain. Let cool. Add the next 6 ingredients. Put about 1/2 cup on each bun; put lettuce on top.

Nutrition Information

- Calories: 425 calories
- Sodium: 734mg sodium
- Fiber: 2g fiber)
- Total Carbohydrate: 26g carbohydrate (5g sugars
- Cholesterol: 57mg cholesterol
- Protein: 19g protein.
- Total Fat: 26g fat (6g saturated fat)

330. Hawaiian Ham Salad Pockets

Serving: 4 servings. | Prep: 15mins | Cook: 0mins | Ready in:

Ingredients

- 1-1/4 cups cubed fully cooked ham
- 3/4 cup unsweetened pineapple tidbits
- 1 large carrot, chopped
- 1/4 cup fat-free mayonnaise
- 1 tablespoon honey mustard
- 4 pita pocket halves
- 4 lettuce leaves

Direction

- Mix together the carrot, pineapple and ham, in a small bowl. Stir in the mustard and mayonnaise until combined. Line a lettuce leaf on each pita half, then fill it with ham salad.

Nutrition Information

- Calories: 194 calories
- Cholesterol: 21mg cholesterol
- Protein: 13g protein. Diabetic Exchanges: 2 starch
- Total Fat: 3g fat (1g saturated fat)
- Sodium: 945mg sodium
- Fiber: 2g fiber)
- Total Carbohydrate: 29g carbohydrate (9g sugars

Nutrition Information

- Calories:
- Sodium:
- Fiber:
- Total Carbohydrate:
- Cholesterol:
- Protein:
- Total Fat:

---

331.   Holiday Sandwich Wreath

Serving: 20 sandwiches. | Prep: 25mins | Cook: 0mins | Ready in:

Ingredients

- 1/4 cup butter, softened
- 20 slices snack rye bread
- 20 slices snack pumpernickel bread
- HAM SALAD:
- 1/2 pound deli ham salad
- 1/4 cup finely chopped celery
- 1/2 teaspoon Worcestershire sauce
- CHICKEN SALAD:
- 1/2 pound deli chicken salad
- 1/4 cup diced peeled apple
- 1 tablespoon sour cream
- Christmas bow, optional

Direction

- Spread butter over 1 side of each slice of bread. Mix the ham salad ingredients in a bowl. Then mix together sour cream, apple and the chicken salad in another bowl.
- Place ham salad on half of the rye bread slices then spread evenly; put the remaining rye on top. Spread chicken salad on half of the pumpernickel bread slices; put the remaining pumpernickel on top. Put sandwiches in a circle on a serving plate. Use a bow to decorate according to your liking.

---

332.   Honeybee Ham Salad Sandwich

Serving: 10-12 servings. | Prep: 25mins | Cook: 0mins | Ready in:

Ingredients

- 1/2 pound ground fully cooked ham
- 1/4 cup mayonnaise
- 2 hard-boiled large eggs, chopped
- 1/4 cup chopped pecans
- 1/4 cup crushed pineapple, drained
- 2 tablespoons honey
- 1 round loaf (1 pound) Italian bread
- 1 round Italian roll (6 inches)
- 2 packages (one 8 ounces, one 3 ounces) cream cheese, softened
- 1 tablespoon heavy whipping cream
- 8 to 10 drops yellow food coloring
- 1/4 cup butter, softened
- 1 can (6 ounces) pitted large ripe olives, drained
- 1 pimiento strip
- 1 celery rib, cut into thirds

Direction

- Mix honey, pineapple, pecans, eggs, mayonnaise, and ham together in a bowl. Cut the loaf and roll in half horizontally. Chop 1/3 off one end of the loaf, cut the smaller part in two.
- Whisk food coloring, cream, and cream cheese together in a bowl until fluffy and light.

Spread over each top of the bread portion and roll. Spread butter over the inside of the bread portion and roll; stuff with ham salad.

- To assemble, put a covered board or a big piece of the loaf on a serving dish to make the bee's body. Put the roll beside the body to make the head. To make the wing, put 2 small pieces of the loaf, the rounded edges opposite each other, above the body.
- Put aside 12 whole olives. Cut the rest of the olives in two lengthwise, use the halved olives to make the strips on the body. Slice 11 olives into pieces. Put one piece on the head to make the eyes, use the rest of the pieces to garnish the wings. Add pimiento to make the mouth. To make the antenna, put the last whole olive on one chunk of celery and push inside the top of head. Put the rest of the celery into the ham salad to make the legs.

Nutrition Information

- Calories: 358 calories
- Total Fat: 24g fat (9g saturated fat)
- Sodium: 739mg sodium
- Fiber: 2g fiber)
- Total Carbohydrate: 27g carbohydrate (5g sugars
- Cholesterol: 80mg cholesterol
- Protein: 10g protein.

---

333.   Hot Ham 'n' Egg Sandwiches

Serving: 8 | Prep: 20mins | Cook: 10mins |Ready in:

Ingredients

- 1 cup finely chopped fully cooked ham
- 2 cups shredded Cheddar cheese
- 1 small onion, chopped
- 1/3 cup chopped stuffed olives
- 2 hard-cooked eggs, chopped
- 1/2 cup chili sauce

- 3 tablespoons mayonnaise
- 8 hot dog buns

Direction

- Mix eggs, olives, onion, cheese and ham in a bowl; mix mayonnaise and chili sauce in. Put 1/3 cupful in every bun; individually wrap in foil. Put on a baking sheet. Bake for 10 minutes till heated through at 400°F.

---

334.   Humpty Dumpty Sandwich Loaf

Serving: 4 servings. | Prep: 15mins | Cook: 25mins | Ready in:

Ingredients

- 1 unsliced loaf (1 pound) Italian bread
- 1/3 cup mayonnaise
- 1/3 cup sweet pickle relish
- 4 teaspoons prepared mustard
- 1 garlic clove, minced
- Pinch pepper
- 4 hard-boiled large eggs, chopped
- 1 cup diced celery
- 1 cup diced fully cooked ham
- 3 tablespoons chopped onion
- 2 tablespoons butter, melted, optional

Direction

- Cut off the top third of the loaf; put aside. Scoop out the loaf bottom, keeping 1-in. shell. Crush the removed part of the bread to measure 3/4 cup; put aside. (Dispose of the rest of the bread or save for later use.) Mix pepper, garlic, mustard, relish, and mayonnaise together in a big bowl. Mix in the saved bread, onion, ham, celery, and eggs. Fill the loaf, replace top.
- To eat immediately, slice into 4.in pieces. To eat hot, use butter to brush and fold in foil. Put

on a cookie sheet and bake at 400° for 25 minutes.

Nutrition Information

- Calories: 613 calories
- Total Carbohydrate: 68g carbohydrate (9g sugars
- Cholesterol: 237mg cholesterol
- Protein: 23g protein.
- Total Fat: 27g fat (6g saturated fat)
- Sodium: 1519mg sodium
- Fiber: 4g fiber)

335. Humpty Dumpty Sandwiches

Serving: 2 servings. | Prep: 10mins | Cook: 0mins | Ready in:

Ingredients

- 1 hard-boiled large egg, chopped
- 1 celery rib, chopped
- 1/3 cup 4% cottage cheese
- 1/4 cup shredded cheddar cheese
- 1 to 1-1/2 teaspoons spicy brown mustard
- 1/4 teaspoon salt
- 1/8 teaspoon pepper
- 4 slices whole wheat bread
- Lettuce leaves

Direction

- Mix together the initial 7 ingredients in a bowl, then spread it on two bread slices. Put lettuce and leftover bread on top.

Nutrition Information

- Calories: 272 calories
- Protein: 16g protein.
- Total Fat: 11g fat (5g saturated fat)
- Sodium: 889mg sodium

- Fiber: 4g fiber)
- Total Carbohydrate: 29g carbohydrate (4g sugars
- Cholesterol: 129mg cholesterol

336. Italian Veggie Turkey Pitas

Serving: 5 servings. | Prep: 15mins | Cook: 0mins | Ready in:

Ingredients

- 1 cup mayonnaise
- 1/2 cup sour cream
- 1 envelope Italian salad dressing mix
- 1/2 teaspoon hot pepper sauce
- 2 cups diced cooked turkey
- 1 cup chopped cauliflowerets
- 1 cup chopped broccoli florets
- 1 cup shredded red cabbage
- 1 celery rib, julienned
- 1 small carrot, julienned
- 1/2 medium green pepper, julienned
- 1 green onion, chopped
- 5 pita breads (6 inches), halved
- Lettuce leaves, optional

Direction

- Mix hot pepper sauce, salad dressing mix, sour cream, and mayonnaise together in a big bowl. Mix in onion, green pepper, carrot, celery, cabbage, broccoli, cauliflower, and turkey. Put on lettuce-lined pita bread if you want.

Nutrition Information

- Calories:
- Protein:
- Total Fat:
- Sodium:
- Fiber:

- Total Carbohydrate:
- Cholesterol:

Serving: 6 servings. | Prep: 25mins | Cook: 0mins | Ready in:

Ingredients

- 1 small zucchini, chopped
- 1 cup cubed provolone cheese (1/2-inch)
- 1 cup cubed hard salami (1/2-inch)
- 1 cup chopped fresh broccoli
- 1 medium tomato, seeded and chopped
- 12 pimiento-stuffed olives, chopped
- 12 pitted ripe olives, chopped
- 4 green onions, chopped
- 1/4 cup prepared zesty Italian salad dressing
- 3 tablespoons hot pepper sandwich relish or chopped pickled hot cherry peppers
- 1 tablespoon prepared Catalina salad dressing
- 6 romaine leaves
- 6 whole wheat tortillas (8 inches)

Direction

- Mix together the first eleven ingredients in a large bowl. When ready to serve, put a romaine leaf on each tortilla, then spoon the filling on top. Fold up bottom and sides of tortilla; if required, use a toothpick to secure.

Nutrition Information

- Calories: 373 calories
- Protein: 15g protein.
- Total Fat: 21g fat (6g saturated fat)
- Sodium: 1298mg sodium
- Fiber: 4g fiber)
- Total Carbohydrate: 29g carbohydrate (4g sugars
- Cholesterol: 31mg cholesterol

338.   Lobster Rolls

Serving: 4 | Prep: 15mins | Cook: | Ready in:

Ingredients

- 1 tablespoon butter, softened
- 4 hot dog buns or kaiser rolls, split
- 4 lettuce leaves
- 1 1/2 pounds cooked and cubed lobster meat
- 2 tablespoons mayonnaise
- 1 teaspoon fresh lime juice
- 1 dash hot pepper sauce (e.g. Tabasco™)
- 2 green onions, chopped
- 1 stalk celery, finely chopped
- salt and pepper to taste
- 1 pinch dried basil, parsley or tarragon

Direction

- Rub the insides of the rolls or buns lightly with butter and then line with lettuce leaves. Reserve.
- Mix together the hot pepper sauce, mayonnaise, pepper, salt and lime juice together in a medium bowl until well combined. Stir in celery and green onion. Lightly stir in the lobster to just coat it without falling apart.
- Fill lobster mixture into the buns and lightly drizzle tarragon, parsley, and basil on top of the filling.

Nutrition Information

- Calories: 369 calories;
- Sodium: 925
- Total Carbohydrate: 25.2
- Cholesterol: 133
- Protein: 39.5
- Total Fat: 11.3

339.   Lobster Shrimp Salad Croissants

Serving: 10 servings. | Prep: 25mins | Cook: 0mins | Ready in:

Ingredients

- 1/2 cup mayonnaise
- 1 tablespoon snipped fresh dill
- 1 tablespoon minced chives
- 1 tablespoon lemon juice
- 1/2 teaspoon salt
- 1/4 teaspoon pepper
- 1/2 pound imitation lobster
- 1/2 pound cooked small shrimp, peeled and deveined and coarsely chopped
- 10 miniature croissants, split

Direction

- Mix together pepper, salt, lemon juice, chives, dill and mayonnaise in a big bowl, then stir in shrimp and lobster. Place on a cover and chill until ready to serve. Serve mixture on the croissants.

Nutrition Information

- Calories: 238 calories
- Sodium: 529mg sodium
- Fiber: 1g fiber)
- Total Carbohydrate: 16g carbohydrate (2g sugars
- Cholesterol: 59mg cholesterol
- Protein: 9g protein.
- Total Fat: 15g fat (5g saturated fat)

340.   Mock Ham Salad Sandwiches

Serving: 8-10 servings. | Prep: 15mins | Cook: 0mins | Ready in:

Ingredients

- 1 pound chunk bologna, ground
- 2 hard-boiled large eggs, finely chopped
- 1/3 cup finely chopped sweet pickles
- 1/2 cup mayonnaise
- Leaf lettuce, optional
- 8 to 10 sandwich buns, split

Direction

- Mix together pickles, onion, eggs and bologna in a bowl. Put in mayonnaise; toss lightly to mix. Put a lid on and chill.
- To serve, put a lettuce leaf on each sandwich bun if you like, and add about 1/3 cup ham salad on top, cover with bun tops.

Nutrition Information

- Calories: 413 calories
- Sodium: 934mg sodium
- Fiber: 2g fiber)
- Total Carbohydrate: 31g carbohydrate (7g sugars
- Cholesterol: 75mg cholesterol
- Protein: 12g protein.
- Total Fat: 27g fat (9g saturated fat)

341.   Mom's Egg Salad Sandwiches

Serving: 6 servings. | Prep: 15mins | Cook: 0mins | Ready in:

Ingredients

- 3 ounces cream cheese, softened
- 1/4 cup mayonnaise

- 1 tablespoon chili sauce
- 1/2 teaspoon salt
- 1/8 teaspoon pepper
- 8 hard-boiled large eggs, chopped
- 1/4 cup chopped green pepper
- 1/4 cup chopped celery
- 2 tablespoons finely chopped onion
- 2 tablespoons diced pimientos, drained
- 1 tablespoon minced fresh parsley
- 12 slices white bread
- 6 lettuce leaves
- 6 slices tomato

Direction

- Mash pepper, salt, chili sauce, mayonnaise and cream cheese in a small-sized bowl. Whisk in parsley, pimientos, onion, celery, green pepper and eggs.
- Layer lettuce, tomato and half a cup of egg salad onto 6 bread slices. Add leftover bread on top.

Nutrition Information

- Calories:
- Protein:
- Total Fat:
- Sodium:
- Fiber:
- Total Carbohydrate:
- Cholesterol:

342.   Nutty Shrimp Salad Sandwiches

Serving: 6 servings. | Prep: 15mins | Cook: 0mins | Ready in:

Ingredients

- 2 cups cooked salad shrimp
- 3 kiwifruit, peeled, sliced and quartered
- 3/4 cup shredded carrots

- 1/2 cup mayonnaise
- 1/2 cup chopped pecans
- 1/8 teaspoon ground nutmeg
- Lettuce leaves
- 3 pita breads (6 inches), halved

Direction

- Mix the first 6 ingredients together in a medium-sized bowl. Use lettuce to line pita halves and put about 1/2 cup of shrimp mixture into each.

Nutrition Information

- Calories:
- Total Fat:
- Sodium:
- Fiber:
- Total Carbohydrate:
- Cholesterol:
- Protein:

343.   Nutty Tuna Sandwiches

Serving: 2-4 servings. | Prep: 10mins | Cook: 0mins | Ready in:

Ingredients

- 1 can (6-1/8 ounces) tuna, drained and flaked
- 1 hard-boiled large egg, chopped
- 1 green onion, sliced
- 1/4 cup chopped salted peanuts
- 1/4 cup prepared ranch dressing
- 2 teaspoons lemon juice
- 4 whole wheat pita pocket halves
- 4 lettuce leaves

Direction

- Mix together lemon juice, dressing, peanuts, onion, egg and tuna in a bowl. Use a lettuce leaf to line each pita half then fill with the tuna mixture.

Nutrition Information

- Calories: 288 calories
- Total Fat: 15g fat (3g saturated fat)
- Sodium: 491mg sodium
- Fiber: 3g fiber)
- Total Carbohydrate: 21g carbohydrate (2g sugars
- Cholesterol: 69mg cholesterol
- Protein: 18g protein.

344. Old Fashioned Egg Salad

Serving: 3 servings. | Prep: 15mins | Cook: 0mins | Ready in:

Ingredients

- 1/4 cup mayonnaise
- 2 teaspoons lemon juice
- 1 teaspoon dried minced onion
- 1/4 teaspoon salt
- 1/4 teaspoon pepper
- 6 hard-boiled large eggs, chopped
- 1/2 cup finely chopped celery

Direction

- Mix together the pepper, salt, onion, lemon juice and mayonnaise in a big bowl. Stir in celery and eggs. Put a cover and let it chill in the fridge.

Nutrition Information

- Calories: 294 calories
- Fiber: 0 fiber)
- Total Carbohydrate: 3g carbohydrate (2g sugars
- Cholesterol: 431mg cholesterol
- Protein: 13g protein.
- Total Fat: 25g fat (5g saturated fat)
- Sodium: 438mg sodium

345. Pear Waldorf Pitas

Serving: 20 mini pitas. | Prep: 20mins | Cook: 0mins | Ready in:

Ingredients

- 2 medium ripe pears, diced
- 1/2 cup thinly sliced celery
- 1/2 cup halved seedless red grapes
- 2 tablespoons finely chopped walnuts
- 2 tablespoons lemon yogurt
- 2 tablespoons mayonnaise
- 1/8 teaspoon poppy seeds
- 20 miniature pita pocket halves
- Lettuce leaves

Direction

- Mix walnuts, grapes, celery and pears in a big-sized bowl. Mix poppy seeds, mayonnaise and yogurt in a different bowl. Place into pear mixture; coat by tossing. Let chill in the refrigerator for 1 hour or overnight.
- Use lettuce to line pita halves; fill each with two tbsp. of pear mixture.

Nutrition Information

- Calories: 67 calories
- Cholesterol: 0 cholesterol
- Protein: 2g protein. Diabetic Exchanges: 1 starch.
- Total Fat: 2g fat (0 saturated fat)
- Sodium: 86mg sodium
- Fiber: 1g fiber)
- Total Carbohydrate: 12g carbohydrate (3g sugars

346. Pear Waldorf Pitas With Poppy Seed Dressing

Serving: 10 servings. | Prep: 10mins | Cook: 0mins | Ready in:

Ingredients

- 2 medium ripe pears, diced
- 1/2 cup thinly sliced celery
- 1/2 cup halved seedless red grapes
- 2 tablespoons finely chopped walnuts
- 2 tablespoons lemon yogurt
- 2 tablespoons mayonnaise
- 1/8 teaspoon poppy seeds
- 10 miniature pita pockets, halved
- Lettuce leaves

Direction

- Mix together the walnuts, grapes, celery and pears in a big bowl. Mix together the poppy seeds, mayonnaise and yogurt in a separate bowl and stir well. Add it to the pear mixture, then toss until coated. Let it chill in the fridge for 1 hour or overnight.
- Line 2 tablespoons of pear mixture and lettuce on pita halves to serve.

Nutrition Information

- Calories: 136 calories
- Cholesterol: 1mg cholesterol
- Protein: 3g protein.
- Total Fat: 4g fat (0 saturated fat)
- Sodium: 172mg sodium
- Fiber: 2g fiber)
- Total Carbohydrate: 23g carbohydrate (6g sugars

347. Perky Ham Salad

Serving: 2 cups. | Prep: 10mins | Cook: 0mins | Ready in:

Ingredients

- 1 can (4-1/4 ounces) deviled ham spread
- 1/2 cup shredded cheddar cheese
- 1/2 cup each finely chopped celery and green onions
- 1/4 cup shredded carrot
- 1/2 cup Miracle Whip
- 2 tablespoons chopped pimiento-stuffed olives
- 2 hard-boiled large eggs, chopped
- 1/2 teaspoon garlic powder
- 1/4 teaspoon pepper

Direction

- Mix all ingredients in a bowl. Let it fully chill. Spread over bread or crackers.

Nutrition Information

- Calories: 294 calories
- Sodium: 535mg sodium
- Fiber: 1g fiber)
- Total Carbohydrate: 4g carbohydrate (1g sugars
- Cholesterol: 150mg cholesterol
- Protein: 11g protein.
- Total Fat: 26g fat (8g saturated fat)

348. Perky Tuna Salad Sandwich

Serving: 6 servings. | Prep: 10mins | Cook: 0mins | Ready in:

Ingredients

- 1 can (6-1/8 ounces) chunk tuna in water, drained and flaked
- 2 hard-boiled large eggs, chopped
- 1 celery rib, chopped
- 1 small onion, chopped
- 1 small carrot, shredded
- 8 medium pitted ripe olives, chopped

- 3 tablespoons mayonnaise
- 1/2 teaspoon salt
- 1/4 teaspoon pepper

Direction

- In a small bowl, mix together all ingredients. Then spread the mixture on bread or cracker.

Nutrition Information

- Calories: 125 calories
- Cholesterol: 82mg cholesterol
- Protein: 10g protein.
- Total Fat: 8g fat (1g saturated fat)
- Sodium: 413mg sodium
- Fiber: 1g fiber)
- Total Carbohydrate: 3g carbohydrate (2g sugars

349. Pesto Egg Salad Sandwiches

Serving: 4 servings. | Prep: 10mins | Cook: 0mins | Ready in:

Ingredients

- 1/2 cup fat-free mayonnaise
- 1/4 cup finely chopped red onion
- 4 teaspoons prepared pesto
- 1/4 teaspoon salt
- 1/8 teaspoon pepper
- 4 hard-boiled large eggs, chopped
- 3 hard-boiled large egg whites, chopped
- 8 slices whole wheat bread, toasted
- 8 spinach leaves

Direction

- Mix together the initial 5 ingredients in a small bowl, then mix in egg whites and eggs gently. Spread it on top of the 4 slices of toast, then put spinach and leftover toast on top.

Nutrition Information

- Calories: 285 calories
- Protein: 18g protein. Diabetic Exchanges: 2 medium-fat meat
- Total Fat: 11g fat (3g saturated fat)
- Sodium: 811mg sodium
- Fiber: 5g fiber)
- Total Carbohydrate: 30g carbohydrate (6g sugars
- Cholesterol: 217mg cholesterol

350. Pesto Dijon Egg Salad Sandwiches

Serving: 4 servings. | Prep: 20mins | Cook: 0mins | Ready in:

Ingredients

- 1/2 cup mayonnaise
- 1/4 cup finely chopped celery
- 1/4 cup finely chopped red onion
- 2 tablespoons honey Dijon mustard
- 4 teaspoons prepared pesto
- 1 garlic clove, minced
- 1/2 teaspoon salt
- 1/4 teaspoon pepper
- 8 hard-boiled large eggs, chopped
- 8 slices whole wheat bread, toasted
- 4 romaine leaves
- 4 slices tomato or 1/2 cup roasted sweet red peppers, cut into strips

Direction

- In a small bowl, mix together the initial 8 ingredients, then stir in the eggs gently. Spread it on top of the 4 slices of toast, then put tomato, lettuce and leftover toast on top.

Nutrition Information

- Calories:

- Sodium:
- Fiber:
- Total Carbohydrate:
- Cholesterol:
- Protein:
- Total Fat:

---

351.   Pineapple Tuna Salad Sandwiches

Serving: 4 servings. | Prep: 15mins | Cook: 0mins | Ready in:

Ingredients

- 1/4 cup unsweetened applesauce
- 2 tablespoons fat-free mayonnaise
- 1/2 cup chopped celery
- 1/2 cup chopped green pepper
- 1/2 cup unsweetened crushed pineapple, drained
- 1/4 cup finely chopped onion
- 1/2 teaspoon salt-free herb seasoning blend
- 1/4 teaspoon garlic powder
- 1/8 teaspoon pepper
- 2 cans (6 ounces each) light water-packed tuna, drained and flaked
- 8 slices Italian bread
- 4 slices tomato
- 4 lettuce leaves

Direction

- Mix together the mayonnaise and applesauce in a small bowl. Stir in the pepper, garlic powder, seasoning blend, onion, pineapple, green pepper and celery, then add tuna and stir well. Spread it on top of the 4 bread slices, then top with tomato, lettuce and leftover bread.

Nutrition Information

- Calories: 310 calories

- Protein: 28g protein. Diabetic Exchanges: 3 lean meat
- Total Fat: 3g fat (1g saturated fat)
- Sodium: 715mg sodium
- Fiber: 3g fiber)
- Total Carbohydrate: 42g carbohydrate (11g sugars
- Cholesterol: 26mg cholesterol

---

352.   Poor Boy Sandwich

Serving: 1 serving. | Prep: 15mins | Cook: 0mins | Ready in:

Ingredients

- 1 French or submarine roll
- 1 tablespoon butter, softened
- 1/4 teaspoon celery seed
- 1 can (6 ounces) tuna, drained and flaked
- 1/4 cup chopped celery
- 1/4 cup chopped fresh parsley
- 3 tablespoons mayonnaise
- 1 tablespoon horseradish
- 1/2 teaspoon grated lemon zest
- 1/8 teaspoon pepper

Direction

- Trim a thin slice off top of roll; put aside. Hollow out the middle, save half a cup of bread and leaving a 1 quarter inch shell. Mix celery seed and butter; spread on the roll inside and on cut surface of top. Mix reserved bread and the leftover ingredients; scoop into roll. Replace top.

Nutrition Information

- Calories: 787 calories
- Total Carbohydrate: 34g carbohydrate (3g sugars
- Cholesterol: 97mg cholesterol
- Protein: 50g protein.

- Total Fat: 49g fat (12g saturated fat)
- Sodium: 1262mg sodium
- Fiber: 3g fiber)

353. Pork Salad Croissants

Serving: 4 servings. | Prep: 15mins | Cook: 0mins | Ready in:

Ingredients

- 1 medium tart apple, diced
- 1/2 cup halved seedless red grapes
- 1/2 cup mayonnaise
- 2 tablespoons chopped walnuts
- 2 tablespoons chutney
- 1/2 teaspoon salt
- 1/4 teaspoon ground ginger
- 2 cups cubed cooked pork tenderloin
- Lettuce leaves
- 4 croissants, split

Direction

- Mix the initial 7 ingredients in a big bowl. Put in pork: coat by tossing. Use lettuce leaf to line the bottom of each croissant. Add roughly three quarters cup of pork salad on top. Replace tops.

Nutrition Information

- Calories: 643 calories
- Protein: 26g protein.
- Total Fat: 43g fat (12g saturated fat)
- Sodium: 915mg sodium
- Fiber: 3g fiber)
- Total Carbohydrate: 38g carbohydrate (12g sugars
- Cholesterol: 112mg cholesterol

354. Pork Salad Rolls

Serving: 6 servings. | Prep: 15mins | Cook: 0mins | Ready in:

Ingredients

- 1/2 cup mayonnaise
- 1 teaspoon Dijon mustard
- 1/2 teaspoon lemon juice
- 1/2 teaspoon seasoned salt
- 1/4 teaspoon pepper
- 3 cups shredded cooked pork
- 1/2 cup thinly sliced celery
- 1/2 cup halved seedless green grapes
- 6 flour tortillas (6 inches) or hard rolls, split
- Lettuce leaves, optional

Direction

- Mix pepper, seasoned salt, lemon juice, mustard, and mayonnaise in a big bowl. Put in the grapes, celery, and pork; coat by tossing. Keep chilled in the refrigerator for no less than 60 minutes.
- Scoop half a cup of pork mixture down the middle of each tortilla; put in lettuce if you want; roll the tortilla up.

Nutrition Information

- Calories: 378 calories
- Sodium: 524mg sodium
- Fiber: 0 fiber)
- Total Carbohydrate: 16g carbohydrate (2g sugars
- Cholesterol: 70mg cholesterol
- Protein: 23g protein.
- Total Fat: 24g fat (4g saturated fat)

355.   Roasted Pepper 'n' Egg Salad Sandwiches

Serving: 2 servings. | Prep: 15mins | Cook: 0mins | Ready in:

Ingredients

- 1/4 cup mayonnaise
- 2 tablespoons diced roasted sweet red pepper
- 1 tablespoon minced fresh parsley
- 1/2 teaspoon Dijon mustard
- 1/2 teaspoon dried oregano
- 1/8 teaspoon pepper
- 3 hard-boiled large eggs, chopped
- 4 slices multigrain bread
- 2 romaine leaves

Direction

- Mix together the initial 6 ingredients in a small bowl, then add eggs; gently stir to blend. Spread it on top of the two bread slices, then put romaine and leftover bread on top.

Nutrition Information

- Calories: 280 calories
- Sodium: 670mg sodium
- Fiber: 4g fiber)
- Total Carbohydrate: 31g carbohydrate (7g sugars
- Cholesterol: 321mg cholesterol
- Protein: 15g protein.
- Total Fat: 11g fat (3g saturated fat)

356.   Salmon Salad Pitas

Serving: 4 servings. | Prep: 15mins | Cook: 10mins | Ready in:

Ingredients

- 1 salmon fillet (1 pound)
- 1/4 cup chopped celery
- 1/4 cup chopped seeded peeled cucumber
- 1/4 cup reduced-fat sour cream
- 1/4 cup fat-free mayonnaise
- 1 tablespoon minced chives
- 1 tablespoon minced fresh dill
- 1 teaspoon Italian seasoning
- 1/4 teaspoon salt
- 1/8 teaspoon white pepper
- 4 romaine leaves
- 4 whole wheat pita pocket halves

Direction

- In a big frying pan, pour water up to 2 inches, then boil. Lower the heat then gently add the salmon. Let it poach for 6 to 12 minutes without cover or until the fish easily flakes using a fork and is firm. Using a slotted spatula, take out the salmon and let it cool.
- Mix together the seasonings, mayonnaise, sour cream, cucumber and celery in a big bowl. Flake the salmon and mix into the salad mixture. Put cover and let it chill in the fridge for a minimum of one hour, then serve it with pita breads lined with lettuce.

Nutrition Information

- Calories: 331 calories
- Protein: 27g protein. Diabetic Exchanges: 3 lean meat
- Total Fat: 15g fat (4g saturated fat)
- Sodium: 522mg sodium
- Fiber: 3g fiber)
- Total Carbohydrate: 22g carbohydrate (3g sugars
- Cholesterol: 74mg cholesterol

357.   Salmon Salad Sandwiches

Serving: 2 servings. | Prep: 10mins | Cook: 0mins | Ready in:

Ingredients

- 3 ounces cream cheese, softened
- 1 tablespoon mayonnaise
- 1 tablespoon lemon juice
- 1 teaspoon dill weed
- 1/4 to 1/2 teaspoon salt
- 1/8 teaspoon pepper
- 1 can (6 ounces) pink salmon, drained, bones and skin removed
- 1/2 cup shredded carrot
- 1/2 cup chopped celery
- Lettuce leaves
- 2 whole wheat buns, split

Direction

- Beat pepper, salt, dill, lemon juice, mayonnaise and cream cheese in a big-sized bowl till become smooth in consistency. Put in then mix well the celery, carrot, and salmon. Add a lettuce leaf and roughly half a cup of salmon salad over each bun.

Nutrition Information

- Calories: 463 calories
- Total Fat: 29g fat (12g saturated fat)
- Sodium: 1158mg sodium
- Fiber: 5g fiber)
- Total Carbohydrate: 28g carbohydrate (5g sugars
- Cholesterol: 87mg cholesterol
- Protein: 25g protein.

358. Seafood Salad Pitas

Serving: 8 servings. | Prep: 20mins | Cook: 0mins | Ready in:

Ingredients

- 2 cups chopped imitation crabmeat (about 10 ounces)
- 1/2 pound cooked medium shrimp, peeled, deveined and chopped (about 1 cup)

- 2 celery ribs, chopped
- 1/2 cup thinly sliced green onions
- 3/4 cup fat-free mayonnaise
- 3/4 teaspoon seafood seasoning
- 1/4 teaspoon salt
- 1/8 teaspoon pepper
- 8 whole wheat pita pocket halves

Direction

- Mix onions, celery, shrimp and crab in a big bowl. Mix pepper, salt, seafood seasoning, and mayonnaise in a small-sized bowl. Add on top of crab mixture; coat by tossing. Keep it covered and let chill in the refrigerator for no less than 2 hours. Scoop into pita halves.

Nutrition Information

- Calories: 162 calories
- Protein: 10g protein. Diabetic Exchanges: 2 starch
- Total Fat: 2g fat (0 saturated fat)
- Sodium: 755mg sodium
- Fiber: 3g fiber)
- Total Carbohydrate: 28g carbohydrate (3g sugars
- Cholesterol: 27mg cholesterol

359. Seafood Salad Sandwiches

Serving: 36 servings | Prep: 25mins | Cook: | Ready in:

Ingredients

- 1 pkg. (12 oz.) imitation crabmeat, flaked
- 1/2 cup finely chopped green peppers
- 1/3 cup shredded carrots
- 1/2 cup KRAFT Real Mayo Mayonnaise
- 1/4 cup GREY POUPON Hearty Spicy Brown Mustard

- 1 pkg. (17-1/4 oz.) frozen puff pastry (2 sheets), thawed
- 1 egg white, lightly beaten
- 2 Tbsp. poppy seed

Direction

- Mix together mustard, mayo, vegetables, and crabmeat. Chill until ready to use.
- Spread the pastry sheet onto a cookie sheet; use egg white to brush. Use poppy seed to drizzle. Slice each sheet into 18 (3x1-1/2-inch) rectangles. Keep the rectangles stick together.
- Bake for 25 minutes. Move the pastry to the wire racks; let it cool down entirely. Split the pastry into rectangles. Cut each rectangle into 2 pieces horizontally. Put 1 Tbsp. of crabmeat on the bottom half of the cut rectangle and put the rectangle top on.

Nutrition Information

- Calories: 90
- Protein: 2 g
- Sugar: 1 g
- Saturated Fat: 1.5 g
- Sodium: 160 mg
- Fiber: 0 g
- Total Carbohydrate: 6 g
- Cholesterol: 3.0011 mg
- Total Fat: 6 g

360. Shamrock Sandwiches

Serving: about 16 sandwiches. | Prep: 35mins | Cook: 0mins |Ready in:

Ingredients

- 1 package (8 ounces) cream cheese, softened
- 1/4 cup mayonnaise
- 2 tablespoons Dijon mustard
- 1 package (2 ounces) thinly sliced deli corned beef, chopped

- 2 tablespoons grated red onion
- 2 teaspoons snipped fresh dill or 3/4 teaspoon dill weed
- 1/4 teaspoon salt
- 1 pound thinly sliced seedless rye bread
- Fresh dill springs, optional

Direction

- Beat mustard, mayonnaise and cream cheese until the mixture gets smooth in a large bowl. Put in salt, dill, onion, corned beef and stir. Cut out 2 shamrocks from each slice of bread using a 2-in. shamrock cookie cutter.
- Spread one to two tablespoonfuls of filling on the bottoms of half of the shamrocks; put remaining shamrocks on top. Use dill to garnish if you like.

Nutrition Information

- Calories: 314 calories
- Cholesterol: 39mg cholesterol
- Protein: 9g protein.
- Total Fat: 18g fat (8g saturated fat)
- Sodium: 783mg sodium
- Fiber: 3g fiber)
- Total Carbohydrate: 29g carbohydrate (5g sugars

361. Shrimp 'n' Slaw Puffs

Serving: 4 servings. | Prep: 15mins | Cook: 0mins |Ready in:

Ingredients

- 1/2 pound cooked small shrimp, peeled and deveined and chopped
- 2 cups coleslaw mix
- 2 tablespoons chopped green onion
- 2 tablespoons chopped sweet yellow pepper
- 1/4 cup coleslaw salad dressing
- 1 tablespoon capers, drained and patted dry

- 1 teaspoon snipped fresh dill or 1/4 teaspoon dill weed
- 1/4 teaspoon salt
- 1/4 teaspoon pepper
- 4 cream puff shells

Direction

- Mix yellow pepper, onion, coleslaw mix, and shrimp together in a big bowl. Mix pepper, salt, dill, capers, and the coleslaw dressing together in a small bowl. Put on the shrimp mixture and lightly mix to combine.
- Let chill until eating. Put 1/2 cup of shrimp salad on each cream puff, just before eating. Replace tops.

Nutrition Information

- Calories: 371 calories
- Protein: 18g protein.
- Total Fat: 23g fat (5g saturated fat)
- Sodium: 920mg sodium
- Fiber: 1g fiber)
- Total Carbohydrate: 21g carbohydrate (5g sugars
- Cholesterol: 247mg cholesterol

362.   Shrimp Egg Salad

Serving: 4 | Prep: 15mins | Cook: | Ready in:

Ingredients

- 1 pound cooked shrimp - peeled, deveined, and chopped
- 4 hard-cooked eggs, chopped
- 4 tablespoons mayonnaise
- 1 teaspoon Dijon mustard
- 1 sprig chopped fresh dill
- 4 leaves green leaf lettuce

Direction

- Mix together mustard, mayonnaise, eggs and shrimp in a medium bowl. Place on lettuce leaves to serve.

Nutrition Information

- Calories: 292 calories;
- Sodium: 429
- Total Carbohydrate: 1.6
- Cholesterol: 439
- Protein: 30.3
- Total Fat: 17.5

363.   Shrimp Salad Croissants

Serving: 8 servings. | Prep: 15mins | Cook: 0mins | Ready in:

Ingredients

- 1 pound cooked small shrimp
- 2 celery ribs, diced
- 2 small carrots, shredded
- 1 cup mayonnaise
- 1/3 cup finely chopped onion
- Dash salt and pepper
- 2 packages (2-1/4 ounces each) sliced almonds
- 8 croissants, split

Direction

- Mix the carrots, celery and shrimp in a big-sized bowl. Mix pepper, salt, onion, and mayonnaise in a small-sized bowl. Add on top of shrimp mixture and coat by tossing.
- Keep it covered and let chill in the refrigerator for at least 2 hours. Just prior to serving, mix in almonds. Serve over croissants.

Nutrition Information

- Calories: 543 calories
- Protein: 19g protein.
- Total Fat: 39g fat (10g saturated fat)

- Sodium: 733mg sodium
- Fiber: 3g fiber)
- Total Carbohydrate: 30g carbohydrate (4g sugars
- Cholesterol: 159mg cholesterol

364. Simon's Famous Tuna Salad

Serving: 5 servings. | Prep: 15mins | Cook: 0mins | Ready in:

Ingredients

- 3 cans (5 ounces each) light water-packed tuna, drained and flaked
- 3/4 cup fat-free mayonnaise
- 1/4 cup chopped celery
- 1/4 cup chopped carrot
- 1/2 teaspoon onion powder
- 1/2 teaspoon garlic powder
- 1/4 teaspoon dill weed
- 10 slices whole wheat bread, toasted
- 5 lettuce leaves

Direction

- Mix together the initial 7 ingredients in a big bowl. Layer a toast slice with lettuce leaf and 1/2 cup tuna salad per sandwich. Put the 2nd slice of toast on top.

Nutrition Information

- Calories: 271 calories
- Total Fat: 4g fat (1g saturated fat)
- Sodium: 852mg sodium
- Fiber: 5g fiber)
- Total Carbohydrate: 29g carbohydrate (6g sugars
- Cholesterol: 29mg cholesterol
- Protein: 29g protein.

365. Smoked Salmon Egg Salad

Serving: 6 servings. | Prep: 10mins | Cook: 0mins | Ready in:

Ingredients

- 3/4 cup mayonnaise
- 1 teaspoon dill weed
- 1/2 teaspoon lemon juice
- 1/4 teaspoon salt
- 1/8 teaspoon pepper
- 6 hard-boiled large eggs, chopped
- 4 ounces smoked salmon, chopped
- 6 croissants, split
- 1-1/2 cups fresh baby spinach

Direction

- Mix the first 5 ingredients together in a big bowl. Mix in salmon and eggs.
- Put 1/3 cup on each croissant bottom; put spinach leaves and replace croissant tops on top.

Nutrition Information

- Calories: 533 calories
- Fiber: 2g fiber)
- Total Carbohydrate: 27g carbohydrate (7g sugars
- Cholesterol: 265mg cholesterol
- Protein: 15g protein.
- Total Fat: 40g fat (11g saturated fat)
- Sodium: 889mg sodium

366. Special Egg Salad

Serving: 6 servings. | Prep: 15mins | Cook: 0mins | Ready in:

Ingredients

- 3 ounces reduced-fat cream cheese
- 1/4 cup fat-free mayonnaise
- 1/2 teaspoon sugar
- 1/4 teaspoon onion powder
- 1/4 teaspoon garlic powder
- 1/8 teaspoon salt
- 1/8 teaspoon pepper
- 6 hard-boiled large eggs, chopped
- 12 slices whole wheat bread, toasted
- 6 lettuce leaves

Direction

- Beat the cream cheese in a small bowl until it becomes smooth. Beat in the pepper, salt, garlic powder, onion powder, sugar and mayonnaise, then fold in the eggs. Put a cover and let it chill in the fridge for an hour. Serve with lettuce on toast.

Nutrition Information

- Calories: 259 calories
- Protein: 13g protein. Diabetic Exchanges: 2 starch
- Total Fat: 10g fat (4g saturated fat)
- Sodium: 528mg sodium
- Fiber: 4g fiber)
- Total Carbohydrate: 30g carbohydrate (0 sugars
- Cholesterol: 225mg cholesterol

367. Special Ham 'n' Cheese Sandwiches

Serving: 2 servings. | Prep: 10mins | Cook: 0mins | Ready in:

Ingredients

- 3 ounces cream cheese, softened
- 2 tablespoons sweet pickle relish
- 1 tablespoon Dijon mustard
- 1/2 cup shredded cheddar cheese

- 2 ounces fully cooked ham, finely chopped
- 4 slices bread or 2 buns

Direction

- Mix mustard, pickle relish, and cream cheese together in a small bowl. Mix in ham and cheese. Spread 1/2 cup in buns or between bread slices.

Nutrition Information

- Calories: 457 calories
- Sodium: 1241mg sodium
- Fiber: 1g fiber)
- Total Carbohydrate: 34g carbohydrate (8g sugars
- Cholesterol: 92mg cholesterol
- Protein: 19g protein.
- Total Fat: 28g fat (16g saturated fat)

368. Special Ham And Cheese Sandwiches

Serving: 3 | Prep: 10mins | Cook: | Ready in:

Ingredients

- 1 (3 ounce) package cream cheese, softened
- 1/2 cup shredded Cheddar cheese
- 2 tablespoons pickle relish
- 2 teaspoons Dijon mustard
- 2 ounces ham, finely chopped
- 6 slices bread

Direction

- Mix mustard, relish, Cheddar cheese, and cream cheese together in a small bowl. Add ham. Split the mixture between 3 bread slices; put the rest of the bread on top to make sandwiches.

369.   Spooky Monster Sandwiches

Serving: 1 dozen. | Prep: 35mins | Cook: 0mins | Ready in:

Ingredients

- 2 cups cubed cooked chicken breast
- 1/2 cup dried cranberries, optional
- 1/2 cup mayonnaise
- 1/4 cup finely chopped onion
- 1/4 cup chopped celery
- 1/4 teaspoon salt
- 1/4 teaspoon pepper
- 12 dinner rolls, split and toasted
- 1 jar (15 ounces) process cheese sauce
- 24 pimiento-stuffed olives
- 12 pimiento strips
- 6 whole baby dill pickles, cut in half lengthwise

Direction

- Mix pepper, salt, celery, onion, mayonnaise, cranberries if you want, and chicken together in a large bowl. Use the chicken mixture to stuff the rolls.
- Heat cheese sauce to melt; sprinkle or pipe over the top of each sandwich to make it look like hair. For each monster sandwich, stick pickles to make fangs, pimiento strips to make noses and olives to make eyes.

Nutrition Information

- Calories: 332 calories
- Total Fat: 20g fat (7g saturated fat)
- Sodium: 1434mg sodium
- Fiber: 2g fiber)
- Total Carbohydrate: 23g carbohydrate (2g sugars
- Cholesterol: 60mg cholesterol
- Protein: 15g protein.

370.   Star Sandwiches

Serving: 8 sandwiches. | Prep: 25mins | Cook: 0mins | Ready in:

Ingredients

- 4 hard-boiled large eggs, diced
- 1/2 cup mayonnaise
- 1 teaspoon Dijon mustard
- 1/4 teaspoon dill weed
- 1/8 teaspoon salt
- 1/8 teaspoon pepper
- 16 slices egg bread or white bread

Direction

- Mix together the pepper, salt, dill, mustard, mayonnaise and eggs in a small bowl. Cut out 16 stars from the bread using a big star-shaped cookie cutter. Spread 1/2 with egg salad, then put leftover bread on top.

Nutrition Information

- Calories: 359 calories
- Cholesterol: 135mg cholesterol
- Protein: 11g protein.
- Total Fat: 17g fat (4g saturated fat)
- Sodium: 457mg sodium
- Fiber: 2g fiber)
- Total Carbohydrate: 39g carbohydrate (2g sugars

371.   Sub Salad

Serving: 8-10 servings. | Prep: 25mins | Cook: 0mins | Ready in:

Ingredients

- 8 ounces hard salami, diced
- 8 ounces fully cooked ham, diced
- 8 ounces pepperoni, diced
- 4 ounces provolone cheese, diced

- 4 ounces American cheese, diced
- 2 medium tomatoes, chopped
- 1 medium red onion, chopped
- 1/2 cup mayonnaise
- 1 tablespoon olive oil
- 1/2 teaspoon garlic salt
- 1/4 teaspoon dried oregano
- French bread slices

Direction

- Mix the first 7 ingredients together in a 2-1/2-qt. serving bowl. Mix oregano, garlic salt, oil, and mayonnaise together in a small bowl. Put on the meat mixture and mix to combine. Put a cover on and chill until eating. Eat with French bread.

Nutrition Information

- Calories: 395 calories
- Total Fat: 34g fat (12g saturated fat)
- Sodium: 1489mg sodium
- Fiber: 1g fiber)
- Total Carbohydrate: 4g carbohydrate (3g sugars
- Cholesterol: 72mg cholesterol
- Protein: 20g protein.

372. Sunny BLT Sandwiches

Serving: 2 servings. | Prep: 20mins | Cook: 0mins | Ready in:

Ingredients

- 4 bacon strips
- 4 hard-boiled large eggs, chopped
- 2 tablespoons 4% cottage cheese
- 1 tablespoon cream cheese, softened
- 2 teaspoons sweet pickle juice
- 1/2 teaspoon prepared mustard
- 1/4 teaspoon onion powder
- 1/8 teaspoon salt

- 1/8 teaspoon pepper
- 1/8 teaspoon Worcestershire sauce
- 4 slices whole wheat bread, toasted
- 2 lettuce leaves
- 2 slices tomato
- 2 slices Swiss cheese (3/4 ounce each)

Direction

- Put bacon in a large skillet and cook over medium heat till crispy. Transfer bacon to paper towels to drain.
- Mix together Worcestershire sauce, pepper, salt, onion powder, mustard, pickle juice, cream cheese, cottage cheese and eggs in large bowl. Arrange lettuce, tomato, cheese slices and bacon in layers on two slices of toast. Put egg salad and remaining toast on top.

Nutrition Information

- Calories: 536 calories
- Protein: 38g protein.
- Total Fat: 30g fat (10g saturated fat)
- Sodium: 1396mg sodium
- Fiber: 4g fiber)
- Total Carbohydrate: 30g carbohydrate (8g sugars
- Cholesterol: 491mg cholesterol

373. Super Duper Tuna Sandwiches

Serving: 4 servings. | Prep: 15mins | Cook: 0mins | Ready in:

Ingredients

- 2 cans (5 ounces each) light water-packed tuna, drained and flaked
- 1/3 cup shredded peeled apple
- 1/3 cup finely shredded cabbage
- 1/3 cup finely shredded carrot
- 3 tablespoons finely chopped celery

- 3 tablespoons finely chopped onion
- 3 tablespoons sweet pickle relish
- 2 tablespoons reduced-fat mayonnaise
- 8 slices whole wheat bread

Direction

- Mix together the initial 8 ingredients in a big bowl. Over the 4 bread slices, spread 1/2 cup of the tuna mixture, then put leftover slices of bread on top.

Nutrition Information

- Calories: 291 calories
- Protein: 29g protein. Diabetic Exchanges: 3 lean meat
- Total Fat: 5g fat (1g saturated fat)
- Sodium: 717mg sodium
- Fiber: 5g fiber)
- Total Carbohydrate: 31g carbohydrate (7g sugars
- Cholesterol: 28mg cholesterol

374. Surprise Sandwich Spread

Serving: 4 servings. | Prep: 15mins | Cook: 0mins | Ready in:

Ingredients

- 2 cups ground fully cooked ham, roast beef or chicken
- 2 hard-boiled large eggs, chopped
- 1/4 cup mayonnaise, ketchup or chili sauce
- 1 teaspoon prepared mustard
- 1/2 teaspoon Worcestershire sauce
- 1/4 teaspoon celery salt
- 1/8 teaspoon onion powder
- 1/8 teaspoon pepper
- 2 tablespoons chopped celery, onion or olives, optional
- 1 tablespoon sweet pickle relish, optional
- 8 slices bread

Direction

- Mix the initial 8 ingredients in a medium-sized bowl. Put in onion or olives and/or relish, with celery if you want. Spread half a cup over four bread slices; add leftover bread on top.

Nutrition Information

- Calories:
- Sodium:
- Fiber:
- Total Carbohydrate:
- Cholesterol:
- Protein:
- Total Fat:

375. Surprise Tuna Salad

Serving: 6 servings. | Prep: 10mins | Cook: 0mins | Ready in:

Ingredients

- 2 cans (6 ounces each) tuna, drained and flaked
- 1 medium apple, peeled and chopped
- 1/2 cup golden raisins
- 1/2 cup Miracle Whip
- 1/3 cup chopped pecans
- 1 tablespoon sweet pickle relish
- 12 bread slices, toasted
- 6 slices Monterey Jack cheese

Direction

- Mix the initial 6 ingredients in a bowl; spread on top of six bread slices. Add leftover bread and a slice of cheese on top of each.

Nutrition Information

- Calories: 476 calories
- Total Fat: 28g fat (7g saturated fat)

- Sodium: 622mg sodium
- Fiber: 3g fiber)
- Total Carbohydrate: 39g carbohydrate (13g sugars
- Cholesterol: 36mg cholesterol
- Protein: 17g protein.

376.   Sweet 'n' Sour Pockets

Serving: 5 servings. | Prep: 10mins | Cook: 0mins | Ready in:

Ingredients

- 1/3 cup mayonnaise
- 1/3 cup sour cream
- 1/2 teaspoon Dijon mustard
- 3/4 cup pineapple tidbits, drained
- 5 pita pocket breads (6 inches), halved
- 10 lettuce leaves
- 10 slices (1 ounce each) fully cooked ham
- 1/2 cup chopped green pepper
- 1/2 cup chopped red onion

Direction

- Mix mustard, sour cream and mayonnaise in a small-sized bowl. Keep it covered and let chill for 60 minutes.
- Just prior to serving, mix in pineapple. Use onion, green pepper, and 2 tbsp. of pineapple mixture, ham, and lettuce to fill each pita half.

Nutrition Information

- Calories: 291 calories
- Fiber: 0 fiber)
- Total Carbohydrate: 49g carbohydrate (0 sugars
- Cholesterol: 30mg cholesterol
- Protein: 16g protein. Diabetic Exchanges: 2-1/2 starch
- Total Fat: 3g fat (0 saturated fat)
- Sodium: 1166mg sodium

377.   Swiss 'n' Asparagus Egg Salad

Serving: 5 servings. | Prep: 25mins | Cook: 5mins | Ready in:

Ingredients

- 8 fresh asparagus,spears, cut into 1/4-inch pieces
- 6 hard-boiled large eggs, chopped
- 1 cup shredded Swiss cheese
- 1/2 cup cubed fully cooked ham
- 3/4 cup mayonnaise
- 1 teaspoon Dijon mustard
- Salt to taste
- 10 slices rye bread

Direction

- In a saucepan, pour in asparagus and 1 inch of water. Boil; let it simmer while uncovered, till tender-crisp, for 5 minutes. Drain and let it cool down. Mix salt, mustard, mayonnaise, ham, cheese, eggs and asparagus in a bowl. Spread over five bread slices, roughly half a cup over each; add the leftover bread on top.

Nutrition Information

- Calories:
- Sodium:
- Fiber:
- Total Carbohydrate:
- Cholesterol:
- Protein:
- Total Fat:

378. Tangy Tuna Bunwiches

Serving: 2 servings. | Prep: 10mins | Cook: 0mins | Ready in:

Ingredients

- 1 can (5 ounces) light water-packed tuna
- 3 tablespoons fat-free mayonnaise
- 1 tablespoon ketchup
- 1/2 teaspoon lemon juice
- 1/2 teaspoon Worcestershire sauce
- 2 sandwich buns, split
- 2 lettuce leaves

Direction

- Mix Worcestershire sauce, lemon juice, ketchup, mayonnaise, and tuna together in a big bowl. Eat on buns with lettuce.

Nutrition Information

- Calories: 336 calories
- Total Fat: 6g fat (3g saturated fat)
- Sodium: 917mg sodium
- Fiber: 3g fiber)
- Total Carbohydrate: 41g carbohydrate (8g sugars
- Cholesterol: 28mg cholesterol
- Protein: 29g protein.

379. Tarragon Crab Sandwiches

Serving: 6 servings. | Prep: 20mins | Cook: 0mins | Ready in:

Ingredients

- 1 package (16 ounces) imitation crabmeat, chopped
- 1/3 cup chopped celery
- 1/3 cup mayonnaise
- 1 tablespoon chopped green onion

- 2 teaspoons minced fresh tarragon
- 2 to 3 drops hot pepper sauce
- 1/8 teaspoon salt
- 1/8 teaspoon pepper
- 12 ready-to-serve fully cooked bacon strips
- 12 slices sourdough bread, toasted
- 6 lettuce leaves
- 6 slices tomato

Direction

- Mix celery and crabmeat together in a big bowl. Mix pepper, salt, pepper sauce, tarragon, onion, and mayonnaise together in a small bowl. Put on the crabmeat mixture and mix to combine.
- Cook bacon as the package directs. Layer on 6 slices of bread with the crab mixture, bacon, tomato, and lettuce. Put the remaining bread on top.

Nutrition Information

- Calories: 591 calories
- Fiber: 4g fiber)
- Total Carbohydrate: 78g carbohydrate (2g sugars
- Cholesterol: 24mg cholesterol
- Protein: 23g protein.
- Total Fat: 20g fat (4g saturated fat)
- Sodium: 1524mg sodium

380. Thanksgiving Sandwiches

Serving: 6 servings. | Prep: 15mins | Cook: 0mins | Ready in:

Ingredients

- 2 cups cubed cooked turkey breast
- 1/2 cup mayonnaise
- 1/2 cup finely chopped fresh or frozen cranberries

- 1 orange, peeled and chopped
- 1 teaspoon sugar
- 1 teaspoon prepared mustard
- 1/2 teaspoon salt
- 1/4 cup chopped pecans
- Lettuce leaves
- 6 rolls or croissants, split

Direction

- Mix salt, mustard, sugar, orange, cranberries, mayonnaise, and turkey in a big-sized bowl. Just prior to serving, mix in pecans. Over each roll, add half cup of turkey mixture and lettuce.

Nutrition Information

- Calories: 458 calories
- Total Fat: 23g fat (5g saturated fat)
- Sodium: 679mg sodium
- Fiber: 3g fiber)
- Total Carbohydrate: 40g carbohydrate (9g sugars
- Cholesterol: 47mg cholesterol
- Protein: 22g protein.

---

381.   Toasted Ham Salad Sandwiches

Serving: 8 servings. | Prep: 20mins | Cook: 15mins | Ready in:

Ingredients

- 1-1/3 cups diced fully cooked ham
- 1-1/3 cups diced cooked chicken
- 1/2 cup diced celery
- 1 can (8 ounces) crushed pineapple, drained
- 1/3 cup mayonnaise
- 3 tablespoons chopped pecans
- 4-1/2 teaspoons chopped green pepper
- 1 teaspoon sliced green onion
- 1/4 teaspoon salt

- Dash pepper
- 16 slices bread
- 8 slices mozzarella cheese
- 6 tablespoons butter, softened

Direction

- Mix together the first 10 ingredients in a bowl. Spread ham mixture, about half a cup on each of eight slices of bread. Put cheese and the remaining bread on top. Use butter to spread on the outsides of sandwiches. Put sandwiches in a large skillet or on a griddle then cook over medium heat until both sides turn golden brown.

Nutrition Information

- Calories: 475 calories
- Sodium: 910mg sodium
- Fiber: 2g fiber)
- Total Carbohydrate: 31g carbohydrate (6g sugars
- Cholesterol: 82mg cholesterol
- Protein: 21g protein.
- Total Fat: 29g fat (12g saturated fat)

---

382.   Triple Tasty Sandwich Spread

Serving: 6 servings. | Prep: 15mins | Cook: 0mins | Ready in:

Ingredients

- 1/2 to 2/3 cup mayonnaise
- 1 tablespoon Dijon mustard
- 1 tablespoon finely chopped onion
- 1 tablespoon minced jalapeno pepper
- 1 teaspoon Worcestershire sauce
- 1/2 pound fully cooked ham, ground
- 1/2 pound Genoa salami, ground
- 1/4 cup finely chopped sweet pickle
- 3 hard-boiled large eggs, chopped

- 12 slices whole wheat bread, toasted

Direction

- In a medium-sized bowl, mix together the first 5 ingredients. Mix in eggs, pickle, salami, and ham. Put about 1/2 cup between slices of whole wheat toast.

Nutrition Information

- Calories: 554 calories
- Total Fat: 38g fat (10g saturated fat)
- Sodium: 1793mg sodium
- Fiber: 4g fiber)
- Total Carbohydrate: 30g carbohydrate (5g sugars
- Cholesterol: 171mg cholesterol
- Protein: 26g protein.

---

383. Tuna Boats

Serving: 4 servings. | Prep: 25mins | Cook: 0mins | Ready in:

Ingredients

- 2 cans (6 ounces each) tuna, drained and flaked
- 1 hard-boiled large egg, chopped
- 3 tablespoons finely chopped celery
- 1 tablespoon finely chopped onion
- 1/2 cup Miracle Whip
- 1 teaspoon sweet pickle relish
- 4 submarine sandwich or hoagie buns
- 4 lettuce leaves
- 4 slices cheddar cheese
- 8 wooden skewers
- Fish-shaped crackers

Direction

- Mix together onion, celery, egg and tuna in a bowl. Put in the Miracle Whip, pickle relish and stir; set aside. Cut a 2-in. wide V-shape in the center of each bun to within 1 inch of the bottom. Get the cut portion out of each bun and keep them for other use. Use a lettuce leaf to line each bun and fill each with tuna mixture.
- Halve each of cheese slices diagonally. For sails, carefully insert a wooden skewer into the top center of each cheese triangle. Slightly bend cheese; push skewer through bottom center of cheese. Insert 2 skewers into each sandwich. Put sandwich on a serving plate. Use fish crackers to sprinkle around boats.

Nutrition Information

- Calories:
- Total Fat:
- Sodium:
- Fiber:
- Total Carbohydrate:
- Cholesterol:
- Protein:

---

384. Tuna Caesar Sandwiches

Serving: 4 servings. | Prep: 20mins | Cook: 0mins | Ready in:

Ingredients

- 2 cans (5 ounces each) white water-packed tuna, drained and flaked
- 1/4 cup marinated quartered artichoke hearts, drained and chopped
- 1/4 cup finely chopped onion
- 1/4 cup reduced-fat mayonnaise
- 3 tablespoons grated Parmesan cheese
- 2 teaspoons lemon juice
- 1 teaspoon Dijon mustard
- 8 slices whole wheat bread, toasted
- 16 cucumber slices
- 8 slices tomato
- 2 cups shredded lettuce

Direction

- Mix together the initial 7 ingredients in a small bowl, then spread the mixture on top of the 4 slices of toast. Put cucumber, tomato, lettuce and leftover toast on top.

Nutrition Information

- Calories: 338 calories
- Fiber: 5g fiber)
- Total Carbohydrate: 30g carbohydrate (6g sugars
- Cholesterol: 38mg cholesterol
- Protein: 27g protein. Diabetic Exchanges: 3 lean meat
- Total Fat: 12g fat (3g saturated fat)
- Sodium: 797mg sodium

---

385. Tuna Caesar Sandwiches For Two

Serving: 2 servings. | Prep: 20mins | Cook: 0mins | Ready in:

Ingredients

- 1 can (5 ounces) albacore white tuna in water
- 2 tablespoons marinated quartered artichoke hearts, drained and chopped
- 2 tablespoons finely chopped onion
- 2 tablespoons reduced-fat mayonnaise
- 4-1/2 teaspoons grated Parmesan cheese
- 1 teaspoon lemon juice
- 1/2 teaspoon Dijon mustard
- 4 slices whole wheat bread, toasted
- 8 cucumber slices
- 4 tomato slices
- 1 cup shredded lettuce

Direction

- Mix together the initial 7 ingredients in a small bowl and spread the mixture on top of the 2

toast slices. Put the cucumber, tomato, lettuce and leftover toast on top.

Nutrition Information

- Calories: 338 calories
- Protein: 27g protein. Diabetic Exchanges: 3 lean meat
- Total Fat: 12g fat (3g saturated fat)
- Sodium: 797mg sodium
- Fiber: 5g fiber)
- Total Carbohydrate: 30g carbohydrate (6g sugars
- Cholesterol: 38mg cholesterol

---

386. Tuna Cheese Sandwiches

Serving: 5 servings. | Prep: 10mins | Cook: 0mins | Ready in:

Ingredients

- 1 can (6 ounces) tuna, drained and flaked
- 1 cup shredded cheddar cheese
- 1/2 cup chopped walnuts
- 1/2 cup mayonnaise
- 1 tablespoon whole milk
- 1 teaspoon lemon juice
- 1/2 teaspoon Worcestershire sauce
- 1/4 teaspoon onion salt
- 1/8 teaspoon pepper
- 10 slices whole wheat bread
- 2-1/2 cups finely shredded lettuce

Direction

- Mix the first 9 ingredients together in a small bowl. Layer about 1/4 cup of the tuna mixture and 1/2 cup of lettuce on 5 slices of bread. Top with remaining bread.

Nutrition Information

- Calories: 501 calories

- Sodium: 741mg sodium
- Fiber: 5g fiber)
- Total Carbohydrate: 27g carbohydrate (4g sugars
- Cholesterol: 43mg cholesterol
- Protein: 23g protein.
- Total Fat: 34g fat (8g saturated fat)

387. Tuna Dill Spread

Serving: 5 servings. | Prep: 10mins | Cook: 0mins | Ready in:

Ingredients

- 1 can (6 ounces) tuna, drained and flaked
- 3 ounces cream cheese, softened
- 1/3 cup finely chopped seeded cucumber
- 2 tablespoons lemon juice
- 1 to 2 tablespoons minced fresh dill
- 1/2 teaspoon salt
- 1/4 teaspoon pepper

Direction

- Mix all ingredients in a bowl; stir them well. Use the mixture to spread on crackers or fill the sandwiches.

Nutrition Information

- Calories: 102 calories
- Total Fat: 6g fat (4g saturated fat)
- Sodium: 402mg sodium
- Fiber: 0 fiber)
- Total Carbohydrate: 1g carbohydrate (1g sugars
- Cholesterol: 29mg cholesterol
- Protein: 10g protein.

388. Tuna Egg Salad

Serving: 3 servings (1-1/4 cups). | Prep: 10mins | Cook: 0mins | Ready in:

Ingredients

- 1 hard-boiled large egg, chopped
- 1 can (3 ounces) light water-packed tuna, drained and flaked
- 1/4 cup chopped celery
- 1/4 cup chopped sweet pickles
- 3 tablespoons reduced-fat mayonnaise
- 2 teaspoons prepared mustard

Direction

- Mix all the ingredients well in a small bowl. Scoop into tomatoes, it can be used with crackers or served as filling of a sandwich.

Nutrition Information

- Calories: 129 calories
- Protein: 11g protein. Diabetic Exchanges: 1-1/2 meat
- Total Fat: 6g fat (0 saturated fat)
- Sodium: 396mg sodium
- Fiber: 0 fiber)
- Total Carbohydrate: 7g carbohydrate (0 sugars
- Cholesterol: 86mg cholesterol

389. Tuna Schooners

Serving: 2-4 servings. | Prep: 15mins | Cook: 0mins | Ready in:

Ingredients

- 1 can (6 ounces) tuna, drained and flaked
- 1/2 cup chopped apple
- 1/4 cup mayonnaise
- 1/4 teaspoon salt
- 4 lettuce leaves
- 2 English muffins, split and toasted

- 8 tortilla chips

Direction

- Mix together salt, mayonnaise, apple and tuna in a large bowl. Put lettuce on muffin halves, place tuna mixture on top. Put tortilla chips in tuna mixture to resemble sails.

Nutrition Information

- Calories: 273 calories
- Sodium: 534mg sodium
- Fiber: 2g fiber)
- Total Carbohydrate: 22g carbohydrate (3g sugars
- Cholesterol: 18mg cholesterol
- Protein: 14g protein.
- Total Fat: 14g fat (2g saturated fat)

390.   Tuna Tea Sandwiches

Serving: 4 tea sandwiches. | Prep: 10mins | Cook: 0mins | Ready in:

Ingredients

- 1 can (6 ounces) light water-packed tuna, drained and flaked
- 1 to 2 tablespoons mayonnaise
- 1/4 teaspoon lemon-pepper seasoning
- 4 tablespoons crumbled goat cheese
- 4 slices multigrain bread, crusts removed
- 4 large fresh basil leaves

Direction

- Mix pepper-lemon, mayonnaise, and tuna in a small-sized bowl. Spread 1 tbsp. goat cheese over each bread slice. Spread 2 slices with tuna mixture; add leftover bread and basil leaves on top. Shape what you want or halve it.

Nutrition Information

- Calories: 191 calories
- Cholesterol: 25mg cholesterol
- Protein: 17g protein.
- Total Fat: 8g fat (4g saturated fat)
- Sodium: 391mg sodium
- Fiber: 2g fiber)
- Total Carbohydrate: 12g carbohydrate (2g sugars

391.   Tune A Piano Sandwiches

Serving: 8-10 servings. | Prep: 35mins | Cook: 0mins | Ready in:

Ingredients

- 17 slices white bread
- 2 slices pumpernickel bread
- 2 cans (6 ounces each) tuna, drained
- 1/2 cup plus 1 tablespoon mayonnaise, divided
- 1/3 cup shredded cheddar cheese
- 3 tablespoons chopped onion
- 3 tablespoons diced celery
- 1/2 teaspoon dill weed
- Salt and pepper to taste

Direction

- Chop crusts off bread. Slice white bread into 1-in strips. Slice pumpernickel bread into 1/2-in. strips then cut each in half widthwise. Mix salt, pepper, dill, celery, onion, cheese, a half cup mayonnaise and tuna in a bowl. Spread the mixture on half of the white bread strips then put the remaining strips on top. Place the strips next to each other on a 3-ft. covered board for "white keys" of keyboard. Use the remaining mayonnaise to spread on 1 side of each pumpernickel bread strip. Arrange the pumpernickel bread strips over the white strips and make sure the mayonnaise side is facing down for "black keys". Repeat patter if required until no bread strip remains.

193

Nutrition Information

- Calories: 251 calories
- Protein: 9g protein.
- Total Fat: 13g fat (2g saturated fat)
- Sodium: 413mg sodium
- Fiber: 1g fiber)
- Total Carbohydrate: 24g carbohydrate (2g sugars
- Cholesterol: 14mg cholesterol

392.   Turkey Salad Croissants

Serving: 6 servings. | Prep: 15mins | Cook: 0mins | Ready in:

Ingredients

- 2 cups cubed cooked turkey
- 1/2 cup chopped celery
- 1/2 cup chopped cashews
- 1/2 cup mayonnaise
- 1/4 cup coarsely chopped radishes
- 2 tablespoons chopped green onions
- 2 tablespoons diced pimientos
- 1 tablespoon lemon juice
- 1 teaspoon dill weed
- 1 teaspoon seasoned salt
- Lettuce leaves
- 6 croissants, split

Direction

- Mix the first 10 ingredients in a big bowl. Put 2/3 cup turkey salad and lettuce on every croissant.

Nutrition Information

- Calories:
- Cholesterol:
- Protein:
- Total Fat:

- Sodium:
- Fiber:
- Total Carbohydrate:

393.   Turkey Salad Puffs

Serving: 4 servings. | Prep: 20mins | Cook: 0mins | Ready in:

Ingredients

- 1-1/2 cups cubed cooked turkey breast
- 1/2 cup chopped peeled mango
- 1/4 cup quartered seedless red grapes
- 1/4 cup pine nuts, toasted
- 2 tablespoons chopped celery
- 5 tablespoons mayonnaise
- 1 teaspoon lemon juice
- 1/2 teaspoon lemon-pepper seasoning
- 1/4 teaspoon garlic powder
- 4 cream puff shells

Direction

- Mix the initial 5 ingredients in a big bowl. Mix garlic powder, lemon-pepper, lemon juice, and mayonnaise in a small bowl. Put on top of turkey mixture and coat by lightly tossing. Keep it chilled in the refrigerator till serving. Just prior to serving, scoop half cup turkey salad into each cream puff shell; replace tops.

Nutrition Information

- Calories: 508 calories
- Sodium: 553mg sodium
- Fiber: 1g fiber)
- Total Carbohydrate: 22g carbohydrate (6g sugars
- Cholesterol: 181mg cholesterol
- Protein: 24g protein.
- Total Fat: 36g fat (6g saturated fat)

394.　　　Turkey Salad Sandwiches

Serving: 6 servings. | Prep: 15mins | Cook: 0mins
| Ready in:

Ingredients

- 10 ounces deli turkey, cubed
- 2 cups torn romaine
- 6 bacon strips, cooked and crumbled
- 1/2 cup shredded Swiss cheese
- 1/2 cup mayonnaise
- 1/3 cup frozen peas, thawed
- 2 green onions, thinly sliced
- 1/4 teaspoon pepper
- 12 slices whole wheat bread

Direction

- Mix the first 8 ingredients together in a big bowl. On every 6 slices of bread, put 2/3 cup of mixture. Put the other rest of the bread slices on top.

Nutrition Information

- Calories: 398 calories
- Cholesterol: 43mg cholesterol
- Protein: 22g protein.
- Total Fat: 22g fat (5g saturated fat)
- Sodium: 1039mg sodium
- Fiber: 5g fiber)
- Total Carbohydrate: 28g carbohydrate (4g sugars

395.　　　Turkey Salad Wraps

Serving: 4 servings. | Prep: 20mins | Cook: 0mins
| Ready in:

Ingredients

- 2 cups cubed cooked turkey breast

- 1 medium sweet onion, chopped
- 3/4 cup chopped celery
- 1/2 cup fat-free plain yogurt
- 1/4 cup reduced-fat mayonnaise
- 1/2 teaspoon garlic salt
- 1/2 teaspoon curry powder
- 2 medium tomatoes, thinly sliced
- 1 cup torn leaf lettuce
- 4 spinach flour tortillas (8 inches), room temperature

Direction

- Mix together the celery, onion and turkey in a big bowl. Whisk the curry, garlic salt, mayonnaise and yogurt together in a separate bowl. Pour it on top of the turkey mixture then toss until coated. On tortillas, layer the tomatoes and lettuce. Put turkey mixture on top, then roll it up and use toothpicks to secure.

Nutrition Information

- Calories: 305 calories
- Sodium: 358mg sodium
- Fiber: 4g fiber)
- Total Carbohydrate: 28g carbohydrate (0 sugars
- Cholesterol: 66mg cholesterol
- Protein: 29g protein. Diabetic Exchanges: 3 lean meat
- Total Fat: 9g fat (2g saturated fat)

396.　　　Turkey Salad On Croissants

Serving: 8 servings. | Prep: 30mins | Cook: 0mins
| Ready in:

Ingredients

- 4 cups cubed cooked turkey breast

- 1 can (8 ounces) sliced water chestnuts, drained and chopped
- 2/3 cup chopped pecans
- 2 celery ribs, sliced
- 2 green onions, sliced
- 1 cup mayonnaise
- 2 teaspoons prepared mustard
- 1/2 teaspoon garlic pepper blend
- 1/4 teaspoon salt
- 8 lettuce leaves
- 8 croissants, split

Direction

- Mix onions, celery, pecans, water chestnuts and turkey in a big bowl. Mix salt, garlic pepper, mustard, mayonnaise; add on top of turkey mixture and coat by tossing. Keep it covered and let chill in the refrigerator till serving. Scoop onto croissants that lined with lettuce.

Nutrition Information

- Calories: 616 calories
- Protein: 27g protein.
- Total Fat: 42g fat (11g saturated fat)
- Sodium: 731mg sodium
- Fiber: 3g fiber)
- Total Carbohydrate: 32g carbohydrate (3g sugars
- Cholesterol: 108mg cholesterol

397.   Turkey Salad On Wheat

Serving: 6 servings. | Prep: 15mins | Cook: 0mins |Ready in:

Ingredients

- 2 cups chopped romaine
- 1-1/4 cups diced cooked turkey
- 1/2 cup shredded Swiss cheese
- 2 green onions, thinly sliced

- 6 bacon strips, cooked and crumbled
- 1/3 cup frozen peas, thawed
- 1/2 cup mayonnaise
- 1/4 teaspoon pepper
- 12 slices whole wheat bread

Direction

- Mix the initial 6 ingredients in a big-sized bowl. Put in pepper and mayonnaise; coat by tossing. Spread over six bread slices; add leftover bread on top.

Nutrition Information

- Calories: 268 calories
- Total Carbohydrate: 31g carbohydrate (0 sugars
- Cholesterol: 36mg cholesterol
- Protein: 20g protein. Diabetic Exchanges: 2 starch
- Total Fat: 8g fat (2g saturated fat)
- Sodium: 618mg sodium
- Fiber: 5g fiber)

398.   Turkey Salad On Wheat Bread

Serving: 2 servings. | Prep: 15mins | Cook: 0mins |Ready in:

Ingredients

- 2/3 cup chopped romaine
- 1/2 cup finely chopped cooked turkey
- 2 bacon strips, cooked and crumbled
- 1 green onion, thinly sliced
- 2 tablespoons frozen peas, thawed
- 2 tablespoons shredded Swiss cheese
- 3 tablespoons mayonnaise
- Dash pepper
- 4 slices whole wheat bread

Direction

- Mix the initial 6 ingredients in a small-sized bowl. Mix in pepper and mayonnaise. Spread on two bread slices; add leftover bread on top.

Nutrition Information

- Calories: 425 calories
- Sodium: 564mg sodium
- Fiber: 4g fiber)
- Total Carbohydrate: 27g carbohydrate (3g sugars
- Cholesterol: 57mg cholesterol
- Protein: 23g protein.
- Total Fat: 25g fat (5g saturated fat)

399. Turkey Waldorf Pita

Serving: 2 servings. | Prep: 10mins | Cook: 0mins | Ready in:

Ingredients

- 1 cup cubed cooked turkey
- 2 celery ribs, chopped
- 1/2 cup chopped tart apple
- 1/2 cup halved seedless grapes
- 1/4 cup chopped walnuts
- 1/4 cup mayonnaise
- 4 lettuce leaves
- 2 pita breads (6 inches), halved

Direction

- Mix mayonnaise, walnuts, grapes, apple, celery, and turkey together in a big bowl. Put lettuce leaf on each pita half and use turkey salad to stuff.

Nutrition Information

- Calories: 636 calories
- Total Fat: 36g fat (5g saturated fat)
- Sodium: 558mg sodium
- Fiber: 4g fiber)

- Total Carbohydrate: 49g carbohydrate (12g sugars
- Cholesterol: 63mg cholesterol
- Protein: 31g protein.

400. Turkey Waldorf Sandwiches

Serving: 16 servings. | Prep: 20mins | Cook: 0mins | Ready in:

Ingredients

- 1 can (20 ounces) unsweetened crushed pineapple
- 3 cups cubed cooked turkey breast
- 1 medium red apple, chopped
- 1 medium green apple, chopped
- 1/2 cup chopped walnuts
- 1 cup sliced celery
- 1 cup fat-free mayonnaise
- 1 tablespoon poppy seeds
- 1 teaspoon grated lemon zest
- 1/2 teaspoon vanilla extract
- 1/2 teaspoon salt-free seasoning blend
- 16 hard rolls, split

Direction

- Strain pineapple, squeeze out the extra juice; keep 1/4 cup of juice, dispose of the rest. Mix celery, walnuts, apples, turkey, and pineapple together in a big bowl.
- Mix the saved pineapple juice, seasoning blend, vanilla, lemon zest, poppy seeds, and mayonnaise together in a small bowl. Put on the turkey mixture and mix thoroughly. Refrigerate. Eat on rolls.

Nutrition Information

- Calories: 314 calories
- Total Carbohydrate: 45g carbohydrate (0 sugars

- Cholesterol: 22mg cholesterol
- Protein: 16g protein. Diabetic Exchanges: 2-1/2 starch
- Total Fat: 8g fat (0 saturated fat)
- Sodium: 475mg sodium
- Fiber: 3g fiber)

- Total Carbohydrate:
- Cholesterol:
- Protein:
- Total Fat:
- Sodium:
- Fiber:

401.   Vegetable Tuna Sandwiches

Serving: 4 servings. | Prep: 15mins | Cook: 0mins | Ready in:

Ingredients

- 6 ounces cream cheese, softened, divided
- 6 tablespoons mayonnaise, divided
- 1/4 teaspoon salt
- 1/8 teaspoon pepper
- 1 can (6 ounces) tuna, drained and flaked
- 3 tablespoons finely chopped celery
- 3 tablespoons finely chopped green pepper
- 1 cup shredded carrots
- 2 tablespoons finely chopped onion
- 8 slices white bread
- 4 slices whole wheat bread

Direction

- Mix together salt, pepper, 3 tablespoons mayonnaise and 3 ounces cream cheese in a large bowl until the mixture gets smooth. Mix in green pepper, celery and tuna.
- Mix together mayonnaise, the remaining cream cheese, onion and carrots in another bowl. Spread 1/3 cup tuna mixture on 4 slices of white bread; then put a slice of whole wheat bread on top. Then spread 1/4 cup of carrot mixture on the whole wheat bread; put a slice of white bread on top.

Nutrition Information

- Calories:

402.   Wake Up Sandwiches

Serving: 2-3 servings. | Prep: 10mins | Cook: 10mins | Ready in:

Ingredients

- 4 ounces cream cheese, softened
- 2 tablespoons milk
- 1 package (2 ounces) thinly sliced deli corned beef, chopped
- 1/2 cup shredded Swiss cheese
- 2 hard-boiled large eggs, chopped
- 3 English muffins, split and toasted
- Sliced hard-boiled large egg, optional
- Minced fresh parsley, optional

Direction

- Mix milk and cream cheese together in a bowl until smooth. Tuck in sliced eggs, cheese, and corned beef. Put 1/3 cup mixture on each muffin half.
- Bake at 450° until cooked through, about 10-12 minutes. Use parsley and sliced eggs to garnish if you want.

Nutrition Information

- Calories: 424 calories
- Protein: 21g protein.
- Total Fat: 25g fat (14g saturated fat)
- Sodium: 784mg sodium
- Fiber: 2g fiber)
- Total Carbohydrate: 29g carbohydrate (4g sugars
- Cholesterol: 216mg cholesterol

403. Waldorf Sandwiches

Serving: 16 servings. | Prep: 20mins | Cook: 0mins | Ready in:

Ingredients

- 1 can (20 ounces) crushed pineapple
- 3 cups cubed cooked chicken
- 1 medium red apple, chopped
- 1 medium green apple, chopped
- 1 cup chopped walnuts
- 1 cup sliced celery
- 1 cup mayonnaise
- 1 tablespoon poppy seeds
- 1 teaspoon sugar
- 1 teaspoon grated lemon zest
- 1/2 teaspoon vanilla extract
- 1/2 teaspoon salt
- Rolls, croissants or pita bread

Direction

- Drain pineapple and press out any excess juice; keep 1/4 cup of juice. Mix together celery, walnuts, apples, chicken and pineapple in a large bowl.
- Mix together reserved pineapple juice, salt, vanilla, lemon zest, sugar, poppy seeds and mayonnaise in a small bowl. Pour the mixture over the chicken mixture and toss well. Refrigerate. Serve on croissants or rolls or in pita bread.

Nutrition Information

- Calories: 233 calories
- Protein: 10g protein.
- Total Fat: 18g fat (2g saturated fat)
- Sodium: 178mg sodium
- Fiber: 1g fiber)
- Total Carbohydrate: 10g carbohydrate (7g sugars

404. Waldorf Turkey Pitas

Serving: 4 servings. | Prep: 15mins | Cook: 0mins | Ready in:

Ingredients

- 2 cups cubed cooked turkey breast
- 2 celery ribs, finely chopped
- 1 medium tart apple, diced
- 1 cup seedless red grapes, halved
- 1/2 cup fat-free mayonnaise
- 2 ounces fresh mozzarella cheese, diced
- 8 whole wheat pita pocket halves
- 2 cups fresh baby spinach

Direction

- Mix together the initial 6 ingredients in a big bowl. Line spinach on pita halves and fill it with the turkey mixture.

Nutrition Information

- Calories: 363 calories
- Sodium: 626mg sodium
- Fiber: 7g fiber)
- Total Carbohydrate: 48g carbohydrate (14g sugars
- Cholesterol: 75mg cholesterol
- Protein: 30g protein.
- Total Fat: 7g fat (3g saturated fat)

405. Waldorf Turkey Salad Sandwiches

Serving: 4 servings. | Prep: 20mins | Cook: 0mins | Ready in:

Ingredients

- 1 cup diced cooked turkey
- 2/3 cup chopped peeled apple
- 1 celery rib, finely chopped
- 1/2 cup chopped walnuts, toasted
- 1/4 cup golden raisins
- 1/3 cup vanilla yogurt
- 1/3 cup mayonnaise
- 1 teaspoon minced fresh tarragon or 1/2 teaspoon dried tarragon
- 1/2 to 1 teaspoon grated orange zest
- 1/8 teaspoon salt
- Dash pepper
- 4 sandwich rolls, split

Direction

- Mix raisins, walnuts, celery, apple and turkey in a big bowl. Mix pepper, salt, orange zest, tarragon, mayonnaise and yogurt. Add on top of turkey mixture, coat by mixing. Scoop a half of a cup onto each roll.

Nutrition Information

- Calories: 547 calories
- Protein: 23g protein.
- Total Fat: 29g fat (5g saturated fat)
- Sodium: 562mg sodium
- Fiber: 4g fiber)
- Total Carbohydrate: 51g carbohydrate (16g sugars
- Cholesterol: 39mg cholesterol

---

406.   Waldorf Turkey Sandwiches

Serving: 4 servings. | Prep: 15mins | Cook: 0mins |Ready in:

Ingredients

- 1/4 cup finely chopped celery
- 3 tablespoons fat-free mayonnaise
- 2 tablespoons fat-free plain yogurt

- 2 tablespoons chopped walnuts
- 1 tablespoon raisins
- 1/8 teaspoon ground nutmeg
- 1/8 teaspoon ground cinnamon
- 1-1/4 cups cubed cooked turkey breast
- 1 small apple, chopped
- 8 slices cinnamon-raisin bread, toasted
- 4 lettuce leaves

Direction

- Mix the first 7 ingredients together in a large bowl. Add apple and turkey, mix to combine. Put a cover on and put in the fridge to chill for a minimum of 1 hour. Put 3/4 cup of turkey mixture on 4 slices of bread, put lettuce leaf and the rest of the bread on top.

Nutrition Information

- Calories: 127 calories
- Fiber: 0 fiber)
- Total Carbohydrate: 9g carbohydrate (0 sugars
- Cholesterol: 26mg cholesterol
- Protein: 12g protein. Diabetic Exchanges: 1-1/2 lean meat
- Total Fat: 5g fat (0 saturated fat)
- Sodium: 114mg sodium

---

407.   Zippy Egg Salad

Serving: 2 | Prep: 10mins | Cook: |Ready in:

Ingredients

- 1/4 cup mayonnaise
- 2 tablespoons grated Parmesan cheese
- 1 tablespoon light soy sauce
- 1/4 lime, juiced
- 1 teaspoon crushed red pepper
- salt and ground black pepper to taste
- 4 hard-cooked eggs, chopped
- 1 stalk celery, finely sliced

Direction

- Whisk the black pepper, salt, red pepper, lime juice, soy sauce, Parmesan cheese and mayonnaise in a bowl.
- Stir celery and eggs into the mayonnaise mixture until well coated.
- Use plastic wrap to cover the bowl and put it in the fridge until chilled prior to serving.

Nutrition Information

- Calories: 389 calories;
- Sodium: 639
- Total Carbohydrate: 5.2
- Cholesterol: 439
- Protein: 15.5
- Total Fat: 34.2

Chapter 5: Grilled Cheese Sandwich Recipes

***

408. "PJ Special" Grilled Cheese

Serving: 1 | Prep: 10mins | Cook: 4mins | Ready in:

Ingredients

- 1 cup shredded extra-sharp Cheddar cheese
- 4 teaspoons horseradish mustard (such as Silver Spring® Beer'n Brat®)
- 2 teaspoons minced garlic
- 1/4 teaspoon salt
- 1/4 teaspoon ground black pepper
- 1 pinch cayenne pepper
- 2 teaspoons softened butter, or to taste
- 2 slices whole grain bread

Direction

- In a bowl, mix together cayenne pepper, pepper, salt, garlic, horseradish mustard and Cheddar cheese.
- Spread over one side of 1 bread slice with one teaspoon of butter. Turn, then evenly spread on the unbuttered side with Cheddar cheese mixture. Place other bread slice on top. Spread on top with one teaspoon of butter.
- Start preheating griddle to medium-high heat. On griddle, put sandwich, then flatten slightly by pressing down, using a spatula. Cook for 2-3 mins or until browned. Turn; keep cooking for 2-3 mins longer or until second side is browned.

Nutrition Information

- Calories: 700 calories;
- Total Fat: 50.1
- Sodium: 1808
- Total Carbohydrate: 31.7
- Cholesterol: 143
- Protein: 36.4

409. Alexa's Gourmet Grilled Cheese

Serving: 2 | Prep: 10mins | Cook: 5mins | Ready in:

Ingredients

- 4 slices marbled rye bread, divided
- 4 teaspoons softened salted butter, or as needed, divided
- 2 teaspoons Dijon mustard, or to taste
- 4 slices shredded sharp Cheddar cheese
- 4 slices Swiss cheese (such as Lorraine®)
- 1 tomato, thinly sliced

- 1 avocado - peeled, pitted, and thinly sliced

Direction

- Place a non-stick pan or cast-iron skillet over high heat until skillet is hot; minimize heat to medium.
- Lay out 2 slices of bread in the hot skillet. Put 1 teaspoon butter under each slice in the skillet; turn over the bread so butter-side is facing-up. Put 1 teaspoon mustard onto each bread slice and spread; put 1 slice Cheddar cheese, 1 slice Swiss cheese, tomato slices, and slices of avocado. Put 1 slice Cheddar cheese, 1 slice Swiss cheese and 1 slice bread, on top of each avocado layer. Put butter onto top of bread piece and spread; turn over sandwich and cook for 2 to 3 minutes until cheeses are slightly melted.
- Place sandwiches to a microwave-safe plate and place in the microwave to heat for no longer than 30 seconds until cheeses are completely melted.

Nutrition Information

- Calories: 860 calories;
- Cholesterol: 133
- Protein: 37.6
- Total Fat: 59.7
- Sodium: 1077
- Total Carbohydrate: 47.2

---

410. Apple Ham Grilled Cheese

Serving: 2 | Prep: 5mins | Cook: 5mins | Ready in:

Ingredients

- 4 slices ham, chopped
- 1 small apple - peeled, cored and finely chopped
- 1 tablespoon mayonnaise

- 2 slices Cheddar cheese
- 4 slices bread
- 2 tablespoons butter
- 2 eggs
- 4 tablespoons milk

Direction

- In a small bowl, combine together mayonnaise, apple and ham, then spread the mixture on 2 bread slices. Put a cheese slice and another bread slice on top of each one.
- In a big skillet, melt butter on moderate heat. In a small bowl, whisk together milk and eggs. Dip both sides of the sandwich into the egg mixture rapidly, then fry sandwiches in pan until turning golden brown, about 1-2 minutes per side. Watch them carefully. The sandwiches should have golden color with cooked egg.

Nutrition Information

- Calories: 513 calories;
- Total Fat: 33.7
- Sodium: 721
- Total Carbohydrate: 35
- Cholesterol: 251
- Protein: 18.5

---

411. Apple And Bacon Grilled Cheese

Serving: 1 | Prep: 10mins | Cook: 5mins | Ready in:

Ingredients

- 2 slices cracked wheat bread
- 2 thin slices aged Cheddar cheese
- 2 slices Honeycrisp apple, or more to taste
- 2 cooked bacon strips

Direction

- Follow the manufacturer's directions; start preheating a sandwich/panini press.
- On a work surface, place one slice of bread. Put bacon slices, 1 slice cheese, apple slices, and remaining 1 slice cheese on the top of bread. Top with remaining bread slice.
- In the preheated panini press, cook sandwich for about 5 minutes until cheese begins to melt and bread is lightly toasted.

Nutrition Information

- Calories: 381 calories;
- Total Fat: 19.2
- Sodium: 876
- Total Carbohydrate: 35.1
- Cholesterol: 50
- Protein: 18.4

412. Aunt Bev's Glorified Grilled Cheese Sandwich

Serving: 1 | Prep: 10mins | Cook: 5mins |Ready in:

Ingredients

- 1 egg
- salt and pepper to taste
- 2 tablespoons butter, divided
- 2 slices Italian bread
- 2 teaspoons mayonnaise
- 2 teaspoons Dijon mustard
- 4 thin slices ham
- 2 slices Swiss cheese

Direction

- Whisk some pepper and salt and egg in a shallow dish big enough to dip the sandwich in; put aside.
- In a skillet, melt 1 tbsp. butter on medium high heat. Spread mustard and mayonnaise on 1 bread slice; layer cheese and ham on the other

slice. To enclose the ingredients, put slices together.
- Quickly and carefully dip each side into beaten egg; put into hot buttered skillet. Cook till bottom is golden brown. Melt the leftover butter in a skillet; flip sandwich. Cook till other side is browned.

Nutrition Information

- Calories: 768 calories;
- Sodium: 1617
- Total Carbohydrate: 28
- Cholesterol: 335
- Protein: 34.8
- Total Fat: 57.3

413. Awesome Grilled Cheese Sandwiches

Serving: 9 | Prep: 10mins | Cook: 15mins |Ready in:

Ingredients

- 18 slices bread
- 4 tablespoons butter
- 9 slices Cheddar cheese

Direction

- Set the oven to 230°C or 450°F to preheat.
- Coat one side of 9 bread slices with butter and put them on a baking sheet with butter-side facing down. Put on each bread slice with cheese. Spread on 9 leftover slices of bread with butter and put them on top of the cheese with buttered-side facing up.
- In the preheated oven, bake for 6-8 minutes. Flip the sandwiches and bake until they turn golden brown, about 6 to 8 more minutes.

Nutrition Information

- Calories: 293 calories;

- Total Fat: 16.2
- Sodium: 553
- Total Carbohydrate: 25.7
- Cholesterol: 43
- Protein: 10.9

414.   Bachelor Grilled Cheese

Serving: 1 | Prep: 2mins | Cook: | Ready in:

Ingredients

- 2 slices white bread
- 2 slices American cheese

Direction

- In a toaster, toast bread until golden. Insert cheese slices between 2 pieces of toasted bread. Using a paper towel, wrap sandwich and microwave for 15 to 20 seconds, or until the cheese becomes melted.

Nutrition Information

- Calories: 346 calories;
- Protein: 16.4
- Total Fat: 19.4
- Sodium: 1185
- Total Carbohydrate: 26.2
- Cholesterol: 53

415.   Bacon, Avocado, And Pepperjack Grilled Cheese Sandwich

Serving: 4 | Prep: 5mins | Cook: 10mins | Ready in:

Ingredients

- 8 (3/4 inch thick) slices sourdough bread
- 1/4 cup butter

- 8 slices cooked thick bacon
- 8 slices pepperjack cheese
- 1 red onion, sliced and separated into rings
- 1 avocado, halved and cut into 1/4-inch slices

Direction

- Place the bread on a work surface and then apply butter on one side of every slice.
- On top of the unbuttered-side of the bread, place slices of avocado, 1 slice of cheese, bacon, onion rings, and another slice of cheese. Place the second slice of bread on top, with buttered-side facing up.
- Over medium heat, cook sandwiches in a skillet, turning once, for about 3 to 5 minutes on each side until each side is golden brown and the cheese has melted.

Nutrition Information

- Calories: 508 calories;
- Cholesterol: 74
- Protein: 17.6
- Total Fat: 33.9
- Sodium: 848
- Total Carbohydrate: 35.1

416.   Bacon, Tomato & Triple Cheese Grilled Cheese

Serving: 2 | Prep: 10mins | Cook: 15mins | Ready in:

Ingredients

- 1/2 pound Dietz & Watson Gourmet Smoked Bacon
- 1/2 pound Dietz & Watson Chicken Bacon
- 4 slices sourdough bread
- 1 (8 ounce) bottle Dietz & Watson Sandwich Spread
- 1/4 pound Dietz & Watson Picante Provolone Cheese, sliced

- 1/4 pound Dietz & Watson Peppadew NY State Cheddar Cheese, sliced
- 1 pound Dietz & Watson Smoked Gouda Cheese, sliced
- 4 slices tomato

Direction

- Cook chicken bacon and bacon as needed.
- Begin with 2 pieces of the sourdough bread. Place sandwich spread on both pieces.
- Layer with 2 ounces of smoked gouda cheese, 2 ounces of peppadew cheese, and 2 ounces of provolone cheese on the bread.
- Place 4 slices of chicken bacon or bacon and 2 pieces of tomato on each sandwich.
- Place the second piece of bread on top.
- You can cook it in a panini press or on a griddle. Cook it until the cheese begins to melt. Serve it warm.

Nutrition Information

- Calories: 1615 calories;
- Protein: 85.1
- Total Fat: 116.1
- Sodium: 4122
- Total Carbohydrate: 65.5
- Cholesterol: 424

---

417.   Broccoli Ham Grilled Cheese Sandwich

Serving: 1 | Prep: | Cook: |Ready in:

Ingredients

- 2 slices whole grain bread
- 1/4 cup Dietz & Watson Yellow NY C-Sharp Cheddar Cheese, grated
- 1/4 cup Dietz & Watson Grated Parmesan Cheese
- 1/4 cup diced Dietz & Watson Branded Cooked Ham*

- 10 small broccoli florets, steamed then diced
- 1/8 teaspoon garlic powder
- Salt, to taste
- Freshly ground black pepper, to taste
- 1 tablespoon olive oil, divided

Direction

- Mix together black pepper, salt, garlic powder, onion powder, steamed broccoli, ham, Parmesan Cheese and grated Cheddar Cheese in a bowl.
- Lay over a bread slice with the cheese mixture then another bread slice on top, pressing down gently.
- Heat a nonstick fry pan on moderately low heat and pour into pan with 1/2 tbsp. of olive oil. Coat the bottom of pan evenly by tilting the pan back and forth, then put into pan with sandwich instantly and place a lid on to cover pan. Cook until the bottom turns golden brown, about 2 to 3 minutes.
- Use a spatula to lift sandwich out of pan carefully, then pour into pan with leftover 1/2 tbsp. of olive oil. Tilt to coat well.
- Flip sandwich back to pan carefully and cook the opposite side, covered, for 2 to 3 minutes more, until the cheese is melted and bottom turns golden brown. Serve warm.

Nutrition Information

- Calories: 1028 calories;
- Total Fat: 39.5
- Sodium: 1646
- Total Carbohydrate: 124.3
- Cholesterol: 74
- Protein: 72.4

---

418.   Cheesy Grilled Cheese

Serving: 1 | Prep: 3mins | Cook: 6mins |Ready in:

Ingredients

- 2 teaspoons butter
- 1 slice Cheddar cheese
- 1 slice Muenster cheese
- 1 slice provolone cheese
- 2 slices rye bread

Direction

- Preheat your oven's broiler.
- Coat one side of each bread slice with butter and put on a baking sheet with butter-side facing down. Put on top of each bread piece with slices of cheese.
- Broil until cheese is bubbly and browned slightly, then take out of the oven and press 2 pieces of bread together, cheese to cheese.

Nutrition Information

- Calories: 555 calories;
- Total Carbohydrate: 32.2
- Cholesterol: 98
- Protein: 26.5
- Total Fat: 35.7
- Sodium: 1082

419.   Chocolate And Brie Grilled Cheese

Serving: 2 | Prep: 15mins | Cook: 5mins | Ready in:

Ingredients

- 2 tablespoons butter, softened
- 4 slices Nature's Own® Perfectly Crafted White Bread
- 3 ounces Brie cheese, sliced
- 2 ounces dark chocolate, coarsely chopped

Direction

- Spread one side of each bread slice with butter, then arrange Brie on the unbuttered side of 2 slices of bread. Put chocolate on top

and then 2 bread slices with buttered-side facing up on top.
- Set a griddle or big skillet on medium heat to preheat. Put sandwiches in the skillet and cook them on medium heat until cheese has melted and bread turns golden, about 5-6 minutes, while turning one time halfway through cooking process.

Nutrition Information

- Calories: 594 calories;
- Protein: 16.5
- Total Fat: 35.5
- Sodium: 771
- Total Carbohydrate: 57
- Cholesterol: 74

420.   Chunky Monkey Grilled Cheese

Serving: 1 | Prep: 15mins | Cook: 5mins | Ready in:

Ingredients

- 2 slices raisin bread
- peanut butter
- 1/2 banana, sliced
- 2 tablespoons chocolate chips, or to taste
- 1/4 cup ricotta cheese
- 1 tablespoon white sugar
- 1 dash ground cinnamon (optional)

Direction

- Place raisin bread in a toaster oven and toast for 2-3 minutes until lightly brown.
- Put peanut butter on toasted bread and spread. Put 1 banana slice on top; put chocolate chips on top of another slice. Cover chocolate chips and banana with ricotta cheese. Dust cinnamon and sugar on top.
- Place in the toaster oven and toast for 3-5 minutes until cheese melts. Slice the sandwich.

Nutrition Information

- Calories: 709 calories;
- Total Fat: 35.9
- Sodium: 359
- Total Carbohydrate: 96.1
- Cholesterol: 0
- Protein: 15.3

---

421.   Egg In A Hole French Toast Grilled Cheese

Serving: 2 | Prep: 15mins | Cook: 4mins |Ready in:

Ingredients

- Batter:
- 3/4 cup half-and-half
- 1 large egg
- 1 tablespoon white sugar
- 1/2 teaspoon ground cinnamon
- 1/2 teaspoon kosher salt
- Sandwiches:
- 4 thin slices white sandwich bread
- 2 slices American cheese
- 2 slices Cheddar cheese
- 2 slices cooked bacon, crumbled
- 1 tablespoon unsalted butter
- 2 large eggs

Direction

- In a bowl, whisk together salt, cinnamon, sugar, one egg and half-and-half, until the batter becomes smooth.
- On a work surface, put 2 slices of bread. Place one American cheese slice and one Cheddar cheese slice, then the crumbled bacon on top of each. Place a second bread piece on top of each, creating the sandwich. Create a 2 inches hole with 2 inches wide glass or biscuit cutter in the middle of every sandwich.

- In a large nonstick frying pan, melt butter over medium-low heat, cover entire of the surface with the butter by tilting the pan. In batter, dip both sandwich rings; cut-out holes until coated evenly.
- Arrange the cut-out holes and dipped sandwich rings in melted butter in the skillet. Break 1 egg immediately into each of ring hole. Cook for 2 minutes per side until cheese has melted softly, the bread turns golden brown and egg white has set.

Nutrition Information

- Calories: 640 calories;
- Sodium: 1578
- Total Carbohydrate: 28.3
- Cholesterol: 391
- Protein: 30.2
- Total Fat: 45.5

---

422.   Elvis' Grilled Cheese Sandwich

Serving: 1 | Prep: 5mins | Cook: 20mins |Ready in:

Ingredients

- 2 slices bacon
- 1 tablespoon smooth peanut butter
- 2 slices soft white bread
- 1 slice American cheese
- 1 tablespoon butter, softened

Direction

- In a big, deep skillet, add bacon and cook on moderately high heat about 10 minutes while flipping sometimes, until browned evenly. Remove bacon slices onto a plate lined with paper towel to drain.
- Spread on a white bread slice with the peanut butter and place on a slice of cheese and bacon to cover. Put another piece of bread on top.

Spread both sides of the sandwich with butter and put into the skillet to pan-fry on moderate heat for 2-3 minutes each side, until cheese is melted and bread turns golden brown. Serve hot.

Nutrition Information

- Calories: 534 calories;
- Cholesterol: 77
- Protein: 21
- Total Fat: 37.7
- Sodium: 1335
- Total Carbohydrate: 29.2

---

423. Gourmet Grilled Cheese

Serving: 4 | Prep: 20mins | Cook: 10mins | Ready in:

Ingredients

- 2 eggs, beaten
- 1 1/2 cups grated Romano cheese
- 1 (8 ounce) package fresh chevre (goat) cheese
- 8 slices bread
- 8 slices tomato

Direction

- In a wide shallow bowl, put beaten eggs; put aside. In a wide shallow dish, put grated Romano cheese; put aside.
- On 1 side of every bread slice, spread goat cheese. Sandwich 2 slices of tomato between 2 bread pieces. Dip both sides in the beaten egg. Let excess drip off; press sandwiches in grated Romano cheese to coat well on each side; put aside. Repeat it for make 4 sandwiches.
- Heat a big nonstick skillet on medium heat; cook sandwiches, 3 minutes per side, till crisp and golden brown.

Nutrition Information

- Calories: 558 calories;
- Total Carbohydrate: 30.7
- Cholesterol: 184
- Protein: 33.9
- Total Fat: 33.2
- Sodium: 1206

---

424. Gourmet Grilled Cheese Sandwiches

Serving: 4 | Prep: 12mins | Cook: 8mins | Ready in:

Ingredients

- 1 (3 ounce) package cream cheese
- 3/4 cup mayonnaise
- 8 ounces shredded Colby-Monterey Jack cheese
- 3/4 teaspoon garlic salt
- 8 slices French bread
- 2 tablespoons butter

Direction

- Mix together garlic salt, shredded cheese, mayonnaise and cream cheese in a medium bowl, then beat the mixture until smooth.
- Set a big skillet on moderate heat to preheat. Spread on four bread slices with cheese mixture and put the other 4 slices of bread on top. Butter each sandwich lightly, on both sides. Put in skillet with sandwiches and grill 4 minutes each side, until both sides are golden brown.

Nutrition Information

- Calories: 783 calories;
- Total Carbohydrate: 32
- Cholesterol: 109
- Protein: 20.6
- Total Fat: 64.9
- Sodium: 1436

425.   Greek Grilled Cheese

Serving: 1 | Prep: 5mins | Cook: 5mins | Ready in:

Ingredients

- 1 1/2 teaspoons butter, softened
- 2 slices whole wheat bread, or your favorite bread
- 2 tablespoons crumbled feta cheese
- 2 slices Cheddar cheese
- 1 tablespoon chopped red onion
- 1/4 tomato, thinly sliced

Direction

- Place a skillet over medium heat. Spread butter on 1 side of each bread slice. Layer feta cheese, Cheddar cheese, red onion, and tomato on the unbuttered side of 1 bread slice. Place the other bread slice atop the filling, buttered side out.
- Fry sandwich, approximately 2 minutes on each side, until golden brown. (The second side takes a shorter time to cook).

Nutrition Information

- Calories: 482 calories;
- Sodium: 876
- Total Carbohydrate: 27.1
- Cholesterol: 92
- Protein: 24.6
- Total Fat: 30.9

426.   Grilled Apple And Swiss Cheese Sandwich

Serving: 1 | Prep: 10mins | Cook: 5mins | Ready in:

Ingredients

- 2 slices whole wheat bread

- 1 1/2 teaspoons olive oil
- 1/2 Granny Smith apple - peeled, cored and thinly sliced
- 1/3 cup shredded Swiss cheese

Direction

- Set a frying pan to preheat on medium heat. Use olive oil to brush one side of each bread slice lightly. In the frying pan, put one bread slice, olive oil side facing down, then lay out the slices of apple evenly on the top. Sprinkle apple with Swiss cheese, then put the leftover bread slice, olive oil side facing up, on top. Let it cook until the bread turns golden brown in color, then turn the sandwich over and let it cook for an additional 1-2 minutes, until the cheese melts and the other side turns golden brown.

Nutrition Information

- Calories: 371 calories;
- Cholesterol: 33
- Protein: 17.3
- Total Fat: 19
- Sodium: 338
- Total Carbohydrate: 33.9

427.   Grilled Brie And Pear Sandwich

Serving: 1 | Prep: 10mins | Cook: 5mins | Ready in:

Ingredients

- 2 tablespoons butter, softened
- 2 thick slices French bread
- 6 thin slices Brie cheese, or more to taste
- 12 fresh thyme leaves, or to taste
- 1 pinch cracked black pepper
- 6 slices pear (such as Bosc)
- salt to taste

Direction

- Butter one side of every bread slice generously.
- Heat skillet on medium heat.
- Put bread slices on hot skillet, butter-side down. On top of every bread piece, put brie cheese slices. Sprinkle cracked black pepper and thyme on top.
- In 1 layer, spread pear slices on brie cheese on one bread slice. Put a pinch of salt on top.
- Flip bread slice without pears on a bread slice with pear slices. Cook sandwich for 2-3 minutes per side until pears and cheese heat through and cheese melts. Put on a plate. Cut to halves.

Nutrition Information

- Calories: 670 calories;
- Total Fat: 41.3
- Sodium: 998
- Total Carbohydrate: 56.5
- Cholesterol: 121
- Protein: 22

---

428.   Grilled Camembert Sandwich

Serving: 1 | Prep: 3mins | Cook: 2mins | Ready in:

Ingredients

- 2 ounces Camembert cheese
- 2 thick slices white bread
- 1 tablespoon whole cranberry sauce
- 1 dash balsamic vinegar
- 1 tablespoon butter, softened

Direction

- Evenly spread 1 bread slice with Camembert cheese. Spread cheese with a thin cranberry sauce layer. Drizzle a few drops of balsamic vinegar over. Place remaining bread slice on top. Spread outer sides of each bread slice with butter.
- Heat a frying pan over moderate heat. Fry sandwich until it is just golden brown, about a few minutes per side. Then slice in 1/2. Enjoy straight away!

Nutrition Information

- Calories: 463 calories;
- Cholesterol: 71
- Protein: 16
- Total Fat: 27.3
- Sodium: 974
- Total Carbohydrate: 38.7

---

429.   Grilled Cheese De Mayo

Serving: 1 | Prep: 10mins | Cook: 5mins | Ready in:

Ingredients

- 1 tablespoon mayonnaise, divided
- 2 slices white bread
- 2 slices American cheese
- 1 slice pepperjack cheese

Direction

- Spread 1 side of a bread slice with a half of the mayonnaise and put in a skillet with mayonnaise-side facing down. Put on top of the bread the American and pepperjack cheeses. Spread 1 side of leftover bread with leftover mayonnaise and put on top of the cheese, mayonnaise-side facing up.
- In the skillet, cook sandwich on medium heat for 2 1/2 minutes each side, until bread turn golden brown and cheese has melted.

Nutrition Information

- Calories: 500 calories;
- Total Fat: 34.9

- Sodium: 1349
- Total Carbohydrate: 27.2
- Cholesterol: 74
- Protein: 19.5

430.   Grilled Cheese Sandwich

Serving: 2 | Prep: 5mins | Cook: 15mins | Ready in:

Ingredients

- 4 slices white bread
- 3 tablespoons butter, divided
- 2 slices Cheddar cheese

Direction

- Place the skillet over medium heat setting and let it heat up. Spread a good amount of butter evenly on one side of a sliced bread. Put the sliced bread onto the preheated skillet with the unbuttered side facing up then put 1 slice of cheese over the unbuttered side of the bread. Spread a good amount of butter evenly on one side of another sliced bread and place it over the cheese with the buttered side facing up. Let the cheese sandwich grill until it turns light brown in color then turn it over onto the other side and keep grilling until the cheese has melted. Do the same process for a slice of cheese, butter and the 2 remaining sliced breads.

Nutrition Information

- Calories: 400 calories;
- Total Fat: 28.3
- Sodium: 639
- Total Carbohydrate: 25.7
- Cholesterol: 76
- Protein: 11.1

431.   Grilled Cheese Shooters

Serving: 18 | Prep: 10mins | Cook: 10mins | Ready in:

Ingredients

- 2 (18.75 ounce) cans tomato bisque (such as Campbell's®)
- 2 tablespoons butter, softened
- 4 slices sourdough bread
- 4 slices aged Cheddar cheese
- toothpicks

Direction

- In a microwave-safe bowl, add a can of tomato bisque. Cook, covered, in the microwave for two and a half to three minutes till hot. Continue with the remaining bisque.
- On every slice of bread, spread butter on one side. On the sides that are not buttered of two slices, lay two slices of Cheddar cheese. Use the other two slices to place on top, buttered-side up, to assemble the sandwiches.
- Heating a large skillet over medium-high heat. Lay sandwiches. Allow to heat for 2-3 minutes till one side gets golden and toasted. Turn and let the other side toast for approximately 2 more minutes. Cut crusts off, if needed. Cut sandwiches into 1 1/2-inch square shapes, there should be 18 squares in total. Secure every square with a toothpick.
- In heat-proof shot glasses, pouring heated soup and place the grilled cheese squares on top.

Nutrition Information

- Calories: 109 calories;
- Sodium: 559
- Total Carbohydrate: 14
- Cholesterol: 12
- Protein: 3.3
- Total Fat: 4.6

432. Grilled Cheese And Peanut Butter Sandwich

Serving: 1 | Prep: 5mins | Cook: 5mins | Ready in:

Ingredients

- 2 slices bread
- 2 tablespoons peanut butter
- 1 slice Cheddar cheese
- 2 teaspoons butter or margarine

Direction

- Heat a skillet on medium heat. Spread on one bread slice with peanut butter and layer over peanut butter with a cheese slice. Put the leftover slice of bread on top. Spread on the outer sides of sandwich with butter and put it in the hot skillet. Fry for 3-5 minutes, until cheese has melted and each side turns golden brown.

Nutrition Information

- Calories: 510 calories;
- Sodium: 723
- Total Carbohydrate: 32
- Cholesterol: 51
- Protein: 19.1
- Total Fat: 35.5

433. Grilled Cheese And Veggie Sandwich

Serving: 4 | Prep: 15mins | Cook: 10mins | Ready in:

Ingredients

- 1 1/2 cups coleslaw mix
- 1/2 cup bean sprouts
- 8 thick slices (3/4 inch thick) sourdough bread
- 3 tablespoons margarine, softened
- 3 tablespoons honey mustard

- 6 ounces sliced Havarti cheese

Direction

- Toss bean sprouts and coleslaw mix together in a medium bowl.
- Spread margarine on one side of each bread slice, and then spread honey mustard on the opposite side of 4 bread slices. Layer coleslaw mixture and cheese on the honey mustard side of 4 bread slices, then put leftover 4 slices of bread on top with margarine side out.
- Cook the sandwiches in a big skillet on medium heat until bread turns golden brown and cheese is melted, about 2 minutes per side.

Nutrition Information

- Calories: 507 calories;
- Total Fat: 27.5
- Sodium: 1008
- Total Carbohydrate: 49.5
- Cholesterol: 56
- Protein: 18.5

434. Grilled Cheese Of The Gods

Serving: 4 | Prep: 10mins | Cook: 6mins | Ready in:

Ingredients

- 1/4 cup butter, softened
- 1 cup freshly grated Parmigiano-Reggiano cheese
- 8 slices cooked bacon
- 4 slices Cheddar cheese
- 8 slices sourdough bread

Direction

- Mash Parmesan cheese and butter together in a small mixing bowl until well incorporated. To build sandwiches, arrange 2 bacon slices and 1 Cheddar cheese slice on half of the bread slices; place the remaining bread slices atop cheese and bacon.

- Bring a large skillet to medium heat on the stove. Spread over top of each sandwich with a small amount of butter. Arrange sandwiches in the heated skillet, buttered side down. Spread the rest of butter on the remaining sides. Cook sandwiches for about 3 minutes on each side, until evenly golden brown. Slice sandwiches diagonally in half to serve.

Nutrition Information

- Calories: 748 calories;
- Cholesterol: 135
- Protein: 43
- Total Fat: 50.1
- Sodium: 2211
- Total Carbohydrate: 30.4

435.   Grilled Cheese With Tomato, Peppers And Basil

Serving: 4 | Prep: 10mins | Cook: 5mins | Ready in:

Ingredients

- 8 (1 ounce) slices bread
- 4 slices Cheddar cheese
- 1 large tomato, sliced
- 2 serrano peppers, seeded and thinly sliced
- 2 teaspoons dried basil
- salt and pepper to taste
- 2 tablespoons butter

Direction

- Coat one side of each bread slice with butter and put 4 slices on a griddle on moderate heat, butter-side facing down.
- Put a cheese slice, a tomato slice and several slices of serrano pepper on each bread piece, then sprinkle dried basil over and use pepper and salt to season to taste. Place a slice of

buttered bread on top of each sandwich, butter-side facing up.

- Grill sandwiches for 2-3 minutes per side, until turn golden brown.

Nutrition Information

- Calories: 327 calories;
- Sodium: 607
- Total Carbohydrate: 31.3
- Cholesterol: 45
- Protein: 12
- Total Fat: 17.1

436.   Grilled Cheese, Cinnamon, And Apple Sandwich

Serving: 1 | Prep: 10mins | Cook: 5mins | Ready in:

Ingredients

- 1 tablespoon softened butter
- 2 slices white bread
- 1 small apple - peeled, cored, and sliced
- 1/2 teaspoon ground cinnamon
- 1 slice American cheese

Direction

- Heat a skillet over medium heat. Brush fully and evenly on a side of each bread slice with butter. Place apple slices on the unbuttered side of one of the bread slices. Sprinkle the apples with cinnamon. Arrange the cheese slice on top of apples. Put on top the bread slice left with the buttered side facing outward. Place gently into the skillet. Cook sandwich about 2 to 3 minutes each side until golden brown.

Nutrition Information

- Calories: 399 calories;
- Total Fat: 22.2

- Sodium: 846
- Total Carbohydrate: 41.3
- Cholesterol: 57
- Protein: 10.5

437. Grilled Goat Cheese And Mango Chutney Sandwich

Serving: 1 | Prep: 5mins | Cook: 5mins | Ready in:

Ingredients

- 2 slices sourdough bread
- 2 ounces goat cheese, or more to taste
- 1 1/2 tablespoons mango chutney (such as Patak's®), or more to taste
- 1 tablespoon butter

Direction

- Spread goat cheese over a side of one slice of bread, do the same with mango chutney on one side of the other slice. Sandwich bread slices around the chutney and goat cheese.
- In a small frying pan, melt the butter over medium-low heat. Cook sandwich in melted butter for 2 -3 minutes per side, sometimes pushing with the back of a spatula to melt the cheese until the bread appears golden brown.

Nutrition Information

- Calories: 516 calories;
- Sodium: 941
- Total Carbohydrate: 41
- Cholesterol: 75
- Protein: 18.3
- Total Fat: 31.8

438. Grilled Havarti And Ham

Serving: 1 | Prep: 10mins | Cook: 12mins | Ready in:

Ingredients

- 4 thin slices smoked honey ham
- 1/4 cup chopped spinach
- salt and ground black pepper to taste
- 2 slices potato bread
- 4 slices Havarti cheese
- 1 tablespoon butter

Direction

- Sauté ham in a skillet on medium high heat for 2 minutes on each side until lightly browned. Transfer cooked ham to a plate.
- Use the same skillet to cook the spinach for 2 minutes until heated through. Season with pepper and salt.
- Put ham on a slice of bread. Add spinach and havarti cheese. Cover with another slice of bread. Let cheese to melt a bit for a minute.
- Use skillet to melt the butter on medium heat. Put the sandwich in the hot butter and cook for 3 minutes on each side until it becomes golden brown.

Nutrition Information

- Calories: 836 calories;
- Total Fat: 60.7
- Sodium: 2347
- Total Carbohydrate: 29.7
- Cholesterol: 217
- Protein: 46.7

439. Grilled Mushroom And Swiss

Serving: 1 | Prep: 10mins | Cook: 10mins | Ready in:

Ingredients

- 1 tablespoon extra-virgin olive oil
- 1/4 cup baby spinach (optional)
- 1/4 cup sliced fresh mushrooms

- salt and ground black pepper to taste
- 2 slices bread
- 1 tablespoon softened butter
- 2 slices Swiss cheese

Direction

- Heat olive oil over medium heat in a skillet. Cook while stirring spinach and mushrooms for about 3 minutes or until spinach is wilted and mushrooms are softened. Sprinkle with pepper and salt to season; put to one side.
- Butter one side of each bread slice. Place 1 bread slice into the skillet, buttered side down. Place Swiss cheese over bread; spoon mushroom mixture over the cheese layer. Place the second bread slice, buttered side up, atop of mushroom mixture. Cook sandwich, flipping once, until both sides turn golden brown. Slice sandwich in half and serve right away.

Nutrition Information

- Calories: 577 calories;
- Protein: 20
- Total Fat: 42.5
- Sodium: 538
- Total Carbohydrate: 29.2
- Cholesterol: 83

440. Grilled SPAM®, Tomato, Cheddar Cheese, And Sweet Onion Sandwiches

Serving: 4 | Prep: 10mins | Cook: 15mins | Ready in:

Ingredients

- 1/4 cup spicy brown mustard
- 8 slices whole wheat bread
- 1 (12 ounce) can fully cooked luncheon meat (such as SPAM®), cut into 1/4 inch slices
- 8 slices Cheddar cheese

- 2 large tomatoes, cut into 1/2-inch slices
- 1 sweet onion, thinly sliced
- 1/4 cup softened butter

Direction

- Spread mustard on 1 side of each bread slices. Put luncheon meat on 1/2 of the bread slices; top each using onion, sliced tomato and 2 Cheddar cheese slices. Put leftover bread slices on onions, mustard side down. Evenly spread butter on outside of each sandwich.
- Heat a big skillet on medium low heat; put sandwiches in skillet. Cook till golden brown; flip sandwiches. Cook, 6 minutes per side, till crisp on one side and golden brown on other. Slightly cool; serve.

Nutrition Information

- Calories: 775 calories;
- Total Carbohydrate: 33.7
- Cholesterol: 150
- Protein: 34.8
- Total Fat: 56.5
- Sodium: 2066

441. Grilled Turkey And Swiss Sandwich

Serving: 1 | Prep: 10mins | Cook: 5mins | Ready in:

Ingredients

- 1 tablespoon mayonnaise
- 2 slices thick-cut rye bread
- 2 slices Swiss cheese
- 2 slices leftover turkey meat, or to taste
- 1/4 cup baby spinach, or to taste

Direction

- Put oven rack about 6-in. from heat source; preheat oven broiler.

- On 1 side of every bread slice, spread mayonnaise; layer Swiss cheese, turkey and spinach onto the mayonnaise side of a bread slice; put 2nd bread slice over. Put sandwich onto a baking sheet.
- In the preheated oven, broil for about 5 minutes till cheese is bubbly and heated through.

Nutrition Information

- Calories: 577 calories;
- Total Fat: 31.6
- Sodium: 655
- Total Carbohydrate: 34.7
- Cholesterol: 100
- Protein: 37.5

---

442. Grown Up Grilled Cheese Sandwich

Serving: 2 | Prep: 10mins | Cook: 10mins | Ready in:

Ingredients

- 2 tablespoons butter, divided
- 4 slices whole wheat bread
- 2 slices white American cheese
- 4 thin slices tomato
- 1/2 avocado, thinly sliced (optional)
- 2 tablespoons chopped fresh basil
- 1 teaspoon red pepper flakes
- 1 pinch garlic salt, or to taste
- 4 ounces fresh mozzarella cheese, thinly sliced
- 2 slices provolone cheese

Direction

- Preheat the skillet over medium heat.
- Coat one side of each of the sliced breads evenly with 1/2 tablespoon of butter. On the unbuttered side of one of the sliced breads, put a layer of 1 slice of American cheese, 2 slices of tomato and 2 slices of avocado. Put red pepper

flakes, garlic salt and half of the basil on top of the avocado layer. Top off with 1 slice of provolone and 1/2 of the mozzarella. Put 1 of the remaining sliced breads on top of the filling with the buttered side facing out.
- Cook the sandwich in the preheated skillet for 3-4 minutes each side until the cheese has melted and the bread is golden brown in color.

Nutrition Information

- Calories: 672 calories;
- Total Fat: 46.7
- Sodium: 1549
- Total Carbohydrate: 32
- Cholesterol: 111
- Protein: 35.8

---

443. Inside Out Grilled Cheese Sandwich

Serving: 1 | Prep: 5mins | Cook: 10mins | Ready in:

Ingredients

- 2 tablespoons butter, divided
- 2 slices white bread
- 1/2 cup shredded extra sharp Cheddar cheese, divided

Direction

- In a nonstick frying pan, melt 1 1/2 tbsp butter on medium low heat. In the frying pan, put the slices of bread over the melted butter.
- On 1 slice of bread, spread approximately 1/4 cup of cheddar cheese, then put the other bread slice, butter side up, over the cheese. Spread approximately 2 tbsp of cheese over the sandwich.
- In the frying pan next to the sandwich, melt the leftover 1/2 tbsp butter. Turn over the sandwich onto the melted butter so that the cheese side faces down. Spread the leftover

cheese over the sandwich. Cook the sandwich for 3-4 minutes, until the cheese on the bottom becomes caramelized and crispy. Turn over the sandwich and let it cook for additional 3-4 minutes, until the cheese becomes caramelized and crispy on the other side.

Nutrition Information

- Calories: 564 calories;
- Total Fat: 43.4
- Sodium: 855
- Total Carbohydrate: 26
- Cholesterol: 120
- Protein: 18.1

---

444.   Italian Grilled Cheese Sandwiches

Serving: 6 | Prep: 8mins | Cook: 7mins | Ready in:

Ingredients

- 1/4 cup unsalted butter
- 1/8 teaspoon garlic powder (optional)
- 12 slices white bread
- 1 teaspoon dried oregano
- 1 (8 ounce) package shredded mozzarella cheese
- 1 (24 ounce) jar vodka marinara sauce

Direction

- Set an oven's broiler to preheat.
- On a baking tray, put 6 bread slices. Scatter a little handful of mozzarella cheese on top of each slice, then put the leftover 6 bread slices on top. Combine the garlic powder and butter, then brush some on top of the sandwiches or spread using the back of a tablespoon. Sprinkle dried oregano on top.
- Put the baking tray under the broiler for 2-3 minutes, until they turn golden brown in color. Take the pan out of the oven, turn the

sandwiches and use butter to brush the other sides, then sprinkle oregano on top. Put sandwiches back into the broiler and cook for around 2 minutes, until they turn golden.

- Halve each of the sandwiches diagonally and serve right away alongside vodka sauce for dipping.

Nutrition Information

- Calories: 394 calories;
- Sodium: 1032
- Total Carbohydrate: 42
- Cholesterol: 46
- Protein: 15
- Total Fat: 18.3

---

445.   Jalapeno Popper Grilled Cheese Sandwich

Serving: 2 | Prep: 10mins | Cook: 10mins | Ready in:

Ingredients

- 2 ounces cream cheese, softened
- 1 tablespoon sour cream
- 10 pickled jalapeno pepper slices, or to taste - chopped
- 2 ciabatta sandwich rolls
- 4 teaspoons butter
- 8 tortilla chips, crushed
- 1/2 cup shredded Colby-Monterey Jack cheese

Direction

- In a small bowl, mix together pickled jalapeno, sour cream, and cream cheese. Let it stand. Preheat a pan on medium heat.
- Halve the roll horizontally, cut off the rounded top of the ciabatta rolls to create a piece with a flat top half. Smear 1 teaspoon of butter on the doughy part of the bottom piece and another teaspoon on the top piece with a flat top. On the unbuttered side of the bottom piece, put

1/2 of the shredded cheese, 1/2 of the crumbled chips, and 1/2 of the cream cheese mixture. Top with half of the bun. Arrange the sandwich in the hot pan. Repeat the process with the remaining sandwich.

- Grill the sandwich for 3-5 minutes until light brown then turn. Keep on grilling until the flip side is golden and the cheese is melted.

Nutrition Information

- Calories: 528 calories;
- Sodium: 1121
- Total Carbohydrate: 40.9
- Cholesterol: 89
- Protein: 16.5
- Total Fat: 34

---

446.   Lazy Chicken Parmesan Grilled Cheese

Serving: 2 | Prep: 10mins | Cook: 25mins | Ready in:

Ingredients

- 2 frozen breaded chicken patties (such as Tyson®)
- 2 tablespoons garlic butter, or to taste
- 4 slices Italian bread
- 1 cup marinara sauce
- 1/2 teaspoon dried basil, or to taste
- 1 pinch garlic salt, or to taste
- 6 thin slices provolone cheese
- 2 tablespoons shredded Parmesan cheese

Direction

- Set oven to 200°C or 400°F. Put chicken patties on a cookie sheet.
- Cook patties in the oven for 20 minutes until crispy and cooked through then cut lengthwise in half.
- Spread 1 side of every bread slice with garlic butter.

- Take a microwavable bowl and mix in garlic salt, basil and marinara sauce. Heat in a microwave for a half a minute to a minute until warm then stir.
- Put 1 bread slice in skillet with the butter-side facing down, put on two slices of provolone cheese, a tablespoon of marinara sauce, two pieces of chicken patty halves overlapping to completely cover the bread, two tablespoons of marinara sauce, a slice of provolone cheese and another bread slice with the butter-side facing up. Cook on medium heat for 2-3 minutes on each side until bread becomes crisp and cheese has melted. Repeat the process for the rest of the ingredients.
- Drizzle parmesan cheese on top of left marinara sauce then serve with sandwiches.

Nutrition Information

- Calories: 752 calories;
- Cholesterol: 111
- Protein: 34.7
- Total Fat: 45.3
- Sodium: 1993
- Total Carbohydrate: 50.2

---

447.   Madame Cristo Grilled Ham And Cheese

Serving: 1 | Prep: 15mins | Cook: 10mins | Ready in:

Ingredients

- For the Egg Batter:
- 1 large egg
- 5 tablespoons heavy cream
- 1/2 teaspoon salt
- 1 pinch cayenne pepper
- 1 pinch freshly grated nutmeg
- 1 teaspoon freshly grated lemon zest
- 4 slices white bread
- 8 thin slices Havarti cheese

- 4 ounces thinly sliced honey baked ham, halved
- 2 tablespoons butter
- 1/2 teaspoon champagne vinegar
- 1 egg
- 1 pinch cayenne pepper

Direction

- In a bowl, mix lemon zest, nutmeg, cayenne pepper, salt, heavy cream and egg till batter is runny and thin.
- Toast bread till light browned; put Havarti cheese on each slice then align ham on top. Bring 2 sandwich halves together; put into batter. Flip many times to evenly coat; put on a plate.
- Boil a big saucepan with 2" water. Meanwhile, melt butter in a pan on medium heat. In hot butter, cook sandwich, 4 minutes per side, till cheese melts and outside is browned.
- Meanwhile, lower saucepan's heat to medium low; put vinegar in. Gently simmer water. Crack egg in a small bowl; slip gently into simmering water, holding bowl right above water's surface. Cook for 2 1/2 - 3 minutes till yolk is thick but not hard and the egg white is firm.
- Put sandwich on a plate; dust cayenne pepper on. Use a slotted spoon to remove the egg from water; dab on a kitchen towel to remove extra water. Put on the sandwich. Dust cayenne pepper on.

Nutrition Information

- Calories: 1527 calories;
- Total Fat: 114.3
- Sodium: 4132
- Total Carbohydrate: 60.6
- Cholesterol: 743
- Protein: 67.1

---

448.   Meatloaf Grilled Cheese Sandwich

Serving: 1 | Prep: 5mins | Cook: 10mins | Ready in:

Ingredients

- 1 slice leftover meatloaf
- 1 tablespoon margarine
- 2 slices bread
- 1 teaspoon ketchup, or to taste
- 3 slices Cheddar cheese
- 1/2 teaspoon prepared yellow mustard, or to taste (optional)

Direction

- Put meatloaf onto a plate that is safe in the microwave; microwave on High to cook, 30 seconds at a time, until the meatloaf is thoroughly heated.
- In a non-stick skillet, melt margarine over medium heat. Put in both slices of bread on top of the melted margarine. Layer the sandwich on bread slice following this order: ketchup, a Cheddar cheese slice, warm slice of meatloaf and mustard. Finish the top of sandwich by flipping the second slice of bread; cook until the sandwich bottom lightly turns browned, approximately 2 minutes.
- Use a spatula to turn the sandwich over and top with 1 Cheddar cheese slice; keep cooking until the cheese slightly melts, approximately 1 minute. Turn the sandwich over and top with remaining slice of cheese; cook until the cheese on the sandwich bottom is crispy and melted, approximately 2 minutes. Flip sandwich over; cook for 2 minutes until cheese is crispy and melted.

Nutrition Information

- Calories: 759 calories;
- Total Carbohydrate: 32.2
- Cholesterol: 173
- Protein: 41.1
- Total Fat: 51.5

- Sodium: 1223

---

449. Mike's Favorite Grilled Cheese

Serving: 1 | Prep: 5mins | Cook: 5mins | Ready in:

Ingredients

- 2 slices bread
- 2 tablespoons butter, divided
- 2 slices processed American cheese

Direction

- Over medium high heat, heat a small-sized skillet. Spread one thin layer of butter on one side of both slices of bread; add 1 slice of bread, with buttered-side-facing-downward, into the hot skillet. Instantly position both slices of cheese over bread and cover it with second slice of bread with butter-side — facing-upward. Once the first side turn browned, flip over and brown the other side. Take out of the heat and allow it to cool down for 2 - 3 minutes prior to serving.

Nutrition Information

- Calories: 549 calories;
- Cholesterol: 114
- Protein: 16.6
- Total Fat: 42.4
- Sodium: 1348
- Total Carbohydrate: 26.2

---

450. Mom's Gourmet Grilled Cheese Sandwich

Serving: 1 | Prep: 5mins | Cook: 5mins | Ready in:

Ingredients

- 2 slices sourdough bread
- 1 tablespoon butter
- 1 tablespoon grated Parmesan cheese
- 1 slice American cheese
- 1 slice Cheddar cheese

Direction

- On moderate heat, heat a skillet. Coat on 1 side of each bread slice with butter. Sprinkle on the buttered sides with Parmesan cheese. Put in the skillet with 1 slice, buttered side facing down, then put on top of it an American cheese slice and a slice of Cheddar cheese. Place the leftover bread slice on top with butter side facing up. Fry until each side is golden.

Nutrition Information

- Calories: 488 calories;
- Protein: 21.3
- Total Fat: 32.1
- Sodium: 1081
- Total Carbohydrate: 29.2
- Cholesterol: 91

---

451. Pesto Grilled Cheese Sandwich

Serving: 1 | Prep: 5mins | Cook: 10mins | Ready in:

Ingredients

- 2 slices Italian bread
- 1 tablespoon softened butter, divided
- 1 tablespoon prepared pesto sauce, divided
- 1 slice provolone cheese
- 2 slices tomato
- 1 slice American cheese

Direction

- Spread butter on 1 side of a bread slice; put on a nonstick skillet, buttered side down on medium heat.
- Spread 1/2 of the pesto sauce on top of the bread slice in skillet. Put American cheese slice, tomato slices and provolone cheese slice on pesto.
- On 1 side of 2nd bread slice, spread leftover pesto sauce; put bread slice on sandwich, pesto side down. Butter the top side of sandwich.
- Fry sandwich gently, flipping once, 5 minutes per side, till both bread sides are golden brown and cheese melts.

Nutrition Information

- Calories: 503 calories;
- Sodium: 1108
- Total Carbohydrate: 24.2
- Cholesterol: 82
- Protein: 20.4
- Total Fat: 36.5

---

452. Pico De Gallo Grilled Cheese Sandwich

Serving: 5 | Prep: 20mins | Cook: 20mins | Ready in:

Ingredients

- Pico de Gallo:
- 1 tomato, diced
- 1/2 white onion, diced
- 2 tablespoons chopped fresh cilantro, or to taste (optional)
- 1/2 lime, juiced
- salt and ground black pepper to taste
- Sandwich:
- 3 tablespoons softened butter, or as needed
- 10 slices white bread
- 10 slices provolone cheese

Direction

- Mix pepper, salt, lime juice, cilantro, onion and tomato in bowl.
- Spread butter on 1 side of every bread slice. Put bread on a work surface, butter side down. Put 1 provolone cheese slice on each bread slice; put pico de gallo on 5 bread-cheese slices. Put leftover bread-cheese slices on each pico de gallo layer, butter side up.
- Heat a skillet on medium heat; grill every sandwich in the hot skillet, 3-4 minutes per side, till golden brown and cheese melts.

Nutrition Information

- Calories: 404 calories;
- Protein: 18.8
- Total Fat: 23.7
- Sodium: 889
- Total Carbohydrate: 29.3
- Cholesterol: 57

---

453. Pleasing Gourmet Grilled Pesto Cheese Sandwiches

Serving: 1 | Prep: 10mins | Cook: 6mins | Ready in:

Ingredients

- 2 teaspoons butter
- 2 slices sourdough bread
- 3 teaspoons pesto sauce
- 1 slice Muenster cheese
- 1 slice provolone cheese
- 1 cup baby spinach leaves
- 1 sprig fresh basil

Direction

- Set a grill to medium heat to preheat and grease the grate lightly.
- Brush 1 side of the bread slices with butter and over the other side with pesto sauce.
- On the preheated grill, arrange the bread with the butter-side down. On 1 slice, lay Muenster

cheese. Top with basil and spinach. Put in the provolone cheese. Use the other slice of bread to cover, pesto-side down.

- Grill for 3-4 minutes each side until golden brown. Diagonally slice the bread and serve warm.

Nutrition Information

- Calories: 499 calories;
- Total Fat: 32.2
- Sodium: 928
- Total Carbohydrate: 30.3
- Cholesterol: 73
- Protein: 22.8

---

454. Quick And Easy Grilled Cheese

Serving: 1 | Prep: 10mins | Cook: 6mins | Ready in:

Ingredients

- 1 tablespoon butter, softened
- 2 slices bread
- 2 slices sharp Cheddar cheese
- 1 tablespoon chopped parsley
- 1 teaspoon chopped basil
- 1 teaspoon oregano
- 1 teaspoon chopped fresh rosemary
- 1 teaspoon chopped fresh dill

Direction

- Spread on one side of each bread piece with 1/2 tsp. of butter, then lie on the side without butter on one of the bread slices with a Cheddar slice. Sprinkle on the unbuttered side of another bread slice with dill, rosemary, oregano, basil and parsley. Sandwich 2 bread slices together, buttered-sides facing outwards.
- Heat a skillet on medium heat. Once skillet is hot, lie the sandwich in the skillet gently, then

cook until cheese is melted, about 3 minutes per side.

Nutrition Information

- Calories: 470 calories;
- Total Carbohydrate: 27.4
- Cholesterol: 90
- Protein: 18.4
- Total Fat: 32.2
- Sodium: 777

---

455. Roasted Raspberry Chipotle Grilled Cheese Sandwich On Sourdough

Serving: 2 | Prep: 5mins | Cook: 5mins | Ready in:

Ingredients

- 4 tablespoons butter, softened
- 4 slices sourdough bread
- 8 Borden® Mild Cheddar Slices
- 4 tablespoons roasted raspberry chipotle sauce

Direction

- Over medium heat, put a skillet.
- Butter 4 bread slices, a tablespoon each. Onto skillet, put 2 bread slices, butter side facing down. Put 2 cheese slices on each.
- Onto every sandwich, scatter 2 tablespoons of roasted raspberry chipotle sauce and put 2 additional cheese slices on top of each.
- Put the leftover bread on top of each, butter side facing up. Allow to grill till bottom is browned lightly; turn sandwiches over. Grill the other side till browned and cheese has melted.

Nutrition Information

- Calories: 708 calories;
- Total Fat: 44

- Sodium: 1049
- Total Carbohydrate: 48.2
- Cholesterol: 121
- Protein: 22.1

456. Spicy Grilled Cheese Sandwich

Serving: 2 | Prep: 2mins | Cook: 3mins | Ready in:

Ingredients

- 2 tablespoons butter or margarine
- 4 slices white bread
- 2 slices American cheese
- 1 roma (plum) tomato, thinly sliced
- 1/4 small onion, chopped
- 1 jalapeno pepper, chopped

Direction

- On low heat, warm a big pan. Smear margarine or butter on one side of 2 bread slices. Put the bread slices buttered-side down on the pan. Layer 1 slice of cheese on each slice and add cuts of jalapeno, onion, and tomato on top. Take the leftover bread slices and butter one side. Arrange it on top of the bread in the skillet with its buttered-side facing up. Turn the sandwich over once the bottom is toasted and cook until the other side is brown.

Nutrition Information

- Calories: 352 calories;
- Cholesterol: 57
- Protein: 10.7
- Total Fat: 22.1
- Sodium: 846
- Total Carbohydrate: 28.2

457. Spicy Ham And Grilled Cheese Sandwich

Serving: 1 | Prep: 5mins | Cook: 6mins | Ready in:

Ingredients

- 2 slices Swiss cheese
- 2 slices deli ham
- 1 green chile pepper
- 2 slices rye bread
- 1 tablespoon butter, softened

Direction

- Preheat the skillet on medium heat.
- Layer cheese, ham and chile pepper on 1 bread slices; top with other slice. Butter both sandwich slices lightly; put into skillet carefully. Grill for about 3 minutes per side till bread looks golden brown and cheese is melted.

Nutrition Information

- Calories: 500 calories;
- Sodium: 616
- Total Carbohydrate: 38.2
- Cholesterol: 83
- Protein: 21.7
- Total Fat: 29.5

458. Sweet Grilled Cheese

Serving: 1 | Prep: 5mins | Cook: 5mins | Ready in:

Ingredients

- 2 slices white bread
- 2 slices American cheese
- 2 teaspoons brown sugar
- 2 teaspoons softened butter

Direction

- Set a skillet over medium heat. Spread 1 side of a piece of bread with butter; place in the heated skillet, buttered side down. Top bread with one piece of cheese, and scatter with brown sugar. Lay another slice of cheese over brown sugar layer. Spread butter over the remaining slice of bread and lay atop cheese, buttered side up. Fry sandwich, 3 to 5 minute on each side, until golden brown.

Nutrition Information

- Calories: 452 calories;
- Cholesterol: 75
- Protein: 16.5
- Total Fat: 27.5
- Sodium: 1245
- Total Carbohydrate: 35.3

---

459. Texas Toast Guacamole Grilled Cheese Sandwich

Serving: 2 | Prep: 15mins | Cook: 4mins | Ready in:

Ingredients

- 2 ripe avocados, halved and pitted
- 1/2 small onion, minced
- 1 tablespoon fresh lime juice
- 1 jalapeno pepper, seeded and minced
- 2 tablespoons chopped fresh cilantro
- 1 clove garlic, minced
- 1/2 teaspoon kosher salt
- freshly ground black pepper to taste
- 1 Roma tomato, finely chopped
- 4 slices Texas toast
- 4 slices Havarti cheese
- 2 teaspoons butter, or to taste

Direction

- In a large bowl, mash avocados. Add in pepper, salt, garlic, cilantro, jalapeno, lime

juice and onion. Mix well. Mix tomato into the guacamole.
- Over 2 bread slices, spread the desired amount of guacamole. Put 2 slices Havarti cheese on top of each bride slices. Cover with the remaining 2 bread slices; apply butter on the outsides.
- Heat skillet to medium-high heat. Cook each side of the sandwiches for about 2-3 minutes until golden brown in color.

Nutrition Information

- Calories: 433 calories;
- Sodium: 1340
- Total Carbohydrate: 30.1
- Cholesterol: 82
- Protein: 16.8
- Total Fat: 28.2

---

460. The Ultimate Apple Cinnamon Grilled Cheese Sandwich

Serving: 2 | Prep: 15mins | Cook: 10mins | Ready in:

Ingredients

- 2 purchased cinnamon buns
- 4 slices aged Cheddar cheese, divided
- 4 slices Brie cheese, divided
- 4 slices deli ham, shredded (divided)
- 1 small apple - peeled, cored, and sliced (divided)
- 2 tablespoons butter
- 2 eggs
- 1/4 cup milk

Direction

- Halve each bun; put slices on a work surface. To make a sandwich, put toppings accordingly: cinnamon bun bottom, 1 Cheddar cheese slice, 1 Brie cheese slice, apple slices, the shredded ham, 1 Brie cheese slice, 1 Cheddar cheese slice, cinnamon bun top. Repeat for another sandwich; press each sandwich together gently.

- In skillet, melt butter on medium heat. Whisk milk and eggs in a bowl.
- In egg mixture, quickly dip both of each sandwich's sides; pan-fry sandwiches, 2 minutes per side, till golden brown on both sides.

Nutrition Information

- Calories: 945 calories;
- Sodium: 1794
- Total Carbohydrate: 43.3
- Cholesterol: 422
- Protein: 46.7
- Total Fat: 66.5

461.   Tomato Bacon Grilled Cheese

Serving: 4 | Prep: | Cook: | Ready in:

Ingredients

- 8 slices bacon
- 1/4 cup butter, softened
- 8 slices white bread
- 8 slices American cheese
- 8 slices tomato

Direction

- Use a deep large skillet to cook bacon over medium high heat. Cook until it becomes evenly brown. Drain and set aside.
- Heat a big skillet over medium heat. Apply butter to one side of each sliced bread. Put about four slices of bread onto the skillet, with the side of butter down. Put a slice of cheese on top, bacon, two slices of tomato then another slice of cheese and bacon. Top with a

slice of bread with butter side out. Fry both sides of the sandwiches until it becomes golden.

Nutrition Information

- Calories: 557 calories;
- Total Fat: 38.7
- Sodium: 1696
- Total Carbohydrate: 28.6
- Cholesterol: 104
- Protein: 23.8

462.   Turkey And Feta Grilled Sandwich

Serving: 1 | Prep: 5mins | Cook: 5mins | Ready in:

Ingredients

- 2 slices smoked deli turkey
- 2 slices wheat bread
- 2 leaves lettuce
- 1 1/2 tablespoons crumbled feta cheese
- 1 tablespoon Italian salad dressing
- 1 tablespoon butter

Direction

- Lay slices of turkey on top of a bread slice. Place lettuce and then feta cheese atop turkey. Smear one side of the second bread slice with Italian salad dressing; place on top of the other slice, dressing-side down.
- Melt butter over medium heat in a skillet. Cook sandwich in melted butter, approximately 2 minutes on each side, until evenly browned.

Nutrition Information

- Calories: 377 calories;
- Total Fat: 21.6
- Sodium: 1418

- Total Carbohydrate: 27.8
- Cholesterol: 66
- Protein: 18.9

463. Twisted Ham And Turkey Grilled Cheese

Serving: 1 | Prep: 15mins | Cook: 12mins | Ready in:

Ingredients

- 2 tablespoons fresh corn kernels
- 2 teaspoons softened butter, divided
- salt and ground black pepper to taste
- 1 teaspoon mayonnaise, or to taste
- 2 thick slices Italian bread
- 2 slices honey ham
- 2 slices honey turkey
- 1 slice Lacy Swiss cheese
- 1 slice Amish Swiss cheese
- 1 slice American cheese
- 2 tablespoons shredded Cheddar cheese, or to taste
- 1 Roma tomato, seeded and chopped
- 1 tablespoon chopped sweet onion
- 1 green onion, chopped

Direction

- In a small bowl, mix the pepper, corn kernels, salt, and 1 tsp. of butter.
- Spread 1/2 tsp. of butter and 1/2 tsp. of mayonnaise on top of each slice of bread. Turn it over and layer the top with turkey ham, honey ham, Lacy Swiss cheese, American cheese, Cheddar cheese, Amish Sweet cheese. Cover the layer with sweet onion, green onion, corn mixture, and tomato. Place the second slice of bread on top to cover them. Spread the remaining 1/2 tsp. of mayonnaise and 1/2 tsp. of butter on outside of the bread slice.
- Place the skillet over medium-low heat and preheat it. Cook each side of the sandwich for 6 minutes, or until the bread appears golden brown and the cheeses are melted.

Nutrition Information

- Calories: 756 calories;
- Total Fat: 40.5
- Sodium: 2270
- Total Carbohydrate: 44.1
- Cholesterol: 155
- Protein: 54.9

464. Ultimate Grilled Cheese Sandwich

Serving: 4 | Prep: 10mins | Cook: 5mins | Ready in:

Ingredients

- 1/4 cup finely chopped Granny Smith apple
- 1 tablespoon finely chopped pecans
- 1 tablespoon creamy salad dressing (such as Miracle Whip®)
- 1 tablespoon sour cream
- 8 slices Colby cheese
- 8 slices sourdough bread
- 4 thick slices ham
- 1/4 cup margarine

Direction

- Combine together the sour cream, salad dressing, pecans, and apple. Reserve. Onto 4 of the bread slices, put a slice of Colby cheese, then add ham, and then remaining slice of cheese and bread. Spread the outside of sandwiches with the margarine.
- Put sandwiches into a large skillet and let it cook for about 3 minutes per side over medium-high heat until the cheese has melted and bread is golden brown on each side. Spread the middle of each sandwich with the apple mixture prior to serving.

Nutrition Information

- Calories: 595 calories;
- Sodium: 1569
- Total Carbohydrate: 33.8
- Cholesterol: 89
- Protein: 29.2
- Total Fat: 38.2

465. Vermont Style Grilled Cheese

Serving: 1 | Prep: 5mins | Cook: 7mins | Ready in:

Ingredients

- 2 links Johnsonville® Fully Cooked Vermont Maple Syrup, Original Recipe or Turkey Breakfast Sausage
- 2 slices bread
- 1 tablespoon butter, softened
- 2 slices processed American cheese
- 4 thin slices apple (optional)

Direction

- Use cooking spray to coat a skillet and heat on medium heat. Slice the sausage links in half lengthwise and put it in a skillet. Let it cook for 2 minutes or until heated through. Transfer the links to the side of the skillet. Spread butter on one side of each bread slice. Put one slice in the skillet, butter side facing down. Layer it with a slice of cheese, sausage, apple, a 2nd slice of cheese and a 2nd slice of bread, butter side facing up. Put cover and let it cook until it the cheese melts and becomes golden brown or for 2-3 minutes per side.

Nutrition Information

- Calories: 612 calories;
- Protein: 23.6
- Total Fat: 43.9
- Sodium: 1657
- Total Carbohydrate: 32.1

- Cholesterol: 114

466. Vidu's Fancy Grilled Cheese

Serving: 4 | Prep: 10mins | Cook: 6mins | Ready in:

Ingredients

- 4 ounces Havarti cheese with dill
- 1 1/2 tablespoons butter
- 8 slices whole-grain bread
- 4 teaspoons mayonnaise
- 4 teaspoons spicy brown mustard

Direction

- Cut Havarti cheese into slices with the thickness of 1/4 inch.
- Coat one side of each bread slice with butter and turn over to spread half of the slices with mayonnaise. Spread the leftover half with mustard and put on Havarti cheese, then put mayonnaise slices to cover, buttered side-up.
- In a skillet, cook sandwiches on medium heat for 3 minutes each side, until browned slightly.

Nutrition Information

- Calories: 334 calories;
- Sodium: 580
- Total Carbohydrate: 22.9
- Cholesterol: 48
- Protein: 13.3
- Total Fat: 21.5

467. Waffle Iron Grilled Cheese Sandwiches

Serving: 2 | Prep: 10mins | Cook: 7mins | Ready in:

Ingredients

- 2 tablespoons mayonnaise
- 2 teaspoons Dijon mustard
- 4 slices whole-grain bread
- 2 ounces shredded pepperjack cheese

Direction

- Preheat waffle iron following the manufacturer's specifications.
- In a bowl, combine Dijon mustard and mayonnaise. Smear mixture on one side of each bread slice. Top the mustard and mayonnaise side of 2 slices of bread with pepperjack cheese. Place the second bread slice on top of the cheese layer to make 2 complete sandwiches.
- In a preheated waffle iron, put in 1 sandwich without pressing it all the way down. Stand by for two minutes until the bread is soft then gently close the waffle iron. Put more pressure on the surface of the waffle iron for 3-4 minutes then close it. Cook for another 2-3 minutes until brown. Repeat these steps with the remaining sandwich.

Nutrition Information

- Calories: 354 calories;
- Total Fat: 22.3
- Sodium: 594
- Total Carbohydrate: 25
- Cholesterol: 36
- Protein: 13.2

---

468.   White Pizza Grilled Cheese

Serving: 1 | Prep: 10mins | Cook: 11mins | Ready in:

Ingredients

- 2 tablespoons butter, softened, divided
- 1/4 small sweet onion, thinly sliced
- 1 teaspoon crushed rosemary
- 1/8 teaspoon onion powder
- 1/8 teaspoon garlic powder
- salt and ground black pepper to taste
- 2 thick slices Italian bread
- 1/4 cup shredded mozzarella cheese
- 1 slice sharp American cheese (such as Cooper®)
- 1 slice provolone cheese

Direction

- In a nonstick skillet, melt butter on medium heat; mix and cook for 5 minutes till onion begins to brown. Put on a plate.
- In a small bowl, mix pepper, salt, garlic powder, rosemary, onion powder and leftover 1 tablespoon of butter. Spread on 1 side of every bread slice.
- Put 1 bread slice in the skillet, buttered side down. Top with provolone cheese, American cheese, mozzarella cheese and onion. Put 2nd bread slice, buttered side up, on top. Cook for 3 minutes till golden brown. Use spatula to flip; cook for 3 more minutes till cheeses melt and second side browns.

Nutrition Information

- Calories: 646 calories;
- Sodium: 1492
- Total Carbohydrate: 32.7
- Cholesterol: 125
- Protein: 25.9
- Total Fat: 46.1

Chapter 6: Ham Sandwich Recipes

***

469.   Big Game Grape Jelly Barbeque Ham Sandwiches

Serving: 12 | Prep: 20mins | Cook: 1hours5mins | Ready in:

Ingredients

- 3/4 cup distilled white vinegar
- 6 tablespoons grape jelly
- 1 1/2 teaspoons paprika
- 1 1/2 teaspoons dry mustard powder
- 6 tablespoons brown sugar
- 1 1/2 (12 ounce) bottles bottled sweet chili sauce (such as Heinz® Premium Chili Sauce)
- 6 tablespoons water
- 3 pounds chipped chopped ham
- 12 sandwich buns, split

Direction

- In a 2 quart saucepan, stir together water, sweet chili sauce in a bottle, brown sugar, mustard powder, paprika, grape jelly, and vinegar on medium heat. Allow to boil then set to a low heat, simmering for 5 minutes.
- Mix in chipped ham and combine with the sauce then refrigerate overnight.
- After that, slowly simmer the ham and sauce on a low heat, stirring now and then, for 1 hour.
- To serve, spoon ham onto sandwich buns.

Nutrition Information

- Calories: 687 calories;
- Total Fat: 25.3
- Sodium: 2169
- Total Carbohydrate: 86.3
- Cholesterol: 51
- Protein: 27.9

470.   Boar's Head Bold® BourbonRidge™ Uncured Smoked Ham And Cheddar Biscuits

Serving: 8 | Prep: 15mins | Cook: 2mins | Ready in:

Ingredients

- 8 biscuits, halved
- 2 tablespoons butter, room temperature
- 4 tablespoons Black Mission fig jam
- 12 ounces Boar's Head Bold® BourbonRidge™ Uncured Smoked Ham
- 12 ounces Boar's Head Sharp Wisconsin Cheddar Cheese, sliced

Direction

- Preheat the broiler. Cut biscuits using a serrated knife horizontally in half. Spread the butter (must be at room temperature) on top half of all the biscuits. Put the broiler until butter is melted and edges turn brown, 1 minute. Transfer the buttered biscuits to a work surface. Keep the broiler on.
- Spread fig jam on the bottom half of all the biscuits and place a folded ham slice and cheese slice on the top of each. Broil 1 minute until the ham is thoroughly heated and the cheese melts. Put biscuit tops on top and enjoy warm.

Nutrition Information

- Calories: 374 calories;
- Sodium: 981
- Total Carbohydrate: 20
- Cholesterol: 76
- Protein: 20.4
- Total Fat: 24.2

471. Boar's Head Bold® BourbonRidge™ Uncured Smoked Ham And Gouda Sandwich

Serving: 2 | Prep: 10mins | Cook: 38mins | Ready in:

Ingredients

- 1 tablespoon extra-virgin olive oil
- 1 large onion, thinly sliced
- Salt and pepper to taste
- Unsalted butter, room temperature
- 4 slices ciabatta, sliced 1/3-inch thick
- 4 ounces Boar's Head Bold® BourbonRidge™ Uncured Smoked Ham, sliced thin
- 3 ounces Boar's Head Sharp Wisconsin Cheddar Cheese, sliced thin
- 1 cup endive, torn into bite-size pieces

Direction

- Put oil in a large nonstick skillet and heat it over medium heat. Add and sauté the onion for 5 minutes. Adjust the heat to medium-low. Cover the skillet and cook the onion for 25 more minutes, stirring constantly until golden and tender. Season it with pepper and salt. Let it cool slightly.
- Spread butter in two bread slices. Arrange the bread on the platter, buttered side down. Top the bread slices with a layer of an onion, cheese, ham, and endive. Place another bread slice on top, buttered slice facing up.
- Place another nonstick skillet over medium heat. Lay the sandwiches and cook each side for 4 minutes, pressing them occasionally using a spatula until the cheese melts and the bread is golden brown. Cut them in half diagonally, serve right away

Nutrition Information

- Calories: 694 calories;
- Sodium: 1508
- Total Carbohydrate: 67
- Cholesterol: 91
- Protein: 30.5
- Total Fat: 32.8

472. Cajun Ham Salad Sandwiches

Serving: 4 | Prep: 20mins | Cook: | Ready in:

Ingredients

- 6 sweet bread and butter pickles
- 1/4 red onion, cut into large chunks
- 2 stalks celery, cut into large chunks
- 10 ounces baked ham, trimmed and cut into 1-inch chunks
- 2 tablespoons mayonnaise
- 1 tablespoon whole-grain Dijon mustard
- 1/2 teaspoon Cajun seasoning (optional)
- 8 slices rye bread
- 8 lettuce leaves

Direction

- In a food processor, combine celery, onion, and pickles, then pulse to make it medium-fine. Add the ham and pulse to make 1/4 inch-diameter pieces.
- In a bowl, stir Cajun seasoning, Dijon mustard, mayonnaise, and the ham mixture.
- Divide the ham salad mixture into 4 rye bread slices and lay 2 lettuce leaves onto each one. Cover with the remaining slices of bread.

Nutrition Information

- Calories: 466 calories;
- Total Carbohydrate: 50.3
- Cholesterol: 42
- Protein: 19
- Total Fat: 20.7
- Sodium: 1806

473. Christy's Awesome Hot Ham And Cheese

Serving: 1 | Prep: 5mins | Cook: 6mins | Ready in:

Ingredients

- 2 slices whole grain bread
- 2 teaspoons butter
- 2 slices Swiss cheese
- 2 thin slices deli ham
- 1 teaspoon mayonnaise
- 1 teaspoon whole grain mustard

Direction

- Put a skillet over medium-high heat to preheat.
- Use 1 teaspoon of butter to spread on 1 side of each bread slice. Add one bread slice to the skillet, unbuttered side up. Arrange ham and Swiss cheese on top. Use mustard and mayonnaise to spread on the unbuttered side of other bread slice; arrange it on top of the sandwich, buttered-side up. Let it cook for 3 minutes each side until the cheese melts and the sandwich is golden brown in color.

Nutrition Information

- Calories: 516 calories;
- Total Fat: 33.5
- Sodium: 747
- Total Carbohydrate: 26.9
- Cholesterol: 87
- Protein: 26.4

474. Easy Ham And Cheese Appetizer Sandwiches

Serving: 12 | Prep: 15mins | Cook: 12mins | Ready in:

Ingredients

- 1 cup butter, softened
- 3 tablespoons poppy seeds
- 1 onion, grated
- 1 tablespoon Worcestershire sauce
- 2 tablespoons prepared Dijon-style mustard
- 2 (12 ounce) packages white party rolls
- 1/2 pound chopped cooked ham
- 5 ounces shredded Swiss cheese

Direction

- Preheat an oven to 175°C/350°F.
- Mix prepped Dijon-style mustard, Worcestershire sauce, onion, poppy seeds and butter in a medium bowl.
- Horizontally halve rolls; put aside tops. Spread butter mixture on bottoms; put Swiss cheese and ham on top. Replace tops.
- Put rolls in a medium baking dish in 1 layer; in preheated oven, bake till cheese melts and rolls are lightly browned for 10-12 minutes.

Nutrition Information

- Calories: 416 calories;
- Protein: 12.1
- Total Fat: 27.2
- Sodium: 748
- Total Carbohydrate: 31.4
- Cholesterol: 63

475. Grilled Ham And Cheese Waffle Sandwiches

Serving: 4 | Prep: 20mins | Cook: | Ready in:

Ingredients

- 1 cup all-purpose flour
- 1 tablespoon sugar
- 1 tablespoon chopped fresh basil
- 1 1/2 teaspoons baking powder

- 1/4 teaspoon salt
- 1 egg, lightly beaten
- 1 cup milk
- 1/2 cup shredded Swiss cheese
- 1/4 cup vegetable oil
- 2 tablespoons Dijon-style mustard
- 1 (16 ounce) package Farmland® Deli-Style Sliced Ham
- 4 slices Swiss cheese
- 1/2 cup arugula or spinach leaves
- 2 tablespoons butter

Direction

- Mix salt, baking powder, basil, sugar and flour in a medium bowl. Add oil, shredded cheese, milk and egg; mix till just moist. Put batter into a lightly greased, preheated waffle iron; follow manufacturer's instructions to bake. Lift waffle off the waffle iron with a fork when done; repeat using the leftover batter to get 8 of 4-in. waffles.
- Spread mustard on waffles for each sandwiches; layer ham, sliced cheese and arugula on 1/2 of the waffles. Top, spread side down, with the leftover waffles.
- Heat a 12-in. skillet or griddle on medium heat then add butter till melted. Put in sandwiches; cook till cheese melts or for 4 minutes, flipping once.

476.   Grilled Leftover Ham And Pineapple Sandwiches

Serving: 4 | Prep: 6mins | Cook: 4mins | Ready in:

Ingredients

- 4 tablespoons cream cheese, softened
- 8 slices white bread
- 1 (8 ounce) can pineapple rings, drained
- 4 slices leftover baked ham
- 2 tablespoons butter

Direction

- Spread 4 bread slices with cream cheese. Put a slice of ham and a slice of pineapple on top the cream cheese. Put the remaining slices of bread over to cover.
- In a big skillet, heat the butter over medium heat. Fry sandwiches with butter until they are golden brown on both sides, approximately 4 minutes in total.

Nutrition Information

- Calories: 347 calories;
- Protein: 10.2
- Total Fat: 17.7
- Sodium: 793
- Total Carbohydrate: 36.7
- Cholesterol: 47

477.   Grilled Roasted Red Pepper And Ham Sandwich

Serving: 1 | Prep: 10mins | Cook: 10mins | Ready in:

Ingredients

- 2 teaspoons mayonnaise, or condiment of your choice (optional)
- 2 slices sourdough bread
- 2 slices provolone cheese
- 2 thin slices ham
- 1/2 roasted red pepper packed in oil, drained and sliced
- 2 teaspoons butter
- 2 teaspoons grated Parmesan or Romano cheese

Direction

- Spread mayonnaise on 1 side of every bread slice. Put 1 provolone cheese slice, ham, red peppers then other cheese slice on 1 bread slice. Top with other bread slice, mayonnaise side facing the filling. Butter outsides of sandwich; sprinkle bit of Parmesan cheese on butter.

- Heat a skillet on medium heat till warm; fry both sides of sandwich till cheese melts and golden brown. You may grill sandwich the same way if you have an indoor grill. Cut sandwich in half; serve.

Nutrition Information

- Calories: 551 calories;
- Total Fat: 35.1
- Sodium: 1749
- Total Carbohydrate: 32.1
- Cholesterol: 84
- Protein: 27.1

478.   Ham Bagels With Honey Mustard Cream Cheese

Serving: 4 | Prep: 15mins | Cook: |Ready in:

Ingredients

- 1/2 cup whipped cream cheese
- 2 tablespoons Dijon mustard
- 1 tablespoon honey
- 4 bagels, split
- 8 slices deli-style ham

Direction

- In a small-sized bowl, combine honey, mustard and cream cheese.
- Spread cream cheese mixture on top of cut sides of 4 bagel halves. Add ham equally on top. Sandwich with the leftover bagel halves.

Nutrition Information

- Calories: 331 calories;
- Total Fat: 7.7
- Sodium: 757
- Total Carbohydrate: 54.5

- Cholesterol: 21
- Protein: 10.4

479.   Ham Broccoli Braid

Serving: 9 | Prep: 20mins | Cook: 25mins |Ready in:

Ingredients

- 2 cups cooked ham, chopped
- 1 cup chopped fresh broccoli
- 1 small onion, chopped
- 1 tablespoon dried parsley
- 2 tablespoons Dijon mustard
- 1 1/2 cups shredded Swiss cheese
- 2 (8 ounce) cans refrigerated crescent roll dough

Direction

- Preheat an oven to 175°C/350°F.
- Mix cheese, mustard, parsley, onion, broccoli and ham well in a big bowl.
- Unroll a crescent roll dough; put flat on medium baking sheet. Seal perforations together to make 1 dough sheet. Cut 1-in. wide trips in towards middle with scissors/knife, beginning on long sides. A solid strip, 3-in. wide down the middle, should be there with cut strips making fringe down each side. Spread filling along middle strip. Fold side strips over the filling, alternating the strips from every side. Twist/pinch to seal.
- In preheated oven, bake till deep golden brown for 20-25 minutes.

Nutrition Information

- Calories: 348 calories;
- Protein: 14.4
- Total Fat: 21.3
- Sodium: 898
- Total Carbohydrate: 22.8
- Cholesterol: 33

480. Ham Pan Sandwiches

Serving: 2 | Prep: 10mins | Cook: 6mins | Ready in:

Ingredients

- 2 eggs
- 3 tablespoons Worcestershire sauce
- 1/2 teaspoon hot pepper sauce (e.g. Tabasco™)
- salt and pepper to taste
- 4 slices sandwich bread
- 6 slices cooked ham
- 3 ounces Cheddar cheese, sliced
- 1 tablespoon vegetable oil

Direction

- Whisk hot pepper sauce, Worcestershire sauce and eggs in medium bowl; season with pepper and salt. Put mixture in shallow wide dish.
- Layer 2 bread slices with even amounts of cheese and sliced ham; put leftover bread slices on top to create sandwiches; press down to secure the filling. Dip sandwiches in egg mixture; turn to coat both of the sides.
- In griddle/frying pan, heat oil on medium heat. Cook sandwiches till cheese melts and sandwiches turn golden brown, 3 minutes per side. Serve hot.

Nutrition Information

- Calories: 665 calories;
- Sodium: 2024
- Total Carbohydrate: 31.3
- Cholesterol: 278
- Protein: 36.4
- Total Fat: 43.3

481. Ham Pineapple Sandwiches

Serving: 12 | Prep: 10mins | Cook: 10mins | Ready in:

Ingredients

- 1 (15 ounce) can crushed pineapple, drained
- 1 cup white sugar
- 1 cup chopped walnuts
- 1 (8 ounce) package cream cheese, softened
- 2 tablespoons milk
- 24 slices whole-grain bread
- 60 thin slices deli ham

Direction

- Mix sugar and pineapple in a saucepan. Bring it to the boil, then cook over medium heat, stirring continuously, until thick, 5-10 minutes. Take away from heat and let cool. Once cool, mix in the walnuts.
- Mix cream cheese until softened in a medium bowl, whisk in enough milk to make it easy to spread. Mix in the pineapple mixture. This step can be made a day in advance if desired.
- On one side of 12 slices of bread, spread 2 tablespoons of the pineapple mixture. Add 5 thin slices of ham on top of each prepared slice. Place the leftover bread slices on top.

Nutrition Information

- Calories: 471 calories;
- Total Fat: 21.4
- Sodium: 1199
- Total Carbohydrate: 49.4
- Cholesterol: 61
- Protein: 21.9

482. Ham Salad Pitas

Serving: 4 | Prep: 15mins | Cook: 4mins | Ready in:

Ingredients

- 1 cup reduced fat sour cream
- 2 tablespoons lemon juice
- 1 teaspoon yellow mustard
- 1 cup cooked ham
- 1 cup mozzarella cheese
- 1/4 cup blanched slivered almonds
- 1/2 cup seedless green grapes, halved
- 3 tablespoons diced green onion
- 4 pita breads, halved

Direction

- In a bowl, mix mustard, lemon juice and sour cream. Add onions, grapes, almonds, cheese and ham; lightly toss to coat.
- Evenly divide ham mixture to pita pockets. Eat as it is or briefly heat. 2 halves at a time, heat for 1 minute in microwave if you want to heat them.

Nutrition Information

- Calories: 460 calories;
- Total Fat: 22.3
- Sodium: 957
- Total Carbohydrate: 42.6
- Cholesterol: 61
- Protein: 22

483.　Ham And Brie Sandwich

Serving: 2 | Prep: 10mins | Cook: 6mins | Ready in:

Ingredients

- 6 slices black forest ham
- 1/2 (8 ounce) wedge Brie cheese, sliced
- 2 tablespoons apricot preserves
- 1 tablespoon Dijon mustard
- 4 thick slices Italian bread
- 1 tablespoon olive oil

Direction

- To assemble the sandwiches, layer on 2 pieces of bread with equal amounts of ham, brie cheese, apricot preserves and mustard. Put the leftover 2 bread slices on top. Use olive oil to brush the top of each sandwich.
- On moderate heat, heat a grill pan. When the pan is hot, lay the sandwiches in pan with oiled side facing down. Brush oil on top of each sandwich, and then cook each side for about 3 minutes, until bread turn golden brown.

Nutrition Information

- Calories: 457 calories;
- Total Carbohydrate: 42.7
- Cholesterol: 57
- Protein: 16.8
- Total Fat: 24.5
- Sodium: 880

484.　Ham And Cheddar Cranberry Melt

Serving: 4 | Prep: 15mins | Cook: 30mins | Ready in:

Ingredients

- 8 slices your favorite bread
- 6 tablespoons butter, softened
- 8 tablespoons coarse-grained mustard
- 1 1/4 pounds Smithfield Ham slices
- 3/4 pound white Cheddar cheese, sliced
- 1 cup whole berry cranberry sauce
- 3 cups assorted salad greens

Direction

- Heat a heavy-bottomed skillet on medium-low heat. Spread butter on 1 side of 2 bread slices and turn the side with butter down. Put 5 ounces of ham slices on top of 1 bread slice and 3 ounces of cheese slices on top of the other bread slice; put them face up onto a skillet and cook for 5-7 minutes until the bread turns brown lightly and the cheese starts to melt. Take sandwich halves out of the skillet and place on a cutting board; do the same with remaining sandwiches.

- Put greens and cranberry sauce over the ham side and top with the cheese side of the bread to finish sandwich; slice the sandwich into 2 parts to serve. The sandwich is best when melty and hot.

Nutrition Information

- Calories: 938 calories;
- Cholesterol: 198
- Protein: 50.3
- Total Fat: 52.6
- Sodium: 2719
- Total Carbohydrate: 68

485.   Ham And Cheese Crescent Roll Ups

Serving: 8 | Prep: 10mins | Cook: |Ready in:

Ingredients

- 1 (8 ounce) can Pillsbury® Refrigerated Crescent Dinner Rolls
- 8 thin slices cooked ham
- 4 thin slices Cheddar cheese, cut into strips

Direction

- Turn the oven to 350° F. Divide dough in eight triangles. Put a piece of ham on every triangle; put 2 pieces of cheese in the middle of the ham. Tuck in the edges of ham even with dough triangle.
- Roll every crescent up, finishing at the tip of the triangle. Put on an ungreased baking sheet with the point down.

- Bake for 15-19 minutes or until golden brown. Remove from the baking sheet right away. Serve hot.

Nutrition Information

- Calories: 164 calories;
- Sodium: 395
- Total Carbohydrate: 11.2
- Cholesterol: 13
- Protein: 5.6
- Total Fat: 10.2

486.   Ham And Cheese Sliders

Serving: 12 | Prep: 15mins | Cook: 24mins |Ready in:

Ingredients

- cooking spray
- 1 (12 count) package Hawaiian sweet rolls
- 1 (6 ounce) package thinly sliced deli ham
- 3/4 pound shredded Swiss cheese
- 1/2 cup unsalted butter
- 1 tablespoon Dijon mustard
- 1 tablespoon poppy seeds
- 2 teaspoons Worcestershire sauce
- 2 teaspoons dried minced onion
- 1/4 teaspoon salt, or to taste
- 1/4 teaspoon ground black pepper, or to taste

Direction

- Set the oven to 175°C or 350°F to preheat. Use aluminum foil to line a 9-in. square baking pan and coat with cooking spray.
- Use a serrated knife to halve attached rolls widthwise into a top and bottom slab, keeping rolls connected. In the prepped pan, position bottom slab.
- Layer evenly over bottom slab of rolls with 1/2 of the ham. Layer on top evenly with Swiss cheese and put over cheese with leftover ham. Use top slab to cover.

- In a microwavable bowl, add butter then heat for a minute in the microwave until melted. Put in pepper, salt, onion, Worcestershire sauce, poppy seeds and mustard, then whisk to mix well.
- Pour over rolls gradually and evenly with the butter mixture, and then use a spatula to spread over tops. There will be some of the mixture pooling at the base of rolls. Use aluminum foil to cover and allow standing for about 5-10 minutes at room temperature.
- In the preheated oven, bake for 20 minutes, until cheese is melted. Take off the cover and keep on baking for 3-5 minutes longer, until browned as you want. Cut into individual sliders.

Nutrition Information

- Calories: 474 calories;
- Total Carbohydrate: 44.8
- Cholesterol: 94
- Protein: 24.1
- Total Fat: 17
- Sodium: 538

---

487. Ham And Pear Panini

Serving: 2 | Prep: 5mins | Cook: 6mins | Ready in:

Ingredients

- 4 slices bread
- 1 tablespoon mustard
- 6 slices ham
- 1 pear, peeled and thinly sliced
- 2 dashes ground black pepper
- 1 cup shredded mozzarella cheese
- 1 tablespoon light margarine (such as I Can't Believe It's Not Butter - Light ®)

Direction

- Slather bustard on two bread slices. Add three ham slices, 1/2 of the pear slices, a pinch of pepper, and half cup of mozzarella cheese on top. Cover with the remaining bread slice. Slather margarine over the outer portions of the sandwich.
- On medium heat, heat a griddle or a pan. Grill sandwiches for 3 mins on each side until cheese melts and the sandwich is golden. Halve the sandwich then serve.

Nutrition Information

- Calories: 357 calories;
- Total Fat: 13.6
- Sodium: 844
- Total Carbohydrate: 40.8
- Cholesterol: 36
- Protein: 18.3

---

488. Ham And Pineapple Fried Sandwiches

Serving: 2 | Prep: 15mins | Cook: 10mins | Ready in:

Ingredients

- 4 slices cooked ham
- 4 slices sourdough bread
- 2 tablespoons cream cheese, softened
- 1/4 cup drained crushed pineapple
- 2 slices provolone or Swiss cheese
- 2 eggs
- 1/2 cup milk
- 2 tablespoons white sugar
- 1 teaspoon butter
- 1 tablespoon vegetable oil

Direction

- On 2 bread slices, spread cream cheese. Layer 1 cheese slice, 2 tablespoons of pineapple and 2 ham slices on the cream cheese. Put 1 more bread slice over each sandwich. Cut crusts off.

- Whisk sugar, milk and eggs in a shallow bowl. Dip both sandwich sides briefly into egg mixture.
- Heat oil and butter in a big skillet on medium heat; put sandwiches in skillet. Fry on each side, 5 minutes per side, till cheese melts and is golden brown. Drain on paper towels; cool for 3 minutes. Serve.

Nutrition Information

- Calories: 541 calories;
- Sodium: 726
- Total Carbohydrate: 49.7
- Cholesterol: 232
- Protein: 22.7
- Total Fat: 28.6

---

489. Ham And Sausage Breakfast Stromboli With Roasted Peppers And Spinach

Serving: 4 | Prep: 20mins | Cook: 10mins | Ready in:

Ingredients

- 1 (14 ounce) package pizza dough
- 1/4 cup pizza sauce
- 4 ounces Farmland® Cubed Ham
- 4 ounces Farmland® Original Breakfast Sausage Links, cooked
- 4 eggs, lightly scrambled
- 2 roasted red peppers, sliced
- 1 cup fresh spinach
- 1/2 cup grated Provolone cheese
- 1 egg mixed with 1 tablespoon water, for egg wash
- 1 teaspoon dried parsley
- 1/4 cup grated Parmesan cheese

Direction

- Preheat your oven to 500°F.

- Roll the pizza dough out to form a rough rectangle and put it onto a baking sheet that is lined with parchment paper.
- Pour the pizza sauce on top of the dough and spread it out evenly keeping 1 inch off the 3 sides of the pizza dough untouched.
- Distribute the ham, sausage, scrambled eggs, peppers, spinach and Provolone cheese evenly on top.
- Use a brush to coat the edges of the dough with egg wash. Fold about 1 inch of the coated sides up and coat it with additional egg wash.
- Roll the pizza lengthwise beginning on the bottom edge of the dough so that it resembles a jelly roll.
- Position the rolled pizza on the baking sheet in such a way that the seam side is facing down; use a brush to coat it with egg wash then sprinkle Parmesan cheese and parsley on top. Carefully cut slashes on top of the pizza roll.
- Put it in the preheated oven and let it bake for 8-10 minutes until it turns golden brown in color.

Nutrition Information

- Calories: 636 calories;
- Sodium: 1767
- Total Carbohydrate: 54.7
- Cholesterol: 262
- Protein: 33.9
- Total Fat: 30.2

---

490. Ham On Ciabatta With Caramelized Mushrooms And Sweet Pea Shoots

Serving: 4 | Prep: 10mins | Cook: 20mins | Ready in:

Ingredients

- 1 loaf ciabatta bread, vertically cut into 4 equal pieces
- 3 tablespoons canola oil

- 1/4 large white onion, thinly sliced
- 1 (8 ounce) package sliced fresh mushrooms
- 1 (8 ounce) package sweet pea shoots, chopped into 2-inch pieces
- 4 slices Muenster cheese
- 12 thin slices deli ham

Direction

- Halve each of 4 ciabatta bread pieces horizontally.
- Heat a skillet on moderately low heat, then put in oil. Cook and stir in the hot oil with onion on low heat for 10-15 minutes, until onion starts to browned slightly and soften. Put in mushrooms then cook and stir for 5-10 minutes longer, until browned and soft. Put in pea shoots and cook for 2-3 minutes, until wilted. Take skillet away from the heat.
- Open the ciabatta pieces to make 4 sandwiches. Arrange among bottom pieces of each sandwich evenly with pea shoot mixture, then put in 3 deli ham slices and 1 Muenster cheese slice. Replace the ciabatta top pieces to form a sandwich.

Nutrition Information

- Calories: 607 calories;
- Sodium: 1402
- Total Carbohydrate: 64.8
- Cholesterol: 51
- Protein: 27.2
- Total Fat: 26.9

491.   Hambuns

Serving: 16 | Prep: | Cook: | Ready in:

Ingredients

- 6 cups diced cooked ham
- 1 (2 pound) loaf processed cheese, cubed
- 1 green onion, chopped

- 1 (2 ounce) can chopped black olives
- 4 hard-cooked eggs, chopped
- 1 cup mayonnaise
- salt and pepper to taste
- 16 hamburger buns

Direction

- Preheat an oven to 175°C/350°F.
- Mix pepper, salt, mayonnaise, eggs, olives, green onion, cheese and ham in big bowl; put into buns. Separately wrap each bun in aluminum foil piece; put wrapped buns on cookie sheet. In preheated oven, bake for 15 minutes then unwrap and serve.

Nutrition Information

- Calories: 557 calories;
- Sodium: 1733
- Total Carbohydrate: 27
- Cholesterol: 132
- Protein: 25.2
- Total Fat: 38.5

492.   Harvey Ham Sandwiches

Serving: 24 | Prep: 30mins | Cook: 10hours | Ready in:

Ingredients

- 1 (6 pound) bone-in ham
- 1 (8 ounce) jar yellow mustard
- 1 pound brown sugar
- 24 dinner rolls, split

Direction

- In a slow cooker or large pot, put ham and cover with enough water. Boil. Lower the heat to low, simmer for 8-10 hours. Remove meat from water. Let cool. When you pick it up it will fall into pieces if it has cooked long enough

When the ham is cool enough to handle, pull it apart into shreds. The ham doesn't need to be the tiny shreds. Put shredded ham into the slow cooker. Stir in brown sugar and mustard. Then cover, set to Low. Cook just until it is heated. Arrange on the dinner rolls. The toppings for sandwich is the personal choice.

Nutrition Information

- Calories: 445 calories;
- Total Carbohydrate: 33.9
- Cholesterol: 65
- Protein: 24.5
- Total Fat: 23.2
- Sodium: 1721

---

493.   Homemade Deviled Ham Sandwiches

Serving: 6 | Prep: 15mins | Cook: | Ready in:

Ingredients

- 1/2 pound cooked ham, cut into chunks
- 1/4 onion, sliced
- 3 tablespoons low-fat creamy salad dressing (such as Miracle Whip Light®)
- 2 teaspoons honey
- 1 teaspoon prepared mustard
- 1 teaspoon Worcestershire sauce
- 1 teaspoon dry mustard powder
- 1 dash hot pepper sauce (such as Tabasco®), or to taste
- 1/2 teaspoon paprika
- 1/8 teaspoon salt
- 1/8 teaspoon ground white pepper

Direction

- In a food processor, add onion and ham, then process until they are chopped finely.
- Remove ham mixture to a bowl, and then mix in thoroughly with white pepper, salt, paprika,

hot pepper sauce, dry mustard powder, Worcestershire sauce, prepared mustard, honey and salad dressing.

- Chill the ham spread with a cover until using.

Nutrition Information

- Calories: 128 calories;
- Total Fat: 8.7
- Sodium: 624
- Total Carbohydrate: 4.6
- Cholesterol: 23
- Protein: 7.4

---

494.   Hot Ham And Cheese Sandwiches

Serving: 8 | Prep: 10mins | Cook: 20mins | Ready in:

Ingredients

- 1/4 cup butter, softened
- 2 tablespoons prepared horseradish mustard
- 2 tablespoons chopped onions
- 1 teaspoon poppy seeds
- 1 teaspoon dill seed
- 8 slices Swiss cheese
- 8 slices cooked ham
- 8 hamburger buns

Direction

- Set the oven to 250°F or 120°C for preheating.
- Mix the dill seed, onions, butter, poppy seeds, and mustard. Fill the insides of the bun with the mixture. Fill each bun with a slice of ham and a slice of cheese.
- Use foil to wrap the buns. Place them inside the preheated oven and bake for 15-20 minutes until the cheese is melted.

Nutrition Information

- Calories: 360 calories;

- Cholesterol: 58
- Protein: 17.4
- Total Fat: 21.7
- Sodium: 715
- Total Carbohydrate: 23.8

495.   Kylie's Ham Delights

Serving: 5 | Prep: 5mins | Cook: 10mins | Ready in:

Ingredients

- 1 pound thinly sliced cooked ham
- 1 (8 ounce) can crushed pineapple
- 5 slices provolone cheese
- 5 large plain croissants

Direction

- In skillet, mix and sauté pineapple and ham on medium heat till most of pineapple juice cooks off. In skillet, separate mixture into 5 sections; put one cheese slice over each. Cook till cheese melts. Serve over warm croissants.

Nutrition Information

- Calories: 622 calories;
- Total Fat: 38.5
- Sodium: 1913
- Total Carbohydrate: 38.4
- Cholesterol: 115
- Protein: 29.7

496.   Mini Ham And Cheese Rolls

Serving: 24 | Prep: 15mins | Cook: 20mins | Ready in:

Ingredients

- 2 tablespoons dried minced onion

- 1 tablespoon prepared mustard
- 2 tablespoons poppy seeds
- 1/2 cup margarine, melted
- 24 dinner rolls
- 1/2 pound chopped ham
- 1/2 pound thinly sliced Swiss cheese

Direction

- Set the oven to 325°F or 165°C for preheating.
- Mix margarine, poppy seeds, onion flakes, and mustard in a small mixing bowl.
- Split each of the dinner rolls. Place the ham and cheese inside to make a sandwich. Put the sandwich in a baking sheet. Pour the poppy seed mixture over the sandwiches.
- Let it bake inside the preheated oven until the cheese melted completely, about 20 minutes. Serve warm.

Nutrition Information

- Calories: 145 calories;
- Sodium: 276
- Total Carbohydrate: 10.2
- Cholesterol: 18
- Protein: 5.7
- Total Fat: 9

497.   Mini Ham, Swiss, Rye Sandwiches With Cranberry Onion Relish

Serving: 44 | Prep: 35mins | Cook: 15mins | Ready in:

Ingredients

- 2 tablespoons vegetable oil
- 2 large onions, cut into medium dice
- 4 teaspoons minced fresh rosemary
- 1/2 teaspoon ground cloves
- 1 (16 ounce) can whole berry cranberry sauce
- 1 (16 ounce) package cocktail rye bread
- 1/4 cup Dijon mustard

- 2 pounds thin ham slices from a baked spiral-cut ham (or substitute Black Forest ham), cut to fit rye bread
- 12 ounces thinly sliced Swiss cheese, cut to fit rye bread Arugula or other baby salad greens
- Toothpicks (optional)

Direction

- In a 12-inch skillet, heat oil over medium-high heat. Put in onions; sauté for 10 - 12 minutes until well-browned. Add in cloves and rosemary; continue to sauté for 1 - 2 more minutes until fragrant. Mix in cranberry sauce, then allow to simmer until heated through. Take away from heat and put aside. (Cranberry-Onion Relish can be cooled, covered up and stored in the fridge up to 2 weeks in advance.)
- To assemble: Working in batches; on a work surface, lay breads and spread with about 1/4 tsp. of mustard and 1 tsp. of cranberry relish. Add a portion of ham, cheese and arugula (optional) on top half the breads, then place the remaining bread slice on top. Halve diagonally each sandwich, sticking a toothpick in each half. (Sandwiches can be wrapped in plastic wrap and a damp paper towel and be stored at room temperature for 2 hours.)

Nutrition Information

- Calories: 114 calories;
- Cholesterol: 19
- Protein: 6.5
- Total Fat: 4.9
- Sodium: 389
- Total Carbohydrate: 10.9

498.   Miso Paste Ham Sandwich

Serving: 1 | Prep: 1mins | Cook: 2mins | Ready in:

Ingredients

- 2 slices whole wheat bread, toasted
- 1 teaspoon miso paste
- 1/2 teaspoon wasabi paste (optional)
- 2 teaspoons mayonnaise
- 2 slices ham
- 1 leaf lettuce
- 1 slice Cheddar cheese

Direction

- Spread on 1 side of a bread slice with miso paste and wasabi paste. Spread on the other slice with mayonnaise. Layer over mayonnaise with ham, lettuce and cheese, then put another bread slice on top, miso-side inside.

Nutrition Information

- Calories: 340 calories;
- Total Fat: 19
- Sodium: 765
- Total Carbohydrate: 27.3
- Cholesterol: 33
- Protein: 15.2

499.   Monte Cristo Sandwich

Serving: 1 | Prep: 5mins | Cook: 15mins | Ready in:

Ingredients

- 2 slices bread
- 1 teaspoon mayonnaise
- 1 teaspoon prepared mustard
- 2 slices cooked ham
- 2 slices cooked turkey meat
- 1 slice Swiss cheese
- 1 egg
- 1/2 cup milk

Direction

- Spread mustard and mayonnaise on bread; alternate turkey, swiss and ham slices on bread.
- Beat milk and egg in small bowl; coat sandwich in milk and egg mixture. Heat greased skillet on medium heat then brown sandwich on both sides and serve hot.

Nutrition Information

- Calories: 641 calories;
- Total Carbohydrate: 33.1
- Cholesterol: 298
- Protein: 48.7
- Total Fat: 33.8
- Sodium: 1308

---

500. Monte Cristo Sandwich The Real One

Serving: 8 | Prep: 10mins | Cook: 5mins | Ready in:

Ingredients

- 1 quart oil for frying, or as needed
- 2/3 cup water
- 1 egg
- 2/3 cup all-purpose flour
- 1 3/4 teaspoons baking powder
- 1/2 teaspoon salt
- 8 slices white bread
- 4 slices Swiss cheese
- 4 slices turkey
- 4 slices ham
- 1/8 teaspoon ground black pepper
- 1 tablespoon confectioners' sugar for dusting

Direction

- Fill a deep fryer with oil up to 5 inches deep. Heat to 180°C/365°F. While heating the oil, prepare the batter. Whisk water and egg together in a medium bowl. Add salt, pepper, baking powder, and flour and whisk together

with the egg mixture until smooth. Place in the refrigerator to set aside.
- On one slice of bread, place a slice of turkey. On another slice of bread, place the slice of ham. Sandwich the two with Swiss cheese in the center. Slice into quarters and keep them secure with toothpicks.
- Dip in the batter and coat all sides of the sandwich. Deep fry until all sides are golden brown. Remove the toothpicks and place them on a serving tray. Before serving, dust confectioners' sugar over on top.

Nutrition Information

- Calories: 305 calories;
- Total Fat: 17.9
- Sodium: 808
- Total Carbohydrate: 23.7
- Cholesterol: 50
- Protein: 12.2

---

501. Monte Cristo Sandwich With Bacon

Serving: 1 | Prep: 15mins | Cook: 20mins | Ready in:

Ingredients

- 2 slices bacon
- 1 teaspoon vegetable oil, or as needed
- 2 tablespoons milk
- 1 egg, beaten
- 1 pinch ground nutmeg
- 2 slices bread
- 1 tablespoon whole berry cranberry sauce, or more to taste
- 2 slices smoked turkey
- 1 slice provolone cheese
- 1 tablespoon brown mustard, or more to taste
- 2 slices cooked ham

Direction

- Cook bacon in big skillet on medium high heat, occasionally turning, for 10 minutes till evenly browned. On paper towels, drain bacon slices. Break every piece in half.
- In skillet, heat oil on medium heat.
- Whisk nutmeg, egg and milk in shallow bowl. In egg mixture, dip every bread slice.
- Cook dipped bread slices in hot oil, 2-3 minutes per side, till French toast browns lightly. Put French toast on work surface; put heat under skillet on medium low.
- Spread cranberry sauce on 1 French toast piece; put bacon, provolone cheese and turkey on top. Spread mustard on other French toast piece; put ham over. Lay over bacon layer to make sandwich, ham-side down.
- Cook sandwich in skillet, 3-4 minutes per side, till sandwich is heated through and cheese is melted.

Nutrition Information

- Calories: 710 calories;
- Sodium: 2496
- Total Carbohydrate: 36.6
- Cholesterol: 285
- Protein: 44.2
- Total Fat: 42.6

502.   Monte Cristo Sandwiches

Serving: 4 | Prep: 15mins | Cook: 10mins | Ready in:

Ingredients

- 3 eggs, beaten
- 1 1/2 cups milk
- 1/2 teaspoon ground cinnamon
- 1/2 teaspoon ground nutmeg
- 8 slices French bread
- 8 ounces honey ham, chopped
- 8 ounces smoked turkey breast, chopped
- 12 slices Swiss cheese

Direction

- Beat milk and eggs in a big bowl; mix nutmeg and cinnamon in.
- Heat a nonstick skillet on medium heat; dip bread slices in egg mixture. Put in skillet; cook till both sides are lightly brown.
- Take bread out of skillet. Use Swiss cheese slice, ham, Swiss cheese, turkey then Swiss cheese over 4 bread slices. Use leftover 4 bread slices to cover. Put sandwiches in skillet; grill till bread is browned and cheese melts. Serve hot.

Nutrition Information

- Calories: 695 calories;
- Total Carbohydrate: 43
- Cholesterol: 278
- Protein: 56.3
- Total Fat: 32.5
- Sodium: 1585

503.   Pittsburgh Ham Barbecue Sandwich

Serving: 8 | Prep: 15mins | Cook: 1hours30mins | Ready in:

Ingredients

- 1 pound chipped chopped ham
- 2 (12 ounce) bottles tomato-based chili sauce
- 1 (12 fluid ounce) can or bottle cola-flavored carbonated beverage
- 1 stalk celery, finely chopped
- 1/2 onion, finely chopped
- 1/2 dill pickle, chopped
- 2 tablespoons brown sugar
- 8 hamburger buns

Direction

- Into a slow cooker, put the chopped ham, dill pickle, chili sauce, onion, cola, brown sugar and celery and stir to combine.
- Cook for 1 1/2 hours on high or cook for 3 hours on low and then serve on buns.

Nutrition Information

- Calories: 288 calories;
- Protein: 12.6
- Total Fat: 11
- Sodium: 1005
- Total Carbohydrate: 34.9
- Cholesterol: 25

---

504.   Sweet Ham Roll Ups

Serving: 4 | Prep: | Cook: |Ready in:

Ingredients

- 4 Mission® Medium Flour Tortillas
- 4 tablespoons fat-free cream cheese
- 1 teaspoon mustard
- 8 thin slices ham
- 4 tablespoons grated Cheddar cheese
- 1 small apple, sliced into toothpick-sized slivers

Direction

- Coat all over surface of each tortilla with 1 tablespoon of cream cheese. Dot a quarter teaspoon of mustard onto each middle of tortilla. Add a quarter of slivered apple, 1 tablespoon of cheese and 2 ham slices on top. Tightly roll up the tortillas into wrap. Firmly wrap in plastic and leave in the fridge.
- Take tortillas out of plastic wrap and halve to serve.

Nutrition Information

- Calories: 259 calories;

- Total Fat: 9
- Sodium: 956
- Total Carbohydrate: 30.8
- Cholesterol: 26
- Protein: 13

---

505.   Sweet And Sour Hot Ham Sandwiches

Serving: 6 | Prep: 20mins | Cook: 15mins |Ready in:

Ingredients

- Crisco® Original No-Stick Cooking Spray
- 1 pound thinly sliced deli-style smoked ham, quartered
- 1 tablespoon Crisco® Pure Vegetable Oil
- 1/2 large yellow onions, cut into very thin wedges
- 3/4 cup chopped green pepper
- 1 (10 ounce) jar Crosse & Blackwell® Premium Ham Glaze
- 1 (8.25 ounce) can crushed pineapple in heavy syrup, undrained
- 1/3 cup firmly packed brown sugar
- 2 tablespoons white vinegar
- 6 kaiser rolls*

Direction

- Use nonstick cooking spray to coat a big skillet, then heat on moderate heat. Sauté a third of ham at a time until it is browned slightly, about 15 second. Take out of the skillet and put into a big bowl.
- In the same skillet, heat oil on moderately low heat, then put in green pepper and onion. Sauté until soft, about 7 minutes.
- Stir in vinegar, brown sugar, undrained pineapple and ham glaze, then heat through. Drizzle over ham in the bowl and toss to coat well. Serve on rolls.

Nutrition Information

- Calories: 412 calories;
- Total Carbohydrate: 64.3
- Cholesterol: 43
- Protein: 17
- Total Fat: 10.7
- Sodium: 1275

Chapter 7: Hoagie Sandwich Recipes

***

506.	Awesome Asparagus Sandwich

Serving: 3 | Prep: 10mins | Cook: 20mins | Ready in:

Ingredients

- 1 bunch fresh asparagus, trimmed
- 1 red bell pepper, seeded and quartered
- 1 tablespoon olive oil
- 3 hoagie rolls
- 6 ounces shredded Swiss cheese
- 1 ripe tomato, sliced
- 3 tablespoons mayonnaise
- 2 tablespoons lemon juice
- 1 teaspoon minced garlic

Direction

- Set the oven to 350°F or 175°C for preheating.
- Toss red pepper and asparagus with the olive oil. Arrange them on a lined baking sheet. Bake for 10 minutes, or until tender. When they are cool enough to handle, start removing the skin from the pepper and cut it into strips.
- Slice the hoagie rolls in half. Arrange them on a baking sheet and toast them inside the oven lightly. Remove halved rolls from the oven.

Sprinkle each halved rolls with cheese. Arrange a few strips of pepper and 4-5 asparagus spears on one side. On the other side of the roll, arrange the tomato slices. Bring the hoagies back inside the oven and bake for 5 minutes, or until the cheese has melted.
- In the meantime, mix garlic, mayonnaise, and lemon juice together in another bowl. Spread the dressing mixture on one side of the roll. Close the sandwich.

Nutrition Information

- Calories: 796 calories;
- Sodium: 951
- Total Carbohydrate: 82.8
- Cholesterol: 57
- Protein: 31.1
- Total Fat: 38.5

507.	BBQ Pulled Pork Sandwich

Serving: 8 | Prep: 1hours30mins | Cook: 3hours30mins | Ready in:

Ingredients

- Coleslaw:
- 1 (16 ounce) package shredded coleslaw mix
- 1/4 cup pickled pepperoncini peppers, chopped
- 1/4 cup diced red onion
- 1/3 cup mayonnaise
- 1/2 lemon, juiced
- 1 tablespoon red wine vinegar
- 1 tablespoon granulated garlic
- 1 teaspoon Dijon mustard
- 1 teaspoon white sugar
- 1 teaspoon salt
- 1/2 teaspoon granulated onion
- 1/4 teaspoon lemon pepper
- Pulled Pork:

- 2 tablespoons kosher salt
- 2 tablespoons ground black pepper
- 2 tablespoons granulated garlic
- 2 tablespoons granulated onion
- 2 tablespoons brown sugar
- 1 tablespoon cayenne pepper
- 1 tablespoon ground nutmeg
- 1 tablespoon ground allspice
- 1 teaspoon ground cinnamon
- 1 (4 pound) pork shoulder roast
- 1/4 cup molasses
- Sauce:
- 3 cups barbeque sauce
- 1 cup strong brewed coffee
- 1 tablespoon molasses
- 1 tablespoon brown sugar
- 1 teaspoon dry mustard
- 1 pinch cayenne pepper, or more to taste
- 4 Italian-style hoagie buns, split lengthwise and toasted
- 1/4 cup onion, chopped (optional)
- 1/4 cup jalapeno pepper, seeded and minced (optional)

Direction

- In a big bowl, mix together lemon pepper, 1/2 teaspoon granulated onion, salt, white sugar, Dijon mustard, 1 tablespoon granulated garlic, red wine vinegar, lemon juice, mayonnaise, red onion, pepperoncini peppers and coleslaw mix. Mix until thoroughly blended. Put a cover on and chill until using.
- Turn the oven to 300°F (150°C) to preheat.
- In a bowl, mix together cinnamon, allspice, nutmeg, 1 tablespoon cayenne pepper, 2 tablespoons brown sugar, 2 tablespoons granulated onion, 2 tablespoons granulated garlic, black pepper and kosher salt.
- In a big roasting pan, put the pork shoulder. Rub between any crevices and on all sides with 1/4 cup molasses. Sprinkle the kosher salt seasoning mixture over and rub onto all sides.
- Put heavy-duty aluminum foil on the pan to tightly cover. In the preheated oven, roast the pork for 3-4 hours until soft and a

thermometer inserted displays 200°F (95°C) when you insert it into the pork. Remove the pork to a cutting board, saving the pan juice, and allow to cool slightly before pulling. Shred the pork shoulder into bite-sized pieces with 2 forks. Remove the meat to a big bowl and mix with some of the pan juices to maintain moistness.

- In a big pot, pour the saved pan juices over medium heat. Add 1 pinch of cayenne pepper, dry mustard, 1 tablespoon brown sugar, 1 tablespoon molasses, coffee and barbeque sauce. Simmer, lower the heat, and cook for 15 minutes. Add the shredded pork and toss for 5 minutes until warm.
- Fill the pork mixture into each hoagie bun. Put 1-2 cups coleslaw on top. Use 1 tablespoon jalapeno and 1 tablespoon jalapeno to garnish.

Nutrition Information

- Calories: 838 calories;
- Total Carbohydrate: 100.1
- Cholesterol: 97
- Protein: 31.2
- Total Fat: 34.7
- Sodium: 3479

---

508.   Carne Asada Sandwich

Serving: 8 | Prep: 40mins | Cook: 20mins | Ready in:

Ingredients

- Chipotle Mayonnaise:
- 1 1/2 cups mayonnaise
- 1/2 cup sour cream
- 1/4 cup chopped fresh cilantro
- 1/4 cup diced green onions
- 1 1/2 tablespoons ground chipotle chile powder
- 1 tablespoon lime juice
- 1 tablespoon garlic basil spread (see footnote for recipe link)

- 1 teaspoon ground cumin
- salt and freshly ground black pepper
- Filling:
- 2 pounds beef tri-tip steak, thinly sliced
- 2 Anaheim chile peppers, diced
- 1 onion, diced
- 1 red bell pepper, diced
- 1 green bell pepper, diced
- 1 lime, juiced
- 1 tablespoon olive oil
- 1 tablespoon minced garlic
- 1 teaspoon red pepper flakes
- 1 teaspoon ground cumin
- 1 teaspoon ground chipotle chile powder
- 1 teaspoon smoked paprika
- 1 teaspoon Mexican oregano
- 1 cup chopped fresh cilantro
- 2 jalapeno peppers, sliced (optional)
- Assembly:
- 4 Italian-style hoagie buns, split lengthwise
- 1/2 pound sliced Asiago cheese, divided
- 1 avocado, sliced - divided
- 1 cup halved cherry tomatoes, divided
- 1/2 cup chopped fresh cilantro, divided

Direction

- In a bowl, mix black pepper, salt, 1 teaspoon cumin, garlic basil spread, 1 tablespoon lime juice, 1 1/2 tablespoon ground chipotle peppers, green onions, 1/2 cup cilantro, sour cream and mayonnaise. Mix till incorporated. Put cover and chill chipotle mayonnaise for a minimum of an hour.
- In a big bowl, mix Mexican oregano, smoked paprika, 1 teaspoon ground chipotle pepper, 1 teaspoon cumin, red pepper flakes, garlic, olive oil, juice of 1 lime, green bell pepper, red bell pepper, onion, Anaheim chili peppers and beef tri-tip; add black pepper and salt to season and mix by tossing. Put the cover and chill beef mixture for a minimum of 4 hours.
- Preheat an oven to 260 °C or 500 °F.
- Over medium-high heat, heat a big pot or Dutch oven. Put beef mixture and allow to cook for 15 to 20 minutes, mixing continuously, till beef browns and onions

soften and turn golden. Mix in jalapeno peppers and a cup chopped cilantro.
- Scatter 2 tablespoons chipotle mayonnaise on every hoagie bun. Into buns, scoop beef mixture and put 2 ounces Asiago cheese on every sandwich top.
- On a baking sheet, put the sandwiches and allow to bake in the prepped oven for 5 minutes till bread is warm and toasted and cheese is melted. Distribute 1/2 cup cilantro, cherry tomatoes and fresh avocado among 4 sandwiches.

Nutrition Information

- Calories: 934 calories;
- Cholesterol: 153
- Protein: 46.2
- Total Fat: 63.4
- Sodium: 1063
- Total Carbohydrate: 46.3

509.   Catfish Po Boy

Serving: 8 | Prep: 30mins | Cook: 10mins | Ready in:

Ingredients

- Coleslaw:
- 1 (16 ounce) package shredded coleslaw mix
- 1/4 cup pickled pepperoncini peppers, chopped
- 1/4 cup diced red onion
- 1/3 cup mayonnaise
- 1/2 lemon, juiced
- 1 tablespoon red wine vinegar
- 1 teaspoon Dijon mustard
- 1 teaspoon white sugar
- 1 teaspoon salt
- 1 tablespoon granulated garlic
- 1/2 teaspoon granulated onion
- 1/4 teaspoon lemon pepper
- Catfish:
- 8 (3 ounce) fillets catfish

- 2 tablespoons hot sauce (such as Tabasco®)
- 1/2 cup Cajun seasoning
- 2 cups all-purpose flour
- 2 cups cornmeal
- 2 cups bread crumbs
- 1 tablespoon granulated garlic
- 1 tablespoon granulated onion
- 1 1/2 teaspoons ground black pepper
- 1/2 teaspoon cayenne pepper
- 1 cup olive oil for frying
- Assembly:
- 4 Italian-style hoagie buns, split lengthwise
- 1 cup remoulade-style sandwich spread (see footnote for recipe link)
- 1 lemon, cut into wedges
- 1 cup cherry tomato halves
- 1/2 cup banana pepper rings

Direction

- In a large bowl, mix together lemon pepper, half teaspoon of granulated onion, half teaspoon of granulated garlic, salt, sugar, Dijon mustard, red wine vinegar, lemon juice, mayonnaise, red onion, pepperoncini peppers and coleslaw mix. Toss to combine thoroughly. Refrigerate, covered, until ready to use.
- Bring catfish fillets into a large shallow baking dish. Add hot sauce onto the top and flip fillets over until coated.
- In a large brown paper bag, blend cayenne pepper, black pepper, 1 tablespoon of granulated onion, 1 tablespoon of granulated garlic, bread crumbs, cornmeal, flour and Cajun seasoning. Put in breadcrumbs. Put the fillets inside and shake lightly until fillets are coated completely.
- In a large skillet, bring olive oil to medium-high heat. Fry coated fillets for about 3 minutes on each side until crispy and browned. Drain on a paper plates lined with paper towel.
- Lather a quarter cup of remoulade-style spread onto each hoagie bun. Top with 2 catfish fillets, following by 1-2 cups of coleslaw. Decorate with dish with banana

pepper rings, cherry tomato halves and lemon wedge.

Nutrition Information

- Calories: 1070 calories;
- Total Carbohydrate: 128.7
- Cholesterol: 72
- Protein: 29.8
- Total Fat: 48.6
- Sodium: 2961

510. Chicken Pesto Sandwich

Serving: 8 | Prep: 30mins | Cook: 20mins | Ready in:

Ingredients

- 4 skinless, boneless chicken breast halves, cut into chunks
- 1 tablespoon olive oil
- 1 tablespoon minced garlic
- 1 teaspoon red pepper flakes
- salt and freshly ground black pepper to taste
- 1 yellow bell pepper, sliced
- 1 onion, sliced
- 1 cup diced zucchini
- 1 teaspoon balsamic vinegar
- 1 cup sliced mushrooms
- 1 tablespoon chopped fresh basil
- 1 cup shredded mozzarella cheese
- 1 cup prepared pesto sauce
- 1/2 cup halved cherry tomatoes
- 4 Italian-style hoagie buns, split lengthwise and toasted
- 1 cup crumbled feta cheese, divided
- 2 tablespoons chopped fresh basil, divided

Direction

- In a large bowl, mix black pepper, salt, red pepper flakes, garlic, olive oil, and chicken; toss to coat.

- Set a large Dutch oven or pot over medium-high heat. Put in chicken mixture and cook for about 5 minutes until chicken starts to brown, stirring frequently. Mix in balsamic vinegar, zucchini, onion, and yellow bell pepper and cook for about 5 minutes until the onion starts to soften.
- Mix 1 tablespoon basil and mushrooms into the chicken mixture and cook for about 5 minutes until mushrooms have softened. Put in pesto sauce and mozzarella cheese; toss to coat. Mix in cherry tomatoes and cook for 2-3 minutes until warmed through.
- Scoop chicken mixture into toasted buns and place 1 1/2 teaspoon basil and 1/4 cup feta cheese on top of each sandwich.

Nutrition Information

- Calories: 525 calories;
- Total Fat: 26.9
- Sodium: 960
- Total Carbohydrate: 41.3
- Cholesterol: 65
- Protein: 29.4

511.   Chicken Sausage Heroes

Serving: 8 | Prep: 20mins | Cook: 25mins | Ready in:

Ingredients

- 1 pound ground chicken
- 1/4 cup grated Parmesan cheese
- 1/2 cup dry bread crumbs
- 1/2 cup oil-packed sun-dried tomatoes, drained and diced
- 1/2 cup chopped Italian flat leaf parsley
- 1 teaspoon fennel seeds
- 1/4 teaspoon freshly ground black pepper
- 1 1/4 teaspoons salt, divided
- 2 tablespoons olive oil, divided
- 1 large sweet onion, sliced
- 3 cloves garlic, slivered

- 1 green bell pepper, cut into strips
- 1 tablespoon red bell pepper, cut into strips
- 2 tablespoons red wine vinegar
- 1 (1 pound) loaf Italian bread, cut in half lengthwise
- 4 (1 ounce) slices provolone cheese

Direction

- Mix 3/4 tsp. salt, pepper, fennel seeds, parsley, sun-dried tomatoes, breadcrumbs, Parmesan cheese and ground chicken in bowl; shape into 8 links.
- Heat 1 tbsp. olive oil in skillet; cook sausage links till juices are clear and chicken is not pink anymore, about 10 minutes.
- Heat leftover 1 tbsp. olive oil in another skillet on medium heat; sauté garlic and onion till tender, about 5 minutes. Mix red bell pepper and green bell pepper in; mix and cook till tender, about 5 minutes. Sprinkle vinegar over; season with leftover 1/2 tsp. salt.
- Put sausages on bottom of bread loaf; cover with veggies. Use provolone cheese to layer. Replace the loaf top to make a long sandwich; cut into slices. Serve

Nutrition Information

- Calories: 514 calories;
- Total Carbohydrate: 85.5
- Cholesterol: 13
- Protein: 17.4
- Total Fat: 13.2
- Sodium: 1198

512.   Chicken, Artichoke Heart, And Parmesan Sandwiches

Serving: 6 | Prep: 30mins | Cook: 40mins | Ready in:

Ingredients

- 6 boneless skinless chicken breast halves
- 2 eggs, lightly beaten
- 1 1/2 cups bread crumbs
- 3 tablespoons olive oil, divided
- 1 small onion, diced
- 2 cloves garlic, chopped
- 1 (10 ounce) can tomato sauce
- 1/2 teaspoon salt
- 3/4 teaspoon black pepper
- 6 hoagie rolls, split lengthwise
- 1 (12 ounce) jar artichoke hearts, drained
- 6 slices mozzarella cheese
- 6 slices red tomato
- 1/2 cup grated Parmesan cheese

Direction

- Set the oven to 400°F (200°C), and start preheating.
- Between two sheets of plastic wrap, arrange each chicken breast, and pound to the thickness of 1/2 inch. Dip breast in lightly beaten eggs, then into bread crumbs to coat evenly.
- In a large skillet, heat 2 tablespoons of oil over medium heat. Cook chicken breasts for approximately 7 minutes per side, until golden brown. Lower the heat if they brown too quickly; make sure that they are cooked through. Remove from heat and arrange on a paper towel-lined plate. Wipe the crumbs out of the skillet.
- In the skillet, heat the remaining 1 tablespoon of oil over medium heat. Put in onions and stir for about 5 minutes, until softened. Put in the garlic and stir for 1 minute. Add tomato sauce. Use pepper and salt for seasoning; simmer without cover, stirring occasionally, about 10 minutes.
- On a baking sheet, place bottom halves of 6 hoagies and the tops on other one, all cut-side up. On each hoagie top and bottom, spread about a tablespoon tomato sauce, saving the remainder. Add a cooked chicken breast on each bottom half. Spoon the rest of tomato sauce over top of each breast. Add one slice each of tomato and mozzarella and artichoke

hearts on top. Sprinkle grated Parmesan cheese on top.
- Bake on the oven's bottom rack till the cheese starts to melt, about 3 minutes. Put the sheet of the hoagie tops on the upper rack; bake for 3-4 minutes, until edges are golden, be careful not to let them burn. Remove both sheets from the oven. Make 6 sandwiches by putting a top on each bottom.

Nutrition Information

- Calories: 898 calories;
- Total Fat: 30
- Sodium: 1980
- Total Carbohydrate: 100.6
- Cholesterol: 150
- Protein: 55.9

---

513. Cuban Sandwich From Smithfield®

Serving: 4 | Prep: 15mins | Cook: 20mins | Ready in:

Ingredients

- 1 pound Smithfield® Original Pork Loin Filet
- 1 pound Smithfield/Farmland® Ham
- 5 tablespoons yellow mustard, divided
- 1 teaspoon salt
- 1/4 teaspoon ground black pepper
- 4 hoagie rolls, split lengthwise
- 5 tablespoons butter, softened
- 2 dill pickles, each cut lengthwise into 4 slices
- 8 slices Swiss cheese

Direction

- Set the oven at 450°F to heat. Coat the entire loin with 1 tbsp. of mustard; add pepper and salt to taste.
- Arrange the pork on a rack in a shallow roasting pan. Roast for about 20 minutes in 450°F oven until the temperature inside the

pork registered 150°F. Let it sit for 10 minutes before cutting thinly.

- Cut hoagie rolls horizontally in half and spread 1 tbsp. of butter on the inside of both halves. Layer the filling ingredients on the sandwich in the following order: sliced roast, sliced ham, remaining 4 tbsp. of mustard, pickles and Swiss cheese.
- Heat a big skillet and coat with 1 tbsp. of butter. Cook the sandwiches in skillet until the cheese melts and the bread is golden brown. You can also use a sandwich press to grill. Cut the sandwiches diagonally in half and serve.

Nutrition Information

- Calories: 830 calories;
- Sodium: 2052
- Total Carbohydrate: 45.4
- Cholesterol: 163
- Protein: 41.1
- Total Fat: 54.1

---

514. Dripping Roast Beef Sandwiches With Melted Provolone

Serving: 4 | Prep: 5mins | Cook: 8mins | Ready in:

Ingredients

- 1 (10.5 ounce) can Campbell's® Condensed French Onion Soup
- 1 tablespoon reduced sodium Worcestershire sauce
- 3/4 pound thinly sliced deli roast beef
- 4 Pepperidge Farm® Classic Soft Hoagie Rolls with Sesame Seeds
- 4 slices diced provolone cheese, cut in half
- 1/4 cup drained hot or mild pickled banana pepper rings

Direction

- Heat an oven to 400°F.
- In a 2-quart saucepan, boil Worcestershire and soup on medium high heat. Add beef; heat through, occasionally mixing.
- Evenly divide beef to rolls; top beef with cheese slices. Put sandwiches on a baking sheet.
- Bake till cheese melts and sandwiches are toasted for 3 minutes. Put soup mixture on sandwiches; top 1 tablespoon of pepper rings on each sandwich.

Nutrition Information

- Calories: 436 calories;
- Total Fat: 17.1
- Sodium: 2146
- Total Carbohydrate: 41
- Cholesterol: 63
- Protein: 32.7

---

515. Easy French Dip Sandwiches

Serving: 4 | Prep: 5mins | Cook: 10mins | Ready in:

Ingredients

- 1 (10.5 ounce) can beef consomme
- 1 cup water
- 1 pound thinly sliced deli roast beef
- 8 slices provolone cheese
- 4 hoagie rolls, split lengthwise

Direction

- Preheat an oven to 175°C/350°F. Open hoagie rolls; lay on a baking sheet.
- In a medium saucepan, heat water and beef consommé on medium high heat to create rich beef broth. Put roast beef in broth; warm for 3 minutes. Put meat on hoagie rolls; put 2 provolone slices on each roll.

- In the preheated oven, bake sandwiches for 5 minutes till cheese just starts to melt. Serves sandwich with the small bowls of warm broth for a dip.

Nutrition Information

- Calories: 548 calories;
- Total Fat: 22.6
- Sodium: 2310
- Total Carbohydrate: 40.5
- Cholesterol: 94
- Protein: 44.6

---

516. Fabulous Zucchini Grinders

Serving: 4 | Prep: 20mins | Cook: 30mins | Ready in:

Ingredients

- Marinara Sauce:
- 1 tablespoon olive oil
- 2 cloves garlic, peeled and coarsely chopped
- 1 pinch crushed red pepper flakes
- 1 tablespoon chopped fresh basil
- 1 teaspoon red wine vinegar
- 1 teaspoon white sugar
- 1 (14.5 ounce) can diced tomatoes
- salt and pepper to taste
- Grinders:
- 1 tablespoon butter
- 2 medium zucchini, cubed
- 1 pinch red pepper flakes
- salt and pepper to taste
- 1 1/2 cups shredded mozzarella cheese
- 4 (6 inch) French or Italian sandwich rolls, split

Direction

- For marinara sauce: In a saucepan on medium heat, heat olive oil. Put in red pepper flakes, basil, and garlic; cook and mix 1-2 minutes until fragrant. Mix in pepper, salt, vinegar,

and sugar. Put in tomatoes with their juices; simmer 15 minutes on low heat. Take away from heat. Transfer to a blender or food processor; puree until smooth.
- Set oven to 175° C (350° F) and start preheating.
- In a skillet on medium heat, melt butter. In butter, cook zucchini until lightly tender and browned. Season with pepper, salt, and red pepper flakes.
- Spoon a generous amount of zucchini mixture into each sandwich roll. Add 1/4 cup marinara sauce to each roll to cover zucchini. Place a handful of shredded mozzarella atop. Close rolls; use aluminum foil to wrap each.
- Place in the preheated oven and bake 15 minutes, till cheese is melted, rolls are soft, and bread is heated through.

Nutrition Information

- Calories: 339 calories;
- Total Carbohydrate: 37.3
- Cholesterol: 35
- Protein: 16.9
- Total Fat: 15.1
- Sodium: 729

---

517. Festival Style Grilled Italian Sausage Sandwiches

Serving: 4 | Prep: 20mins | Cook: 10mins | Ready in:

Ingredients

- 4 (4 ounce) links hot Italian sausage
- 1 red bell pepper, halved and seeded
- 1 small onion, peeled and cut in half crosswise
- 2 teaspoons olive oil
- salt and pepper to taste
- 1 tablespoon olive oil
- 4 (6 inch) sandwich rolls, split and toasted

Direction

- Set an outdoor grill for medium heat and start preheating. Coat the grate lightly with oil and place 4 inches from the heat source.
- Use a fork to pierce in several places of the sausages, then put aside. Cut the bottoms off the onion halves to let them sit flat on the grill. Brush 2 teaspoons of olive oil over onion halves and bell pepper.
- On the prepared grill, arrange peppers, onions, and sausages. Turn and cook the sausages until juices from them run clear and the sausages are browned nicely. Cook the vegetables until they become tender and the peppers are charred slightly. Take the sausages and vegetables out of the grill.
- Fill a paper bag with the peppers, seal, and let it slightly cool. Then remove the charred skin from the peppers and throw away; cut the peppers into strips. Cut the onion halves into slices. Put pepper and salt to taste, and a tablespoon of olive oil into a bowl. Add onions and peppers, then toss them until coated evenly. In the sandwich rolls, arrange the sausages, then place the onion and pepper mixture on top to serve.

Nutrition Information

- Calories: 631 calories;
- Total Fat: 33.7
- Sodium: 1258
- Total Carbohydrate: 56.2
- Cholesterol: 61
- Protein: 27

518. Giardino Grinder

Serving: 8 | Prep: 20mins | Cook: 25mins | Ready in:

Ingredients

- 1 tablespoon olive oil
- 1 onion, sliced
- 2 eggplants, peeled and sliced into rings
- 2 zucchini, peeled and sliced
- 1 cup sliced mushrooms
- salt
- 2 tablespoons Marsala wine
- 3 ciabatta sandwich rolls, sliced horizontally
- 1/4 cup garlic basil spread (see footnote for recipe link)
- 1/4 cup garlic roasted tomato spread (see footnote for recipe link)
- 1/4 cup artichoke aioli (see footnote for recipe link)
- 1 pound shredded mozzarella cheese

Direction

- Set the oven to 500°F (260°C) for preheating.
- In a Dutch oven or large pot, heat the olive oil over medium heat. Cook and stir the onion for 5 minutes until it starts to turn translucent and soften. Add the eggplant. Cook for 1 minute until the eggplant already absorbed some oil. Stir in zucchini. Cook for 1-2 minutes until softened. Stir in salt and mushrooms. Cook and stir for 3-4 minutes until the mushrooms have softened.
- Add Marsala wine to the eggplant mixture. Bring the mixture to a boil while scraping all the browned bits in the pan's bottom. Cook for 2-3 minutes until the wine has slightly reduced.
- Spread 1 tbsp. of garlic basil spread, 1 tbsp. of artichoke aioli, and 1 tbsp. of garlic roasted tomato sauce on each of the ciabatta rolls. Place 1/4 pound of mozzarella cheese on the top. Divide the eggplant mixture among the 4 sandwiches evenly.
- Arrange sandwiches onto the baking sheet. Bake inside the preheated oven for 3-4 minutes until the bread has toasted and the cheese has melted.

Nutrition Information

- Calories: 672 calories;
- Total Fat: 17
- Sodium: 1373
- Total Carbohydrate: 97.7

- Cholesterol: 36
- Protein: 30.9

---

519. Grilled Margherita® Pepperoni On Focaccia With Sun Dried Tomato Olio

Serving: 4 | Prep: 5mins | Cook: 10mins | Ready in:

Ingredients

- Sun-dried Tomato Olio:
- 6 tablespoons sun-dried tomato pesto
- 2 tablespoons mayonnaise
- 1 tablespoon extra-virgin olive oil
- 8 ounces sliced Margherita® Sandwich Pepperoni
- 4 focaccia rolls (3.5 oz. each), sliced in half
- 6 ounces sliced aged provolone cheese
- 2 cups baby arugula

Direction

- To make the sun-dried tomato olio: Put olive oil, mayonnaise and the sun-dried tomato pesto together in a small bowl then stir well until they really blend.
- Fry the Margherita® Pepperoni over low heat in a medium saucepan for 1 to 2 minutes per side or till edges start to curl.
- Grill or toast sliced focaccia until it gets crispy.
- Layer pepperoni and cheese on the bottom slices of focaccia bread. Make sure there are equal pepperoni and cheese among the 4 sandwiches. For melted cheese, put built sandwich bottoms on a baking sheet. Put the baking sheet into an oven and bake at 225° till cheese melts, about 3-5 minutes.
- Get sandwich bottoms out of oven. Lay sun-dried tomato olio on pepperoni and melted cheese, then put baby arugula on top, lastly make a whole sandwich by closing with top half of bread.

Nutrition Information

- Calories: 694 calories;
- Total Fat: 48.4
- Sodium: 1746
- Total Carbohydrate: 33.9
- Cholesterol: 83
- Protein: 28.9

---

520. Hot Buffalo Chicken, Bacon, And Cheese Sandwich

Serving: 8 | Prep: 10mins | Cook: 30mins | Ready in:

Ingredients

- 6 slices bacon
- 1/2 cup mayonnaise
- 1/4 cup sour cream
- 2 tablespoons hot buffalo wing sauce
- 1 loaf Italian bread, cut in half lengthwise
- 3 cups shredded meat from a rotisserie chicken
- 8 slices pepperjack cheese
- 1/4 cup roasted red bell peppers, drained and sliced (optional)

Direction

- Turn oven to 325°F (165°C) to preheat.
- Cook bacon over medium-high heat in a large, deep skillet until all sides are browned, flipping occasionally. Transfer bacon to a plate lined with paper towels to drain.
- In a small mixing bowl, stir together hot sauce, sour cream, and mayonnaise. Spread mayonnaise mixture onto both halves of the bread. Arrange chicken on the bottom bread half. Place bacon and then cheese over chicken. Fold the top half of the bread over the bottom to close the sandwich; use foil to wrap sandwich.
- Bake in the preheated oven for 20 to 25 minutes. If desired, arrange one layer of red pepper slices atop cheese and bacon. Slice sandwich into slices to serve.

Nutrition Information

- Calories: 566 calories;
- Sodium: 988
- Total Carbohydrate: 44.3
- Cholesterol: 77
- Protein: 27.9
- Total Fat: 30.1

---

521.   Hot Pat

Serving: 8 | Prep: 20mins | Cook: 15mins | Ready in:

Ingredients

- 1 tablespoon canola oil
- 1 head cabbage, chopped
- 2 tablespoons garlic basil spread (see footnote for recipe link)
- 1 cup sauerkraut
- 1/2 cup sweet hot mustard
- 1 pound sliced pastrami
- 2 cups shredded Swiss cheese
- 4 Italian-style hoagie buns, split lengthwise and toasted
- 1/4 cup spicy brown mustard
- 16 slices Swiss cheese
- 1/2 onion, diced
- 2 tomatoes, cut into wedges

Direction

- Heat oil over medium heat in a Dutch oven or large pot; cook while stirring garlic basil spread and cabbage in heated oil for about 5 minute or until cabbage starts to become tender. Stir in pastrami, sweet hot mustard, and sauerkraut; cook while stirring for 3 to 4 minutes until hot. Add 2 cups shredded Swiss cheese; cook for 2 to 3 minutes or until cheese melts.
- Spread 1 tablespoon spicy brown mustard onto each hoagie bun. Place 4 slices of Swiss

cheese over mustard layer and divide pastrami mixture equally among the sandwiches. Scatter with diced onion and place tomato wedges on top.

Nutrition Information

- Calories: 679 calories;
- Protein: 43.6
- Total Fat: 33.8
- Sodium: 1301
- Total Carbohydrate: 51.1
- Cholesterol: 116

---

522.   Italian Cheesesteak Sandwich

Serving: 4 | Prep: 15mins | Cook: 15mins | Ready in:

Ingredients

- 1 tablespoon butter
- 1 medium onion, thinly sliced
- 1 cup sliced fresh mushrooms
- 1 green bell pepper, thinly sliced
- 1 pinch salt
- 1 clove garlic, minced
- 1/2 pound very thinly sliced or shaved steak
- 1 (24 ounce) jar RAGÚ® Old World Style® Traditional Sauce
- 1 teaspoon dried Italian seasoning
- 1/2 teaspoon crushed red pepper flakes
- 4 Italian bread rolls
- 1 clove garlic
- 1 tablespoon extra-virgin olive oil
- 1/3 pound provolone or fresh mozzarella cheese, sliced
- 1/2 cup fresh basil leaves, torn

Direction

- In a big skillet, melt butter on medium heat. Add a pinch of salt, green peppers, mushrooms and onions; sauté for 2-3 minutes till veggies start to soften. Add minced garlic; cook for 1 minute.

- Push vegetables to 1 side of skillet; add sliced meat in open area. Sauté for 2-3 minutes till not pink.
- Heat Ragu Old World Style Traditional Sauce, crushed red pepper and Italian seasoning in another saucepan on medium heat.
- Put oven rack 6-inches away from heat source; preheat oven's broiler.
- Lengthwise, slice rolls. Put on a baking sheet, opened. Toast under broiler on low heat for 30 seconds; watch carefully to not burn. Take out of oven; rub cut side of whole garlic clove on toasted roll sides. Lightly brush with olive oil.
- Fold the cheese slices in meat and pepper/onion mix; mix till cheese starts to melt. Divide to toasted roll bottoms. Put a generous spoonful of Ragu sauce on top; save the rest for dipping if you want.
- Sprinkle fresh basil on; immediately serve.

Nutrition Information

- Calories: 608 calories;
- Sodium: 1450
- Total Carbohydrate: 57.7
- Cholesterol: 64
- Protein: 29.7
- Total Fat: 28.5

---

523.   Italian Heroes

Serving: 4 | Prep: 10mins | Cook: | Ready in:

Ingredients

- 1 (14 ounce) can marinated artichoke hearts, drained
- 2 cloves garlic, peeled
- 1/4 cup extra-virgin olive oil
- 4 (6 inch) French sandwich rolls
- 3/4 cup sliced roasted red peppers
- 2 cups arugula leaves or spring mix

- 8 ounces thinly sliced hard salami
- 8 ounces thinly sliced provolone cheese
- 4 pepperoncini peppers, drained and chopped (optional)
- 1/2 cup sliced black olives (optional)
- 1/2 red onion, thinly sliced (optional)

Direction

- Process olive oil, garlic and artichoke hearts till smooth in a food processor/blender. Season to taste with pepper and salt.
- Lengthwise, slice sandwich rolls in halve; pull most of soft bread out from bottom and top. On each side of every roll, spread artichoke paste. Put layers of onion, olives, pepperoncini, provolone cheese, salami, arugula and red peppers on rolls. Press the sandwiches together; tightly wrap with aluminum foil.
- Put sandwiches in the fridge; put something heavy over like a plate with cans on top or weighted containers over it (i.e, cottage cheese). Chill for a maximum of 3 hours then unwrap; halve and serve.

Nutrition Information

- Calories: 1068 calories;
- Sodium: 3762
- Total Carbohydrate: 96.3
- Cholesterol: 95
- Protein: 48.3
- Total Fat: 56

---

524.   Italian Smoked Sausage Sandwich

Serving: 4 | Prep: 5mins | Cook: 15mins | Ready in:

Ingredients

- 1 (14 ounce) package Hillshire Farm® Smoked Sausage, cut into 1-inch pieces

- 1/2 cup thinly sliced yellow onion
- 1 cup thinly sliced red bell pepper
- 1 cup tomato sauce
- 4 hoagie buns
- 1 cup shredded mozzarella cheese

Direction

- Set oven to 425°F to preheat.
- Bring a large skillet to medium-high heat. Cook peppers, onions and sausage into the tomato sauce, stirring frequently, for 8 to 10 minutes. Scoop sausage mixture into buns and arrange on a baking sheet; add shredded cheese over the top. Bake in the preheated oven just until cheese is melted, for 3 to 5 minutes.

Nutrition Information

- Calories: 822 calories;
- Total Carbohydrate: 80
- Cholesterol: 80
- Protein: 31.9
- Total Fat: 39.9
- Sodium: 2104

525.   Italian Subs Restaurant Style

Serving: 8 | Prep: 20mins | Cook: | Ready in:

Ingredients

- 1 head red leaf lettuce, rinsed and torn
- 2 medium fresh tomatoes, chopped
- 1 medium red onion, chopped
- 6 tablespoons olive oil
- 2 tablespoons white wine vinegar
- 2 tablespoons chopped fresh parsley
- 2 cloves garlic, chopped
- 1 teaspoon dried basil
- 1/4 teaspoon red pepper flakes
- 1 pinch dried oregano

- 1/2 pound sliced Capacola sausage
- 1/2 pound thinly sliced Genoa salami
- 1/4 pound thinly sliced prosciutto
- 1/2 pound sliced provolone cheese
- 4 submarine rolls, split
- 1 cup dill pickle slices

Direction

- Toss onion, tomatoes and lettuce in a big bow. Whisk oregano, red pepper flakes, basil, garlic, parsley, white wine vinegar and olive oil in another bowl. Put on salad; toss to evenly coat. Refrigerate for 1 hour.
- Spread submarine rolls open; evenly layer provolone cheese, prosciutto, salami and capicola on each roll. Put some salad and pickle slices as many as desired on top. Close rolls; serve.

Nutrition Information

- Calories: 708 calories;
- Protein: 29.2
- Total Fat: 47.3
- Sodium: 2083
- Total Carbohydrate: 40.4
- Cholesterol: 79

526.   Joanne's Super Hero Sandwich

Serving: 6 | Prep: 20mins | Cook: | Ready in:

Ingredients

- 1/2 cup olive oil
- 1 tablespoon lemon juice
- 3 tablespoons tarragon vinegar
- 3 cloves garlic, minced
- 2 tablespoons chopped fresh parsley
- 2 teaspoons dried oregano
- 1/2 teaspoon black pepper
- 1 cup black olives, chopped

- 1 cup mushrooms, chopped
- 1 (1 pound) loaf round, crusty Italian bread
- 1/2 pound sliced deli turkey meat
- 1/2 pound sliced ham
- 1/4 pound sliced salami
- 1/2 pound sliced mozzarella cheese
- 6 leaves lettuce
- 1 tomato, sliced

Direction

- Mix together garlic, vinegar, lemon juice and olive oil in a medium bowl. Add pepper, oregano and parsley to season. Whisk in mushrooms and olives. Put aside.
- Cut off the top half of the bread. Spoon out the inside part while leaving 1/2" of the outside wall. Scoop two-thirds of olive mixture into the bottom of the bread. Place layers of turkey, ham, salami, mozzarella, lettuce and tomato. Transfer the rest of olive mixture over and put back the top half of the bread. Use plastic wrap to wrap securely, then leave in the fridge overnight.

Nutrition Information

- Calories: 683 calories;
- Cholesterol: 92
- Protein: 34.3
- Total Fat: 40.2
- Sodium: 2182
- Total Carbohydrate: 46.1

527. Johnsonville Italian Sausage, Onions & Peppers Skillet

Serving: 4 | Prep: 20mins | Cook: 15mins | Ready in:

Ingredients

- 1 (22 ounce) package frozen Johnsonville® Mild Italian Sausage Slices

- 1 medium green bell pepper, thinly sliced
- 1 medium red bell pepper, thinly sliced
- 1 medium onion, thinly sliced
- 2 cloves garlic, minced
- 1 tablespoon olive oil
- 1 (14.5 ounce) can diced tomatoes with basil, garlic and oregano
- 1/4 teaspoon red pepper flakes
- Hoagie or sub rolls (optional)

Direction

- In a big skillet, sauté garlic, onion, peppers, and sausage in oil, about 10 minutes till vegetables are tender.
- Put in pepper flakes and tomatoes; stir and cook until heated through, about 5 minutes.
- Serve on rolls if wished.

Nutrition Information

- Calories: 516 calories;
- Protein: 31
- Total Fat: 49
- Sodium: 2119
- Total Carbohydrate: 26.2
- Cholesterol: 111

528. Lamb Grinder

Serving: 4 | Prep: 1hours | Cook: 1hours55mins | Ready in:

Ingredients

- Roast Lamb:
- 1/4 cup kosher salt
- 1/4 cup freshly ground black pepper
- 1/4 cup Italian seasoning
- 2 tablespoons dried rosemary
- 2 tablespoons granulated garlic
- 2 tablespoons granulated onion
- 1 tablespoon lemon pepper
- 1 (4 pound) boneless leg of lamb

- 1 lemon, juiced
- 1 tablespoon olive oil
- 1 tablespoon red wine
- 1 tablespoon Worcestershire sauce
- 2 cups dry white wine
- 2 cups chicken stock
- 4 cloves garlic, crushed
- 3 bay leaves
- 2 tablespoons capers
- 2 anchovy fillets, diced (optional)
- Horseradish Cream:
- 1 cup sour cream
- 1/4 cup prepared horseradish
- 2 tablespoons sweet hot mustard
- 1 tablespoon garlic basil spread (see footnote for recipe link)
- Filling:
- 2 tablespoons olive oil
- 2 onions, sliced
- 1/4 cup Marsala wine
- 1 cup sliced mushrooms
- 1/2 cup Kalamata olives, pitted and sliced in half
- 2 tablespoons minced garlic
- 2 teaspoons chopped fresh rosemary
- 2 teaspoons red pepper flakes
- Assembly:
- 4 Italian-style hoagie buns, split lengthwise
- 1 head romaine lettuce, chopped - divided
- 2 cups halved cherry tomatoes, divided
- 1 cup shredded Asiago cheese, divided
- 1 cup crumbled feta cheese, divided

Direction

- Set the oven at 325°F (165°C) and start preheating.
- In a small bowl, mix together lemon pepper, granulated onion, granulated garlic, dried rosemary, Italian seasoning, black pepper and kosher salt.
- In a large roasting pan, put lamb. Rub Worcestershire sauce, red wine, 1 tablespoon of olive oil and lemon juice between any crevices and on all sides. Sprinkle the kosher salt mixture over and rub on all sides. Transfer anchovies, capers, bay leaves, 4 crushed garlic

cloves, chicken stock and white wine into the bottom of the roasting pan.
- Use heavy-duty aluminum foil to cover the pan tightly; roast the lamb for 1 1/2-2 hours in the preheated oven, till tender but still pink in the center. An instant-read thermometer should register 130°F (54°C) when inserted into the center of the meat.
- Take the lamb away and place on a cutting board; let cool slightly before slicing. Move the meat into a large bowl; toss with some of the pan juices to remain its moisture. Set the remaining pan juice aside.
- Turn the oven temperature up to 500°F (260°C).
- In a small bowl, stir together garlic basil spread, mustard, horseradish and sour cream till well combined. Refrigerate with a cover.
- Place a Dutch oven or a large pot on medium-high heat; heat 2 tablespoons of olive oil; cook while stirring onions for around 12 minutes, or till beginning to turn golden and soften. Put in Marsala wine; cook for around 5 minutes, or till reduced.
- Mix in red pepper flakes, fresh rosemary, 2 tablespoons of minced garlic, Kalamata olives and mushrooms; cook while stirring for around 5 minutes, or till the mushrooms are softened. Put in the reserved pan juices and the lamb slices. Cook while stirring to mix for around 10 minutes, or till heated through.
- Spread horseradish sauce over each hoagie bun. Spoon the lamb mixture into the buns; top each sandwich with a quarter of the lettuce, cherry tomatoes, Asiago cheese, and feta cheese. Serve accompanied with the remaining pan juices for a dipping.

Nutrition Information

- Calories: 1614 calories;
- Cholesterol: 270
- Protein: 84.9
- Total Fat: 81.5
- Sodium: 8796
- Total Carbohydrate: 110.6

529.   Meatball Grinder

Serving: 8 | Prep: 1hours | Cook: 40mins | Ready in:

Ingredients

- Meatballs:
- 1 cup soft bread crumbs
- 1 cup dry bread crumbs
- 1/2 cup milk
- 1 pound ground beef
- 1 pound sweet Italian sausage
- 1 cup prepared marinara sauce
- 2 eggs
- 1 tablespoon minced garlic
- 1 tablespoon Italian seasoning
- 1 teaspoon red pepper flakes
- 1 cup olive oil for frying
- 1 cup prepared marinara sauce
- Filling:
- 1 tablespoon olive oil
- 1 onion, sliced
- 1 red bell pepper, sliced
- 1 serrano pepper, sliced
- 2 tablespoons Marsala wine
- salt and ground black pepper to taste
- Assembly:
- 4 Italian-style hoagie buns, split lengthwise
- 1 cup mascarpone cheese, divided
- 1/4 cup garlic basil spread (see footnote for recipe link)
- 4 cups shredded mozzarella cheese, divided
- 1/2 cup chopped fresh basil, divided
- 1/2 cup grated Parmesan cheese, divided

Direction

- Start preheating the oven to 500°F (260°C).
- In a large bowl, combine dry breadcrumbs, milk and soft breadcrumbs. Let soak for 10 minutes until breadcrumbs absorb most of milk. Put in red pepper flakes, Italian seasoning, garlic, eggs, one cup of the marinara sauce, Italian sausage and ground beef. Mix until combined thoroughly. Shape into 16 large meatballs.
- In a Dutch oven or large pot, heat one cup of the olive oil over medium-high heat. Cook meatballs for 10 minutes until browned. Place onto the baking sheet. Bake in prepared oven for 10 minutes until middle is no longer pink.
- In a large saucepan, simmer one cup of the marinara sauce over medium heat. Put in cooked meatballs; heat through for 5 minutes.
- In a large skillet, heat one tablespoon of the olive oil over medium-high heat. In hot oil, cook while stirring serrano pepper, red bell pepper, and onion for 5-6 minutes until onion has soften. Put in black pepper, salt, and Marsala wine; cook for 10 minutes until the onion is golden and the wine is evaporated.
- Spread a quarter cup of mascarpone cheese and one tablespoon of the garlic basil spread over each hoagie bun. Arrange 4 meatballs and 1 spoonful of the marinara sauce over top. Sprinkle one cup of the mozzarella cheese over each sandwich.
- Put the sandwiches into the baking sheet. Bake in prepared oven for 5 minutes until the buns are toasted and cheese melts. Add a quarter of the onion mixture on top of each sandwich; decorate every sandwich with 2 tablespoons Parmesan cheese and 2 tablespoons basil.

Nutrition Information

- Calories: 986 calories;
- Total Fat: 60.6
- Sodium: 1789
- Total Carbohydrate: 64.6
- Cholesterol: 189
- Protein: 44.7

530.   Meatball Sub Sandwich

Serving: 4 | Prep: 30mins | Cook: 30mins | Ready in:

Ingredients

- 5 Ball Park® Tailgaters Brat Buns
- 1 pound lean ground beef
- 1/4 cup milk
- 1 egg
- 2 tablespoons grated Parmesan cheese
- 1 teaspoon Italian seasoning
- 1/2 teaspoon onion powder
- 1/2 teaspoon garlic powder
- salt and pepper to taste
- 1 (24 ounce) jar marinara sauce
- 1 cup arugula
- 4 tablespoons shredded mozzarella cheese
- Chopped fresh basil or crushed red pepper for garnish

Direction

- Set oven to 425°F to preheat.
- Toast 1 bun until it turns golden brown; put into a blender and chop until finely crumbly.
- Transfer bread crumbs to a large bowl and pour in milk. Allow to soak for 5 minutes.
- Mix pepper, salt, garlic powder, onion powder, Italian seasoning, Parmesan, eggs and ground beef into the bread crumb mixture until thoroughly incorporated.
- Distribute mixture into 16 golf ball-sized meatballs, and arrange on a greased baking pan.
- Bake meatballs in the preheated oven for 10 minutes.
- While baking meatballs, heat marinara sauce over medium-high heat in a large pot. Put in cooked meatballs and simmer for 15 minutes.
- In the meantime, toast the rest of buns; divide over the top of each bun with spinach or arugula, meatballs and mozzarella.
- Garnish on top with crushed red pepper (optional) and chopped basil. Enjoy!

Nutrition Information

- Calories: 768 calories;
- Protein: 35.7
- Total Fat: 34
- Sodium: 1363

- Total Carbohydrate: 75.2
- Cholesterol: 143

---

531. Mediterranean Chicken Sandwich

Serving: 8 | Prep: 40mins | Cook: 20mins | Ready in:

Ingredients

- 4 skinless, boneless chicken breast halves , cut into cubes
- 1 tablespoon olive oil
- 1 tablespoon minced garlic
- 1 teaspoon red pepper flakes
- 1 pinch salt and freshly ground black pepper to taste
- 1 yellow bell pepper, diced
- 1 onion, diced
- 1/4 cup pitted kalamata olives, diced
- 1/4 cup capers, drained
- 1 cup halved cherry tomatoes
- 1 pound shredded mozzarella cheese
- 1 cup crumbled feta cheese
- 4 Italian-style hoagie buns, split lengthwise and toasted
- 1/4 cup artichoke aioli (see footnote for recipe link)
- 1/4 cup chopped fresh basil

Direction

- In a big bowl, mix together black pepper, salt, red pepper flakes, garlic, olive oil and chicken; mix to coat.
- Place a Dutch oven or a big pot on medium-high heat. Add the chicken mixture and cook for 5 minutes until the middle of the chicken is not pink anymore, tossing often. Add onion and yellow bell pepper, cook for 5 minutes until the onion starts to get tender. Stir in capers and olives until blended. Mix in mozzarella cheese until melted. Take away from the heat and mix in feta cheese.

- Spread 1 tablespoon artichoke aioli over each hoagie roll. Evenly divide the chicken mixture between the 4 sandwiches. Sprinkle 1 tablespoon basil over each sandwich.

Nutrition Information

- Calories: 494 calories;
- Sodium: 1185
- Total Carbohydrate: 40.6
- Cholesterol: 85
- Protein: 34.7
- Total Fat: 20.8

532.   Muffuletta

Serving: 4 | Prep: 20mins | Cook: |Ready in:

Ingredients

- 1 cup pitted kalamata olives
- 1 cup pitted green olives
- 1/2 cup fresh basil leaves
- 1 tablespoon finely chopped garlic
- 1/4 cup olive oil
- 1 (1 pound) loaf Italian bread
- 1/2 pound thinly sliced Genoa salami
- 1/2 pound thinly sliced provolone cheese
- 3 tomatoes, sliced
- 1 large red onion, thinly sliced

Direction

- In a food processor/blender, process oil, garlic, basil, green olives and kalamata olives till chopped coarsely.
- Cut top from bread loaf; hollow center out. Leave 1/2-inch of crust. Evenly spread olive mixture inside of loaf; layer onion, tomatoes, cheese and salami till loaf is full.
- Put bread top on; press down lightly. Use plastic wrapping to tightly wrap. Refrigerate for at least 2 hours up to 1 day. Crosswise, slice to 1 1/2-inch pieces; serve.

Nutrition Information

- Calories: 1016 calories;
- Total Fat: 63.2
- Sodium: 3698
- Total Carbohydrate: 71.7
- Cholesterol: 96
- Protein: 40.2

533.   Muffuletta Sandwich

Serving: 4 | Prep: 15mins | Cook: |Ready in:

Ingredients

- 1 (1 pound) loaf fresh Italian bread
- 1/3 cup olive oil
- 1/3 cup grated Parmesan cheese
- 1 tablespoon dried basil
- 1 tablespoon dried oregano
- 8 oil-cured black olives, pitted and chopped
- 8 pitted green olives, chopped
- 1/4 pound thinly sliced salami
- 1/4 pound thinly sliced ham
- 1/2 pound provolone cheese, sliced
- 1/4 pound mozzarella cheese, sliced

Direction

- Cut the bread in two lengthwise. Sprinkle olive oil on each side. Drizzle both sides with basil, oregano and Parmesan cheese.
- On the lower half, layer chopped green olives and chopped black olives, add the salami, ham, mozzarella, and provolone. Finish with the top layer of bread. Slice into 4 portions.

Nutrition Information

- Calories: 975 calories;
- Total Fat: 59.9
- Sodium: 2790
- Total Carbohydrate: 61.3

- Cholesterol: 107
- Protein: 46.2

---

534.   Murica Dogs

Serving: 6 | Prep: 15mins | Cook: 20mins | Ready in:

Ingredients

- 6 Italian sausage links
- 2 teaspoons vegetable oil, or as needed
- 1 jalapeno pepper, diced small
- 3 tablespoons butter, or to taste, divided
- 1 large white onion, minced
- 2/3 cup kimchi, cut into thin strips
- 6 hoagie rolls, split lengthwise

Direction

- In a skillet, put the sausages; add enough water to cover sausages by 2/3 in the skillet. Boil the water. Cover and cook the sausages for 8-10 minutes until the middle is no longer pink, flipping every few minutes. The instant-read thermometer should register 160°F (70°C) when inserted into middle.
- In a separate skillet, add sufficient oil to just cover bottom, then heat over the medium-high heat. In hot oil, sauté the jalapeno pepper for 3-4 minutes until it has softened.
- In skillet, melt 2 tablespoons of the butter with jalapeno pepper. When the butter becomes hot, cook the onion until softened in the hot butter for 4-5 minutes. Lower the heat to medium-low, put in kimchi. Cook for 1-2 minutes until soft.
- Place the skillet with the sausages over medium heat. Add the onion mixture to skillet with sausages.
- Put now-empty skillet back to the medium heat. In skillet, melt enough butter to completely cover the bottom. Working in batches, grill the hoagie buns in skillet, if needed, putting butter between the batches, for 2-3 minutes on each side until toasted.
- Put 1 sausage into every toasted bun. Spoon over every sausage with the vegetable mixture.

Nutrition Information

- Calories: 732 calories;
- Sodium: 1848
- Total Carbohydrate: 74.4
- Cholesterol: 60
- Protein: 27
- Total Fat: 35.5

---

535.   Pittsburgh Style Sandwich

Serving: 1 | Prep: 10mins | Cook: 20mins | Ready in:

Ingredients

- 10 strips frozen French fried potatoes
- 2 slices Italian bread
- 5 slices deli cooked roast beef
- 2 slices provolone cheese
- 2 slices tomato
- 1/4 cup prepared coleslaw

Direction

- Preheat an oven and then prepare the French fries as directed on the package.
- Onto the Italian bread, spread a layer of freshly cooked fries, roast beef, coleslaw, provolone cheese, and tomato. Serve right away.

Nutrition Information

- Calories: 613 calories;
- Cholesterol: 111
- Protein: 49.3
- Total Fat: 25.3
- Sodium: 2397
- Total Carbohydrate: 47.6

536. Ponzu Chicken Sandwich

Serving: 8 | Prep: 30mins | Cook: 25mins | Ready in:

Ingredients

- 1 cup prepared ponzu sauce
- 1 cup chopped fresh cilantro
- 1/2 cup pineapple juice
- 4 fresh mint leaves, chopped
- 4 cloves garlic, crushed
- 1 tablespoon grated fresh ginger
- 1 tablespoon toasted sesame oil
- 1 tablespoon chili oil
- 1 teaspoon brown sugar
- 3 skinless, boneless chicken breast halves, cut into chunks
- 1 tablespoon olive oil
- 1 onion, sliced
- 1 red bell pepper, sliced
- 1 jalapeno pepper, sliced
- salt and freshly ground black pepper to taste
- 1 small head cabbage, shredded
- 4 Italian-style hoagie buns, split lengthwise and toasted
- 12 slices Swiss cheese
- 1/4 cup chopped fresh cilantro, divided
- 1 tablespoon sesame seeds, divided
- 1 tablespoon chile-garlic sauce (such as Sriracha®), or to taste - divided
- 1 lime, cut into wedges

Direction

- Prepare the oven by preheating to 500°F (260°C).
- In a large bowl, mix brown sugar, chili oil, sesame oil, fresh ginger, garlic, mint leaves, pineapple juice, 1 cup cilantro, and ponzu sauce. Put in chicken and toss to coat.
- Take the chicken from ponzu sauce mixture, set aside marinade. Set a large Dutch oven or pot over medium-high heat. Put in chicken and cook for about 5 minutes until browned, stirring frequently. Mix in black pepper, salt, jalapeno pepper, red bell pepper, onion, and olive oil. Stir and cook for about 5 minutes until the onion has turned translucent and softened.
- Put reserved marinade into chicken mixture and bring to a boil. Mix in cabbage and cook for 4-5 minutes until slightly wilted.
- Place chicken mixture into toasted hoagie buns using a slotted spoon and put 3 slices Swiss cheese on each top of the sandwich.
- Transfer sandwiches to a baking sheet and put in the preheated oven and bake for about 5 minutes until buns are toasted and cheese melts. Decorate each sandwich with 1/4 of the chile-garlic sauce, 1/4 of the sesame seeds, and 2 tablespoons cilantro. Serve with lime wedges.

Nutrition Information

- Calories: 516 calories;
- Total Fat: 21.7
- Sodium: 1354
- Total Carbohydrate: 52.3
- Cholesterol: 61
- Protein: 28.2

537. Portabella Basil Sub

Serving: 1 | Prep: 23mins | Cook: 7mins | Ready in:

Ingredients

- 1 tablespoon butter
- 1/4 cup chopped red shallots
- 2 tablespoons chopped fresh basil leaves
- 1 tablespoon minced fresh garlic
- 1 teaspoon hot paprika
- 1 teaspoon salt
- 1 teaspoon fresh ground black pepper
- 1 cup fresh spinach leaves
- 1/4 cup diced portabella mushroom caps
- 1/4 cup diced yellow bell pepper

- 1 tablespoon sweet Jamaican pepper sauce (such as Pickapeppa Sauce ®)
- 1 tablespoon balsamic vinegar
- 1 hoagie roll, split lengthwise

Direction

- In a lidded skillet, heat butter on medium heat until melted; cook, stirring, garlic, basil and red shallots for about 60 seconds until aromatic. Mix in pepper, salt and hot paprika. Add in yellow bell pepper, portabella mushrooms and spinach, whisk several times; cover and lower the heat to medium-low. Cook mixture for about 4 minutes until mushrooms and spinach are wilted and peppers are tender.
- Take off the lid of the skillet and add in balsamic vinegar, along with pepper sauce. Raise the heat to medium; simmer and let mixture thicken a little for about 2 minutes.
- Scoop hot mushroom mixture over the split hoagie roll; serve.

Nutrition Information

- Calories: 568 calories;
- Sodium: 3200
- Total Carbohydrate: 85.8
- Cholesterol: 31
- Protein: 15.4
- Total Fat: 18.9

538.   Pulled Pork Pesto Sandwich

Serving: 8 | Prep: 1hours | Cook: 3hours27mins | Ready in:

Ingredients

- Pulled Pork:
- 1/4 cup kosher salt
- 1/4 cup freshly ground black pepper

- 1/4 cup Italian seasoning
- 2 tablespoons dried rosemary
- 2 tablespoons granulated garlic
- 2 tablespoons granulated onion
- 1 tablespoon red pepper flakes
- 1 tablespoon lemon pepper
- 1 (4 pound) pork shoulder roast
- 1 lemon, juiced
- 1 tablespoon olive oil
- 1 tablespoon red wine vinegar
- 1 tablespoon Worcestershire sauce
- 2 cups dry white wine
- 1 cup chicken stock
- 4 cloves garlic, crushed
- Filling:
- 1 tablespoon olive oil
- 2 goat horn peppers, or other hot green chiles, sliced
- 1 red bell pepper, sliced
- 1 onion, sliced
- 1 tablespoon Italian seasoning
- 1 teaspoon red pepper flakes
- salt and freshly ground black pepper to taste
- 1 cup sliced mushrooms
- 1/4 cup garlic basil spread (see footnote for recipe link)
- 1/4 cup Marsala wine
- 1 cup prepared pesto sauce
- Assembly:
- 4 Italian-style hoagie buns, split lengthwise
- 2 cups shredded mozzarella cheese, divided
- 1 cup halved cherry tomatoes, divided
- 1/2 cup chopped fresh basil, divided

Direction

- Turn the oven to 300°F (150°C) to preheat.
- In a bowl, mix together lemon pepper, 1 tablespoon red pepper flakes, granulated onion, granulated garlic, rosemary, 1/4 cup Italian seasoning, 1/4 cup black pepper and kosher salt.
- In a big roasting pan, put the pork shoulder. Rub between any crevices and on all sides with Worcestershire sauce, red wine vinegar, 1 tablespoon olive oil and lemon juice. Sprinkle the kosher salt mixture over and rub onto all

266

sides. Add 4 crushed garlic cloves, chicken stock and white wine to the bottom of the roasting pan.

- Put heavy-duty aluminum foil onto the pan to cover tightly. In the preheated oven, roast the pork for 3-4 hours until soft and an inserted thermometer displays 200°F (95°C). Remove the pork to a cutting board and let it cool slightly, and then pull it. Shred the pork shoulder into bite-sized pieces with 2 forks. Remove the meat to a big bowl and mix with some of the pan juices so it stays moist.
- Raise the oven temperature to 500°F (260°C).
- In a Dutch oven or a big pot, heat 1 tablespoon olive oil over medium-high heat. In the hot oil, stir and cook black pepper, salt, 1 teaspoon red pepper flakes, 1 tablespoon Italian seasoning, onion, red bell pepper and goat horn peppers for 12 minutes until the onion starts to turn golden and gets tender.
- Mix in Marsala wine, garlic basil spread and mushrooms and cook for 5 minutes until the mushrooms are tender and the wine decreases. Stir pesto sauce and pulled pork into the vegetables and thoroughly heat for 10 minutes. Put the pork mixture into hoagie buns using a spoon and put 1/2 cup mozzarella cheese on top of each.
- On a baking sheet, put the sandwiches and put in the hot oven to bake for 5 minutes until the bread has toasted and the cheese has melted. Put basil and cherry tomatoes on top.

Nutrition Information

- Calories: 885 calories;
- Sodium: 4083
- Total Carbohydrate: 52.9
- Cholesterol: 118
- Protein: 43.9
- Total Fat: 50.3

539. Pulled Pork Pub Subs

Serving: 4 | Prep: 5mins | Cook: 4hours10mins | Ready in:

Ingredients

- 1 (23 ounce) Smithfield® Garlic & Herb Seasoned Pork Sirloin
- 1 cup shredded provolone cheese, or as needed
- 2 tablespoons chopped fresh oregano
- 4 bakery sub rolls

Direction

- In a slow cooker, use water to just cover meat's top. Cook for 6 hours on medium/low or for 4 hours on high. You may use an oven on low temperature the same way.
- Use a fork to gently shred meat; fill rolls up.
- Top with some oregano/spices you like and cheese. Bake on a sheet pan with a sprinkle of spices for 10 minutes at 350° till subs are warmed through and cheese melts. Serve warm.

Nutrition Information

- Calories: 676 calories;
- Total Carbohydrate: 74.7
- Cholesterol: 102
- Protein: 47.3
- Total Fat: 21.5
- Sodium: 1692

540. Real N'awlins Muffuletta

Serving: 8 | Prep: 40mins | Cook: | Ready in:

Ingredients

- 1 cup pimento-stuffed green olives, crushed
- 1/2 cup drained kalamata olives, crushed
- 2 cloves garlic, minced

- 1/4 cup roughly chopped pickled cauliflower florets
- 2 tablespoons drained capers
- 1 tablespoon chopped celery
- 1 tablespoon chopped carrot
- 1/2 cup pepperoncini, drained
- 1/4 cup marinated cocktail onions
- 1/2 teaspoon celery seed
- 1 teaspoon dried oregano
- 1 teaspoon dried basil
- 3/4 teaspoon ground black pepper
- 1/4 cup red wine vinegar
- 1/2 cup olive oil
- 1/4 cup canola oil
- 2 (1 pound) loaves Italian bread
- 8 ounces thinly sliced Genoa salami
- 8 ounces thinly sliced cooked ham
- 8 ounces sliced mortadella
- 8 ounces sliced mozzarella cheese
- 8 ounces sliced provolone cheese

Direction

- Olive salad: mix canola oil, olive oil, vinegar, black pepper, basil, oregano, celery seed, cocktail onions, pepperoncini, carrot, celery, capers, cauliflower, garlic, kalamata olives and green olives in a medium bowl; put mixture in a glass jar/other nonreactive container. Put more oil to cover if needed. Cover container/jar; refrigerate at least overnight.
- Sandwiches: horizontally, cut bread loaves in half; hollow some excess bread out to create room for filling. Spread equal amounts of olive salad and oil on each bread pieces. Layer 1/2 of provolone, mozzarella, mortadella, ham and salami on bottom half of every loaf. Put top half on every loaf; slice sandwich to quarters.
- Immediate serve or tightly wrap and refrigerate for several hours to merge flavors and soak olive salad into bread.

Nutrition Information

- Calories: 987 calories;
- Total Fat: 62.8

- Sodium: 3465
- Total Carbohydrate: 63.2
- Cholesterol: 97
- Protein: 41.4

---

541. Roast Beef Subs With Balsamic Onions And Brie Cheese

Serving: 4 | Prep: 10mins | Cook: 35mins | Ready in:

Ingredients

- 1 pound top round beef, cut into 1-inch pieces
- 1 tablespoon Worcestershire sauce
- 2 teaspoons Montreal steak seasoning
- 1 tablespoon extra-virgin olive oil
- 2 small sweet onions, sliced
- 1/3 cup balsamic vinegar
- 1/4 teaspoon salt
- 1/4 teaspoon cracked black pepper
- 1 teaspoon canola oil
- 4 (6 inch) submarine sandwich roll, split
- 6 ounces Brie cheese, torn into pieces

Direction

- In a bowl, stir together Montreal steak seasoning, beef and Worcestershire sauce. While preparing the other items, marinate the beef.
- In skillet, heat olive oil over high heat. In the hot oil, cook while stirring the onions for 15 mins or until golden brown. Put in black pepper, salt and balsamic vinegar. Lower the heat to low, then cook at a simmer for 10 mins or until mixture has syrup-like texture and little liquid remains.
- Start preheating outdoor grill to 400°F (200°C). Oil grate lightly.
- Take the steak pieces out of marinade; shake any excess off. Put away remaining marinade. In a bowl, combine canola oil and beef; coat by tossing.

- Start preheating the oven to 200°F (95°C).
- On hot grill, cook the beef slices for 4-6 mins on each side, until they are juicy in middle and reddish-pink and begin to firm, turning frequently. The instant-read thermometer should register 130°F (54°C) when inserted into middle.
- Place the rolls on the baking sheet. Put the onions into bottom of sandwich rolls. Put in beef. Add Brie cheese over the beef.
- Heat in the prepared oven for 5 mins or until cheese melts.

Nutrition Information

- Calories: 575 calories;
- Total Fat: 26.7
- Sodium: 1380
- Total Carbohydrate: 45.7
- Cholesterol: 99
- Protein: 35.9

542.   Roasted Eggplant Subs

Serving: 4 | Prep: 15mins | Cook: 20mins | Ready in:

Ingredients

- 1 Reynolds® Oven Bag, large size
- Reynolds® Parchment Paper
- 1 tablespoon all-purpose flour
- 1 (1 pound) eggplant, quartered and sliced 1/4 inch thick
- 1 tablespoon olive oil
- 1/2 teaspoon salt
- 1/4 teaspoon black pepper
- 1 medium red onion, thinly sliced
- 4 whole wheat Italian-style rolls, split
- 4 ounces reduced-fat feta cheese, crumbled
- 2 ounces reduced-fat cream cheese
- 1/2 cup sliced roasted red pepper
- 1 cup baby romaine lettuce or mixed greens

Direction

- Set the oven to 350°F for preheating. Make sure it won't exceed up to 400°F. In a Reynolds® Large Oven Bag, place the flour and shake the bag. Set the bag in a 2-inches deep roasting pan.
- Drizzle the olive oil all over the eggplant. Sprinkle it with salt and pepper.
- Place the red onion and eggplant in the bag. Seal the bag using its corresponding tie. Make six 1/2-inch slits on top of the bag to let the steam escape. Tuck the ends of the bag in pan.
- Place the pan inside the oven. Make sure there is a space for the bag to expand while roasting to avoid touching the racks, heating elements, or walls. The bag must hang over the pan.
- Roast for 20 minutes until the vegetables turn tender.
- Use a Reynolds® Parchment Paper to line the baking sheet. Arrange the rolls onto the prepared baking sheet, cut-sides up. Mix the cream cheese and feta in a small bowl. Pour the cheese mixture over the cut sides of the roll tops. Bake inside the oven during the last 5 minutes of roasting.
- Get the eggplant and rolls from the oven. Cut the top of the oven bag open to serve. Take note to always set the bag over the pan. Arrange the onion and eggplant onto the roll bottoms. Place the romaine and red peppers on top. Enclose the sandwiches with the cheese-topped halves.

Nutrition Information

- Calories: 380 calories;
- Total Fat: 13.9
- Sodium: 1146
- Total Carbohydrate: 49.4
- Cholesterol: 18
- Protein: 16.5

543. Roasted Pork Banh Mi (Vietnamese Sandwich)

Serving: 1 | Prep: 25mins | Cook: 7mins | Ready in:

Ingredients

- 1/4 cup julienned (2-inch matchsticks) daikon radish
- 1/4 cup julienned (2-inch matchsticks) carrots
- 1 tablespoon seasoned rice vinegar
- 1/4 cup mayonnaise
- 1 teaspoon hoisin sauce, or to taste
- 1 teaspoon sriracha hot sauce, or more to taste
- 1 crusty French sandwich roll
- 4 ounces cooked pork roast, thinly sliced
- 2 ounces smooth pate, thinly sliced
- 6 thin spears English cucumber, diced
- 6 thin slices jalapeno pepper, or more to taste
- 1/4 cup cilantro leaves

Direction

- Set the oven for preheating to 400°F. Prepare a baking sheet lined with aluminum foil.
- Mix together the carrot and julienned daikon with seasoned rice vinegar and toss to coat well. Let the mixture stand for 15 to 20 minutes until the vegetables are a bit wilted. Drain. Place inside the fridge or just set aside.
- Combine together the sriracha, hoisin sauce and mayonnaise in a small bowl.
- Slice the French roll on the side just enough to open it like a book. To accommodate the filling better, scoop out some of the bread from the top half if preferred.
- Scoop a mayo mixture and spread the interior surfaces of the roll generously. Arrange the roll placing cut side up in the prepared baking sheet. Bake inside the preheated oven for about 7 minutes until edges begins to get brown, crisp, and heated through.
- Assemble sliced pork, jalapeno, cucumber, picked daikon and carrots, pate and cilantro leaves in the roll. Cut evenly into 2 portions and serve.

Nutrition Information

- Calories: 1263 calories;
- Sodium: 1994
- Total Carbohydrate: 91.3
- Cholesterol: 188
- Protein: 54.2
- Total Fat: 75.9

544. Roasted Red Pepper Sub

Serving: 3 | Prep: 10mins | Cook: 5mins | Ready in:

Ingredients

- 1 baguette, cut into 3 sub-size portions and then sliced open lengthwise
- 2 tablespoons olive oil
- 1 (8 ounce) can roasted red peppers, drained and chopped
- 2 tablespoons creamy goat cheese
- 2 teaspoons balsamic vinegar, or to taste
- 1/4 cup arugula
- 1/4 cup torn fresh basil leaves, or to taste

Direction

- Cut each baguette segment into lengthwise. Use olive oil to brush on the cut sides. Place in the toaster and toast for 2-4 minutes, to your wished darkness.
- In a saucepan over medium heat, heat red peppers for 2-3 minutes until hot.
- Place goat cheese onto the cut sides of each baguette piece and spread to thick layers. Scatter red peppers onto 3 of the baguette pieces. Drizzle balsamic vinegar over the red peppers; put basil and arugula on top. Put the rest segments of baguette on top of the fillings to complete the sandwiches.

Nutrition Information

- Calories: 452 calories;
- Sodium: 1034

- Total Carbohydrate: 68.7
- Cholesterol: 4
- Protein: 15.5
- Total Fat: 13

---

545.   Saucy Cheese Steak Hoagies

Serving: 6 | Prep: 5mins | Cook: 15mins | Ready in:

Ingredients

- 1 (24 ounce) jar Ragu® Old World Style® Traditional Pasta Sauce
- 1 tablespoon olive oil
- 2 cloves garlic, pressed
- 1 green bell pepper, sliced
- 1 red bell pepper, sliced
- 1 small yellow onion, sliced
- 1/2 pound deli sliced Angus roast beef
- 6 slices provolone cheese
- 6 hoagie buns

Direction

- Preheat an oven to 450°. Put sauce in a small saucepan; cover. Heat till just warm on low heat.
- Sauté onion, peppers, garlic and olive oil in a big skillet on medium high heat for 3-5 minutes till vegetables are soft. Remove vegetables from pan. Put roast beef in the skillet; sauté for 2-3 minutes till heated through on medium high heat.
- Make sandwiches: Lengthwise, open each hoagie bun; divide the roast beef slices on rolls. Top with 1 provolone cheese slice, 1/4 cup of Ragu Old World Style Traditional sauce and vegetables. Heat leftover sauce for dip if you want.
- Put hoagies on a baking sheet; bake till cheese melts for 3-5 minutes. Serve while hot.

Nutrition Information

- Calories: 637 calories;
- Protein: 28.6
- Total Fat: 20.3
- Sodium: 2075
- Total Carbohydrate: 83.5
- Cholesterol: 38

---

546.   Sausage Grinder

Serving: 8 | Prep: 15mins | Cook: 35mins | Ready in:

Ingredients

- 8 Italian sausage links
- 1 (16 ounce) jar marinara sauce for dipping
- 2 tablespoons olive oil
- 1 onion, sliced
- 1 red bell pepper, sliced
- 1 jalapeno pepper, sliced
- 1 goat horn pepper or other hot green chile, sliced
- 4 Italian-style hoagie buns, split lengthwise
- 1 (8 ounce) container mascarpone cheese, divided
- 1/4 cup garlic basil spread, divided (see footnote for recipe link)
- 1/2 cup grated Parmesan cheese

Direction

- Bring water in a large pot to a boil; cook sausages in boiling water for 10 to 12 minutes until inside is no longer pink. Drain off water and put to one side.
- Place marinara sauce over medium-low heat in a small saucepan; cook for about 5 minutes or until warmed through. Turn heat to low and keep the sauce warm while preparing sandwiches.
- Heat olive oil over medium-high heat in a large skillet. Cook while stirring goat horn pepper, jalapeno pepper, red bell pepper, and onion in heated oil for 7 to 8 minutes or until onion is tender and starts to turn golden.

Transfer onion mixture to a plate and put to one side.

- Put sausages in the hot skillet; cook for about 10 minutes, tossing often, until evenly browned and warmed through.
- Spread 1 tablespoon garlic basil spread and 1/4 cup mascarpone cheese onto each hoagie bun. Arrange 2 sausages on top and spread with onion mixture. Scatter with 2 tablespoons Parmesan cheese. Pour marinara sauce into small bowls for dipping.

Nutrition Information

- Calories: 715 calories;
- Total Fat: 46.7
- Sodium: 1675
- Total Carbohydrate: 48.4
- Cholesterol: 85
- Protein: 26

547.   Sausage, Pepper, And Onion Sandwiches

Serving: 25 | Prep: 15mins | Cook: 6hours15mins | Ready in:

Ingredients

- 5 pounds Italian sausage links
- 2 (28 ounce) cans whole peeled tomatoes
- 1 (28 ounce) can crushed tomatoes
- 1 (29 ounce) can tomato sauce
- 1/4 cup grated Parmesan cheese
- 1 tablespoon garlic powder
- 1 tablespoon Italian seasoning
- 1 tablespoon white sugar
- 1 tablespoon onion powder
- 4 large green bell peppers, thickly sliced
- 3 large onions, thickly sliced
- 25 (6 inch) Italian-style hoagie buns

Direction

- If needed, slice the sausages apart into separate links, then arrange the sausage links into a large skillet on medium, brown all sides of the sausage links. Put aside the sausages and save the pan drippings.
- Add tomato sauce, crushed tomatoes, and the whole tomatoes into a large saucepan covered with a lid; stir in onion powder, sugar, Italian seasoning, garlic powder, and the grated Parmesan cheese. Boil; then put in onions, green peppers, pan drippings, and the cooked sausages. Turn down the heat to low, put a cover on and bring to a simmer for 6 hours until the sauce becomes thick and the vegetables become very tender. Place on Italian hoagie buns and serve.

Nutrition Information

- Calories: 479 calories;
- Sodium: 1491
- Total Carbohydrate: 50.9
- Cholesterol: 36
- Protein: 20.6
- Total Fat: 21.5

548.   School Lunch Bagel Sandwich

Serving: 1 | Prep: 10mins | Cook: 5mins | Ready in:

Ingredients

- 1 tablespoon herb and garlic flavored cream cheese
- 1 multigrain bagel, split and toasted
- 2 thin slices Cheddar cheese
- 2 slices dill pickle
- 1/4 cup shredded carrot
- 1 leaf lettuce

Direction

- On toasted bagel, spread the cream cheese. Layer on one half of bagel with Cheddar cheese, pickle slices, lettuce and carrot, then put the leftover bagel half on top. Halve each sandwich and use aluminum foil or plastic wrap to wrap. Arrange the sandwich together with an ice park in a lunch bag.

Nutrition Information

- Calories: 474 calories;
- Sodium: 1055
- Total Carbohydrate: 66.8
- Cholesterol: 44
- Protein: 20
- Total Fat: 16

---

549.   Scrambled Egg And Pepperoni Submarine Sandwich

Serving: 1 | Prep: 5mins | Cook: 5mins | Ready in:

Ingredients

- 1 submarine sandwich roll, split
- 1 slice American cheese
- 2 tablespoons butter or margarine, softened
- 3 egg, beaten
- 1 pinch salt
- 1 clove garlic, minced
- 12 slices pepperoni sausage

Direction

- Over medium heat, heat a large skillet. Spread over cut sides of submarine sandwich roll with one tablespoon margarine or butter. Put roll into heated skillet, the buttered side down. Cook until toasted lightly. Take out roll from skillet. Then add cheese onto one of the toasted surfaces. Put aside.
- In hot skillet, melt remaining butter. Put in pepperoni and garlic. Cook while stirring until they are soft. Mix in beaten eggs. Then cook

while stirring with pepperoni until scrambled and firm. Spread onto cheese on roll with egg mixture. Place other roll half on top. Enjoy!

Nutrition Information

- Calories: 1034 calories;
- Cholesterol: 671
- Protein: 42.5
- Total Fat: 64.3
- Sodium: 1949
- Total Carbohydrate: 70.5

---

550.   Seitan Philly Cheese Steak Sandwiches

Serving: 4 | Prep: 15mins | Cook: 20mins | Ready in:

Ingredients

- 2 tablespoons olive oil, divided
- 1 onion, cut into matchstick-size pieces
- 1 green bell pepper, cut into matchstick-size pieces
- 1 red bell pepper, cut into matchstick-size pieces
- 1 (4 ounce) package mushrooms, sliced
- 1 (10 ounce) package seitan, thinly sliced
- salt and ground black pepper to taste
- 4 hoagie rolls, split lengthwise
- 4 slices provolone cheese

Direction

- Preheat an oven to 220 degrees C (425 degrees F).
- Over medium heat, heat one tablespoon of oil in a skillet. Cook while stirring red bell pepper, onion, and green bell pepper for about 5 to 10 minutes and until the onion becomes translucent. Add the mushrooms and then cook while stirring for 5 to 10 minutes until tender. Pour the vegetable mixture into a bowl.

- Over medium heat, add the remaining olive oil into the skillet. Add the seitan and then cook while turning often for about 5 to 10 minutes until turned brown on all sides. Place back the vegetable mixture into skillet and then combine with seitan. Add pepper and salt.
- Spread the hoagie rolls into baking sheet and then add the seitan-veggie mixture. Add one provolone cheese slice on top of filling of every sandwich.
- Heat the sandwiches for about 5 minutes until the cheese has melted.

Nutrition Information

- Calories: 688 calories;
- Sodium: 1208
- Total Carbohydrate: 84.1
- Cholesterol: 20
- Protein: 36.8
- Total Fat: 22.7

---

551.   Sicilian Steak Sandwich

Serving: 8 | Prep: 30mins | Cook: 15mins | Ready in:

Ingredients

- Artichoke Aioli:
- 1 (6.5 ounce) jar marinated artichoke hearts, drained
- 2 tablespoons mayonnaise
- 2 tablespoons grated Parmesan cheese
- 1 teaspoon lemon zest
- 1/2 lemon, juiced
- 1/4 teaspoon red pepper flakes
- salt and ground black pepper to taste
- Filling:
- 2 tablespoons olive oil
- 1 1/2 pounds beef tri-tip steak, thinly sliced
- 1 teaspoon Italian seasoning
- 1 onion, sliced thin
- 1 yellow bell pepper, sliced into strips

- 1 orange bell pepper, sliced into strips
- 1/4 cup pickled sweet and hot pepper rings
- 1/4 cup garlic basil spread (see footnote for recipe link)
- 1 cup sliced mushrooms
- 1 tablespoon capers
- 1 tablespoon Marsala wine
- 1 anchovy fillet (optional)
- 12 slices aged provolone cheese
- 1/4 cup crumbled Gorgonzola cheese
- Assembly:
- 4 Italian-style hoagie buns, split lengthwise
- 1/4 cup chopped fresh basil

Direction

- In a blender or a food processor, mix together black pepper, salt, red pepper flakes, lemon juice, lemon zest, Parmesan cheese, mayonnaise, and artichoke hearts. Process until smooth. Put a cover on and chill until using.
- In a Dutch oven or a big pot, heat olive oil over medium-high heat. Mix tri-tip steak slices into the hot oil and cook for 3 minutes until they start to turn brown, tossing continually. Sprinkle black pepper, salt and Italian seasoning over. Add garlic basil spread, sweet hot peppers, orange pepper, yellow pepper, and onion; stir and cook for 5 minutes until the onion starts to get tender. Mix in anchovy fillet, Marsala wine, capers, and mushrooms and cook for 5 minutes until the wine has vaporized and mushrooms are brown.
- Top the hot beef mixture with Gorgonzola cheese and provolone cheese and lightly fold for 2 minutes until the cheese melts. Take the cheese-beef mixture away from heat.
- Spread approximately 1/4 cup artichoke aioli onto each hoagie bun. Put the cheese-beef mixture into the buns and use basil to garnish.

Nutrition Information

- Calories: 681 calories;
- Sodium: 1087
- Total Carbohydrate: 44.9

- Cholesterol: 108
- Protein: 43.7
- Total Fat: 36.4

---

552. Slow Cooker 3 Ingredient French Dips

Serving: 8 | Prep: 5mins | Cook: 7hours | Ready in:

Ingredients

- 1 (3 pound) beef brisket
- 1 envelope onion soup mix
- 1 (14 ounce) can beef broth
- 8 large French rolls, split

Direction

- In a slow cooker, put in beef brisket. In a small bowl, blend onion soup mix into beef broth; pour over the brisket.
- Cook for 7 to 9 hours on low.
- Transfer brisket to a cutting board and slice into pieces. Fill rolls with beef. For dipping, pour juices from slow cooker into 5 separate bowls to serve with the sandwiches.

Nutrition Information

- Calories: 501 calories;
- Total Fat: 5.9
- Sodium: 2273
- Total Carbohydrate: 79.8
- Cholesterol: 34
- Protein: 31.5

---

553. Slow Cooker Cheese Steaks

Serving: 6 | Prep: 10mins | Cook: 4hours10mins | Ready in:

Ingredients

- 2 pounds beef tri tip steak
- 1 cup beef stock
- 1 tablespoon red wine vinegar
- 1 tablespoon Worcestershire sauce
- 2 teaspoons olive oil
- 1 large onion, sliced
- 1 large green pepper, sliced
- 8 ounces sliced fresh mushrooms
- 12 slices white American cheese
- 6 French or Italian sandwich rolls, split

Direction

- Put the beef in the slow cooker crock. Drizzle Worcestershire, vinegar and beef stock over the beef. Cook for 3 to 4 hours on Low, until beef is cooked to medium. Remove cooked beef from broth then put aside. Reserve the broth.
- Preheat the oven at 175°C (350°F).
- Heat oil over medium to high heat in a big skillet. Cook mushrooms in oil until they start softening; put in green pepper and onion. Cook and mix for 5 minutes, until the vegetables are soft.
- Slice the beef thinly. Split beef and vegetables among the rolls evenly. Top 2 slices cheese over each sandwich; enclose in foil.
- Put sandwiches in the preheated oven and heat for 10 minutes; until cheese is melted. If desired, serve hot sandwiches with reserved beef broth.

Nutrition Information

- Calories: 652 calories;
- Sodium: 1221
- Total Carbohydrate: 32.1
- Cholesterol: 191
- Protein: 58.9
- Total Fat: 33.9

554. Slow Cooker Italian Beef Hoagies

Serving: 6 | Prep: 20mins | Cook: | Ready in:

Ingredients

- PAM® Original No-Stick Cooking Spray
- 1 (2 pound) boneless beef chuck roast
- 1/2 teaspoon salt
- 1/2 teaspoon dried Italian seasoning
- 1/4 teaspoon ground black pepper
- 1 cup lower sodium beef broth
- 1 (14.5 ounce) can Hunt's® Diced Tomatoes, undrained
- 6 hoagie rolls, split lengthwise and toasted
- 6 thin slices provolone cheese, cut in half
- 1/2 cup giardiniera
- 1/4 cup mild yellow banana pepper rings

Direction

- Grease cooking spray over the inside of a large skillet and a 4 1/2-quart slow cooker. Place the skillet over medium-high heat until hot. Season beef with pepper, Italian seasoning, and salt; cook, turning one time, until all sides are browned, about 3 to 5 minutes. Pour beef in the greased slow cooker.
- Pour broth into the skillet, whisking to dissolve any browned bits from the bottom of the skillet; stream over beef the cooker. Pour undrained tomatoes over beef. Cook on high setting for 4 to 6 hours or low setting for 8 to 10 hours, until beef is very tender. Take beef out of the slow cooker and shred using two forks; pour back into the cooker.
- For serving: lay 2 pieces of cheese on the bottom of each roll. Place shredded beef, peppers, and giardiniera evenly over cheese. If desired, enjoy with the cooking juices for dipping.

Nutrition Information

- Calories: 697 calories;
- Cholesterol: 82
- Protein: 35.9
- Total Fat: 28.2
- Sodium: 1486
- Total Carbohydrate: 72.5

555. Slow Cooker Sausage With Sauce

Serving: 6 | Prep: 5mins | Cook: 6hours | Ready in:

Ingredients

- 8 (4 ounce) links fresh Italian sausage
- 1 (26 ounce) jar spaghetti sauce
- 1 green bell pepper, seeded and sliced into strips
- 1 onion, sliced
- 6 hoagie rolls, split lengthwise (optional)

Direction

- In a slow cooker, place onion, green pepper, spaghetti sauce, and Italian sausage links. Stir to cover everything with sauce.
- Cook with a cover for 6 hours on Low. Place on hoagie rolls and enjoy.

Nutrition Information

- Calories: 1024 calories;
- Protein: 35.5
- Total Fat: 57.4
- Sodium: 2356
- Total Carbohydrate: 88.2
- Cholesterol: 117

556. Stromboli Grinder

Serving: 8 | Prep: 20mins | Cook: 15mins | Ready in:

Ingredients

- 1 (16 ounce) jar marinara sauce
- 1 tablespoon olive oil
- 1 onion, sliced
- 1 red bell pepper, sliced
- 1 jalapeno pepper, sliced
- 1 goat horn pepper, or other hot green chile, sliced
- 16 slices salami
- 16 slices pepperoni
- 4 Italian-style hoagie buns, split lengthwise
- 1 (8 ounce) container mascarpone cheese, divided
- 1/4 cup garlic basil spread, divided (see footnote for recipe link)
- 1 pound mozzarella cheese, shredded

Direction

- Set oven to 500°F (260°C) to preheat.
- Put marinara sauce in a small saucepan over medium-low heat; cook for about 5 minutes or until warmed through. Turn heat down to low and keep warm while you prepare sandwiches.
- Heat olive oil over medium-high heat in a large skillet; cook, stirring, goat horn pepper, jalapeno pepper, red bell pepper, and onion in heated oil, for 7 to 8 minutes, until onion is tender and starts to become golden. Transfer onion mixture to a plate and put to one side.
- Cook pepperoni and salami in the hot skillet, for about 2 minutes on each side, until crispy.
- Spread 1 tablespoon garlic spread and 1/4 cup mascarpone cheese over each hoagie bun. Place 4 slices each of pepperoni and salami on top of each roll. Scatter with mozzarella cheese and onion mixture.
- Arrange sandwiches on a baking sheet; bake for about 5 minutes in the preheated oven until bread is toasted and cheese is melted. Spread each sandwich with 1/2 cup warm marinara sauce before serving.

Nutrition Information

- Calories: 793 calories;
- Protein: 37

- Total Fat: 50.1
- Sodium: 2215
- Total Carbohydrate: 48.6
- Cholesterol: 133

---

557.   Sublime Oxford Sandwich

Serving: 2 | Prep: 20mins | Cook: 5mins | Ready in:

Ingredients

- 4 slices whole grain bread
- 4 tablespoons goat cheese
- 1/2 cucumber, thinly sliced
- 4 cherry tomatoes, thinly sliced
- 1/4 red bell pepper, finely chopped
- 1 tablespoon finely chopped fresh basil
- 1 teaspoon fig preserves

Direction

- Toast the bread. Slather goat cheese on 1/2 of the slices of bread.
- Put cucumber and slices of tomato over the goat cheese. Add basil and chopped red bell pepper on top.
- Scatter a few figs over the layer of red bell peppers. Place the leftover two bread slices on top.

Nutrition Information

- Calories: 212 calories;
- Total Fat: 6.7
- Sodium: 296
- Total Carbohydrate: 28
- Cholesterol: 11
- Protein: 10.9

558. The America Sandwich

Serving: 12 | Prep: 30mins | Cook: 30mins | Ready in:

Ingredients

- 1 pound bacon
- 4 (1 pound) loaves sourdough bread
- 8 ounces processed cheese, sliced
- 1 pound sliced cooked roast beef
- 1 pound sliced smoked ham
- 8 ounces sliced American cheese
- 2 sticks butter, sliced
- 1 cup Dijon mustard
- 1 cup mayonnaise
- 4 cups canned gravy, or to taste

Direction

- Set the oven to 350°F (175°C) for preheating.
- Cook the bacon in a large and deep skillet over medium-high heat for 10 minutes, flipping occasionally until well browned. Transfer the slices of bacon on a paper towel-lined plate and let them drain.
- Slowly create a slit down the middle of the bread loaf. Using a spoon, scoop its interior out, creating a pocket in the bread loaf. Line the created pocket with 2 processed cheese food slices. Divide the slices of cooked bacon into four. Stuff each loaf of bread with 1/4 of the bacon.
- Arrange the ham and sliced roast beef on the microwave-safe plates. Drop a pat of butter onto the top slices. Cook them inside the microwave oven that is set on high for 30 seconds until the butter has melted. Fill each loaf with 1/4 of the buttered meat slices lightly. Arrange the sliced American cheese on top. Stuff the top of each loaf with a few pats of butter.
- Spread the remaining butter all over the outer portion of each loaf. Drizzle mayonnaise and dollops of Dijon mustard all over the top of the stuffing generously.
- Arrange the loaves on a baking sheet. Bake the loaves inside the preheated oven for 30 minutes until the filling is melted and hot and the bread is toasted. Make sure to check them always to keep them from burning.
- Simmer the gravy over low heat. Get the sandwiches from the oven. Slice the sandwiches into serving portions. Drizzle generous amount of hot gravy all over the top of each serving.

Nutrition Information

- Calories: 1074 calories;
- Total Carbohydrate: 95.5
- Cholesterol: 139
- Protein: 47.7
- Total Fat: 55.9
- Sodium: 3844

559. The Dipper

Serving: 8 | Prep: 20mins | Cook: 20mins | Ready in:

Ingredients

- 1 tablespoon olive oil
- 1 onion, sliced
- 1 tablespoon garlic basil spread (see footnote for recipe link)
- 1 tablespoon Italian seasoning
- 1 cup pickled sweet and hot pepper rings
- 1 cup sliced mushrooms
- 2 tablespoons Marsala wine
- 1 cup beef broth
- 2 pounds sliced roast beef
- 4 ciabatta sandwich rolls, sliced horizontally
- 1/4 cup garlic basil spread, divided (see footnote for recipe link)
- 1/4 cup prepared horseradish sauce, divided
- 12 slices Swiss cheese, divided

Direction

- Set oven to 260°C (or 500°F) and start preheating.

- In a Dutch oven or a large pot, bring olive oil to medium heat. Cook, stirring, Italian seasoning, 1 tablespoon of garlic basil spread and onion in hot oil for 4-5 minutes until onion is tender. Mix in mushrooms and pepper rings; cook, stirring, mushrooms for about 5 minutes until soft.
- Add in Marsala wine and boil, while scraping browned bits from the pan's bottom. Pour in roast beef and beef broth; stir beef for 3-4 minutes until cooked.
- Lather 1 tablespoon of horseradish sauce and 1 tablespoon of garlic basil spread onto each ciabatta roll. Add 3 Swiss cheese slices on top.
- Bring sandwiches to a baking sheet and bake for 3-4 minutes in prepared oven until bread is heated through and cheese is melted. Stack beef-onion mixture onto each sandwich with a slotted spoon, then add 1-2 tablespoons of pan juices onto the filling. Pour the leftovers of pan juices into small bowls for dipping purpose.

Nutrition Information

- Calories: 976 calories;
- Total Fat: 28.4
- Sodium: 2723
- Total Carbohydrate: 123.1
- Cholesterol: 94
- Protein: 55.5

560.   Toasted Cuban Sandwich

Serving: 8 | Prep: 30mins | Cook: 15mins | Ready in:

Ingredients

- Chipotle Mayonnaise:
- 1 1/2 cups mayonnaise
- 1/2 cup sour cream
- 1/4 cup chopped fresh cilantro
- 1/4 cup diced green onions
- 1 1/2 tablespoons ground chipotle peppers
- 1 tablespoon lime juice

- 1 tablespoon garlic basil spread (see footnote for recipe link)
- 1 teaspoon ground cumin
- salt and ground black pepper to taste
- Fillings:
- 2 tablespoons olive oil
- 2 sweet onions, sliced
- 1 teaspoon red pepper flakes
- 1 teaspoon dried oregano
- 2 jalapeno peppers cut into rings, divided
- 4 ciabatta sandwich rolls, sliced horizontally
- 1/4 cup sweet hot mustard, divided
- 1/2 pound sliced Swiss cheese, divided
- 1/2 pound sliced deli roast pork loin, divided
- 1/2 pound sliced ham, divided
- 2 dill pickles, cut into strips lengthwise - divided

Direction

- in a small bowl, mix mayonnaise, green onions, black pepper, ground chipotle peppers, garlic basil spread, lime juice, sour cream, cumin, cilantro and salt. Mix until combined. Cover the bowl and chill for at least 1 hour.
- Preheat the oven to 260 degrees C (500 degrees F).
- over medium-high heat, heat olive oil in large skillet and then mix oregano, onions, and red pepper flakes into the hot oil for about 5 minutes until the onions start to soften. Season to taste with ground black pepper and salt. Place in half jalapeno pepper rings and let cook for 2 to 3 minutes until they start to soften. Save the remaining jalapeno rings.
- Spread 2 tablespoons chipotle mayonnaise and 1 tablespoon sweet hot mustard onto each ciabatta roll. Divide evenly the remaining jalapeno rings, Swiss cheese slices, dill pickles, slices of pork loin, and ham among the 4 sandwiches. Add cooked onion mixture on top.
- Put the sandwiches in a baking sheet and then bake for 4 to 5 minutes in the preheated oven until the cheese has melted and the bread is toasted and warm.

Nutrition Information

- Calories: 671 calories;
- Total Carbohydrate: 26.9
- Cholesterol: 85
- Protein: 24.2
- Total Fat: 52.7
- Sodium: 927

561. Tomato Basil Mozzarella Melt

Serving: 6 | Prep: 15mins | Cook: 16mins | Ready in:

Ingredients

- 6 Sister Schubert's® Mini Baguettes
- 1/2 cup prepared pesto
- 12 slices fresh mozzarella cheese, or more if desired
- 4 Roma tomatoes, sliced
- Salt and pepper to taste
- Fresh basil leaves

Direction

- Arrange 6 Sister Schuberts Mini Baguettes on a baking sheet and bake rolls as followed the direction on package. Let baguettes cool down.
- Lower the oven temperature to 375°F.
- Carefully halve each Sister Schubert's Mini Baguette horizontally. Spread pesto over a side of each baguette. Keep layering with fresh mozzarella and tomatoes, then scatter pepper and salt over. Wrap a large piece of aluminum foil around each sandwich, arrange packages on the baking sheet and bake for 7 to 10 minutes or until sandwiches are warm and the cheese is melted. Remove the wrap around sandwiches, open and put in fresh basil leaves. Serve.

562. Tuna Coney Dogs

Serving: 4 | Prep: 15mins | Cook: 10mins | Ready in:

Ingredients

- 4 ounces American cheese, cubed
- 3 hard-cooked eggs, chopped
- 1 (5 ounce) can tuna, drained and flaked
- 2 tablespoons chopped green bell pepper
- 2 tablespoons chopped onion
- 2 tablespoons chopped pimento-stuffed green olives
- 2 tablespoons chopped sweet pickles
- 1/2 cup mayonnaise
- 4 hot dog buns

Direction

- Start preheating oven to 300°F (150°C).
- Combine sweet pickles, olives, onion, bell pepper, tuna, eggs and cheese in medium bowl. Mix in the mayonnaise until coating everything evenly. Generously spoon into hot dog buns; cover each sandwich with aluminum foil.
- Bake Coneys in prepared oven for 10 mins or until the cheese melts and the filling is heated through.

Nutrition Information

- Calories: 533 calories;
- Total Fat: 37.6
- Sodium: 1014
- Total Carbohydrate: 24.9
- Cholesterol: 206
- Protein: 23.6

563.   Tuna, Avocado And Bacon Sandwich

Serving: 2 | Prep: 6mins | Cook: 4mins | Ready in:

Ingredients

- 4 slices bacon
- 1 (5 ounce) can solid white tuna packed in water
- 1/2 teaspoon Dijon mustard
- 1/2 teaspoon prepared horseradish
- 1 tablespoon sweet pickle relish
- 1 tablespoon minced red onion
- 1/4 teaspoon paprika
- black pepper to taste
- 2 hoagie buns, split
- 1 avocado - peeled, pitted and sliced
- 1 tomato, sliced
- 2 slices provolone cheese
- 2 lettuce leaves

Direction

- Place bacon on a microwavable plate lined with a paper towel. Microwave for 4 minutes or until crispy.
- In a bowl, combine tuna, relish, Dijon mustard, horseradish, and red onion. Add paprika and pepper to taste. Separate mixture between hoagie buns. Place 1/2 an avocado, 1/2 tomato, a slice of Provolone cheese, 1 lettuce leaf, and 2 slices of bacon in each sandwich.

Nutrition Information

- Calories: 845 calories;
- Sodium: 1561
- Total Carbohydrate: 84
- Cholesterol: 58
- Protein: 44.3
- Total Fat: 37.4

564.   Tuscan Style Sausage Sandwiches

Serving: 4 | Prep: 15mins | Cook: 15mins | Ready in:

Ingredients

- 1 pound hot Italian sausage links or sweet Italian sausage links, sliced
- 1 small onion, sliced
- 1 (10 ounce) package frozen chopped spinach, thawed and squeezed dry
- 1 (24 ounce) jar RAGÚ® Sauce
- 1 (16-inch) loaf Italian bread or French bread, cut into 4 pieces

Direction

- Brown sausage in a large non-stick skillet on medium-high heat. Mix in mushrooms, spinach and onion. Cook while stirring sausage occasionally until done, 5 minutes. Whisk in sauce until heated through.
- Open each piece of sandwich and spread in sausage mixture evenly. If preferred, top with crushed red pepper flakes.

Nutrition Information

- Calories: 760 calories;
- Protein: 33.6
- Total Fat: 28.9
- Sodium: 2256
- Total Carbohydrate: 90.3
- Cholesterol: 61

Chapter 8: Panini Sandwich Recipes

***

565.   Barbeque Chicken Paninis

Serving: 4 | Prep: 15mins | Cook: 5mins | Ready in:

Ingredients

- 1 (2 pound) rotisserie chicken, boned and shredded
- 4 slices Cheddar cheese
- 8 slices crispy cooked bacon, halved
- 1/2 cup barbeque sauce
- 4 Kaiser rolls, halved

Direction

- Preheat a panini press to medium-high heat and coat its surface slightly with oil.
- Layer the bottom of each Kaiser roll with shredded chicken, a Cheddar cheese slice, 4 half-slices of bacon and barbeque sauce, then put another half of each roll on top.
- In the prepped panini press, grill sandwiches for 5 minutes, until rolls turn golden brown and cheese has melted.

Nutrition Information

- Calories: 648 calories;
- Total Fat: 33.6
- Sodium: 1125
- Total Carbohydrate: 32.9
- Cholesterol: 155
- Protein: 50.3

566.   Basic Grilled Panini

Serving: 1 | Prep: 10mins | Cook: 6mins | Ready in:

Ingredients

- 1 tablespoon extra-light olive oil, or as needed
- 2 slices Italian bread

- 2 tablespoons mayonnaise
- 2 slices Cheddar cheese
- 3 slices deli ham, or more to taste
- 1 slice firm-ripe tomato
- 1 thin slice onion
- cooking spray

Direction

- Drizzle over one side of each bread slice with olive oil. Spread on the other side of each slice with one tablespoon of mayonnaise. Top with the Cheddar cheese, the ham, the tomato, and the onion in a pile. Place other slice of bread on top, the mayonnaise side facing down.
- Over medium-high heat, heat a grill pan; lightly spray cooking spray over. Put the sandwich onto grill, using a heavy pan to weigh it down. Cook for 3-5 mins on each side or until grill marks appear and cheese melts.

Nutrition Information

- Calories: 802 calories;
- Total Fat: 63.2
- Sodium: 1840
- Total Carbohydrate: 26.7
- Cholesterol: 118
- Protein: 32.2

567.   Chef John's Cuban Sandwich

Serving: 2 | Prep: 15mins | Cook: 6mins | Ready in:

Ingredients

- 1/4 cup mayonnaise
- 1/4 cup mustard
- 1 pinch cayenne pepper
- 1 (8 ounce) loaf Cuban bread
- 8 slices Swiss cheese
- 6 thin slices smoked fully-cooked ham
- 1 1/2 cups cooked pulled pork, heated

- 1 large dill pickle, sliced thinly lengthwise
- 2 tablespoons butter, or as needed

Direction

- In a mixing bowl, stir cayenne, mustard, and mayonnaise together to make sauce.
- Cut off ends of the bread. Slice loaf into 2 portions and split bread evenly to make bottoms and tops of 2 individual sandwiches. Spread mayo/mustard sauce liberally onto both sides of each half.
- Separate sandwich components evenly onto 2 bottom halves following this order: 2 slices Swiss cheese, 3 slices ham, hot cooked pork, pickle slices and 2 additional slices of Swiss cheese. Place the top halves over the filling.
- Melt butter over medium heat in a heavy skillet. Lay sandwiches in a skillet; press sandwiches with a heavy weight (you can use foil-wrapped bricks or another skillet). Toast sandwiches, for 3 to 4 minutes on each side, until filling is heated through and bread is crispy.

Nutrition Information

- Calories: 1473 calories;
- Sodium: 4077
- Total Carbohydrate: 85.4
- Cholesterol: 287
- Protein: 88.2
- Total Fat: 85.2

568.   Chicken Parmesan Panini

Serving: 4 | Prep: 10mins | Cook: 15mins | Ready in:

Ingredients

- 1/4 cup flour
- 1 teaspoon garlic powder
- 1/2 teaspoon salt
- 1/4 teaspoon black pepper

- 1 egg, beaten
- 1 cup panko bread crumbs
- 1/4 cup Parmesan cheese
- 4 small chicken cutlets*
- 2 tablespoons olive oil
- 4 slices fresh mozzarella cheese
- 1/4 cup Parmesan cheese
- 8 thick slices artisanal-style bread
- 1 (24 ounce) jar RAGÚ® Old World Style® Traditional Sauce

Direction

- In a shallow bowl, combine pepper, salt, garlic powder, and flour. Put the beaten egg in another bowl. Combine Parmesan cheese and panko bread crumbs in a third shallow bowl.
- Place each piece of chicken in the flour and dredge, coating both sides; shake off the excess. Dunk chicken in beaten egg, and then into the breadcrumbs and press, ensuring that both sides are well coated. Place on a plate.
- Put olive oil in a large skillet and heat over medium-high heat. Add chicken and pan fry for about 4 minutes each side until the juices run clear and not pink in the center.
- Put the chicken on bread slices. Scatter about 1/4 cup Ragu® Old World Style® Traditional Sauce over each piece of chicken. Place a tablespoon of Parmesan cheese and a slice of cheese on top. Put the rest bread slices on top. Heat in a large skillet or a Panini press until the cheese melts. Heat the rest of the sauce for dipping.

Nutrition Information

- Calories: 646 calories;
- Total Fat: 24.3
- Sodium: 1792
- Total Carbohydrate: 68.5
- Cholesterol: 125
- Protein: 42.6

569. Chicken Pesto Paninis

Serving: 4 | Prep: 15mins | Cook: 5mins | Ready in:

Ingredients

- 1 focaccia bread, quartered
- 1/2 cup prepared basil pesto
- 1 cup diced cooked chicken
- 1/2 cup diced green bell pepper
- 1/4 cup diced red onion
- 1 cup shredded Monterey Jack cheese

Direction

- Start preheating a panini grill.
- Horizontally cut each quarter of the focaccia bread in half. Spread pesto on each half. Layer equal portions of the chicken, the bell pepper, the onion and the cheese onto the bottom halves. Place the rest of focaccia halves on top to have 4 sandwiches.
- Place paninis in the prepared grill and grill until cheese is melted and focaccia bread turns golden brown, about 5 minutes.

Nutrition Information

- Calories: 641 calories;
- Total Fat: 29.4
- Sodium: 1076
- Total Carbohydrate: 60.9
- Cholesterol: 61
- Protein: 32.4

570. Ciabatta Panini

Serving: 4 | Prep: 10mins | Cook: 5mins | Ready in:

Ingredients

- 8 slices provolone cheese
- 4 ciabatta rolls, split
- 12 slices pancetta
- 2 cups baby spinach leaves
- 1 large tomato, sliced
- 2 roasted red bell peppers, sliced
- 1/2 small red onion, thinly sliced
- 1/4 cup olive oil
- 2 tablespoons red wine vinegar
- salt and ground black pepper to taste

Direction

- Heat up a panini press and lightly grease the grates.
- Arrange a slice of provolone cheese on both bottom and top pieces of ciabatta bread. Arrange 3 slices pancetta and one-quarter cup of spinach over 4 bottom slices of bread. Divide onion, bell peppers, and tomato evenly among the sandwiches. Drizzle approximately 1 teaspoon each vinegar and olive oil onto each sandwich; sprinkle with pepper and salt to taste. Top with the top pieces of ciabatta rolls and brush evenly with the rest of olive oil.
- Arrange sandwiches on the preheated panini grill; close then press tightly on top. Cook for about 5 minutes or until cheese is melted and sandwiches are golden brown.

Nutrition Information

- Calories: 661 calories;
- Total Fat: 42.6
- Sodium: 1700
- Total Carbohydrate: 37.7
- Cholesterol: 69
- Protein: 31.5

571. Deluxe Pizza Panini

Serving: 4 | Prep: 20mins | Cook: 5mins | Ready in:

Ingredients

- 1 teaspoon butter
- 2 tablespoons sliced fresh mushrooms

- 1/2 cup tomato sauce
- 4 ciabatta rolls, split
- 2 cloves garlic, minced
- 1 tablespoon dried oregano
- 8 slices hot Genoa salami
- 8 slices roasted ham
- 2 tablespoons diced red onion
- 2 tablespoons chopped roasted red pepper
- 2 tablespoons chopped black olives
- 4 leaves basil, chopped
- 4 slices provolone cheese

Direction

- In a small skillet, melt butter over medium-high heat; add mushrooms and sauté for 5-7 minutes until soft. Take away from heat and cool.
- Turn on a panini press to preheat following the manufacturer's directions.
- Spread the tomato sauce in an even layer over the cut sides of each ciabatta roll. Sprinkle over each roll with equal amounts of oregano and garlic. On each roll, arrange 2 salami slices side by side, put 2 slices ham on top. Distribute basil, olives, red pepper, mushrooms and red onion among 4 sandwiches and evenly spread on top of the meats. Complete by putting provolone cheese on top and sandwiching roll halves around the fillings.
- On the preheated panini press, cook the sandwiches for 5 minutes until the middle is warm, the cheese melts, and the bread has dark brown grill marks.

Nutrition Information

- Calories: 652 calories;
- Sodium: 2696
- Total Carbohydrate: 36.9
- Cholesterol: 111
- Protein: 37.1
- Total Fat: 38.9

572.   Eggplant Panini

Serving: 4 | Prep: 15mins | Cook: 15mins | Ready in:

Ingredients

- 1 baby eggplant, cut into 1/4-inch slices
- salt and ground black pepper to taste
- 1/4 cup olive oil, divided
- 1 loaf flat bread, sliced horizontally and cut into 4 equal pieces
- 1/2 (12 ounce) jar roasted red bell peppers, drained and sliced
- 4 ounces shredded mozzarella cheese
- 1/4 cup roasted garlic hummus

Direction

- Sprinkle salt and pepper all over the slices of eggplant. Allow them to stand for 2 minutes.
- Put 2 tbsp. of olive oil into the skillet and heat it over medium-high. Cook half of the eggplant for 2-3 minutes per side until golden brown. Do the same with the remaining eggplant and olive oil.
- Follow the manufacturer's directions on how to preheat the panini press.
- On the bottom of each flatbread, layer the following in particular order: eggplant, roasted red pepper, and mozzarella cheese. Stuff the inside of each top piece of flatbread with 1 tbsp. of hummus. Place it over the mozzarella layer, making it a panini.
- Grill each panini onto the preheated panini press for 7 minutes until the cheese has melted and cooked through.

Nutrition Information

- Calories: 401 calories;
- Total Fat: 21.7
- Sodium: 625
- Total Carbohydrate: 41.5
- Cholesterol: 18
- Protein: 15.7

573.   Grilled Cuban Bunini Sandwich

Serving: 4 | Prep: 20mins | Cook: 6hours | Ready in:

Ingredients

- 4 Ball Park® Hamburger Buns
- Dijon mustard
- 12 slices dill pickle
- 1/2 cup sliced red onion
- Cuban pulled pork (recipe below)
- 8 slices Black Forest ham
- 8 slices Swiss cheese
- olive oil
- Cuban Pulled Pork:
- 1 tablespoon kosher salt
- 1/2 teaspoon garlic powder
- 1/2 teaspoon onion powder
- 2 teaspoons ground cumin
- 2 teaspoons dried oregano
- 1 teaspoon crushed red pepper
- 1 teaspoon whole black peppercorns
- 1 bay leaf
- 1 orange, zested and juiced
- 1 lime, zested and juiced
- 1 yellow onion, sliced
- 5 whole garlic cloves, peeled
- 3 pounds pork shoulder

Direction

- In a bowl, mix together juices, lime/orange zest, bay leaf, peppercorns, crushed red pepper, oregano, cumin, onion powder, garlic powder, and salt.
- In the bottom of a slow cooker, put garlic cloves and sliced onions. Put pork shoulder on top and add the spice and juice mixture onto the meat. Set the slow cooker for 6-8 hours on Low. Once done, take the pork out of the cooker and allow to cool slightly. Then break the pork into thick chunks with 2 forks. Put the leftover juices on the pork to keep warm.
- Start preheating a panini press as the manufacturer instructs.
- Spread two sides of each hamburger bun with Dijon mustard. Layer pickles, red onions, 1/2 cup pulled pork per sandwich, sliced ham, and Swiss cheese from bottom to top.
- Brush olive oil on the bun's outsides and put in the panini press until the cheese melts.

Nutrition Information

- Calories: 897 calories;
- Total Fat: 52.3
- Sodium: 2851
- Total Carbohydrate: 38.5
- Cholesterol: 230
- Protein: 68.3

574.   Grilled Panini Sandwich Without A Panini Maker

Serving: 1 | Prep: 5mins | Cook: 6mins | Ready in:

Ingredients

- 1 teaspoon mayonnaise, or to taste
- 2 (1 inch thick) slices Italian bread
- 3 slices deli ham
- 2 slices provolone cheese
- 1 slice roasted red bell pepper

Direction

- Spread one side of each slice of bread with mayonnaise. Layer the bread with ham, provolone cheese and roasted red bell pepper, then place another slice of bread on top of the sandwich, mayonnaise-side facing down.
- Heat grill pan on medium heat and put sandwich into pan, then place another heavy pan on top of sandwich. Put on top 2 heavy cans and compress the sandwich by pressing down cans. Lower heat to medium and cook about 3-4 minutes. Turn the sandwich and

replace both pan and cans. Cook for 3-4 minutes longer, until cheese has melted.

Nutrition Information

- Calories: 589 calories;
- Sodium: 2122
- Total Carbohydrate: 45.1
- Cholesterol: 89
- Protein: 35.7
- Total Fat: 28.8

---

575.   Grilled Turkey Cuban Sandwiches

Serving: 6 | Prep: 15mins | Cook: 2hours | Ready in:

Ingredients

- Non-stick cooking spray
- 1 (3 pound) Butterball® Boneless Breast of Turkey Roast, thawed
- 2 cloves garlic, peeled, sliced
- 1 tablespoon canola oil
- 1 tablespoon ground cumin
- 2 teaspoons salt
- 1 teaspoon coarsely ground black pepper
- 2 loaves Cuban, French or Italian bread (15 inches long)
- 1/4 cup honey mustard
- 1/2 pound smoked ham
- 1/2 pound sliced Swiss cheese
- 12 sandwich-style dill pickle slices

Direction

- Preheat grill to medium indirect heat. Brush or spray the grate of an outdoor gas grill using oil. Remove the gravy packet of the packaged turkey and set it aside for another use. Dry turkey with paper towels. To easily remove the string netting, lift it and position on roast. Using a knife, make one inch apart small cuts all over the surface of the turkey. Slide 1 garlic

slice in every cut and lightly brush the skin with oil. Make a rub of salt, pepper and cumin, sprinkle it all over the turkey. Position the turkey on the grate with a drip pan. Close lid. Cook the turkey until thermometer inserted into the center of the roast reaches 170 degrees F. This may take about 1 1/4 to 1 3/4 hours. Allow to rest for 10 minutes. Discard the string netting. Carve half of turkey in six portions 1/8 inches thick. Freeze uncarved turkey. Cut the bread loaf into 3 pieces and cut each in half to make six sandwiches. Spread 2 teaspoon mustard on the bottom half of each bread. Layer sliced turkey, cheese, ham and pickles on top of it. Put the top half of the bread and press each sandwich lightly to flatten. Wrap each sandwich tightly with foil. On the preheated grill grate, grill the sandwiches for 3 to 5 minutes per side, with a heavy iron skillet or a brick on top of it. Best served warm.

Nutrition Information

- Calories: 1066 calories;
- Total Fat: 34.4
- Sodium: 2712
- Total Carbohydrate: 95.1
- Cholesterol: 202
- Protein: 91.6

---

576.   Harissa Fried Halloumi Panini

Serving: 4 | Prep: 15mins | Cook: 30mins | Ready in:

Ingredients

- 3 tablespoons olive oil, divided
- 1 medium yellow bell pepper, chopped
- 1 red onion, cut into thin wedges
- 2 tablespoons harissa sauce, or more to taste
- 8 (1/4 inch thick) slices eggplant
- 1/4 teaspoon salt, divided
- 1/4 teaspoon ground black pepper, divided

- 8 ounces Halloumi cheese, cut into 8 slices
- 8 slices multigrain seeded sandwich bread
- 4 tablespoons softened butter

Direction

- Put 1 tbsp. of oil in a large skillet and heat it over medium heat. Add the onion and bell pepper. Cook for 8 minutes until tender. Once done, place them in a separate skillet and mix in harissa sauce.
- Brush 2 tbsp. of oil on both sides of slices of eggplant. Sprinkle the slices with 1/8 tsp. of black pepper and 1/8 tsp. of salt. Place half of the eggplant slices into the skillet. Cook each side for 3 minutes until tender and browned. Do the same with the remaining slices. Keep the slices warm.
- Sprinkle leftover 1/8 tsp. of black pepper and 1/8 tsp. of salt into the Halloumi. Place half of the Halloumi into the skillet and cook each side for 2 minutes. Do the same with the remaining slices.
- Layer 4 slices of bread with bell pepper mixture, Halloumi, and slices of eggplant. Place the remaining slices of bread on top. Coat the outsides of the sandwiches with butter.
- Arrange 2 sandwiches into the large skillet. Use a plate that is weighted with food cans to cover the sandwiches. Cook each side for 2 minutes until toasted and heated through. Do the same with the remaining sandwiches.

Nutrition Information

- Calories: 381 calories;
- Sodium: 490
- Total Carbohydrate: 34
- Cholesterol: 31
- Protein: 8.8
- Total Fat: 24.4

577.   Hatch Chile Turkey Panini

Serving: 1 | Prep: 10mins | Cook: 10mins | Ready in:

Ingredients

- 8 ounces Dietz & Watson Hatch Chile Turkey
- 3 ounces Dietz & Watson Hatch Chile Cheese
- 2 slices white bread
- 1/2 cup wilted spinach
- 1/4 cup julienned red onion
- 2 shishito peppers
-

Direction

- Stack your ingredients like this: bread, the spinach, Dietz & Watson Hatch Chile Cheese, the Dietz & Watson Hatch Turkey, the red onions, and the bread. Press for five minutes in a panini press. On a preheated outdoor grill on medium heat, grill the shishito peppers one to two minutes each side or until the skin blisters. Serve the panini topped with grilled shishito peppers.

Nutrition Information

- Calories: 743 calories;
- Total Carbohydrate: 41.1
- Cholesterol: 207
- Total Fat: 28.4
- Protein: 75.6
- Sodium: 3054

578.   Panzanella Panini

Serving: 1 | Prep: 10mins | Cook: 5mins | Ready in:

Ingredients

- 1 French deli roll, split
- 1 teaspoon balsamic vinegar
- 2 slices mozzarella cheese

- 1 small tomato, sliced
- 4 fresh basil leaves
- olive oil

Direction

- Preheat a skillet on the medium low heat.
- Drizzle cut sides of roll along with balsamic vinegar. Layer 1 mozzarella cheese slice, tomato slices, basil leaves, and the leftover mozzarella cheese slice over the roll. Close the sandwich; using olive oil to rub the outside of sandwich.
- Put sandwich into the preheated skillet; press by add another heavy skillet on top of it. Cook for roughly 3 minutes till bread becomes toasted and golden. Turn the sandwich over; place the skillet on top. Cook second side for roughly extra 2 minutes till becomes toasted.

Nutrition Information

- Calories: 402 calories;
- Protein: 18.5
- Total Fat: 24.1
- Sodium: 613
- Total Carbohydrate: 29.9
- Cholesterol: 36

579.   Peanut Butter And Chocolate Panini

Serving: 4 | Prep: 10mins | Cook: 15mins | Ready in:

Ingredients

- 1 teaspoon butter
- 1/2 cup crunchy peanut butter
- 8 slices firm bread
- 1/2 cup semi-sweet chocolate chips

Direction

- Preheat the panini press following the direction of manufacturer to medium low heat. Coat the inside surfaces using butter.
- Spread 1-2 tablespoons of the peanut butter onto 1/2 of the bread slices; use 1-2 tablespoons of the chocolate chips to cover the peanut butter. Add the second bread slice on top of each, make 4 sandwiches.
- Grill each sandwich in panini press for 2-4 minutes or till the chocolate melts and the bread toasts.

Nutrition Information

- Calories: 433 calories;
- Total Fat: 25.1
- Sodium: 507
- Total Carbohydrate: 45.5
- Cholesterol: 3
- Protein: 12.5

580.   Portobello, Eggplant, And Roasted Red Pepper Panini

Serving: 4 | Prep: 40mins | Cook: 20mins | Ready in:

Ingredients

- 2 red bell peppers
- 4 portobello mushroom caps
- 1 cup fat-free balsamic vinaigrette
- 4 (1/2 inch thick) slices eggplant, peeled
- 1 teaspoon garlic powder
- 1 teaspoon onion powder
- 2 teaspoons grated Parmesan cheese
- 8 slices focaccia bread
- 1/4 cup fat free ranch dressing
- 4 thin slices Swiss cheese
- 4 thin slices Asiago cheese

Direction

- Set the oven's broiler to preheating. Position the oven rack 6-inches away from the heat source. Use an aluminum foil to line the baking sheet.

- Slice the peppers in half, starting from top to bottom. Remove their seeds, stem, and ribs. Arrange the peppers onto the prepared baking sheet, cut-sides down.
- Cook the peppers under the preheated broiler for 5 minutes until the skin of the peppers turn blistered and blackened. Toss the peppers into the bowl and cover them tightly with a plastic wrap. Let the peppers steam as they cool for 20 minutes. Once the peppers are cool, remove their skins; discard. Refrigerate them overnight.
- In a resealable plastic bag, add the Portobello mushroom caps and drizzle them with the balsamic vinegar. Squeeze any excess air out; seal. Allow them to marinate inside the fridge overnight.
- The next day, follow the manufacturer's instructions on how to preheat the electric double-sided grill, just like the George Foreman® grill. Sprinkle onion powder and garlic powder all over the slices of eggplant.
- Take the Portobello mushrooms out of the marinade. Discard the leftover marinade from the Portobello mushrooms. Cook the mushrooms on the preheated grill for 4-5 minutes until tender. Cook also the slices of eggplant onto the preheated grill for 4-5 minutes until tender. Transfer them onto the plate. Sprinkle them with Parmesan cheese; put aside.
- In assembling the sandwiches, spread the ranch dressing onto each focaccia slice. Set the cheese slice on each bread piece. Distribute the slices of eggplant, a Portobello mushroom, and roasted peppers among the four bread slices. Place the remaining bread on each top.
- Coat the double-sided grill with cooking spray. Cook the sandwiches for 4-5 minutes until they are already hot in the center, the bread turns golden brown, and the cheese has melted.

Nutrition Information

- Calories: 679 calories;
- Total Carbohydrate: 100.5
- Cholesterol: 46
- Protein: 28.1
- Total Fat: 19
- Sodium: 1779

---

581. Ratatouille Sandwich

Serving: 2 | Prep: 30mins | Cook: 16mins | Ready in:

Ingredients

- Sauce:
- 1 red bell pepper, sliced
- 1 tomato, chopped
- 1 clove garlic, minced
- 1 teaspoon dried oregano, or to taste
- salt and ground black pepper to taste
- Sandwich:
- 1 eggplant, sliced
- 1 zucchini, sliced
- 1 tomato, sliced
- 1 red onion, sliced
- 4 teaspoons olive oil
- 4 slices sourdough bread
- 4 slices mozzarella cheese

Direction

- Follow the manufacturer's directions on how to preheat the panini press.
- Place the slices of red bell pepper onto the panini press and grill them on high heat for 5 minutes until soft. Place the grilled slices into the blender.
- Toss the garlic and chopped tomato into the blender. Blend the mixture for 2 minutes until the sauce that is formed is smooth. Season the sauce with black pepper, salt, and oregano.
- Grill the tomato, slices of onion, zucchini, and eggplant onto the panini press for 3 minutes per side until they are softened.
- Drizzle bread slices with olive oil. Flip the bread over and spread a generous amount of

sauce on it. Arrange 2 bread slices onto the panini press, oil-side down. Add a slice of mozzarella cheese. Place the eggplant mixture on top. Set the second slice of mozzarella cheese on the top. Place the second bread slice on the top, oil-side up.

- Grill it over medium-high for 5 minutes until the cheese has melted and golden.

Nutrition Information

- Calories: 524 calories;
- Sodium: 777
- Total Carbohydrate: 64.2
- Cholesterol: 36
- Protein: 26.1
- Total Fat: 20.7

582. Roast Beef Panini With Caramelized Shallots And Roquefort

Serving: 6 | Prep: 10mins | Cook: 15mins | Ready in:

Ingredients

- 3 tablespoons unsalted butter
- 6 large shallots, sliced
- salt and black pepper to taste
- 2 French baguettes, halved lengthwise
- 2 tablespoons Dijon mustard, or to taste
- 1 cup Roquefort cheese, crumbled
- 1 pound thinly sliced deli roast beef
- 1/2 cup cold heavy cream
- 1 1/2 tablespoons finely shredded horseradish root
- 1 pinch salt and white pepper to taste

Direction

- In a skillet over medium heat, melt butter. Mix in sliced shallots; cook while stirring for 10 mins or until golden-brown and very tender.

Season with black pepper and salt to taste. Put aside.

- Start preheating panini press following the manufacturer's directions.
- Spread Dijon mustard over cut sides of baguettes, then evenly sprinkle with the Roquefort cheese. Portion roast beef among bottom pieces. Spread over roast beef with shallots. Add the top pieces on top. Slice each baguette into 2-3 pieces to fit the panini machine.
- Grill sandwiches for 4 mins on the prepared press until cheese has melted and bread is crisp and golden. In a metal bowl, beat heavy cream to form the soft peaks while sandwiches are cooking. Stir in horseradish. Season to taste with white pepper and salt.
- Once done, slice each sandwich in 1/2. Enjoy with the horseradish cream.

Nutrition Information

- Calories: 652 calories;
- Total Fat: 23.3
- Sodium: 1983
- Total Carbohydrate: 77.3
- Cholesterol: 96
- Protein: 34.7

583. Roasted Vegetable Panini Bites

Serving: 2 | Prep: | Cook: | Ready in:

Ingredients

- 2 slices rustic Italian bread
- 4 ounces BelGioioso Fresh Mozzarella cheese, sliced
- Roasted tomatoes
- Roasted zucchini
- Roasted asparagus
- Roasted mushrooms
- Fresh basil leaves

- 2 ounces prosciutto

Direction

- Between the 2 pieces of bread, arrange all ingredients. Press and grill sandwich to make a tasty panini. Slice panini into bite-sized pieces to serve.

Nutrition Information

- Calories: 322 calories;
- Protein: 18.9
- Total Fat: 20
- Sodium: 844
- Total Carbohydrate: 15.5
- Cholesterol: 65

---

584. Tubby's Pesto Panini

Serving: 2 | Prep: 20mins | Cook: 16mins | Ready in:

Ingredients

- 1/4 cup packed fresh basil leaves
- 1/4 cup olive oil
- 4 cloves garlic, minced
- 2 tablespoons grated Romano cheese
- 1 teaspoon dried oregano
- 1 teaspoon ground black pepper
- 2 skinless, boneless chicken breast halves
- 2 tablespoons creamy Caesar salad dressing
- 6 (1/4 inch thick) slices Italian bread with sesame seeds (also known as Scali)
- 1/2 cup shredded iceberg lettuce
- 2 thin slices smoked mozzarella

Direction

- Start preheating outdoor grill for medium heat; oil grate lightly.
- In a blender, put pepper, oregano, Romano cheese, garlic, oil and basil. Blend for half a minute on High, until they become smooth; if necessary, put in more oil.

- Grill the chicken for 5 mins on each side or until the juices run clear. Do not turn the grill off.
- Spoon onto 2 bread slices with one tablespoon of Caesar dressing. Put lettuce and 1 more bread slice on top of each. Thickly spread pesto over the second bread slice. Place one cooked chicken breast, one smoked mozzarella slice, and the remaining bread on top of each sandwich.
- Grill the sandwiches for 3 mins on each side or until bread has been toasted and cheese melts.

Nutrition Information

- Calories: 587 calories;
- Sodium: 523
- Total Carbohydrate: 20
- Cholesterol: 85
- Protein: 32.5
- Total Fat: 41.5

---

585. Tuna Panini Melt

Serving: 2 | Prep: 10mins | Cook: 3mins | Ready in:

Ingredients

- 1 (5 ounce) can solid white albacore tuna in water (such as Bumble Bee®)
- 1 tablespoon mayonnaise
- 1 tablespoon balsamic vinegar
- 1 tablespoon chopped onion
- 1 dill pickle, chopped
- 4 slices sourdough bread
- 2 slices American cheese

Direction

- In a bowl, combine the dill pickle, balsamic vinegar, tuna, mayonnaise and onion.
- Put tuna mixture evenly on 2 sliced breads. Place American cheese and top with the remaining 2 sliced breads.

- Use a panini press to cook the sandwiches for 3-4 minutes until the cheese has melted and the bread is crispy.

Nutrition Information

- Calories: 381 calories;
- Protein: 28.4
- Total Fat: 15.8
- Sodium: 865
- Total Carbohydrate: 30.7
- Cholesterol: 48

586.   Turkey Avocado Panini

Serving: 2 | Prep: 17mins | Cook: 8mins | Ready in:

Ingredients

- 1/2 ripe avocado
- 1/4 cup mayonnaise
- 2 ciabatta rolls
- 1 tablespoon olive oil, divided
- 2 slices provolone cheese
- 1 cup whole fresh spinach leaves, divided
- 1/4 pound thinly sliced mesquite smoked turkey breast
- 2 roasted red peppers, sliced into strips

Direction

- In a bowl, mash the mayonnaise and the avocado together until mixed thoroughly.
- Preheat the panini sandwich press.
- To prepare the sandwiches, divide in half the flat way the ciabatta rolls and then use olive oil to polish the bottom of every roll. Onto the panini press, put the bottoms of the rolls with the olive oil side facing down. On each sandwich, put a sliced roasted red pepper, a provolone cheese slice, half the chopped turkey breast, and half spinach leaves. On the cut surface of each top, lay half of the mixture of avocado and then put top of the roll onto

the sandwich. Use olive oil to polish the top of the roll.
- Cover the panini press and then cook for about 5 to 8 minutes until bun is crisp and toasted, cheese has melted and has golden brown grill marks.

Nutrition Information

- Calories: 723 calories;
- Total Fat: 51.3
- Sodium: 1720
- Total Carbohydrate: 42.1
- Cholesterol: 62
- Protein: 25.3

587.   Turkey And Avocado Panini

Serving: 2 | Prep: 10mins | Cook: 10mins | Ready in:

Ingredients

- 4 slices artisan bread such as ciabatta
- 2 teaspoons honey Dijon salad dressing
- 1/2 cup baby spinach leaves
- 1/4 pound sliced oven-roasted deli turkey breast
- 1/4 red onion, cut into strips
- 1 ripe avocado from Mexico, peeled, pitted and thickly sliced
- Salt and pepper to taste
- 1/4 cup crumbled soft goat cheese
- Non-stick cooking spray

Direction

- Put honey Dijon dressing on one side of the sandwiches and put baby spinach leaves on top. Put a layer of turkey breast and red onion on top of the spinach.
- Meanwhile, put avocado slices on the other half of the sandwich. Sprinkle salt and pepper for added taste. Sprinkle goat cheese on top of

the avocado slices. Combine sandwiches together to close.

- Follow the instructions on the manufacturer's manual on how to preheat a Panini press. Apply cooking spray onto Panini press. Put sandwiches into the press then close. Cook bread for 5-8 minutes until crisp and toasted, with grill marks, while the cheese starts to melt.

Nutrition Information

- Calories: 469 calories;
- Total Fat: 23.8
- Sodium: 1250
- Total Carbohydrate: 45.5
- Cholesterol: 37
- Protein: 22.1

---

588. Turkey And Bacon Panini With Chipotle Mayonnaise

Serving: 4 | Prep: 20mins | Cook: 20mins | Ready in:

Ingredients

- 8 slices bacon
- 1 tablespoon butter
- 2 cloves garlic, minced
- 1/2 red onion, thinly sliced
- 3 cups fresh spinach leaves
- 1/2 cup reduced-fat mayonnaise
- 2 chipotle peppers in adobo sauce, minced
- 1 teaspoon adobo sauce from chipotle peppers
- 8 (4 inch) pieces focaccia bread
- 4 slices provolone cheese
- 1/2 pound sliced deli turkey meat

Direction

- Preheat the panini press following manufacturer's directions.
- In a big, deep skillet, put the bacon, and allow to cook over medium-high heat for 10 minutes,

flipping from time to time, till equally browned. Let the bacon slices drain on plate lined with paper towel. Meantime, in a big skillet, melt butter over medium heat. Cook and mix onion and garlic till the onion for 10 minutes has become translucent and softened. Mix in spinach and let cook for 3 minutes longer till wilted.

- Meanwhile, in a small bowl, mix together the adobo sauce, minced chipotle peppers and mayonnaise. Scatter mayonnaise on 4 focaccia bread slices. Onto the 4 slices, put a cheese slice, then distribute the turkey between sandwiches. Onto every sandwich, put 2 bacon strips and place spinach mixture on top. Onto the sandwiches, put the leftover bread slices.
- In the prepped panini grill, cook the sandwiches following manufacturer's instructions for 5 minutes till golden brown and crispy.

Nutrition Information

- Calories: 699 calories;
- Protein: 34.5
- Total Fat: 33.2
- Sodium: 2276
- Total Carbohydrate: 65.1
- Cholesterol: 81

Chapter 9: Sloppy-Joes Sandwich Recipes

***

589.   Bar B Q

Serving: 10 | Prep: 15mins | Cook: 30mins | Ready in:

Ingredients

- 3 pounds lean ground beef
- 1 (10.75 ounce) can condensed tomato soup
- 1 (10.5 ounce) can condensed French onion soup
- 1/2 cup ketchup
- 1/2 cup packed brown sugar
- 10 hamburger buns

Direction

- In a big skillet, brown ground beef on medium heat then drain fat.
- Add in French onion soups and tomato. Fill water into each can until 1/4 full to rinse the cans out. Pour into the meat mixture. Add in brown sugar and ketchup then combine thoroughly.
- Allow to simmer about half hour then serve on hamburger buns.

Nutrition Information

- Calories: 480 calories;
- Protein: 29.3
- Total Fat: 21.5
- Sodium: 844
- Total Carbohydrate: 41.7
- Cholesterol: 83

590.   Best Ever Sloppy Joes

Serving: 6 | Prep: 15mins | Cook: 30mins | Ready in:

Ingredients

- 2 pounds ground beef chuck
- 1 large diced onion
- 1 large diced green pepper
- 1 celery stalk, diced

- 1 1/2 (10.75 ounce) cans tomato soup
- 1 teaspoon cumin
- 1/4 teaspoon Worcestershire sauce
- salt and pepper to taste (optional)
- 6 hamburger buns
- 1 cup shredded Cheddar cheese

Direction

- Heat a big frying pan on medium heat. Into the frying pan, crumble the ground beef and cook until turning brown. Add celery, pepper, and onion and cook until tender. Mix in pepper, salt, Worcestershire sauce, ground cumin, and tomato soup; simmer until hot. Spoon the meat onto hamburger buns, put Cheddar cheese on top.

Nutrition Information

- Calories: 485 calories;
- Sodium: 839
- Total Carbohydrate: 36
- Cholesterol: 89
- Protein: 28.1
- Total Fat: 25.2

591.   Bubba's Sloppy Joes

Serving: 12 | Prep: 45mins | Cook: 50mins | Ready in:

Ingredients

- 3 tablespoons butter
- 6 cloves garlic, minced
- 1 large sweet onion (such as Vidalia®), chopped
- 1 large green bell pepper, chopped
- 1/4 cup chopped fresh cilantro
- 2 pounds ground beef
- 1/4 cup brown sugar
- 2 tablespoons prepared yellow mustard (such as Colman's®)
- 1 tablespoon Worcestershire sauce

- 1 teaspoon Italian seasoning
- 1 teaspoon onion powder
- 3/4 teaspoon Greek seasoning (such as Cavender's®), or more to taste
- 1/2 teaspoon hamburger seasoning (such as McCormick® Grill Mates®), or more to taste
- 1/2 teaspoon garlic powder
- 1/2 teaspoon ground black pepper
- 1/2 teaspoon smokehouse maple seasoning (such as McCormick® Grill Mates®), or more to taste
- 1/4 teaspoon hickory smoked salt (such as McCormick®), or more to taste
- 2 pinches ground nutmeg, or more to taste
- 2 cups barbeque sauce (such as Sweet Baby Ray's®)
- 1 cup ketchup
- 2 tablespoons apple cider vinegar
- 12 hamburger buns

Direction

- In a skillet, heat butter on medium until melted. In hot butter, cook, stirring, garlic for 1-2 minutes until aromatic. Mix cilantro, green pepper and onion into the garlic; cook, stirring, for another 5-10 minutes until onion is tender.
- In a large skillet, cook and stir ground beef on medium heat for 5-10 minutes until browned; degrease. Raise to medium-high heat. Whisk in nutmeg, smoked salt, smokehouse maple seasoning, black pepper, garlic powder, hamburger seasoning, Greek seasoning, onion powder, Italian seasoning, Worcestershire sauce, mustard and brown sugar; cook for 4-6 minutes until boiled through.
- Mix in onion mixture, then reduce heat until simmering.
- Add apple cider vinegar, ketchup and barbeque sauce into beef mixture; stir, then simmer, covered, for half an hour until sauce is thick. Fill hamburger buns with beef, then serve.

Nutrition Information

- Calories: 401 calories;
- Sodium: 1141
- Total Carbohydrate: 49.7
- Cholesterol: 55
- Protein: 17.3
- Total Fat: 14.6

592.   Dallas Style Sloppy Joes

Serving: 5 | Prep: 20mins | Cook: 25mins | Ready in:

Ingredients

- 1 1/2 pounds lean ground beef
- 1 yellow onion, chopped
- 1 red bell pepper, chopped
- sea salt and ground black pepper to taste
- 1 1/2 cups ketchup
- 3 tablespoons apple cider vinegar
- 3 tablespoons Worcestershire sauce
- 3 tablespoons brown sugar
- 3 tablespoons yellow mustard
- 3 tablespoons hickory flavored barbecue sauce
- 2 tablespoons grated Parmesan cheese
- 5 large hamburger buns, toasted

Direction

- In a large skillet, cook ground beef over medium heat for 5-7 minutes or until brown completely. Put in the bell pepper and onion, season with black pepper and sea salt. Cook for 7 minutes, until vegetables soften.
- Stir in barbeque sauce, mustard, brown sugar, Worcestershire sauce, vinegar and ketchup. Turn the heat to low, simmer for 10 minutes or until mixture thicken. Put in Parmesan cheese. Place on toasted hamburger buns. Enjoy!

Nutrition Information

- Calories: 530 calories;
- Sodium: 1531
- Total Carbohydrate: 59.4

- Cholesterol: 85
- Protein: 29.6
- Total Fat: 19.5

---

593. Delish Sloppy Joes

Serving: 8 | Prep: 10mins | Cook: 10mins | Ready in:

Ingredients

- 2 pounds ground beef
- 1 (10.75 ounce) can condensed tomato soup (such as Campbell's®)
- 2 tablespoons brown sugar, or to taste
- 1/4 teaspoon Worcestershire sauce, or to taste
- 2 tablespoons distilled white vinegar
- 8 hamburger buns, split and toasted

Direction

- Place a large skillet over medium-high heat; add ground beef and stir well. Cook beef, stirring, until no longer pink inside, evenly browned, and crumbly. Drain beef and discard any excess drippings.
- Whisk in vinegar, Worcestershire sauce, brown sugar, and condensed tomato soup. Cook, stirring, approximately 5 minutes until thick. Adjust seasoning if necessary. Spoon beef mixture onto toasted hamburger buns to serve.

Nutrition Information

- Calories: 363 calories;
- Protein: 23.3
- Total Fat: 16.1
- Sodium: 520
- Total Carbohydrate: 30
- Cholesterol: 69

---

594. Emily's Famous Sloppy Joes

Serving: 8 | Prep: 10mins | Cook: 20mins | Ready in:

Ingredients

- 1 1/2 pounds ground beef
- 1 onion, chopped
- 1 red bell pepper, chopped
- 1 (6 ounce) can tomato paste
- 1 cup water
- 3 cloves garlic, minced
- 1 tablespoon chili powder
- 1 teaspoon paprika
- 1 teaspoon ground cumin
- 1 teaspoon distilled white vinegar
- 3 tablespoons brown sugar
- 1 teaspoon dried oregano
- 1/2 teaspoon salt
- 1/2 teaspoon ground black pepper
- 8 hamburger buns, split

Direction

- Over medium-high heat, sauté ground beef for 5 minutes in a big skillet. Put the red bell pepper and onion in; sauté until onion is soft, 5 minutes. Remove the fat.
- Mix water and tomato paste. Stir well until paste dissolves. Add chili powder, garlic, paprika, vinegar, brown sugar, cumin, oregano, pepper, and salt. Heat for 5 to 10 minutes or until mixture becomes like a thick stew.

Nutrition Information

- Calories: 328 calories;
- Total Fat: 12.6
- Sodium: 617
- Total Carbohydrate: 34.2
- Cholesterol: 52
- Protein: 19.4

595. Family Favorite Sloppy Joes

Serving: 6 | Prep: 10mins | Cook: 25mins | Ready in:

Ingredients

- 1 pound ground beef
- 1 cup ketchup
- 1/2 (12 ounce) bottle chili sauce
- 1/2 cup dark brown sugar
- 1/4 cup grated Parmesan cheese, or to taste
- 1 teaspoon sweet pickle relish
- 1 teaspoon minced onion
- 1 teaspoon Worcestershire sauce

Direction

- Place a large skillet over medium-high heat. In the hot skillet, cook and stir beef for approximately 5 to 7 minutes until crumbly and browned; drain and discard grease. Mix into ground beef chili sauce, ketchup, Parmesan cheese, brown sugar, relish, Worcestershire sauce, and onion; simmer for 20 to 25 minutes until flavors blend and heated through.

Nutrition Information

- Calories: 264 calories;
- Total Fat: 10.2
- Sodium: 597
- Total Carbohydrate: 29.4
- Cholesterol: 50
- Protein: 14.8

596. Grandma's Sloppy Joes

Serving: 4 | Prep: 10mins | Cook: 45mins | Ready in:

Ingredients

- 1 pound ground beef
- 1 cup chopped onion
- 1 cup chopped green bell pepper
- 1 tablespoon brown sugar
- 1 tablespoon vinegar
- 1 cup ketchup
- 2 tablespoons prepared mustard
- 1/2 teaspoon ground cloves
- 1 teaspoon salt
- 4 hamburger buns, split

Direction

- Mix green pepper, onion, and ground beef in a large skillet on medium heat. Cook until the meat is browned, the drain all the excess grease. Stir in mustard, ketchup, vinegar, and brown sugar, flavor with salt and cloves. Bring to a simmer on low heat for half an hour. Place on hamburger buns and serve.

Nutrition Information

- Calories: 429 calories;
- Total Fat: 16.2
- Sodium: 1648
- Total Carbohydrate: 47
- Cholesterol: 69
- Protein: 24.9

597. Hodie's Sloppy Joes

Serving: 6 | Prep: 10mins | Cook: 25mins | Ready in:

Ingredients

- 1 pound ground beef
- 1/2 cup chopped onion
- 1 (8 ounce) can tomato sauce
- 1/3 cup ketchup
- 2 tablespoons brown sugar
- 1 tablespoon apple cider vinegar

Direction

- In a skillet, cook and stir chopped onion and ground beef on medium heat until onions are translucent and beef is browned thoroughly. Drain the grease off the skillet and put back the skillet on medium heat. Whisk in vinegar, brown sugar, ketchup and tomato sauce. Lower heat to medium-low and let simmer for 20 minutes.

Nutrition Information

- Calories: 280 calories;
- Total Fat: 20.2
- Sodium: 398
- Total Carbohydrate: 11.1
- Cholesterol: 64
- Protein: 13.5

598. Homemade Sloppy Joes

Serving: 6 | Prep: 15mins | Cook: 55mins | Ready in:

Ingredients

- 1 1/2 pounds extra lean ground beef
- 1/2 onion, diced
- 2 cloves garlic, minced
- 1 green pepper, diced
- 1 cup water
- 3/4 cup ketchup
- 1 dash Worcestershire sauce
- 2 tablespoons brown sugar
- 1 teaspoon Dijon mustard
- 1 1/2 teaspoons salt, or to taste
- 1/2 teaspoon ground black pepper
- 1 cup water
- cayenne pepper to taste (optional)

Direction

- In a big skillet, put in the onion and ground beef. Set the heat setting to medium heat and let the mixture cook for about 10 minutes while continuously stirring it until the ground beef turned brown in color and are formed into small crumbles.

- Add in the green bell pepper and the garlic and mix everything together; let the mixture cook for 2-3 minutes while stirring it until it becomes soft. Pour in 1 cup of water and give it a mix, scrape any browned flavor bits off the bottom of the skillet and let it dissolve in the mixture.
- Add in the brown sugar, black pepper, ketchup, salt, Worcestershire sauce and Dijon mustard and mix well. Pour in another 1 cup of water and allow the mixture to get back to a simmer. Lower the heat setting to low heat and let the mixture simmer for about 40 minutes while stirring it from time to time until the mixture becomes thick in consistency and the cooking liquid has evaporated. Add in black pepper, cayenne pepper and salt to taste.

Nutrition Information

- Calories: 251 calories;
- Sodium: 1002
- Total Carbohydrate: 14.4
- Cholesterol: 69
- Protein: 21.5
- Total Fat: 11.9

599. Kendra's Maid Rite Sandwiches

Serving: 16 | Prep: 10mins | Cook: 35mins | Ready in:

Ingredients

- 2 pounds ground beef
- 1 chopped onion
- 3/4 cup ketchup
- 2 tablespoons brown sugar
- 2 tablespoons distilled white vinegar
- 1 tablespoon Worcestershire sauce
- 2 teaspoons prepared yellow mustard
- 1/2 teaspoon salt
- 16 hamburger buns, warmed

Direction

- Over medium-high heat, heat a large skillet; mix in onion and ground beef. Cook while stirring until beef is no longer pink, crumbly and browned evenly. Drain; remove all the excess grease. Mix in salt, mustard, Worcestershire sauce, vinegar, brown sugar and ketchup. Simmer. Lower the heat to medium-low and simmer, covered, for 20 more minutes. Place on the warmed buns to serve.

Nutrition Information

- Calories: 244 calories;
- Cholesterol: 34
- Protein: 13.4
- Total Fat: 8.9
- Sodium: 483
- Total Carbohydrate: 27

---

600. Kid Pleasing Sloppy Joes

Serving: 6 | Prep: 10mins | Cook: 20mins | Ready in:

Ingredients

- 1 pound ground beef
- 1 small onion, chopped
- 1 cup ketchup
- 2 tablespoons cider vinegar
- 2 tablespoons brown sugar
- 1 tablespoon Worcestershire sauce
- 1 teaspoon mustard

Direction

- Heat a big frying pan on medium-high heat. In the hot frying pan, stir and cook onion and beef for 5-7 minutes until the beef is fully browned. Drain and dispose the fat. Reheat the frying pan.
- Mix mustard, Worcestershire sauce, brown sugar, vinegar, and ketchup into the beef

mixture, simmer for 15-20 minutes until the liquid has thickened, stirring occasionally.

Nutrition Information

- Calories: 199 calories;
- Total Fat: 9
- Sodium: 540
- Total Carbohydrate: 16.4
- Cholesterol: 46
- Protein: 13.5

---

601. Maddog's Venison Sloppy Joes

Serving: 4 | Prep: 20mins | Cook: 23mins | Ready in:

Ingredients

- 3 tablespoons vegetable oil, divided
- 1 yellow onion, diced
- 1 red bell pepper, diced
- 1 jalapeno pepper, diced
- 1 pound ground venison
- 1 pinch ground black pepper, or to taste
- 1 pinch ground cayenne pepper, or to taste
- 1 pinch grill seasoning (such as Montreal Steak Seasoning®), or to taste
- 1 pinch garlic salt, or to taste
- 1 dash Worcestershire sauce
- 1 vine-ripened tomato, diced
- 2 tablespoons barbeque sauce, or more to taste
- 2 tablespoons ketchup (such as Heinz®), or more to taste
- 2 teaspoons tomato paste, or more to taste
- 2 teaspoons hot sauce, or more to taste
- 4 hamburger buns, split
- 1 (8 ounce) package shredded sharp Cheddar cheese

Direction

- Heat 1 1/2 tbsp. oil on medium heat in a big skillet. Add jalapeno, red bell pepper and onion; mix and cook for 5-8 minutes till soft.
- Heat leftover 1 1/2 tbsp. oil on medium heat in another skillet. Add venison; mix and cook for 4-5 minutes till lightly browned. Mix in Worcestershire sauce, garlic salt, grill seasoning, cayenne pepper and black pepper; cook for 4-5 minutes till venison is browned.
- Pulse hot sauce, tomato paste, ketchup, barbeque sauce and tomato till sauce is combined in a food processor.
- Simmer sauce, venison mixture and onion mixture in a saucepan for 10-15 minutes till flavors merge. Divide to buns; put cheddar cheese over.

Nutrition Information

- Calories: 622 calories;
- Total Fat: 33.7
- Sodium: 1018
- Total Carbohydrate: 36.7
- Cholesterol: 144
- Protein: 42.3

---

602.   Mark's Nearly Famous Sloppy Joes

Serving: 10 | Prep: 30mins | Cook: 4hours | Ready in:

Ingredients

- 2 1/2 pounds ground beef
- 1 large onion, chopped
- 1/4 green bell pepper, chopped
- 2 stalks celery, chopped
- 1 (10.75 ounce) can condensed chicken gumbo soup
- 1 (6 ounce) can tomato paste
- 2 tablespoons brown sugar
- 4 tablespoons lemon juice
- 1 1/2 tablespoons yellow mustard
- 1/2 cup ketchup

- 1/2 cup barbecue sauce
- 6 tablespoons white vinegar
- 2 tablespoons Worcestershire sauce
- 1 teaspoon liquid smoke flavoring
- 1/2 teaspoon dried parsley
- 1/2 teaspoon black pepper
- 1 teaspoon salt

Direction

- Cook ground beef till evenly brown in a big heavy skillet; drain well.
- Mix together brown sugar, tomato paste, condensed gumbo soup, celery, bell pepper and onion in a slow cooker; mix in vinegar, barbeque sauce, ketchup, mustard and lemon juice. Season with salt, black pepper, parsley, liquid smoke and Worcestershire sauce; mix in browned beef.
- Cover; cook for 4-6 hours on low, occasionally mixing. Skim off excess fat.

Nutrition Information

- Calories: 439 calories;
- Total Fat: 31.2
- Sodium: 1017
- Total Carbohydrate: 18.7
- Cholesterol: 97
- Protein: 20.9

---

603.   Midwest Loose Meats

Serving: 12 | Prep: 15mins | Cook: 55mins | Ready in:

Ingredients

- 3 pounds ground beef
- 3 cups chicken broth
- 3 tablespoons Worcestershire sauce
- 3 tablespoons spicy brown mustard
- 1 teaspoon salt
- 1 teaspoon ground black pepper
- 1/4 cup yellow mustard, or as needed

- 12 hamburger buns, split
- 24 dill pickle slices

Direction

- Over medium-high heat, heat large skillet. Cook while stirring until beef is no longer pink, browned evenly and crumbly. Drain; remove all the excess grease. Mix in pepper, salt, brown mustard, Worcestershire sauce and chicken broth. Boil. Lower the heat to low, simmer, uncovered, for half an hour until liquid is evaporated.
- In the meantime, start preheating oven to 300°F (150°C).
- Spread on top half of each bun with preferred amount of the yellow mustard. On bottom half, arrange two slices of pickle. Spoon 2-3 tablespoons ground beef mixture over. Place the other bun half on top to create the sandwich. Do again until all the sandwiches are complete.
- Individually cover every sandwich in aluminum foil. Put into the baking sheet. Bake in prepared oven for 10 minutes to warm through the bread.

Nutrition Information

- Calories: 341 calories;
- Total Fat: 16.1
- Sodium: 1069
- Total Carbohydrate: 23.9
- Cholesterol: 70
- Protein: 23.4

604.   Momma's Sloppy Joes

Serving: 6 | Prep: 15mins | Cook: 40mins | Ready in:

Ingredients

- 1 pound ground turkey
- 1 cup ketchup
- 2 tablespoons white sugar

- 2 tablespoons white vinegar
- 2 tablespoons yellow mustard

Direction

- In a large skillet over medium heat, place the turkey; cook until browned evenly, allow to drain.
- Mix the sugar, ketchup, mustard, and vinegar in a large saucepan over medium heat. Add in the turkey. Cook for around 30 minutes, stirring often.

Nutrition Information

- Calories: 170 calories;
- Sodium: 547
- Total Carbohydrate: 14.5
- Cholesterol: 56
- Protein: 15.9
- Total Fat: 6

605.   Neat Sloppy Joes

Serving: 8 | Prep: 20mins | Cook: 30mins | Ready in:

Ingredients

- 2 pounds lean ground beef
- 1/2 cup chopped onion
- 1 cup chopped celery
- 1 (10.75 ounce) can condensed tomato soup
- 1/4 cup ketchup
- 1 tablespoon white vinegar
- 1/4 cup packed brown sugar
- 1 1/2 teaspoons Worcestershire sauce
- 1/2 teaspoon salt
- 1/4 teaspoon garlic powder
- 8 hamburger buns

Direction

- In a big skillet, put ground beef on moderate heat. Cook till equally browned, mixing to break up. You can use potato masher to remove all lumps. Put in celery and onion, put on pan cover, and cook for 5 minutes till transparent and tender. Let any grease drain.

- Into the mixture of beef, mix Worcestershire sauce, brown sugar, vinegar, ketchup and undiluted tomato soup. Add garlic powder and salt to season. On low heat, heat to simmer, and cook till well heated, mixing often to avoid it from burning on bottom.
- Scoop mixture of hot beef onto buns, which can be toasted first, serve.

Nutrition Information

- Calories: 407 calories;
- Total Carbohydrate: 37
- Cholesterol: 74
- Protein: 26.2
- Total Fat: 16.7
- Sodium: 774

---

606.   Nonie's Best BBQ

Serving: 12 | Prep: 10mins | Cook: 30mins | Ready in:

Ingredients

- 1 (14 ounce) bottle ketchup
- 1/2 cup water
- 1/4 cup white sugar
- 1 tablespoon brown sugar
- 1 tablespoon red wine vinegar
- 1 tablespoon prepared yellow mustard
- 1 teaspoon salt
- 1/4 teaspoon ground black pepper
- 1/4 teaspoon paprika
- 2 pounds ground beef
- 2 teaspoons minced onion
- 12 hamburger buns, split

Direction

- Whisk paprika, pepper, salt, mustard, vinegar, brown sugar, white sugar, water and ketchup

in a big saucepan; simmer on medium high heat. Lower heat to medium low; simmer for 15 minutes.

- Meanwhile, heat big skillet on medium high heat; mix and cook onion and ground beef in hot skillet till not pink, evenly browned and beef is crumbly. Drain extra grease; discard. Mix beef into simmering barbeque sauce; simmer for 10 minutes. Put onto buns; serve.

Nutrition Information

- Calories: 314 calories;
- Total Carbohydrate: 35.5
- Cholesterol: 47
- Protein: 17
- Total Fat: 11.5
- Sodium: 863

---

607.   Philly Cheese Steak Sloppy Joes

Serving: 4 | Prep: 15mins | Cook: 20mins | Ready in:

Ingredients

- 1 pound lean ground beef
- 1/2 red bell pepper, thinly sliced
- 1/2 green bell pepper, thinly sliced
- 1/2 yellow onion, thinly sliced
- 1 clove garlic, minced
- 1 cup cold water
- 1 tablespoon cornstarch
- 2 teaspoons beef bouillon granules
- 1 teaspoon Worcestershire sauce
- salt and ground black pepper to taste
- 3/4 cup shredded mozzarella cheese
- 4 whole wheat hamburger buns, split

Direction

- Over medium-high heat, heat a large skillet. Cook while stirring beef in the hot skillet for 5-7 minutes until crumbly and browned. Add garlic, onion and bell peppers; sauté until they start tenderizing, about 5 more minutes.

- In a bowl, stir together Worcestershire sauce, bouillon, cornstarch and water. Add to beef mixture in skillet. Use a lid to cover and lower the heat to low. Simmer for 7-10 minutes until the veggies become tender and the sauce is thickened. Sprinkle with pepper and salt to taste. Add mozzarella cheese, cover until melted, about 2 minutes. Stir to mix well.
- Serve buns topped with beef mixture, Sloppy Joe-style.

Nutrition Information

- Calories: 747 calories;
- Sodium: 1628
- Total Carbohydrate: 82.1
- Cholesterol: 93
- Protein: 44.4
- Total Fat: 27.6

---

608.   Picadillo

Serving: 12 | Prep: 30mins | Cook: 1hours | Ready in:

Ingredients

- 2 tablespoons olive oil
- 7 cloves garlic, chopped
- 1 1/2 cups chopped onion
- 1 1/2 cups chopped green bell pepper
- 3 pounds lean ground beef
- 1 (5 ounce) jar green olives, pitted and halved
- 5 ounces capers, rinsed and drained
- 1/4 cup white vinegar
- 1 teaspoon salt
- 1 teaspoon freshly ground black pepper
- 1 teaspoon ground cinnamon
- 1 teaspoon ground cloves
- 2 dried bay leaves
- 1/4 teaspoon hot sauce
- 6 cups canned tomatoes, half-drained

Direction

- Heat 1 tbsp. olive oil in a big stockpot on medium heat. Sauté green pepper, onion and garlic until onions are transparent. Put onion mixture into a bowl. Put aside. Heat leftover olive oil in the same pot. Brown ground beef.
- Mix hot sauce, bay leaves, cloves, cinnamon, pepper, salt, vinegar, capers and olives in another saucepan. Simmer for 10 minutes on medium heat.
- Put onion mixture and olive mixture into the pot with ground beef. Add 1/2 drained tomatoes. Cook on medium heat for 1 hour. Occasionally stir.

Nutrition Information

- Calories: 292 calories;
- Sodium: 1064
- Total Carbohydrate: 9.8
- Cholesterol: 74
- Protein: 23.6
- Total Fat: 18

---

609.   Pork Rites (Taverns)

Serving: 12 | Prep: 5mins | Cook: 25mins | Ready in:

Ingredients

- 2 pounds ground pork
- 1 cup ketchup
- 1/2 cup water
- 2 tablespoons vinegar
- 1 tablespoon brown sugar
- 1 teaspoon dry mustard
- 1 teaspoon salt
- 12 hamburger buns

Direction

- Place a large skillet on medium-high heat. Cook while stirring ground pork in the hot skillet for 5-7 minutes, or till crumbly and browned; drain and discard any grease.

- Combine salt, dry mustard, brown sugar, vinegar, water and ketchup into the ground beef; simmer the mixture; cook for 20 minutes. Serve on hamburger buns.

Nutrition Information

- Calories: 303 calories;
- Sodium: 696
- Total Carbohydrate: 27.8
- Cholesterol: 49
- Protein: 17.5
- Total Fat: 13.2

610. Pumpkin Joes

Serving: 40 | Prep: 15mins | Cook: 1hours | Ready in:

Ingredients

- 5 pounds ground beef
- 1/2 large onion, diced
- 1 tablespoon pumpkin pie spice
- 1 teaspoon dried thyme
- 1/2 teaspoon ground dried rosemary
- salt to taste
- 1 3/4 tablespoons Worcestershire sauce
- 1 tablespoon hot pepper sauce, or to taste
- 2 (10.75 ounce) cans condensed tomato soup
- 1 1/2 (10.75 ounce) cans condensed cream of celery soup
- 1 (29 ounce) can pure pumpkin
- 40 hamburger buns

Direction

- On medium heat, cook onion and ground beef for 10mins in a big pan until the beef is crumbly and beginning to brown, crumbling the meat while cooking.
- Drain the fat from the ground beef; mix in pumpkin, pumpkin pie spice, celery soup,

thyme, tomato soup, rosemary, hot pepper sauce, Worcestershire sauce, and salt. Stir until well blended.

- Boil the mixture; lower heat and let it simmer for 45mins to an hour until the mixture is thick and the flavors have combined.

Nutrition Information

- Calories: 251 calories;
- Sodium: 514
- Total Carbohydrate: 26.5
- Cholesterol: 36
- Protein: 13.8
- Total Fat: 9.7

611. Ruby Drive Sloppy Joes

Serving: 6 | Prep: 5mins | Cook: 30mins | Ready in:

Ingredients

- 1 pound ground beef
- 1 1/2 cups ketchup
- 1 cup chunky salsa
- 2 tablespoons brown sugar
- 1 tablespoon Worcestershire sauce
- 2 tablespoons white vinegar
- 2 tablespoons Dijon mustard
- 1 teaspoon hot sauce
- 6 potato rolls

Direction

- Place a big frying pan on medium-high heat and mix in ground beef. Stir and cook until the beef is not pink anymore, evenly brown, and crumbly. Strain and dispose any excess fat.
- Mix in hot sauce, Dijon mustard, white vinegar, Worcestershire sauce, brown sugar, salsa, and ketchup. Simmer and cook over low heat, whisking sometimes, about 20-30 minutes. Enjoy on potato rolls.

Nutrition Information

- Calories: 382 calories;
- Total Fat: 15.2
- Sodium: 1338
- Total Carbohydrate: 46.2
- Cholesterol: 46
- Protein: 17.4

---

612.   Runza Burgers

Serving: 10 | Prep: 10mins | Cook: 30mins | Ready in:

Ingredients

- 1 1/2 pounds lean ground beef
- 3 cloves garlic, minced
- 1 onion, chopped
- 1 small head cabbage, shredded
- 1 (14 ounce) can beef broth
- 2 tablespoons Worcestershire sauce
- 2 tablespoons yellow mustard
- salt and pepper to taste
- 10 hamburger buns, split

Direction

- In a big skillet, brown ground beef on high heat, then drain fat. Stir in cabbage, onion and garlic, then cook until vegetables are soft and wilted. Stir in mustard, Worcestershire sauce and beef broth. Cook on medium heat without a cover until it is reduced to the consistency of a sloppy joe. Use pepper and salt to season.
- Put on top of meat mixture with hamburger buns, then cover the skillet and steam for a minute. To serve, fill beef and cabbage mixture into steamed buns.

Nutrition Information

- Calories: 284 calories;
- Total Fat: 10.8
- Sodium: 493
- Total Carbohydrate: 27.9

- Cholesterol: 45
- Protein: 18.3

---

613.   Saucy Smoked Sausage Sandwich

Serving: 6 | Prep: 10mins | Cook: 12mins | Ready in:

Ingredients

- 1/4 medium onion
- 1 large carrot
- 2 stalks celery
- 1 (14 ounce) package Hillshire Farm® Smoked Sausage, diagonally cut into 1/4-inch slices
- 1/2 cup ketchup
- 1 1/2 tablespoons Worcestershire sauce
- 2 tablespoons dark brown sugar
- 6 slices Cheddar cheese
- 6 brioche or hamburger buns

Direction

- Cut celery, onion and carrot into equal size pieces. In the food processor, pulse until they are finely chopped.
- Heat a large non-stick skillet over medium heat. Cook the smoked sausage until brown. Put in celery, onion and carrot; cook for about 5 mins or until soft.
- Put in brown sugar, ketchup and Worcestershire sauce. Cook, stirring occasionally, for 6 to 7 mins.
- Pour the filling onto buns with the cheese. Serve.

Nutrition Information

- Calories: 510 calories;
- Total Carbohydrate: 37.8
- Cholesterol: 71
- Protein: 19.6
- Total Fat: 30.6
- Sodium: 1269

614.   Sloppy Joe Mamas

Serving: 6 | Prep: 15mins | Cook: 2hours15mins | Ready in:

Ingredients

- 1 tablespoon olive oil, or more if needed
- 1/2 onion, chopped
- 2 cloves garlic
- 2 pounds lean ground beef
- 1/2 cup Mexican-style hot tomato sauce (such as El Pato Salsa de Chile Fresco®)
- 1/2 cup ketchup
- 3 tablespoons brown sugar
- 3 tablespoons Worcestershire sauce
- 2 tablespoons mustard
- 2 tablespoons cider vinegar
- 1/2 teaspoon chili powder

Direction

- Heat olive oil on medium high heat in a big skillet; sauté garlic and onion in hot oil for 5-7 minutes till browned. Add ground beef; mix and cook for 7-10 minutes till beef browns completely. Drain grease from skillet; discard. Put beef mixture into slow cooker.
- Mix chili powder, cider vinegar, mustard, Worcestershire sauce, ketchup, brown sugar and Mexican-style hot tomato sauce into beef mixture.
- Cook for 1 hour on high or for 2 hours on low.

Nutrition Information

- Calories: 374 calories;
- Cholesterol: 99
- Protein: 29.5
- Total Fat: 21
- Sodium: 550
- Total Carbohydrate: 15.6

615.   Sloppy Joe With Ground Turkey

Serving: 6 | Prep: 15mins | Cook: 20mins | Ready in:

Ingredients

- 1 teaspoon extra-virgin olive oil
- 2 cloves garlic, minced
- 1 1/2 pounds ground turkey
- 1 tomato, chopped
- 1 small onion, chopped
- 3/4 green bell pepper, chopped
- 2 tablespoons chopped fresh parsley
- 1 pinch red pepper flakes
- salt and ground black pepper to taste
- 4 ounces tomato paste
- 1 lemon, juiced
- 6 hamburger buns, split and toasted
- 6 slices American cheese (optional)

Direction

- Over medium heat, in a pot, heat olive oil. Cook while stirring garlic in hot oil for about 2 minutes until fragrant. Break ground turkey into the pot. Use lid to cover the pot; cook meat for 2-3 minutes until the outside turns brown. Using a slivered wooden spoon, break meat up into very small pieces; keep cooking while stirring for 3-5 minutes until nearly browned completely.
- Stir red pepper flakes, parsley, green bell pepper, onion and tomato into turkey mixture; season with black pepper and salt; cook for 3-4 minutes until tomato is softened. Add lemon juice and tomato paste; stir to coat vegetables with tomato paste. Use lid to cover pot, lower the heat to low; cook for 7-10 minutes until vegetables become tender. Top with cheese and serve on toasted hamburgers buns.

Nutrition Information

- Calories: 435 calories;

- Total Fat: 20.6
- Sodium: 878
- Total Carbohydrate: 29.5
- Cholesterol: 110
- Protein: 33.8

---

616.   Sloppy Sams

Serving: 4 | Prep: 15mins | Cook: 35mins | Ready in:

Ingredients

- 3 cups water
- 1 cup lentils, rinsed
- salt to taste (optional)
- 1 cup chopped onion
- 3 tablespoons olive oil
- 2 cups chopped tomato
- 2 cloves garlic, minced
- 1/2 (6 ounce) can tomato paste
- 1/2 cup ketchup
- 1 teaspoon mustard powder
- 1 tablespoon chili powder
- 3 tablespoons molasses
- 1 dash Worcestershire sauce
- salt and ground black pepper to taste
- 4 hamburger buns, split

Direction

- In a saucepan, combine lentils and water; if wanted, season with salt to taste. Heat to a boil on high heat; decrease to medium-low heat, put on cover and allow to simmer 30 minutes, mixing occasionally, until tender.
- At the same time, in a big skillet on medium heat, cook olive oil together with onions for 4 minutes, till onions have become translucent and softened. Add in garlic and tomatoes and cook 5 minutes. Mix in Worcestershire sauce, molasses, chili powder, mustard powder, ketchup, and tomato paste; allow to simmer until thickened, about 5-10 minutes.
- Drain lentils and save the cooking liquid. Mix lentils into the sauce mixture; if necessary,

pouring in water or cooking liquid to have your wished "sloppy joe" consistency. Arrange on buns and serve.

Nutrition Information

- Calories: 517 calories;
- Cholesterol: 0
- Protein: 19.3
- Total Fat: 13.9
- Sodium: 782
- Total Carbohydrate: 82.2

---

617.   Spicy Beef Sloppy Joes

Serving: 6 | Prep: 20mins | Cook: 4hours | Ready in:

Ingredients

- 2 pounds lean ground beef
- 2 (16 ounce) jars salsa
- 3 cups sliced fresh mushrooms
- 1 1/2 cups shredded carrots
- 1 1/2 cups finely chopped red or green bell pepper
- 1/3 cup tomato paste
- 2 teaspoons dried basil, crushed
- 1 teaspoon dried oregano, crushed
- 1/2 teaspoon salt
- 1/4 teaspoon cayenne pepper
- 4 cloves garlic, minced
- 6 kaiser rolls, split and toasted
- 1 Reynolds® Slow Cooker Liner

Direction

- Cook the beef on medium heat in a skillet until it turns brown, stirring to crumble the meat into pieces. Drain off the fat.
- Use a Reynolds® Slow Cooker Liner to line a 5- or 6-quart slow cooker. Open the slow cooker liner and arrange it inside a slow cooker bowl. Fit the liner against the sides and

bottom of the bowl snugly; then pull the top of the liner to overlap the rim of the bowl.

- In the slow cooker, mix beef with the remaining ingredients excluding kaiser rolls.
- Put a cover on and cook for 8-10 hours on Low or 4-5 hours on High.
- Remove the lid carefully to release the steam. Remove sloppy joes right out of the slow cooker to serve, topping each Kaiser roll with meat. Don't transport or lift the liner containing food. Allow the slow cooker to cool completely, remove all excess liquid, then take the liner out and toss.

Nutrition Information

- Calories: 500 calories;
- Total Fat: 20.8
- Sodium: 1539
- Total Carbohydrate: 40.6
- Cholesterol: 105
- Protein: 38.7

618. Super Easy Sloppy Joes

Serving: 6 | Prep: 10mins | Cook: 20mins | Ready in:

Ingredients

- 3 pounds ground beef
- 1 cup chopped yellow onion
- 1 cup finely chopped celery
- 1 (12 ounce) bottle tomato-based chili sauce
- 1/4 cup apple cider vinegar
- 1/4 cup packed brown sugar
- 1 teaspoon prepared yellow mustard (optional)

Direction

- In a Dutch oven or a big pot, crumble ground beef over medium-high heat. Cook until turning brown evenly, mixing often. Strain off

the fat. Add celery and onion, and cook for 3 minutes until the onion is soft.
- Lower the heat to medium and add chili sauce. Mix in sugar and vinegar. Add mustard (if using). Simmer until the mixture reaches the thickness you want. Enjoy with buns.

Nutrition Information

- Calories: 536 calories;
- Total Fat: 35.4
- Sodium: 233
- Total Carbohydrate: 13.7
- Cholesterol: 139
- Protein: 38.1

619. Terri's Sloppy Joes

Serving: 6 | Prep: 5mins | Cook: 30mins | Ready in:

Ingredients

- 1 1/2 pounds ground beef
- 1 small onion, chopped
- 3/4 cup ketchup
- 1/4 cup barbeque sauce
- 1 tablespoon vinegar
- 1 tablespoon prepared mustard
- 1 tablespoon white sugar

Direction

- In a big frying pan, stir and cook onion and ground beef over medium heat for 10 minutes until the onion is tender and the beef is fully brown.
- Mix white sugar, mustard, vinegar, barbeque sauce, and ketchup into the ground beef mixture, simmer for 15 minutes.

Nutrition Information

- Calories: 260 calories;
- Total Fat: 13.5

- Sodium: 546
- Total Carbohydrate: 14.6
- Cholesterol: 69
- Protein: 19.8

---

620. Turkey Joes

Serving: 5 | Prep: 10mins | Cook: 20mins | Ready in:

Ingredients

- 2 tablespoons olive oil
- 1 yellow onion, diced
- 1 1/4 pounds ground turkey
- 1 cup ketchup
- 1 tablespoon red wine vinegar
- 1 tablespoon Worcestershire sauce
- 1 tablespoon Dijon mustard
- 1 tablespoon brown sugar
- 1 tablespoon chili powder

Direction

- Over medium heat, in a large skillet, heat oil; cook while stirring onion in hot oil for 5-7 minutes until translucent. Break ground turkey into small pieces; add to skillet; cook while stirring, breaking the turkey more into smaller pieces, for 7-10 minutes until browned completely.
- Stir chili powder, brown sugar, Dijon mustard, Worcestershire sauce, vinegar, and ketchup into the turkey; cook at a simmer for about 10 minutes until thick and hot.

Nutrition Information

- Calories: 302 calories;
- Sodium: 726
- Total Carbohydrate: 21.3
- Cholesterol: 84
- Protein: 24
- Total Fat: 14.4

---

621. Vegetarian Sloppy Joes

Serving: 6 | Prep: 20mins | Cook: 20mins | Ready in:

Ingredients

- 1/4 cup vegetable oil
- 1/2 cup minced onion
- 2 (8 ounce) packages tempeh
- 1/2 cup minced green bell pepper
- 2 cloves garlic, minced
- 1/4 cup tomato sauce
- 1 tablespoon vegetarian Worcestershire sauce
- 1 tablespoon honey
- 1 tablespoon blackstrap molasses
- 1/4 teaspoon cayenne pepper
- 1/4 teaspoon celery seed
- 1/4 teaspoon ground cumin
- 1/4 teaspoon salt
- 1/2 teaspoon ground coriander
- 1/2 teaspoon dried thyme
- 1/2 teaspoon oregano
- 1/2 teaspoon paprika
- 1 pinch ground black pepper
- hamburger buns

Direction

- Over medium-low heat, heat the oil in a deep, 10-inch frying pan. Cook the onion in the oil until it becomes translucent. Break the tempeh into small pieces into the frying pan, then cook and stir until they turn golden brown. Add the garlic and green pepper, then cook for 2-3 minutes more.
- Mix in the black pepper, paprika, oregano, thyme, coriander, salt, cumin, celery seed, cayenne pepper, molasses, honey, Worcestershire sauce and tomato sauce, then mix. Simmer for another 10-15 minutes. To serve, spoon hot mixture on the hamburger buns.

Nutrition Information

- Calories: 384 calories;
- Total Carbohydrate: 37.3
- Cholesterol: 0
- Protein: 18.3
- Total Fat: 19.6
- Sodium: 425

622. White Sloppy Joes

Serving: 6 | Prep: 10mins | Cook: 10mins | Ready in:

Ingredients

- 1 pound ground beef
- 1 (10.75 ounce) can condensed cream of mushroom soup
- 3 tablespoons milk
- 4 tablespoons sour cream
- 1 teaspoon liquid smoke flavoring
- salt and pepper to taste
- 6 hamburger buns, split

Direction

- Place the ground beef in a big skillet atop medium-high heat. Cook while stirring to crumble until they are browned evenly. Drain the excess grease off. Stir in liquid smoke, milk, and undiluted cream of mushroom soup. Turn the heat down to low and cook until just hot. Stir in the sour cream and season with pepper and salt. Take it off the heat and serve them on hamburger buns.

Nutrition Information

- Calories: 331 calories;
- Total Carbohydrate: 25.8
- Cholesterol: 51
- Protein: 17.7
- Total Fat: 17
- Sodium: 621

623. Zippy Sloppy Joes

Serving: 8 | Prep: 20mins | Cook: 15mins | Ready in:

Ingredients

- 2 pounds extra lean ground beef
- 1 onion, diced
- 4 cloves garlic, minced
- 2 jalapeno chile peppers, seeded and minced
- 1 red bell pepper, diced
- 1 (12 ounce) jar Crosse & Blackwell® Seafood Cocktail Sauce
- 2 tablespoons molasses
- 2 tablespoons brown sugar
- 1 teaspoon chipotle seasoning
- Salt and pepper to taste
- 8 whole wheat buns

Direction

- In large skillet, brown onions and meat over medium-high heat, until browned, or for about 5 minutes. Drain the drippings from the pan. Discard.
- In pan, put red pepper, jalapeno peppers and garlic to beef. Cook, stirring occasionally, about 5 minutes more. Stir in pepper, salt, seasoning, sugar, molasses and cocktail sauce. Lower the heat to low, simmer for 5 minutes. Place on buns to serve.

Nutrition Information

- Calories: 537 calories;
- Total Fat: 21.3
- Sodium: 870
- Total Carbohydrate: 59.6
- Cholesterol: 77
- Protein: 29.1

Chapter 10: Turkey Sandwich Recipes

***

624.   Awesome Turkey Sandwich

Serving: 1 | Prep: 10mins | Cook: | Ready in:

Ingredients

- 2 slices whole wheat bread, toasted (optional)
- 1 tablespoon mayonnaise
- 2 teaspoons Dijon-style prepared mustard
- 3 slices smoked turkey breast
- 2 tablespoons guacamole
- 1/2 cup mixed salad greens
- 1/4 cup bean sprouts
- 1/4 avocado - peeled, pitted and sliced
- 3 ounces Colby-Monterey Jack cheese, sliced
- 2 slices tomato

Direction

- Spread over one slice of toast with mayonnaise, then spread over the other with the mustard. On one side, arrange the sliced turkey. Spread over the turkey with guacamole. Then pile on the cheese, avocado, bean sprouts and salad greens. Ending with the tomato slices, then top with the rest of the slice of toast.

Nutrition Information

- Calories: 804 calories;
- Sodium: 1988
- Total Carbohydrate: 41.4
- Cholesterol: 124
- Protein: 37.9
- Total Fat: 56.6

625.   Black Friday Sandwich

Serving: 1 | Prep: 10mins | Cook: | Ready in:

Ingredients

- 1 tablespoon canned jellied cranberry sauce
- 1 tablespoon mayonnaise
- 1/4 teaspoon celery seed
- 2 slices bread
- 1 tablespoon mashed leftover sweet potato casserole with marshmallow topping
- 1 tablespoon gravy (optional)
- 1 tablespoon dry leftover stuffing
- 1/4 cup shredded leftover cooked turkey
- 1 tablespoon coarsely chopped leftover green bean casserole
- 1 tablespoon chopped French-fried onions

Direction

- In a bowl, use a fork to mash cranberry sauce until it becomes smooth. Put in celery seed and mayonnaise; blend through. Spread sauce on top of bread slices.
- Spread over 1 slice of bread with sweet potato casserole.
- In a bowl, mash together stuffing and gravy. Put in turkey and mix. Scoop the mixture on top of the sweet potatoes; put onions and green bean casserole over. Top with second slice of bread.

Nutrition Information

- Calories: 489 calories;
- Total Fat: 25.5
- Sodium: 804
- Total Carbohydrate: 47.8
- Cholesterol: 34
- Protein: 15.6

626. Croissant Club Sandwich

Serving: 4 | Prep: 15mins | Cook: 5mins | Ready in:

Ingredients

- 2 avocados, peeled and pitted
- 1/2 teaspoon garlic salt
- 1/2 teaspoon lemon juice
- 1/4 teaspoon dried oregano
- 4 croissants, split
- 8 slices smoked deli turkey breast
- 4 slices Swiss cheese
- 8 slices cooked bacon
- 8 slices tomato
- 4 lettuce leaves
- 4 teaspoons spicy brown mustard, or to taste

Direction

- Preheat oven to 350°F (175°C).
- Use potato masher or a fork to mash avocado in a bowl. Stir in oregano, lemon juice, and garlic salt.
- On a work surface, arrange split croissants. On bottom half of each croissant, place 2 slices turkey. Layer 1 slice Swiss cheese and 2 bacon slices over. Place each croissant top over bacon layer. Place sandwiches on a baking sheet.
- Bake for approximately 5 to 7 minutes in the preheated oven until cheese is melted.
- Open each sandwich and place 2 tomato slices and 1 lettuce leaf on top. On each croissant top, spread lightly 1/4 the avocado mixture and 1 teaspoon mustard. Place each top back to each sandwich.

Nutrition Information

- Calories: 636 calories;
- Cholesterol: 100
- Protein: 29
- Total Fat: 41
- Sodium: 1725
- Total Carbohydrate: 41.4

627. Fiesta Turkey Tavern

Serving: 5 | Prep: 10mins | Cook: 40mins | Ready in:

Ingredients

- 2 tablespoons olive oil
- 1 1/4 pounds ground turkey
- 1 cup finely chopped white onion
- 1 clove garlic, minced
- 1/4 teaspoon ground black pepper
- 1 1/2 tablespoons prepared yellow mustard, divided
- 1/8 teaspoon cayenne pepper
- 1/8 teaspoon chili powder
- 1 cup water
- 1/4 cup finely chopped jalapeno
- 5 hamburger buns

Direction

- Over medium-low heat, heat olive oil; cook while stirring ground turkey with a back of a wooden spoon to break the meat into small crumbles as it cooks. When meat is about half browned, stir in black pepper, garlic and onion; cook while stirring until no longer pink and turkey is browned evenly and crumbly.
- Stir in a tablespoon of prepared mustard, water, chili powder, and cayenne pepper. Boil the mixture, lower the heat; simmer while stirring for about 20 minutes until water evaporates. Stir in the rest of mustard and chopped jalapeno; cook for about 5 more minutes until heated through. Scoop mixture onto hamburger buns.

Nutrition Information

- Calories: 356 calories;
- Sodium: 361
- Total Carbohydrate: 25.5
- Cholesterol: 84

- Protein: 26.8
- Total Fat: 16.4

628.   Grilled Hot Turkey Sandwiches

Serving: 4 | Prep: 10mins | Cook: 10mins | Ready in:

Ingredients

- 4 tablespoons mayonnaise
- 2 tablespoons salsa
- 2 green onions, chopped
- 8 slices sourdough bread
- 1/2 pound deli-sliced turkey
- 4 slices pepperjack cheese
- 4 tablespoons butter

Direction

- In a small bowl, combine green onions, salsa and mayonnaise together. Spread evenly on each bread slice with seasoned mayonnaise. Layer on four slices with turkey and cheese, then place leftover bread on top to form 4 sandwiches.
- In a big skillet, melt 2 tbsp. of butter on moderate heat. Fry in butter with sandwiches until toasted slightly. Put into the skillet with leftover butter and flip sandwiches over. Cook until bread turn brown and cheese has melted.

Nutrition Information

- Calories: 515 calories;
- Cholesterol: 89
- Protein: 21.7
- Total Fat: 33.5
- Sodium: 1373
- Total Carbohydrate: 32.7

629.   Grilled Turkey Reubens

Serving: 2 | Prep: 5mins | Cook: 5mins | Ready in:

Ingredients

- 4 slices rye bread
- 2 tablespoons extra-virgin olive oil
- 4 teaspoons mayonnaise
- 4 teaspoons hot chicken wing sauce
- 2 slices Swiss cheese
- 1/2 cup sauerkraut
- 8 slices deli turkey

Direction

- Prepare a big frying pan and preheat over medium heat.
- On one side of each bread slice, lightly coat with olive oil and lay out the bread slices on a plate with the oiled side facing down. On each slice, spread a teaspoon of hot sauce and a teaspoon of mayonnaise. Put 1/4 cup of sauerkraut and a slice of Swiss cheese on top of the two bread slices. On the other two slices of bread, put turkey then put the two halves together to create a sandwich.
- In the preheated frying pan, fry the sandwiches until the cheese melts and the bread becomes golden brown on each side.

Nutrition Information

- Calories: 575 calories;
- Protein: 32.1
- Total Fat: 32.8
- Sodium: 2343
- Total Carbohydrate: 38.3
- Cholesterol: 75

630.   Jive Turkey Burgers

Serving: 8 | Prep: 15mins | Cook: 15mins | Ready in:

Ingredients

- 2 tablespoons olive oil
- 1 small onion, diced
- 1 large clove garlic, minced
- 1 pound ground turkey
- 1 pound turkey sausage, casings removed
- 1 egg
- 3 tablespoons chopped fresh flat-leaf (Italian) parsley
- salt and ground black pepper to taste (optional)

Direction

- Over medium heat, in a skillet, heat olive oil; cook while stirring garlic and onion for about 3 minutes until fragrant and soft; take out of the heat.
- In a large bowl, stir together pepper, salt, onion mixture, parsley, egg, turkey sausage and ground turkey. Measure 8 equal portions by an ice cream scoop; pat each into a burger shape gently.
- Over medium-low heat, in a large skillet, pan fry the burgers for about 4 minutes on each side until browned and the inside of the pink is no longer pink. The inserted instant-read meat thermometer into the burgers' center should register at least 160°F (70°F).

Nutrition Information

- Calories: 224 calories;
- Protein: 22.5
- Total Fat: 14.6
- Sodium: 538
- Total Carbohydrate: 1.2
- Cholesterol: 111

---

631. Low Carb Bacon Lettuce Turkey Wraps

Serving: 4 | Prep: 10mins | Cook: |Ready in:

Ingredients

- 4 large lettuce leaves
- 1/4 cup mayonnaise
- 8 slices bacon
- 12 slices deli smoked turkey
- 4 slices Swiss cheese
- (8-inch) lengths of baking string

Direction

- Use paper towels to dry the lettuce leaves. Spread each leaf with 1 tbsp. of mayonnaise.
- Arrange the bacon between paper towels set on a microwave-safe plate. Heat it inside the microwave for 4-6 minutes, or until crispy.
- Place 3 turkey slices, 1 Swiss cheese slice, and 2 bacon slices on top of each lettuce. Roll each lettuce up and use a length of baking string to tie each wrap.

Nutrition Information

- Calories: 395 calories;
- Protein: 30
- Total Fat: 27.7
- Sodium: 1381
- Total Carbohydrate: 6.1
- Cholesterol: 87

---

632. Shredded Turkey Barbecue

Serving: 8 | Prep: 15mins | Cook: 10hours |Ready in:

Ingredients

- 2 bone-in turkey thighs without skin
- 2 (16 ounce) cans baked beans
- 1 1/2 cups finely chopped onion
- 1 cup barbecue sauce
- 1 tablespoon prepared yellow mustard
- 1 teaspoon ground cumin
- 1 teaspoon salt

- 8 potato rolls

Direction

- In a slow cooker, put salt, cumin, yellow mustard, barbecue sauce, onion, baked beans, and turkey thighs. Turn the cooker to Low, and cook for 10-12 hours. Take the turkey thighs out, and use 2 forks to shred the meat. Dispose the bones. Put the shredded turkey meat back into the slow cooker. For serving, put onto each potato roll with sauce and approximately half a cup of shredded turkey.

Nutrition Information

- Calories: 385 calories;
- Sodium: 1320
- Total Carbohydrate: 60.7
- Cholesterol: 69
- Protein: 25.8
- Total Fat: 5.8

633.   The Earl's Sandwich

Serving: 1 | Prep: 4mins | Cook: 1mins | Ready in:

Ingredients

- 2 slices American cheese
- 2 slices white bread, toasted
- 3 slices deli-style sliced turkey breast
- 2 tablespoons Russian salad dressing

Direction

- On a toasted bread slice, put American cheese. Microwave on High for 15 to 20 seconds till cheese has melted. Onto the melted cheese, put the turkey. On 1 side of the leftover toasted bread slice, scatter the Russian dressing. Set over the turkey, dressing-side facing down to make a sandwich.

Nutrition Information

- Calories: 535 calories;
- Sodium: 2472
- Total Carbohydrate: 38.7
- Cholesterol: 88
- Protein: 30.8
- Total Fat: 28.8

634.   The Hot Brown

Serving: 4 | Prep: 20mins | Cook: 1hours10mins | Ready in:

Ingredients

- For the Turkey (Enough for 4 portions):
- 2 pounds boneless turkey breast with skin on
- 1 tablespoon kosher salt
- 1 teaspoon herbes de Provence
- 1 teaspoon oil
- 8 slices bacon
- 2 tablespoons salted butter
- 2 tablespoons all-purpose flour
- 2 cups heavy cream
- salt and freshly ground black pepper to taste
- 1 pinch cayenne pepper, or to taste
- 1/2 cup grated Pecorino Romano cheese
- 1 pinch freshly grated nutmeg
- For 4 Hot Browns:
- 8 slices white bread, toasted
- 12 slices tomato
- 8 tablespoons grated Pecorino Romano cheese, or to taste
- 1 pinch paprika, or to taste
- 4 teaspoons chopped Italian parsley, or to taste

Direction

- Preheat your oven to 350°F (175°C).
- Coat the flesh side of the turkey breast evenly with herbes de Provence and 1/2 of the kosher salt. Spread the leftover half of the kosher salt in the skin side of the turkey breast to taste. In

a greased baking dish, put in the seasoned turkey, skin-side up.

- Put in the preheated oven and let it roast for 45-60 minutes until an inserted instant-read thermometer on the meat indicates 148°F (64°C).
- Cover the bottom of a baking sheet with aluminum foil and put in the bacon. Take the roasted turkey out from the oven and allow it to cool down.
- Put the bacon in the preheated oven and let it cook for 10-15 minutes until it is cooked halfway through.
- Put the butter in a pot and let it melt on medium heat. Add in the flour and mix until well-blended. Let the roux mixture cook while occasionally stirring it for 3 minutes until it smells similar to a cooked pie crust. Add in all the cream at once and whisk it. Let it cook for 5 minutes until the Mornay sauce has begun to boil and its consistency is thick. Switch off the heat right away.
- Put black pepper, cayenne pepper and salt into the Mornay sauce to taste. Add in 1/2 cup of Pecorino Romano cheese and mix until everything is well-blended. Put in the nutmeg and give it a quick mix.
- Slice the turkey into fat slices. Remove the turkey skin.
- Put the 2 sliced breads over each other and cut off the edges. Cut 1 of the bread slices into 2 triangles. Put a small baking dish on top of a sheet pan and arrange the bread in the baking dish. Put 3 turkey slices on top of the bread layer. Put 3 sliced tomatoes in between the slices of turkey. Pour 1/4 of the Mornay sauce evenly on top and sprinkle it with 2 tablespoons of Pecorino Romano cheese. Dust it off with paprika and place the half-cooked bacon across the very top. Do the same procedure with the rest of the ingredients thrice more.
- Place the oven rack around 6 inches away from the source of heat then preheat the broiler in your oven.
- Put in the preheated oven broiler and let it cook under the broiler for 5 minutes until the

top turns nicely brown in color and the bacon is crispy. Put it on a plate lined with table napkin and garnish it with parsley.

Nutrition Information

- Calories: 1280 calories;
- Cholesterol: 400
- Protein: 88.7
- Total Fat: 85.4
- Sodium: 2841
- Total Carbohydrate: 36.6

---

635.   The Munroe Melt

Serving: 1 | Prep: 5mins | Cook: 5mins | Ready in:

Ingredients

- 1 crusty sandwich roll, split
- 1 tablespoon prepared Dijon mustard mayonnaise blend
- 2 slices deli turkey
- 1 slice Swiss cheese
- 2 slices deli ham
- 1 tablespoon mayonnaise
- 2 slices deli roast beef
- 2 slices tomato
- 1 slice Muenster cheese

Direction

- Preheat the broiler of the oven. Use aluminum foil to line the baking sheet.
- Open the sandwich roll on prepped baking sheet. Spread the mustard-mayonnaise blend on one half of the roll and add ham, Swiss cheese and turkey on top.
- Spread 1 tbsp. of mayonnaise on the other half of the roll and add Muenster cheese, slices of tomato and roast beef.
- Broil the sandwich open-faced till the ham starts to crisp around edges, cheese has melted

and starts to turn bubbly. Take sandwich out of oven and bring both sides together.

Nutrition Information

- Calories: 835 calories;
- Sodium: 2372
- Total Carbohydrate: 76.1
- Cholesterol: 109
- Protein: 47.1
- Total Fat: 38.1

Chapter 11: Roll-Up Sandwich Recipes

***

| 636. | Apple Bacon Wraps |

Serving: 4 | Prep: 10mins | Cook: 10mins | Ready in:

Ingredients

- 6 slices bacon, cut in half
- 4 (10 inch) flour tortillas
- 1/4 cup honey
- 1/2 cup shredded Cheddar cheese (optional)
- 8 slices deli ham
- 1 Granny Smith apple, cut into thin bite-size pieces

Direction

- In a big skillet, add bacon and cook on moderately high heat for 10 minutes while turning sometimes, until browned evenly. Remove bacon slices to paper towels to drain.
- On a work surface, put a tortilla and drizzle down the middle of tortilla with a tbsp. of honey, then place 3 bacon pieces on top. Layer

over bacon with 2 tbsp. of Cheddar cheese and put 2 slices of ham and 1/4 of the sliced apples on top, then roll tortilla around the filling. Do the same process to make 3 more wraps.

Nutrition Information

- Calories: 569 calories;
- Sodium: 1580
- Total Carbohydrate: 58.1
- Cholesterol: 62
- Protein: 25.1
- Total Fat: 26.4

| 637. | Avocado, Cream Cheese, And Egg Burrito |

Serving: 2 | Prep: 10mins | Cook: 10mins | Ready in:

Ingredients

- 1 avocado, peeled and pitted
- 2 tablespoons cream cheese, softened
- 2 flour tortillas
- 1 teaspoon vegetable oil, or as needed
- 3 eggs
- salt and ground black pepper to taste

Direction

- Beat cream cheese and avocado till smooth in a bowl; spread on tortillas.
- In a skillet, heat oil on medium heat; mix and cook eggs in the hot oil for 5 minutes till set and scrambled. Put eggs on tortillas; season with pepper and salt. Roll tortillas around eggs; put in the hot skillet for 5 minutes till tortillas are crisp.

Nutrition Information

- Calories: 498 calories;
- Protein: 16.8
- Total Fat: 33

- Sodium: 467
- Total Carbohydrate: 36.8
- Cholesterol: 295

638.   Baked Tofu Spinach Wrap

Serving: 2 | Prep: 3mins | Cook: 2mins | Ready in:

Ingredients

- 2 (10 inch) whole wheat tortillas
- 1 (7.5 ounce) package hickory flavor baked tofu
- 1/2 cup shredded sharp Cheddar cheese
- 1 cup fresh baby spinach
- 1 tablespoon Ranch dressing
- 1 tablespoon grated Parmesan cheese, or to taste

Direction

- On a paper plate, arrange tortillas next to each other. Cut tofu into slices; arrange them into the middle of each tortilla. Use cheese to sprinkle on top of tofu. Use damp paper towel to cover; put into the microwave and heat until the cheese melts, about 45 seconds.
- Stack spinach on top of each tortilla; drizzle with Ranch dressing. Top with a sprinkle of Parmesan cheese; roll tortillas to cover the filling to serve.

Nutrition Information

- Calories: 449 calories;
- Cholesterol: 40
- Protein: 35.2
- Total Fat: 20.4
- Sodium: 567
- Total Carbohydrate: 33.9

639.   Basil Avocado Chicken Salad Wraps

Serving: 4 | Prep: 20mins | Cook: | Ready in:

Ingredients

- 2 ripe avocados - peeled, pitted, and mashed
- 1 lime, juiced
- 2 tablespoons chopped fresh basil
- 1/2 teaspoon garlic salt
- 1/2 teaspoon ground black pepper
- 4 cups chopped cooked chicken
- 1/4 cup raisins
- 1/4 cup chopped walnuts
- 2 heads Bibb lettuce, leaves separated

Direction

- In a bowl, combine pepper, garlic salt, basil, lime juice and mashed avocados. Put walnuts, raisins and chicken into the avocado mixture; stir to coat evenly. Scoop chicken mixture into lettuce leaves, then roll leaves around the filling.

Nutrition Information

- Calories: 471 calories;
- Sodium: 311
- Total Carbohydrate: 21.6
- Cholesterol: 105
- Protein: 42.7
- Total Fat: 25.5

640.   Beach Goers' Wraps

Serving: 4 | Prep: 20mins | Cook: 10mins | Ready in:

Ingredients

- 2 peaches
- 1/2 mango
- 6 slices fresh or canned DOLE® Pineapple

- Olive oil for brushing
- 2 teaspoons raspberry vinegar
- 1/4 teaspoon salt
- Ground black pepper, to taste
- 1 (13 ounce) package DOLE All Natural Endless Summer™ Kit
- 4 (10 inch) wraps or tortillas

Direction

- Slice the peaches in 1/2. Discard the seed. Slice into 1/4-inch. Slice the mango half into 1/2-inch slices. Brush pineapple, peaches and mango slices with oil. Grill on each side until they are tender. Slightly cool, then slice into chunks. Toss salt, pepper, and raspberry vinegar over the fruit, to taste.
- In large bowl, mix all the ingredients (but not Summer Vinaigrette) in the salad kit. Put in the fruit chunks, then mix well. Toss with the dressing.
- Heat wraps in the microwave for half a minute. Lay out the wraps, then equally divide the salad filling. Fold over 1 end; wrap sides over the filling.

Nutrition Information

- Calories: 485 calories;
- Total Carbohydrate: 61
- Cholesterol: 5
- Protein: 10.1
- Total Fat: 27.1
- Sodium: 880

---

641.   Beef And Blue Cheese Wrap

Serving: 1 | Prep: 10mins | Cook: |Ready in:

Ingredients

- 4 ounces thinly sliced deli roast beef
- 1 (8 inch) flour tortilla

- 2 romaine lettuce leaves
- 1/4 cup red bell pepper strips
- 2 tablespoons crumbled blue cheese
- 2 tablespoons blue cheese salad dressing, or to taste

Direction

- On flour tortilla, place roast beef slices; put blue cheese salad dressing, blue cheese, red bell pepper leaves, and lettuce leaves on top. Roll around the ingredients with the tortilla.

Nutrition Information

- Calories: 522 calories;
- Total Fat: 28.7
- Sodium: 2065
- Total Carbohydrate: 34
- Cholesterol: 72
- Protein: 33

---

642.   Beef And Swiss Wrap

Serving: 2 | Prep: 10mins | Cook: |Ready in:

Ingredients

- 2 multi grain wraps
- 2 tablespoons Neufchatel cheese
- 2 leaves romaine lettuce
- 1 cup fresh spinach
- 6 slices deli sliced roast beef
- 2 slices reduced-fat Swiss cheese
- 6 cherry tomatoes, halved
- ground black pepper to taste

Direction

- In the microwave, heat wraps on high for half a minute.
- Spread on the right side of one wrap (the side that will fold in last) with 1 tbsp. of Neufchatel cheese, approximately two-thirds of the way down that side. Layer into the center of each

wrap with half of the romaine, spinach, beef, Swiss cheese and tomatoes, leaving a third of the wrap open at bottom. Fold that third up over the bottom of fillings, then fold in the left side and roll toward the right to allow Neufchatel to seal the wrap together. Do same manner for the 2nd wrap.

Nutrition Information

- Calories: 311 calories;
- Sodium: 1254
- Total Carbohydrate: 32.6
- Cholesterol: 64
- Protein: 33.6
- Total Fat: 8.7

643.   Buffalo Or Barbeque Chicken And Rice Wraps

Serving: 4 | Prep: 10mins | Cook: | Ready in:

Ingredients

- 1 cup UNCLE BEN'S® Ready Rice® Whole Grain Brown
- 1 cup shredded cooked chicken breast
- 1/4 cup Buffalo-style hot pepper sauce (such as Frank's® Red Hot®)
- 1/2 cup shredded Cheddar cheese
- 1/2 cup shredded lettuce
- 4 (8 inch) whole-wheat tortillas
- 1 cup baby carrots
- 1 cup celery sticks
- 1 cup reduced fat ranch dressing, divided

Direction

- Cook the rice following the package instructions.
- In a bowl, combine buffalo sauce and shredded chicken.
- Cover a microwave-safe plate with a damp paper towel, then place the tortillas over it and

microwave for 20 to 30 seconds on High until pliable and warm.

- Evenly divide the rice into quarters and spread each quarter over 1 tortilla, leaving a margin of 1/2 inch around the edges. Spread the chicken mixture over the rice and sprinkle 2 tablespoons of shredded Cheddar cheese on top. Place shredded lettuce on top.
- Fold in the sides and lightly roll the tortilla up. Repeat with leftover tortillas. When serving, diagonally cut each wrap in half. If serving later, wrap in aluminum foil and store in refrigerator.
- Serve each with celery sticks and baby carrot and a dip of about 1/4 cup ranch dressing.

Nutrition Information

- Calories: 402 calories;
- Total Carbohydrate: 62.6
- Cholesterol: 45
- Protein: 20.1
- Total Fat: 10.8
- Sodium: 1475

644.   California Club Chicken Wraps

Serving: 2 | Prep: 15mins | Cook: 1mins | Ready in:

Ingredients

- Chipotle Mayonnaise:
- 1/2 cup mayonnaise
- 1/2 cup plain yogurt
- 2 chipotle chiles in adobo sauce, finely chopped
- Wraps:
- 2 large spinach tortillas
- 1/2 cup shredded lettuce, or to taste
- 1 1/2 cups shredded Monterey Jack cheese
- 1 Haas avocado - peeled, pitted, and diced
- 4 slices cooked bacon, chopped
- 1 red onion, finely chopped

- 1 tomato, chopped
- 2 cooked chicken breasts, cut into chunks

Direction

- In a bowl, whisk together chipotle chiles, mayonnaise, and yogurt.
- Cook the tortillas in the microwave for about 30 seconds until pliable and warm.
- Put one tablespoon of chipotle mayonnaise down the middle of each tortilla. Put the following ingredients in the middle of each tortilla in this order: 1/2 the lettuce, 1/2 the Monterey Jack cheese, 1/2 the avocado, 1/2 the bacon, 1/2 the red onion, 1/2 the tomato, and 1/2 the chicken. Roll the opposing edges of the tortilla so as to overlap the filling. Fold one of the opposing edges all over the filling to form a wrap.

Nutrition Information

- Calories: 1525 calories;
- Total Fat: 104
- Sodium: 2053
- Total Carbohydrate: 82.7
- Cholesterol: 186
- Protein: 69.3

645.　　　Caribbean Wrap

Serving: 4 | Prep: 35mins | Cook: | Ready in:

Ingredients

- 2 cups shredded breast meat from a rotisserie chicken
- 2 cups cubed mango
- 1 cup low-sodium black beans, rinsed and drained
- 1/2 cup chopped red onion
- 2 2/3 tablespoons chopped fresh cilantro
- 8 cloves garlic, chopped
- 1 pinch red pepper flakes

- 4 (8 inch) low-fat whole wheat tortillas
- 8 cups mixed salad greens
- 3 tablespoons Italian salad dressing, or to taste
- 1/2 cup roasted macadamia nuts

Direction

- In a large bowl, mix together red pepper flakes, garlic, cilantro, red onion, black beans, mango and chicken.
- Distribute the chicken mixture into tortillas. Roll up the tortillas.
- In a large bowl, toss salad greens with dressing; use macadamia nuts for garnish. Serve each wrap with 2 cups of salad.

Nutrition Information

- Calories: 490 calories;
- Total Fat: 25.5
- Sodium: 492
- Total Carbohydrate: 47.3
- Cholesterol: 55
- Protein: 28

646.　　　Chicken Curry And Turmeric Salad Wrap

Serving: 5 | Prep: 15mins | Cook: | Ready in:

Ingredients

- 1/2 cup light mayonnaise (such as Fred Meyer®)
- 1 lime, juiced
- 1 tablespoon Madras curry powder
- 1 tablespoon ground turmeric
- 1/2 teaspoon ground cayenne pepper
- 1 pound cubed cooked chicken breast tenders (such as Foster Farms®)
- 1 Honeycrisp apple, chopped
- 1/2 cup raw slivered almonds, chopped
- 5 whole-wheat tortillas (such as Mission®)

Direction

- In a bowl, mix together cayenne pepper, turmeric, curry powder, lime juice, and mayonnaise. Fold in almonds, apple, and chicken.
- Put a scoop of mixture in the center of each tortilla in a line. Fold the tortilla's opposing edges, overlapping the filling. Roll one of the opposing edges around the filling.

Nutrition Information

- Calories: 432 calories;
- Protein: 31.6
- Total Fat: 21.2
- Sodium: 446
- Total Carbohydrate: 36.5
- Cholesterol: 76

647. Chicken Salad Wraps

Serving: 6 | Prep: 10mins | Cook: | Ready in:

Ingredients

- 2 (10 ounce) cans chunk chicken, drained and flaked
- 1/4 cup chopped onion
- 1/4 cup mayonnaise
- 4 tablespoons fresh salsa
- salt and pepper to taste
- 6 (10 inch) flour tortillas
- 12 lettuce leaves

Direction

- Mix pepper, salt, salsa, mayonnaise, onion and chicken in a small bowl.
- Line 2 lettuce leaves on each tortilla; evenly divide chicken salad on each tortilla. Roll up/wrap.

Nutrition Information

- Calories: 464 calories;
- Total Fat: 14.8
- Sodium: 934
- Total Carbohydrate: 42.5
- Cholesterol: 61
- Protein: 27.2

648. Crispy Vegetable Turkey Wrap

Serving: 1 | Prep: 15mins | Cook: | Ready in:

Ingredients

- 3 ounces HORMEL® NATURAL CHOICE® Oven Roasted Deli Turkey
- 1/4 cup Swiss chard, chopped
- 3 sprigs daikon radish sprouts
- 1 medium red bell pepper, cut into matchsticks
- 1 medium yellow bell pepper, cut into matchsticks
- 1 medium orange bell pepper, cut into matchsticks
- 1 (6 inch) whole grain tortilla or flatbread
- 2 tablespoons rice wine vinegar
- 1 1/2 teaspoons soy sauce
- 1 teaspoon honey
- salt and ground black pepper to taste

Direction

- On a flat surface or a plate, place a tortilla.
- Spread Swiss chard, sprouts and pepper in a layer on the tortilla.
- In the middle of the wrap, evenly pile the turkey.
- Stir honey, pepper and salt to taste, soy sauce and vinegar together in a small bowl; pour on top of the turkey.
- Fold the tortilla sides to the middle. Fold from the bottom up to the top of the tortilla.

Nutrition Information

- Calories: 295 calories;
- Protein: 22.5
- Total Fat: 2.9
- Sodium: 1473
- Total Carbohydrate: 50.9
- Cholesterol: 38

---

649.   Curried Chipotle Potato, Spinach And Cheese Wraps

Serving: 2 | Prep: 10mins | Cook: 25mins | Ready in:

Ingredients

- 4 small red potatoes
- 2 tablespoons olive oil
- curry paste, to taste
- 2 tablespoons cream
- 4 slices Muenster cheese
- 2 (10 inch) flour tortillas
- 2 cups baby spinach, rinsed and dried
- 1/4 cup chipotle salsa, or to taste

Direction

- Boil a small pot of salted water. In boiling water, let the potatoes cook for 15 minutes till soft yet remain firm. Allow to drain, then cool and cut.
- In a big skillet, heat the olive oil over medium-high heat; put the potatoes and let cook till warm. Mix in cream and curry paste over low heat. On every tortilla, put 2 cheese slices and microwave separately for 15 to 25 seconds till melted.
- For assembling, evenly distribute the spinach and potatoes among tortillas and put chipotle salsa to taste. In microwave, heat for 20 seconds, then seal tortillas surrounding the filling.

Nutrition Information

- Calories: 883 calories;

- Total Fat: 41.9
- Sodium: 986
- Total Carbohydrate: 102
- Cholesterol: 75
- Protein: 26.5

---

650.   Dan's Meat Wrap

Serving: 1 | Prep: 9mins | Cook: 1mins | Ready in:

Ingredients

- 1 (10 inch) flour tortilla
- 4 slices roast beef
- 1/2 cup shredded Cheddar-Monterey Jack cheese blend
- 1/2 cup shredded lettuce
- 1/2 cup chopped tomato
- 1/4 cup chopped onion
- 4 black olives
- 2 tablespoons Italian-style salad dressing

Direction

- Add tortilla onto a dish. Keep it covered tortilla with roast beef, then cheese. Microwave till melted the cheese for 45 seconds. Drizzle with olives, onion, tomato, and lettuce. Add 3 to 4 splashes Italian dressing on top. Roll them up.

Nutrition Information

- Calories: 699 calories;
- Sodium: 2616
- Total Carbohydrate: 53.1
- Cholesterol: 105
- Protein: 42.7
- Total Fat: 35.8

651.   Easy Lentil Feta Wraps

Serving: 6 | Prep: 15mins | Cook: 20mins | Ready in:

Ingredients

- 6 (8 inch) whole wheat tortillas
- 3 tablespoons olive oil
- 2 cloves garlic, minced
- 2 shallots, finely chopped
- 1/2 pound fresh mushrooms, sliced
- 1/4 cup dry white wine
- 1 (15 ounce) can brown lentils
- 1 (4 ounce) package feta cheese, crumbled
- 1/4 cup chopped kalamata olives
- 1/2 cup chopped tomatoes

Direction

- Set an oven to 120°C (250°F) and start preheating. Use aluminum foil to wrap the tortillas, then put in the oven to warm until they become soft, for 10 minutes.
- In a saucepan, heat olive oil over medium heat, then sauté mushrooms, shallots, and garlic until they are browned slightly, for 5 minutes. Add the wine and loosen all browned bits from the bottom of the saucepan. Stir in lentils and cook until they are just heated through, 2 minutes.
- Spoon a portion of the lentil mixture into each tortilla, then roll or fold them. Put tomatoes, olives, and feta cheese on top.

Nutrition Information

- Calories: 309 calories;
- Total Fat: 13
- Sodium: 614
- Total Carbohydrate: 42.1
- Cholesterol: 17
- Protein: 12.8

652.   Emmi's Banana Wraps

Serving: 4 | Prep: 10mins | Cook: | Ready in:

Ingredients

- 4 teaspoons peanut butter
- 2 tablespoons honey
- 1/4 cup shredded coconut
- 1/2 cup granola
- 1 banana, peeled and halved lengthwise
- 2 large whole wheat tortillas

Direction

- In a bowl, mix together honey and peanut butter until they become smooth. Stir in granola and coconut. Halve the mixture and spread each half over the tortillas. Put in half of banana in the middle of tortilla and roll it up. Cut the rolls in two and serve.

Nutrition Information

- Calories: 325 calories;
- Protein: 9.3
- Total Fat: 11
- Sodium: 318
- Total Carbohydrate: 59.3
- Cholesterol: 0

653.   Fish Taco Cabbage Wraps

Serving: 4 | Prep: 20mins | Cook: 20mins | Ready in:

Ingredients

- 1 pound cod fillets, cut into 1-inch cubes
- 1 tablespoon canola oil
- 3 dried red chile peppers
- salt and ground black pepper to taste
- 1/4 cup mayonnaise
- 1 tablespoon wasabi paste

- 2 tablespoons chopped fresh cilantro
- 8 large green cabbage leaves
- 1 tablespoon chopped fresh cilantro

Direction

- Pat fish dry using paper towels.
- On medium heat, in a big nonstick skillet, heat dried red chiles with canola oil. In the hot oil, cook fish for roughly 3 minutes on each side till fish edges are a bit browned and flesh becomes opaque. Use black pepper and salt to drizzle fish. Take away from heat, drain off, and get rid of peppers.
- In a bowl, mix 2 tbsp. of cilantro, wasabi paste and mayonnaise. Scoop a few fish tbsp. into a cabbage leaf and wrap leaf around fish; repeat with leftover fish and leaves. Use a sprinkling of cilantro to decorate each roll. Serve alongside wasabi mayonnaise.

Nutrition Information

- Calories: 208 calories;
- Total Carbohydrate: 10
- Cholesterol: 45
- Protein: 20.9
- Total Fat: 9.2
- Sodium: 267

---

654.   Grilled Steak And Fresh Mozzarella Flatbread

Serving: 4 | Prep: 10mins | Cook: 15mins | Ready in:

Ingredients

- 1 pound beef top sirloin center filets, cut 1 inch thick, tied
- 1 1/2 teaspoons lemon pepper
- 2 cups packed fresh baby spinach
- 1/4 pound fresh mozzarella cheese, cut into 1/2 inch pieces
- 2 tablespoons chopped fresh basil

- 1 1/2 teaspoons balsamic vinegar
- 4 naan breads (Indian flatbread) or pita breads

Direction

- Press the lemon pepper equally onto the steaks. Put the steaks on to the grid on medium and ash-covered coals. Let grill, covered, 12 - 17 minutes on medium heat on the pre-heated gas grill, 12 - 16 minutes for medium-rare on 145 degrees F to the medium on 160 degrees F to the doneness, flip once in a while.
- At the same time, mix the basil, cheese and spinach in the big bowl. Sprinkle with the balsamic vinegar; coat by tossing and put aside.
- Take the steak out of the grill and allow it to rest for 5 minutes. Add the naan onto the grill; let grill, covered, till turning brown a bit or for 1 - 3 minutes, flip one time.
- Carve the steaks into the slices. Add the naan on top equally with the slices of steak and spinach mixture.

Nutrition Information

- Calories: 500 calories;
- Total Carbohydrate: 45.7
- Cholesterol: 93
- Protein: 34.2
- Total Fat: 19.5
- Sodium: 578

---

655.   Healthy Sweet Potato Wraps

Serving: 6 | Prep: 15mins | Cook: 20mins | Ready in:

Ingredients

- 2 sweet potatoes, peeled and cut into bite-size pieces
- 2 tablespoons extra virgin olive oil

- 1 cup broccoli florets
- 1 (15 ounce) can lentils, drained and rinsed
- 1 tablespoon cumin
- 1 1/2 teaspoons cayenne pepper, or to taste
- 1 teaspoon garlic salt
- 2 tomatoes, chopped
- 6 tablespoons barbeque sauce, divided
- 6 whole wheat Lebanese-style pita bread rounds

Direction

- In a large pot, add sweet potatoes and cover with water; bring it to a boil. Lower the heat to medium-low; simmer in about 8 minutes, until tender. Drain.
- In a large skillet, heat olive oil over medium-high heat. Cook and stir broccoli in hot oil in the skillet for about 3-5 minutes, until tender yet still crisp. Mix salt, cayenne pepper, cumin, lentils and sweet potatoes into the broccoli; cook in about 5 minutes, until heated through. Put in diced tomatoes and cook for about 3 minutes, until hot.
- Drizzle 1 tablespoon of barbeque sauce into each of pita round. Scoop approximately 1 cup of sweet potato mixture into each pita; then wrap each pita, folding up the pita's bottom first, and then the sides. If needed, secure with toothpicks.

Nutrition Information

- Calories: 356 calories;
- Total Fat: 5.6
- Sodium: 888
- Total Carbohydrate: 65.2
- Cholesterol: 0
- Protein: 11.4

---

656. Hot Dog Roll Up

Serving: 4 | Prep: 2mins | Cook: 2mins | Ready in:

Ingredients

- 4 (6 inch) Mission® Fajita Flour Tortillas
- 4 all beef hot dogs
- 4 slices processed American cheese

Direction

- Put hot dogs between 2 paper towels. Then microwave for 20 seconds on high. Discard from the towels. Keep them hot.
- On middle each tortilla, lay 1 slice of the American cheese.
- Top each cheese slice with the hot dogs. Roll up every tortilla/cheese/hot dog by rolling simply from 1 end to other.
- In the microwave, arrange all 4 hot dog roll ups. Cook until the tortillas are warm and cheese melts fully, about 10-12 seconds longer.
- Discard from the microwave. Enjoy every per hot dog roll up whole.

Nutrition Information

- Calories: 355 calories;
- Total Fat: 24.7
- Sodium: 1225
- Total Carbohydrate: 18.3
- Cholesterol: 50
- Protein: 14.3

---

657. Hummus And Artichoke Wrap

Serving: 1 | Prep: 10mins | Cook: | Ready in:

Ingredients

- 3 tablespoons hummus
- 1 large whole-wheat sandwich wrap
- 3 marinated artichoke hearts, cut into small pieces
- 1/4 cup shredded fat-free mozzarella cheese
- 1 roasted red bell pepper, cut into small pieces

- 1 cup fresh spinach leaves

Direction

- Spread sandwich wrap with hummus. Top the hummus with red bell pepper pieces and artichoke hearts. Scatter bell pepper and artichokes with the mozzarella cheese; place spinach on top. Roll sandwich wrap around ingredients. Enjoy.

Nutrition Information

- Calories: 497 calories;
- Total Fat: 15.2
- Sodium: 1572
- Total Carbohydrate: 88.4
- Cholesterol: 18
- Protein: 25

---

658.   Keto And Gluten Free Spinach, Feta, And Tomato Wraps For Two

Serving: 2 | Prep: 10mins | Cook: 10mins | Ready in:

Ingredients

- Keto wraps:
- 3 eggs
- 1/2 cup almond milk
- 1/4 cup coconut flour
- 1 pinch sea salt
- cooking spray
- Filling:
- 2 cups baby spinach
- 1/2 cup feta cheese, crumbled
- 3 chopped sun-dried tomatoes
- 1 teaspoon olive oil

Direction

- In a bowl, combine almond milk and eggs until well blended.

- In another bowl, mix salt, and coconut flour together. Mix with the egg mixture for 2 mins until it forms into a soft and smooth batter. Set aside for 5 mins.
- On medium-high heat, heat an 8-in pan; use cooking spray to grease. Scoop in half of the batter; twirl the pan to spread it out distribute batter in a thin layer. Cook for 3 mins until the base is light brown and the top is not wet. Loosen the wrap by sliding a spatula on the edges of the wrap; turn and cook the other side for a minute until light brown. Repeat with the leftover batter.
- In the middle of the wraps, arrange the sun-dried tomatoes, feta cheese, and spinach. Pour olive oil over the filling. Make the wraps by rolling from one side to another.

Nutrition Information

- Calories: 416 calories;
- Total Fat: 24.5
- Sodium: 1910
- Total Carbohydrate: 30
- Cholesterol: 302
- Protein: 24.4

---

659.   Kickin' Turkey Club Wrap

Serving: 4 | Prep: 5mins | Cook: | Ready in:

Ingredients

- 4 (6 inch) flour tortillas
- 1/2 (8 ounce) tub PHILADELPHIA Spicy Jalapeno Cream Cheese Spread
- 4 lettuce leaves
- 8 slices OSCAR MAYER Deli Fresh Smoked Turkey Breast
- 4 slices OSCAR MAYER Bacon, cooked, drained
- 1 avocado, sliced
- 1/2 red pepper, sliced into thin strips

Direction

- Using cream cheese, spread on tortillas.
- Add the remaining ingredients on top, roll up.

---

660. Leftover Pork Roast BBQ Wrap

Serving: 2 | Prep: 10mins | Cook: 15mins | Ready in:

Ingredients

- 1/2 pound cooked pork roast, shredded
- 2 (10 inch) flour tortillas
- 1/4 cup barbeque sauce
- 4 slices Cheddar cheese, halved
- 1/2 small onion, thinly sliced into rings
- salt and ground black pepper to taste

Direction

- Turn the oven to 350°F (175°C) to preheat.
- On each tortilla, scoop 1/2 the shredded pork; put pepper, salt, 1/2 the onion rings, 4 Cheddar cheese halves, and 2 tablespoons barbeque sauce on top of each. Fold opposite edges of every tortilla, overlapping the filling. Roll around the filling with one of the opposing edges to make a burrito-shape. Tightly wrap aluminum foil around each and put on a baking sheet.
- Bake for 15-20 minutes in the preheated oven until the fully cooked and the cheese melts. Halve every wrap and enjoy.

Nutrition Information

- Calories: 668 calories;
- Protein: 49.7
- Total Fat: 28.8
- Sodium: 1212
- Total Carbohydrate: 49.6
- Cholesterol: 142

---

661. Make Ahead Lunch Wraps

Serving: 16 | Prep: 30mins | Cook: 35mins | Ready in:

Ingredients

- 2 cups uncooked brown rice
- 4 cups water
- 4 (15 ounce) cans black beans
- 2 (15.5 ounce) cans pinto beans
- 1 (10 ounce) can whole kernel corn
- 1 (10 ounce) can diced tomatoes and green chiles
- 16 (10 inch) flour tortillas
- 1 pound shredded pepperjack cheese

Direction

- In a saucepan, combine water and rice and bring to a boil. Turn heat to low and cover. Simmer until tender or for 35 to 40 minutes. Move it away from heat. Let it cool.
- In a strainer or a colander, put pinto beans and black beans, then, rinse. Put diced tomatoes with green chilies and corn. Mix by tossing it. Put into big bowl and mix cheese and rice in.
- Evenly distribute mixture into tortillas, roll up then, wrap with plastic wrap individually. Put into a big freezer bag and let it freeze. As needed, reheat in the microware for snack or lunch.

Nutrition Information

- Calories: 557 calories;
- Protein: 22.9
- Total Fat: 16
- Sodium: 1312
- Total Carbohydrate: 80.8
- Cholesterol: 30

662. Mediterranean Lamb Meatball Sandwiches With Yogurt Sauce

Serving: 4 | Prep: 25mins | Cook: 18mins | Ready in:

Ingredients

- Lamb Meatballs:
- 1 small onion
- 1 cup fresh mint leaves
- 3 cloves garlic
- 1 pound ground lamb
- 3 tablespoons ground sweet paprika
- 1 tablespoon ground cumin
- 1 teaspoon salt
- 1 teaspoon ground black pepper
- cooking spray
- 1/4 cup vegetable oil, or as needed
- Yogurt Sauce:
- 1 (6 ounce) container Greek yogurt
- 2 tablespoons tahini
- 1 1/2 teaspoons lemon juice
- 4 sheets lavash bread
- 1 (4 ounce) package crumbled feta cheese
- 1 cup shredded lettuce
- 1/2 cup diced fresh tomatoes
- 1/2 cup cucumber matchsticks

Direction

- Process garlic, mint and onion till minced in a food processor. Add pepper, salt, cumin, paprika and lamb; process till smooth.
- Shape 1 1/2 tsp. lamb mixture to ball; to make 20 meatballs, repeat with leftover lamb mixture.
- Preheat an oven to 190°C/375°F; use cooking spray to grease a baking sheet.
- Put 1/4-in. oil in a big skillet; heat till bubbles form around wooden spoon's end dipped into oil on medium heat. Add 1/2 meatballs; cook for 1-2 minutes per side till browned. Put onto prepped baking sheet; repeat with leftover meatballs.
- In preheated oven, bake for 10 minutes till center isn't pink.
- To make yogurt sauce, mix lemon juice, tahini and yogurt in a bowl.
- In a line down the middle of every lavash sheet, put 2-3 tbsp. yogurt sauce; add 5 meatballs, 2 tbsp. cucumber, 2 tbsp. tomato, 1/4 cup lettuce and 2-3 tbsp. feta cheese. Fold sides and 1 end of lavash up, to roll into the wraps.

Nutrition Information

- Calories: 850 calories;
- Total Carbohydrate: 71.2
- Cholesterol: 110
- Protein: 41.2
- Total Fat: 46.5
- Sodium: 1475

663. Merrick's PBJ N' Banana Burritos

Serving: 1 | Prep: 5mins | Cook: | Ready in:

Ingredients

- 2 tablespoons smooth natural peanut butter
- 1 whole wheat tortilla
- 1 banana
- 1 tablespoon apricot jelly
- 1 teaspoon honey

Direction

- Place the peanut butter evenly on the center of tortilla; put the apricot jelly on top of the peanut butter. Arrange the banana on top of the peanut butter and jelly layers. Pour the honey on the banana. Tuck the two edges of the tortilla over the top of the banana and roll the other two edges of tortilla over mixture to make a burrito.

Nutrition Information

- Calories: 459 calories;
- Total Carbohydrate: 79.1
- Cholesterol: 0
- Protein: 13
- Total Fat: 16.9
- Sodium: 314

- Calories: 403 calories;
- Total Fat: 10.6
- Sodium: 1883
- Total Carbohydrate: 45.3
- Cholesterol: 90
- Protein: 30.6

664. Mexican Black Bean And Turkey Wraps

Serving: 4 | Prep: 10mins | Cook: 35mins | Ready in:

Ingredients

- 1 large onion, diced
- 1 pinch sea salt
- 1 pinch cayenne pepper
- 1 pound lean ground turkey
- 1 dash garlic powder
- 1 (15 ounce) can black beans, drained and rinsed
- 1 cup water
- 1 large green bell pepper, diced
- 1 (4 ounce) can chopped green chiles
- 6 tablespoons taco seasoning mix
- 1 cup cooked brown rice

Direction

- Heat a big skillet over medium-high heat and sauté onions with cayenne pepper and sea salt until they are softened, 7 minutes. Add in garlic powder and ground turkey, then cook while stirring for 5 minutes until the meat is no longer pink. Add taco seasoning, green chiles, green bell pepper, water, and black beans, mixing well. Bring heat down to low and allow to simmer, covered, for 10-15 minutes until the flavors combine.
- Stir in the cooked rice and simmer until heated through, around 3-5 minutes. Take off the heat and allow to sit for 10 minutes.

Nutrition Information

665. Mexican Roll Ups

Serving: 6 | Prep: 15mins | Cook: | Ready in:

Ingredients

- 6 (12 inch) whole wheat tortillas
- 6 leaves romaine lettuce
- 1 1/4 pounds sliced roast beef
- 1 cup chopped tomatoes
- 1 cup chopped red bell pepper
- 2 tablespoons olive oil
- 3 tablespoons red wine vinegar
- 2 tablespoons ground cumin

Direction

- Tear off approximately a 15-inch piece of aluminum foil or wax paper for each roll-up. Set the tortilla on foil or the paper. Position a romaine lettuce leaf atop the tortilla. For each tortilla, put in about 3 ounces of beef atop the lettuce. Distribute the cumin, yellow and red bell peppers, vinegar, oil and tomatoes over each tortilla.
- To encase the filling, start rolling the foil or paper over the tortilla. Roll till the sandwich is totally rolled up. Peel back the foil or paper to eat.

Nutrition Information

- Calories: 419 calories;
- Total Fat: 9.8
- Sodium: 1635
- Total Carbohydrate: 73.7
- Cholesterol: 45

- Protein: 27.8

666. Red Bird Wrap

Serving: 4 | Prep: 30mins | Cook: 25mins | Ready in:

Ingredients

- 2 tablespoons red wine vinegar
- 1 1/2 tablespoons seedless raspberry jam
- 1 tablespoon extra-virgin olive oil
- 1/8 teaspoon freshly ground black pepper
- 1 tomato, seeded and coarsely chopped
- 1 cup fresh spinach leaves - stems removed, leaves rolled, and finely sliced
- 1/4 cup shredded Italian cheese blend (Parmesan, Romano, and Asiago)
- 1 tablespoon extra-virgin olive oil
- 4 (8 inch) whole wheat tortillas
- 2 tablespoons extra-virgin olive oil
- 2 skinless, boneless chicken breast halves
- 4 cremini mushrooms, coarsely chopped
- 1/2 red bell pepper, chopped
- 1 green onion, chopped

Direction

- In a bowl, mix black pepper, 1 tablespoon olive oil, raspberry jam, and red wine vinegar until smooth. Use plastic wrap to cover the bowl and keep in the refrigerator for at least 30 minutes to enhance the flavors.
- In a bowl, lightly toss Italian cheese blend, spinach, and tomato. Dot 3 tablespoons raspberry dressing over the mixture and toss again.
- Put 1 tablespoon olive oil in a large skillet set over medium heat; put a tortilla into the skillet and cook for about 45 seconds until small brown spots dot the bottom of the tortilla.
- Turn tortilla over and cook for 45 seconds until it begins to slightly puff up.
- Place the warmed tortilla onto a paper towel-lined plate.
- Continue with the rest of the tortillas; pile them on the paper plate with paper towels between each.
- Put 2 tablespoons olive oil in the skillet set over medium-high heat; put chicken breasts into hot oil and pan-fry for about 5 minutes each side, until not pink inside and lightly browned. Reserve the chicken.
- Stir and cook green onion, red bell pepper, and cremini mushrooms in the same skillet set over medium heat for 5-8 minutes, until mushrooms released their juice and have softened.
- Place the mushroom mixture to a paper towel-lined plate to get rid of excess moisture.
- Cut chicken breasts thinly, then chop into pieces, about 1/2-inch.
- Place chopped chicken back to the hot skillet and stir and cook for 3-5 minutes until chicken turns light brown.
- For assembling, put a warm tortilla on a plate. Dust with 1/4 of the chopped chicken.
- Dot 1 teaspoon of the raspberry dressing over the chicken.
- Place 1/4 of the mushroom mixture and 1/4 of the tomato-cheese mixture on top.
- Fold the tortilla over the fillings and serve.

Nutrition Information

- Calories: 350 calories;
- Sodium: 335
- Total Carbohydrate: 35.7
- Cholesterol: 39
- Protein: 19.5
- Total Fat: 17.6

667. Roast Beef And Avocado Wraps

Serving: 6 | Prep: 20mins | Cook: | Ready in:

Ingredients

- 1 (4 ounce) package cream cheese, softened
- 1 teaspoon ground cumin
- 1 clove garlic, minced
- 1/8 teaspoon dried red pepper flakes
- 6 tomato and oregano tortillas
- 6 lettuce leaves - rinsed and dried
- 12 slices deli sliced roast beef
- 1 avocado, cubed
- 1 tomato, seeded and chopped
- 1 cup shredded Colby-Monterey Jack cheese

Direction

- In a bowl, mix chili flakes, garlic, cumin and cream cheese until blended well.
- Spread each tortilla with a thin cream cheese mixture layer, separating evenly. On every tortilla, put 1 lettuce leaf. Then place 2 slices of the roast beef on top. Evenly sprinkle cheese, tomatoes, and avocado over. Beginning at one end, roll up every tortilla gently into a tight tube. Diagonally slice in 1/2. Arrange 2 pieces on six serving plates.

Nutrition Information

- Calories: 533 calories;
- Cholesterol: 70
- Protein: 26.1
- Total Fat: 26.6
- Sodium: 1388
- Total Carbohydrate: 48.4

668. Salt And Spice Pork Wrap

Serving: 1 | Prep: 5mins | Cook: 10mins | Ready in:

Ingredients

- 1 (5 ounce) boneless pork loin chop
- 1/2 tablespoon onion salt
- 1 teaspoon cayenne pepper
- fresh-ground black pepper
- 1 teaspoon vegetable oil

- 1 (12 inch) flour tortilla
- 3 tablespoons salsa or guacamole
- 1/2 cup shredded Cheddar cheese

Direction

- Add pepper, cayenne and onion salt to pork chop for seasoning. In a skillet, heat vegetable oil over medium heat. Put in pork chop. Cook for 4 mins on each side until both sides are lightly browned. Cut the pork chop into 1/4-in. strips, put back to skillet, cook until no longer pink.
- Smear the middle of tortilla with guacamole or salsa; sprinkle Cheddar cheese over. Top the cheese with the pork strips. Then roll up the tortilla into a wrap.

Nutrition Information

- Calories: 798 calories;
- Protein: 43.9
- Total Fat: 39.3
- Sodium: 4141
- Total Carbohydrate: 66.5
- Cholesterol: 107

669. Sesame Lime Steak Wraps

Serving: 4 | Prep: 15mins | Cook: 15mins | Ready in:

Ingredients

- 1/2 pound eye of round, thinly sliced
- 1/4 cup lime juice
- 1/4 cup honey
- 1 tablespoon vegetable oil
- 2 teaspoons toasted sesame seeds
- 2 teaspoons reduced-sodium soy sauce
- 1 teaspoon sesame oil
- 1 teaspoon finely chopped fresh ginger root
- 4 leaves red leaf lettuce - rinsed, dried and torn

- 4 (8 inch) flour tortillas

Direction

- In a shallow bowl, arrange the sliced beef. Mix grated ginger, sesame oil, soy sauce, sesame seeds, oil, honey, and lime juice in a jar. Tightly seal the lid and shake it until mixed thoroughly. Pour onto the beef and marinate for half an hour.
- Start heating a nonstick skillet until it becomes very hot. Pour the marinade and beef into the pan and sauté on high heat until the steak turns brown evenly. Use a slotted spoon to take the beef out. Carry on boiling marinade and stir often to avoid burning for 5 minutes until it reduces by half. Return the steak slices to the marinade, combine thoroughly and put aside to slightly cool.
- Top the tortillas with the lettuce leaves and divide steak slides equally among all the tortillas. Fold up the bottom of the tortilla by one-third, then roll tightly from the side until it is wrapped.

Nutrition Information

- Calories: 401 calories;
- Sodium: 355
- Total Carbohydrate: 46.9
- Cholesterol: 35
- Protein: 16.1
- Total Fat: 17

---

670. Slow Cooker Buffalo Chicken Wraps

Serving: 12 | Prep: 25mins | Cook: | Ready in:

Ingredients

- PAM® Original No-Stick Cooking Spray
- 2 1/2 pounds boneless, skinless chicken breasts
- 1 (15 ounce) can Manwich® Original Sloppy Joe Sauce
- 1/4 cup hot pepper sauce
- 2 tablespoons firmly packed brown sugar
- 2/3 cup nonfat plain Greek yogurt
- 2 tablespoons ranch dip mix
- 2 cups thinly sliced celery
- 1 1/2 cups carrots, chopped
- 12 (12 inch) flour tortillas
- 3 cups shredded romaine or Bibb lettuce
- Blue cheese crumbles (optional)

Direction

- Coat the inside of a 4.5-quart slow cooker with cooking spray; put the chicken in. In small bowl, stir brown sugar, Manwich and hot sauce together; pour onto the chicken. Cook on HIGH for 3-4 hours or LOW for 4-5 hours, until the chicken is tender.
- In medium bowl, stir ranch powder and yogurt together. Mix in carrot and celery until well combined. Put aside. Take the chicken out of the slow cooker. Use 2 forks to shred the chicken and put back to the sauce in slow cooker.
- If desired, build wraps with blue cheese, a quarter cup of shredded lettuce, a quarter cup of celery slaw and half a cup of chicken. Enjoy immediately!

Nutrition Information

- Calories: 516 calories;
- Total Fat: 12.3
- Sodium: 1144
- Total Carbohydrate: 69.1
- Cholesterol: 52
- Protein: 29.9

---

671. Smoked Turkey Tortilla Wraps

Serving: 10 | Prep: 10mins | Cook: 10mins | Ready in:

Ingredients

- 10 whole wheat flour tortillas
- 10 slices smoked turkey, cut into thin strips
- 1 avocado - peeled, pitted and sliced
- 1/2 cup sour cream, for topping
- 1/2 cup Cheddar cheese

Direction

- In a big skillet set over medium heat, heat flour tortillas until slightly browned. Divide avocado, cheese, turkey strips and sour cream among the tortillas. Fold in half before serving.

Nutrition Information

- Calories: 211 calories;
- Sodium: 509
- Total Carbohydrate: 28.9
- Cholesterol: 24
- Protein: 9.9
- Total Fat: 9.8

---

672.   Spicy Bacon Cheeseburger Turkey Wraps

Serving: 7 | Prep: 5mins | Cook: 8mins | Ready in:

Ingredients

- 1 pound lean ground turkey
- 2 tablespoons Worcestershire sauce (such as French's®)
- 1 tablespoon Cajun seasoning, or to taste
- 1/4 cup bacon bits (such as Hormel®)
- 2 tablespoons diced jalapeno pepper
- 1 tablespoon minced garlic
- 7 light flatbreads (such as Flatout®)
- Condiments:
- 28 dill pickle slices
- 3 1/2 cups fresh spinach
- 7 slices pepper Jack cheese (such as Borden®)

Direction

- In a bowl, mix the turkey with the Cajun seasoning and the Worcestershire sauce.
- In a skillet, cook minced garlic, jalapeno pepper and bacon bits over medium-high heat for 4 mins or until the bacon bits begin to stick. Put in turkey mixture and cook while stirring for 4 mins or until it is no longer pink.
- In each flatbread, add 2 ounces of turkey mixture. In each wrap, put four slices of pickle, half a cup of spinach and one slice of the pepper Jack cheese.

Nutrition Information

- Calories: 273 calories;
- Total Fat: 13
- Sodium: 1080
- Total Carbohydrate: 20.1
- Cholesterol: 66
- Protein: 27.4

---

673.   Spicy Chipotle Turkey Wraps

Serving: 4 | Prep: 15mins | Cook: | Ready in:

Ingredients

- 1/2 cup mayonnaise
- 1 tablespoon chopped chipotle chile in adobo sauce
- 2 teaspoons adobo sauce from chipotle peppers
- 4 (10 inch) whole wheat tortillas
- 1/2 pound sliced smoked turkey
- 1 (8 ounce) package Shredded Monterey jack cheese
- 1 avocado - peeled, pitted and sliced
- 4 romaine lettuce leaves

Direction

- In a small bowl, mix the chipotle chile, adobo sauce, and mayonnaise. Spread the mixture onto the tortillas evenly. Distribute the Monterey jack cheese, romaine lettuce, avocado, and turkey onto each of the tortillas. Fold the bottom of each of the tortilla snugly to cover the filling; fold their left and right edges. Roll up to the top edge to form a tight cylinder. Before serving, cut the wrap in half.

Nutrition Information

- Calories: 729 calories;
- Protein: 30.9
- Total Fat: 52.4
- Sodium: 1454
- Total Carbohydrate: 47.3
- Cholesterol: 93

---

674.   Spicy Polynesian Wrap

Serving: 10 | Prep: 20mins | Cook: 30mins | Ready in:

Ingredients

- 2 pounds skinless, boneless chicken breast halves - cut into 1 inch strips
- 1 (14 ounce) can coconut milk
- 1 cup uncooked long grain white rice
- 2 cups water
- 1 1/2 cups all-purpose flour
- 1 1/2 tablespoons curry powder
- 1 tablespoon garlic salt
- 3/4 cup vegetable oil
- 2 limes
- 10 (10 inch) flour tortillas
- 1/2 cup shredded coconut
- 1/2 cup chopped green onions

Direction

- In a bowl, place coconut milk and the chicken, and marinate in the refrigerator for 1 hour.

- Bring the rice and water to a boil in a pot. Put on the cover, lower the heat to low, and let it simmer for 20 minutes.
- Combine garlic salt, curry powder and the flour in a small bowl. Drain the chicken, and get rid of marinade. Dip the chicken to coat in the flour mixture.
- In a skillet, heat the oil over medium heat, and cook the coated chicken strips for 5 minutes on each side, or until golden brown and juices run clear. Squeeze lime juice over chicken, and get rid of limes.
- Put equal amounts of rice, green onions, coconut and chicken on each tortilla. Wrap burrito style.

Nutrition Information

- Calories: 735 calories;
- Total Carbohydrate: 70.9
- Cholesterol: 55
- Protein: 31
- Total Fat: 36.5
- Sodium: 1048

---

675.   Spicy Turkey Wraps With Strawberry Salsa

Serving: 4 | Prep: 45mins | Cook: 5mins | Ready in:

Ingredients

- 2 pounds turkey tenderloins, cut into 1/2 inch slices
- 1 (1 ounce) package Southwest marinade seasoning
- 1 pound strawberries, diced
- 1/2 cup finely chopped red onion
- 1/4 cup finely chopped cilantro
- 1 jalapeno pepper, seeded and minced
- 1 tablespoon fresh lime juice
- 1 teaspoon sea salt
- fresh ground pepper
- 1 tablespoon vegetable oil

- 4 (10 inch) jalapeno and cheese flavored tortillas
- 2 cups fresh baby spinach
- 1 cup crumbled blue cheese

Direction

- Toss turkey and Southwest marinade seasoning together in a medium bowl to coat, then let stand about 15 minutes.
- In the meantime, stir together lime juice, jalapeno pepper, cilantro, red onion and diced strawberries in a bowl to prepare for a strawberry salsa. Use pepper and salt to season to taste, then put aside.
- In a big skillet, heat vegetable oil on moderately high heat. Put in turkey and cook for 5 minutes, until firm and browned slightly. Once done, microwave the tortillas about a half minute.
- For assembly, split cooked turkey evenly onto each tortilla. Put strawberry salsa, blue cheese and spinach on top of tortilla, then roll into a wrap.

Nutrition Information

- Calories: 725 calories;
- Total Fat: 20.8
- Sodium: 2625
- Total Carbohydrate: 57.3
- Cholesterol: 189
- Protein: 74.8

---

676. Taco Turkey Wraps

Serving: 36 | Prep: 15mins | Cook: | Ready in:

Ingredients

- 2/3 cup sour cream
- 1/2 cup pico de gallo salsa, drained
- 2 tablespoons taco seasoning
- 6 (8 inch) flour tortillas

- 1 cup shredded Mexican cheese blend
- 1/2 pound thinly sliced deli turkey breast

Direction

- In a bowl, combine taco seasoning, pico de gallo and sour cream; spread the mixture onto each flour tortilla. Sprinkle Mexican cheese blend over the top of sour cream mixture layer. Add turkey on top. Roll each of the tortillas around the filling. Wrap aluminum foil around each portions then place in the fridge for 8 hours to overnight.
- Discard the aluminum foil and cut cross-wise each wrap into slices of 3/8-inch. Place the slices on a plate.

Nutrition Information

- Calories: 59 calories;
- Total Fat: 2.8
- Sodium: 198
- Total Carbohydrate: 5.5
- Cholesterol: 8
- Protein: 2.7

---

677. Thanksgiving Any Day Rollups

Serving: 3 | Prep: 15mins | Cook: | Ready in:

Ingredients

- 1 (8 ounce) package reduced-fat cream cheese
- 1/2 (8 ounce) package shredded Cheddar cheese
- 12 meatless turkey-flavored deli slices (such as Tofurky®), chopped
- 1/3 cup dried cranberries
- 1/4 cup pecans
- 1 celery stick, chopped
- 2 green onions, chopped
- 1 tablespoon chopped fresh chives
- salt and ground black pepper to taste

- 3 large flour tortillas

Direction

- In food processor, combine Cheddar cheese and cream cheese. Then process until they are blended. Put in black pepper, salt, chives, green onions, celery, pecans, cranberries and meatless turkey slices. Process until they become smooth.
- Spread each tortilla with the cream cheese mixture, then roll up. Enjoy immediately or place in the refrigerator until serving time.

Nutrition Information

- Calories: 773 calories;
- Total Fat: 39.2
- Sodium: 1196
- Total Carbohydrate: 69.5
- Cholesterol: 82
- Protein: 36.9

678. Tor Tunas

Serving: 4 | Prep: 10mins | Cook: |Ready in:

Ingredients

- 2 (5 ounce) cans tuna, drained
- 3 tablespoons mayonnaise
- 1 1/2 tablespoons pickle relish
- 1 tablespoon chopped onion
- 1 tablespoon chopped celery
- 1 teaspoon lemon juice, or to taste
- 1 pinch garlic salt, or to taste
- 4 leaves lettuce (optional)
- 4 (8 inch) flour tortillas, warmed

Direction

- In a bowl, combine mayonnaise, tuna, celery, pickle relish, garlic, lemon juice and onion. Put a lettuce leaf on each tortilla. Put the mixture across the center of each tortilla. Fold the

opposite edges of tortilla to overlap the filling. Roll in burrito style one of the opposing edges around the filling.

Nutrition Information

- Calories: 317 calories;
- Total Carbohydrate: 30.2
- Cholesterol: 23
- Protein: 20.6
- Total Fat: 12.3
- Sodium: 455

679. Tortilla Filled With Lunchmeat

Serving: 1 | Prep: 10mins | Cook: |Ready in:

Ingredients

- 1 (12 inch) flour tortilla
- 2 tablespoons whipped cream cheese
- 3 slices ham
- 1 banana pepper, seeded and sliced

Direction

- On one side of the tortilla, add cream cheese and spread it out evenly. Top with layer of slices of ham. Arrange banana pepper slices so that it is in the center of the tortilla and forms a straight line. Roll up the tortilla into cylinder shape.

Nutrition Information

- Calories: 437 calories;
- Cholesterol: 20
- Protein: 11.4
- Total Fat: 15.2
- Sodium: 839
- Total Carbohydrate: 63.5

680. Tortilla Moo Shu Pork

Serving: 6 | Prep: 15mins | Cook: 45mins | Ready in:

Ingredients

- 1 (1 pound) pork tenderloin
- salt and ground black pepper to taste
- 1/2 cup hoisin sauce
- 2 tablespoons soy sauce
- 2 tablespoons Asian (toasted) sesame oil
- 1 tablespoon cornstarch
- 3 tablespoons chopped fresh ginger
- 2 tablespoons chopped green onion
- 3 cloves garlic, minced
- 6 (7 inch) flour tortillas
- 1 (16 ounce) package coleslaw mix
- 1/2 (10 ounce) package carrots, chopped

Direction

- Set oven to 350°F (175°C) to preheat.
- Season pork with pepper and salt; place on a large baking sheet.
- Bake seasoned pork for 20 to 30 minutes in the preheated oven until center is slightly pink. An instant-read thermometer inserted into the center should register at least 145°F (63°C). Shred cooked pork.
- In a mixing bowl, combine cornstarch, sesame oil, soy sauce, and hoisin sauce.
- Bring a large skillet to medium heat on the stove; sauté shredded pork, garlic, green onion, and ginger until vegetables are aromatic. Stir in hoisin sauce mixture. Simmer, covered, for about 20 minutes until sauce thickens and pork is very tender.
- Arrange tortillas on a microwaveable plate; place a damp paper towel over tortillas to cover.
- Heat for half a minute in the microwave until warm. Spoon approximately 1/2 cup pork mixture in the middle of each tortilla. Top with shredded carrots and coleslaw mix; fold tortillas in half to serve.

Nutrition Information

- Calories: 385 calories;
- Total Fat: 12.5
- Sodium: 923
- Total Carbohydrate: 49.3
- Cholesterol: 39
- Protein: 18.1

681. Turkey And Grape Wraps

Serving: 4 | Prep: 15mins | Cook: | Ready in:

Ingredients

- 4 cups chopped cooked turkey
- 2 cups red seedless grapes, halved
- 1/2 cup grated Parmesan cheese
- 1/2 cup mayonnaise
- salt and ground black pepper to taste
- 4 (8 inch) flour tortillas
- 4 large fresh spinach leaves

Direction

- In a bowl, mix the Parmesan cheese, mayonnaise, grapes, and turkey lightly until well-combined. Season the mixture with salt and pepper to taste. Arrange 4 tortillas onto the work surface and garnish the middle of each tortilla with 1 leaf of spinach. Fill each spinach leaf with 1/4 of the turkey fillings with a spoon, forming them in a line. Fold each tortilla's bottom to hold the filling; wrap tightly. Allow the tops to remain open.

Nutrition Information

- Calories: 697 calories;
- Sodium: 651
- Total Carbohydrate: 43.1
- Cholesterol: 126
- Protein: 50.2
- Total Fat: 35.6

682.　Turkey, Cranberry, And Spinach Roll Ups

Serving: 4 | Prep: 20mins | Cook: | Ready in:

Ingredients

- 1 (8 ounce) package cream cheese, at room temperature
- 4 large whole-wheat sandwich wrap
- 1/4 cup sweetened dried cranberries (such as Craisins®), or to taste
- 12 slices turkey lunch meat
- 1 cup fresh spinach, or to taste

Direction

- On one side of each sandwich wrap, put 1/4 of cream cheese onto the center. Drizzle 1 tablespoon of cranberries onto the cream cheese. Put 3 slices of turkey on each wrap. Put 1/4 cup of spinach on top of the turkey.
- Tightly roll the wrap around the filling starting with one edge of a wrap to form a cylinder; slice into 1 1/4-inch cuts and position onto a serving platter.

Nutrition Information

- Calories: 547 calories;
- Cholesterol: 96
- Protein: 28.2
- Total Fat: 22.6
- Sodium: 1743
- Total Carbohydrate: 77.8

683.　Yam And Kale Wrap

Serving: 2 | Prep: 15mins | Cook: 20mins | Ready in:

Ingredients

- 4 large kale leaves, cut into small pieces
- 1/2 cup balsamic vinaigrette
- 2 tablespoons soy sauce
- 2 yams, quartered
- 1/2 (15 ounce) can black beans, rinsed and drained
- 1 1/2 teaspoons olive oil
- 1/4 cup crumbled feta cheese
- 2 (9 inch) whole wheat tortillas, warmed

Direction

- Mix soy sauce, balsamic vinaigrette and kale in a bowl. Cover; marinate for 1 hour in the fridge.
- Boil a big pot of water. Add yam pieces; cook for 15 minutes till soft when fork pierces it. Drain; cool. Cut to cubes when yams can get handled.
- Warm black beans for 2-5 minutes in a small saucepan on medium heat.
- Take kale from vinaigrette mixture; mix and cook olive oil and kale in a skillet on medium heat for 2 minutes till dark green.
- On each tortilla, put 1/2 yams; top yams with black beans, kale and feta cheese. Fold tortilla's bottoms partially over filling; roll to wrap filling in tortillas.

Nutrition Information

- Calories: 813 calories;
- Cholesterol: 28
- Protein: 24.4
- Total Fat: 30.2
- Sodium: 2843
- Total Carbohydrate: 126

684.　Zingy Pesto Tuna Wrap

Serving: 1 | Prep: 15mins | Cook: | Ready in:

Ingredients

- 1 (5 ounce) can albacore tuna in water, drained and flaked
- 2 tablespoons mayonnaise
- 1 tablespoon basil pesto sauce
- 1 teaspoon lemon juice
- 1 pinch ground black pepper
- 1 (10 inch) flour tortilla
- 4 leaves lettuce
- 1 slice provolone cheese
- 5 pitted kalamata olives, cut in half

Direction

- In a bowl, stir pepper, lemon juice, pesto, mayonnaise and tuna lightly together until combined well.
- Microwave tortilla for 5-10 seconds on High until pliable and warmed.
- Place tuna mixture on top of tortilla and spread; top with kalamata olives, provolone cheese and lettuce leaves. Fold bottom of tortilla up about 2 inches to enclose filling; roll the tortilla into a compact wrap tightly.

Nutrition Information

- Calories: 834 calories;
- Total Carbohydrate: 42.3
- Cholesterol: 94
- Protein: 49.9
- Total Fat: 51.2
- Sodium: 1806

Chapter 12: Awesome Sandwich Recipes

***

685.   A Plus Fair Corn Dogs

Serving: 20 | Prep: 15mins | Cook: 4mins |Ready in:

Ingredients

- 1 quart oil for deep frying
- 1 cup all-purpose flour
- 2/3 cup yellow cornmeal
- 1/4 cup white sugar
- 1 1/2 teaspoons baking powder
- 1 teaspoon salt
- 2 tablespoons bacon drippings
- 1 egg, beaten
- 1 1/4 cups buttermilk
- 1/2 teaspoon baking soda
- 2 pounds hot dogs
- wooden sticks

Direction

- In a deep fryer, heat oil to 365°F (185°C).
- Mix flour, sugar, salt, baking powder, and cornmeal in a big bowl. Mix in melted bacon drippings. Create a well in the middle. Pour in buttermilk, egg and baking soda. Stir until well blended and everything is smooth.
- Use paper towels to dry the hotdogs to make sure batter will stick to them. Skewer the hotdogs with wooden sticks. Dip them one at a time, into the batter, removing any excess batter by shaking. Deep fry the hotdogs in batches, do not overcrowd fryer. Cook until browned. Remove excess oil with paper towels. Serve.

Nutrition Information

- Calories: 261 calories;
- Protein: 6.9
- Total Fat: 19.7
- Sodium: 724
- Total Carbohydrate: 13.6
- Cholesterol: 35

686. Adrienne's Overnight Barbecued Beef Sandwiches

Serving: 10 | Prep: 20mins | Cook: 10hours | Ready in:

Ingredients

- 1 large onion, chopped
- 1/2 cup brown sugar
- 1 teaspoon ground black pepper
- 1/4 teaspoon salt
- 1 teaspoon chili powder
- 1 teaspoon paprika
- 1 teaspoon dried oregano
- 2 cloves garlic, minced
- 1 cup ketchup
- 1/2 cup water
- 1/2 cup white vinegar
- 2 tablespoons canola oil
- 2 tablespoons Worcestershire sauce
- 3 drops liquid smoke flavoring
- 1 (3 pound) beef brisket
- 2 teaspoons cornstarch
- 10 whole-wheat buns

Direction

- Combine liquid smoke, Worcestershire sauce, canola oil, white vinegar, water, ketchup, garlic, oregano, paprika, chili powder, salt, pepper, brown sugar, and onion in a slow cooker and stir. Place the pieces of beef into the sauce and cook on low setting for 10 hours.
- Take the beef out of the sauce, keeping sauce in the slow cooker, and use two forks to shred them. Take out 1/4 cup sauce from the slow cooker and pour in a bowl. Whisk cornstarch into sauce and stir it back into the slow cooker. Add the shredded beef and stir. Serve this hot on whole-wheat buns.

Nutrition Information

- Calories: 973 calories;
- Total Carbohydrate: 95.9
- Cholesterol: 98
- Protein: 39.8
- Total Fat: 49.2
- Sodium: 1231

687. Amazing Southwest Cilantro Lime Mango Grilled Chicken Sandwiches

Serving: 8 | Prep: 1hours20mins | Cook: 20mins | Ready in:

Ingredients

- MARINADE
- 1/4 cup finely chopped fresh cilantro
- 1 clove garlic, minced
- 1/4 jalapeno chile pepper, seeded and minced
- 2 tablespoons finely grated fresh lime zest
- 1 1/2 teaspoons salt
- 1/2 teaspoon onion powder
- 1/4 teaspoon ground black pepper
- 1/4 teaspoon chipotle chile powder
- 1 tablespoon olive oil
- 1 pound chicken breast tenderloins or strips
- SALSA
- 1 medium tomato, chopped
- 1 small sweet onion, finely chopped
- 2 tablespoons finely chopped fresh cilantro
- 1/2 jalapeno chile pepper, seeded and minced
- 1 clove garlic, finely chopped
- 1/4 teaspoon ground black pepper
- 1/4 teaspoon sea salt
- 1/8 teaspoon chipotle chile powder
- 1 tablespoon fresh lime juice
- GRILLED VEGETABLES
- 1 sweet onion cut into 1/2-inch slices
- 1 red bell pepper, quartered
- 1 tablespoon olive oil
- 1/4 teaspoon salt
- 1/2 teaspoon minced garlic
- LIME MAYONNAISE
- 1/2 cup mayonnaise
- 2 tablespoons fresh lime juice
- 16 thick slices French bread
- 2 mangos - peeled, seeded, and sliced

- 8 slices Monterey Jack cheese

Direction

- For marinade: in a small bowl, add a tablespoon of the olive oil, a quarter teaspoon of chipotle chile powder, a quarter teaspoon of black pepper, onion powder, one and a half teaspoons salt, lime zest, a quarter jalapeno, 1 clove minced garlic and a quarter cup of cilantro. Stir until well combined. Put chicken breast tenderloins into large resealable plastic bag. Add marinade to the bag with chicken, then seal. Coat by shaking the bag. Place in the refrigerator for 60 mins.
- For salsa: In a bowl, combine a tablespoon of lime juice, 1/8 teaspoon of chipotle pepper, sea salt, a quarter teaspoon of black pepper, a clove garlic, half of jalapeno, 2 tablespoons cilantro, a small onion and tomato. Wrap with the plastic wrap, then place in the refrigerator.
- To prepare grilled vegetables, in a bowl, toss red peppers and onions with a clove of garlic, a tablespoon of the olive oil and a quarter teaspoon of salt. Put aside.
- For lime mayonnaise: Whisk 2 tablespoons lime juice and mayonnaise together; wrap with the plastic wrap, then place in the refrigerator.
- Start preheating outdoor grill for medium-high heat.
- Grill marinated chicken on prepared grill for 8-10 mins or until juices run clear and the chicken is no longer pink in middle. Grill onions and red pepper for 8-10 mins or until golden brown and tender. Take vegetables and chicken out of the grill. Slice grilled pepper into thin strips.
- Spread one and a half teaspoons of prepared lime mayonnaise over each bread slice. Layer sliced mango, a tablespoon of the prepared salsa, the grilled chicken tenderloins, the grilled peppers, the grilled onions, and finally 1 slice of Monterey Jack cheese in 1/2 of the pieces of bread. Top off with remaining bread slices. Put sandwiches back to the grill, flipping when bottom turns golden brown

- Put sandwiches back to the grill. Grill for about 2 mins each side or until cheese melts and bread is toasted.

Nutrition Information

- Calories: 555 calories;
- Sodium: 1292
- Total Carbohydrate: 54
- Cholesterol: 63
- Protein: 29.4
- Total Fat: 25.2

688. Apple Cider Pulled Pork With Caramelized Onion And Apples

Serving: 6 | Prep: 10mins | Cook: 6hours20mins | Ready in:

Ingredients

- 3 (12 fluid ounce) bottles hard apple cider
- 1/4 cup brown sugar
- 1 (2 pound) pork tenderloin
- 1/2 cup butter
- 1 large onion, cut into strips
- 1/2 cup brown sugar
- 1/2 teaspoon ground cinnamon
- 1/2 teaspoon onion powder
- salt and ground black pepper to taste
- 2 large Granny Smith apples - peeled, cored, and sliced
- 6 hard rolls, split

Direction

- In a slow cooker, mix together 1/4 cup brown sugar and hard apple cider; stir until dissolved. Add the pork tenderloin.
- Cook the tenderloin on Low for 6 hours until very soft. Use a fork to shred the pork.
- During the last 20 minutes of cooking the roast, in a big skillet, melt butter over

medium-low heat; cook while mixing the onion for 10 minutes until thoroughly browned.

- Mix together onion powder, cinnamon and half a cup of brown sugar; use pepper and salt to season. Mix the sugar mixture and apples into the cooked onion. Put a cover on and cook for another 10 minutes until the sauce is thick and the apples are soft.
- Put the onion-apple sauce and pork on the rolls using a spoon and enjoy.

Nutrition Information

- Calories: 653 calories;
- Total Fat: 22.8
- Sodium: 408
- Total Carbohydrate: 67.4
- Cholesterol: 125
- Protein: 31.9

689. Apple, Bacon, And Cheddar Panini

Serving: 1 | Prep: 10mins | Cook: 4mins | Ready in:

Ingredients

- 2 tablespoons butter, or to taste
- 3 slices bread
- 1/4 cup shredded Cheddar cheese
- 4 slices cooked bacon
- 1/4 apple, peeled and sliced thinly

Direction

- Set a panini press for preheating.
- Spread butter over 2 of the bread slices. Put a slice, buttered-side-down on the panini press. Place Cheddar cheese on the bread; top with unbuttered bread. Top with apple and bacon; cover with the extra bread slice, buttered side-up. Close the press and cook for 4 minutes, until panini appears browned.

Nutrition Information

- Calories: 665 calories;
- Total Carbohydrate: 43.4
- Cholesterol: 117
- Protein: 22
- Total Fat: 45
- Sodium: 1405

690. Apple Kraut Tuna Sandwich

Serving: 2 | Prep: 15mins | Cook: | Ready in:

Ingredients

- 1 (5 ounce) can tuna in water, drained
- 1/4 cup sauerkraut
- 1/4 cup finely chopped apple
- 2 tablespoons Dijon mustard
- 1 tablespoon red wine vinegar
- 4 slices whole wheat bread, toasted

Direction

- In a bowl, combine red wine vinegar, tuna, Dijon mustard, sauerkraut, and apple. Spread on the toasted wheat bread; serve.

Nutrition Information

- Calories: 243 calories;
- Total Fat: 2.5
- Sodium: 792
- Total Carbohydrate: 30
- Cholesterol: 19
- Protein: 23.6

691. Applesauce Sandwich

Serving: 1 | Prep: 5mins | Cook: 5mins | Ready in:

Ingredients

- 1 tablespoon butter
- 2 slices bread
- 3 tablespoons applesauce

Direction

- On low heat, heat a skillet. Spread on one side of each bread slice with butter. Put slices of bread in the skillet with buttered-side down. Split onto both bread slices with the applesauce and spread to the edges.
- Cook for 5 minutes, until they are browned slightly. Fold slices together and allow to cool about 5 minutes. Slice into quarters.

Nutrition Information

- Calories: 254 calories;
- Sodium: 423
- Total Carbohydrate: 30.5
- Cholesterol: 31
- Protein: 4
- Total Fat: 13.2

692. Arepas

Serving: 12 | Prep: 15mins | Cook: 11mins | Ready in:

Ingredients

- 2 1/2 cups milk
- 1 1/2 cups arepas flour (such as P.A.N.®)
- 1/2 cup grated Monterey Jack cheese
- 1 teaspoon kosher salt
- 1/2 teaspoon freshly ground black pepper
- 1/4 cup unsalted butter, cut into pieces
- 1 tablespoon honey
- vegetable oil

- 1 (6 ounce) package cooked chicken, shredded, or to taste
- 1/2 (8 ounce) package Monterey Jack cheese, sliced, or to taste
- 1/2 avocado, sliced, or to taste

Direction

- Place milk in a pot and bring to a simmer. Take away from the heat and mix in butter.
- In a large bowl, mix black pepper, kosher salt, grated Monterey Jack cheese, and arepas flour. Put in the honey and hot milk mixture; whisk until blended. Allow the mixture to sit for 1-2 minutes until the milk is soaked up enough for a soft dough. The dough will keep on stiffen.
- Shape the dough into 12 balls (about 2-in diameter). Place between palms and flatten them into arepa patties, 3 1/2- to 4-inch, with a thickness of about 1/3-inch.
- In a large nonstick skillet, put oil and heat over medium heat. Put in 3-4 arepas at a time, and fry for about 3 minutes per side until lightly golden brown. Cut each arepa in half crosswise and fill a portion of chicken, avocado, and sliced Monterey Jack cheese between the halves.

Nutrition Information

- Calories: 222 calories;
- Protein: 10.1
- Total Fat: 13.8
- Sodium: 266
- Total Carbohydrate: 14.7
- Cholesterol: 37

693. Asian Inspired Sloppy Joes

Serving: 4 | Prep: 20mins | Cook: 10mins | Ready in:

Ingredients

- Sloppy Joes:
- 1 tablespoon sesame oil
- 1 pound ground pork
- 3 scallions, trimmed and thinly sliced
- 1 (1 inch) piece minced fresh ginger root
- 1 stalk lemongrass, tough outer stalks removed, inner stalks thinly sliced
- 1 teaspoon garlic powder
- 1/4 cup reduced-sodium soy sauce
- 3 tablespoons ketchup
- salt and ground black pepper to taste
- Wasabi Slaw:
- 1 (10 ounce) package shredded cabbage
- 2 tablespoons wasabi-flavored mayonnaise (such as Trader Joe's®)
- 1 tablespoon rice vinegar
- 1 tablespoon lime juice
- 4 whole-wheat hamburger buns

Direction

- In a big skillet, heat sesame oil over medium heat. Put in pork; cook and mix for 5 to 7 minutes till pork is not pink anymore. Put in garlic powder, lemongrass, ginger and scallions; cook and mix for 2 to 3 minutes till aromatic.
- Lower heat to low. Mix in ketchup and soy sauce. Cook for 3 to 5 minutes till mixture thickens slightly and flavors incorporate. Spice with pepper and salt.
- In a big bowl, mix together lime juice, rice vinegar, wasabi mayonnaise and cabbage; combine slaw by tossing.
- Divide all bread roll and fill with pork mixture. Put atop with slaw prior to serve.

Nutrition Information

- Calories: 769 calories;
- Total Fat: 32.5
- Sodium: 1593
- Total Carbohydrate: 84.6
- Cholesterol: 79
- Protein: 38

694.   Asparagus Sandwiches

Serving: 48 | Prep: 20mins | Cook: | Ready in:

Ingredients

- 1 (10 ounce) can asparagus tips, drained
- 1/2 cup mayonnaise
- 2 tablespoons finely chopped onion
- 1 pinch seasoning salt
- 1 (1 pound) loaf soft, sliced white bread

Direction

- Allow the asparagus spears to absorb excess liquid on the paper towels. Combine the seasoning salt, onion, and mayonnaise together in small bowl. Remove crusts from bread slices, and spread mayonnaise mixture thinly on each slice. Top the slice with a spear and roll it up. Slice each roll in half and place on a serving tray. Use a plastic wrap to cover and put in the fridge until serving.

Nutrition Information

- Calories: 43 calories;
- Total Fat: 2.2
- Sodium: 99
- Total Carbohydrate: 5
- Cholesterol: < 1
- Protein: 0.9

695.   Authentic Mexican Torta Tortas Ahogadas

Serving: 12 | Prep: 40mins | Cook: 2hours30mins | Ready in:

Ingredients

- 16 cloves garlic, minced
- 2 tablespoons minced fresh oregano

- 2 teaspoons salt
- 2 teaspoons ground black pepper
- 9 pounds boneless pork butt
- 4 dried chipotle chili peppers
- 6 tablespoons vegetable oil
- 8 cloves garlic, minced
- 4 onions, chopped
- 20 Roma tomatoes, chopped
- 1 cup water
- 5 teaspoons minced fresh oregano
- 1/4 teaspoon white sugar
- salt, to taste
- 12 Mexican bolillo rolls, lightly toasted, cut in half lengthwise
- 2 pickled jalapeno peppers, sliced

Direction

- Preheat the oven to 245 °C or 475 °F.
- In a bowl, combine pepper, 2 teaspoons of salt, 2 tablespoons of minced oregano and 16 cloves of minced garlic. On pork butt, massage the garlic mixture, and in a shallow roasting pan, put the pork.
- In the prepped oven, allow to roast for 20 minutes, then lower oven temperature to 175 °C or 350 °F. Keep on roasting for 2 hours and 15 minutes till pork is soft and not pink in the middle anymore. A pricked instant-read thermometer into the middle should register 63 °C or 145 °F. Using 2 layers of aluminum foil, cover the meat, and let rest for 20 minutes in warm area prior shredding or coarse chopping. Set pan drippings aside.
- In a bowl, put the chipotle peppers, and submerge in hot water. Let the peppers soak till for 3 minutes tender; allow to drain. Reserve. In a skillet over medium heat, heat vegetable oil. Mix in chopped onions and 8 cloves minced garlic; cook and mix for 5 minutes till the onion has turned translucent and softened. Mix in salt to taste, sugar, 5 teaspoons of oregano, chipotle chili peppers, 1 cup of water and Roma tomatoes. Put the leftover drippings from pan. Allow to simmer over low heat without cover for 15 to 20 minutes, mixing often.

- Into the blender, put the chipotle sauce, fill the pitcher midway full or less. Using a folded kitchen towel, press down the blender lid, and cautiously on the blender, get the sauce moving with a several quick pulses prior keeping it on puree. Working in batches, puree till smooth and transfer into clean pot. Incase blender is not available, use stick blender instead and in the skillet, puree the sauce. Drain sauce through a sieve.
- To serve: to form a shallow bowl, remove the inner part of each bolillo for chopped pork. Spoon approximately 2 tablespoons of chipotle sauce on the base of every roll, then set chopped pork on top of sauce. Put a few pickled jalapeno slices, next by top half of roll on top of every sandwich. Put approximately quarter cup more of chipotle sauce on top of the whole sandwich.

Nutrition Information

- Calories: 867 calories;
- Total Fat: 41
- Sodium: 571
- Total Carbohydrate: 75.1
- Cholesterol: 135
- Protein: 47.7

696. Authentic Turkish Doner Kebab

Serving: 4 | Prep: 10mins | Cook: 1hours20mins | Ready in:

Ingredients

- 1 teaspoon all-purpose flour
- 1 teaspoon dried oregano
- 1/2 teaspoon salt
- 1/2 teaspoon garlic powder
- 1/2 teaspoon onion powder
- 1/2 teaspoon dried Italian herb seasoning
- 1/4 teaspoon ground black pepper

- 1/4 teaspoon cayenne pepper
- 1 1/4 pounds ground lamb

Direction

- Preheat the oven to 350°F (175°C).
- In a large bowl mix flour, salt, garlic powder, oregano, onion powder, Italian seasoning, cayenne pepper, and black pepper. Add the ground lamb to the mixture and knead thoroughly for about 3 minutes, until evenly combined.
- Shape the seasoned meat and transfer it to a loaf pan placed on the baking sheet.
- Bake for about 1 hour and 20 minutes in the preheated oven, turning the loaf halfway to allow even browning.
- Once done, wrap loaf in tinfoil, set aside and let it rest for about 10 minutes. Cut as thinly as possible, making the kebab pieces.

Nutrition Information

- Calories: 283 calories;
- Total Fat: 19.3
- Sodium: 370
- Total Carbohydrate: 1.5
- Cholesterol: 95
- Protein: 24.4

697.   Avocado Breakfast Toast

Serving: 2 | Prep: 10mins | Cook: 12mins | Ready in:

Ingredients

- 4 slices turkey bacon
- 2 tablespoons butter
- 2 slices bread
- 1 avocado
- 1 1/2 tablespoons lemon juice
- 2 teaspoons minced garlic
- 2 teaspoons ground turmeric
- 2 teaspoons ground cumin
- 2 teaspoons garlic salt
- 1 dash cayenne pepper
- salt and ground black pepper to taste
- 1 small Roma tomato, chopped
- 2 eggs
- 2 slices Colby-Monterey Jack cheese

Direction

- On medium heat, heat a pan. Put in bacon and fry for 5 minutes until the bacon is a bit crunchy. Move the bacon to a cutting board. Keep the grease in the skillet. Chop up bacon into small pieces.
- Spread butter on each side of the bread slices.
- In a bowl, combine pepper, avocado, salt, lemon juice, cayenne pepper, minced garlic, garlic salt, turmeric, and cumin until the avocado mixture is creamy. Fold in tomato and chopped bacon until mixed through.
- On medium heat, heat the bacon grease in the pan. Cook over-easy eggs by breaking the eggs in the pan and frying for 3 minutes until the whites are solid. Gently turn the eggs by sliding a spatula underneath. Cook for another minute. Sprinkle the eggs with pepper and salt to season. Move the eggs to the corner of the pan.
- Lower the heat and arrange the buttered bread in the pan. Lightly toast for one minute. Flip the bread and put a slice of cheese on the toasted parts. Generously spread the avocado mixture over the cheese. Put a lid on the pan for the cheese to melt faster. Cook for another 2 minutes until the bottom of the bread is golden. Place the toast on a plate and top with the over-easy eggs.

Nutrition Information

- Calories: 585 calories;
- Total Fat: 45.7
- Sodium: 2663
- Total Carbohydrate: 28.3
- Cholesterol: 260
- Protein: 20.6

698. Avocado Chicken Lettuce Wraps

Serving: 4 | Prep: 10mins | Cook: 40mins | Ready in:

Ingredients

- 2 boneless, skinless chicken breasts
- 2 tablespoons olive oil
- 2 teaspoons mango lime seasoning blend
- 1 large avocado - peeled, pitted, and diced
- 2 tablespoons lime juice, or more to taste
- 2 tablespoons hot salsa (optional)
- 1 tablespoon chopped fresh cilantro, or more to taste
- 1 tablespoon garlic powder
- salt and ground black pepper to taste
- 1 head romaine lettuce, leaves separated

Direction

- Set an oven to preheat to 150°C (300°F).
- Use olive oil to coat the chicken breasts and sprinkle both sides with lime and mango seasoning. Put it in a shallow baking dish and cover it using aluminum foil.
- Let the chicken bake for 40-45 minutes in the preheated oven, until an inserted instant-read thermometer in the middle registers at least 74°C (165°F) and it has no visible pink color in the middle. Take it out of the oven and let it cool for about 10 minutes, until easy to handle.
- Chop the chicken into small pieces and put it in a big bowl. Add black pepper, salt, garlic powder, cilantro, salsa, lime juice and avocado, then stir well to blend. To make the wraps, serve it on top of the lettuce leaves.

Nutrition Information

- Calories: 264 calories;
- Protein: 15.2
- Total Fat: 18.9
- Sodium: 381
- Total Carbohydrate: 11.5

699. Avocado Toast With Cauliflower Mash

Serving: 3 | Prep: 10mins | Cook: 7mins | Ready in:

Ingredients

- 2 cups cauliflower florets
- 1/3 cup olive oil
- 1/2 cup grated Parmesan cheese
- 1 teaspoon lemon juice
- 1 teaspoon ground black pepper
- 1 teaspoon cayenne pepper
- 2 slices whole-grain bread
- 1 tablespoon light mayonnaise (optional)
- 1 avocado, thinly sliced

Direction

- On medium heat, put cauliflower in a pan; pour in olive oil. Cook and stir the cauliflower for 5-7 mins until nearly golden. In a blender, blend black pepper, cooked cauliflower, lemon juice, and Parmesan cheese for 10-15 secs until the texture is like mashed potatoes.
- Toast the bread for two minutes; slather light mayonnaise on the bread slices evenly. Slather cauliflower mixture evenly on the toasts; top with slices of avocado.

Nutrition Information

- Calories: 460 calories;
- Total Fat: 40.2
- Sodium: 336
- Total Carbohydrate: 18.7
- Cholesterol: 13
- Protein: 10.3

700. Avocado Toast With Pickled Radishes

Serving: 2 | Prep: 15mins | Cook: 7mins | Ready in:

Ingredients

- Pickled Radishes:
- 3/4 cup white vinegar
- 3/4 cup water
- 3 tablespoons honey
- 2 teaspoons salt
- 1 bunch radishes, cubed
- 1/2 teaspoon whole mustard seeds
- 1 pinch ground black pepper
- 1 bay leaf
- Seasoning Mix:
- 1 pinch coarse sea salt
- 1 pinch furikake (Japanese nori seasoning) (optional)
- 1 pinch toasted sesame seeds
- Toast:
- 1 avocado, cut into 1/4-inch dice
- 2 slices whole-grain bread
- 1 bunch sprouted cilantro
- 1 lemon wedge

Direction

- In a small pot, combine salt, vinegar, honey, and water; boil. Take off heat.
- In a lidded pint jar, put in bay leaf radishes, black pepper, and mustard seeds; pour in hot vinegar mixture. Cool to room temperature and secure with a lid. Refrigerate for a minimum of two hours.
- For the seasoning mix, combine sesame seeds, coarse sea salt, and furikake in a small bowl.
- Toast bread for 2 mins until light brown; add 1/2 of the avocado on top of each slice. Arrange a few pickled radishes and 1/2 of the seasoning mix on top. Garnish with some cilantro and squeeze in lemon juice on the top.

Nutrition Information

- Calories: 363 calories;
- Protein: 7.5
- Total Fat: 16.8
- Sodium: 2700
- Total Carbohydrate: 55.4
- Cholesterol: 0

701. BBQ Chicken Sandwiches

Serving: 12 | Prep: 15mins | Cook: 4hours | Ready in:

Ingredients

- 2 (4 pound) whole chickens, cut up
- 1 1/2 cups ketchup
- 3/4 cup prepared mustard
- 5 tablespoons brown sugar
- 5 tablespoons minced garlic
- 5 tablespoons honey
- 1/4 cup steak sauce
- 4 tablespoons lemon juice
- 3 tablespoons liquid smoke flavoring
- salt and pepper to taste
- 12 hamburger buns
- 3 cups prepared coleslaw (optional)

Direction

- In a big pot, cover chicken with enough water. Boil. Cook for about 3 hours until chicken easily comes off the bone. Create sauce as chicken cooks.
- Mix liquid smoke, lemon juice, steak sauce, honey, garlic, brown sugar, mustard and ketchup in a saucepan on medium heat. Season with pepper and salt. Bring to a gentle boil. Simmer for about 10 minutes. Put aside to merge flavors.
- When chicken is finished, take away meat from bones then shred/chop to small pieces. Put in pan with sauce. Cook for about 15 minutes to let sauce flavors soak into chicken. On buns, spoon barbequed chicken. If you like, top it with coleslaw.

Nutrition Information

- Calories: 662 calories;
- Total Fat: 29
- Sodium: 956
- Total Carbohydrate: 51.4
- Cholesterol: 137
- Protein: 47.9

| 702. | BBQ Chicken And Bacon Bread |

Serving: 6 | Prep: 25mins | Cook: 30mins |Ready in:

Ingredients

- 1 egg
- 1/4 cup water
- 3 cooked skinless, boneless chicken breast halves, chopped
- 6 slices bacon - cooked and crumbled
- 1 small green bell pepper, chopped
- 1 1/2 cups honey barbecue sauce, divided
- 1 (8 ounce) package shredded Cheddar-Monterey Jack cheese blend, divided
- all-purpose flour for rolling
- 1 (11.5 ounce) can refrigerated crusty French loaf dough

Direction

- Start preheating oven to 350°F (175°C). Whisk water and egg. Put aside.
- Combine one cup shredded cheese blend, one cup of the barbecue sauce, bell pepper, bacon and chicken. Meat should be coated with barbecue sauce. Pour in more sauce if mixture gets too dry.
- On a smooth, clean, well-floured surface, unroll the dough. Roll out or spread to 1/4-in. thickness, retaining the rectangular shape. Spread down center of dough with chicken mixture. Add rest of cheese and more barbecue sauce over top. Fold 1 side of the dough over the mixture. Brush the folded

dough edge with egg wash. Fold the other dough side over, sealing with the egg wash. Seal both ends of the loaf with the egg wash well; then brush over the bread top.

- On an oiled baking sheet, place bread carefully. Bake in prepared oven for 25-35 minutes until golden brown. Let cool slightly. Slice and serve.

Nutrition Information

- Calories: 503 calories;
- Sodium: 1472
- Total Carbohydrate: 53.2
- Cholesterol: 111
- Protein: 30.5
- Total Fat: 18.2

| 703. | BBQ Pork For Sandwiches |

Serving: 12 | Prep: 15mins | Cook: 4hours30mins |Ready in:

Ingredients

- 1 (14 ounce) can beef broth
- 3 pounds boneless pork ribs
- 1 (18 ounce) bottle barbeque sauce

Direction

- Add a can of beef broth into the slow cooker, then put in boneless pork ribs. Cook on high heat for 4 hours until meat can be shredded easily. Transfer the meat and shred with 2 forks. It may seem that it's not successful right away, but it will.
- Start preheating the oven at 350°F (175°C). Place the shredded pork to a Dutch oven or iron skillet and blend in barbeque sauce.
- Bake in the prepared oven for 30 minutes until heated thoroughly.

Nutrition Information

- Calories: 355 calories;
- Total Fat: 18.1
- Sodium: 623
- Total Carbohydrate: 15.2
- Cholesterol: 83
- Protein: 30.2

---

704.   BLT Dogs

Serving: 4 | Prep: 15mins | Cook: 5mins | Ready in:

Ingredients

- 1 small tomato, seeded and chopped
- 4 slices cooked bacon, crumbled
- 3 tablespoons diced dill pickles
- 1 tablespoon mayonnaise
- 1 tablespoon sour cream
- 4 hot dogs
- 4 hot dog buns
- 2 lettuce leaves, thinly sliced, or as desired
- 1 green onion top, thinly sliced, or as desired

Direction

- In a bowl, combine the sour cream, mayonnaise, pickles, bacon and tomato, then use plastic wrap to cover it and let it chill in the fridge for around 4 hours for the flavors to combine.
- Boil a pot of water and let the hot dogs cook for 5-10 minutes, until it is completely warmed, then drain.
- In each of the bun, put a hot dog and put the tomato-bacon mixture on top of each. Put green onion and lettuce on each to garnish.

Nutrition Information

- Calories: 341 calories;
- Protein: 11.9
- Total Fat: 21.2
- Sodium: 968

- Total Carbohydrate: 25.1
- Cholesterol: 33

---

705.   Baby Greens And Goat Cheese Wrap

Serving: 1 | Prep: 10mins | Cook: | Ready in:

Ingredients

- 1 (12 inch) whole wheat tortilla
- 1 cup mixed baby salad greens
- 4 cherry tomatoes, chopped
- 2 tablespoons crumbled goat cheese
- 2 tablespoons diced roasted red peppers
- 1/2 tablespoon shredded mozzarella cheese
- balsamic vinegar to taste
- olive oil to taste

Direction

- Lay out the tortilla flat and arrange the baby greens across. Sprinkle evenly across the greens the goat cheese, mozzarella cheese, cherry tomatoes, and roasted red pepper. Drizzle with balsamic vinegar and olive oil.
- To enclose the filling, fold the tortilla bottom up about 2 inches and roll the wrap tightly.

Nutrition Information

- Calories: 381 calories;
- Protein: 15.4
- Total Fat: 11.5
- Sodium: 787
- Total Carbohydrate: 74.1
- Cholesterol: 13

706.   Bacon Mollete With Black Beans, Eggs And Salsa Fresca

Serving: 2 | Prep: 15mins | Cook: 15mins | Ready in:

Ingredients

- 4 slices Farmland® Bacon, cooked
- 2 Mexican bolillo rolls or baguettes, sliced in half horizontally
- 4 eggs, fried
- 1/2 cup Cotija cheese, crumbled
- Cilantro for garnish
- Black Bean Spread:
- 2 tablespoons vegetable oil
- 1/2 cup diced yellow onion
- 1 jalapeno pepper, seeds removed, diced
- 2 garlic cloves, sliced
- 1 (15 ounce) can black beans, rinsed and drained
- 1/2 teaspoon ground cumin
- 1 lime, juiced
- 1 cup chicken stock
- Salsa Fresca:
- 2 ripe tomatoes, seeds removed, diced
- 1/4 cup diced red onion
- 1/2 jalapeno pepper, seeds removed, diced
- 1/4 cup fresh cilantro, minced
- 1 lime, juiced
- salt and pepper to taste

Direction

- To make black bean spread: put a medium sauté pan on medium heat and heat vegetable oil. Place in jalapenos and garlic. Sauté until soft then place in garlic. Cook for another 2 minutes.
- Place lime juice, cumin, and black beans in and mix. Cook until the beans are fully warmed.
- Move to a blender and blend it until smooth. Place in enough chicken stock to get your ideal spreading consistency.
- Salsa Fresca: mix all the ingredients except the seasonings in a mixing bowl. Season with pepper and salt.

- Serving: Lightly toast bread in a toaster or oven.
- Cover the bottom half with the black bean spread then bacon. Put fried eggs on top. Garnish using more cilantro, cheese, and salsa fresca. Place the other bread half on the top.

Nutrition Information

- Calories: 1043 calories;
- Cholesterol: 381
- Protein: 49.2
- Total Fat: 42.7
- Sodium: 2165
- Total Carbohydrate: 119.8

707.   Bacon, Apple And Brie Panini

Serving: 2 | Prep: 10mins | Cook: 6mins | Ready in:

Ingredients

- 2 tablespoons butter, room temperature
- 2 slices bread
- 1 teaspoon Dijon mustard (optional)
- 3 slices Brie cheese
- 1 Fuji apple, thinly sliced
- 4 strips cooked bacon

Direction

- On medium-high heat, heat a panini press following the manufacturer's directions.
- Butter one side of each bread slice. Turn one slice over, then spread on the mustard. Put in cheese. Top cheese with the apple slices. Top with bacon layer. Put on the other bread slice, buttered side facing up.
- Arrange sandwich in panini press, then press down. Grill for 3 mins on each side or until browned lightly.

Nutrition Information

- Calories: 587 calories;
- Total Fat: 42.6
- Sodium: 1599
- Total Carbohydrate: 23.5
- Cholesterol: 121
- Protein: 27.3

---

708.   Baked Eggplant Sandwiches

Serving: 4 | Prep: 15mins | Cook: 30mins | Ready in:

Ingredients

- 2 tablespoons olive oil, divided
- 2 cups panko bread crumbs
- 2 teaspoons salt
- 1/2 teaspoon ground black pepper
- 1 cup all-purpose flour
- 1 egg
- 1/4 cup water
- 1 large long eggplant, cut crosswise into 1/3 inch thick slices
- 1/2 cup finely chopped onion
- 3 cloves garlic, minced
- 5 ounces fresh goat cheese
- 1 cup shredded sharp provolone cheese
- 2 tablespoons chopped fresh parsley
- 2 tablespoons chopped fresh basil leaves
- ground black pepper to taste
- 1/2 cup pomegranate molasses

Direction

- Preheat the oven to 450°F (230°C). Coat olive oil on two big baking sheets.
- Stir together in a medium bowl the salt, panko crumbs, and 1/2 teaspoon pepper. Whisk together the egg and water in another bowl. In a third bowl, place the flour. Coat each eggplant slice with flour, shake the excess off, then dip into the egg, and lastly cover with

panko crumbs. Arrange on the oiled baking sheets.
- In the preheated oven, bake about 12 minutes, then turn the slices and bake until golden brown for another 12 minutes. Remove from the oven and cool slightly, but keep the oven on.
- Heat over medium heat 1 tablespoon oil in a skillet while the eggplant is cooking. Add the onion; stir and cook until nearly tender, then add the garlic. Cook for 1 minute. Put off the heat and stir in the provolone cheese, parsley, goat cheese, and basil. Add pepper to season.
- Split the cheese blend onto 8 eggplant pieces (half). Spread to cover, then place the remaining slices of eggplant on top; press to compact. Put them back on the baking sheets.
- Bake in the preheated oven for about 15 minutes until the eggplant is crisp. Place onto each serving plate two sandwiches; drizzle with pomegranate molasses.

Nutrition Information

- Calories: 620 calories;
- Total Fat: 29.7
- Sodium: 1922
- Total Carbohydrate: 74
- Cholesterol: 97
- Protein: 28.4

---

709.   Baked Hawaiian Roll Sandwiches

Serving: 4 | Prep: 10mins | Cook: 15mins | Ready in:

Ingredients

- 4 Hawaiian bread rolls, split
- 4 tablespoons lingonberry jam
- 4 slices deli ham
- 4 slices deli Swiss cheese
- 1/2 cup melted butter
- 1/4 cup dried onion flakes

- 1/4 cup white sugar
- 2 tablespoons poppy seeds
- 2 tablespoons sesame seeds
- 1 tablespoon honey mustard

Direction

- Prepare the oven by preheating to 350°F (175°C). Use parchment paper to line a baking sheet.
- On the prepared baking sheet, put the bottoms of buns. Then layer lingonberry jam, the ham, and the Swiss cheese evenly on each. Add honey mustard, sesame seeds, poppy seeds, sugar, onion flakes, and melted butter evenly to each. Put back the tops of buns.
- Place in preheated oven and bake for 15-20 minutes until cheese is dissolved and buns become toasty.

Nutrition Information

- Calories: 780 calories;
- Cholesterol: 143
- Total Fat: 37.7
- Protein: 28.6
- Sodium: 828
- Total Carbohydrate: 72.3

710. Balsamic Avocado Toast

Serving: 1 | Prep: 5mins | Cook: 1mins | Ready in:

Ingredients

- 1 slice French bread
- 2 teaspoons balsamic vinegar
- 1/4 avocado, sliced
- 1 dash paprika, or to taste
- salt and freshly cracked black pepper to taste

Direction

- Toast the French bread lightly for a minute, and then sprinkle on the toasted bread with vinegar.
- Layer on the bread with slices of avocado, then sprinkle on top with pepper, salt and paprika.

Nutrition Information

- Calories: 169 calories;
- Protein: 4.4
- Total Fat: 7.9
- Sodium: 578
- Total Carbohydrate: 21.9
- Cholesterol: 0

711. Bandito Slow Cooker Chili Dogs

Serving: 20 | Prep: 15mins | Cook: 4hours | Ready in:

Ingredients

- 2 (16 ounce) packages hot dogs
- 2 (15 ounce) cans chili without beans
- 1 (10.75 ounce) can condensed Cheddar cheese soup
- 3 tablespoons ketchup
- 1 (4 ounce) can chopped green chilies, drained
- 20 hot dog buns
- 1 cup shredded Cheddar cheese
- 1/4 cup chopped onion, or to taste
- 1 1/2 cups crushed corn chips (such as Fritos®)

Direction

- Put hot dogs in a slow cooker. In a bowl, mix chopped green chilies, ketchup, Cheddar cheese soup, and chili; pour over the hot dogs. Next, cover the cooker, set to Low, and cook for 4-5 hours (if desired, you can cook longer).
- Serve hot dogs on buns with about 2 tablespoons crushed corn chips, 1 tablespoon of shredded Cheddar cheese, 1 teaspoon of

chopped onion, and a large spoonful of chili on top of them.

Nutrition Information

- Calories: 385 calories;
- Total Fat: 21.4
- Sodium: 1172
- Total Carbohydrate: 33.1
- Cholesterol: 39
- Protein: 14.7

712.   Banh Mi

Serving: 2 | Prep: 30mins | Cook: 20mins | Ready in:

Ingredients

- 1/2 cup rice vinegar
- 1/4 cup water
- 1/4 cup white sugar
- 1/4 cup carrot, cut into 1/16-inch-thick matchsticks
- 1/4 cup white (daikon) radish, cut into 1/16-inch-thick matchsticks
- 1/4 cup thinly sliced white onion
- 1 skinless, boneless chicken breast half
- garlic salt to taste
- ground black pepper to taste
- 1 (12 inch) French baguette
- 4 tablespoons mayonnaise
- 1/4 cup thinly sliced cucumber
- 1 tablespoon fresh cilantro leaves
- 1 small jalapeno pepper - seeded and cut into 1/16-inch-thick matchsticks
- 1 wedge lime

Direction

- In a saucepan over medium heat, add sugar, water and rice vinegar; bring to a boil. Stir for 1 minute to dissolve the sugar. Let it cool.
- In a bowl, add onion, radish and carrot; pour the vinegar mixture over. Let it stand for at

least 30 minutes. Remove excess vinegar mixture after marinated.

- When marinating the vegetables, turn on the oven's broiler to preheat. Position the rack 6 inches away from heat. Use oil to lightly grease a slotted broiler pan.
- Use pepper and garlic salt to sprinkle on chicken breast; put on the slotted pan to broil for 6 minutes on each side, flipping once, until the surface turns brown and the center of breast is no longer pink. Take the chicken out; cut into bite-size pieces.
- Cut the baguette in 2 lengthwise; remove the center to make space for filing. Put baguette halves under broiler for 2-3 minutes to toast a bit.
- For banh mi assembling: Use mayonnaise to spread out on each half of the toasted baguette. Use jalapeno pepper, cilantro leaves, radish, onion, pickled carrot, cucumber slices and broiled chicken to fill the cavity of bottom half of the bread. Use a wedge of lime to squeeze over the filling; use the other half of the baguette to top.

Nutrition Information

- Calories: 657 calories;
- Sodium: 990
- Total Carbohydrate: 85.2
- Cholesterol: 43
- Protein: 24
- Total Fat: 25.2

713.   Banh Mi Style Vietnamese Baguette

Serving: 2 | Prep: 20mins | Cook: 25mins | Ready in:

Ingredients

- 2 portobello mushroom caps, sliced
- 2 teaspoons olive oil
- salt and pepper to taste

- 1 carrot, sliced into sticks
- 1 daikon (white) radish, sliced into sticks
- 1 cup rice vinegar
- 1/2 cup fresh lime juice
- 1/2 cup cold water
- 1/2 cup chilled lime juice
- 2 teaspoons soy sauce
- 1 teaspoon nuoc mam (Vietnamese fish sauce)
- 1/2 teaspoon toasted sesame oil
- 2 tablespoons canola oil
- 2 teaspoons minced garlic
- 1/3 cup white sugar
- 1/3 cup cold water
- 1 jalapeno pepper, thinly sliced
- 8 sprigs fresh cilantro with stems
- 1 medium cucumber, sliced into thin strips
- 2 sprigs fresh Thai basil
- 2 (7 inch) French bread baguettes, split lengthwise

Direction

- Set the oven to 450°F (230°C) for preheating. Arrange the mushrooms on a baking sheet. Drizzle with a bit of olive oil and spice up with pepper and salt. Roast the mushroom for about 25 minutes inside the prepped oven. Let it cool slightly, and cut into strips.
- Meanwhile, put a water in a saucepan and let it boil. Drop the radish sticks and carrot into the boiling water and remove after a few seconds, and submerge them in an ice water placed in a bowl to prevent the vegetables from cooking. In another bowl, stir a half cup of lime juice, rice vinegar and half cup cold water together. Place the radish and carrot to the vinegar and lime marinade and allow soaking for 15 minutes, much longer if it's convenient.
- Make the sandwich sauce: Combine together 1/3 cup water, the remaining lime juice, fish sauce, 1/3 cup sugar, sesame oil, soy sauce and canola oil, mix in a small bowl,.
- To arrange the sandwiches, drizzle a bit of a sandwich sauce on each half of the French loaves. Put the roasted mushrooms on the bottom half of each roll and drizzle with a

little more sauce. Top it off with a couple sticks of carrot and radish (without the marinade), a few slices of jalapeno, basil, cilantro and cucumber. Place the other half of the bread on top to close. Serve.

Nutrition Information

- Calories: 760 calories;
- Total Fat: 22.8
- Sodium: 1282
- Total Carbohydrate: 128.4
- Cholesterol: 0
- Protein: 19.5

---

714. Barbecue Beef For Sandwiches

Serving: 16 | Prep: 5mins | Cook: 2hours45mins | Ready in:

Ingredients

- 4 pounds boneless chuck roast
- 1 onion, chopped
- 2 tablespoons butter
- 3 tablespoons distilled white vinegar
- 12 ounces chile sauce
- 2 tablespoons brown sugar
- 1 teaspoon mustard powder
- 2 tablespoons Worcestershire sauce
- 1/2 teaspoon freshly ground black pepper
- 1 teaspoon salt
- 1/8 teaspoon ground cayenne pepper
- 3 cloves garlic, minced

Direction

- In a big covered pan, add the roast. Roast at 165°C or 325°F until meat shreds easily and falls apart, about 2 hours.
- Melt butter in a big skillet on moderate heat. Put in onions and sauté until translucent.

- Stir in chili sauce and vinegar. Fill water into empty chili sauce bottle and shake, then pour the liquid into skillet. Mix in garlic, cayenne pepper, salt, black pepper, Worcestershire sauce, mustard and brown sugar. Cook sauce on low heat while stirring frequently, until thickened.
- Shred roasted beef using 2 forks. Stir in the sauce in skillet with the meat and simmer for half an hour.

Nutrition Information

- Calories: 200 calories;
- Cholesterol: 53
- Protein: 14.4
- Total Fat: 13.3
- Sodium: 207
- Total Carbohydrate: 4.9

---

715.   Barbeque Tempeh Sandwiches

Serving: 4 | Prep: 10mins | Cook: 15mins | Ready in:

Ingredients

- 1 cup barbecue sauce, your choice
- 1 (8 ounce) package tempeh, crumbled
- 1 tablespoon vegetable oil
- 1 red bell pepper, seeded and chopped
- 1 green bell pepper, seeded and chopped
- 1 medium onion, chopped
- 4 kaiser rolls, split and toasted

Direction

- In a medium bowl, add the barbeque sauce. Crumble the tempeh into the sauce; marinate lightly for about 10 minutes.
- In a skillet, heat oil over medium heat. Put in the onion and green and red peppers. Cook and stir often until tender. Mix in barbeque sauce and tempeh; heat through.

- Scoop tempeh mixture onto kaiser rolls, then serve.

Nutrition Information

- Calories: 375 calories;
- Protein: 15.2
- Total Fat: 11.5
- Sodium: 925
- Total Carbohydrate: 54.7
- Cholesterol: 0

---

716.   Beef Gyro

Serving: 5 | Prep: 15mins | Cook: 5mins | Ready in:

Ingredients

- 2 (8 ounce) containers plain yogurt
- 2 cucumbers - peeled, seeded, and diced
- 3 tablespoons olive oil, divided
- 1 tablespoon chopped fresh dill
- 1/2 lemon, juiced
- 3 cloves garlic, peeled
- salt and ground black pepper to taste
- 1 (1 pound) beef top sirloin steak, cut into thin strips
- 5 pita bread rounds
- 1 tomato, chopped
- 1/2 small onion, thinly sliced
- 1 (4 ounce) package crumbled feta cheese
- 1/2 cup shredded lettuce
- 1 (2.25 ounce) can sliced ripe olives, drained

Direction

- In a blender, process pepper, salt, garlic, lemon juice, dill, 2 tablespoons of olive oil, cucumbers and yogurt until tzatziki sauce is blended thoroughly.
- In a large skillet, bring the rest 1 tablespoon of olive oil to medium heat; cook, stirring, beef in hot oil for 5-10 minutes until no pink meat remains.

- Stack steak, tomato, onion, feta cheese, lettuce, olives and tzatziki sauce in the exact order onto half of each pita. Fold edge of each pita over the filling, then use a toothpick to secure.

Nutrition Information

- Calories: 497 calories;
- Sodium: 732
- Total Carbohydrate: 41.5
- Cholesterol: 74
- Protein: 28.9
- Total Fat: 24.1

---

717.   Beef Salad Sandwich Filling

Serving: 4 | Prep: 15mins | Cook: | Ready in:

Ingredients

- 1 cup chopped cooked beef
- 2 stalks celery, chopped
- 1 carrot, diced
- 1/4 cup chopped onion
- 3 tablespoons mayonnaise
- 1/4 teaspoon salt
- 1/8 teaspoon ground black pepper
- 1/8 teaspoon garlic powder

Direction

- In a bowl, mix garlic powder, black pepper, salt, mayonnaise, onion, carrot, celery and beef together till mixed completely.

Nutrition Information

- Calories: 228 calories;
- Total Carbohydrate: 3.4
- Cholesterol: 46
- Protein: 13.2
- Total Fat: 17.8
- Sodium: 261

---

718.   Beef On Weck

Serving: 6 | Prep: 10mins | Cook: 10mins | Ready in:

Ingredients

- 3 cups prepared au jus sauce
- 2 pounds thinly sliced roast beef
- 6 Kaiser rolls, split
- 2 teaspoons kosher salt
- 2 teaspoons caraway seeds
- 1/4 cup prepared horseradish

Direction

- Set the oven to 150°C or 300°F to preheat.
- In a saucepan, warm the au jus sauce on moderate heat, then put in roast beef and allow to it to warm up at the same time. While soaking the meat, on a baking sheet, put the rolls, cut-side facing down. Use water to brush lightly over tops and sprinkle with caraway seeds as well as salt.
- In the preheated oven, bake for about 10 minutes, until rolls are toasted. Serve sliced beef on the rolls with au jus and horseradish alongside.

Nutrition Information

- Calories: 315 calories;
- Total Fat: 6.8
- Sodium: 2479
- Total Carbohydrate: 27.6
- Cholesterol: 73
- Protein: 36.2

---

719.   Beefy Rice Salad Sandwiches

Serving: 6 | Prep: 15mins | Cook: 25mins | Ready in:

Ingredients

- 1 1/2 cups rice, cooked
- 1/2 small onion, finely chopped
- 1/2 red bell pepper, finely chopped
- 1 tablespoon olive oil
- 3/4 pound lean ground beef
- 1/2 teaspoon dried thyme, crushed
- 1/2 avocado - peeled, pitted and diced
- 1/4 cup chopped fresh parsley
- salt and pepper to taste
- 3 tablespoons olive oil
- 3 tablespoons seasoned rice vinegar
- 3 pita bread rounds, cut in half
- lettuce leaves
- tomato slices

Direction

- Wash rice in a fine mesh strainer under cold running water until no longer cloudy. Put to a medium saucepan and put 2 1/2 cups water to cover. Make it boil, covered, and minimize heat to low. Simmer for 15 minutes, separate from the heat and allow to stand for at least 10 minutes, or until all liquid has vaporized. Reserve to cool.
- Then cook bell pepper and onion in 1 tablespoon oil on medium high heat until softened. Put thyme and ground beef, and cook until well browned, occasionally whisking and minimizing heat if needed.
- Mix together in a bowl the parsley, avocado, meat mixture and cooked rice.
- Mix desired amount of pepper and salt, rice vinegar, and olive oil in another bowl. Put over rice mixture, and lightly toss. Then line each pita half with tomato and lettuce, ad pack each with rice mixture. Serve cold or warm. Have fun!

Nutrition Information

- Calories: 501 calories;
- Total Fat: 20.1
- Sodium: 736
- Total Carbohydrate: 61.5
- Cholesterol: 34
- Protein: 17.3

---

720.   Beer And Bourbon Pulled Pork Sandwiches

Serving: 6 | Prep: 15mins | Cook: 8hours30mins | Ready in:

Ingredients

- 1 tablespoon paprika
- 2 teaspoons onion powder
- 2 teaspoons garlic powder
- 2 teaspoons dried oregano
- 2 teaspoons ground thyme
- 1 teaspoon salt
- 1 pinch ground black pepper, or to taste
- 1 (3 pound) pork roast, cut into 3-inch chops
- 2 1/2 tablespoons canola oil, divided
- 1 1/2 teaspoons butter
- 2 onions, sliced
- 1 (12 fluid ounce) can or bottle wheat beer, divided
- 1 pinch salt
- 1 teaspoon liquid smoke flavoring
- 3/4 cup barbeque sauce
- 1 1/2 teaspoons Worcestershire sauce
- 5 cloves garlic, minced
- 2 (1.5 fluid ounce) jiggers bourbon whiskey
- 3 dashes hot pepper sauce
- 6 crusty bread rolls, split

Direction

- In a small bowl, mix together salt, thyme, oregano, garlic powder, onion powder and paprika; use black pepper to season.
- Blot paper towels onto the pork chops to dry, and then rub the paprika mixture over.
- In a non-stick skillet, heat approximately 2 tablespoons canola oil over medium-high heat. Working in batches, fry the pork chops for 5 minutes on each side until turning brown.

Remove the browned pork chops to a slow cooker.

- Clean the skillet by wiping and heat butter and the leftover 1 1/2 teaspoon canola oil over medium heat; stir and cook 1 pinch of salt, 1/2 bottle beer and onions for 10 minutes until the onions are lightly brown and soft. Pour in the liquid smoke. Spread over the pork with the onions.
- In a bowl, combine hot sauce, bourbon, garlic, Worcestershire sauce, the leftover beer and barbeque sauce; add onto the pork.
- Cook the pork on Low for 8 hours until very soft. Shred and distribute the pork over the rolls to create sandwiches.

Nutrition Information

- Calories: 514 calories;
- Sodium: 1041
- Total Carbohydrate: 41.7
- Cholesterol: 82
- Protein: 31.6
- Total Fat: 18.5

---

721. Best Grilled Vegetable Sandwich

Serving: 2 | Prep: 15mins | Cook: 5mins | Ready in:

Ingredients

- 1/2 zucchini, cut crosswise into 1/2-inch slices
- 1/2 small eggplant, cut crosswise into 1/2-inch slices
- 1 red bell pepper, quartered
- 1/2 teaspoon salt
- 1 1/2 teaspoons olive oil
- ground black pepper to taste
- 1 small whole-grain baguette, cut into two halves and split lengthwise
- 1/4 cup basil pesto
- 4 ounces fresh baby mozzarella, sliced
- 2 plum tomatoes, sliced

Direction

- In a bowl, mix together red bell pepper, eggplant, and zucchini. Sprinkle over the mixture with salt. Put the vegetables aside to tenderize for a minimum of 3 hours.
- Start preheating the oven to medium heat and lightly grease the grate with oil.
- Strain liquid from the vegetable mixture. Brush olive oil over the vegetables to coat, use black pepper to season.
- Put the vegetables on the hot grill and cook for 2-3 minutes each side until soft. Remove to a bowl and put aside.
- In a toaster oven, toast the cut sides of baguette for 2-3 minutes until they turn golden brown. Evenly spread over the toasted surface with the basil pesto. Evenly put the grilled vegetables on both of the baguette halves. Put plum tomato slices and sliced mozzarella on top of each; put the leftover baguette pieces on top of the sandwich and enjoy.

Nutrition Information

- Calories: 714 calories;
- Sodium: 1918
- Total Carbohydrate: 79.8
- Cholesterol: 46
- Protein: 35.1
- Total Fat: 29.4

---

722. Best Ever Fried Chicken Sandwiches

Serving: 4 | Prep: 15mins | Cook: 20mins | Ready in:

Ingredients

- 1 1/2 cups all-purpose flour, divided
- 1 egg
- 1/4 cup ranch dressing mix (such as Hidden Valley®)
- 2 chicken breasts

- 1 cup vegetable oil
- 1/2 cup mayonnaise
- 1/4 cup sriracha sauce
- 4 potato rolls
- 16 dill pickle chips

Direction

- Preheat an oven to 175°C/350°F.
- In small bowl, put 1/2 cup flour.
- Use fork to beat egg in shallow bowl.
- In bowl, put 1 cup flour; mix ranch dressing in.
- Split chicken breasts to make 4 pieces; use plain flour to coat each piece. Dip in egg; coat in flour-ranch mixture. Put on wire rack placed above a rimmed baking sheet.
- In big saucepan, heat oil till nearly boiling. Add 2 chicken pieces and fry for 5 minutes, turning once, till lightly golden. Put chicken back on wire rack; repeat with leftover 2 chicken pieces.
- In preheated oven, bake chicken for 10 minutes till juices run clear.
- Mix sriracha sauce and mayonnaise in small bowl then spread on rolls. On each roll, put 4 pickle slices; put 1 chicken piece over each sandwich.

Nutrition Information

- Calories: 655 calories;
- Cholesterol: 92
- Protein: 22.7
- Total Fat: 34.1
- Sodium: 1652
- Total Carbohydrate: 63.7

723. Bohemian Kebab Wraps

Serving: 8 | Prep: 30mins | Cook: 10mins | Ready in:

Ingredients

- 4 (4 ounce) beef skirt steaks, cut into 1-inch cubes
- 2 large yellow onions, cut into 1-inch pieces
- 2 large green bell peppers, cut into 1-inch pieces
- 2 large red bell peppers, cut into 1-inch pieces
- 1 large yellow bell pepper, cut into 1-inch pieces
- 8 wooden skewers, soaked in water
- 1 teaspoon salt
- 1 teaspoon ground black pepper
- 1 teaspoon paprika
- 12 (10 inch) flour tortillas
- 1 cup butter, melted
- 1 clove garlic, crushed

Direction

- Thread onions, beef steak, yellow bell peppers, green bell peppers, and red bell peppers until about 1 inch is left vacant on the skewer. Sprinkle with paprika, salt, and pepper.
- Set an outdoor grill on high to pre-heat. Lightly oil the grille. Cook for about 8 minutes or until steak is brown on all sides. A meat thermometer inserted into the center of the meat should read 160 degrees F (70 degrees C).
- Place tortillas on a microwave-safe plate and cover with a damp towel. Heat tortillas in the microwave at 30-second intervals until heated through. Take the meat and vegetables off the skewers and into the tortillas and roll them up.
- Thoroughly mix butter and garlic in a small bowl. Serve in individual cups to dip.

Nutrition Information

- Calories: 664 calories;
- Total Fat: 27.4
- Sodium: 993
- Total Carbohydrate: 69.9
- Cholesterol: 79
- Protein: 17.8

724.   Bologna Salad Sandwich Spread I

Serving: 48 | Prep: 20mins | Cook: | Ready in:

Ingredients

- 4 eggs
- 1 (16 ounce) package bologna
- 1 (16 ounce) jar creamy salad dressing
- 1 cup sweet pickle relish

Direction

- In a medium saucepan, place eggs and cover with cold water. Bring water to a boil and immediately take away from the heat. Cover up and allow the eggs to stand in hot water for 10 - 12 minutes. Take away from hot water, cool down, peel off and chop.
- In a meat grinder, grind eggs and bologna with a medium blade.
- In a large bowl, combine the bologna mixture with desired amount of sweet pickle relish and creamy salad dressing. Place in the fridge for chilling, about 2 - 3 hours or until chilled.

Nutrition Information

- Calories: 64 calories;
- Sodium: 236
- Total Carbohydrate: 3.1
- Cholesterol: 24
- Protein: 2
- Total Fat: 4.8

725.   Bologna Salad Sandwich Spread II

Serving: 24 | Prep: 20mins | Cook: | Ready in:

Ingredients

- 4 eggs
- 1 1/2 pounds unsliced bologna
- 6 medium sweet pickles
- 1/4 cup mayonnaise

Direction

- In a medium saucepan, place eggs and cover with cold water. Let it come to a boil and remove immediately from heat. Cover up and allow the eggs to sit in hot water for 10 - 12 minutes. Take away from water, cool down and peel the shell off.
- Put sweet pickles, bologna and eggs in a food processor. Blend until having a spreadable consistency.
- Place the mixture into a medium bowl. Stir in enough mayonnaise to make a smooth mixture. Cover up and chill in the fridge until serving.

Nutrition Information

- Calories: 123 calories;
- Protein: 4.6
- Total Fat: 10.8
- Sodium: 332
- Total Carbohydrate: 1.7
- Cholesterol: 48

726.   Breakfast Rounds

Serving: 8 | Prep: 10mins | Cook: 3mins | Ready in:

Ingredients

- 1/2 cup peanut butter
- 4 English muffins, split and toasted
- 1 red apple, cored and sliced
- 1/4 cup packed brown sugar
- 2 tablespoons margarine
- 1/4 teaspoon ground cinnamon

Direction

- On each English muffin half, spread 1 tbsp. of peanut butter. Put several apple slices on top of each. Melt together cinnamon, margarine and brown sugar in the microwave while stirring often until smooth. Drizzle over apple slices with cinnamon mixture.

Nutrition Information

- Calories: 219 calories;
- Total Fat: 11.3
- Sodium: 204
- Total Carbohydrate: 25.2
- Cholesterol: 0
- Protein: 6.4

---

727. Brittany's Turkey Burgers

Serving: 8 | Prep: 15mins | Cook: 10mins | Ready in:

Ingredients

- 2 pounds ground turkey
- 1 green apple, chopped
- 1/4 cup chopped fresh mushrooms, or to taste
- 3 scallions, or more to taste, chopped
- 3 tablespoons barbeque sauce
- 2 tablespoons spicy mango chutney, or more to taste
- 2 tablespoons red pepper jelly
- 2 dashes Worcestershire sauce, or to taste
- 1 pinch seasoned salt, or to taste
- 1 pinch garlic powder, or to taste
- ground black pepper to taste

Direction

- Set grill to medium heat and start preheating; oil the grate lightly.
- In a large bowl, using hand, mix black pepper, garlic powder, seasoned salt, Worcestershire sauce, red pepper jelly, chutney, barbeque sauce, scallions, mushrooms, green apple and ground turkey; form into 8 patties.

- Cook turkey burgers on the prepared grill for about 4 minutes on each side until the center is no longer pink and juices run clear. The inserted instant-read thermometer into the center should register at least 165°F (74°C).

Nutrition Information

- Calories: 206 calories;
- Total Fat: 8.6
- Sodium: 163
- Total Carbohydrate: 10
- Cholesterol: 84
- Protein: 22.8

---

728. Broiled, Marinated Tofu Sandwich

Serving: 5 | Prep: 15mins | Cook: 25mins | Ready in:

Ingredients

- 1 pound firm tofu
- 1/4 cup olive oil
- 1/2 teaspoon ground cumin
- 1/2 teaspoon chili powder
- 1/2 teaspoon dried oregano
- 2 cloves garlic, minced
- 1/4 cup white wine vinegar
- 1/4 cup dry white wine
- 10 slices whole wheat bread
- 1/4 cup mayonnaise
- 5 Roma tomatoes, sliced
- 1 cup arugula
- 1 red onion, thinly sliced
- salt and ground black pepper to taste

Direction

- Slice tofu into 10 thin slices. Arrange on a baking sheet, put on a separate baking sheet to cover, and top with something heavy (a big food can for example) to weigh down. Strain for a minimum of 30 minutes to remove the excess liquid.

- In a small cast-iron skillet, heat olive oil over medium heat. In the hot oil, toast oregano, chili powder, and ground cumin for 2-3 minutes until the spices are fragrant.
- Remove the spice and oil mixture to a saucepan over medium heat, then mix in white wine, white wine vinegar, and minced garlic. Simmer, and then take the marinade away from heat.
- In a glass dish, put the strained tofu and add the marinade over. Put on plastic wrap to cover; chill for a minimum of 8 hours.
- Put the oven rack approximately 6-in. from the heat source and turn on the oven's broiler to preheat.
- Take the tofu out of the marinade; use paper towels to blot dry and put on the broiler rack. Broil all sides for 6 minutes each side until the skin is crunchy.
- To assemble, spread over one side of each bread slice with mayonnaise. On 5 of the bread slices, put 2 tofu slices; put black pepper, salt, red onion, arugula, sliced tomato, and the leftover bread slices on top.

Nutrition Information

- Calories: 482 calories;
- Sodium: 354
- Total Carbohydrate: 33.4
- Cholesterol: 4
- Protein: 22.9
- Total Fat: 29.6

---

729. Buff Chick (Buffalo Chicken Stromboli)

Serving: 5 | Prep: 20mins | Cook: 15mins | Ready in:

Ingredients

- cooking spray

- 3 cups shredded cooked chicken
- 3/4 cup crumbled blue cheese
- 1/3 (8 ounce) package cream cheese
- 1/4 cup hot sauce, or more as needed
- 1 (10 ounce) container refrigerated thin crust pizza dough (such as Pillsbury®)

Direction

- Start preheating the oven to 400°F (200°C). Coat a baking sheet with the cooking spray.
- In a bowl, mix together hot sauce, cream cheese, blue cheese and chicken.
- Unroll the pizza dough on baking sheet. Spread the chicken mixture in line down the middle of dough. Cover around the chicken mixture with the dough, tucking and pinching together the seams.
- Bake in prepared oven for 15-20 mins or until the crust turns golden brown. Allow the Stromboli to cool for a few mins before cutting.

Nutrition Information

- Calories: 429 calories;
- Total Fat: 19.3
- Sodium: 1053
- Total Carbohydrate: 28
- Cholesterol: 95
- Protein: 33.5

---

730. Buffalo Chicken Phyllo Wraps

Serving: 2 | Prep: 15mins | Cook: 30mins | Ready in:

Ingredients

- 2 (5 ounce) skinless, boneless chicken breast halves
- 1/4 cup hot pepper sauce (such as Frank's RedHot®)
- 6 sheets phyllo dough

- 1 tablespoon olive oil
- salt and pepper to taste
- 1/2 cup hot pepper sauce (such as Frank's RedHot®)
- 2 tablespoons distilled white vinegar
- 1/2 cup light garlic-flavored cream cheese
- 1 tablespoon olive oil

Direction

- In a shallow dish, mix 1/4 cup of hot sauce and chicken; place in the refrigerator to marinate for 1 hour. Coat a 9x13-in. baking dish with grease.
- Set the oven at 350°F (175°C) and start preheating. Lay phyllo sheets on a work surface; use a damp towel to cover to prevent from drying out.
- Place a small skillet on medium heat; heat 1 tablespoon of olive oil. Take the chicken out of the hot sauce; season with pepper and salt. Cook the chicken in the oil for 3-5 minutes per side, till the juices run clear. Take away from the heat and shred. In a large bowl, combine cream cheese, vinegar, the remaining 1/2 cup of hot sauce and the shredded chicken. Mix till creamy. Let the mixture cool for around 5 minutes.
- Take 1 phyllo sheet away from the stack; fold lengthwise in half. Use oil to brush lightly. On the bottom of the folded phyllo, place 2 heaping tablespoons of the chicken mixture, around 1 in. from the bottom. Fold the bottom of the phyllo over the filling; fold in each side; roll wrap to the end of the phyllo sheet. Repeat with the remaining chicken mixture and phyllo sheets.
- Arrange the phyllo rolls in the prepared baking dish. Bake for 20-25 minutes in the preheated oven, till the phyllo is flaky and browned.

Nutrition Information

- Calories: 579 calories;
- Cholesterol: 111
- Protein: 40

- Total Fat: 29.9
- Sodium: 2934
- Total Carbohydrate: 37.6

731.   Buffalo Chicken Sandwiches

Serving: 4 | Prep: 5mins | Cook: 15mins | Ready in:

Ingredients

- 4 skinless, boneless chicken breast halves
- 1 (2 ounce) bottle hot pepper sauce
- 1 (5 ounce) bottle green hot pepper sauce
- 2 teaspoons paprika, divided
- 1 red onion, sliced in rings
- 4 slices tomato
- 4 leaves lettuce
- 4 thick slices French baguette, halved

Direction

- Preheat oven to Broil.
- Put the chicken onto a broiling pan lined with foil. Pour the green hot pepper sauce and hot pepper sauce over all, then sprinkle paprika on top. Top with the onion slices.
- Broil until the chicken juices run clear and meat is no longer pink, about 15 minutes.
- Place each half of the breast on the bottom half of a sliced baguette and top with tomato and lettuce followed by the top half of baguette to serve.

Nutrition Information

- Calories: 236 calories;
- Cholesterol: 67
- Protein: 27.8
- Total Fat: 4.2
- Sodium: 1561
- Total Carbohydrate: 20.5

732. Buffalo Tempeh Sliders

Serving: 18 | Prep: 30mins | Cook: 12mins | Ready in:

Ingredients

- 3 (8 ounce) packages tempeh, cut into 2-inch strips
- 2 (12 fluid ounce) bottles Buffalo wing sauce (such as Frank's® RedHot)
- 1 tablespoon vegetable oil
- 1 cup crumbled blue cheese, or more to taste
- 1 cup chopped fresh cilantro
- 1 large green bell pepper, diced
- 2 stalks celery, diced, or more to taste
- 1/4 red onion, diced
- 1 (5.3 ounce) container Greek yogurt, or as needed
- 18 pita pockets, or more to taste

Direction

- In a large bowl, lay tempeh and pour in Buffalo sauce to cover. Put aside for marinating for 10-20 minutes.
- Take tempeh out of Buffalo sauce, keep sauce for later use. In a large skillet, heating oil over medium-high heat. Cooking tempeh in batches, in a single layer, for approximately 3 minutes on each side till browned lightly and thoroughly heated. Pouring over tempeh with some of Buffalo sauce again to coat.
- In a large bowl, combine onion, celery, green bell pepper, cilantro and blue cheese. Mixing in enough Greek yogurt till topping just holds together.
- Into pita pockets, evenly distributes tempeh pieces; place a spoonful of topping on top. Place the remaining Buffalo sauce on top.

Nutrition Information

- Calories: 288 calories;
- Sodium: 1257
- Total Carbohydrate: 37.9

- Cholesterol: 7
- Protein: 14.8
- Total Fat: 9.4

733. Buffalo Tofu Sandwiches

Serving: 2 | Prep: 25mins | Cook: 16mins | Ready in:

Ingredients

- 1 (8 ounce) container tofu, frozen for at least 36 hours
- 2/3 cup cornflake crumbs
- 1/3 teaspoon cayenne pepper
- 1/3 cup all-purpose flour
- 1/4 cup egg substitute (such as Egg Beaters®)
- 2 tablespoons canola oil
- 2 tablespoons buttery spread (such as Smart Balance®)
- 3 tablespoons hot sauce, or to taste

Direction

- In a microwave-safe bowl, put tofu; heat for 10 minutes on the defrost setting. Slice into 4 slices, each with a maximum of 1/2-in. thickness.
- On a cutting board lined with paper towels, place the tofu slices next to each other. Wrap around the tofu with paper towel. Top with a dish; put a 3-5-pound weight on the dish (you can also use a water-filled container). Press the tofu for 20-30 minutes; strain and dispose the collected water.
- In a bowl, combine cayenne pepper and corn flakes. In 2 different bowls, put egg substitute and flour.
- In a skillet, heat oil over medium-high heat. Into the flour, the egg substitute, and then the corn flake mixture, dredge the tofu slices. In the skillet, immediately put the slices. Cook for 3 minutes each side until turning light brown and crunchy. Put on a dish lined with paper towels to strain. Remove the excess crumbs and oil from the skillet.

- In the skillet, melt buttery spread over low heat. Turn the heat off and stir in hot sauce. In the sauce, quickly dip the tofu to coat both sides.

Nutrition Information

- Calories: 496 calories;
- Cholesterol: 0
- Protein: 16.2
- Total Fat: 28.7
- Sodium: 942
- Total Carbohydrate: 46.4

- In the preheated oven, bake until warm all the way through, about 8 minutes. Bake for about 12-15 minutes in case you use frozen sandwiches.

Nutrition Information

- Calories: 442 calories;
- Total Fat: 28.3
- Sodium: 1097
- Total Carbohydrate: 23.8
- Cholesterol: 74
- Protein: 22.2

---

734. Bunwiches

Serving: 16 | Prep: 20mins | Cook: 12mins | Ready in:

Ingredients

- 1/2 cup butter or margarine, softened
- 2 tablespoons mayonnaise
- 2 tablespoons prepared mustard
- 1/4 cup chopped onion
- 2 tablespoons poppy seeds
- salt and pepper to taste
- 1 (2 pound) 2 inch thick ham steak
- 16 slices Swiss cheese
- 16 hamburger buns, split

Direction

- Set the oven to 175°C or 350°F to preheat.
- Combine poppy seeds, if wanted, onion, mustard, mayonnaise and margarine or butter in a small bowl, then use pepper and salt to season. Spread over the cut sides of buns with a thin layer of the mayonnaise mixture. Put on the bottom half of each bun with 1 cheese slice, then place several ham slices on top. Use aluminum foil to wrap each sandwich separately. The sandwiches now can be frozen or chilled in a plastic bag.

---

735. Cabbage Burgers

Serving: 18 | Prep: 1mins | Cook: 20mins | Ready in:

Ingredients

- 3 (1 pound) loaves frozen bread dough, thawed
- 5 pounds ground beef
- 1/4 cup water
- 1 large head cabbage, chopped
- 1 large onion, chopped
- 2 cloves garlic, chopped
- salt and freshly ground black pepper to taste
- 2 tablespoons butter, melted

Direction

- Preheat an oven to 190 ° C or 375 ° F. Split every frozen bread dough loaf into 6 portions, and roll into rounds. Reserve.
- Into a big pot, break ground beef up on moderate heat. Cook and mix till equally browned. Let the grease drain. Put in garlic, onion, cabbage and water. Cook on moderately-low heat, mixing as necessary, till cabbage become soft. Season to taste with pepper and salt. You may use more pepper than the salt. Let any extra liquids to drain, and reserve.

- Roll dough rounds on a slightly floured area into about 5-inch squares. Into the middle, put approximately 3/4 cup of cabbage burger, fold over with dough and press to enclose. Put on baking sheet, seam side facing down.
- In the prepped oven, bake till golden brown for 15 to 18 minutes. Take out of oven, and brush with liquified butter. Serve while hot.

Nutrition Information

- Calories: 468 calories;
- Protein: 29.7
- Total Fat: 19.2
- Sodium: 518
- Total Carbohydrate: 41.2
- Cholesterol: 80

---

736. Calgary Dinner

Serving: 6 | Prep: 15mins | Cook: 15mins | Ready in:

Ingredients

- 1 (12 ounce) loaf French bread
- 1 pound lean ground beef
- 1/2 cup chopped celery
- 1 (8 ounce) container reduced-fat sour cream
- 1 (1.25 ounce) envelope dry onion soup mix
- 1 tomato, sliced (optional)
- 2 cups shredded mozzarella and Cheddar cheese blend

Direction

- Place oven rack in a 6"-distance away from the heat and start preheating the oven's broiler.
- Slice French bread lengthwise and remove the soft bread inside to hollow the loaf; put bread pieces aside for another purpose.
- Bring a skillet to medium-high heat. Cook, stirring, celery and beef in the heated skillet for 5-7 minutes until beef is crumbled and browned; drain and remove the grease.

- Mix soup mix and sour cream into beef mixture; cook for about 3 minutes until cooked through. Pour mixture into prepared bread; place tomato slices onto the meat, then evenly scatter in cheese blend and bring filled bread onto a baking sheet.
- Broil bread for about 3 minutes until cheese is bubbly and melted.

Nutrition Information

- Calories: 501 calories;
- Sodium: 1206
- Total Carbohydrate: 39.8
- Cholesterol: 86
- Protein: 29.3
- Total Fat: 25.1

---

737. California Club Turkey Sandwich

Serving: 1 | Prep: 10mins | Cook: | Ready in:

Ingredients

- 1 tablespoon cream cheese, or to taste
- 2 slices toasted whole wheat bread
- 1 tablespoon sunflower seeds
- 3 slices avocado
- 1 teaspoon mayonnaise
- 3 slices smoked turkey, or to taste

Direction

- Put cream cheese on one piece of toast. Sprinkle sunflower seeds over the cream cheese and put slices of avocado over the seeds.
- Then on the other piece of toast, spread mayonnaise. Lay out slices of turkey over the mayonnaise. Then place turkey side of sandwich along with the avocado side of the sandwich.

Nutrition Information

- Calories: 526 calories;
- Cholesterol: 55
- Protein: 23.7
- Total Fat: 34.4
- Sodium: 1068
- Total Carbohydrate: 34.6

---

738. **California Grilled Veggie Sandwich**

Serving: 4 | Prep: 30mins | Cook: 20mins | Ready in:

Ingredients

- 1/4 cup mayonnaise
- 3 cloves garlic, minced
- 1 tablespoon lemon juice
- 1/8 cup olive oil
- 1 cup sliced red bell peppers
- 1 small zucchini, sliced
- 1 red onion, sliced
- 1 small yellow squash, sliced
- 2 (4-x6-inch) focaccia bread pieces, split horizontally
- 1/2 cup crumbled feta cheese

Direction

- In a bowl, mix together lemon juice, minced garlic, and mayonnaise, then keep in the refrigerator.
- Set the grill to high heat.
- Use olive oil to brush both sides of the vegetables and brush the grate. Place the zucchini and bell peppers closest to the grill's middle, set the squash and onion pieces around them. Cook for around 3 minutes, turn, and cook for 3 more minutes. The bell peppers may take a bit longer to cook. Take away from the grill and put aside.
- Spread some mayonnaise mixture onto the cut-sides of the bread, then sprinkle each with feta cheese. Place them on the grill with the

cheese-side up and cover with the lid for 2-3 minutes to warm the bread and melt the cheese slightly. Carefully watch so the bottoms won't burn. Take away from the grill and layer with vegetables to make open-faced grilled sandwiches.

Nutrition Information

- Calories: 393 calories;
- Total Fat: 23.8
- Sodium: 623
- Total Carbohydrate: 36.5
- Cholesterol: 22
- Protein: 9.2

---

739. **California Melt**

Serving: 4 | Prep: 15mins | Cook: 2mins | Ready in:

Ingredients

- 4 slices whole-grain bread, lightly toasted
- 1 avocado, sliced
- 1 cup sliced mushrooms
- 1/3 cup sliced toasted almonds
- 1 tomato, sliced
- 4 slices Swiss cheese

Direction

- Set the oven broiler to preheat.
- On a baking sheet, lay out the toasted bread, then put slices of tomato, almonds, mushrooms and 1/4 cup of avocado on top of each bread slice, then top each with Swiss cheese slice.
- Broil the open-face sandwiches for about 2 minutes, until starts to bubble and the cheese has melted. Serve the sandwiches while it's still warm.

Nutrition Information

- Calories: 335 calories;
- Total Carbohydrate: 21.1
- Cholesterol: 26
- Protein: 15.6
- Total Fat: 22.5
- Sodium: 170

740.   Campbell's® Slow Cooked Pulled Pork Sandwiches

Serving: 12 | Prep: 15mins | Cook: 8hours10mins |Ready in:

Ingredients

- 1 tablespoon vegetable oil
- 3 1/2 pounds boneless pork shoulder roast, netted or tied
- 1 (10.5 ounce) can Campbell's® Condensed French Onion Soup
- 1 cup ketchup
- 1/4 cup cider vinegar
- 3 tablespoons packed brown sugar
- 12 round sandwich rolls or hamburger rolls, split

Direction

- Heat oil on medium high heat in a 10-in. skillet. Add pork; cook till all sides brown well.
- Mix brown sugar, vinegar, ketchup and soup in a 5-qt. slow cooker. Add pork; turn to coat.
- Cover; cook on low till pork is fork tender for 8-9 hours.
- Transfer pork from cooker onto cutting board; stand for 10 minutes. Shred pork using 2 forks; put pork into cooker.
- Divide sauce mixture and pork to rolls.

Nutrition Information

- Calories: 344 calories;
- Sodium: 684

- Total Carbohydrate: 31.2
- Cholesterol: 53
- Protein: 17.9
- Total Fat: 16.1

741.   Campfire Reubens

Serving: 4 | Prep: 15mins | Cook: 30mins |Ready in:

Ingredients

- 8 slices pumpernickel bread
- 1 cup Thousand Island dressing
- 3/4 pound deli sliced corned beef
- 1/2 pound sliced Swiss cheese
- 1 cup sauerkraut

Direction

- Preheat grill to low heat.
- Cut 4 big aluminum foil squares; on each foil piece, put 2 bread slices side by side. Spread thousand island dressing on bread slices. Divide sauerkraut, Swiss cheese and corned beef evenly to bread. Put 2nd bread slice over to create sandwich. Snugly wrap foil around sandwich to create sealed packet.
- On preheated grill, put packets; cook for 30 minutes, turning every 10 minutes, till cheese melts and bread toasts lightly.

Nutrition Information

- Calories: 777 calories;
- Total Fat: 48.9
- Sodium: 2637
- Total Carbohydrate: 50.7
- Cholesterol: 128
- Protein: 37.4

742. Carrie's Garlic Pesto Tuna Salad Sandwiches

Serving: 4 | Prep: 10mins | Cook: |Ready in:

Ingredients

- 2 (5 ounce) cans tuna in water, drained
- 2 tablespoons mayonnaise
- 1 tablespoon prepared mustard
- 2 tablespoons basil pesto
- 2 cloves garlic, minced
- 8 slices rye bread
- 8 leaves lettuce
- 1 large ripe tomato, sliced

Direction

- Combine garlic, pesto, mustard, mayonnaise and tuna in a medium bowl.
- Layer slices of tomato, lettuce and tuna between the bread slices; make four of these, then serve.

Nutrition Information

- Calories: 342 calories;
- Sodium: 600
- Total Carbohydrate: 34.6
- Cholesterol: 24
- Protein: 23.8
- Total Fat: 11.9

743. Carrot Cake Sandwich

Serving: 1 | Prep: 10mins | Cook: |Ready in:

Ingredients

- 1 cinnamon-raisin English muffin, halved
- 3 baby carrots, shredded
- 1 pinch ground nutmeg
- 1 tablespoon crunchy peanut butter
- 1 tablespoon whipped cream cheese
- 1/4 cup clover sprouts (optional)

Direction

- Toast together both halves of English muffin lightly.
- Put grated carrots in a little bowl; drizzle with nutmeg.
- Put peanut butter on 1 side of the English muffin.
- Apply cream cheese on the other side of English muffin. Place sprouts and carrots on top. Put together both sides making a sandwich.

Nutrition Information

- Calories: 297 calories;
- Total Fat: 14.6
- Sodium: 340
- Total Carbohydrate: 33.6
- Cholesterol: 16
- Protein: 10.3

744. Cauliflower Cheesy Bites

Serving: 4 | Prep: 15mins | Cook: 35mins |Ready in:

Ingredients

- 1 head cauliflower, stemmed and cut into small florets
- 1/2 cup grated Parmesan cheese
- 1 egg
- 1 teaspoon Italian herb seasoning
- 1/2 cup shredded Parmesan cheese
- 4 slices white Cheddar cheese

Direction

- Set the oven at 450°F (230°C) and start preheating. Using a silicone mat or parchment paper, line a baking sheet.

- In a food processor, put cauliflower florets; pulse into crumbs, around half the size of rice grains.
- Transfer the cauliflower into a large microwave-safe bowl. Microwave for around 2 minutes, till tender and soft. Take out and stir. Microwave again for 3 minutes. Take out and stir again so that all the grains are cook evenly. Microwave for around 5 minutes, till almost dry. Combine and microwave for around 5 minutes, till the cauliflower clumped up and looks dry.
- Mix in seasoning, egg and Parmesan cheese till the cauliflower mixture forms a smooth paste. Divide into 8 equal portions; move to the baking dish. Using your fingers and knuckles, pat into square 'bread' slices, around 1/2-inch thick.
- Bake in the preheated oven for 15-18 minutes, till the slices turn golden brown. Allow to cool for a few minutes. Using a good spatula, slide off the baking dish carefully.
- Top 4 cauliflower bread slices with 1 slice of Cheddar cheese. Carefully top with the other 4 slices.
- Put sandwiches into a toaster oven; broil for 5-10 minutes, till the bead is toasted and the cheese completely melts.

Nutrition Information

- Calories: 255 calories;
- Total Fat: 16.5
- Sodium: 542
- Total Carbohydrate: 9.1
- Cholesterol: 94
- Protein: 19.2

745. Cheesy Bacon Slider Bake

Serving: 12 | Prep: 15mins | Cook: 30mins | Ready in:

Ingredients

- 1 (18 ounce) package Hawaiian sweet rolls
- 2 cups shredded Cheddar cheese, divided
- 1 pound ground beef
- 1 small onion, chopped
- 1/2 (14 ounce) can diced tomatoes with garlic and onion
- 1 1/2 teaspoons Dijon mustard
- 1 1/2 teaspoons Worcestershire sauce
- 1/4 teaspoon salt
- 1/4 teaspoon ground black pepper
- 12 bacon strips, cooked and crumbled
- Glaze:
- 1/2 cup butter
- 2 tablespoons brown sugar
- 1 tablespoon Dijon mustard
- 2 teaspoons Worcestershire sauce
- 1 tablespoon sesame seeds

Direction

- Prepare the oven by preheating to 350°F (175°C). Prepare a 9x13-inch baking pan that is greased.
- On a flat work surface, put the rolls without separating. Slice horizontally in half. Lay out on bottom half in prepared pan. Dust 1 cup cheddar cheese over the top.
- Place in preheated oven and bake for 3-5 minutes until cheese is dissolved.
- Stir and cook onion and beef in a skillet for 5-8 minutes until beef is browned. Strain grease. Mix in pepper, salt, 1 1/2 teaspoons Worcestershire sauce, 1 1/2 Dijon mustard, and tomatoes. Then cook for 1-2 minutes until completely blended.
- Scoop beef mixture on rolls. Dust the bacon and the rest of 1 cup cheddar cheese over the top. Then cover with top half of the rolls.
- In a microwave-safe bowl, mix 2 teaspoons Worcestershire sauce, 1 tablespoon Dijon mustard, brown sugar, and butter. Then cover and place in a microwave on high for approximately 1 minute until butter is dissolved. Whisk until combined and drop on rolls. Dust sesame seeds on the top.
- Place in preheated oven and bake for 20-25 minutes, without cover, until golden brown.

Nutrition Information

- Calories: 417 calories;
- Total Fat: 21.5
- Sodium: 641
- Total Carbohydrate: 28.3
- Cholesterol: 92
- Protein: 21.6

---

746.   Cheesy Bacon Ultimate Dogs

Serving: 4 | Prep: 10mins | Cook: 10mins | Ready in:

Ingredients

- 1 teaspoon prepared yellow mustard
- 4 hot dogs, butterflied
- 2 ounces cheddar cheese, sliced into 8 matchsticks
- 4 strips thick-cut bacon
- 8 toothpicks
- 4 hot dog buns, split
- 1 large (5 inch) dill pickle, sliced into 8 long strips

Direction

- Start preheating the grill to medium heat. Oil grate lightly.
- Smear inside each butterflied hot dog with a quarter teaspoon of mustard. Inside each hot dog, place two Cheddar cheese matchsticks.
- Use a toothpick to secure one end of bacon strip to one end of hot dog. Tightly cover entire hot dog with bacon strip; using another toothpick, secure the far end. Do the same with the remaining hot dogs.
- On the prepared grill, cook 4-5 mins on each side or until the bacon has been cooked through and hot dogs have been heated.
- Put each cooked hot dog on a bun. Place 2 slices of pickle on top.

Nutrition Information

- Calories: 463 calories;
- Total Fat: 32.8
- Sodium: 1491
- Total Carbohydrate: 24.9
- Cholesterol: 58
- Protein: 16.2

---

747.   Chef John's Turkey Sloppy Joes

Serving: 6 | Prep: 10mins | Cook: 30mins | Ready in:

Ingredients

- 2 tablespoons butter
- 1 onion, diced
- salt and ground black pepper to taste
- 1 1/4 pounds ground turkey
- 1/2 cup cold water
- 3/4 cup ketchup
- 1 1/2 tablespoons brown sugar
- 1/2 teaspoon cayenne pepper, or to taste
- 1/2 teaspoon Worcestershire sauce
- 1/2 teaspoon unsweetened cocoa powder
- 1 cup water, or as needed
- 6 hamburger buns, split
- 1/3 cup chopped green onions
- 1/2 cup shredded white Cheddar cheese

Direction

- In a heavy skillet, liquify the butter over moderate heat. Put the onion; cook and mix for 5 minutes till onion begins to brown. Add black and salt to season.
- Into the onions, mix 1/2 cup cold water and ground turkey. Cook and mix for 2 minutes, crumbling up the meat, till it starts to brown. Put the black pepper, salt, cayenne pepper, brown sugar and ketchup. Cook and mix for 5 minutes till liquid decreases. Mix in cocoa

powder and Worcestershire sauce. Cook for 20 minutes to half an hour, mixing often and pouring in up to 1 cup of water if necessary, till meat is cooked completely and liquid is cooked down and thick.

- Preheat an oven's broiler and place oven rack approximately 6-inch away from heat source. Let the hamburger buns toast for 2 to 3 minutes till golden.
- Take turkey mixture off heat and add in Cheddar cheese and green onions. Serve over toasted hamburger buns.

Nutrition Information

- Calories: 394 calories;
- Cholesterol: 90
- Protein: 25.9
- Total Fat: 16.5
- Sodium: 724
- Total Carbohydrate: 36.8

---

748. Cheggy Salad Sandwiches

Serving: 5 | Prep: 20mins | Cook: |Ready in:

Ingredients

- 2 (10 ounce) cans chunk chicken, drained
- 4 hard-cooked eggs, chopped
- 1/4 cup Parmesan curls, shaved with a vegetable peeler
- 1/4 cup chopped pine nuts
- 2 tablespoons sweet dill pickle relish
- 1/4 cup chopped white onion
- 1/3 cup mayonnaise
- 1/3 cup cole slaw dressing
- salt and freshly ground black pepper to taste
- 10 slices sandwich bread
- 5 lettuce leaves
- 5 slices ripe tomato
- 2 avocados, sliced
- 5 slices Monterey Jack cheese

Direction

- Lightly mix pepper and salt to taste, coleslaw dressing, mayonnaise, chopped onion, pickle relish, pine nuts, parmesan cheese, eggs and canned chicken in a big bowl; cover. Refrigerate to blend flavors for 30 minutes.
- Assemble sandwiches: On each of 5 sandwich bread slices, spread generous serving; put Monterey jack cheese, sliced avocado, sliced tomato and lettuce leaves on salad. Put leftover sandwich bread slices over.

Nutrition Information

- Calories: 810 calories;
- Protein: 45.6
- Total Fat: 57.1
- Sodium: 1328
- Total Carbohydrate: 30.4
- Cholesterol: 280

---

749. Chicago Inspired Italian Beef Sandwich

Serving: 4 | Prep: 15mins | Cook: 1hours10mins |Ready in:

Ingredients

- 1 1/2 pounds boneless beef chuck, cut into 2-inch pieces
- salt and ground black pepper to taste
- 1 tablespoon vegetable oil
- 6 cloves garlic, sliced
- 2 tablespoons white vinegar
- 1 tablespoon dried oregano
- 1 1/2 teaspoons salt, or to taste
- 1 teaspoon dried thyme
- 1 teaspoon dried rosemary
- 1 teaspoon freshly ground black pepper
- 1 bay leaf
- 1/4 teaspoon red pepper flakes, or to taste
- 3 cups chicken broth, or as needed

- 4 ciabatta rolls, sliced in half
- 1 cup chopped giardiniera (pickled Italian vegetables)
- 2 teaspoons chopped fresh flat-leaf parsley

Direction

- Spice beef with a pinch of black pepper and salt. In a heavy pot, heat vegetable oil over high temperature. Cook and stir beef 5 to 8 minutes in hot oil until brown.
- Mix red pepper flakes, bay leaf, a teaspoon of black pepper, rosemary, thyme, 1 1/2 teaspoons of salt, oregano, vinegar and garlic in beef. Pour a sufficient amount of chicken broth into the beef mixture to cover the meat by 1 inch and gently boil.
- Put the lid over the pot, lower the heat to low and simmer 1 to 1 1/2 hours until the meat is fork-tender.
- Use a strainer or slotted spoon to transfer the meat to a different pot; pour about a quarter cup of meat broth into the pot. Gently break the meat into smaller pieces with a wooden spoon. Cover the pot with aluminium foil or a lid and keep it warm.
- Remove excess fat from top of the remaining broth in the first pot; add salt and pepper to taste. Use aluminium or a lid to cover the pot and keep the broth warm.
- Place halves of roll out on a work surface and pour 2-3 tablespoons meat broth over each half. Add a generous portion of meat and 1 spoonful pickled vegetables over the top of bottom half of roll. Put tops on sandwich. Do the same with remaining pickled vegetables, meat, broth and buns to make 3 additional sandwiches.
- Pour the hot meat broth into ramekins and finish each ramekin with half teaspoon of parsley on top. Serve sandwiches with hot broth to dip.

Nutrition Information

- Calories: 406 calories;
- Total Fat: 15.7

- Sodium: 1399
- Total Carbohydrate: 35.7
- Cholesterol: 79
- Protein: 29.3

---

750.   Chicken Brown Rice Sloppy Joes

Serving: 6 | Prep: 15mins | Cook: 20mins | Ready in:

Ingredients

- 1 (2-cup) bag UNCLE BEN'S® Boil-in-Bag Whole Grain Brown Rice
- 1/2 tablespoon olive oil
- 1 pound ground chicken
- 1 cup onion, diced
- 1/4 cup diced green bell pepper
- 1 clove garlic, minced
- 1/2 teaspoon salt
- 1/2 teaspoon ground black pepper
- 1/4 cup water
- 3/4 cup ketchup
- 2 tablespoons brown sugar
- 1 teaspoon Worcestershire sauce
- 1 teaspoon mustard
- 1 teaspoon white vinegar
- 6 whole-wheat hamburger buns

Direction

- Cook rice following the package instructions.
- Meanwhile, start preparing the sloppy joes.
- Place a large skillet over medium heat and heat the oil, then add chicken to the hot oil. Separate the chicken by stirring, then add garlic, peppers, onions, and salt and pepper. Cook for 5 minutes, until the chicken is done and the onions turn translucent. Combine vinegar, mustard, Worcestershire sauce, brown sugar, ketchup, and 1/4 cup of water in a small bowl or measuring cup.
- Once the rice is done, drain excess liquid out and transfer the rice to the skillet. Pour the liquid ingredients into the rice and meat

mixture and stir until thoroughly combined. Simmer for 5 minutes for the flavors to combine.

- Serve on whole-wheat buns to assemble the sloppy joe.

Nutrition Information

- Calories: 344 calories;
- Sodium: 810
- Total Carbohydrate: 50
- Cholesterol: 46
- Protein: 23.3
- Total Fat: 5.7

751.   Chicken Cheese Steak

Serving: 4 | Prep: 20mins | Cook: 18mins |Ready in:

Ingredients

- 2 tablespoons vegetable oil, divided
- 1 green bell pepper, chopped
- 1 onion, chopped
- 1 pound ground chicken
- salt and ground black pepper to taste
- 4 slices American cheese
- 2 long sandwich rolls, halved lengthwise

Direction

- On medium-high heat, pour 1 tablespoon of oil in a non-stick pan and heat. Cook and stir onion and green bell pepper in the heated oil for 8-10 minutes until tender.
- In a separate non-stick pan, heat the leftover tablespoon of oil on medium-high heat. Cook and stir chicken in the pan for 8-10 minutes until crumbly and the chicken is not pink. Mix in black pepper, green bell pepper, salt, and onion. Add cheese slices on top. Cook for 2-3 minutes until the cheese melts.
- Distribute the chicken mixture evenly on top of the sliced rolls.

Nutrition Information

- Calories: 501 calories;
- Total Carbohydrate: 38.4
- Cholesterol: 92
- Protein: 38.8
- Total Fat: 20.6
- Sodium: 915

752.   Chicken Chutney Sandwiches With Curry

Serving: 6 | Prep: 15mins | Cook: |Ready in:

Ingredients

- 1 roasted chicken, bones and skin removed, meat shredded
- 3/4 cup cranberry and apple chutney
- 1/4 cup whipped cream cheese
- 2 teaspoons curry powder
- 6 croissants, split

Direction

- Stir together the curry powder, cream cheese, chutney and chicken. Spread onto the split croissants. Serve.

Nutrition Information

- Calories: 450 calories;
- Total Fat: 20
- Sodium: 527
- Total Carbohydrate: 40.3
- Cholesterol: 109
- Protein: 26.9

753.   Chicken Cordon Bleu Ish Grilled Sandwich

Serving: 1 | Prep: 5mins | Cook: 10mins | Ready in:

Ingredients

- 2 slices bread
- 2 tablespoons margarine, divided
- 2 slices Swiss cheese
- 1 cooked chicken breast half
- 1 tablespoon barbecue sauce
- 2 slices honey-cured deli ham

Direction

- Spread margarine on 1 side of each bread slice; put a bread slice into a nonstick skillet, margarine-side down, on medium heat.
- Put a Swiss cheese slice, cooked chicken breast, barbecue sauce layer, ham slices then the leftover Swiss cheese slice on top of bread slice in the skillet. Put other bread slice over sandwich, margarine-side up.
- Fry sandwich gently for about 5 minutes per side till both sides of bread is golden brown and cheese is gooey and melted, flipping once.

Nutrition Information

- Calories: 744 calories;
- Total Fat: 43.1
- Sodium: 1262
- Total Carbohydrate: 35.6
- Cholesterol: 139
- Protein: 52.8

754.   Chicken Creole With Chile Cream Sauce

Serving: 4 | Prep: | Cook: 20mins | Ready in:

Ingredients

- 4 skinless, boneless chicken breasts
- 2 teaspoons Creole or Cajun seasoning
- 1 tablespoon olive oil
- 1 (10.75 ounce) can Campbell's® Condensed Cream of Chicken Soup (Regular or 98% Fat Free)
- 1/2 cup water
- 1 (4 ounce) can chopped green chilies
- 1 teaspoon lime juice
- 1/4 cup sour cream
- Hot cooked regular long-grain white rice

Direction

- Add Creole seasoning to chicken.
- Heat the oil in a skillet, then add chicken and let cook until browned.
- Add lime juice, chiles, water, and soup. Bring to boil. Let cook on low heat for about 5 minutes or until done.
- Mix in the sour cream and heat through. Then serve atop rice.

Nutrition Information

- Calories: 366 calories;
- Total Fat: 14
- Sodium: 1159
- Total Carbohydrate: 31.1
- Cholesterol: 73
- Protein: 27.7

755.   Chicken Parmesan Sliders

Serving: 16 | Prep: 30mins | Cook: 28mins | Ready in:

Ingredients

- Marinara Sauce:
- 1 tablespoon olive oil
- 1/2 cup diced onions
- 3 cloves garlic, chopped
- 1 (28 ounce) can whole peeled plum tomatoes, crushed by hand or mashed

- 1 teaspoon salt
- 1 teaspoon dried oregano
- 1 teaspoon dried basil
- 1/2 teaspoon fennel seeds
- 1/2 teaspoon dried thyme
- 1/4 teaspoon red pepper flakes
- Chicken:
- 4 skinless, boneless chicken breast halves
- 2 cups panko bread crumbs
- 3 eggs, beaten
- 1 cup all-purpose flour
- 1/3 cup grated Parmesan cheese
- 1/2 teaspoon salt
- 1/2 teaspoon dried oregano
- 1/2 teaspoon dried basil
- 1/4 teaspoon ground black pepper
- 1/4 cup olive oil, or as needed
- salt as needed
- To Serve:
- 1 cup shredded mozzarella cheese
- 16 slider buns

Direction

- In a saucepan, heating garlic, onions, and olive oil over medium-high heat. Let it sauté for 6-8 minutes, occasionally stirring till translucent. Adding red pepper flakes, thyme, fennel seeds, basil, oregano, salt, and tomatoes; stirring to mix. Lower the heat. Allow to cook for 15 minutes over low heat. If necessary, adjusting seasoning; keeping warm.
- On a cutting board, lay chicken. Cut each breast into two thin cutlets lengthwise; cut each cutlet into two smaller pieces.
- Heat oven to 230°C (450°F) beforehand. On a baking sheet, lay a cooling rack and put aside.
- In separate shallow dishes, pouring eggs and panko. In the third shallow dish, combine a quarter teaspoon of black pepper, half a teaspoon of basil, half a teaspoon of oregano, half a teaspoon of salt, Parmesan cheese, and flour.
- In a large skillet over medium-high heat, heating olive oil. First, dredge chicken pieces into flour mixture, then dip into eggs, and lastly panko. Pan-frying the chicken for 2-3

minutes on each side till the center is not pink anymore, juices are clear, and browned lightly. When insert an instant-read thermometer into the center, it should read no less than 74°C (165°F). Transferring to the cooling rack; use salt to lightly drizzle over.
- Use a tablespoon mozzarella cheese and two tablespoons marinara sauce to place on top of each piece of chicken on cooling rack.
- In the preheated oven, allow to bake for 3-5 minutes till cheese melts. Removing from oven; laying chicken on buns.

Nutrition Information

- Calories: 182 calories;
- Total Carbohydrate: 18.6
- Cholesterol: 57
- Protein: 12.2
- Total Fat: 8.1
- Sodium: 461

756.   Chicken Shawarmas

Serving: 4 | Prep: 15mins | Cook: 10mins | Ready in:

Ingredients

- 1 clove garlic, minced
- 1/2 cup mayonnaise
- 2 tablespoons unsalted butter
- 2 large skinless, boneless chicken breast halves - cut into bite-size pieces
- 1 1/2 teaspoons garam masala
- 4 pita bread rounds
- 4 dill pickle spears

Direction

- In small bowl, stir mayonnaise and garlic together. Put aside. In a skillet, heat butter over medium-high heat. In hot butter, cook while stirring the chicken until the outside is white. Sprinkle the garam masala over. Keep

cooking for 4 mins or until the middle is no longer pink and the outside is browned lightly.
- Spread garlic mayonnaise over pita rounds. Portion chicken among pitas. Put 1 pickle spear into each. Then fold; enjoy.

Nutrition Information

- Calories: 516 calories;
- Total Carbohydrate: 29.7
- Cholesterol: 92
- Protein: 31.2
- Total Fat: 29.8
- Sodium: 591

---

757. Chicken Souvlaki Gyro Style

Serving: 4 | Prep: 30mins | Cook: 20mins | Ready in:

Ingredients

- Souvlaki Marinade:
- 3/4 cup balsamic vinaigrette salad dressing
- 3 tablespoons lemon juice
- 1 tablespoon dried oregano
- 1/2 teaspoon freshly ground black pepper
- 4 skinless, boneless chicken breast halves
- Tzatziki Sauce (cucumber sauce):
- 1/2 cup seeded, shredded cucumber
- 1 teaspoon kosher salt
- 1 cup plain yogurt
- 1/4 cup sour cream
- 1 tablespoon lemon juice
- 1/2 tablespoon rice vinegar
- 1 teaspoon olive oil
- 1 clove garlic, minced
- 1 tablespoon chopped fresh dill
- 1/2 teaspoon Greek seasoning
- kosher salt to taste
- freshly ground black pepper to taste
- 4 large pita bread rounds

- 1 heart of romaine lettuce, cut into 1/4 inch slices
- 1 red onion, thinly sliced
- 1 tomato, halved and sliced
- 1/2 cup kalamata olives
- 1/2 cup pepperoncini
- 1 cup crumbled feta cheese

Direction

- Combine half a teaspoon of black pepper, oregano, juice from half a lemon and balsamic vinaigrette in a small bowl. Transfer chicken into a big resealable plastic bag. Pour marinade onto the chicken, seal, and leave in the fridge for 60 minutes minimum.
- Set an outdoor grill to high heat and start preheating.
- Mix 1 teaspoon of kosher salt with shredded cucumber and let it rest for a minimum of 5 minutes. Combine olive oil, rice vinegar, 1 tablespoon of lemon juice, sour cream and yogurt in a medium bowl. Add Greek seasoning, fresh dill and garlic to season. Squeeze out any excess water in the cucumber, then mix into the sauce. Add pepper and kosher salt to taste. Leave in the fridge until ready to serve.
- Take chicken out of the marinade and transfer to preheated grill. Remove the leftover marinade. Cook chicken for about 8 minutes for each side until juices run clear. Take chicken away from the heat, allow to stand for about 10 minutes, then slice into thin strips.
- Arrange pita rounds on the grill, and cook, while flipping often to prevent burning until warm, for about 2 minutes. Lay pepperoncini, olives, tomato, onion, lettuce, sliced chicken and warmed pita on a serving platter. Place feta cheese and tzatziki sauce in different bowls to serve on the side. Stuff chicken and toppings into pita pockets, then serve.

Nutrition Information

- Calories: 764 calories;
- Sodium: 3170

- Total Carbohydrate: 55.9
- Cholesterol: 133
- Protein: 44.4
- Total Fat: 40.5

758.   Chicken Verde Sandwiches

Serving: 6 | Prep: 10mins | Cook: 8hours | Ready in:

Ingredients

- 2 pounds frozen boneless chicken breast
- 10 ounces prepared pizza sauce
- 1 cup salsa verde (such as Herdez®)
- 1/2 cup sour cream
- 6 kaiser rolls
- 6 ounces shredded Cheddar cheese
- 6 ounces sour cream
- 12 dashes hot sauce, or to taste

Direction

- In a slow cooker, mix salsa verde, prepared pizza sauce, and the frozen boneless chicken breast. Put a cover on, select Low and cook for 8-10 hours.
- Pull the chicken meat apart with 2 forks until shredded completely. Add 1/2 cup of sour cream into the chicken mixture and stir. Pour the chicken mixture onto the rolls. To serve, put 2 dashes of hot sauce, 1 ounce of sour cream, and 1 ounce of the shredded Cheddar cheese atop each sandwich.

Nutrition Information

- Calories: 523 calories;
- Total Carbohydrate: 30.8
- Cholesterol: 129
- Protein: 42.6
- Total Fat: 24.2
- Sodium: 922

759.   Chicken, Feta Cheese, And Sun Dried Tomato Wraps

Serving: 4 | Prep: 15mins | Cook: 30mins | Ready in:

Ingredients

- 2 (4 ounce) skinless, boneless chicken breast halves
- 1/4 cup sun-dried tomato dressing
- 8 sun-dried tomatoes (not oil packed)
- 1 cup boiling water
- 1/3 cup crumbled feta cheese
- 4 cups loosely packed torn fresh spinach
- 4 (10 inch) whole wheat tortillas
- 1/4 cup sun-dried tomato dressing

Direction

- In a large resealable plastic bag, combine 1/4 cup dressing and chicken breasts. Let seal, and allow several hours to refrigerate.
- Preheat grill for high heat. In a small bowl, combine hot water and sun-dried tomatoes. Leave aside for around 10 minutes, let drain, and cut tomatoes into thin slices.
- Oil grill grate lightly. Discard marinade; and on grill, place chicken. Cook for 12 to 15 minutes till done, turning once.
- Cut chicken into strips; and in a medium bowl, place spinach, feta, and sliced tomatoes. Toss with the rest 1/4 cup dressing. Between the four tortillas, distribute mixture, and wrap. Cut in half and enjoy while it is cold, or place briefly back on grill till the tortilla turns crispy and warm.

Nutrition Information

- Calories: 324 calories;
- Protein: 20.7
- Total Fat: 14.2
- Sodium: 902
- Total Carbohydrate: 34.1
- Cholesterol: 44

760.   Chickpea "Tuna" Salad Sandwiches

Serving: 4 | Prep: 15mins | Cook: | Ready in:

Ingredients

- Chickpea "Tuna" Salad:
- 1/2 sheet nori (dried seaweed), torn into small pieces
- 1 (15 ounce) can no-salt-added chickpeas, drained and rinsed
- 1/4 cup vegan mayonnaise
- 1/3 cup minced or finely grated carrot
- 1/3 cup finely diced celery
- 2 tablespoons dried minced onion
- 2 tablespoons fresh dill
- 1/2 teaspoon salt
- black pepper to taste
- Sandwiches:
- 8 slices whole wheat bread, toasted
- 1/4 cup vegan mayonnaise
- 8 lettuce leaves
- 8 tomato slices

Direction

- In a blender, pulse nori until having a fine powder. Put aside and allow the dust to settle.
- In a big bowl, use a potato masher with small holes (chickpeas will slip through mashers with zigzag or bigger holes) or a sturdy fork to mash chickpeas until mostly crumbled. Make sure to not over mash. The chickpeas should maintain some texture.
- Mix in mayo and mash a bit more. Mix in pepper, salt, dill, onion, celery, carrot, and nori powder. Put a cover on and refrigerate for a minimum of 15 minutes and a maximum of 3 days.
- To prepare sandwiches, generously spread mayo over the toast (approximately 1 1/2 teaspoons each slice). Put between each slice

the tomato, lettuce, and salad. Slice the sandwiches into two diagonally.

Nutrition Information

- Calories: 360 calories;
- Total Carbohydrate: 43.6
- Cholesterol: 0
- Protein: 11.8
- Total Fat: 16
- Sodium: 690

761.   Chili Dogs With Cheese

Serving: 8 | Prep: 10mins | Cook: 10mins | Ready in:

Ingredients

- 8 beef franks
- 8 hot dog buns, split
- 1 (15 ounce) can HORMEL® Chili No Beans, heated
- Shredded cheese
- Sliced green onions (optional)

Direction

- Cook franks following the package instructions.
- Put the franks into buns; then scoop over the franks with the hot chili. If desired, add green onions and cheese over top.

Nutrition Information

- Calories: 340 calories;
- Total Fat: 18.9
- Sodium: 999
- Total Carbohydrate: 27.6
- Cholesterol: 39
- Protein: 14.4

762. Chinese Pork Buns

Serving: 12 | Prep: 30mins | Cook: 27mins | Ready in:

Ingredients

- First Dough:
- 1/2 cup water
- 2 teaspoons instant yeast
- 2 teaspoons white sugar
- 2 cups cake flour, divided
- Pork Filling:
- 2/3 cup water
- 3 slices fresh ginger root, peeled and minced
- 1 spring onion, minced
- 1 tablespoon oyster sauce
- 1 tablespoon white sugar
- 1 tablespoon all-purpose flour
- 1 tablespoon corn flour
- 1 tablespoon sesame oil
- 1 pinch ground white pepper to taste
- 7 ounces Chinese barbeque pork, cut into very thin slices
- Second (Sweet) Dough:
- 1/2 cup corn flour
- 3/8 cup cake flour
- 1 tablespoon baking powder
- 3/8 cup white sugar
- 2 1/2 tablespoons cooking oil

Direction

- In a large bowl, mix 1 tsp. of cake flour, a half cup of water, 2 tsp. of sugar, and yeast. Set aside for 20 minutes until the top of the mixture begins to form a white foam layer. Stir in the remaining cake flour (2 cups minus the 1 tsp.), and use chopsticks to gently blend the mixture until it forms a dough. Massage the dough until smooth and cover it with plastic wrap. Put the dough in a warm area and leave it for 4-6 hours.
- Put a saucepan over medium-low heat and stir in ginger, oyster sauce, all-purpose flour, white pepper, 2/3 cup of water, 1 tbsp. of sugar, spring onion, 1 tbsp. of corn flour, and sesame oil. Cook and stir for 5 minutes until the mixture has thickened. Let it cool at room temperature before storing it inside the refrigerator.
- Add the chilled filling over the pork and combine well.
- Sieve 3/8 cup of cake flour, baking powder, and 1/2 cup of corn flour into a bowl. Stir in cooking oil and 3/8 cup of sugar and mix them thoroughly. Add this mixture into the dough and knead it carefully until smooth. Make a ball out of this dough and cover it with an inverted bowl. Set aside for 10 minutes.
- Divide the dough into 12-15 pieces and roll each to make a ball. Press down each ball into rounds and spoon at least 1-2 tbsp. of the filling into each center. Fold the round to seal the fillings inside. It's still acceptable if the top is a little bit thick, it will assist in creating the top flower look.
- Use parchment paper to line the bamboo steamers. Arrange the buns on top and place it in a warm place for 5 minutes. Lock the lids tightly.
- In a large skillet or wok, boil about 1 1/2-2 quarts of water for 10 minutes. Transfer the steamers in the wok or large skillet. Steam the buns over medium heat for 12-15 minutes until cooked through.

Nutrition Information

- Calories: 217 calories;
- Total Fat: 5
- Sodium: 142
- Total Carbohydrate: 35.5
- Cholesterol: 12
- Protein: 7.2

763. Chipotle Chicken Sandwich

Serving: 4 | Prep: 15mins | Cook: 30mins | Ready in:

Ingredients

- 2 teaspoons olive oil
- 4 skinless, boneless chicken breast halves
- 1 tablespoon red wine vinegar
- 1 tablespoon fresh lime juice
- 1/2 teaspoon white sugar
- salt and ground black pepper to taste
- 1 green onion, chopped
- 1 clove garlic, minced
- 1/2 teaspoon dried oregano
- 1/3 cup light mayonnaise
- 1 tablespoon canned chipotle peppers in adobo sauce, seeded and minced
- 1 1/2 tablespoons chopped green onion
- 1 1/2 tablespoons sweet pickle relish
- 8 slices sourdough bread
- 4 slices mozzarella cheese
- 1 cup torn lettuce

Direction

- In a big skillet over medium heat, heat olive oil. Pan-fry chicken breasts for 10 minutes on each side, until browned and not pink inside anymore.
- Sprinkle the chicken breasts with oregano, garlic, 1 chopped green onion, black pepper, salt, sugar, lime juice, and red wine vinegar. Pan-fry 5 more minutes on each side, till green onion is soft. Remove chicken breasts to plate; keep warm.
- In a blender, put chipotle pepper and light mayonnaise; process until smooth. Pour into a bowl, mix in sweet pickle relish and 1 1/2 tablespoons of chopped green onion.
- Toast the sourdough bread slices.
- On each of 4 bread slices, layer 1/4 cup lettuce then a chicken breast and a slice of mozzarella cheese. Spread chipotle mayonnaise on remaining slices, arrange over top for making sandwiches. Serve warm.

Nutrition Information

- Calories: 451 calories;
- Sodium: 757

- Total Carbohydrate: 35.2
- Cholesterol: 92
- Protein: 37.7
- Total Fat: 17.3

---

764. Chipotle Roast For Tacos And Sandwiches

Serving: 6 | Prep: 5mins | Cook: 5hours15mins | Ready in:

Ingredients

- 1 (3 pound) boneless beef chuck roast
- 2 teaspoons chili powder
- 2 teaspoons ground cumin
- 1 teaspoon salt
- 1 teaspoon ground black pepper
- 1 cup beef broth
- 1 cup sliced onion
- 1 (7 ounce) can green salsa (salsa verde)
- 1 (4 ounce) can chopped green chilies
- 3 chipotle peppers in adobo sauce, chopped
- 1 tablespoon minced garlic

Direction

- Put the chuck roast in the crock of a slow cooker. Season with cumin, pepper, salt, and chili powder. Add green salsa, chopped chipotle peppers, garlic, green chiles, onion, and beef broth in the crock.
- Cook for 5 hours on high or 7-8 hours on low.
- Use 2 forks to shred beef in the slow cooker. Keep cooking for another 15-20 minutes on high.

Nutrition Information

- Calories: 290 calories;
- Total Carbohydrate: 7.8
- Cholesterol: 105
- Protein: 32.1
- Total Fat: 13.6

- Sodium: 960

- Protein: 92.1

765. Classic Cuban Midnight (Medianoche) Sandwich

Serving: 4 | Prep: 15mins | Cook: 8mins | Ready in:

Ingredients

- 4 sweet bread rolls
- 1/2 cup mayonnaise
- 1/4 cup prepared mustard
- 1 pound thinly sliced cooked ham
- 1 pound thinly sliced fully cooked pork
- 1 pound sliced Swiss cheese
- 1 cup dill pickle slices
- 2 tablespoons butter, melted

Direction

- Split sandwich rolls to half. Liberally spread mayonnaise and mustard onto cut sides. Put an equal amount of the Swiss cheese, ham and the pork on each sandwich, specifically in that order. Put several pickles on each one. Put the roll's top on the sandwich. Brush melted butter on tops.
- In a sandwich press heated on medium high heat, press each sandwich. Use a big skillet on medium high heat and press down sandwiches using a skillet/sturdy plate if you don't have a sandwich press. You can use some indoor grills too. Cook, keeping sandwiches pressed, for 5-8 minutes. Flip once to evenly brown if using a skillet. Diagonally sliced. Serve hot.

Nutrition Information

- Calories: 1453 calories;
- Total Fat: 88.4
- Sodium: 3309
- Total Carbohydrate: 69.1
- Cholesterol: 275

766. Cobb Sandwich

Serving: 4 | Prep: 25mins | Cook: | Ready in:

Ingredients

- 1/2 cup mayonnaise
- 1/4 cup blue cheese dressing
- 8 slices multigrain bread
- 2 cooked chicken breasts, sliced
- 1 ripe avocado, sliced
- 8 slices cooked bacon
- 2 hard boiled eggs, chopped
- 4 lettuce leaves

Direction

- Mix bleu cheese dressing and mayonnaise to prep sandwich spread; spread 2 tbsp. on 1 side of every bread slice. Put 1/4 each of lettuce, hard boiled eggs, bacon, avocado and chicken over 4 of prepped bread pieces. Put another bread slice over each sandwich; serve with leftover blue cheese spread alongside.

Nutrition Information

- Calories: 811 calories;
- Total Fat: 56.1
- Sodium: 908
- Total Carbohydrate: 29.6
- Cholesterol: 204
- Protein: 46.3

767. Corned Beef Rolls

Serving: 8 | Prep: 15mins | Cook: 15mins | Ready in:

Ingredients

- 1 (12 ounce) can corned beef
- 1/3 cup ketchup
- 2 tablespoons prepared yellow mustard
- 2 tablespoons Worcestershire sauce
- 1 onion, chopped
- 1 (8 ounce) package shredded white Cheddar cheese
- 8 hot dog buns

Direction

- Set oven to 350° F (175° C) to preheat.
- In a saucepan, mash in the corned beef, and stir in white Cheddar cheese, onion, Worcestershire sauce, mustard and ketchup on medium heat. Heat to boiling, then lower heat to medium-low, and simmer for about 10 minutes until the onion is translucent and soft and the cheese melts. Use about 1/2 cup of the mixture to fill each hot dog bun, and wrap each filled bun using aluminum foil. Put the wrapped buns onto a baking sheet.
- In the prepared oven, bake for about 15 minutes until buns are lightly toasted. If preferred, make a large batch of filled and wrapped buns, keep them in the freezer. Bake frozen for 35 minutes before serving.

Nutrition Information

- Calories: 365 calories;
- Sodium: 1000
- Total Carbohydrate: 27.8
- Cholesterol: 65
- Protein: 23.1
- Total Fat: 17.6

768. Corned Beef Special Sandwiches

Serving: 4 | Prep: | Cook: | Ready in:

Ingredients

- 1/3 cup Russian salad dressing
- 8 slices Jewish rye bread
- 1 pound thin-sliced corned beef
- 1/2 pound prepared coleslaw

Direction

- Spread one side of each of 4 slices of bread with a quarter of the Russian salad dressing, then put 4-oz. of corned beef and 2-oz. of coleslaw on top of each slice. Put the leftover bread slices on top to finish the sandwich construction. Prior to serving, cut sandwiches diagonally in half.

Nutrition Information

- Calories: 443 calories;
- Cholesterol: 78
- Protein: 28.4
- Total Fat: 16.7
- Sodium: 2152
- Total Carbohydrate: 45.4

769. Corny Cheese Toasties

Serving: 1 | Prep: 5mins | Cook: 10mins | Ready in:

Ingredients

- 2 slices bread
- 1 tablespoon butter
- 1 teaspoon mayonnaise
- 1 slice canned corned beef
- 1 slice American processed cheese

Direction

- Preheat a skillet over medium heat. Spread 1 side of each slice of bread with butter. Spread mayonnaise on the un-buttered sides. Arrange 1 slice of bread in the skillet, buttered side down. Layer with corned beef and cheese slices on bread. Lay the remaining slice of bread, buttered side up. Cook until cheese is melted and toast turns golden brown, about 5 minutes per side.

Nutrition Information

- Calories: 414 calories;
- Protein: 15
- Total Fat: 26.6
- Sodium: 1126
- Total Carbohydrate: 28.1
- Cholesterol: 70

---

770.   Cramer Family Stuffed Crawfish Bread

Serving: 24 | Prep: 15mins | Cook: 1hours | Ready in:

Ingredients

- 1/4 cup butter
- 1 onion, chopped
- 1/2 (12 fluid ounce) can evaporated milk, or as needed
- 2 pounds processed cheese food (such as Velveeta®), cubed
- 3/4 pound cooked and peeled whole crawfish tails
- 24 brown and serve pistolette rolls
- 2 quarts vegetable oil for frying

Direction

- In a saucepan, melt butter over medium heat. Sauté onion for 5 minutes, until it is translucent and softened. Add the cheese, evaporated milk, and crawfish tails. Cook and stir for 5 more minutes, until the sauce is smooth, and the cheese melts. Poke a hole into every pistolette roll using the end of a spoon. Stuff the rolls with a tablespoon of crawfish filling each.
- In a large saucepan or a deep-fryer, heat oil to 375°F (190°C).

- Cook the rolls in the hot oil, in batches. Cook them for 3 minutes per batch, until golden brown. Drain excess oil with paper towels. Serve while hot.

Nutrition Information

- Calories: 317 calories;
- Protein: 12.8
- Total Fat: 21.3
- Sodium: 661
- Total Carbohydrate: 18.9
- Cholesterol: 54

---

771.   Cranberry Thanksgiving Turkey Sandwich

Serving: 1 | Prep: 5mins | Cook: | Ready in:

Ingredients

- 2 slices wheat bread
- 2 tablespoons mayonnaise
- 1/4 cup shredded lettuce
- 4 ounces sliced Butterball® Maple Honey Turkey
- 2 tablespoons whole berry cranberry sauce

Direction

- Spread mayonnaise over each bread slice.
- Place the lettuce and the turkey, then the cranberry sauce, finally the remaining bread slice on top.

Nutrition Information

- Calories: 512 calories;
- Cholesterol: 61
- Protein: 26
- Total Fat: 26.9
- Sodium: 1348
- Total Carbohydrate: 47.8

772.　Crawfish Pistolettes

Serving: 20 | Prep: 30mins | Cook: 20mins | Ready in:

Ingredients

- 1/4 cup butter
- 1 cup finely chopped onions
- 1/2 cup chopped green bell pepper
- 1/4 cup chopped green onions
- 3 cloves garlic, minced
- 1 cup evaporated milk
- 1 (8 ounce) package processed cheese, cubed
- 1/2 teaspoon butter
- 2 (16 ounce) packages cooked and peeled whole crawfish tails
- 1/2 teaspoon salt
- 1/2 teaspoon ground black pepper
- 1/2 teaspoon garlic powder
- 1 teaspoon Cajun seasoning
- 2 cups vegetable oil for frying
- 20 brown and serve pistolette rolls

Direction

- In a saucepan, melt 1/4 cup butter over medium heat. Sauté and stir green onions, chopped onion, garlic and bell pepper for 5 minutes, until the onion is translucent and tender. Add the evaporated milk and let it simmer. Add processed cheese and cook until it melts. Lower the heat to low and keep the mixture warm.
- In the meantime, take another skillet and melt half a teaspoon of butter over medium heat. Toss in the crawfish tails. Sprinkle with salt, garlic powder, pepper, and Cajun seasoning to taste. Stir and cook for 3-5 minutes, until the crawfish tails start to curl and are hot. Mix the tails into the cheese sauce. Cook for another five minutes.
- In a large pan, heat oil at 350°F (175°C).
- Fry the pistolette rolls in the hot oil until they turn completely golden brown. Drain them on a paper towel-lined platter. Let them cool down. Once you can handle them, slice a slit in

one of the ends of the rolls. Using a spoon handle, make a pocket inside the roll and stuff it with the crawfish mixture. Serve while hot.

Nutrition Information

- Calories: 221 calories;
- Cholesterol: 69
- Protein: 13
- Total Fat: 10.7
- Sodium: 435
- Total Carbohydrate: 18.2

773.　Cream Cheese Filled Croissants

Serving: 8 | Prep: 10mins | Cook: 15mins | Ready in:

Ingredients

- 1 (4 ounce) package cream cheese, softened
- 1/4 cup vanilla yogurt
- 1/8 cup white sugar
- 3 large strawberries, diced
- 1 (8 ounce) package refrigerated dinner roll dough

Direction

- Set the oven at 190°C (375°F) to preheat. Grease a baking dish.
- In a bowl, stir sugar, yogurt, and cream cheese until smooth. Add strawberries and fold into the cheese mixture.
- Divide the crescent roll dough into 8 triangles. Scoop into the middle of each triangle with the cream cheese mixture; beginning at the smallest end, roll the dough around the filling. Pinch to seal up and arrange in the greased baking dish.
- In the preheated oven, bake for 13-15 minutes, until puffed and golden-brown.

Nutrition Information

- Calories: 184 calories;
- Sodium: 267
- Total Carbohydrate: 17.1
- Cholesterol: 16
- Protein: 3.5
- Total Fat: 11

---

774. Creamy Peanut Towers

Serving: 9 | Prep: 5mins | Cook: | Ready in:

Ingredients

- 2 slices white bread
- 2 tablespoons butter
- 4 tablespoons peanut butter
- 1 teaspoon white sugar
- 1 slice whole wheat bread

Direction

- Coat a slice of white bread with butter, then spread over the layer of butter on the bread slice with peanut butter. Sprinkle over the top peanut butter layer with sugar.
- Place on top of the white bread with a slice of wheat bread, then repeat the layering of butter, peanut butter as well as sugar. Place on top of the wheat bread with a slice of white bread.
- Divide the layered slices into 9 pieces then insert toothpicks into the pieces and serve.

Nutrition Information

- Calories: 89 calories;
- Sodium: 104
- Total Carbohydrate: 6
- Cholesterol: 7
- Protein: 2.7
- Total Fat: 6.5

---

775. Creamy Strawberry Sandwiches

Serving: 20 | Prep: 10mins | Cook: | Ready in:

Ingredients

- 2 (8 ounce) packages cream cheese, softened
- 1 (16 ounce) package fresh strawberries, hulled
- 1 loaf sliced white bread
- 1/2 cup chopped pecans, or more to taste (optional)

Direction

- In a food processor, place strawberries and cream cheese, then pulse the mixture until smooth. Spread half of the bread with cream cheese mixture and sprinkle pecans over. Top with leftover slices of bread to make sandwiches.

Nutrition Information

- Calories: 165 calories;
- Protein: 3.8
- Total Fat: 10.6
- Sodium: 221
- Total Carbohydrate: 14.2
- Cholesterol: 25

---

776. Crunchy Curry Tuna Sandwich

Serving: 2 | Prep: 15mins | Cook: | Ready in:

Ingredients

- 1 (5 ounce) can tuna, drained
- 1 tablespoon mayonnaise
- 2 tablespoons peanuts
- 2 tablespoons raisins
- 1 stalk celery, finely chopped

- 2 teaspoons curry powder
- salt to taste
- ground black pepper to taste
- 1 pinch white sugar, or to taste
- 1 pinch garlic powder, or to taste
- 1 pinch cayenne pepper, or to taste
- chopped onion (optional)
- chopped green onion (optional)
- 4 slices bread

Direction

- Combine mayonnaise, peanuts, celery, raisins, and tuna in a mixing bowl. Drizzle with salt, black pepper, cayenne pepper, sugar, garlic powder, cayenne pepper and curry powder. Add in green onions and onion. Serve on cut bread.

Nutrition Information

- Calories: 353 calories;
- Protein: 22.9
- Total Fat: 12.2
- Sodium: 576
- Total Carbohydrate: 39.2
- Cholesterol: 22

---

777.   Cuban Midnight Sandwich

Serving: 4 | Prep: 20mins | Cook: 5mins | Ready in:

Ingredients

- 1 cup mayonnaise
- 5 tablespoons Italian dressing
- 4 hoagie rolls, split lengthwise
- 4 tablespoons prepared mustard
- 1/2 pound thinly sliced deli turkey meat
- 1/2 pound thinly sliced cooked ham
- 1/2 pound thinly sliced Swiss cheese
- 1 cup dill pickle slices
- 1/2 cup olive oil

Direction

- Mix Italian dressing and mayonnaise in a small bowl; on hoagie rolls, spread mixture. Spread mustard on each roll; put layers of turkey, ham and cheese on each roll. Put dill pickle slices on top of each. Close sandwiches; brush olive oil on bottoms and tops.
- On medium high heat, heat a nonstick skillet. Put sandwiches into skillet; cook sandwiches, pressing down with an aluminum foil-covered plate, for 2 minutes. Flip; cook till cheese melts or for another 2 minutes. Take off the heat; put on plates. Diagonally halve.

Nutrition Information

- Calories: 1096 calories;
- Total Fat: 84.4
- Sodium: 3110
- Total Carbohydrate: 44.1
- Cholesterol: 127
- Protein: 43.3

---

778.   Cucumber Sandwich

Serving: 1 | Prep: 10mins | Cook: | Ready in:

Ingredients

- 2 thick slices whole wheat bread
- 2 tablespoons cream cheese, softened
- 6 slices cucumber
- 2 tablespoons alfalfa sprouts
- 1 teaspoon olive oil
- 1 teaspoon red wine vinegar
- 1 tomato, sliced
- 1 leaf lettuce
- 1 ounce pepperoncini, sliced
- 1/2 avocado, mashed

Direction

- Put a tablespoon of cream cheese on each slice of bread. On a single bread, put a single layer of cucumber slices. Add sprouts then drizzle with vinegar and oil. Add a layer of tomato slices, pepperoncini and lettuce. Spread mashed avocado on the other slice of bread. Close the two slices together then serve right away.

Nutrition Information

- Calories: 496 calories;
- Total Fat: 32.5
- Sodium: 1024
- Total Carbohydrate: 46.3
- Cholesterol: 32
- Protein: 11.4

779.   Cucumber Sandwiches I

Serving: 15 | Prep: 15mins | Cook: | Ready in:

Ingredients

- 1 (8 ounce) package whipped cream cheese
- 1 (.7 ounce) package dry Italian-style salad dressing mix
- 1 (1 pound) loaf cocktail rye bread
- 1 cucumber, thinly sliced

Direction

- Combine dry Italian-style dressing mix and whipped cream cheese in a small bowl. On cocktail rye bread slices, spread out even amounts of the mixture. Put a cucumber slice on top.

Nutrition Information

- Calories: 48 calories;
- Total Carbohydrate: 1.9
- Cholesterol: 14
- Protein: 0.8
- Total Fat: 4.3
- Sodium: 277

780.   Cucumber Sandwiches III

Serving: 35 | Prep: 20mins | Cook: | Ready in:

Ingredients

- 1 (8 ounce) package cream cheese, softened
- 1/2 cup mayonnaise
- 1 (.7 ounce) package dry Italian salad dressing mix
- 2 loaves French bread, cut into 1 inch slices
- 2 medium cucumbers, sliced
- 1 pinch dried dill weed

Direction

- Mix Italian dressing mix, mayonnaise and cream cheese together in a medium bowl. Chill in the refrigerator at least 6 hours or preferably up to overnight.
- Spread slices of French bread with cream cheese blend. Place a cucumber slice on top, then top with dill. You can make as few or many as you want. Keep cream cheese mixture in the refrigerator for about 1 week and you can use them over and over again!

Nutrition Information

- Calories: 123 calories;
- Total Fat: 5.2
- Sodium: 297
- Total Carbohydrate: 15.6
- Cholesterol: 8
- Protein: 3.6

781.   Cyprus Gyro Burger

Serving: 4 | Prep: 1hours | Cook: 10mins | Ready in:

Ingredients

- 3/4 cup peeled, seeded, and shredded cucumber
- 2 1/4 cups plain yogurt
- cheesecloth
- 2 1/2 teaspoons fresh lemon juice
- 1 tablespoon olive oil
- 4 cloves garlic, minced
- 1 tablespoon fresh dill, chopped
- 1 red onion, thinly sliced
- 1 teaspoon lemon juice
- 1 teaspoon ground sumac
- 1 pound ground beef
- 1 small sweet onion, minced
- 1 1/4 teaspoons crushed red pepper flakes
- 1/2 tablespoon ground coriander
- 1/2 tablespoon ground cumin
- 1 tablespoon Urfa biber
- 1 tablespoon butter, softened
- 1/2 red bell pepper, chopped
- 1 teaspoon kosher salt, or to taste
- 2 tablespoons olive oil
- 4 hamburger buns

Direction

- Dry the grated cucumber by sandwiching it between two heavy-duty paper towel or a kitchen towel. Pat it dry and set aside. Remove the excess moisture of the yogurt by enveloping it in a larger square of cheesecloth, twist the ends to close then squeezing out the excess water.
- In a bowl, combine the strained yogurt and 2 1/2 teaspoon of lemon juice. Trickle in slowly 1 tablespoon of olive while whisking continually until well incorporated. Stir in the garlic, dill and drained cucumbers. Cover and set aside in the refrigerator.
- On another bowl, combine the red onions, sumac and 1 teaspoon lemon juice. Cover and refrigerate.
- Combine ground beef, minced onion, red pepper flakes, coriander, cumin, urfa biber, and butter on separate bowl. Using your hands mix the mixture gently until well combined.
- Using a blender, puree the bell peppers. Discard any excess liquid. Set aside. Then pour the pureed bell pepper into the mixture and season with kosher salt. Mix well. Portion the meat mixture into 4 equal parts. Form the 4 portions into a patty that is slightly larger than the bun as it will shrink during grilling.
- Preheat the outdoor grill on high heat and lightly grease its grate.
- Brush the patties with 2 tablespoons of olive oil and grill on direct heat for about 5 minutes on each side or depending on your preferred doneness. Arrange the burger on the bun, topping it with the cucumber and yogurt tzatziki, and the lemon, red onion, sumac mixture.

Nutrition Information

- Calories: 574 calories;
- Sodium: 910
- Total Carbohydrate: 41.3
- Cholesterol: 85
- Protein: 31.6
- Total Fat: 31.4

---

782. Dad's Homemade Corn Dogs

Serving: 8 | Prep: 20mins | Cook: 10mins | Ready in:

Ingredients

- 1 cup yellow cornmeal
- 1 cup all-purpose flour
- 1/4 cup white sugar
- 4 teaspoons baking powder
- 1/4 teaspoon salt
- 1/8 teaspoon ground black pepper
- 1 cup whole milk
- 1 large egg
- 16 large hot dogs

- 4 cups vegetable oil for frying
- 16 skewers

Direction

- In a bowl, combine pepper, salt, baking powder, white sugar, four, and cornmeal, then stir in egg and milk until smooth, then keep in the refrigerator until the batter chills.
- Boil a big pot of water and cook the hot dogs for 7 minutes until heated through. Allow the hot dogs to rest for 10 minutes, then dry on a paper towel.
- Heat oil using a big saucepan or a deep-fryer to 175 degrees C or 350 degrees F. Insert a skewer into each of the hot dogs.
- Pour batter into a big drinking glass and dip the hot dogs until coated well.
- Fry 2-3 hot dogs at a time for 3 minutes in hot oil until browned lightly, then drain on paper towels.

Nutrition Information

- Calories: 545 calories;
- Total Carbohydrate: 35.5
- Cholesterol: 71
- Protein: 15
- Total Fat: 38
- Sodium: 1347

783.   Dan's Favorite Chicken Sandwich

Serving: 2 | Prep: 15mins | Cook: 35mins | Ready in:

Ingredients

- 2 skinless, boneless chicken breast halves
- 2 tablespoons barbeque sauce
- 4 slices bacon
- 2 hoagie rolls, split lengthwise
- 2 tablespoons Ranch dressing
- 4 slices Swiss cheese

- 1 small avocado - peeled, pitted and diced

Direction

- Set oven to 190°C or 375°F. Apply cooking spray to a baking dish. For the chicken breasts, brush each side with barbeque sauce then place them in baking dish. Place two bacon slices on each chicken breast.
- Let the chicken bake for 25 minutes until juices are clear. Remove excess oil from the bacon strips with paper towels. Cut the breasts lengthwise in two.
- Prepare and heat oven's broiler. Spread Ranch dressing to both halves of every hoagie roll. On one side of every roll, put two breast halves. Put two strips bacon on each left roll half. Place 1 slice of Swiss cheese on every half.
- Place halves on cookie sheet. Broil them for 2-5 minutes until the cheese melts and is bubbling. Put avocado slices on chicken hoagie halves and put bacon halves on top; then serve.

Nutrition Information

- Calories: 1063 calories;
- Total Carbohydrate: 84.8
- Cholesterol: 143
- Protein: 59.8
- Total Fat: 53.3
- Sodium: 1663

784.   Darra's Famous Tuna Waldorf Salad Sandwich Filling

Serving: 4 | Prep: 15mins | Cook: 5mins | Ready in:

Ingredients

- 1/2 cup mayonnaise
- 1 tablespoon prepared Dijon-style mustard
- 1/4 teaspoon curry powder
- salt and pepper to taste
- 1 (5 ounce) can tuna, drained

- 1 shallot, finely chopped
- 1 Granny Smith apple, cored and diced
- 1/4 cup chopped walnuts
- 1/2 cup diced celery
- 1 teaspoon sweet pickle relish
- 4 large croissants
- 4 leaves lettuce
- 4 slices Swiss cheese

Direction

- Combine pepper, salt, curry powder, mustard, and mayonnaise in a medium-sized bowl. Add pickle relish, celery, walnuts, apple, shallot, and tuna and mix until all ingredients are covered with dressing.
- Toast the croissants lightly. Divide in half, on the bottom half of the croissant put a lettuce leaf and fill with tuna salad. Put a slice of Swiss cheese and the top half of croissant on top. Eat with potato chips and a dill pickle. Enjoy!

Nutrition Information

- Calories: 695 calories;
- Cholesterol: 91
- Protein: 23.1
- Total Fat: 48.9
- Sodium: 844
- Total Carbohydrate: 42.4

---

785.   Dash's Donair

Serving: 4 | Prep: 30mins | Cook: 1hours15mins | Ready in:

Ingredients

- 1 teaspoon salt
- 1 teaspoon ground oregano
- 1 teaspoon all-purpose flour
- 1/2 teaspoon ground black pepper
- 1/2 teaspoon Italian seasoning

- 1/2 teaspoon garlic powder
- 1/2 teaspoon onion powder
- 1/4 teaspoon cayenne pepper
- 1 pound ground beef
- 1 (12 fluid ounce) can evaporated milk
- 3/4 cup white sugar
- 2 teaspoons garlic powder
- 4 teaspoons white vinegar, or as needed

Direction

- Start preheating oven to 350°F (175°C). Mix cayenne pepper, onion powder, garlic powder, Italian seasoning, black pepper, flour, oregano and salt together in a small bowl or cup.
- In large bowl, put ground beef. Blend in spice mixture with your hands. You must do this in a steel mixing bowl and on a sturdy surface if you want the smooth texture of meat like the one in a real donair shop. Pick up meat, and throw down about 20 times with force, kneading before throwing the next. It helps to hold the meat together better when slicing.
- Form the meat into a loaf, and place it on a broiler pan. If you do not have one, a baking sheet will do.
- Bake for 75 mins in the prepared oven, turning the loaf over about half way through. This will ensure even cooking. Serve, or allow the meat to chill before slicing and reheating.
- For donair sauce: in medium bowl, mix garlic powder, sugar and evaporated milk together. Whisk in white vinegar gradually, until thickened to preferred consistency; put in one teaspoon at once.

Nutrition Information

- Calories: 489 calories;
- Sodium: 748
- Total Carbohydrate: 49.5
- Cholesterol: 98
- Protein: 26
- Total Fat: 20.9

786.   Detroit Style Coney Dogs

Serving: 4 | Prep: 10mins | Cook: 10mins | Ready in:

Ingredients

- 4 hot dogs with natural casings
- 1 hot dog rolls, sliced
- 1 small onion, diced
- 1 (10 ounce) can chile sauce without beans
- 4 tablespoons prepared yellow mustard, or to taste

Direction

- Set the outdoor grill on medium-high heat.
- Cook hot dogs in the preheated grill for 5-8mins until brown or until your preferred doneness; turn the hotdogs once. Grill the hot dog rolls lightly.
- Put the chile sauce in a small microwaveable bowl; cook in a microwave for a minute then stir. Cook for another minute.
- Arrange hot dogs on buns; add onion, chile sauce, and a tablespoon of mustard on top to taste.

Nutrition Information

- Calories: 266 calories;
- Cholesterol: 30
- Protein: 10.4
- Total Fat: 18
- Sodium: 877
- Total Carbohydrate: 16.3

787.   Dill Cream Cheese, Roast Beef And Cucumber Sandwiches

Serving: 5 | Prep: 20mins | Cook: | Ready in:

Ingredients

- 1/2 cucumber, peeled and grated
- 1 (8 ounce) package cream cheese, softened
- 3 tablespoons chopped fresh dill
- salt and ground black pepper to taste
- 10 slices dense white bread
- 1/2 cucumber, peeled and thinly sliced
- 1 pound deli roast beef, thinly sliced

Direction

- Place grated cucumber in a kitchen towel to wrap then squeeze out all the liquid from the cucumber. Put cucumber in a bowl.
- Combine dill, cream cheese, salt and black pepper into the grated cucumber.
- Spread the mixture over slices of bread.
- Divide cucumber slices and roast beef on five slices of bread. Place another slice of bread with spread side facing down on top to create 5 sandwiches.

Nutrition Information

- Calories: 398 calories;
- Total Carbohydrate: 28.9
- Cholesterol: 93
- Protein: 25.8
- Total Fat: 20.1
- Sodium: 1394

788.   Divine Summertime Chicken Sandwich

Serving: 2 | Prep: 10mins | Cook: 20mins | Ready in:

Ingredients

- 4 ounces cream cheese, softened
- 4 teaspoons dried dill weed, divided
- 4 tablespoons minced garlic, divided
- 2 tablespoons butter, softened
- 2 skinless, boneless chicken breast halves
- 1 small tomato, diced
- 1 leaf lettuce

- 4 thick slices French bread

Direction

- Combine 2 tbsps. garlic, cream cheese, and 2 tbsps. dill in a medium bowl; set aside.
- On medium heat, melt 1/2 of the butter in a pan. Sprinkle the remaining dill and garlic over the chicken breast halves. Cook until the juices are clear, and the chicken is firm for 8 mins on each side. Take the breasts out of the pan; set aside.
- Slather the leftover butter on one side of each bread slices; toast in the pan until golden. Slather the cream cheese mixture on the other side of the bread slices. Arrange lettuce, chicken breasts, and tomato to make a sandwich.

Nutrition Information

- Calories: 671 calories;
- Protein: 39
- Total Fat: 35.7
- Sodium: 773
- Total Carbohydrate: 49.6
- Cholesterol: 160

---

789. Drowned Beef Sandwich With Chipotle Sauce (Torta Ahogada)

Serving: 4 | Prep: 15mins | Cook: 20mins | Ready in:

Ingredients

- 12 ounces chipotle cooking sauce (such a Knorr®)
- 1 (14 ounce) can reduced-sodium beef broth
- 1/4 cup chopped fresh cilantro (optional)
- 2 tablespoons vegetable oil
- 1 onion, thinly sliced
- 3 cloves garlic, minced
- 1 pound thinly sliced deli roast beef

- 4 bolillo rolls, halved and lightly toasted
- 4 sprigs fresh cilantro, or to taste (optional)

Direction

- In a saucepan, mix 1/4 cup chopped cilantro, beef broth and chipotle cooking sauce; boil. Turn heat to medium-low and let simmer for 10 minutes, mixing from time to time.
- In a skillet, heat oil over medium-high heat; sauté onion for 5 minutes till tender. Into the onion, mix the garlic and allow to cook for a minute. Put the 1/4 cup chipotle sauce mixture and roast beef and let cook for 2 minutes, mixing continuously, till heated through.
- Into 4 bowls, scoop the rest of chipotle sauce mixture for dipping. Onto the base half of every bun, scoop roast beef mixture, put 1 cilantro sprig on top, and put the top bun on each. Into the sauce, dip the sandwiches.

Nutrition Information

- Calories: 569 calories;
- Cholesterol: 56
- Protein: 37.1
- Total Fat: 14.8
- Sodium: 2009
- Total Carbohydrate: 71.1

---

790. E A G L E S Swirl Sandwich

Serving: 4 | Prep: 10mins | Cook: 25mins | Ready in:

Ingredients

- 1 tablespoon vegetable oil
- 1/2 cup sliced onion
- 1/2 cup sliced fresh mushrooms
- 1 clove garlic, minced
- 1 (10 ounce) can refrigerated pizza crust dough

- 4 ounces thinly sliced American cheese
- 4 ounces thinly sliced deli roast beef
- 1 egg white
- 1 tablespoon water
- 1/8 teaspoon Italian seasoning

Direction

- Preheat an oven to 175 degrees C (350 degrees F).
- Over medium heat, heat oil in a skillet until hot and then add garlic, mushrooms, and onion into the hot oil. Cook while stirring for about 5 minutes until tender. Reserve to cool a bit.
- Roll out pizza crust dough to form a 12x9 inch rectangle onto a surface that is lightly floured. Then cover with layers of roast beef slices, veggies and cheese to within half inch of the edges. , Fold across to the other side beginning from the longest side of dough and then seal by pinching the seam. Transfer to a greased baking sheet with the seam side down. Use a fork to whisk together water and egg white and then rub this mix over the roll. Drizzle Italian seasoning atop the roll.
- Bake for about 25 minutes or until turned golden brown. Cool a bit, chop and serve.

Nutrition Information

- Calories: 369 calories;
- Sodium: 1192
- Total Carbohydrate: 36.7
- Cholesterol: 40
- Protein: 19.7
- Total Fat: 15.7

791.   Easiest Slow Cooker French Dip

Serving: 8 | Prep: 5mins | Cook: 8hours | Ready in:

Ingredients

- 3 pounds beef sirloin roast
- 1 (1 ounce) packet dry au jus mix
- 1 cup water
- 8 (1 ounce) slices provolone cheese
- 8 hoagie rolls, split lengthwise

Direction

- Add beef roast to the slow cooker. Whisk au jus mix and water together; add on top of roast. Keep covered and cook on Low heat for 6 - 8 hours.
- Take roast out of slow cooker and shred/slice. Open hoagie rolls and add the provolone cheese and beef on top. Serve with the small bowls of hot au jus from slow cooker.

Nutrition Information

- Calories: 756 calories;
- Sodium: 1463
- Total Carbohydrate: 70.5
- Cholesterol: 110
- Protein: 46.8
- Total Fat: 30

792.   Easy Beef Shawarma

Serving: 4 | Prep: 20mins | Cook: 5mins | Ready in:

Ingredients

- Shawarma:
- 1 tablespoon olive oil
- 1 pound beef top sirloin, thinly sliced
- 1 tablespoon shawarma seasoning
- 1 teaspoon ground allspice
- 1/2 teaspoon salt
- Tahini Sauce:
- 1/2 cup tahini
- 3 tablespoons plain yogurt
- 1/2 lemon, juiced
- 1/2 teaspoon salt
- 1 (10 ounce) package large flour tortillas

- 2 tomatoes, halved and sliced
- 1 onion, thinly sliced

Direction

- Heat the olive oil on medium heat in the big skillet. Put in half tsp. of the salt, allspice, shawarma seasoning and beef; cook, flip once in a while, for 3-5 minutes or till the beef turns brown and softens.
- Stir together half tsp. of the salt, lemon juice, yogurt and tahini in the small-sized bowl till creamy.
- Spread 1 - 2 tbsp. of the tahini sauce in middle of each tortilla. Split the slices of onion, slices of tomato and slices of beef equally between the tortillas. Roll up the tortillas.
- Pre-heat the Panini press based on the direction of the manufacturer. Press the rolled tortillas with the seam side-down for roughly 2 minutes or till the grill marks are appeared. Chop each tortilla into 4-5 pieces.

Nutrition Information

- Calories: 637 calories;
- Total Fat: 35.7
- Sodium: 1122
- Total Carbohydrate: 50.3
- Cholesterol: 61
- Protein: 31.2

793.   Easy Chicken Gyro

Serving: 6 | Prep: 20mins | Cook: 20mins | Ready in:

Ingredients

- 1 (16 ounce) container Greek yogurt
- 1 cucumber, peeled and coarsely chopped
- 1 1/2 teaspoons dried dill weed
- 2 cloves garlic, minced
- 1 teaspoon distilled white vinegar
- 1 teaspoon lemon juice

- 1 tablespoon extra-virgin olive oil
- salt and ground black pepper to taste
- 4 cloves garlic, minced
- lemon, juiced
- 2 teaspoons red wine vinegar
- 2 tablespoons extra-virgin olive oil
- 1 tablespoon dried oregano
- 1 1/4 pounds skinless, boneless chicken breast halves - cut into strips
- 6 (6 inch) pita bread rounds
- 1 teaspoon olive oil
- 1 tomato, diced
- 1 red onion, thinly sliced
- 1/2 head iceberg lettuce, chopped

Direction

- Bring black pepper, salt, 1 Tbsp. of olive oil, 1 tsp. of lemon juice, white vinegar, 2 cloves of garlic, dill weed, cucumber and Greek yogurt into a blender. Blend until smoothened; put aside.
- Stir oregano, 2 Tbsp. of olive oil, red wine vinegar, juice of one lemon, 4 cloves of minced garlic together in a large ceramic or glass bowl. Add black pepper and salt to taste.
- Mix chicken strips into the mixture and toss until coated evenly. Wrap bowl with plastic and leave in the fridge to marinate for 60 minutes.
- Start preheating the oven's broiler and place oven rack in a 6" distance from the heat.
- Take chicken out of the marinade and let the excess drip off. Put the rest of the marinade away. Transfer chicken to a large baking sheet.
- Broil the chicken for 2-4 minutes on each side in the prepared oven until browned a little and no pink meat remains in the middle.
- Bring cooked chicken to a plate and let rest for 5 minutes.
- In a large skillet, bring 1 tsp. of olive oil to medium heat; toast pita bread in skillet for about 2 minutes each until softened and warmed.
- Place lettuce, onion, tomatoes, yogurt sauce and chicken strips onto warmed pita bread.

Nutrition Information

- Calories: 441 calories;
- Sodium: 398
- Total Carbohydrate: 39.3
- Cholesterol: 71
- Protein: 30.3
- Total Fat: 18.3

794.   Easy Chicken Parmesan Sandwich

Serving: 1 | Prep: 5mins | Cook: 2mins | Ready in:

Ingredients

- 6 frozen chicken nuggets
- 2 tablespoons tomato sauce
- 1 hamburger bun, split
- 1 slice American cheese
- 1 tablespoon grated Parmesan cheese

Direction

- On a microwave-safe dish, position chicken nuggets. Cook in the microwave oven for 2 minutes, or until the middle of the nuggets are hot.
- On hamburger buns spread about 1 tablespoon of tomato sauce on one piece of the bun, then top with 1 slice of American cheese. Place chicken nuggets over the cheese. Pour the rest of the tomato sauce over chicken nuggets; top with Parmesan cheese. Put the other hamburger bun on and finish the sandwich.

Nutrition Information

- Calories: 569 calories;
- Sodium: 1484
- Total Carbohydrate: 40.6
- Cholesterol: 97
- Protein: 30.4

- Total Fat: 31.5

795.   Easy Peezy Sweet Toasted Cheese Sandwich

Serving: 4 | Prep: 5mins | Cook: 5mins | Ready in:

Ingredients

- 1 (4 roll) package Hawaiian bread rolls, split
- 8 slices Cheddar cheese
- white sugar, or to taste

Direction

- Put a slice of Cheddar cheese on top of every bread roll half.
- Then place the topped rolls in the toaster oven to toast for 5-7 minutes until cheese is dissolved.
- Dust sugar on the dissolved cheese.

Nutrition Information

- Calories: 500 calories;
- Total Fat: 18.8
- Sodium: 563
- Total Carbohydrate: 43
- Cholesterol: 100
- Protein: 28.1

796.   Eggplant Sandwiches

Serving: 2 | Prep: 20mins | Cook: 10mins | Ready in:

Ingredients

- 1 small eggplant, halved and sliced
- 1 tablespoon olive oil, or as needed
- 1/4 cup mayonnaise
- 2 cloves garlic, minced
- 2 (6 inch) French sandwich rolls

- 1 small tomato, sliced
- 1/2 cup crumbled feta cheese
- 1/4 cup chopped fresh basil leaves

Direction

- Preheat the oven's broiler. Coat slices of eggplant with olive oil and then transfer them onto a broiling pan or baking sheet. Put pan about 6 inches away from the heat. Cook for 10 minutes under the broiler or until toasted and tender.
- Slice French rolls lengthwise and then toast. Mix together the garlic and mayonnaise in a cup or small bowl. Pour this mixture onto the toasted bread. Then fill the rolls with basil leaves, tomato, eggplant slices, and feta cheese.

Nutrition Information

- Calories: 802 calories;
- Cholesterol: 44
- Protein: 23.8
- Total Fat: 39.5
- Sodium: 1460
- Total Carbohydrate: 91.3

797.   Eggplant And Pepper Parmesan Sandwiches

Serving: 4 | Prep: 15mins | Cook: 10mins |Ready in:

Ingredients

- 1 eggplant, seeded and cut lengthwise into 1/4 inch slices
- 1 red bell pepper, sliced into thin strips
- salt and pepper to taste
- 1 French baguette
- 2 ounces soft goat cheese
- 1/4 cup tapenade (olive spread)
- 1/4 cup grated Parmesan cheese

Direction

- Start preheating the oven broiler.
- In a medium-sized baking sheet, put red bell pepper and eggplant, and use pepper and salt to season. Broil until turning light brown and soft, about 5-10 minutes.
- Slice baguette in half lengthwise. Spread goat cheese onto the bottom half, and then spread with tapenade. Layer with red pepper and eggplant, and then sprinkle Parmesan cheese over. Put on the top half of the baguette to cover. Slice into 4 pieces. Enjoy cold or hot.

Nutrition Information

- Calories: 461 calories;
- Total Fat: 9.6
- Sodium: 1018
- Total Carbohydrate: 74.7
- Cholesterol: 13
- Protein: 20.3

798.   Ellie's Fresh Vegetable Sandwich

Serving: 1 | Prep: 15mins | Cook: 5mins |Ready in:

Ingredients

- 2 slices whole wheat bread, toasted
- 2 tablespoons honey mustard salad dressing
- 1/2 cup alfalfa sprouts
- 2 slices tomato
- 1/4 cup chopped broccoli
- 2 tablespoons sliced fresh mushrooms
- 4 slices cucumber
- 1 slice Swiss cheese

Direction

- Toast both sides of 2 slices of bread to a light golden brown.

On each slice of toast, smear one tablespoon of honey mustard dressing. Add alfalfa sprouts, tomato slices, chopped broccoli, sliced mushrooms, and sliced cucumber on top of one toast slice. Lay Swiss cheese onto vegetables and put second slice of toast on top to make a sandwich.

Nutrition Information

- Calories: 455 calories;
- Cholesterol: 31
- Protein: 19
- Total Fat: 25.4
- Sodium: 497
- Total Carbohydrate: 41.9

799.   Elvis Sandwich

Serving: 1 | Prep: 10mins | Cook: 10mins | Ready in:

Ingredients

- 3 tablespoons peanut butter
- 2 slices white bread
- 1 banana, peeled and sliced
- 3 slices cooked bacon
- 1 1/2 teaspoons butter

Direction

- Spread 1 side of 1 bread slice with peanut butter. Place the sliced banana on top, followed by the cooked bacon slices. Wrap in other bread slice. Spread outside of sandwich with butter.
- Over medium heat, heat the skillet. Fry each side of sandwich for 4 minutes total until peanut butter melts and sandwich turns golden brown.

Nutrition Information

- Calories: 676 calories;

- Total Fat: 40.2
- Sodium: 1025
- Total Carbohydrate: 62.1
- Cholesterol: 36
- Protein: 24.1

800.   Eric's Lobster Rolls

Serving: 6 | Prep: 20mins | Cook: 12mins | Ready in:

Ingredients

- 2 stalks celery, finely chopped
- 2 green onions, finely chopped
- 1 lemon juice, or more to taste
- 2 tablespoons seafood seasoning (such as Old Bay®)
- 2 tablespoons blackening seasoning
- water to cover
- 2 lobster tails
- 1/2 pound peeled, deveined raw shrimp
- 2 cups seafood salad
- 4 ounces Cajun crab dip
- 6 small croissants

Direction

- Trim green onion ends and celery, put in a pot. Add blackening seasoning, seafood seasoning, and 2 tablespoons lemon juice. Add water to cover, boil it.
- Mix shrimp and lobster tails into the boiling water. Cook for 7 minutes until they rose to the top. Strain. Remove the shell from lobster meat, slice the meat into bite-sized pieces. In a bowl, put shrimp and lobster meat. Chill until cool.
- Remove green onions and celery to a bowl. Add crab dip and seafood salad. Drizzle over the top with the leftover lemon juice. Stir in shrimp and the cooled lobster meat. Use a small amount of additional lemon juice to season.
- Split croissants and stuff with the shrimp and lobster salad.

Nutrition Information

- Calories: 392 calories;
- Protein: 28.5
- Total Fat: 19.4
- Sodium: 1739
- Total Carbohydrate: 24.8
- Cholesterol: 170

801. Falafel Pita Sandwich With Tahini Sauce

Serving: 6 | Prep: 20mins | Cook: 10mins |Ready in:

Ingredients

- 12 frozen falafel
- 1/4 cup tahini
- 1/4 cup water
- 2 tablespoons lemon juice
- 2 cloves garlic, minced
- 1/4 teaspoon ground paprika
- 6 whole wheat pitas
- 1 head lettuce, shredded
- 1 tomato, cut into thin wedges
- 1/2 cucumber, peeled and sliced
- 1 low-sodium dill pickle, sliced
- 1/4 small red onion, thinly sliced
- 3 teaspoons harissa, or to taste (optional)

Direction

- Set the oven to 230°C or 450°F to preheat and put on a baking sheet with falafel.
- In the preheated oven, bake for 8-10 minutes, until heated through.
- In a bowl, whisk together paprika, garlic, lemon juice, water and tahini while baking falafel.
- Cut 1 inch off the top of each pita to make a pocket, then put into each pita with 2 falafel along with equal quantity of red onion, pickle, cucumber, tomato and lettuce. Drizzle some

harissa and 1 tbsp. of tahini sauce over each pita.

Nutrition Information

- Calories: 361 calories;
- Total Carbohydrate: 53.4
- Cholesterol: 0
- Protein: 12.6
- Total Fat: 12.7
- Sodium: 576

802. Faye's Pulled Barbecue Pork

Serving: 11 | Prep: 10mins | Cook: 3hours30mins |Ready in:

Ingredients

- 6 pounds Boston butt roast
- 4 cloves garlic, minced
- 2 teaspoons seasoning salt
- 2 teaspoons ground black pepper
- 1/8 tablespoon cayenne pepper
- 1 onion, chopped
- 3 cups barbecue sauce

Direction

- To taste, rub cayenne pepper, pepper, seasoning salt and garlic on roast.
- Put roast in big Dutch oven; fill with water halfway. Add onion; put on rolling boil on high heat. Lower heat; simmer. Cook for at least 3-4 hours, varies on roast's size, till meat falls off bone.
- Put hot roast in serving bowl; put preferred barbecue sauce on top. Mix till blended well; serve with your favorite buns.

Nutrition Information

- Calories: 694 calories;

- Sodium: 1091
- Total Carbohydrate: 26.5
- Cholesterol: 176
- Protein: 42.8
- Total Fat: 44.8

803. Flatbread Sandwiches With Hillshire Farm® Smoked Sausage And Watermelon Salsa

Serving: 4 | Prep: 10mins | Cook: 10mins | Ready in:

Ingredients

- 1 cup chopped seeded watermelon
- 1 cup chopped multicolor cherry tomatoes
- 1/4 cup thinly sliced green onion
- 1/4 cup chopped fresh basil
- 2 tablespoons lime juice
- 1/4 teaspoon salt
- 1/8 teaspoon ground black pepper
- 1 (14 ounce) package Hillshire Farm® Smoked Sausage
- 4 flatbreads
- Lime wedges

Direction

- To make Watermelon Salsa: mix together pepper, salt, lime juice, basil, green onion, tomatoes and watermelon in a medium bowl, then toss to coat well. Put aside.
- On the rack of a charcoal or gas grill, arrange the sausage to grill directly on moderate heat, then cover and grill until heated through (160°F), while turning one time, about 7-9 minutes. Put on grill rack over heat with flatbreads. Grill about 1-2 minutes while flipping one time, until toasted slightly.
- To serve, slice the grilled sausage, then split among toasted flatbreads with sausage slices. Put the Watermelon Salsa on top and serve along with lime wedges.

Nutrition Information

- Calories: 501 calories;
- Protein: 17.8
- Total Fat: 29.2
- Sodium: 1270
- Total Carbohydrate: 39.9
- Cholesterol: 62

804. Frankly Super Supper

Serving: 4 | Prep: 20mins | Cook: 20mins | Ready in:

Ingredients

- 1 (16 ounce) package hot dogs
- 8 slices sourdough bread
- 1/2 cup butter, softened
- 4 slices sharp Cheddar cheese, or to taste
- 20 dill pickle slices, or to taste

Direction

- Cut hot dogs lengthwise, keeping the skin intact to hold the two halves together.
- Heat a skillet on medium heat; in hot skillet, cook the hot dogs for 2-3 minutes per side, or till crispy and cooked through. Drain on a plate lined with paper towels.
- On a sheet of waxed paper, arrange bread slices; on 1 side of each slice, spread butter. Turn over and spread butter on the other sides. Lay a slice of Cheddar cheese onto each of 4 slices of bread; top each cheese slice with 1 hot dog and pickle slices. Place a sourdough slice on top of each hot dog.
- Heat a skillet on medium heat; put the sandwiches into the hot skillet, 1 by 1; cook for 2-3 minutes per side, or till the bread is toasted and the cheese melts. While cooking, lay a heavy plate on the sandwiches to add weight to them, if needed. Diagonally slice the sandwiches to serve.

Nutrition Information

- Calories: 838 calories;
- Protein: 26
- Total Fat: 66.5
- Sodium: 2390
- Total Carbohydrate: 34.6
- Cholesterol: 150

Nutrition Information

- Calories: 490 calories;
- Total Fat: 11.4
- Sodium: 2444
- Total Carbohydrate: 71.4
- Cholesterol: 27
- Protein: 24.7

805. French Canadian Dip

Serving: 10 | Prep: 15mins | Cook: 30mins | Ready in:

Ingredients

- 2 tablespoons butter
- 1 1/2 cups sliced onion
- 3 garlic cloves, crushed
- 8 1/2 cups beef stock
- 1 cup soy sauce
- 2 tablespoons Worcestershire sauce
- 2 bay leaves
- 1 1/4 pounds Montreal smoked meat (smoked brisket)
- 1/3 pound thinly sliced Canadian bacon
- 10 (7 inch) baguettes, slit lengthwise but still attached

Direction

- In a big pot, heat butter on moderate heat, then cook and stir garlic and onion for 5 minutes, until onion is translucent and soft.
- Put into the onion mixture with Worcestershire sauce, soy sauce, beef stock and bay leaves. Put in 1 Canadian bacon slice at a time and Montreal smoked meat, then bring to a boil. Lower heat and simmer for about 20 minutes.
- Take the meat out of stock with tongs and arrange them inside sandwich baguettes evenly. Get rid of bay leaves and scoop into separate bowls with stock as dipping. Serve hot.

806. French Toast And Spam Sandwiches

Serving: 4 | Prep: 5mins | Cook: 30mins | Ready in:

Ingredients

- 1 (12 ounce) container fully cooked luncheon meat (e.g. Spam)
- 5 eggs
- 1/2 cup milk
- 8 slices white bread

Direction

- Cut meat to 8 slices; cook in big skillet till both sides are brown. Take out of skillet; keep warm.
- Beat milk and eggs in shallow dish. Quickly dip bread in egg mixture to coat both sides. 2 at a time, fry in skillet till both sides are done. Wrap 1 meat piece with 1 French toast slice.

Nutrition Information

- Calories: 498 calories;
- Sodium: 1590
- Total Carbohydrate: 29.8
- Cholesterol: 294
- Protein: 23.8
- Total Fat: 31.3

807. Fried Bacon Wrapped Hot Dog

Serving: 8 | Prep: 10mins | Cook: 10mins | Ready in:

Ingredients

- 8 hot dogs
- 8 slices bacon
- oil for frying
- 8 hot dog buns, split and toasted

Direction

- Use bacon strip to wrap each hotdog; use toothpick to secure. While heating oil, refrigerate wrapped hot dogs.
- Heat oil to 175°C/350°F in big saucepan/deep fryer.
- Working in batches, fry hotdogs in preheated oil for 2-5 minutes till bacon, turns brown and become crispy; drain on paper towel-lined plate. Place hot dogs in toasted buns to serve.

Nutrition Information

- Calories: 412 calories;
- Cholesterol: 34
- Protein: 11.8
- Total Fat: 30.1
- Sodium: 911
- Total Carbohydrate: 23.1

808. Fried Green Tomato Sandwich

Serving: 2 | Prep: 15mins | Cook: 15mins | Ready in:

Ingredients

- 6 (1/4 inch thick) slices green tomato
- 1 egg, beaten
- 1 cup yellow cornmeal
- 1/4 cup cooking oil
- 2 tablespoons butter
- 4 slices sourdough bread
- 6 (1/4 inch thick) slices red tomato
- 2 slices pepperjack cheese
- 2 tablespoons pickled jalapeno slices

Direction

- Plunge slices of green tomato in beaten egg, tent in cornmeal to coat and shake to remove the excess. In a large skillet, heat the oil on medium heat. Add tomato slices once the oil becomes hot. Cook for 2-3 minutes per side until each side turns golden brown. Take out of the skillet and transfer onto paper towels to drain.
- Use a paper towel to wipe the skillet and put it on medium heat. Spread the butter over one side of each bread slice. In the skillet, arrange 1/2 of the slices, butter side down. Stack several jalapeno slices, a slice of pepper jack cheese, 3 slices of a red tomato, and 3 slices of green tomato in reverse order on each piece of bread in the skillet. Add the rest of bread slices on top with the butter on outside. Cook until the bottom turns golden. Turn over the sandwiches, then cook until the other side turns golden brown.

Nutrition Information

- Calories: 859 calories;
- Protein: 18.1
- Total Fat: 47.9
- Sodium: 739
- Total Carbohydrate: 90.4
- Cholesterol: 128

809. Fried Scrapple Sandwiches

Serving: 4 | Prep: 5mins | Cook: 10mins | Ready in:

Ingredients

- 3 tablespoons vegetable oil
- 4 (1/4 inch thick) slices fresh scrapple
- 8 slices bread, toasted
- 2 teaspoons prepared spicy mustard

Direction

- In a big nonstick skillet, heat the vegetable oil over medium-low heat. Cook each side of the scrapple for 5 to 7 minutes until browned and crispy on both sides. Drain extra grease from the scrapple slices by placing them on a paper towel-lined plate. Put a slice on a piece of toasted bread, then spread with mustard and put another piece of bread on top.

Nutrition Information

- Calories: 294 calories;
- Cholesterol: 31
- Protein: 10.1
- Total Fat: 12.3
- Sodium: 1040
- Total Carbohydrate: 35.7

810.   Frosted Sandwich Loaf

Serving: 24 | Prep: 1hours | Cook: | Ready in:

Ingredients

- 2 cups fully cooked ground ham
- 1/2 cup creamy salad dressing (e.g. Miracle Whip)
- 3 tablespoons sweet pickle relish
- 1 tablespoon grated onion
- 2 cups ground bologna
- 3 tablespoons sweet pickle relish
- 1/2 cup creamy salad dressing (e.g. Miracle Whip)
- 1 (8 ounce) package cream cheese, softened
- 1/3 cup finely chopped walnuts
- 3 tablespoons pimento-stuffed green olives, chopped

- 2 tablespoons milk
- 2 cups shredded Cheddar cheese
- 1 (8 ounce) package cream cheese, softened
- 3 tablespoons creamy salad dressing (e.g. Miracle Whip)
- 1/8 teaspoon onion salt
- 1/8 teaspoon garlic salt
- 1/8 teaspoon celery salt
- 2 (8 ounce) packages cream cheese, softened
- 3 tablespoons milk, or as needed
- 1 (1 pound) loaf white bread, sliced horizontally
- 4 medium sweet pickles, chopped
- 1 (2 ounce) bottle diced pimento, drained

Direction

- Mix onion, 3 tbsp. relish, 1/2 cup salad dressing and ground ham in a small bowl. Put aside in the fridge.
- Mix 1/2 cup salad dressing, 3 tbsp. relish and ground bologna together in another bowl. Put aside in the fridge.
- Stir 2 tbsp. milk, green olives, walnuts and 1 package cream cheese together in a 3rd bowl. Put aside in the fridge.
- Mix celery salt, garlic salt, onion salt, 3 tbsp. salad dressing, 1 package cream cheese and cheddar cheese together in a 4th bowl. Put aside in the fridge.
- Spread ham spread on the bottom of bread slice. Top using another slice. Cover the following slice using bologna spread. Top it with another slice. Spread the following slice with nut spread. Top with another bread slice. Top cheddar cheese spread on this slice. Top using another bread slice. Use a knife/big spatula to smooth sides and refrigerate for about 30 minutes prior to "frosting" so it will be easier.
- Mix 2 leftover packages of cream cheese and enough milk together so it's spreadable. Frost loaf sides first then frost the top. Decorate with pimentos and sweet pickles to your preference.

Nutrition Information

- Calories: 352 calories;
- Protein: 11.8
- Total Fat: 27.3
- Sodium: 654
- Total Carbohydrate: 15.1
- Cholesterol: 74

---

811. Fruit N' Nut Sandwich

Serving: 4 | Prep: | Cook: | Ready in:

Ingredients

- 1 (8 ounce) package Neufchatel cheese, softened
- 1/4 cup crushed pineapple
- 4 tablespoons sliced almonds
- 8 slices whole-grain bread

Direction

- Combine together crushed pineapple and softened Neufchatel cheese in a small bowl.
- On a bread slice, spread cheese mixture and a quarter of the pineapple. Put 1 tbsp. of almonds on top and use another bread slice to cover, forming a sandwich. Do the same process with leftover ingredients.

Nutrition Information

- Calories: 328 calories;
- Total Fat: 18.3
- Sodium: 442
- Total Carbohydrate: 27.6
- Cholesterol: 43
- Protein: 13.8

---

812. Ghost Sandwich

Serving: 1 | Prep: 5mins | Cook: | Ready in:

Ingredients

- 2 slices bread
- 1 teaspoon peanut butter
- 1 teaspoon strawberry jelly
- 2 miniature semisweet chocolate chips

Direction

- Let the bread toast, then evenly spread the peanut butter onto one of the toasted bread slices and jelly on the other toasted bread. Join the 2 breads together to form a sandwich. Use a big cookie cutter to cut out a ghost from the peanut butter-jelly sandwich. Use 2 chocolate chips to form the eyes of the ghost sandwich.

Nutrition Information

- Calories: 182 calories;
- Total Fat: 4.4
- Sodium: 365
- Total Carbohydrate: 30.8
- Cholesterol: 0
- Protein: 5.2

---

813. Giant Bundt® Muffuletta Sandwich

Serving: 8 | Prep: 20mins | Cook: 30mins | Ready in:

Ingredients

- 1 serving cooking spray
- 2 (11 ounce) cans refrigerated French bread dough (such as Pillsbury®)
- 1/3 cup olive oil
- 1 tablespoon Italian herbs
- 1 (8 ounce) package sliced provolone cheese
- 1/2 (8 ounce) package sliced mozzarella cheese

- 1 (8 ounce) package thinly sliced deli ham
- 1 (4 ounce) package thinly sliced deli salami
- 10 green olives, sliced
- 10 black olives, sliced
- 1/2 cup sliced fire-roasted red peppers
- 1 teaspoon olive oil
- 1 teaspoon sesame seeds

Direction

- Preheat an oven to 175°C/350°F. Use cooking spray to grease a fluted tube pan/Bundt.
- Take bread dough out of the package; pinch edges together to make a ring. Put the ring in the prepared pan.
- In the preheated oven, bake for 30-35 minutes till golden brown. Put pan on a wire rack; cool for 20 minutes.
- Halve cooled bread with a serrated bread knife.
- In a small bowl, mix Italian herbs and 1/3 cup of olive oil. Use a pastry brush to brush on cut bread sides.
- Put red peppers, black and green olives, salami, ham, mozzarella cheese and provolone cheese on the bottom half of bread. Use top half of bread to cover; brush 1 teaspoon of olive oil on top. Scatter sesame seeds over; cut to slices. Serve.

Nutrition Information

- Calories: 530 calories;
- Total Fat: 30.2
- Sodium: 1695
- Total Carbohydrate: 38.2
- Cholesterol: 59
- Protein: 25.3

814.   Good And Easy Sloppy Joes

Serving: 6 | Prep: 5mins | Cook: 15mins | Ready in:

Ingredients

- 1 pound ground beef
- 1 (12 ounce) bottle chili sauce
- 2 tablespoons mustard
- 2 tablespoons brown sugar
- 1 tablespoon vinegar

Direction

- Bring a large skillet to medium-high heat. In the prepared skillet, cook, while stirring the beef for 7-10 minutes until it is crumbly and browned, then strain and throw away the grease. Put the beef and skillet back on the stove and lower heat to medium-low.
- Whisk vinegar, brown sugar, mustard and chili sauce into the ground beef and simmer for 5-10 minutes until the sauce is thickened.

Nutrition Information

- Calories: 163 calories;
- Sodium: 175
- Total Carbohydrate: 6
- Cholesterol: 47
- Protein: 13.1
- Total Fat: 9.3

815.   Gourmet Chicken Sandwich

Serving: 4 | Prep: 10mins | Cook: 15mins | Ready in:

Ingredients

- 4 skinless, boneless chicken breast halves - pounded to 1/4 inch thickness
- ground black pepper to taste
- 1 tablespoon olive oil
- 1 teaspoon minced garlic
- 2 tablespoons mayonnaise
- 2 teaspoons prepared Dijon-style mustard
- 1 teaspoon chopped fresh rosemary

- 8 slices garlic and rosemary focaccia bread

Direction

- Add pepper on 1 side of each chicken cutlet. In a big skillet, heat the oil and cook the garlic in oil until it becomes brown, then add the chicken pepper-side facing down. Sauté the chicken for about 12-15 minutes, until the juices run clear and cooked through.
- Mix together the rosemary, mustard and mayonnaise in a small bowl. Mix together and spread the mixture on four focaccia bread slices. Put one chicken cutlet on each of the slices, then put on another slice of bread.

Nutrition Information

- Calories: 522 calories;
- Total Fat: 15.7
- Sodium: 826
- Total Carbohydrate: 58
- Cholesterol: 70
- Protein: 34.6

---

816. Grandma's Pork And Bean Sandwiches

Serving: 4 | Prep: 5mins | Cook: 5mins | Ready in:

Ingredients

- 4 slices white bread
- 4 slices processed cheese
- 6 slices bacon, cut in half
- 1 (15 ounce) can baked beans with pork

Direction

- Preheat the broiler of the oven.
- Position slices of bread onto the aluminum foil-lined broiling pan. Scoop roughly half a cup of beans to each bread piece. Use 1 cheese slice to cover each pile of beans. Add three

half-slices of bacon to each sandwich so that they don't hang over the edge.
- Broil in the oven for 5 minutes or till cheese melts and bacon is cooked. Watch carefully! You should leave the door of the oven cracked near the 5 minute mark to let some oven heat out.

Nutrition Information

- Calories: 354 calories;
- Sodium: 1205
- Total Carbohydrate: 37.6
- Cholesterol: 45
- Protein: 17.9
- Total Fat: 15.3

---

817. Greek Pita Pockets

Serving: 4 | Prep: 15mins | Cook: 10mins | Ready in:

Ingredients

- 1/2 cup Greek-style (thick) unflavored yogurt
- 1 lemon, juiced
- 4 ounces bulk pork sausage
- 1 small onion, diced
- 1/3 cup Greek olives, diced
- 3/4 cup wild mushrooms, chopped
- 1 cup fresh baby spinach leaves, packed
- 6 eggs, beaten
- 2/3 cup Nikos® feta cheese crumbles
- 2 pitas, halved crosswise

Direction

- Combine lemon juice and yogurt in a small bowl; put aside.
- Cook sausage, stirring often and crumbling, on medium-high heat for 2 minutes in a non-stick skillet. Put in mushrooms, olives and onion, then cook for another 4 minutes.
- Put in spinach leaves and cook for about 1-3 minutes until vegetables give up all liquid and

the sausage is cooked through. Crack in eggs and cook while stirring constantly until almost dry. Take off the heat and whisk in feta.

- Pack feta-egg mixture into each pita half. Serve at once with lemon yogurt.

Nutrition Information

- Calories: 382 calories;
- Cholesterol: 317
- Protein: 21
- Total Fat: 23.4
- Sodium: 896
- Total Carbohydrate: 23.4

---

818.   Grilled Bacon Apple Sandwich

Serving: 2 | Prep: 5mins | Cook: 20mins | Ready in:

Ingredients

- 6 slices maple-cured bacon
- 5 tablespoons peanut butter
- 4 slices whole wheat bread
- 5 tablespoons apricot jelly
- cayenne pepper to taste
- 1 Granny Smith apple, cored and thinly sliced
- 3 tablespoons softened butter

Direction

- Cook bacon over medium-high heat in a large, deep skillet for about 10 minutes, flipping sometimes, until browned on all sides. Transfer bacon slices to a plate lined with paper towel to drain.
- Smear peanut butter onto 2 slices of bread; put to one side. Spread the remaining 2 slices of bread with apricot jelly; sprinkle with cayenne pepper to season. Place half of each of cooked bacon and sliced apple atop each bread slice covered with apricot jam. Place the peanut butter-spread bread slices on top.

- Bring a large skillet to medium heat on the stove. Spread the outside of the sandwiches with butter; set into the heated skillet. Cook until crispy and golden browned; flip over; keep cooking until the other side turns golden brown, approximately 4 minutes on each side.

Nutrition Information

- Calories: 832 calories;
- Protein: 28.5
- Total Fat: 51.3
- Sodium: 1233
- Total Carbohydrate: 72.6
- Cholesterol: 76

---

819.   Grilled Chicken Cordon Bleu Sandwiches

Serving: 1 | Prep: 5mins | Cook: 5mins | Ready in:

Ingredients

- 2 slices whole wheat bread
- 2 tablespoons butter, softened
- 1 tablespoon sour cream
- 2 slices Swiss cheese
- 1 thick slice deli cooked chicken breast meat
- 1 slice deli ham

Direction

- Spread margarine or butter on the outsides of the slices of bread. Spread sour cream onto the insides of the slices of bread. Then layer sandwich as follows: Bread slice, cheese slice, chicken, ham, second slice of cheese, second slice of bread.
- On medium heat, gill sandwich in a small-sized skillet till melted the cheese and thoroughly heated the meat.

Nutrition Information

- Calories: 692 calories;
- Protein: 33.4
- Total Fat: 49.8
- Sodium: 1246
- Total Carbohydrate: 27.7
- Cholesterol: 149

820.   Grilled Chicken Pineapple Sliders

Serving: 6 | Prep: 1hours | Cook: 15mins | Ready in:

Ingredients

- 1 lemon, juiced
- 1 lime, juiced
- 1 tablespoon cider vinegar
- salt and black pepper to taste
- 3 skinless, boneless chicken breast halves - cut in half
- 6 pineapple rings
- 2 tablespoons teriyaki sauce
- 6 slices red onion
- 6 Hawaiian bread rolls - split and toasted
- 6 lettuce leaves - rinsed and dried

Direction

- In a big ceramic or glass bowl, mix pepper, salt, cider vinegar, lime juice, and lemon juice. Mix in the chicken and toss to equally coat.
- Use plastic wrap to cover the bowl, then store in the refrigerator for 1 hour to marinate.
- Prepare an outdoor grill by preheating to medium-high and put oil on the grate lightly.
- Take the chicken from the marinade, then shake off the excess. Get rid of the rest of the marinade. Place the chicken on the griller then grill for 5-7 minutes per side, or until juices are clear once the chicken is pricked with a fork. Then place the pineapple on a grill for 2-3 minutes each side, or until heated well and grills marks form. On the bottom half of a toasted roll, put 1 teaspoon teriyaki sauce and spread; then put a lettuce leaf, a piece of

chicken, a pineapple round, and a slice of onion. Put back the top and continue with the rest of the rolls.

Nutrition Information

- Calories: 397 calories;
- Cholesterol: 74
- Protein: 27.3
- Total Fat: 1.5
- Sodium: 505
- Total Carbohydrate: 58.2

821.   Grilled Chicken Salad Sandwich

Serving: 4 | Prep: 15mins | Cook: | Ready in:

Ingredients

- 1 cup mayonnaise
- 1/8 teaspoon ground black pepper
- 1/8 teaspoon garlic powder
- 1/8 teaspoon celery salt
- 4 cups chopped leftover grilled chicken
- 2 celery stalks, sliced
- 1/2 cup sweetened dried cranberries
- 2/3 cup salted cashews
- 8 slices bread, toasted
- 4 tablespoons mayonnaise
- 4 large red leaf lettuce leaves
- 1 ripe tomato, sliced

Direction

- Whip celery salt, garlic powder, pepper and 1 cup of mayonnaise together until blended. In a big bowl, mix cashews, cranberries, celery and chicken. Top the chicken mixture with mayonnaise mixture and stir until well mixed.
- Spread each toasted bread slice with 1/2 tablespoon of mayonnaise. Distribute chicken salad evenly into 4 of the toast slices; put a slice of tomato and a lettuce leaf on top of

each. Top with the remaining toast slices to finish each sandwich.

Nutrition Information

- Calories: 1078 calories;
- Total Fat: 77.4
- Sodium: 1048
- Total Carbohydrate: 50
- Cholesterol: 131
- Protein: 46.9

822.   Grilled Flank Steak And Sriracha Mayo

Serving: 4 | Prep: 1hours30mins | Cook: 18mins | Ready in:

Ingredients

- Marinade:
- 1/3 cup Kikkoman Less Sodium Soy Sauce
- 4 medium cloves garlic, minced or pressed through a garlic press
- 2 tablespoons minced fresh rosemary
- 2 pounds flank steak, uncut
- 1 loaf flat rustic bread
- 2 cups arugula
- 2 tablespoons Kikkoman Sriracha Hot Chili Sauce
- 3 tablespoons mayonnaise
- 2 cups arugula
- Brie cheese

Direction

- In a blender, pulse all of the marinade ingredients until forming a rough paste, scraping down the container of the blender as necessary.
- In a gallon-sized zipper-lock bag, mix together meat and marinade; force out as much air as you can and close the bag. Chill for 60

minutes, turning the bag over after 30 minutes to evenly marinate the meat.

- Strain and dispose the marinade. Grill the steak over medium-high heat until the meat achieves the doneness you want, about 7-9 minutes per side. Let sit prior to cutting, about 10 minutes.
- Bring the steaks to a cutting board, put on a foil to partially tent and let sit for 5 minutes. Very thinly cut the steaks on the bias. Separate loaf, brush over the inside with a small amount of oil, and grill until partially toasted and warm, about 1 minute. Combine mayonnaise and Kikkoman Sriracha Sauce; put on the toasted bread and smear. Make a sandwich with brie, arugula, and sliced steak.

Nutrition Information

- Calories: 879 calories;
- Total Carbohydrate: 65.1
- Cholesterol: 132
- Protein: 52.2
- Total Fat: 44.4
- Sodium: 3047

823.   Grilled Gyro Burgers

Serving: 6 | Prep: 30mins | Cook: 14mins | Ready in:

Ingredients

- 2 (8 ounce) containers plain yogurt, divided
- 1 (1 ounce) package dry Ranch-style dressing mix
- 1 cucumber, peeled, seeded, and chopped
- 1 1/2 pounds ground beef
- 1/4 cup diced onion
- 6 pita bread rounds
- 2 cups torn lettuce leaves
- 1 tomato, seeded and diced

Direction

- Combine an envelope of ranch dressing mix with 1 container of plain yogurt in a medium bowl. Transfer 1/2 of the mixture to another bowl. Add diced cucumber and pour in the remaining container of plain yogurt into one of the bowls; stir to combine. Chill the bowl, covered. Preheat the grill and lightly grease the grate.
- Stir 1/4 cup onion and ground beef into the remaining 1/2 of the yogurt mixture. Form the mixture into 6 hamburger patties.
- Grill burgers over medium heat, flipping once, about 7 minutes per side.
- Slice of 1/4 end of the pita pockets; fill with diced tomatoes, creamy cucumber sauce, grill burger, and torn lettuce.

Nutrition Information

- Calories: 590 calories;
- Total Fat: 32.1
- Sodium: 782
- Total Carbohydrate: 44.3
- Cholesterol: 101
- Protein: 28.9

824. Grilled Maple Turkey Sandwich

Serving: 1 | Prep: 5mins | Cook: 10mins | Ready in:

Ingredients

- 3 strips bacon
- 4 ounces sliced deli-style maple turkey
- 2 tablespoons butter, softened
- 2 slices raisin black bread
- 4 slices Swiss cheese
- 2 tablespoons honey mustard

Direction

- Cook bacon till crisp in a skillet on medium heat. Remove; drain over paper towels. Drain

the bacon grease from the skillet. Put maple turkey in skillet; briefly cook long just enough to heat through.
- Butter both bread sides. Layer 1 slice with 2 Swiss cheese slices then bacon and maple turkey. Drizzle honey mustard; top with the leftover 2 Swiss cheese slices. Top with the leftover bread slices; halve sandwich. Put sandwich halves back into the skillet; cook on medium heat for 4-5 minutes till cheese starts to melt, flipping once.

Nutrition Information

- Calories: 1102 calories;
- Total Carbohydrate: 51.7
- Cholesterol: 243
- Protein: 65.1
- Total Fat: 72.8
- Sodium: 2809

825. Grilled Mediterranean Vegetable Sandwich

Serving: 6 | Prep: 20mins | Cook: 40mins | Ready in:

Ingredients

- 1 eggplant, sliced into strips
- 2 red bell peppers
- 2 tablespoons olive oil, divided
- 2 portobello mushrooms, sliced
- 3 cloves garlic, crushed
- 4 tablespoons mayonnaise
- 1 (1 pound) loaf focaccia bread

Direction

- Start by preheating the oven to 400°F (200°C).
- Brush 1 tablespoon olive oil over red bell peppers and eggplant; use extra if needed, according to the sizes of the vegetables. Put on a cookie sheet and put in the preheated oven to roast. Roast the eggplant for 25 minutes

until soft, roast the peppers until it turns black. Take out of the oven and put aside to cool.

- In the meantime, heat 1 tablespoon olive oil and stir and cook mushrooms until soft. Mix crushed garlic into the mayonnaise. Cut focaccia lengthwise into two. Spread over 1 or 2 halves with the mayonnaise mixture.
- Peel the skin from the prepared peppers, scoop out the core, and cut. Put mushrooms, peppers, and eggplant on the focaccia. Wrap plastic wrap around the sandwich, top the sandwich with a cutting board and put several canned foods on to weight it down. Let the sandwich stand before cutting and enjoying, for 2 hours.

Nutrition Information

- Calories: 356 calories;
- Total Fat: 14.8
- Sodium: 500
- Total Carbohydrate: 48.3
- Cholesterol: 3
- Protein: 9

---

826. Grilled Mushroom Sandwich With Citrus Mayo

Serving: 4 | Prep: 10mins | Cook: 15mins | Ready in:

Ingredients

- 2 tablespoons olive oil
- 1/4 cup balsamic vinegar
- 1 clove garlic, minced
- 4 portobello mushroom caps
- 1/3 cup mayonnaise
- 2 tablespoons orange juice
- 1 (12 ounce) jar roasted red bell peppers
- 4 rolls sourdough bread
- 4 slices smoked Gouda cheese
- 1 (10 ounce) bag mixed salad greens

Direction

- Beat garlic, balsamic vinegar and olive oil until combined thoroughly. In a resealable bag, transfer on top of the mushroom caps to coat, then seal the bag and let it marinate for half an hour. Stir orange juice and mayonnaise together, then put aside.
- Set an outdoor grill on medium heat and start preheating.
- Take the mushroom caps out of the marinade, then shake off to remove the excess. On a square piece of foil, arrange each mushroom cap upside down. Top with the roasted peppers, then seal. Cook on the prepared grill, turning from time to time, for 15 minutes until tender. Slice open the sourdough rolls once the mushrooms are almost finished, then grill on the sliced sides until golden brown.
- Spread orange mayonnaise over the sliced sides of the rolls and place the mixed greens, Gouda cheese, roasted pepper, and mushrooms into layers to assemble the sandwiches.

Nutrition Information

- Calories: 519 calories;
- Protein: 17
- Total Fat: 30.3
- Sodium: 848
- Total Carbohydrate: 49.2
- Cholesterol: 39

---

827. Grilled Peanut Butter And Banana Sandwich

Serving: 1 | Prep: 2mins | Cook: 10mins | Ready in:

Ingredients

- cooking spray
- 2 tablespoons peanut butter
- 2 slices whole wheat bread
- 1 banana, sliced

Direction

- Heat a griddle or frying pan on medium heat and use cooking spray to coat. On one side of each bread slice, spread 1 tbsp. of peanut butter. On the peanut buttered side of one slice, put the slices of banana, then place the other slice on top and firmly press together. Fry the sandwich for around 2 minutes per side, until it turns golden brown on each side.

Nutrition Information

- Calories: 437 calories;
- Sodium: 422
- Total Carbohydrate: 56.8
- Cholesterol: 0
- Protein: 16.8
- Total Fat: 18.7

828.　Grilled Peanut Butter And Jelly Sandwich

Serving: 1 | Prep: 5mins | Cook: 8mins |Ready in:

Ingredients

- 2 teaspoons butter
- 2 slices white bread
- 1 teaspoon peanut butter
- 2 teaspoons any flavor fruit jelly

Direction

- Heat a skillet or griddle to 175°C to 350°F.
- Spread on one side of each bread slice with butter, then spread on the unbuttered side of 1 bread slice with peanut butter while the other with jelly. Put on the griddle with a slice, buttered-side facing down. Place other slice on top so that jelly as well as peanut butter is in the middle. Cook until heated through and turn golden, about 4 minutes per side.

Nutrition Information

- Calories: 273 calories;
- Total Fat: 12.5
- Sodium: 427
- Total Carbohydrate: 35.5
- Cholesterol: 22
- Protein: 5.3

829.　Grilled Pineapple Chicken Sandwiches

Serving: 2 | Prep: 5mins | Cook: 15mins |Ready in:

Ingredients

- 4 slices canned pineapple
- 1 tablespoon honey mustard
- 2 skinless, boneless chicken breast halves
- 1 red bell pepper, thinly sliced
- 2 sandwich rolls, split

Direction

- Put the pineapple slices and chicken breasts together on the grill rack. Broil or grill them until the chicken has no pink left in the middle and the juices are running clear. During the process, baste the fruit and meat with honey mustard from time to time. It is ready when an inserted thermometer comes out from the centre registers 165°F (74°C). Put the chicken on sandwich rolls. Before serving, put red bell pepper rings and pineapple slices atop.

Nutrition Information

- Calories: 437 calories;
- Sodium: 468
- Total Carbohydrate: 58.6
- Cholesterol: 69
- Protein: 35.2
- Total Fat: 7.2

830.　Grilled Pork Belly BLT With Fried Tomatoes And Avocado

Serving: 4 | Prep: 30mins | Cook: 20mins | Ready in:

Ingredients

- 1 cup soy sauce
- 1 cup mirin
- Salt and ground white pepper to taste
- 1 pound skinless pork belly, thinly sliced
- 1 cup milk
- 2 eggs, beaten
- 1 1/2 cups all-purpose flour
- 2 teaspoons salt
- 2 teaspoons ground black pepper
- 2 teaspoons steak seasoning blend
- 2 large red tomatoes, thickly sliced
- 3 tablespoons butter
- 3 tablespoons olive oil
- 2 ripe avocados from Mexico, peeled, pitted and sliced
- 4 leaves green leaf lettuce
- 8 slices crusty artisan bread, toasted
- 1 tablespoon mayonnaise

Direction

- In a mixing bowl, mix together white pepper, salt, mirin, and soy sauce. Toss in pork slices until well coated with marinade. Chill, covered, for half an hour to overnight.
- Take pork out of the fridge. Strain pork and pour off used marinade. Heat a grill pan and grease with vegetable oil. Lay pork slices on the heated grill, cook, flipping every 3 to 4 minutes, until well seared. Transfer pork to paper towels to drain.
- Place milk into a shallow bowl. In a shallow dish, combine seasoned salt, pepper, salt, and flour to make dredging. Whisk eggs well in a separate bowl. Immerse tomato slices into milk, coat with flour mixture, then eggs. Dredge with flour again until evenly coated.
- Heat olive oil and butter over medium-high heat in a frying pan. Fry tomato slices in heated oil-butter, about 2 minutes on each side, until golden brown. Place tomatoes in warm oven until serving, if needed.
- To assemble sandwiches, spoon mayonnaise over bread slices, spread. Layer on half of the slices respectively with lettuce, avocado slices, grilled pork belly, and then fried tomato slices. Top with the rest of bread slices.

Nutrition Information

- Calories: 1124 calories;
- Total Fat: 56.8
- Sodium: 6653
- Total Carbohydrate: 107.4
- Cholesterol: 163
- Protein: 37.7

831.　Grilled Portobello With Basil Mayonnaise Sandwich

Serving: 6 | Prep: 10mins | Cook: 10mins | Ready in:

Ingredients

- 1/3 cup balsamic vinegar
- 1/4 cup olive oil
- 1 tablespoon minced garlic
- 6 portobello mushroom caps
- 1/2 cup mayonnaise
- 1 tablespoon Dijon mustard
- 1 teaspoon lemon juice
- 2 tablespoons chopped fresh basil
- 6 kaiser rolls, split, toasted
- 1 tablespoon butter
- 6 leaves lettuce
- 6 tomato slices

Direction

- Set the outdoor grill over medium heat for preheating. Put oil onto the grate lightly. In a small bowl, mix the balsamic vinegar, garlic, and olive oil.

- Place the Portobello mushrooms onto the baking sheet or tray, arranging them gill-side up. Coat the mushrooms with some of the vinegar mixture. Let them marinate for 3-5 minutes.
- Arrange the marinated mushrooms onto the preheated grill gill-side down. Grill each side of the mushrooms for 4 minutes, coating both sides with the remaining marinade until tender.
- In a small bowl, mix the Dijon mustard, basil, lemon juice, and mayonnaise. Spread butter onto the toasted Kaiser rolls. Spread the rolls with the mayonnaise mixture. Distribute the mushrooms, slices of tomato, and lettuce evenly until you have a total of 6 sandwiches.

Nutrition Information

- Calories: 412 calories;
- Total Carbohydrate: 35.6
- Cholesterol: 12
- Protein: 8.3
- Total Fat: 27.7
- Sodium: 417

---

832.   Grilled Spaghetti Sandwich

Serving: 2 | Prep: 10mins | Cook: 15mins | Ready in:

Ingredients

- 1/4 cup butter
- garlic powder, or to taste
- 2 hoagie rolls
- 8 thin slices mozzarella cheese
- 2 cups cold cooked spaghetti
- 1 cup spaghetti sauce

Direction

- Melt butter in a big pan; add in garlic powder.
- Slice a crust off the base and top of every hoagie roll. Slather garlic-flavored butter on the cut sides.
- Divide rolls and place slices of mozzarella cheese on the insides. In a bowl, combine spaghetti sauce and spaghetti; split among the hoagie rolls. Top roll over around the pasta mixture and cheese.
- In the pan, grill sandwiches for 5 mins on each side until the cheese completely melts.

Nutrition Information

- Calories: 1377 calories;
- Sodium: 2132
- Total Carbohydrate: 167.6
- Cholesterol: 135
- Protein: 55
- Total Fat: 52.7

---

833.   Grilled Tofu Sandwich Filling

Serving: 10 | Prep: 5mins | Cook: 5mins | Ready in:

Ingredients

- 1 (16 ounce) package firm tofu
- 1 cup honey mustard sauce
- 2 tablespoons vegetable oil

Direction

- Turn on the oven's broiler to preheat.
- Quarter the tofu cake. Cut each piece very thinly, and on a paper towel, lay the tofu strips and blot them dry to remove excess liquid. In a bowl, put the dry strips and pour in honey mustard sauce to cover. Put a cover on the bowl and chill for at least 3 hours, tossing sometimes.

- Broil for 5 minutes, and then turn the tofu over and broil until the tofu is hot, about 5 minutes more.

Nutrition Information

- Calories: 109 calories;
- Sodium: 202
- Total Carbohydrate: 12
- Cholesterol: < 1
- Protein: 4.7
- Total Fat: 6.4

---

834. Grilled Turkey Asparagus Pesto Paninis

Serving: 2 | Prep: 20mins | Cook: 20mins | Ready in:

Ingredients

- Pesto:
- 2 cups chopped fresh basil
- 1/2 cup grated Parmesan cheese
- 1/4 cup extra-virgin olive oil
- 2 garlic cloves
- coarse salt and freshly ground black pepper to taste
- 1/4 cup pine nuts
- Panini:
- 8 fresh asparagus spears, trimmed, or more to taste
- 2 tablespoons butter, softened
- 4 slices soft oatmeal bread (such as Pepperidge Farm®)
- 4 slices provolone cheese
- 1/4 pound sliced deli turkey meat

Direction

- In a blender or food processor, blend basil, olive oil, garlic, Parmesan cheese, salt and pepper until smooth. Scrape the sides occasionally. Pulse in pine nuts until just chopped. Brush the grate lightly with oil and

set grill on preheat to medium low. Grill the asparagus for 5 to 10 minutes until tender, directly or on a grill pan. Butter one side on the bread slice about 1 1/2 teaspoon. On the opposite side, spread pesto depending on your liking. On the pesto side of the two bread slices, layer turkey and provolone cheese topping with pesto-side down of the other bread slice. Grill sandwiches directly, 6 minutes per side and cook until cheese melts and color is golden brown. Cut in half and serve.

Nutrition Information

- Calories: 961 calories;
- Total Fat: 72.7
- Sodium: 1878
- Total Carbohydrate: 37.2
- Cholesterol: 110
- Protein: 43.1

---

835. Grilled Venison Scape Sandwich

Serving: 4 | Prep: 10mins | Cook: 15mins | Ready in:

Ingredients

- 1 1/2 pounds venison, slightly frozen and sliced into 1/16-inch slices
- 8 garlic scapes, minced
- 1/3 cup canola oil
- 1/4 cup soy sauce
- 4 hamburger buns, split
- 4 slices sharp Cheddar cheese (optional)

Direction

- Put venison strips into bowl. Sprinkle garlic scapes. Put soy sauce and canola oil in; stir well. Cover bowl. Marinate venison for minimum of 1 hour.

- Preheat a grill fitted with a fine grate grill topper on medium heat.
- Spread venison evenly on grill topper. Occasionally mix to cook meat evenly for 10-15 minutes till not pink.
- On grill's warming rack, warm hamburger buns. Divide venison to buns. Put cheddar cheese on top.

Nutrition Information

- Calories: 623 calories;
- Protein: 45.7
- Total Fat: 33.8
- Sodium: 1381
- Total Carbohydrate: 33.1
- Cholesterol: 149

836.   Guinness® Dogs

Serving: 8 | Prep: 10mins | Cook: 15mins | Ready in:

Ingredients

- 1 teaspoon butter
- 1/2 yellow onion, chopped
- 1 (12 fluid ounce) bottle Irish stout beer (such as Guinness®)
- 1/2 cup butter
- 1 teaspoon garlic powder
- 1/2 teaspoon hot sauce
- 8 hot dogs

Direction

- In a fry pan, heat 1 tsp of butter on medium heat, then cook and stir the onion for about 10 minutes in melted butter, until the liquid has been released and the onion becomes soft. Add hot sauce, garlic powder, half a cup of butter and beer into the onion, then boil until the beer starts to froth. Lower the heat and put in the hot dogs into the beer mixture, then let

it simmer for 5-8 minutes, until the hot dogs become heated through.

Nutrition Information

- Calories: 250 calories;
- Total Fat: 24.5
- Sodium: 598
- Total Carbohydrate: 2.4
- Cholesterol: 54
- Protein: 5.5

837.   Gyroll

Serving: 4 | Prep: 25mins | Cook: 35mins | Ready in:

Ingredients

- 1 tablespoon olive oil
- 1 pound ground lamb
- 6 cloves garlic, crushed
- 1 large onion, sliced
- 1 tablespoon dried oregano
- 2/3 teaspoon ground cumin
- 2 teaspoons salt
- 2 teaspoons freshly ground black pepper
- 1 dash hot pepper sauce
- 2/3 cup chopped fresh parsley
- 1 pound pizza crust dough
- 6 ounces feta cheese
- 1/2 zucchini, diced
- 8 ounces chopped black olives
- 1/2 teaspoon garlic powder

Direction

- Preheat oven to 450 °F (230 °C).
- In a large skillet, heat oil over medium-high heat. Brown the meat with onion, garlic, cumin, oregano, salt, hot pepper sauce and pepper. Add in parsley when meat is almost done, and cook till the parsley wilts. Take away mixture from heat and allow to cool.

- Roll pizza dough out to form a rectangle of 18 x 12 inches (with the long side laid out left-to-right in front of you). Evenly spread out black olives, zucchini and feta cheese over the dough, leaving 3 inches from the edges of the crust uncovered. Spread the top with the cooled meat mixture, but still keep the edges of dough uncovered.
- Beginning with the edge closest to you, roll up the whole thing till it is all rolled up. You can do this by using the uncovered edge of dough at the end as a 'strip' to stick to the roll and seal it, making sure that both ends are pressed down and sealed. Sprinkle with garlic powder and bake in the preheated oven for 5 minutes. Then, decrease heat to 350 °F (175 °C) and bake for about 30 minutes until it has the color of golden brown.

Nutrition Information

- Calories: 694 calories;
- Total Fat: 32.9
- Sodium: 2952
- Total Carbohydrate: 66.6
- Cholesterol: 95
- Protein: 32.5

838.   Gyros Burgers

Serving: 4 | Prep: 10mins | Cook: 15mins | Ready in:

Ingredients

- 1/2 pound lean ground beef
- 1/2 pound lean ground lamb
- 1/2 onion, grated
- 2 cloves garlic, pressed
- 1 slice bread, toasted and crumbled
- 1/2 teaspoon dried savory
- 1/2 teaspoon ground allspice
- 1/2 teaspoon ground coriander
- 1/2 teaspoon salt
- 1/2 teaspoon ground black pepper

- 1 dash ground cumin

Direction

- Set the outdoor grill on medium heat; preheat and oil lightly the grill grate.
- Mix together the ground lamb, garlic, ground beef, bread crumbs, and onion in a big bowl. Sprinkle on allspice, salt, cumin, pepper, savory, and coriander. Massage mixture until stiff. Mold mixture in 4 thin patties about 1/8-1/4 inch in thickness.
- For 5-7 minutes per side, cook the patties until thoroughly cooked.

Nutrition Information

- Calories: 338 calories;
- Sodium: 408
- Total Carbohydrate: 5.7
- Cholesterol: 84
- Protein: 20.3
- Total Fat: 25.4

839.   Harvest Breakfast Pitas

Serving: 4 | Prep: 20mins | Cook: 1hours1mins | Ready in:

Ingredients

- 1 cup peeled, seeded, and cubed butternut squash
- 1 cup peeled and cubed sweet potatoes
- 1 tablespoon olive oil
- 1 teaspoon salt
- 1 teaspoon ground black pepper
- 2 links apple chicken sausage (such as Aidells®), thinly sliced and quartered
- 4 eggs
- 2 cups fresh baby spinach
- 1 tablespoon red pepper flakes, or to taste
- 1 cup canned black beans, rinsed
- 2 tablespoons goat cheese, or to taste

- 2 large whole-wheat pita breads, toasted and halved

Direction

- Start preheating oven to 375°F (190°C).
- In a storage container, mix pepper, salt, olive oil, sweet potatoes and butternut squash. Shake well, covered with lid, until fully coated. Put vegetables onto the baking sheet.
- Bake in the prepared oven for 45 minutes or until vegetables are easily pierced with the fork.
- In a large skillet, put in chicken sausage. Cook over medium-high heat for about 10 minutes or until evenly browned, turning occasionally. Lower heat to medium-low, then add red pepper flakes, spinach and eggs. Cook and stir for 5 mins or until the eggs are set. Mix in black beans and cook for a minute, until heated through. Put in goat cheese.
- Fill the pita breads with baked vegetables and scrambled eggs.

Nutrition Information

- Calories: 328 calories;
- Total Fat: 15.8
- Sodium: 1047
- Total Carbohydrate: 30.5
- Cholesterol: 241
- Protein: 17.6

---

840. Hawaiian Sandwiches

Serving: 8 | Prep: 20mins | Cook: 10mins | Ready in:

Ingredients

- 16 slices bacon
- 8 slices toasted white bread
- 1 (20 ounce) can sliced pineapple, drained
- 8 slices Cheddar cheese

Direction

- In a big, deep skillet, put the bacon. Then cook on medium-high heat until equally brown. Strain and reserve.
- On a baking sheet, put 8 toast slices. Add a cheese slice, 2 slices of bacon, and a pineapple slice on each. Then broil until cheese is dissolved. Then serve right away.

Nutrition Information

- Calories: 491 calories;
- Total Fat: 35.4
- Sodium: 819
- Total Carbohydrate: 27.1
- Cholesterol: 68
- Protein: 15.5

---

841. Hawaiian Tuna Sandwich

Serving: 4 | Prep: 10mins | Cook: 15mins | Ready in:

Ingredients

- 4 hamburger buns, split
- 2 tablespoons butter
- 1 (5 ounce) can tuna chunks in olive oil
- 1 tablespoon lemon juice
- salt and freshly ground black pepper to taste
- 1 dash chili powder
- 1 cup shredded lettuce
- 1 cup shredded mozzarella cheese
- 4 canned pineapple rings

Direction

- Prepare the oven by preheating to 350°F (175°C). Then toast hamburger buns, and use butter to spread on cut sides.
- Strain half of the oil from tuna. In a small bowl, mix chili powder, pepper, salt, lemon juice, the rest of the oil, and tuna. Then fill every toasted bun with the tuna salad, a pineapple ring, mozzarella cheese, and shredded lettuce.

- Transfer sandwiches on a baking sheet, then heat for about 10-12 minutes until cheese dissolves.

Nutrition Information

- Calories: 349 calories;
- Sodium: 617
- Total Carbohydrate: 32.5
- Cholesterol: 39
- Protein: 20.1
- Total Fat: 15.1

842.   Healthier BBQ Pork For Sandwiches

Serving: 12 | Prep: 15mins | Cook: 4hours30mins |Ready in:

Ingredients

- 1 (14 ounce) can beef broth
- 3 pounds boneless pork ribs
- 1 cup shredded carrot
- 4 1/2 fluid ounces barbeque sauce
- 4 1/2 ounces mesquite sauce

Direction

- In the slow cooker, pour the beef broth and add the pork ribs. Let it cook for about 4 hours on High, until the meat easily shreds. Take out the meat and use 2 forks to shred it.
- Set an oven to preheat to 175°C (350°F). Move the shredded pork to a frying pan or Dutch oven and mix in the mesquite sauce, barbecue sauce and carrots.
- Let it bake in the preheated oven for about 30 minutes, until heated through.

Nutrition Information

- Calories: 313 calories;
- Cholesterol: 83

- Protein: 30.3
- Total Fat: 18.1
- Sodium: 290
- Total Carbohydrate: 5.1

843.   Hearty Meatball Sandwich

Serving: 6 | Prep: 15mins | Cook: 1hours5mins |Ready in:

Ingredients

- 1 1/2 pounds lean ground beef
- 1/3 cup Italian seasoned bread crumbs
- 1/2 small onion, chopped
- 1 teaspoon salt
- 1/2 cup shredded mozzarella cheese, divided
- 1 tablespoon cracked black pepper
- 1 teaspoon garlic powder
- 1/2 cup marinara sauce
- 3 hoagie rolls, split lengthwise

Direction

- Set oven to 175° C (350° F) and start preheating.
- In a medium bowl, combine 1/2 mozzarella cheese, garlic powder, salt and pepper, onion, bread crumbs, and ground beef. Shape into a log and put on an 8x8-in. baking dish.
- Place in the preheated oven and bake till the center is not pink anymore, about 50 minutes. Let sit 5 minutes; cut into 1/2-in. slices. Arrange some slices on each hoagie roll, pour in marinara sauce to cover then sprinkle with the rest of mozzarella cheese.
- Use aluminum foil to wrap each sandwich; bring back to the oven until cheese is melted and bread is slightly toasted, about 15 minutes. Let sit for 15 minutes. Enjoy. Each sandwich can serve two.

Nutrition Information

- Calories: 491 calories;
- Total Carbohydrate: 43.1
- Cholesterol: 75
- Protein: 29.3
- Total Fat: 21.4
- Sodium: 1068

844.   Homemade Lunch Combination

Serving: 1 | Prep: 10mins | Cook: |Ready in:

Ingredients

- 6 wheat crackers (such as Wheat Thins®)
- 3 slices reduced-sodium turkey
- 2 slices reduced-fat Cheddar cheese, quartered
- 1 romaine lettuce leaf, torn into large pieces (optional)
- 1 roma tomato, sliced (optional)

Direction

- Put crackers in a small, closable plastic bag. Put the Cheddar cheese squares and turkey in another closable plastic bag. Put the lettuce and tomato in a third closable plastic bag.
- Serve by piling up Cheddar cheese, turkey, lettuce, and tomato on the wheat crackers.

Nutrition Information

- Calories: 296 calories;
- Total Fat: 9.7
- Sodium: 890
- Total Carbohydrate: 17.7
- Cholesterol: 49
- Protein: 35.6

845.   Honduran Baleadas

Serving: 8 | Prep: 25mins | Cook: 2mins |Ready in:

Ingredients

- Tortillas:
- 2 cups all-purpose flour
- 1 cup water
- 1/2 cup vegetable oil
- 1 egg
- 1/2 teaspoon salt
- Filling:
- 2 cups refried beans, warmed
- 1 avocado, sliced
- 1/2 cup crumbled queso fresco (fresh white cheese)
- 1/4 cup crema fresca (fresh cream)

Direction

- In a big bowl, combine salt, egg, vegetable oil, water and flour; knead till dough is smooth and no sticky anymore.
- Shape the dough into 8 golf ball-sized balls. Put cover and allow to sit for 20 minutes.
- Expand every dough round into a thick tortilla.
- Over medium -high heat, heat a big skillet. Cook every tortilla for a minute each side till slightly puffed and browned.
- Arrange queso fresco, avocado and refried beans on top of tortillas. Sprinkle with crema over; fold the tortillas in 1/2 on top of the filling.

Nutrition Information

- Calories: 390 calories;
- Total Fat: 23.1
- Sodium: 368
- Total Carbohydrate: 36.9
- Cholesterol: 43
- Protein: 10.1

846. Hot Curried Tuna Sandwiches

Serving: 4 | Prep: 10mins | Cook: 3mins | Ready in:

Ingredients

- 1 (5 ounce) can tuna, drained
- 1/4 cup finely chopped celery
- 1/4 cup chopped green onion
- 2 tablespoons mayonnaise
- 1 tablespoon lemon juice
- 1/2 teaspoon curry powder, or to taste
- 2 English muffins, split, toasted and buttered
- 4 thin slices Cheddar cheese

Direction

- Preheat the oven's broiler.
- Stir curry powder, lemon juice, mayonnaise, green onion, celery and tuna together in a moderate-sized bowl. Scoop onto each English muffin half an even amount of the mix, then put a cheese slice on top of each. Put the sandwiches on a baking sheet.
- Broil until toasty and cheese has melted, or 2-3 minutes. Serve hot.

Nutrition Information

- Calories: 213 calories;
- Total Carbohydrate: 14.5
- Cholesterol: 27
- Protein: 14
- Total Fat: 10.9
- Sodium: 246

847. Hot Dogs With Pineapple Bacon Chipotle Slaw

Serving: 8 | Prep: 30mins | Cook: 8mins | Ready in:

Ingredients

- 1 head green cabbage, finely shredded
- 1 cup finely shredded red cabbage
- 3/4 cup finely chopped pineapple
- 1 large carrot, finely shredded
- 5 slices cooked bacon, chopped
- 1/2 red onion, grated
- 1/4 cup chopped fresh parsley
- 3/4 cup mayonnaise
- 1/4 cup apple cider vinegar
- 3 chipotle chiles in adobo sauce, pureed
- 2 tablespoons white sugar
- 1 tablespoon honey
- 1 tablespoon Dijon mustard
- 1/2 teaspoon onion powder
- 1/2 teaspoon garlic powder
- 1/2 teaspoon celery salt
- 1/2 teaspoon salt
- 1/2 teaspoon ground black pepper
- 8 kosher all-beef hot dogs
- 8 hot dog buns

Direction

- In a big bowl, mix parsley, red onion, bacon, carrot, pineapple, red cabbage and green cabbage.
- In a bowl, beat pepper, salt, celery salt, garlic powder, onion powder, Dijon mustard, honey, sugar, chipotle puree, apple cider vinegar and mayonnaise till well incorporates. Put on top of cabbage mixture and toss thoroughly. Allow to sit for a minimum of 15 minutes prior serving.
- Preheat the outdoor grill for high heat and grease grate lightly. Grill the hot dogs for 7 minutes in all till golden brown on every side. Put to plate. On the grill, put the buns cut-side facing down and let grill for 20 seconds till lightly golden brown.
- In the buns, put the hot dogs and cabbage slaw over.

Nutrition Information

- Calories: 519 calories;
- Cholesterol: 36

- Protein: 13.1
- Total Fat: 33.4
- Sodium: 1269
- Total Carbohydrate: 43.1

---

848. Hot Shredded Chicken Sandwiches

Serving: 12 | Prep: 5mins | Cook: 20mins | Ready in:

Ingredients

- 1 (3 pound) chicken - cooked, deboned and shredded
- 2 (10.75 ounce) cans condensed cream of mushroom soup
- 1/2 teaspoon poultry seasoning
- 1/4 (16 ounce) package buttery round crackers, crushed
- 12 hamburger buns

Direction

- Over medium heat, mix crushed crackers, shredded chicken, poultry seasoning, and condensed soup in a large saucepan. Cook while stirring often for 15 to 20 minutes until the mixture is hot. Serve on top of the buns.

Nutrition Information

- Calories: 367 calories;
- Total Fat: 16.5
- Sodium: 707
- Total Carbohydrate: 30.6
- Cholesterol: 56
- Protein: 22.5

---

849. Indian Tacos

Serving: 6 | Prep: 20mins | Cook: 20mins | Ready in:

Ingredients

- 2 cups all-purpose flour
- 1 tablespoon baking powder
- 1/2 teaspoon white sugar
- 1/2 teaspoon salt
- 1 1/2 cups lukewarm water
- 2 cups oil for frying, or as needed
- 1 pound ground beef
- 1 (1.25 ounce) package chili seasoning mix
- 1 (15 ounce) can kidney beans, drained
- 2 cups shredded Cheddar cheese
- 2 cups chopped iceberg lettuce
- 2 tomatoes, chopped
- 1 cup sour cream

Direction

- Whisk salt, sugar, baking powder and flour in big bowl; mix water in just till somewhat sticky dough forms. Put aside to rest as oil preheats.
- Heat oil to 190°C/375°F in deep-fryer/big saucepan.
- Divide dough to 6 even portions; flatten every portion to round disc to same size of your palm.
- Fry dough discs in hot oil, one by one, for 2 minutes till 1 side turns brown. Use tongs to flip; cook for 1 more minute till both sides turn brown. On paper towels, drain fry bread; repeat with leftover dough.
- Mix and cook ground beef in skillet on medium heat; mix kidney beans and chili seasoning in. Cook for 5 minutes till heated through.
- On plate, put fry bread; put a portion of chili mixture, sour cream, tomatoes, lettuce and shredded cheddar cheese over each.

Nutrition Information

- Calories: 696 calories;
- Total Carbohydrate: 50.5
- Cholesterol: 103
- Protein: 32.6
- Total Fat: 40.9

- Sodium: 1371

850. Instant Pot® Pulled Chicken

Serving: 10 | Prep: 10mins | Cook: 1hours | Ready in:

Ingredients

- 2 teaspoons kosher salt
- 1 1/2 teaspoons smoked paprika
- 1 teaspoon garlic powder
- 1/2 teaspoon onion powder
- 1/2 teaspoon ground black pepper
- 2 1/2 pounds skinless, boneless chicken breasts, or more to taste
- 1 cup water
- 1 teaspoon hickory-flavored liquid smoke
- 10 hamburger buns, or as needed
- 1 cup barbeque sauce

Direction

- In a bowl, combine pepper, salt, paprika, onion powder, and garlic powder. Slice the chicken in 3-4- inch pieces and transfer to a big zip top bag. Add the salt mixture on chicken; seal and shake to cover completely.
- In a multi-function cooker like an Instant Pot®, pour water and arrange the wire rack. Place the chicken on top of rack; secure lid. Put the cooker on Meat/Poultry mode and put timer for 50 minutes. Let the pressure build for 10-15 minutes.
- Let the pressure out naturally in accordance with the cooker's manual, 10 minutes.
- Put the chicken in a bowl and shred with 2 forks. Mix in with shredded chicken liquid smoke and half cup of liquid from cooker. Serve the chicken on buns with barbeque sauce on top.

Nutrition Information

- Calories: 282 calories;
- Total Fat: 5.1
- Sodium: 953
- Total Carbohydrate: 31.2
- Cholesterol: 59
- Protein: 25.8

851. Italian "Stuffed" Toast (Toast Farcito)

Serving: 2 | Prep: 10mins | Cook: 3mins | Ready in:

Ingredients

- 2 slices prosciutto
- 2 slices fontina cheese
- 4 slices thinly sliced sandwich bread
- 1/4 cup chopped giardiniera (pickled Italian vegetables)
- 2 hot pickled peppers (optional)

Direction

- Follow the manufacturer's directions to bring panino press to a heat.
- Put 1 fontina cheese and 1 prosciutto slice over a bread slice; do the same with other bread slice, fontina cheese and the leftover prosciutto. Put half of giardiniera over each cheese layer and top with 2 other bread slices to make 2 sandwiches.
- Cook each panino for about 3 minutes in the press until bread is heated through and cheese is melted. Serve alongside hot pickled peppers.

Nutrition Information

- Calories: 310 calories;
- Sodium: 887
- Total Carbohydrate: 29
- Cholesterol: 46
- Protein: 14.2
- Total Fat: 15.1

852.   Italian Style Beef Sandwiches

Serving: 6 | Prep: 10mins | Cook: 5hours | Ready in:

Ingredients

- 2 1/2 cups water
- 1 packet dry onion soup mix
- 2 tablespoons Worcestershire sauce
- 1 teaspoon garlic powder
- 1 teaspoon dried marjoram
- 1 teaspoon dried thyme
- 1 teaspoon dried oregano
- 4 pounds chuck roast
- 1 (10 ounce) package frozen bell pepper stir-fry mix

Direction

- Mix the oregano with thyme, marjoram, garlic powder, Worcestershire sauce, soup blend and water in a slow cooker.
- Put in the stir-fry blend and meat. Cook on high setting for half a day or on low setting for the whole day until the meat falls apart. Pull meat apart, then mix all together.

Nutrition Information

- Calories: 634 calories;
- Cholesterol: 197
- Protein: 59
- Total Fat: 40.7
- Sodium: 389
- Total Carbohydrate: 4.7

853.   Jamaican Turkey Sandwich

Serving: 6 | Prep: 35mins | Cook: 6hours | Ready in:

Ingredients

- Pulled Turkey:
- 1/2 cup chopped celery
- 1/3 cup chopped green onion
- 1 (2 pound) skinless, boneless turkey breast, cut into 8 ounce chunks
- 1/2 cup juice from canned pineapple
- 1/4 cup sweet chile sauce
- 3 tablespoons distilled white vinegar
- 2 tablespoons water
- 1 tablespoon beef bouillon granules
- 2 teaspoons garlic powder
- 6 canned pineapple rings
- Coleslaw Topping:
- 1/4 cup mayonnaise
- 1 tablespoon lemon juice
- 2 tablespoons chopped fresh parsley
- 1/2 cup chopped onion
- 2 cups chopped cabbage
- 1 cup shredded Cheddar cheese
- salt and black pepper to taste
- 6 Kaiser rolls, split

Direction

- In the bottom of a slow cooker, sprinkle green onions and celery; top with turkey chunks. Mix together garlic powder, beef bouillon, water, vinegar, sweet chile sauce, and pineapple juice; pour over the turkey. On the turkey chunks, put pineapple rings.
- Cook on Low for 6-7 hours until the turkey is easy to pull apart.
- In the meantime, prepare the coleslaw: In a mixing bowl, combine onion, parsley, lemon juice, and mayonnaise. Add Cheddar cheese and cabbage, season with pepper and salt to taste. Put a cover on and chill in the fridge while the turkey is cooking.
- When the turkey is soft, use 2 forks to shred. On a Kaiser roll, stack a pineapple ring and

some of the shredded turkey, put coleslaw on top and enjoy.

Nutrition Information

- Calories: 524 calories;
- Total Fat: 16.5
- Sodium: 808
- Total Carbohydrate: 42.8
- Cholesterol: 133
- Protein: 49.4

854. Jeff's Sloppy Joes

Serving: 8 | Prep: 10mins | Cook: 10mins |Ready in:

Ingredients

- 2 tablespoons olive oil
- 1 cup chopped onion
- 2 cloves garlic, minced
- 1/2 cup chopped green bell pepper
- 1 stalk celery, chopped
- 1/2 teaspoon dried oregano
- 1 pound ground beef
- 1/2 pound Italian sausage
- 1 (12 fluid ounce) can or bottle chili sauce
- 2 tablespoons red wine vinegar
- 1 tablespoon Worcestershire sauce
- 2 teaspoons brown sugar
- salt and pepper to taste

Direction

- In a large skillet, heat the oil over medium heat. Add the oregano, onion, green bell pepper, garlic and celery. Sauté for approximately 5 minutes until onion is softened. Remove to a plate and set aside.
- Combine the sausage and ground beef in the same skillet and sauté over medium high heat for around 10 minutes until browned well. Mix in chili sauce, the reserved onion mixture, brown sugar, Worcestershire sauce and

vinegar, then mix well. Add pepper and salt to taste.

Nutrition Information

- Calories: 235 calories;
- Sodium: 296
- Total Carbohydrate: 8.9
- Cholesterol: 46
- Protein: 14.9
- Total Fat: 15.4

855. Kid Approved Bento Toolbox Lunch

Serving: 1 | Prep: 15mins | Cook: |Ready in:

Ingredients

- 2 tablespoons peanut butter, or to taste
- 1 (7 inch) whole wheat tortilla
- 1 apple, sliced
- 4 grape tomatoes, or to taste
- 4 yellow grape tomatoes, or to taste
- 3 celery sticks, or to taste
- 4 baby carrots, or to taste
- 2 tablespoons ranch dressing, or to taste

Direction

- Spread the peanut butter over the tortilla. Arrange the apple slices from the end to end and down to the middle of the tortilla. Roll it up tightly and divide into small pieces.
- Assemble the bento box with the tortillas pieces, golden tomatoes, carrots, celery, and grape tomatoes. Serve them together with ranch dressing.

Nutrition Information

- Calories: 476 calories;
- Total Fat: 33.1
- Sodium: 719

- Total Carbohydrate: 42.5
- Cholesterol: 8
- Protein: 13.8

856. Kings Flat Iron Steak Sandwich

Serving: 4 | Prep: 20mins | Cook: 15mins | Ready in:

Ingredients

- 4 sandwich rolls, partially split
- 4 teaspoons softened butter
- 2 teaspoons garlic powder
- 2 tablespoons vegetable oil
- 4 (4 ounce) thinly-cut flat iron steaks
- 1/2 cup fresh spinach leaves
- 1 tomato, sliced
- 1 avocado, sliced
- 8 thick slices fresh mozzarella cheese
- 2 teaspoons balsamic vinegar, for drizzling

Direction

- Prepare an oven broiler for high heat.
- Open the sandwich rolls; spread 1 teaspoon of softened butter over each roll. Scatter approximately 1/2 teaspoon garlic powder over each buttered sandwich roll.
- Broil the sandwich rolls under the preheated broiler until edges are slightly charred, about 5 minutes. Put to one side.
- Bring a large, heavy skillet to high heat on the stove, and put in vegetable oil. Once oil just starts to smoke, add the flat iron steaks and sear quickly for about 3 minutes until browned. Turn the steaks over, and sear the remaining side for 3 more minutes; immediately take steaks out of the pan, or reduce the burner temperature and cook until desired doneness is reached. Put steaks to one side and keep warm.
- To build the sandwich roll, place spinach leaves, tomato, and avocado slices, respectively, on one side, and 2 mozzarella

cheese slices on the other side. Scatter approximately 1/2 teaspoon balsamic vinegar over the avocado and tomato side, and lay a hot browned steak on the mozzarella cheese. Fold each sandwich carefully and serve.

Nutrition Information

- Calories: 890 calories;
- Sodium: 1134
- Total Carbohydrate: 43.2
- Cholesterol: 161
- Protein: 59.5
- Total Fat: 54.5

857. Lebanese Chicken Shawarma

Serving: 4 | Prep: 15mins | Cook: 10mins | Ready in:

Ingredients

- 1 cup plain yogurt
- 1/4 cup lemon juice
- 2 tablespoons olive oil
- 1 tablespoon tomato paste
- 3 cloves garlic, minced
- 1 teaspoon ground cumin
- 1 teaspoon ground coriander
- 1/2 teaspoon salt
- 1/2 teaspoon ground black pepper
- 1/4 teaspoon red pepper flakes
- 2 pounds skinless, boneless chicken breasts, cut into 1/2-inch strips

Direction

- In a bowl, combine red pepper flakes, pepper, salt, coriander, cumin, garlic, tomato paste, olive oil, lemon juice and yogurt together. Stir in chicken strips. Use plastic wrap to cover the bowl; put into the refrigerator overnight or for 8 hours to marinate.

- Position the rack 6 inches away from heat source; turn on the oven's broiler to preheat.
- Take the chicken out of the bowl; on a broiling pan, arrange in a single layer. Throw away excess marinade.
- Put the chicken into the oven's broiler to broil for 10 minutes until juices run clear, flipping once. An instant-read thermometer should register at least 165°F (74°C) when inserted into the center.

Nutrition Information

- Calories: 365 calories;
- Sodium: 480
- Total Carbohydrate: 7.9
- Cholesterol: 133
- Protein: 51
- Total Fat: 13.4

858.   Leftover Dog Pile

Serving: 1 | Prep: 10mins | Cook: 5mins | Ready in:

Ingredients

- 2 hot dogs
- 3/4 cup chili with beans
- 1 slice bread
- 1/4 cup shredded Cheddar cheese, divided
- 1 tablespoon chopped onion
- 2 tablespoons prepared yellow mustard

Direction

- In a microwave safe plate, put some hotdogs and put in the microwave to cook for 1 to 2 minutes to heat. Microwave for chili placed in a microwave safe bowl for 1 to 2 minutes to heat. Cut the hotdogs to half vertically, and put in the bread slice cut-side bottom. Put the cheese that's left, onion mustard and the chili.

Nutrition Information

- Calories: 892 calories;
- Protein: 38.8
- Total Fat: 66
- Sodium: 3092
- Total Carbohydrate: 40.5
- Cholesterol: 150

859.   Leftover Meatloaf Sandwich

Serving: 1 | Prep: 5mins | Cook: 5mins | Ready in:

Ingredients

- 2 slices leftover meatloaf
- 4 thin slices Cheddar cheese
- 1 teaspoon mayonnaise, or to taste
- 1 teaspoon ketchup, or to taste
- 1 teaspoon mustard, or to taste (optional)
- 2 slices bread, toasted

Direction

- In a nonstick pan over medium heat, add meatloaf slices. Add 2 slices of Cheddar cheese on top of each loaf. Cook for 3-5 minutes until the bottom of meatloaf is browned and it is heated through. Turn 1 piece of meatloaf over the other so that the cheese is in the center.
- Spread mustard, ketchup and mayonnaise over the toast. Sandwich the toast with cheesy meatloaf to serve.

Nutrition Information

- Calories: 689 calories;
- Sodium: 1047
- Total Carbohydrate: 40.2
- Cholesterol: 206
- Total Fat: 34.4
- Protein: 52.8

860.   Leftover Salmon Lunch Wrap

Serving: 2 | Prep: 15mins | Cook: 11mins | Ready in:

Ingredients

- 1 (15 ounce) can black beans, drained
- 1 (3 ounce) fillet cooked salmon
- 2 (6 inch) flour tortillas
- 1 red bell pepper, thinly sliced
- 1 green bell pepper, thinly sliced
- 1 small avocado, halved and sliced

Direction

- On medium-low heat, cook black beans in a small pan for 5 minutes until the beans are warmed through.
- In a covered skillet, reheat the leftover salmon, 3-5 minutes on each side over medium-low heat. Cut into bite-size pieces.
- Place an even amount of black beans and salmon on each tortilla. Add avocado slices, green bell pepper, and red bell peppers. Wrap up the tortillas and serve.

Nutrition Information

- Calories: 519 calories;
- Protein: 28.2
- Total Fat: 17.7
- Sodium: 1054
- Total Carbohydrate: 65.2
- Cholesterol: 23

861.   Lemon Dill Tuna Melt Sandwiches

Serving: 6 | Prep: 10mins | Cook: 5mins | Ready in:

Ingredients

- 6 slices white bread

- 2 (5 ounce) cans tuna, drained
- 1/4 cup mayonnaise, or to taste
- 1 tablespoon lemon juice
- 1 tablespoon finely chopped lemon zest
- 1 tablespoon finely chopped fresh dill
- 1 large tomato, thinly sliced
- 6 slices Swiss cheese

Direction

- Position an oven rack around 6 in. from the heat; preheat the oven's broiler. Arrange bread on a baking sheet, in a single layer.
- Lightly toast the bread on both sides in the preheated oven for around 1 minute per side.
- In a bowl, mix dill, lemon zest, lemon juice, mayonnaise and tuna together. Evenly spread the tuna mixture over each slice of bread. Place tomato slices atop the tuna mixture; sprinkle Swiss cheese on top.
- Turn the baking sheet back to the oven; broil for 3-5 minutes longer, or till the cheese is melted.

Nutrition Information

- Calories: 296 calories;
- Total Fat: 16.4
- Sodium: 300
- Total Carbohydrate: 16.1
- Cholesterol: 42
- Protein: 20.6

862.   Lemony Avocado Toast

Serving: 2 | Prep: 20mins | Cook: 2mins | Ready in:

Ingredients

- 1 avocado, chopped
- 4 radishes, minced
- 3 tablespoons minced cilantro, or to taste
- olive oil
- 1 squeeze lime juice

- 1 squeeze lemon juice
- 1 dash salt and ground black pepper to taste
- 2 slices bread
- 1/2 cup alfalfa sprouts, or to taste

Direction

- In a bowl, mix pepper, salt, lemon juice, lime juice, olive oil, cilantro, radishes and avocado. Crush roughly, keeping a few chunks of avocado.
- Then toast the bread for about 2 minutes until it is crispy and nice. Put avocado mixture over the bread and spread equally. Put sprouts and add salt to taste.

Nutrition Information

- Calories: 261 calories;
- Total Fat: 18.2
- Sodium: 378
- Total Carbohydrate: 23.1
- Cholesterol: 0
- Protein: 5.1

---

863.   Lentil Sloppy Joes

Serving: 10 | Prep: 20mins | Cook: 40mins | Ready in:

Ingredients

- 1 tablespoon coconut oil
- 1/2 cup finely chopped onion
- 1/3 cup finely chopped green bell peppers
- 3 1/4 cups water
- 2 cups truRoots® Organic Sprouted Green Lentils
- 1 1/2 cups ketchup
- 2 teaspoons mustard
- 2 tablespoons brown cane sugar
- 2 teaspoons apple cider vinegar
- 1/2 teaspoon fine sea salt
- 1/4 teaspoon black pepper
- 5 small (4 inch) pita pockets, halved

Direction

- In a large saucepan, over medium-high heat, melt coconut oil. Add peppers and onion. Sauté until softened. Add water. Bring to a boil over high heat. Lower to simmer. Stir in lentils. Cook until lentils become tender or for 25-30 minutes.
- Add pepper, salt, vinegar, brown sugar, mustard and ketchup. Simmer while stirring occasionally until slightly thickened or for 10 minutes.
- Serve in pitas.

Nutrition Information

- Calories: 213 calories;
- Cholesterol: 0
- Protein: 10.1
- Total Fat: 2.5
- Sodium: 587
- Total Carbohydrate: 40.6

---

864.   Loose Meat On A Bun, Restaurant Style

Serving: 12 | Prep: 10mins | Cook: 50mins | Ready in:

Ingredients

- 3 pounds ground beef
- 1/4 cup minced onion
- 3 tablespoons Worcestershire sauce
- 4 cups beef broth
- 1 teaspoon salt
- 1 teaspoon ground black pepper
- 2 teaspoons butter
- 12 hamburger buns, split

Direction

- Crumble onion and ground beef into a big skillet over moderately high heat. Cook the mixture until beef is not pink anymore while stirring to break up lumps. Drain off grease and bring skillet back to the stove. Put in butter, pepper, salt, beef broth and Worcestershire sauce. Bring the mixture to a boil then set the heat to low and simmer without a cover for 40 minutes, until liquid is nearly completely gone. Take away from the heat, place on a cover and allow to rest about 15 minutes prior to serving on buns.

Nutrition Information

- Calories: 341 calories;
- Total Fat: 16.4
- Sodium: 810
- Total Carbohydrate: 22.9
- Cholesterol: 71
- Protein: 23.6

---

865. Lorraine's Club Sandwich

Serving: 1 | Prep: 5mins | Cook: 5mins | Ready in:

Ingredients

- 2 slices bacon
- 3 slices bread, toasted
- 3 tablespoons mayonnaise
- 2 leaves lettuce
- 2 (1 ounce) slices cooked deli turkey breast
- 2 slices tomato

Direction

- In a heavy skillet, place bacon. Cook until evenly brown on medium-high heat. Drain on paper towels.
- Spread mayonnaise on each slice of bread. On a slice of toast, place lettuce and turkey. Cover with a slice of toast, then bacon and tomato. Cover with the last slice of toast.

Nutrition Information

- Calories: 818 calories;
- Protein: 22.4
- Total Fat: 61.7
- Sodium: 1874
- Total Carbohydrate: 44.2
- Cholesterol: 76

---

866. Lunch Box Hot Hot Dogs

Serving: 1 | Prep: 5mins | Cook: 10mins | Ready in:

Ingredients

- 1 all-beef hot dog
- 1 hot dog bun
- 1 packet ketchup
- 1 packet prepared yellow mustard
- 2 tablespoons shredded Cheddar cheese

Direction

- Assemble your child's lunch box by packing the Cheddar cheese, ketchup, hotdog bun and mustard.
- Preheat your kid's insulated water bottle by pouring in boiling water. Let it sit, 15-20 minutes. Let the kettle heat while your kids get ready for school. Before they leave, throw out the water and pour more boiling water. The preheating makes the water bottle stay hot longer. Put hotdog into the water and seal the lid.
- When your child takes their lunch, they can get the hotdog out of the bottle and put it on the bun. Drizzle with mustard, cheese and ketchup for a hot lunch.

Nutrition Information

- Calories: 384 calories;
- Total Fat: 24.4
- Sodium: 1083
- Total Carbohydrate: 25.6

- Cholesterol: 48
- Protein: 15

867. Lunch Box Pita Pockets

Serving: 1 | Prep: 10mins | Cook: | Ready in:

Ingredients

- 1/2 cup deli ham, chopped
- 1/2 cup shredded lettuce
- 1/4 cup shredded carrot
- 1/4 cup Ranch dressing
- 1 pita bread round, cut in half

Direction

- In a resealable plastic bag, place the carrot, lettuce, and ham. In a small resealable container, pour the ranch dressing. Use a plastic wrap to wrap the pita bread. Place the ranch dressing, pita bread, and ham mixture in a lunch bag or box together with a spoon.
- Fill each pita half with the ham mixture using a spoon to assemble the pita pocket. Drizzle the ranch dressing over the top.

Nutrition Information

- Calories: 558 calories;
- Sodium: 1744
- Total Carbohydrate: 36.6
- Cholesterol: 55
- Protein: 17.1
- Total Fat: 37.7

868. M's Sloppy Joe Sauce

Serving: 4 | Prep: 20mins | Cook: 15mins | Ready in:

Ingredients

- 1 tablespoon extra-virgin olive oil
- 1 large onion, diced
- 1 green bell pepper, diced
- 1 tablespoon minced garlic
- 1 pound ground turkey
- 1 cup canned pureed tomatoes
- 1/4 cup barbeque sauce (such as KC Masterpiece®)
- 2 tablespoons ketchup
- 2 tablespoons white vinegar
- 2 tablespoons Worcestershire sauce
- 1 tablespoon brown mustard
- 1 tablespoon chile-garlic sauce (such as Sriracha®)

Direction

- In a frying pan, heat olive oil over medium heat. In the hot oil, cook bell pepper and onion for 5 minutes until they start to get tender. Add ground turkey or garlic to the frying pan, stir and cook for 5-7 minutes until the turkey is brown and very crumbly.
- Mix chile-garlic sauce, mustard, Worcestershire sauce, vinegar, ketchup, barbeque sauce, and pureed tomatoes into the turkey mixture. Simmer for another 7-10 minutes until fully heated.

Nutrition Information

- Calories: 287 calories;
- Total Fat: 12.4
- Sodium: 865
- Total Carbohydrate: 21
- Cholesterol: 84
- Protein: 24.6

869. Make Ahead Cheesy Joe's

Serving: 16 | Prep: 20mins | Cook: 20mins | Ready in:

Ingredients

- 2 pounds ground beef
- 1 large onion, finely chopped
- 1 (10 ounce) jar sweet pickle relish, drained
- 16 hamburger buns, split
- 2 (15 ounce) jars processed cheese sauce (such as Cheez Whiz®)

Direction

- On moderately-high heat, heat a big skillet and mix in onion and ground beef. Cook and mix till beef is not pink anymore, equally browned and crumbly. Let drain and throw any extra grease. Mix in relish.
- On every bun half, scatter processed cheese sauce, put a scoop mixture of meat among halves. Wrap foil on every sandwich and freeze or refrigerate till using. Bake in prepped to 175 ° C or 350 ° F oven till hot for 5 to 10 minutes if chilled and 20 minutes in case frozen.

Nutrition Information

- Calories: 397 calories;
- Protein: 19.7
- Total Fat: 20.1
- Sodium: 1291
- Total Carbohydrate: 33.6
- Cholesterol: 74

---

870. Maple Tuna Olive Toastie

Serving: 4 | Prep: 10mins | Cook: 15mins | Ready in:

Ingredients

- 2 tablespoons butter
- 1/2 large sweet red onion, thinly sliced
- 1 tablespoon maple syrup
- 2 (5 ounce) cans tuna, drained
- 2 tablespoons creamy salad dressing (such as Miracle Whip®)

- salt and ground black pepper to taste
- 1 (12 ounce) loaf Italian olive bread
- 8 ounces shredded Cheddar cheese

Direction

- Melt butter over medium heat in a small frying pan; cook onion in melted butter, stirring while cooking, for 3 minutes. Turn heat to medium-low, whisk in maple syrup, and cook for 7 to 10 minutes or until onions are tender and golden.
- Position oven rack approximately 8 inches away from the heat source and turn oven's broiler on to preheat.
- In a mixing bowl, toss tuna with salad dressing; sprinkle with pepper and salt to season. Cut bread loaf horizontally in half, then cut both pieces in half lengthways, making 4 equal portions. Arrange bread on a baking sheet, crust-side down. Place tuna mixture, onion, and cheddar cheese in separate layers over pieces of bread.
- Broil for about 5 minutes in the preheated oven until cheese bubbles.

Nutrition Information

- Calories: 624 calories;
- Sodium: 1019
- Total Carbohydrate: 49.3
- Cholesterol: 96
- Protein: 37.9
- Total Fat: 29.9

---

871. Marsala Pork Chop Sandwich With Hot And Sweet Dipping Sauce

Serving: 6 | Prep: 15mins | Cook: 10mins | Ready in:

Ingredients

- 1 cup Marsala wine

- 2 cups honey
- 4 cloves garlic, minced
- 4 small pork chops, cut into thin strips
- Dipping Sauce:
- 1 cup rice vinegar
- 1 cup white sugar
- 2 cloves garlic, minced
- 1/2 teaspoon salt
- 1/2 teaspoon red pepper flakes
- 6 French rolls, split
- 1/4 head lettuce, chopped

Direction

- In a bowl, mix together 4 minced garlic cloves, honey, and wine; put in the pork. Put the pork in the fridge to marinate, about 8 hours or overnight.
- In a saucepan, boil vinegar; add sugar and cook for 2-3 minutes until melted. Add red pepper flakes, salt, and 2 minced garlic cloves; whisk until the dipping sauce has evenly blended.
- Remove the marinade and pork to a saucepan on medium heat, cook while stirring for 5-10 minutes until the pork has fully cooked.
- In French rolls, put the pork mixture and top with lettuce. Enjoy the sandwiches with the dipping sauce.

Nutrition Information

- Calories: 819 calories;
- Sodium: 525
- Total Carbohydrate: 160.5
- Cholesterol: 42
- Protein: 20.9
- Total Fat: 9.8

---

872.   Mary Pat's Tuna Melt

Serving: 2 | Prep: 20mins | Cook: 4mins | Ready in:

Ingredients

- 1 (5 ounce) can olive-oil packed tuna, undrained
- 1/4 cup mayonnaise
- 1 teaspoon Dijon mustard
- 1 dill pickle, chopped
- 2 tablespoons minced red onion
- 4 slices rustic whole-grain bread
- 4 slices Irish Cheddar cheese
- 2 tablespoons whipped cream cheese, divided
- 1 cup coarsely crushed potato chips (such as Utz®)
- 2 tablespoons mayonnaise, divided

Direction

- In a small bowl, combine Dijon mustard, quarter cup mayonnaise, tuna, red onion, and pickle. Slather mixture on two bread slices; add two slices Cheddar cheese on top.
- Slather a tablespoon of cream cheese over the leftover two bread slices; put over the Cheddar cheese.
- Pour crushed chips in a bowl. Slather 1 1/2tsp mayonnaise on top of every tuna melt then push the top down into crushed chips. Do the same on the other side.
- On medium-high heat, toast tuna melts in a heated dry grill pan for 2 mins on each side until golden.

Nutrition Information

- Calories: 1042 calories;
- Total Fat: 76.6
- Sodium: 1806
- Total Carbohydrate: 46.5
- Cholesterol: 107
- Protein: 43.5

---

873.   Meatball Sandwich

Serving: 4 | Prep: 20mins | Cook: 20mins | Ready in:

Ingredients

- 1 pound ground beef
- 3/4 cup bread crumbs
- 2 teaspoons dried Italian seasoning
- 2 cloves garlic, minced
- 2 tablespoons chopped fresh parsley
- 2 tablespoons grated Parmesan cheese
- 1 egg, beaten
- 1 French baguette
- 1 tablespoon extra-virgin olive oil
- 1/2 teaspoon garlic powder
- 1 pinch salt, or to taste
- 1 (14 ounce) jar spaghetti sauce
- 4 slices provolone cheese

Direction

- Preheat an oven to 175°C/350°F.
- By hand, mix egg, Parmesan cheese, parsley, garlic, Italian seasoning, breadcrumbs, and ground beef gently in a medium bowl. Form to 12 meatballs; put in a baking dish.
- In the preheated oven, bake till cooked through for 15-20 minutes. Meanwhile, lengthwise, cut baguette in half. Remove some bread from the inside to create a well for meatballs. Brush olive oil on; season with salt and garlic powder. Slip baguette into oven at final 5 minutes of meatball's time till lightly toasted.
- As bread toasts, warm spaghetti sauce in saucepan on medium heat. When meatballs are done, transfer meatballs into sauce with a slotted spoon; put on baguette. Top with provolone cheese slices. Put in oven to melt the cheese for 2-3 minutes. Slightly cool; cut to servings. Serve.

Nutrition Information

- Calories: 781 calories;
- Cholesterol: 141
- Protein: 43.6
- Total Fat: 31.9
- Sodium: 1473
- Total Carbohydrate: 78.2

874.   Mexican Steak Torta

Serving: 4 | Prep: 20mins | Cook: 15mins | Ready in:

Ingredients

- 1 pound sirloin steak
- 1 tablespoon garlic salt
- 1 teaspoon ground black pepper
- 1 teaspoon ground cumin
- ground cayenne pepper to taste
- 4 kaiser rolls, split
- 1/4 cup mayonnaise
- 1/2 cup refried beans
- 1 large avocado, thinly sliced
- 1 large tomato, sliced
- 2 cups shredded lettuce
- crumbled cotija cheese (optional)

Direction

- Start preheating outdoor grill to medium-high heat; oil grate lightly. Season the steak with cayenne pepper, cumin, black pepper and garlic salt.
- Grill the steak on prepared grill for 5 mins on each side, until medium-rare. Transfer from the heat onto cutting board. Wrap in foil.
- Over medium-high heat, set a large skillet. Spread mayonnaise over both halves of each roll. Brown rolls for 3 mins or until golden, the mayonnaise-side down. In a bowl, warm refried bean in microwave on High for one minute. Slice sirloin steak thinly into strips.
- Spread over bottom half of each roll with a thin layer of beans. Layer with the steak, the avocado and the tomato, then the lettuce. If preferred, sprinkle cheese over top. Close sandwich with the top of roll.

Nutrition Information

- Calories: 546 calories;
- Sodium: 1886
- Total Carbohydrate: 36.4

- Cholesterol: 64
- Protein: 29.4
- Total Fat: 32.3

Serving: 8 | Prep: 20mins | Cook: 50mins |Ready in:

Ingredients

- 1 pound ground beef
- 1/2 cup chopped onion
- 1/2 cup chopped green pepper
- 1/2 cup crushed butter-flavored crackers
- 1 egg
- 1 teaspoon Worcestershire sauce
- 1 teaspoon chopped garlic
- 1 teaspoon seasoned salt
- 1 teaspoon ground black pepper
- 1 (26.5 ounce) can spaghetti sauce
- 1/2 cup shredded mozzarella cheese
- 1/3 cup grated Parmesan cheese
- 8 dinner rolls, split

Direction

- Preheat the oven to 175 degrees C/350 degrees F.
- In a big bowl, mix egg, crackers, green pepper, onion and ground beef. Season with pepper, seasoned salt, garlic and Worcestershire sauce. Mix well. Form mixture to 8 meatballs. Put meatballs in a 9x13-in. baking dish.
- Bake meatballs for 20 minutes in preheated oven. Put spaghetti sauce into a big saucepan. Simmer on low heat. Mix baked meatballs into simmering sauce. Don't turn off the oven. Simmer sauce for about 20 minutes until meatballs cook fully.
- Between each roll, put 1 meatball, a bit of sauce, and a sprinkle of parmesan and mozzarella. Put sandwiches in the hot oven. Bake for about 7 minutes until cheeses melt.

Nutrition Information

- Calories: 351 calories;
- Protein: 18
- Total Fat: 16.4
- Sodium: 821
- Total Carbohydrate: 32.2

875.   Meyer Lemon Avocado Toast

Serving: 2 | Prep: 10mins | Cook: 3mins |Ready in:

Ingredients

- 2 slices whole grain bread
- 1/2 avocado
- 2 tablespoons chopped fresh cilantro, or more to taste
- 1 teaspoon Meyer lemon juice, or to taste
- 1/4 teaspoon Meyer lemon zest
- 1 pinch cayenne pepper
- 1 pinch fine sea salt
- 1/4 teaspoon chia seeds

Direction

- Toast bread slices for 3 to 5 minutes until they reach desired doneness.
- In a bowl, mash avocado; mix in sea salt, cayenne pepper, Meyer lemon zest, Meyer lemon juice, and cilantro. Serve toasted bread with avocado mixture spread and topped with chia seeds.

Nutrition Information

- Calories: 72 calories;
- Total Fat: 1.2
- Sodium: 271
- Total Carbohydrate: 11.8
- Cholesterol: 0
- Protein: 3.6

- Cholesterol: 68

Mini Philly Cheesesteaks

Serving: 12 | Prep: 30mins | Cook: 30mins | Ready in:

Ingredients

- Cheese Sauce:
- 2 tablespoons butter, or as needed
- 2 tablespoons all-purpose flour, or as needed
- 1 cup cold milk
- 2 ounces shredded provolone cheese, or more to taste
- 1 pinch ground nutmeg
- 1 pinch cayenne pepper
- salt to taste
- 1 (12 ounce) skirt steak
- salt and freshly ground black pepper to taste
- 3 tablespoons olive oil, divided, or as needed
- 1/4 cup water
- 1/3 cup diced onion
- 1/3 cup diced sweet peppers
- 2 baguettes, or as needed, cut into 48 1/2-inch thick slices
- 1/4 cup shredded provolone cheese, or as needed

Direction

- Preheat the oven to 200 degrees C/400 degrees F. Line aluminum foil on baking sheets.
- In a skillet, melt butter on medium high heat. In hot butter, whisk flour in. Cook, constantly whisking, for about 1 minute until flour taste cooks off and mixture is pale. Put milk into flour mixture. Cook, constantly whisking, for 3-6 minutes until mixture thickens and is hot. Add salt, cayenne pepper, nutmeg and 2-oz. provolone cheese. Mix until cheese melts completely. Take off from heat.
- Season steak with ground black pepper and salt all over.
- In a skillet, heat 1 tbsp. olive oil on medium high heat. Cook steak in the hot oil,

occasionally turning, for 5-7 minutes until meat is pink on the inside and slightly firm. Put meat on a plate.
- Put back skillet on heat. Pour water into skillet. Boil as you scrape browned food bits off the pan's bottom using a wooden spoon. Pour liquid from skillet on steak. Cool the steak to room temperature. Dice the meat. In a big bowl, put meat and the accumulated juices from plate.
- In a skillet, heat 1 tbsp. oil on medium high heat. Sauté peppers and onions in hot oil for about 5 minutes until slightly translucent and softened.
- Mix onions and peppers mixture into the diced meat. Season with pepper and salt.
- On prepped baking sheet, spread bread slices out. Drizzle leftover olive oil on top. Flip slices to make the oiled side face down. On each slice, spread a thick layer of the cheese mixture. Spoon meat mixture on cheese. On top of every slice, sprinkle provolone cheese.
- Bake in preheated oven for 12-15 minutes until cheese melts and it's brown.

Nutrition Information

- Calories: 280 calories;
- Sodium: 489
- Total Carbohydrate: 34.8
- Cholesterol: 18
- Protein: 12.9
- Total Fat: 9.9

Mini Spam Sandwiches

Serving: 20 | Prep: 20mins | Cook: | Ready in:

Ingredients

- 10 slices white bread, lightly toasted
- 1/2 cup creamy salad dressing, e.g. Miracle Whip ™

- 1 (12 ounce) container Spam™ sliced into 1/4 inch thick slices
- 10 slices Cheddar cheese
- 10 thin pineapple slices

Direction

- On one side of every bread slice, scatter a thin layer of salad dressing. Put 2 slices of Spam next to each other on five of the bread slices. They should perfectly cover the slices. Over every layer of Spam, put two slices of cheese, to cover the entire bread slice. Put slices of pineapple on the cheese, snipping it to a square to fit in the sandwiches. Place the rest of the slices of bread on top with salad dressing inside. Snip crusts if you wish, then slice every sandwich into 4 even squares.

Nutrition Information

- Calories: 174 calories;
- Protein: 6.9
- Total Fat: 11.3
- Sodium: 453
- Total Carbohydrate: 11.5
- Cholesterol: 29

879.   Mizuna, Cheese, And Sausage Sandwich Toast

Serving: 2 | Prep: 15mins | Cook: 5mins | Ready in:

Ingredients

- 2 slices ham
- 1 bunch mizuna, roots removed, cut into 2-inch pieces
- 1/4 onion, sliced
- 4 slices bread
- 2 slices mozzarella cheese
- 2 Vienna sausages, thinly sliced
- 1 tablespoon butter, or as needed

Direction

- Arrange ham, mizuna, and onion on top of two bread slices; top with mozzarella cheese. Place sausage slices evenly on top of the cheese; cover with two remaining bread slices.
- Preheat the sandwich maker following the manufacturer's directions. Spread melted butter on plates.
- Cook sandwiches in the sandwich maker for 5 mins until crispy. Halve sandwiches then serve.

Nutrition Information

- Calories: 380 calories;
- Cholesterol: 63
- Protein: 20.5
- Total Fat: 18.2
- Sodium: 1110
- Total Carbohydrate: 34.8

880.   Mock Sliders

Serving: 24 | Prep: 15mins | Cook: 1mins | Ready in:

Ingredients

- 1 (12 ounce) can corned beef, chopped
- 1 (8 ounce) container sour cream
- 1 (1 ounce) envelope dry onion soup mix
- 2 (8 ounce) packages dinner rolls
- 1 (16 ounce) jar dill pickle slices, drained

Direction

- Mix dry onion soup mix, sour cream and corned beef in medium bowl.
- Horizontally cut rolls in half; spread corned beef mixture on bottoms. Replace tops.
- Microwave on high heat for 30-45 seconds till moist and hot; before serving, put dill pickle slices over.

Nutrition Information

- Calories: 62 calories;
- Protein: 4.3
- Total Fat: 4.1
- Sodium: 489
- Total Carbohydrate: 1.9
- Cholesterol: 16

881.　Most Excellent Sandwich

Serving: 4 | Prep: 10mins | Cook: 10mins | Ready in:

Ingredients

- 4 slices whole wheat bread, toasted
- 1/2 (8 ounce) package cream cheese, room temperature
- 1 medium tomato, sliced
- 1 (5 ounce) package alfalfa sprouts
- 1 cup shredded mozzarella cheese

Direction

- Turn the oven to 175°C (350° F).
- With aluminum foil, line a baking sheet. Put cream cheese on each piece of bread, and place cheese side up on baking sheet. Put the tomato slices on cream cheese. Garnish with alfalfa sprouts, and then drizzle generously with mozzarella cheese.
- Bake for 10 minutes in the oven until the cheese melts, and sandwiches are hot.

Nutrition Information

- Calories: 256 calories;
- Cholesterol: 49
- Protein: 14.3
- Total Fat: 15.4
- Sodium: 395
- Total Carbohydrate: 15.9

882.　Mr. Head's Spicy Tuna Melt

Serving: 2 | Prep: 15mins | Cook: 10mins | Ready in:

Ingredients

- 2 teaspoons vegetable oil
- 1/2 cup chopped onion
- 1/2 cup chopped celery
- 1 pinch kosher salt
- 2 (5 ounce) cans tuna, packed in olive oil, drained
- 1 tablespoon spicy brown mustard
- 1 tablespoon mayonnaise
- 2 pinches cayenne pepper
- 1 teaspoon Cajun style blackened seasoning (Old Bay® recommended)
- 1 pinch dried parsley
- 1 teaspoon hot pepper sauce (e.g. Tabasco™)
- 2 slices pepperjack cheese
- 4 slices Italian bread

Direction

- In a skillet, heat the vegetable oil over medium heat. Add celery and onions, then flavor with a bit of kosher salt. Cook and stir until soft, about 5 minutes.
- Stir the sautéed onion and celery, mayonnaise, mustard, and tuna in a medium bowl. Flavor with hot pepper sauce, parsley, blackened seasoning, and cayenne. Scoop onto 1/2 of the bread slices. Place a slice of pepper jack cheese on top of each bread slice, then the leftover slices of bread.
- Spread onto the outsides of the sandwich with butter. Over medium heat, fry sandwich in a skillet until the outside is golden brown and cheese is melted, about 5 minutes total.

Nutrition Information

- Calories: 743 calories;
- Total Fat: 51.2
- Sodium: 1647
- Total Carbohydrate: 27.2

- Cholesterol: 108
- Protein: 43.5

883. Muffuletta Paninis

Serving: 8 | Prep: 20mins | Cook: 3mins | Ready in:

Ingredients

- 1 cup pimento-stuffed green olives, drained
- 1/2 cup chopped Kalamata olives
- 1/4 cup diced red onions
- 1/4 lemon, juiced
- 2 marinated artichoke hearts, drained
- 1 tablespoon chopped fresh basil
- 2 teaspoons olive oil
- 2 teaspoons capers, drained
- 1/2 teaspoon roasted garlic
- cooking spray
- 8 slices provolone cheese, or to taste
- 8 thin slices ham, or to taste
- 8 slices Genoa salami, or to taste
- 1 loaf crusty Italian bread, sliced

Direction

- In a food processor, process garlic, capers, olive oil, basil, artichoke hearts, lemon juice, red onions, Kalamata olives and stuffed olives till chopped coarsely; refrigerate it for 8 hours – overnight.
- Spray cooking spray on a panini press; preheat grill.
- On 4 bread slices, layer 1 provolone cheese slice, 1 spoonful of olive salad, 2 ham slices, 2 salami slices, 1 more spoonful of olive salad and 1 extra provolone cheese slice. Top with 4 extra slices to make 4 sandwiches; put sandwiches in preheated panini press. Grill for 3-5 minutes each till bread is toasted; cut sandwiches into half.

Nutrition Information

- Calories: 528 calories;
- Total Fat: 26.8
- Sodium: 2252
- Total Carbohydrate: 46.9
- Cholesterol: 56
- Protein: 24.4

884. Mushroom Artichoke Sandwich

Serving: 2 | Prep: 10mins | Cook: 15mins | Ready in:

Ingredients

- 1 (12 inch) French baguette
- 1 tablespoon olive oil
- 12 ounces fresh mushrooms, sliced
- 1 (14 ounce) can quartered artichoke hearts in water, drained
- 2 tablespoons grated Parmesan cheese
- 2 teaspoons garlic and onion seasoning
- salt and pepper to taste

Direction

- Heat the oven to 350°F (175°C).
- Slice lengthwise the baguette in half, split open, and toast in the oven for 7 - 9 minutes, till slightly browned.
- In a skillet, heat the olive oil over medium heat; cook and stir the artichoke hearts and mushrooms for about 10 minutes, until the mushrooms start to brown and their liquid is released. Mix in onion seasoning, garlic and Parmesan cheese, and pepper and salt; cook and stir for about 5 minutes longer, until the mixture thickens.
- Fill the mushroom filling into the toasted bread, close the sandwich, cut in half and serve.

Nutrition Information

- Calories: 466 calories;

- Protein: 22.7
- Total Fat: 10.5
- Sodium: 1893
- Total Carbohydrate: 73.4
- Cholesterol: 4

- Calories: 214 calories;
- Sodium: 240
- Total Carbohydrate: 10.9
- Cholesterol: 77
- Protein: 18.1
- Total Fat: 11.6

885.   Mushroom Sliders

Serving: 6 | Prep: 10mins | Cook: 15mins | Ready in:

Ingredients

- 1 pound lean ground beef, or more to taste
- 1 large egg
- 1 small onion, finely chopped
- 1 cup finely chopped mushrooms
- 1 teaspoon ground black pepper
- 1/2 teaspoon garlic salt
- salt to taste
- 6 portobello mushrooms, or more to taste
- 1 green bell pepper, halved and seeded
- 1 red bell pepper, halved and seeded
- 1 yellow bell pepper, halved and seeded

Direction

- Set an outdoor grill to medium-high heat to preheat and lightly grease the grate.
- In a bowl, mix ground beef, chopped mushrooms, onion, and egg; season with salt, garlic salt, and pepper as you mix. Shape the mixture into 2-inch patties.
- On the preheated grill, grill the patties for 5-7 minutes per side or until browned and reached the desired doneness. Insert an instant-read meat thermometer into the center and it should show at least 70°C (160°F).
- On the grill, grill yellow bell pepper, red bell pepper, green bell pepper, and portobello mushrooms until softened for 3-5 minutes each side. Use 2 mushrooms as the 'bun' for the burgers.

Nutrition Information

886.   My Favorite Sloppy Joes

Serving: 6 | Prep: 10mins | Cook: 40mins | Ready in:

Ingredients

- 1 pound lean ground beef
- 1 cup ketchup
- 1/4 cup dried minced onion
- 3 tablespoons brown sugar, or to taste
- 2 tablespoons spicy brown mustard
- 1 tablespoon Worcestershire sauce, or more to taste
- 1 tablespoon liquid smoke flavoring
- 1 teaspoon minced garlic
- 1 cup beef broth
- salt and ground black pepper to taste

Direction

- In a skillet, cook while stirring the ground beef on medium heat until the meat turns crumbly and brown, roughly 10 minutes; drain the extra grease. Mix in garlic, smoke flavoring, Worcestershire sauce, mustard, brown sugar, dried onion, and ketchup, then stir until the brown sugar dissolves.
- Stir in the beef broth and boil. Turn the heat down to low and simmer until it thickens, around 30 minutes. Season with black pepper and salt.

Nutrition Information

- Calories: 247 calories;
- Sodium: 743
- Total Carbohydrate: 19.6

- Cholesterol: 50
- Protein: 16.1
- Total Fat: 12

887.   My Sloppy Joes

Serving: 4 | Prep: 15mins | Cook: 15mins | Ready in:

Ingredients

- 1 tablespoon olive oil
- 1 pound ground beef
- 1/2 onion, finely chopped
- 1/2 cup finely chopped green bell pepper
- 1/2 cup finely chopped celery
- 1/2 cup finely chopped carrot
- 1 (10.75 ounce) can chicken gumbo soup
- 1/2 cup chili sauce
- 1 tablespoon prepared yellow mustard
- 1 teaspoon onion salt

Direction

- In a big skillet, heat olive oil on medium heat. Cook and stir the hot oil with beef for 5-7 minutes, until crumbly and browned, then drain and get rid of grease. Turn the skillet back to heat.
- Stir the ground beef with carrot, celery, bell pepper and onion, then cook and stir for 5-7 minutes, until vegetables are soft. Add in onion salt, yellow mustard, chili sauce and chicken gumbo soup, then lower heat to medium-low. Stir the beef mixture and simmer for 5 minutes, until the sauce is thickened.

Nutrition Information

- Calories: 332 calories;
- Total Carbohydrate: 19.4
- Cholesterol: 73
- Protein: 22.5
- Total Fat: 18.3

- Sodium: 1623

888.   Not So Sloppy Hot Dogs

Serving: 8 | Prep: 20mins | Cook: 30mins | Ready in:

Ingredients

- 1 pound lean ground beef
- 1/2 cup chopped celery
- 1/4 cup chopped onion
- 1/2 (10.75 ounce) can condensed tomato soup
- 2 1/2 tablespoons ketchup
- 2 tablespoons packed brown sugar
- 1 1/2 teaspoons white vinegar
- 3/4 teaspoon Worcestershire sauce
- 1 tablespoon taco seasoning mix
- 1/4 teaspoon garlic powder
- 1/4 teaspoon salt
- 8 hot dogs
- 8 hot dog buns, split and toasted

Direction

- Prepare a large skillet over medium-high heat. Cook while stirring beef in heated skillet for 5 to 7 minutes or until crumbly and browned; drain and discard drippings. Add onion and celery to the skillet, cook, covered, for about 5 minutes, until vegetables are tender.
- Stir Worcestershire sauce, vinegar, brown sugar, ketchup, and tomato soup into ground beef mixture; season mixture with salt, garlic powder, and taco seasoning. Simmer everything for 15 to 20 minutes, stirring often, until flavors have melded.
- Bring lightly salted water in a large pot to a boil; add hot dogs and cook for 5 to 10 minutes or until cooked through. Use tongs to take hot dogs out of the water.
- Set each hot dog into a toasted bun; spoon ground beef mixture atop hot dog to serve.

Nutrition Information

- Calories: 407 calories;
- Total Fat: 22.4
- Sodium: 1066
- Total Carbohydrate: 30.7
- Cholesterol: 57
- Protein: 19.7

889.   Nova Scotia Style Donair

Serving: 15 | Prep: 40mins | Cook: 2hours30mins | Ready in:

Ingredients

- 4 pounds ground beef
- 1 pound ground lamb
- 5 teaspoons all-purpose flour (optional)
- 4 teaspoons salt
- 5 teaspoons dried oregano
- 2 1/2 teaspoons dry mustard
- 2 1/2 teaspoons garlic powder
- 2 1/2 teaspoons cracked black pepper
- 2 1/2 teaspoons cayenne pepper
- 2 teaspoons crushed dried chile pepper
- 1 1/2 teaspoons paprika
- 1 teaspoon Italian seasoning
- Sauce:
- 1 (12 fluid ounce) can evaporated milk
- 3/4 cup white sugar
- 2 teaspoons garlic powder
- 3 tablespoons white vinegar, or as needed
- 15 pita bread rounds
- 2 tomatoes, chopped, or more to taste
- 1 onion, chopped

Direction

- Start preheating the oven to 300°F (150°C). Coat a large baking pan with sides with oil.
- In a bowl, put Italian seasoning, paprika, chile pepper, cayenne pepper, black pepper, 2 1/2 teaspoons of garlic powder, dry mustard, oregano, salt, flour, lamb and beef. Using your hands, knead all the ingredients together for 10 mins until the paste forms. Shape meat

mixture into a large loaf form. Put into prepared pan.
- Bake in prepared oven for 120 mins or until the middle is no longer pink. The instant-read thermometer should register at least 160°F (70°C) when inserted into middle. Take out meat from the oven. Allow meat to cool completely on drip rack to let fat and juices drain. Place meat in the refrigerator for 6 hours or up to overnight.
- In a small bowl, stir together 2 teaspoons of garlic powder, sugar and evaporated milk. Stir in the vinegar gradually until the mixture has just thickened.
- Slice the donair meat into 1/8-1/4-in. thick strips. In a skillet, fry the meat strips over medium-high heat, in single-sandwich batches, until the edges of meat start to crisp. Take out of the pan. Rub one pita round quickly and lightly with water. In the same frying pan, fry pita for one min or until it is just warm, turning once.
- Spread half a tablespoon sauce mixture over the pita. Place donair meat on top. Decorate with more sauce, tomato, and onion; do the same with the remaining pita and meat.

Nutrition Information

- Calories: 511 calories;
- Sodium: 1004
- Total Carbohydrate: 44.9
- Cholesterol: 103
- Protein: 32.7
- Total Fat: 21.6

890.   Octodogs

Serving: 6 | Prep: 10mins | Cook: 1mins | Ready in:

Ingredients

- 6 hot dogs

Direction

- Boil water in a saucepan.
- Slice hotdogs in two. To make the 'tentacles' of the octodog, slit 3 cuts on one side of every hotdog, leave 1/3 of the rounded top of the hotdog for the 'head'. Flip hotdog over and slit three more cuts to make 8 'tentacles'.
- Boil the octodogs in water for one minute until cooked thoroughly and the 'tentacles' curl up.

Nutrition Information

- Calories: 148 calories;
- Total Carbohydrate: 1.8
- Cholesterol: 24
- Total Fat: 13.3
- Protein: 5.1
- Sodium: 513

---

891.   Orange Chicken And Vegetable Stir Fry

Serving: 4 | Prep: 10mins | Cook: 20mins | Ready in:

Ingredients

- 2 tablespoons cornstarch
- 1 3/4 cups Swanson® Chicken Stock
- 2 tablespoons soy sauce
- Vegetable cooking spray
- 1 pound skinless, boneless chicken breast, cut into strips
- 2 cloves garlic, minced
- 3 cups cut-up fresh vegetables (see Note)
- 1/2 cup orange marmalade
- 4 cups hot cooked rice, cooked without salt

Direction

- In a small bowl, combine soy sauce, stock and cornstarch until smoothened.
- Grease a 12" non-stick skillet and bring to medium-high heat for 60 seconds. Put in

chicken and stir-fry, stirring frequently, until well-browned.
- Add in vegetables and garlic, then sauté until tenderly crisped, 5 minutes.
- Whisk in marmalade and cornstarch mixture. Cook, stirring, until mixture is boiled through and thickened. Serve on top of rice.

Nutrition Information

- Calories: 478 calories;
- Sodium: 758
- Total Carbohydrate: 80.1
- Cholesterol: 65
- Protein: 31.4
- Total Fat: 3.3

---

892.   Oven SPAM® Sandwiches

Serving: 8 | Prep: 15mins | Cook: 10mins | Ready in:

Ingredients

- 1 (12 ounce) can fully cooked luncheon meat (such as SPAM®), cubed
- 3/4 (1 pound) loaf processed cheese food (such as Velveeta®), cubed
- 2 tablespoons sweet pickle relish
- 1/2 cup creamy salad dressing (such as Miracle Whip®)
- 8 hamburger buns, split

Direction

- Set the oven to 175°C or 350°F to preheat.
- In a bowl, stir salad dressing, relish, processed cheese and luncheon meat together. Scoop into the sandwich buns with filling and use aluminum foil to wrap each sandwich separately. Put sandwiches onto a baking sheet.
- In the preheated oven, bake for 10-15 minutes, until buns are toasted and the filling is hot.

Nutrition Information

- Calories: 443 calories;
- Total Fat: 28.4
- Sodium: 1509
- Total Carbohydrate: 29.5
- Cholesterol: 68
- Protein: 17

---

893.   PBM Sandwich

Serving: 1 | Prep: 4mins | Cook: 1mins | Ready in:

Ingredients

- 2 tablespoons peanut butter
- 2 slices bread
- 2 1/2 tablespoons marshmallow cream (such as Marshmallow Fluff®)

Direction

- Spread peanut butter on a bread slice. Spread marshmallow crème on another bread slice. With the toppings side facing up, place the breads on a microwave-safe plate. Place plate inside microwave and heat for 30 seconds on high power. Place the 2 slices of bread together, then serve.

Nutrition Information

- Calories: 373 calories;
- Protein: 12.1
- Total Fat: 18.1
- Sodium: 502
- Total Carbohydrate: 43.5
- Cholesterol: 0

---

894.   PDQ Hot Beef Sandwiches

Serving: 12 | Prep: 20mins | Cook: 3hours30mins | Ready in:

Ingredients

- 1 tablespoon vegetable oil
- 1 (4 pound) beef chuck roast
- 1 cup chili sauce
- 1/2 cup water
- 1/2 cup white vinegar
- 1 tablespoon chili powder
- salt and pepper to taste
- 1 teaspoon garlic powder, or to taste
- 2 teaspoons white sugar

Direction

- Pour vegetable oil into a big Dutch oven on medium-high heat. Put in the roast and wait until brown on all sides.
- Lower the heat to medium-low, then add vinegar, water, and chili sauce. Sprinkle with garlic powder, salt, pepper, chili powder and white sugar to season it. Simmer in medium-low heat until meat is flaccid, for 3 hours. Take beef out, and put in the fridge overnight. Store sauce, and refrigerate.
- Slice or mince the beef into pieces, put in a big pot on the stove with sauce. Grill it, then serve with sandwich buns or alone.

Nutrition Information

- Calories: 424 calories;
- Cholesterol: 109
- Protein: 26.5
- Total Fat: 31.8
- Sodium: 412
- Total Carbohydrate: 6.9

895.　　　Pan Basquaise

Serving: 4 | Prep: 10mins | Cook: 10mins | Ready in:

Ingredients

- 4 tablespoons olive oil, divided
- 4 large red bell peppers - roasted, peeled and sliced
- 1 (5 ounce) can tuna, drained
- salt and freshly ground black pepper to taste
- 2 tablespoons white wine vinegar
- 4 tablespoons chopped fresh parsley, divided
- 3 cloves garlic, minced
- 2 (8 ounce) loaves French baguette
- 4 hard-cooked eggs, sliced
- 8 kalamata olives, pitted and halved

Direction

- Set the oven at 375°F (190°C) and start preheating.
- Place a large skillet over medium-high heat and heat 3 tablespoons of olive oil. Sauté red peppers in hot oil for 2-3 minutes. Mix in tuna; flavor with pepper and salt. Put in garlic, 2 tablespoons of parsley and vinegar. Cook till the vinegar is evaporated, 2-3 minutes. Take away from the heat; set aside.
- Slice bread lengthwise in half; then, slice into 4-in. pieces crosswise. Toast the bread in the oven till crisp and warm, but not brown. Remove onto a serving platter. Transfer the red pepper tuna mixture on top of each piece. Garnish with a halved olive and sliced egg. Drizzle the remaining olive oil over all; sprinkle the remaining parsley on top.

Nutrition Information

- Calories: 638 calories;
- Total Fat: 23.6
- Sodium: 947
- Total Carbohydrate: 76.1
- Cholesterol: 221
- Protein: 29.7

896.　　　Panini Sandwiches

Serving: 4 | Prep: 10mins | Cook: 10mins | Ready in:

Ingredients

- 4 Sister Schubert's Dinner Yeast Rolls, split
- Plain or sundried tomato mayonnaise (see below)
- 4 slices roast turkey or ham
- 4 slices Swiss, Monterey Jack, or Gruyere cheese
- 8 small slices red onion
- 1 cup fresh spinach leaves or several fresh basil leaves (optional)
- Salt and freshly ground black pepper
- Butter
- Sundried Tomato Mayonnaise:
- 1/4 cup mayonnaise
- 2 finely chopped sundried tomatoes
- Salt and freshly ground black pepper

Direction

- Start preheating the panini machine or grill pan to medium heat.
- Spread one tablespoon of mayonnaise over middle of each roll. Assemble the sandwiches with the remaining ingredients (but not butter). Add pepper and salt to season.
- Spread over bottom and top of each roll with small amount of the butter. Put sandwich either onto panini machine or into pan, then grill. Cook for 5-7 mins.
- (Using pan lid, press the sandwich down if using a pan. Cook the sandwiches until the bread has been toasted, about 3-4 mins per side.)
- For mayonnaise: in small bowl, whisk all the ingredients together. Place in the refrigerator until ready to use.

Nutrition Information

- Calories: 464 calories;

- Protein: 17.4
- Total Fat: 26.6
- Sodium: 742
- Total Carbohydrate: 40.8
- Cholesterol: 60

897.   Peanut Butter Chocolate Waffle Sandwich

Serving: 1 | Prep: 10mins | Cook: 5mins | Ready in:

Ingredients

- 2 frozen waffles
- 1 cup chocolate chips, or to taste
- 2 tablespoons peanut butter

Direction

- In the toaster oven, add waffles and cook for 2-3 minutes, until they are halfway done. Spread waffles with chocolate chips and turn back to toaster oven to cook for 2-3 minutes, until chocolate is melted.
- Use a toothpick or fork to spread chocolate evenly around waffle. Spread chocolate layer with peanut butter. Close the waffles together to create a sandwich.

Nutrition Information

- Calories: 1195 calories;
- Sodium: 614
- Total Carbohydrate: 142.5
- Cholesterol: 10
- Protein: 19.7
- Total Fat: 73.6

898.   Peanut Butter Cup Grilled Sandwich

Serving: 2 | Prep: 5mins | Cook: 5mins | Ready in:

Ingredients

- 2 teaspoons margarine
- 2 slices white bread
- 1 1/2 tablespoons peanut butter
- 2 tablespoons semisweet chocolate chips

Direction

- Spread 1 tsp. margarine on 1 side of each bread slice; put margarine sides together to avoid putting margarine on your hands while spreading peanut butter then spread peanut butter on 1 bread slice. Sprinkle chocolate chips on peanut butter; remove other bread slice from back of peanut butter slice. Put margarine side out on chocolate chips and peanut butter.
- In skillet on medium heat, fry sandwich for 2-3 minutes till each side is golden brown; slightly cool. Cut in half.

Nutrition Information

- Calories: 222 calories;
- Total Fat: 13.9
- Sodium: 272
- Total Carbohydrate: 21.7
- Cholesterol: 0
- Protein: 5.5

899.   Peanut Butter Hot Dogs

Serving: 2 | Prep: 5mins | Cook: | Ready in:

Ingredients

- 2 tablespoons peanut butter
- 2 slices whole wheat bread
- 1 banana, peeled

Direction

- On one side of each slice of bread, spread a tablespoon of peanut butter. Split the banana in two and put 1/2 on the middle of each slice of bread with peanut butter. Enclose the bread around each of the bananas so you can eat it like a hotdog.

Nutrition Information

- Calories: 218 calories;
- Cholesterol: 0
- Protein: 8.4
- Total Fat: 9.3
- Sodium: 209
- Total Carbohydrate: 28.4

900.   Peanut Butter And Apple Sandwich

Serving: 1 | Prep: 2mins | Cook: | Ready in:

Ingredients

- 2 slices whole wheat bread
- 1 tablespoon peanut butter, or to taste
- 1 small apple - peeled, cored and shredded

Direction

- Put a thin layer of peanut butter on a slice of bread. Put shredded apple onto the peanut butter. Spread peanut butter on another slice of bread the combine the two slices to make a sandwich then serve right away.

Nutrition Information

- Calories: 291 calories;
- Total Fat: 10.3
- Sodium: 344
- Total Carbohydrate: 41.3
- Cholesterol: 0

- Protein: 11.7

901.   Pepperoni Filled Bread

Serving: 8 | Prep: 5mins | Cook: 10mins | Ready in:

Ingredients

- 1 cup shredded mozzarella cheese
- 1 cup pepperoni sausage, chopped
- 1/4 cup minced onion
- 2 tablespoons chopped parsley
- 3 tablespoons olive oil
- 4 hero sandwich rolls, split lengthwise
- 1 tablespoon olive oil
- 2 tablespoons grated Parmesan cheese

Direction

- Preheat oven to 190 degrees C (375 degrees F).
- Mix olive oil, parsley, onion, pepperoni and Mozzarella cheese in bowl. Spread over cut surface of rolls. Brush tops of rolls using 1 tbsp. of oil and drizzle with Parmesan cheese.
- Bake till thoroughly heated and turns golden for 10 minutes in the preheated oven.

Nutrition Information

- Calories: 350 calories;
- Total Fat: 25.2
- Sodium: 737
- Total Carbohydrate: 17.4
- Cholesterol: 42
- Protein: 13.6

902.   Pesto Shrimp Sandwich

Serving: 4 | Prep: 5mins | Cook: 10mins | Ready in:

Ingredients

- 1 (16 inch) French baguette
- 1 tablespoon softened butter, divided
- 4 romaine lettuce leaves
- 1 pound cooked salad shrimp
- 6 tablespoons prepared pesto sauce

Direction

- Set an oven to 200 0 F (95 0 C) and preheat.
- Slice the baguette into 4 equal pieces and put in the oven to warm.
- In a bowl, combine together the cooked shrimp and pesto sauce.
- To make the sandwiches, halve each piece of warmed bread and spread butter over the cut sides. Place one lettuce leaf and same amounts of pesto and shrimp in each sandwich to serve.

Nutrition Information

- Calories: 441 calories;
- Total Fat: 16
- Sodium: 870
- Total Carbohydrate: 38
- Cholesterol: 236
- Protein: 35.6

903.   Philly Cheese Steak Dog

Serving: 8 | Prep: 10mins | Cook: 15mins | Ready in:

Ingredients

- 1 tablespoon olive oil
- 1/2 large onion, diced
- 1/2 pound shaved rib-eye, chopped
- 8 hot dogs
- 8 hot dog buns
- 1 (8 ounce) jar processed cheese spread (such as Cheese Whiz®)

Direction

- Over medium heat, heat olive oil in a skillet and add onion. Cook while stirring for 5 to 10

minutes until tender. Place the onion into a bowl. Cook while stirring rib-eye in the same skillet for 5 to 10 minutes until no red color remains in meat and the liquid is evaporated. Mix the onion into the cooked rib-eye.
- Bring water to boil in a pot and then cook the hot dogs in the boiling water for 5 to 10 minutes until cooked through.
- Put each of the cooked hot dog into a bun. Scoop the rib-eye mixture on top of hot dog. Add cheese spread on top.

Nutrition Information

- Calories: 445 calories;
- Sodium: 1319
- Total Carbohydrate: 26.9
- Cholesterol: 56
- Protein: 18.3
- Total Fat: 29

904.   Philly Steak Sandwich

Serving: 4 | Prep: 15mins | Cook: 25mins | Ready in:

Ingredients

- 1 pound beef sirloin, cut into thin 2 inch strips
- 1/2 teaspoon salt
- 1/2 teaspoon black pepper
- 1/2 teaspoon paprika
- 1/2 teaspoon chili powder
- 1/2 teaspoon onion powder
- 1/2 teaspoon garlic powder
- 1/2 teaspoon dried thyme
- 1/2 teaspoon dried marjoram
- 1/2 teaspoon dried basil
- 3 tablespoons vegetable oil
- 1 onion, sliced
- 1 green bell pepper, julienned
- 3 ounces Swiss cheese, thinly sliced
- 4 hoagie rolls, split lengthwise

Direction

- Into a large bowl, put the beef. Combine together marjoram, salt, pepper, thyme, paprika, chili powder, basil, onion powder, and garlic powder in a small bowl. Drizzle on top of beef.
- Over medium-high heat, heat 1/2 of the oil in a skillet, add beef and then sauté to your desired doneness. Take out from the pan. Heat remaining oil in skillet, add green pepper and onion and sauté them.
- Preheat the oven using broiler setting.
- Distribute the meat between bottoms of four rolls, then spread a layer of green pepper and onion and add sliced cheese on top. Transfer onto cookie sheet and then broil until the cheese has melted. The cover using tops of rolls before serving.

Nutrition Information

- Calories: 641 calories;
- Total Fat: 38.4
- Sodium: 717
- Total Carbohydrate: 39.5
- Cholesterol: 96
- Protein: 35.3

---

905. Phoritto (Pho + Burrito)

Serving: 8 | Prep: 25mins | Cook: 20mins | Ready in:

Ingredients

- 1 tablespoon vegetable oil
- 1 1/2 onion, thinly sliced
- 3 jalapeno peppers, thinly sliced
- 2 (14 ounce) cans beef-flavored pho broth
- 1 pound frozen ribeye steak, thinly sliced
- 10 ounces thin rice noodles (vermicelli-style)
- 8 burrito-size flour tortillas
- 1 (8 ounce) jar chili-garlic sauce
- 1 (8 ounce) package bean sprouts
- 2 tablespoons hoisin sauce, or to taste
- 1 bunch Thai basil

- 1 bunch cilantro
- 1 lime, sliced

Direction

- In a large saucepan, heat oil over medium heat. Put in onions; cook while stirring for 5 mins until softened. Put in jalapenos; cook while stirring for 5 mins until dark green. Discard from the heat.
- In a saucepan, heat broth over medium-high heat. In the hot broth, cook ribeye slices in batches for 10-20 seconds each batch until medium-rare.
- Boil water in a large pot. Put in noodles and cook for 3-5 mins at a boil until tender. Then drain.
- On a microwave-safe plate, put the tortillas. Heat for 20-25 seconds until warm in microwave.
- Divide cilantro, Thai basil, hoisin sauce, bean sprouts, chili-garlic sauce, noodles, ribeye slices and jalapeno and onion mixture among the warmed tortillas. Add small amount of the broth over top. Fold the opposing tortillas edges over the filling. Then roll up into the burritos. Enjoy with the lime slices.

Nutrition Information

- Calories: 446 calories;
- Total Fat: 11.9
- Sodium: 1940
- Total Carbohydrate: 68.4
- Cholesterol: 20
- Protein: 15

---

906. Piggy Wiggys

Serving: 8 | Prep: 10mins | Cook: 15mins | Ready in:

Ingredients

- 1 (10 ounce) can refrigerated crescent roll dough

- 1 (16 ounce) package cocktail sausages

Direction

- Turn oven to 375°F (190°C) to preheat. Lightly oil a large baking sheet.
- Split crescent rolls apart; flatten them then cut into triangles that measure 1 1/2 inches on each side. Wrap each triangle around 1 sausage. Arrange wrapped sausages on the greased baking sheet.
- Bake for 15 minutes in the preheated oven until golden.

Nutrition Information

- Calories: 317 calories;
- Total Fat: 24.4
- Sodium: 824
- Total Carbohydrate: 14.8
- Cholesterol: 37
- Protein: 9.9

---

907.   Pita Love

Serving: 8 | Prep: 20mins | Cook: 10mins | Ready in:

Ingredients

- 1/2 tablespoon extra virgin olive oil
- 1 cup fresh bean sprouts, rinsed and drained
- 1/4 cup chopped green onion
- 1/8 cup sliced fresh mushrooms
- 1/8 cup sliced black olives
- 1/8 cup sliced carrots
- 1/8 cup sliced celery
- 1/4 teaspoon ground ginger
- 1/2 teaspoon salt
- 1/4 teaspoon ground black pepper
- 1 cup cooked black beans, rinsed and drained
- 4 whole wheat pita breads, cut into quarters
- 1/8 cup sunflower seeds
- 2 cups shredded Monterey Jack cheese
- 1/2 cup sour cream, for topping

- 1/4 cup chopped fresh chives

Direction

- In a big skillet, heat olive oil on medium-high heat. Sauté together olives, mushrooms, onions and bean sprouts for 3 minutes, until soft. Lower heat to low and put in pepper, salt, ginger, celery and carrots. Cook the mixture for several minutes longer to make flavors combine. The celery as well as carrots should remain crisp. Stir into the skillet with sunflower seeds and black beans, then cook just until heated through. Take away from the heat.
- In the meantime, use a toothpick to prop open each pita, then put inside with some of the shredded cheese and microwave until cheese is melted, about half a minute. Put aside.
- Scoop into the pita triangles with vegetable mixture and get rid of toothpicks. Use chives and sour cream to decorate.

Nutrition Information

- Calories: 265 calories;
- Total Carbohydrate: 24.7
- Cholesterol: 31
- Protein: 12.8
- Total Fat: 13.6
- Sodium: 613

---

908.   Pita Parcels

Serving: 2 | Prep: 10mins | Cook: 5mins | Ready in:

Ingredients

- 2 oval pita breads
- 2 tablespoons mayonnaise
- 2 tablespoons corn relish
- 3 leaves lettuce, chopped
- 10 frozen chicken nuggets, thawed

Direction

- Preheat oven to broil/grill.
- Split open pita pockets carefully; put them onto serving plates. Spread inside of pitas with mayonnaise then corn relish; use lettuce to fill each pocket. Put aside.
- In preheated oven, broil/grill chicken nuggets till juices are clear and cooked through for 2-3 minutes per side.
- In pita pockets, put chicken nuggets; serve hot.

Nutrition Information

- Calories: 537 calories;
- Sodium: 889
- Total Carbohydrate: 51.1
- Cholesterol: 60
- Protein: 21.1
- Total Fat: 27.6

---

909.   Pittsburgh Ham Barbecues

Serving: 8 | Prep: 10mins | Cook: 20mins | Ready in:

Ingredients

- 1/2 cup butter
- 1 small onion, finely chopped
- 2 cups ketchup
- 1/3 cup distilled white vinegar
- 1/2 cup water
- 3 tablespoons brown sugar
- 2 teaspoons prepared yellow mustard
- 2 tablespoons Worcestershire sauce
- 1 1/2 pounds chipped chopped ham
- 8 kaiser rolls, split
- 1 cup pickle relish (optional)

Direction

- Preheat the oven to 135 degrees C (275 degrees F).
- Over medium-high heat, heat butter in a large skillet and add onions. Cook while stirring for

about 5 minutes until translucent. Into the skillet with onions, mix in Worcestershire sauce, ketchup, brown sugar, vinegar, mustard and water. Let to simmer for around ten minutes. Mix in ham and cook for 5 to 7 minutes more until the sauce is bubbling and heated through.
- As the ham simmers, heat Kaiser Rolls in the preheated oven for 5 to 7 minutes until toasted.
- To assemble the sandwiches, distribute the ham mixture among toasted Kaiser Rolls and add pickle relish on top. Serve while still hot.

Nutrition Information

- Calories: 526 calories;
- Protein: 17.5
- Total Fat: 27.2
- Sodium: 2278
- Total Carbohydrate: 56.6
- Cholesterol: 68

---

910.   Pittsburgh Style Chipped Ham Barbeque

Serving: 12 | Prep: 5mins | Cook: 10mins | Ready in:

Ingredients

- 2 (12 ounce) bottles chili sauce (such as Heinz®)
- 1 cup brown sugar
- 3 pounds chipped chopped ham (such as Isaly's®)

Direction

- Over medium heat, mix brown sugar and chili sauce in a large skillet until sugar dissolves and mixture comes to a simmer. Mix in ham and heat to boil. Serve while still hot.

Nutrition Information

- Calories: 318 calories;
- Protein: 16.4
- Total Fat: 18.2
- Sodium: 1433
- Total Carbohydrate: 23.4
- Cholesterol: 51

---

911. Pork Tenderloin Sliders With Spicy Mango Slaw

Serving: 8 | Prep: 15mins | Cook: 20mins | Ready in:

Ingredients

- 1 Smithfield® Golden Rotisserie Pork Tenderloin
- 2 cups shredded cabbage
- 1 mango, thinly sliced
- 1/2 cup chopped cilantro
- 2 tablespoons olive oil
- 1 lime, juiced
- 2 teaspoons sriracha sauce, or to taste
- 1 pinch salt
- 8 slider buns

Direction

- Toss cilantro, mango and cabbage together in a medium bowl.
- In an oven, roast tenderloin for 25-30 minutes at 425°F, until the temperature inside the tenderloin reaches 150°F. Take out of the oven and allow to rest about 5 minutes then slice.
- Whisk together salt, sriracha, lime juice and olive oil in a small bowl, then drizzle over cabbage mixture and toss to coat well.
- For assembling the sandwiches, cut the rolls in half then place a few rounds of pork and a heap of the spicy mango slaw on top.

Nutrition Information

- Calories: 217 calories;
- Total Fat: 6.5
- Sodium: 546
- Total Carbohydrate: 166.8
- Cholesterol: 41
- Protein: 16.7

---

912. Portabella Mushroom Burgers From Reynolds Wrap®

Serving: 6 | Prep: | Cook: 6mins | Ready in:

Ingredients

- 1 sheet Reynolds Wrap® Non-Stick Aluminum Foil
- 3 tablespoons butter, melted
- 2 cloves garlic, minced
- 6 large portabella mushrooms
- 6 slices provolone cheese
- 6 hamburger buns
- Sauce:
- 1 cup light sour cream
- 2 tablespoons red wine vinegar
- 1/4 cup Dijon mustard
- 2 teaspoons sugar
- 1/8 teaspoon cayenne pepper

Direction

- Preheat a grill to medium high heat; create drainage holes in Reynolds Wrap Nonstick Aluminum Foil sheet with a big fork; put aside.
- Mix garlic and butter; use mixture to baste mushroom caps. Put foil on a grill grate, nonstick/dull side facing up. Put mushrooms on foil immediately.
- Grill for 6-8 minutes, flipping once, uncovered, till mushrooms are tender and browned. Put 1 cheese slice on each mushroom at the final grilling minute.
- Mix pepper, sugar, mustard, vinegar and sour cream in a small microwave safe bowl for sauce. Microwave till warm for 30 seconds on

high. Serve sauce on burgers in buns. If desired, add tomato and lettuce.

Nutrition Information

- Calories: 325 calories;
- Sodium: 846
- Total Carbohydrate: 31.7
- Cholesterol: 41
- Protein: 13.7
- Total Fat: 15.5

---

913. Prawn Banh Mi

Serving: 6 | Prep: 20mins | Cook: | Ready in:

Ingredients

- 1 large carrot, peeled and shredded
- 1 stalk celery, chopped
- 2 scallions (green onions), chopped
- 1/4 cup rice vinegar
- 1/3 cup chopped fresh cilantro
- 3 tablespoons low-fat mayonnaise
- 3 tablespoons low-fat plain yogurt
- 1 tablespoon lime juice
- 1/8 teaspoon cayenne pepper
- 3 (12 inch) French baguettes, cut into halves
- 1 pound frozen cooked prawns, thawed and tails removed
- 18 thin slices cucumber, or more to taste

Direction

- In a bowl, mix scallions, celery and carrot together. Add vinegar over vegetable mixture; toss to coat; put aside to marinate.
- In a bowl, combine cayenne pepper, lime juice, yogurt, mayonnaise and cilantro together. Spread onto bottom piece of each baguette with about 2 teaspoons of cilantro sauce.
- Use a slotted spoon to take the vegetables from vinegar; get rid of the vinegar. On

baguette pieces, scoop vegetables over cilantro sauce layer.
- Stir prawns in the rest of cilantro sauce; place 10 prawns over vegetable layer, then cucumber slices on top. Add top piece of baguette over cucumber layer to form a sandwich.

Nutrition Information

- Calories: 388 calories;
- Sodium: 886
- Total Carbohydrate: 60.9
- Cholesterol: 148
- Protein: 28.2
- Total Fat: 3.3

---

914. Pretzel Reuben Sandwich

Serving: 6 | Prep: 15mins | Cook: 10mins | Ready in:

Ingredients

- 6 Sister Schubert's® Soft Pretzel Rolls
- 1 pound cooked and thinly sliced corned beef
- 6 slices Swiss cheese
- 1 cup chopped cabbage
- 1/4 cup Marzetti® Thousand Island Dressing

Direction

- On a baking sheet, put 6 Sister Schubert's Soft Pretzel Rolls and bake the roll following the package instructions. Let the rolls cool. Raise the oven heat to 350°. Halve the rolls horizontally.
- On the bottom half of each roll, put Swiss cheese and sliced corned beef and fold the top part of the roll over to cover. Wrap aluminum foil around each sandwich and put it on a baking sheet. Bake until the sandwich is warm and the cheese melts, about 8-10 minutes. As the sandwiches bake, in a small bowl, combine dressing and cabbage.

- Take the sandwiches out of the aluminum foil, carefully open each sandwich and top the meat with some cabbage salad. Lightly press the sandwiches back together again. If you want, enjoy with additional dressing.

Nutrition Information

- Calories: 409 calories;
- Protein: 26.4
- Total Fat: 20
- Sodium: 1426
- Total Carbohydrate: 31.8
- Cholesterol: 80

---

915. Pulled Pork Grilled Cheese

Serving: 8 | Prep: | Cook: | Ready in:

Ingredients

- BBQ sauce:
- 2 tablespoons Borden® Butter
- 1 medium yellow onion, diced
- 1 jalapeno chile pepper, diced (optional)
- 1 cup ketchup
- 1/2 cup brown sugar
- Liquid smoke, to taste
- Sandwich:
- 1 (3 pound) pork shoulder roast
- 1 (1 pound) loaf sourdough bread, sliced
- 16 slices Borden® Singles Sensations® Extra Sharp Cheddar
- 4 tablespoons Borden® Butter

Direction

- Use a medium skillet to melt the butter on medium heat and sauté the onions in until they become soft. Stir in liquid smoke, sugar, ketchup, and jalapenos, then boil. Turn the heat down to medium-low and simmer until

the sauce thickens to the consistency you want, around 1 hour.
- Smoke the pork shoulder using a hot smoker set at 210 degrees Fahrenheit for 3-5 hours, or until the internal temperature of the meat reads 150 degrees Fahrenheit. Take it out of the smoker and wrap in foil, then place in the refrigerator overnight.
- Discard the excess fat from the pork and use 2 forks to shred the remaining meat into a big bowl, then mix in the barbecue sauce.
- Brown 2 buttered sourdough bread slices in a griddle or pan set on medium heat and place 1 cheese onto each slice. Top with the pulled pork mixture, another cheese slice, and a bread slice. Turn the sandwiches over once the bottom slice browns, then brown the top side as well.

Nutrition Information

- Calories: 687 calories;
- Sodium: 1421
- Total Carbohydrate: 58
- Cholesterol: 120
- Protein: 32.6
- Total Fat: 35.9

---

916. Quick Vegan Veggie Sandwich

Serving: 1 | Prep: 20mins | Cook: 5mins | Ready in:

Ingredients

- 1 tablespoon extra-virgin olive oil
- 1 small garlic clove, finely chopped
- 1/2 small tomato, finely chopped
- 1/4 green bell pepper, finely chopped
- 1/4 red onion, finely chopped
- salt and ground black pepper to taste
- 2 slices multigrain bread
- 1 tablespoon hummus spread

- 1 tablespoon vegan mayonnaise (such as Follow Your Heart® Vegenaise)
- salt and ground black pepper to taste
- 4 sun-dried tomatoes packed in oil, drained and chopped
- 2 leaves lettuce, or more to taste

Direction

- In a frying pan, heat garlic and olive oil on medium for a minute. Put in onion, bell pepper and tomato. Cook for 4 minutes until soft. Flavor with pepper and salt, then take away from the heat.
- Toast the bread slices while cooking the vegetables. Spread hummus over one slice. Spread the vegan mayonnaise over the other, the flavor lightly with pepper and salt.
- Arrange the cooked vegetables, lettuce, and sun-dried tomatoes on a slice, then put the remaining slice on top. Halve the sandwich.

Nutrition Information

- Calories: 293 calories;
- Sodium: 661
- Total Carbohydrate: 38.2
- Cholesterol: 0
- Protein: 10.7
- Total Fat: 12.3

917. Quick And Easy Pizza Burgers

Serving: 8 | Prep: 20mins | Cook: 20mins | Ready in:

Ingredients

- 1 1/2 pounds lean ground beef
- 1 pound chopped cooked ham
- 1 pound American cheese, cut into pieces
- 1 (14 ounce) jar pizza sauce
- 1 tablespoon dried oregano
- 8 hamburger buns, split, or as desired

Direction

- Heat a big frying pan on medium-high heat. In the hot frying pan, stir and cook beef for 5-7 minutes until crumbly and brown; strain and dispose the fat. Allow the ground beef to cool until easy to work with.
- Set the oven to 350°F (175°C) to preheat.
- In a food processor, process American cheese and ham until finely chopped. In a big bowl, combine oregano, pizza sauce, American cheese and ham, and ground beef. Spread this mixture over bottom half of every hamburger bun and put tops over filling. On a baking sheet, put the hamburgers.
- Bake for 15-20 minutes in the preheated oven until the buns turn pale brown and the cheese melts in burgers.

Nutrition Information

- Calories: 669 calories;
- Sodium: 2126
- Total Carbohydrate: 27.6
- Cholesterol: 137
- Protein: 42.4
- Total Fat: 42.2

918. R. B. Miller's Gyro Meat

Serving: 8 | Prep: 30mins | Cook: 1hours15mins | Ready in:

Ingredients

- 1 pound ground beef chuck (80% lean)
- 1 pound boneless lamb chops, cubed
- 1 cup minced onion
- 4 teaspoons minced garlic
- 1 teaspoon ground marjoram
- 1 1/2 teaspoons ground rosemary
- 2 teaspoons sea salt
- 1 teaspoon ground black pepper

Direction

- Using the meat grinder's coarse plate, grind the lamb cubes and ground chuck twice to combine well. In a food processor, pulse pepper, onion, salt, garlic, rosemary, and marjoram until finely ground. In a bowl, combine the onions mixture and ground meat; use a fine plate to grind again. Press the mixture in a 3-in by 7-in loaf pan; use plastic wrap to tightly wrap. Chill overnight.
- Preheat the oven to 165°C or 325°Fahrenheit.
- Take and discard the plastic wrap from the pan. Bake gyro meat for an hour in the preheated oven until the internal temperature reads 60°C or 140°Fahrenheit. Drain the collected liquid in the pan then take the loaf out of the pan. Put the meat on a rack placed on top of a baking sheet to collect the drips. Bake for another 15-30 minutes until the internal temperature reads 75°C or 165°Fahrenheit. Take it out of the oven. Let it sit for 15 minutes before cutting. The cooked loaf should be quite dry and firm.

Nutrition Information

- Calories: 226 calories;
- Cholesterol: 71
- Protein: 19.6
- Total Fat: 14.7
- Sodium: 501
- Total Carbohydrate: 2.7

919. Reuben Sandwich I

Serving: 1 | Prep: | Cook: 5mins | Ready in:

Ingredients

- 2 slices rye bread
- 1 tablespoon butter, softened
- 2 ounces thinly sliced corned beef
- 2 ounces sauerkraut

- 1 slice mozzarella cheese

Direction

- Over medium heat, heat a medium skillet. Butter the bread on one side and then put one slice of the bread in skillet with the buttered side facing down. Spread a layer of mozzarella, corned beef, and sauerkraut onto the bread. Place the remaining slice of bread on top. Cook, flipping once, until the bread turns browned, cheese has melted and the sandwich is heated through. Serve right away.

Nutrition Information

- Calories: 489 calories;
- Total Fat: 28.8
- Sodium: 1683
- Total Carbohydrate: 34.4
- Cholesterol: 103
- Protein: 23

920. Reuben Sandwich II

Serving: 4 | Prep: 15mins | Cook: 2mins | Ready in:

Ingredients

- 1 tablespoon chili sauce
- 1/3 cup mayonnaise
- 1/4 cup butter, softened
- 8 slices rye bread
- 1/2 pound thinly sliced corned beef
- 1/2 pound sliced Swiss cheese
- 1 pound sauerkraut

Direction

- Preheat an oven broiler.
- Mix mayonnaise and chili sauce till smooth; spread butter and mayonnaise mixture on bread slices. Layer sauerkraut, Swiss and corned beef on 4 slices; put leftover slices over. Put onto baking sheet under the preheated

broiler; broil for 2 minutes, turning once, till browned.

Nutrition Information

- Calories: 738 calories;
- Total Carbohydrate: 40.6
- Cholesterol: 128
- Protein: 29.2
- Total Fat: 51.5
- Sodium: 1977

921. Ricotta And Tomato Sandwich

Serving: 2 | Prep: 5mins | Cook: 5mins |Ready in:

Ingredients

- 2 tomatoes, sliced
- 1/2 cup ricotta cheese
- 1/4 teaspoon Italian seasoning, or to taste
- 2 tablespoons mayonnaise
- 4 slices multigrain bread, toasted
- 2 slices provolone cheese

Direction

- Preheat oven broiler; put oven rack 6-inches away from heat source. Line parchment paper on a baking sheet.
- Put tomato slices on the prepared baking sheet; top every slice with ricotta cheese. Sprinkle Italian seasoning on ricotta cheese; put under the preheated broiler for 5 minutes till cheese starts to brown.
- Spread 1 tablespoon of mayonnaise on each of 2 toasted multigrain bread slices. Put leftover 2 toast pieces and provolone cheese slices on top. Put broiled tomatoes on provolone cheese; put bread, mayonnaise above tomatoes, to complete sandwich.

Nutrition Information

- Calories: 296 calories;
- Total Carbohydrate: 22.4
- Cholesterol: 29
- Protein: 11.7
- Total Fat: 19.6
- Sodium: 563

922. Rowing Team's Turkey Reuben Wraps

Serving: 4 | Prep: 15mins | Cook: |Ready in:

Ingredients

- 2 cups shredded cabbage
- 1 cup shredded carrots
- 1/2 cup thousand island salad dressing
- 3 tablespoons cider vinegar
- 4 (10 inch) whole wheat tortillas
- 1/4 cup thousand island salad dressing (optional)
- 4 romaine lettuce leaves
- 12 ounces sliced deli turkey meat
- 8 thin slices Gruyere cheese or Swiss cheese

Direction

- Mix the carrots, half cup salad dressing, cider vinegar and cabbage in a big bowl.
- Apply to each tortilla 1 tbsp. salad dressing if desired. Line every wrap with 1 lettuce leaf and 3 oz. turkey down the middle of lettuce. Put 2 pieces of cheese over the turkey. Top with three-quarter cup of cabbage mixture.
- Crease the base of the tortilla tightly over the filling, then crease in the right and left sides. Roll the wrap up to make a tight barrel. Do the same with remaining ingredients. Enclose in plastic wrap or sandwich wrappers and keep in the fridge until ready to serve. Just before serving, slice each wrap in two across the center with a slightly tilted cut.

Nutrition Information

- Calories: 582 calories;
- Sodium: 2011
- Total Carbohydrate: 59.3
- Cholesterol: 83
- Protein: 29.6
- Total Fat: 31.3

923.   Saint Paddy's Irish Sandwich

Serving: 6 | Prep: 20mins | Cook: 2hours30mins | Ready in:

Ingredients

- 1 (3 pound) corned beef brisket with spice packet
- 2 tablespoons olive oil
- 1 tablespoon balsamic vinegar
- 1 tablespoon spicy brown mustard
- 1/2 teaspoon salt
- 1/2 teaspoon ground black pepper
- 1/2 medium head cabbage, cored and sliced thin
- spicy brown mustard
- 12 slices sourdough bread, lightly toasted

Direction

- In a Dutch oven or a big pot, put corned beef and add water to cover. Add the spice packet from the corned beef. Put a cover on the pot and boil, and then lower the heat to simmer. Simmer until soft, about 50 minutes each pound. Take the meat out and let sit for 15 minutes. Cut the meat across the grain.
- In a small bowl, combine pepper, salt, mustard, balsamic vinegar, and olive oil. In a big bowl, put shredded cabbage and add the dressing; mix to blend the dressing with the cabbage.
- Spread mustard in 1 layer onto 6 toasted bread slices. On each slice, put corned beef and some

shredded cabbage and put the leftover bread slices on top.

Nutrition Information

- Calories: 461 calories;
- Total Fat: 24.8
- Sodium: 1757
- Total Carbohydrate: 34
- Cholesterol: 97
- Protein: 25.4

924.   Salmon Cake Sliders And Garlic Aioli

Serving: 12 | Prep: 30mins | Cook: 10mins | Ready in:

Ingredients

- Salmon Cakes:
- 1 pound salmon, chopped
- 1/2 cup finely chopped bell pepper
- 1/4 cup olive oil mayonnaise
- 1/4 cup dry bread crumbs
- 1 green onion, finely chopped
- 1 tablespoon lemon juice
- 1 tablespoon finely chopped cilantro
- 1 teaspoon spicy brown mustard
- 1 teaspoon hot sauce
- 1 teaspoon Worcestershire sauce
- 1/2 teaspoon seafood seasoning (such as Old Bay®)
- 1/4 teaspoon garlic powder
- salt and ground black pepper to taste
- 1 egg
- 2 tablespoons vegetable oil, or as needed
- 12 slider-size burger buns, split
- Aioli:
- 1 cup mayonnaise
- 1 tablespoon freshly squeezed lemon juice
- 1 tablespoon finely chopped cilantro
- 1 teaspoon kosher salt
- 1 clove garlic, minced

Direction

- In a large bowl, mix together pepper, salt, garlic powder, seafood seasoning, Worcestershire sauce, hot sauce, mustard, a tablespoon of cilantro, a tablespoon of lemon juice, green onion, bread crumbs, olive oil mayonnaise, bell pepper, and salmon.
- In a small bowl, whisking egg; pouring over salmon mixture and mixing till incorporated evenly. Shape salmon mixture into twelve patties.
- In a large skillet, heating vegetable oil over medium heat. Cooking salmon patties in batches for approximately 5 minutes on each side till browned lightly. In each slider bun, lay a patty.
- To make aioli, in a bowl, mix together garlic, a teaspoon of kosher salt, a tablespoon of cilantro, a tablespoon of lemon juice, and mayonnaise. Spreading over the salmon patties with aioli.

Nutrition Information

- Calories: 324 calories;
- Sodium: 400
- Total Carbohydrate: 161.1
- Cholesterol: 45
- Protein: 10.6
- Total Fat: 23.3

---

925. Sausage Sandwich With Sauteed Apple Slices

Serving: 2 | Prep: 5mins | Cook: 20mins | Ready in:

Ingredients

- 3 links pork sausage
- 2 tablespoons butter
- 1 large Granny Smith apples - peeled, cored and sliced
- 2 slices whole wheat bread

- 1 tablespoon butter, softened
- 1/4 cup maple syrup

Direction

- Slice the sausages lengthwise into 2 equal pieces. Put the halved sausages in a skillet and let it cook slowly for about 15 minutes until it is thoroughly cooked and has turned brown in color, flip it frequently and drain off any excess drippings as it accumulates.
- Put 2 tablespoons of butter in a separate skillet and let it heat up over low heat setting. Put in the apple slices and let it cook while flipping it frequently until it has softened and turns nicely brown in color. Make sure that the apple slices and sausages are ready at the same time.
- Toast the bread then coat one side with softened butter. Drain off any excess oil from the cooked sausages then put it onto the buttered toast. Put the cooked apple slices on top of the sausages then drizzle maple syrup all over the top. Serve it right away.

Nutrition Information

- Calories: 473 calories;
- Sodium: 475
- Total Carbohydrate: 53.4
- Cholesterol: 76
- Protein: 8.9
- Total Fat: 26.3

---

926. Savory Panettone

Serving: 8 | Prep: 30mins | Cook: 40mins | Ready in:

Ingredients

- Panettone:
- 2 eggs
- 1 1/2 teaspoons salt
- 1/2 cup lukewarm milk

- 2 1/2 tablespoons lukewarm milk, or more as needed
- 1/2 ounce compressed fresh yeast
- 1 teaspoon white sugar
- 2 cups Italian-style tipo 00 flour
- 2 cups strong bread flour
- 1/4 cup lukewarm water
- 6 tablespoons butter, at room temperature
- Tuna Filling:
- 1 (3 ounce) can tuna, drained
- 3 tablespoons mayonnaise
- Tapenade:
- 1/4 cup sliced black olives
- 2 tablespoons extra-virgin olive oil
- 2 anchovy fillets
- 1 tablespoon capers
- Cheese Filling:
- 2 ounces cubed ham
- 3 tablespoons cream cheese
- 3/4 cup cooked shrimp
- 4 lettuce leaves
- 4 slices mozzarella cheese
- 3 slices prosciutto, or more to taste

Direction

- Lightly beat salt and eggs in a bowl.
- Mix sugar, yeast, and 1/2 cup and 2 1/2 tablespoons of lukewarm milk. Let stand for 5 minutes till foamy.
- In a bowl, mix bread flours and tipo 00 together; create a well in middle. Add yeast mixture and beaten eggs; mix using a fork. Add water; mix again to get a sticky ball. A little at a time, knead butter in dough.
- Put dough on a floured work surface; vigorously knead for 10 minutes till smooth. Put in a lightly floured bowl. Use a damp, clean cloth to cover. Let rest for 1 1/2 hours till doubled in volume in a warm place.
- On floured surface, turn dough out. Stretch a piece out; fold over top. Repeat with other dough section, working your way around circle. Put dough in paper panettone mold. Use plastic wrap to cover. Let rise for 2 hours till dough reaches rim of mold in a warm place.

- Preheat an oven to 175°C/350°F. Use some water to fill a baking dish; put on bottom oven rack to keep panettone moist while baking.
- Brush some milk over panettone; put mold on flat baking sheet.
- In the preheated oven, bake for 40-45 minutes till a skewer inserted in the middle exits clean. Cool for a few minutes on a wire wrap. Use 2 long wooden skewers to pierce side, near bottom, to stick out opposite side. Gently flip panettone; set skewers on rim of tall pot. Cool panettone for 5 hours minimum upside down so it won't collapse.
- Mix mayonnaise and tuna till smooth in a bowl. Blend capers, anchovy fillets, olive oil and olives till smooth in another bowl. Mix ham and cream cheese in a 3rd bowl.
- Gently remove skewers from panettone. Lengthwise, slice, including top, to get 6 slices. Lay bottom slice onto a serving plate; spread tuna mixture on. Use lettuce and shrimp to cover. Press over the 2nd slice and add the 3rd slices. On top, spread olive mixture and use mozzarella cheese to cover. Press on 4th slice. On top, spread cream cheese mixture then use prosciutto to cover. Use top slice to cover.
- Use plastic wrap to wrap panettone. Before serving, refrigerate for 1 hour minimum. From top to bottom, cut to wedges.

Nutrition Information

- Calories: 418 calories;
- Total Fat: 25.7
- Sodium: 986
- Total Carbohydrate: 27.9
- Cholesterol: 122
- Protein: 18.3

---

927.   Schnitzel Sandwich

Serving: 4 | Prep: 20mins | Cook: 20mins | Ready in:

Ingredients

- 2 skinless, boneless chicken breasts, halved lengthwise
- salt and ground black pepper to taste
- 1 cup all-purpose flour
- 2 eggs
- 1 cup dry bread crumbs
- 5 tablespoons vegetable oil
- 4 sandwich rolls, split
- 2 tablespoons mayonnaise
- lemon, juiced
- 4 dashes hot pepper sauce (such as Tabasco®) (optional)
- 4 leaves chopped romaine lettuce
- 1 tablespoon mustard

Direction

- Position chicken between 2 sheets of heavy plastic on a solid, flatten surface; use the smooth side of a meat mallet to pound meat firmly to an even thickness. Sprinkle liberally with pepper and salt.
- Put flour into a large, flat dish. In a shallow mixing bowl, whisk eggs well. Spread bread crumbs into a separate large, flat dish.
- Dredge each chicken piece in flour, immerse in beaten eggs, and press into breadcrumbs to coat.
- Set oven to 200°F (95°C) to preheat.
- Heat oil over medium-low heat in a large skillet. Working in batches, cook breaded chicken in heated oil, about 5 minutes on each side, until center is no longer pink and outside turns golden brown. Remove chicken to a paper towel-lined oven-safe plate to drain. Keep chicken warm in the oven.
- Spread the bottom half of each sandwich roll with mayonnaise; place 1 piece of breaded chicken over mayonnaise layer, and top with a couple of drops of lemon juice, 1 dash hot sauce, and 1 lettuce leaf. Smear the top half of each sandwich roll with mustard. Lay the top halves atop lettuce to complete sandwiches.

Nutrition Information

- Calories: 914 calories;

- Total Fat: 35.3
- Sodium: 1164
- Total Carbohydrate: 112.3
- Cholesterol: 119
- Protein: 34.1

---

928.   Seattle Style Turkey Lettuce Wraps

Serving: 4 | Prep: 20mins | Cook: | Ready in:

Ingredients

- 1 (16 ounce) package JENNIE-O® Lean Ground Turkey
- 2 cloves garlic, chopped
- 1 tablespoon fresh grated ginger
- 2 tablespoons HOUSE OF TSANG® ginger-flavored soy sauce
- 1 tablespoon brown sugar
- 1/4 cup chopped green onions
- 1 red bell pepper, chopped
- 1/2 cup chopped fresh mint leaves
- 1 head butter lettuce

Direction

- Cook turkey following packaging directions. Cook to well done all the time, a meat thermometer should register 165°F.
- Put in the red bell pepper, green onions, brown sugar, soy sauce, ginger and garlic. Let cook for 7 minutes or till garlic is tender.
- Mix in the mint leaves. Quickly transfer the meat to shallow dish and refrigerate for an hour.
- Take core off head of lettuce; part, rinse and dry the leaves.
- In lettuce cups, scoop refrigerated turkey mixture.

Nutrition Information

- Calories: 165 calories;

- Cholesterol: 46
- Protein: 28
- Total Fat: 1.7
- Sodium: 443
- Total Carbohydrate: 9.3

---

929. Sensational Steak Sandwich

Serving: 4 | Prep: 30mins | Cook: 4hours20mins | Ready in:

Ingredients

- 2 tablespoons olive oil
- 1 pound thinly sliced sirloin steak strips
- 8 ounces sliced fresh mushrooms
- 1 green bell pepper, seeded and cut into strips
- 1 medium onion, sliced
- 10 slices provolone cheese
- 1 loaf French bread
- 1 (14 ounce) can beef broth
- 1/2 teaspoon salt
- 1/2 teaspoon ground black pepper
- 1/2 teaspoon garlic powder
- 2 tablespoons Worcestershire sauce
- 1/8 teaspoon red pepper flakes
- 1/4 cup Pinot Noir or other dry red wine
- 1/2 cup prepared horseradish (optional)
- 1/2 cup brown mustard (optional)

Direction

- In a large skillet, heat the oil over medium heat. Put in the beef, then cook until browned. Put in the onion, bell pepper and mushrooms; cook and mix for around 5 minutes, until beginning to turn tender.
- In a slow cooker, blend the red wine, red pepper flakes, Worcestershire sauce, pepper, salt, and beef broth. Move the vegetables and beef to the slow cooker, then stir to combine. Cook while covered on High for 3 - 4 hours, till the beef becomes extremely softened.

- Preheat the oven to 425° F (220° C). Drain the liquid from the slow cooker, reserve for dipping. Cut lengthwise the French bread loaf like a submarine sandwich. Mix the mustard and horseradish together; spread onto the inner of the loaf. On both sides of the loaf, position slices of provolone cheese, fill with vegetables and beef. Seal the loaf, then wrap aluminum foil around the entire sandwich.
- In the preheated oven, bake for 10 - 15 minutes. Bake without the aluminum foil for crunchier bread. Cut into servings. Serve with the juices reserved from the slow cooker as dipping.

Nutrition Information

- Calories: 908 calories;
- Total Fat: 40.6
- Sodium: 2586
- Total Carbohydrate: 78.8
- Cholesterol: 109
- Protein: 55.7

---

930. Shooter Sandwich

Serving: 6 | Prep: 25mins | Cook: 20mins | Ready in:

Ingredients

- 1 loaf hearty country bread, unsliced
- 3 tablespoons vegetable oil, divided
- 1 (3 pound) boneless beef round steak, 2 inches thick
- 1 onion, thinly sliced
- 2 cups sliced fresh mushrooms
- 1 clove garlic, minced, or to taste
- salt to taste
- ground black pepper to taste
- garlic salt to taste

Direction

- For lid, cut thick slice from top of loaf; use gingers to pull bread middle out of crust and leave thick shell. Keep removed bread for another time.
- Heat 1 tbsp. vegetable oil in big heavy skillet on high heat till oil smokes slightly; lay beef round steak in hot skillet. Cook for 5-8 minutes per side to get medium-rare or till inside reaches preferred degree of doneness and outside of meat is crusty and browned. Remove steak; put aside.
- Heat leftover 2 tbsp. vegetable oil in skillet; mix and cook garlic, mushrooms and onion for 5-8 minutes till mushrooms give up juice and onions are translucent. Take off heat; put aside.
- Lay cooked steak in hollowed-out bread loaf; pile garlic, mushrooms and onions over steak. Put bread lid on; use aluminum foil to wrap whole loaf. Put loaf on baking sheet; put heavy flat weight over loaf like heavy skillet/board. Weight top using jars of water or several bricks.
- Put loaf and its weights in the fridge; chill and press sandwich for 6 hours minimum. Bring to room temperature to serve; cut loaf slices off.

Nutrition Information

- Calories: 516 calories;
- Sodium: 635
- Total Carbohydrate: 42.9
- Cholesterol: 78
- Protein: 34.3
- Total Fat: 22.3

931.   Shrimp Po' Boys

Serving: 4 | Prep: | Cook: | Ready in:

Ingredients

- Vegetable oil for deep-frying
- 4 French rolls, split and hinged
- 4 tablespoons melted butter
- 1 teaspoon minced garlic
- 3 eggs, beaten
- 2 tablespoons Creole seasoning
- 3/4 cup all-purpose flour
- 2 pounds jumbo shrimp, peeled and deveined
- 2 cups Kikkoman Panko Bread Crumbs
- 2 cups shredded lettuce
- Remoulade sauce:
- 1/2 cup mayonnaise
- 1 tablespoon horseradish
- 1 teaspoon pickle relish
- 1 teaspoon minced garlic
- 1/2 teaspoon cayenne pepper
- 2 tablespoons Kikkoman Ponzu Lime

Direction

- Mix garlic and butter then spread on rolls; toast till brown in oven. Heat oil to 360° in 2-qt. saucepan. Mix flour and creole seasoning; dredge shrimp into the flour, then egg and roll in panko. Working in batches, fry shrimp till golden brown. Smear remoulade sauce on all four rolls; put shrimp over then the shredded lettuce.
- Remoulade sauce: Mix ponzu, cayenne pepper, minced garlic, pickle relish, horseradish and mayo in bowl.

Nutrition Information

- Calories: 1257 calories;
- Total Carbohydrate: 127.3
- Cholesterol: 526
- Protein: 73.2
- Total Fat: 50
- Sodium: 2641

932.   Simple Stromboli

Serving: 3 | Prep: 10mins | Cook: 30mins | Ready in:

Ingredients

- 1/2 pound bulk pork sausage (optional)
- 1 (1 pound) loaf frozen bread dough, thawed
- 4 slices hard salami
- 4 slices thinly sliced ham
- 4 slices American cheese
- 1 cup shredded mozzarella cheese
- salt and ground black pepper to taste
- 1 egg white, lightly beaten

Direction

- Preheat the oven to 220°Celcius or 425°F
- On medium-high heat, heat a big pan; add sausage. Cook and stir for about 10 minutes until evenly brown, crumbly, and the sausage is not pink anymore; drain. Get rid of the excess grease.
- In a baking sheet, ungreased, flatten the bread dough to 3/4 -in thick. Layer the middle of the dough with ham, salami, and slices of American cheese. Top with cooked sausage, mozzarella cheese, pepper, and salt. Wrap the dough up to enclose the ingredients, seal by pressing the edges together to avoid leaks. Slather the surface with egg white.
- Bake in the 425°F preheated oven for 17-20 minutes until the dough is light brown and cooked.

Nutrition Information

- Calories: 1065 calories;
- Total Fat: 54.6
- Sodium: 3633
- Total Carbohydrate: 77.8
- Cholesterol: 162
- Protein: 59

933.   Simple Tuna Melt

Serving: 1 | Prep: 3mins | Cook: 7mins | Ready in:

Ingredients

- 1 (5 ounce) can tuna, drained and flaked
- 2 tablespoons mayonnaise
- 1 pinch salt
- 1 teaspoon balsamic vinegar
- 1 teaspoon Dijon mustard
- 2 slices whole wheat bread
- 2 teaspoons chopped dill pickle
- 1/4 cup shredded sharp Cheddar cheese

Direction

- Set the oven at 375°F (190°C) and start preheating. Toast bread slices in the oven while it preheats and while preparing tuna salad.
- Meanwhile, for the tuna salad, in a small bowl, combine dill pickle, mustard, balsamic vinegar, salt, mayonnaise and tuna till well-blended. Take the bread away from the oven; pile the tuna mixture onto one slice. Sprinkle the other slice of bread with cheese.
- Bake in the preheated oven till the tuna is heated through and the cheese is melted, 7 minutes. Top the tuna side of the sandwich with the cheese side. Cut in half. Serve immediately.

Nutrition Information

- Calories: 608 calories;
- Sodium: 1028
- Total Carbohydrate: 26.8
- Cholesterol: 78
- Protein: 46.8
- Total Fat: 34.2

934.   Simple Tuna Melts

Serving: 4 | Prep: 5mins | Cook: 10mins | Ready in:

Ingredients

- 1 (5 ounce) can tuna, drained
- 1/2 small onion, minced

- pepper to taste
- 12 slices pickled jalapeno
- 2 English muffins, split
- 4 slices Cheddar cheese

Direction

- Set the oven at 350°F (175°C) and start preheating.
- Combine black pepper, minced onion and tuna in a small bowl. Distribute the mixture onto 4 halves of English Muffins. Place 3 slices of jalapenos on each muffin half. Place a slice of Cheddar cheese on top. Arrange on a baking sheet.
- Bake for 10 minutes in the preheated oven, or till the cheese starts to bubble.

Nutrition Information

- Calories: 224 calories;
- Protein: 17.5
- Total Fat: 10.2
- Sodium: 444
- Total Carbohydrate: 15.4
- Cholesterol: 39

---

935. Skillet Garlic Chicken Dinner

Serving: 4 | Prep: 5mins | Cook: 40mins | Ready in:

Ingredients

- Vegetable cooking spray
- 4 skinless, boneless chicken breast halves
- 2 cloves garlic, minced
- 1 3/4 cups Swanson® Chicken Stock
- 3/4 cup uncooked regular long-grain white rice
- 1 (16 ounce) bag frozen vegetable combination (broccoli, cauliflower, carrots)
- 1/3 cup grated Parmesan cheese
- Paprika

Direction

- Use the cooking spray to spray a skillet (12 inches) and heat over medium-high heat for approximately 1 minute. Stir in garlic and the chicken; cook for around 10 minutes till the chicken is well browned on both sides. Take the chicken out of the skillet.
- In the skillet, stir the vegetables, rice and stock and heat to a boil. Lower to low heat. Cook while covered for 15 minutes. Blend in the cheese.
- Place the chicken back to the skillet. Use paprika to sprinkle the chicken. Cook while covered for 10 minutes till the rice is tender and the chicken is cooked through.

Nutrition Information

- Calories: 390 calories;
- Protein: 36.4
- Total Fat: 6.4
- Sodium: 441
- Total Carbohydrate: 46.3
- Cholesterol: 75

---

936. Slaw Dogs

Serving: 4 | Prep: 10mins | Cook: 10mins | Ready in:

Ingredients

- 4 hot dogs
- 4 hot dog buns, split
- 1 cup prepared creamy coleslaw
- 1/4 cup Carolina-style barbeque sauce
- 2 teaspoons Dijon mustard, or to taste

Direction

- Grill hot dogs for 5 to 8 minutes until browned and heated through. An instant-read thermometer pierced into the center should register 165°F (74°C).

- Grill buns with the cut side down for approximately 1 minute or until lightly golden.
- Put hot dogs into buns; spoon coleslaw and barbeque sauce over top. Drizzle mustard on top to complete.

Nutrition Information

- Calories: 334 calories;
- Total Fat: 16.5
- Sodium: 968
- Total Carbohydrate: 35.5
- Cholesterol: 28
- Protein: 9.8

937. Sloppy Joe Sandwiches

Serving: 2 | Prep: 5mins | Cook: 40mins | Ready in:

Ingredients

- 1/2 pound ground beef
- 1/2 onion, chopped
- 1/2 cup ketchup
- 2 tablespoons water
- 1 tablespoon brown sugar
- 1 teaspoon Worcestershire sauce
- 1 teaspoon prepared mustard
- 1 teaspoon white vinegar
- 1 teaspoon chili powder
- 1/4 teaspoon garlic powder
- 1/4 teaspoon onion powder
- 1/4 teaspoon salt
- 2 hamburger buns, split

Direction

- Take a big frying pan and heat it over medium high heat. Stir fry onion and ground beef for about 10 minutes until beef becomes crumbly, no longer pink and evenly brown. Remove excess grease. Mix in salt, onion powder, garlic powder, chili powder, vinegar, mustard,

Worcestershire sauce, brown sugar, water and ketchup.
- Boil beef mixture over high heat. Lower the heat to low and let it simmer, covered, for 30-40 minutes until the sauce becomes thick. Put on buns and serve.

Nutrition Information

- Calories: 467 calories;
- Total Fat: 20.3
- Sodium: 1339
- Total Carbohydrate: 47.8
- Cholesterol: 69
- Protein: 24

938. Sloppy Joes I

Serving: 6 | Prep: 10mins | Cook: 1hours | Ready in:

Ingredients

- 1 pound lean ground beef
- 1 (10.75 ounce) can condensed chicken gumbo soup
- 2 tablespoons ketchup
- 1 tablespoon yellow mustard
- 1 1/4 cups water
- salt to taste
- ground black pepper to taste

Direction

- In a big frying pan, brown meat over medium heat. Strain any fat from the pan.
- Mix in pepper, salt, water, yellow mustard, ketchup, and soup. Heat to medium-low, simmer without a cover until the mixture has thickened and absorbed the liquid, about 60 minutes.

Nutrition Information

- Calories: 229 calories;

- Sodium: 524
- Total Carbohydrate: 4.8
- Cholesterol: 58
- Protein: 14.7
- Total Fat: 16.3

939. Sloppy Juan

Serving: 8 | Prep: 30mins | Cook: 30mins | Ready in:

Ingredients

- Chipotle Mayo:
- 1 1/2 cups mayonnaise
- 1/2 cup sour cream
- 1/4 cup chopped fresh cilantro
- 1/4 cup diced green onions
- 1 1/2 tablespoons chipotle chili powder
- 1 tablespoon garlic basil spread (see footnote for recipe link)
- 1 tablespoon lime juice
- 1 teaspoon ground cumin
- salt and freshly ground black pepper to taste
- 1 tablespoon olive oil
- 1 pound ground chorizo
- 1 pound ground beef
- 1 teaspoon ground coriander
- 1 head cabbage, chopped
- 1 green bell pepper, diced
- 1 yellow bell pepper, diced
- 1 orange bell pepper, diced
- 1 jalapeno pepper, seeded and minced (optional)
- 1 cup water, or as needed
- 1/4 cup brown sugar
- 2 tablespoons chili powder
- 1/4 cup chopped fresh cilantro
- 1 lime, juiced
- 4 Italian-style hoagie buns, split lengthwise and toasted
- 1 tablespoon olive oil
- 8 eggs

Direction

- In small bowl, combine cumin, garlic basil spread, one tablespoon of lime juice, chipotle chili powder, green onions, a quarter cup cilantro, sour cream and mayonnaise. Mix until combined. Then season with black pepper and salt. Place in the refrigerator for at least 60 mins with a cover.
- In a large pot or Dutch oven, heat one tablespoon of the olive oil over medium heat; cook while stirring coriander, ground beef, and chorizo for 15 mins until the meat has been browned. Drain, then remove the fat. Add black pepper and salt to season.
- Stir water, jalapeno, orange bell pepper, yellow bell pepper, green bell pepper and cabbage into the chorizo mixture. Cook while stirring for 10 mins or until peppers are softened. Put in chili powder and brown sugar; cook while stirring for 10 mins or until the sauce becomes thick and water has evaporated.
- Sprinkle onto chorizo mixture with juice of one lime and a quarter cup of cilantro. Take away from the heat.
- Spread one tablespoon of the chipotle mayo over each hoagie bun. Distribute chorizo mixture evenly among four sandwiches.
- In a nonstick skillet, heat one tablespoon of olive oil over medium heat. Then fry eggs for 2 mins on each side; if necessary, fry 2-4 at once, until the whites are set but yolks are still soft. Top each sandwich with 2 eggs.

Nutrition Information

- Calories: 1077 calories;
- Total Fat: 77.5
- Sodium: 1519
- Total Carbohydrate: 58.9
- Cholesterol: 292
- Protein: 39

940. Slow Cooker BBQ Flat Iron Steak Sandwiches

Serving: 4 | Prep: 15mins | Cook: 5hours | Ready in:

Ingredients

- 1/2 cup ketchup
- 1/2 cup Italian dressing
- 2 tablespoons soy sauce
- 1 tablespoon molasses
- 2 pounds flat iron steak, cubed
- 1 tablespoon dried chopped onion
- 4 hoagie rolls, split lengthwise and toasted
- 1 cup prepared coleslaw (optional)

Direction

- In a small bowl, mix molasses, soy sauce, Italian dressing and ketchup. Put steak into slow cooker. Sprinkle on onions. Put ketchup mixture on steak.
- Put slow cooker on high. Cook for an hour. Lower heat to low. Keep cooking for about 4 hours until meat is tender. Serve it on hoagie buns. Put 1/4 cup coleslaw on top (optional) for Southern barbecue flavor.

Nutrition Information

- Calories: 987 calories;
- Total Fat: 42.7
- Sodium: 2186
- Total Carbohydrate: 89.8
- Cholesterol: 159
- Protein: 60

941. Slow Cooker Barbequed Pork For Sandwiches

Serving: 12 | Prep: 10mins | Cook: 7hours | Ready in:

Ingredients

- 2 1/2 pounds boneless pork roast
- salt and ground black pepper to taste
- 2 cups strong brewed coffee
- 2 tablespoons Worcestershire sauce
- 2 tablespoons bourbon whiskey
- 10 cloves garlic
- 3 cups beef broth
- 1 cup water
- 1 small onion, diced
- 1 pinch crushed red pepper flakes
- 2 (12 ounce) bottles barbeque sauce

Direction

- Use pepper and salt to season roast. In a slow cooker, put seasoned roast, Worcestershire sauce, coffee, red pepper flakes, onion, water, beef broth, garlic and bourbon whiskey, then set to low setting. Cook for 3-4 hours. Take garlic cloves out of the cooker and use a fork to mash them, then bring mashed garlic back to the slow cooker. Cook for 3-4 hours more.
- Remove roast to a big cutting board and get rid of liquid. Use 2 forks to shred the roast into strands, then bring the meat back to slow cooker. Stir in barbecue sauce and keep on cooking for 1-3 hours on low setting.

Nutrition Information

- Calories: 224 calories;
- Total Fat: 9.2
- Sodium: 914
- Total Carbohydrate: 22.3
- Cholesterol: 37
- Protein: 10.6

942. Slow Cooker Ground Beef Barbecue

Serving: 20 | Prep: 10mins | Cook: 6hours15mins | Ready in:

Ingredients

- 3 pounds lean ground beef
- 1 large onion, chopped
- 2 cloves garlic, minced
- 5 stalks celery, finely chopped
- 1 1/2 teaspoons salt
- 1/2 teaspoon ground black pepper
- 1 tablespoon cider vinegar
- 2 tablespoons prepared mustard
- 1/4 cup firmly packed brown sugar
- 3 1/2 cups ketchup

Direction

- In a big skillet, add ground beef on moderate heat then cook for 15 minutes while breaking up meat as it cooks, until browned. Get rid of excess grease.
- In a slow cooker, add ketchup, brown sugar, mustard, cider vinegar, black pepper, salt, celery, garlic, onion and cooked meat, then stir to mix together. Set the cooker on low setting and cook for about 6-8 hours.

Nutrition Information

- Calories: 188 calories;
- Total Fat: 8.5
- Sodium: 710
- Total Carbohydrate: 14.5
- Cholesterol: 45
- Protein: 13.9

---

943.   Slow Cooker Pulled Pork Roast

Serving: 8 | Prep: 10mins | Cook: 10hours | Ready in:

Ingredients

- 1 (3 1/2) pound pork butt roast
- 1 tablespoon chili powder
- 1 tablespoon vegetable oil
- 2 teaspoons pepper
- 2 teaspoons ground cumin

- 2 teaspoons coriander
- 2 teaspoons paprika
- 1 teaspoon allspice
- 1/2 teaspoon salt
- 2 cloves garlic, minced
- 1 1/2 cups Heinz Tomato Ketchup
- 1 cup Heinz® Apple Cider Vinegar
- 1/2 cup fancy molasses
- 1/3 cup Heinz® Mustard
- 2 teaspoons cornstarch
- Soft rolls

Direction

- Discard all string from the roast and trim away excess fat. In a bowl, put chili powder; mix in garlic, salt, allspice, paprika, coriander, cumin, pepper, chili and oil to form a paste. Rub all over the whole pork; thoroughly work the spice mixture into the meat. Let the meat marinate for a minimum of 30 minutes or overnight. Remove the roast to a slow cooker.
- Stir together mustard, molasses, vinegar and ketchup. Add the mixture onto the roast and cook on low until very soft, or about 8-10 hours.
- Remove the roast to a big bowl; remove any fat you can see. Separate the meat into long strands with 2 forks. Pour off 1 1/2 cups of the cooking juices and drain into a saucepan. Mix in cornstarch and boil. Cook until bubbly and thick while whisking. Put the shredded meat back into the slow cooker, mix to blend with the leftover cooking juices. Put the meat on soft rolls to enjoy, drizzle the thickened sauce mixture over to taste.

Nutrition Information

- Calories: 503 calories;
- Total Carbohydrate: 49.3
- Cholesterol: 78
- Protein: 24.8
- Total Fat: 22.8
- Sodium: 934

944.   Slow Cooker Spicy Buffalo Ranch Chicken

Serving: 8 | Prep: 5mins | Cook: 6hours | Ready in:

Ingredients

- 3 pounds chicken breast
- 1 (12 ounce) bottle hot pepper sauce (such as Frank's RedHot®)
- 1 (1 ounce) package dry ranch dressing mix (such as Hidden Valley Ranch®)
- 2 (4 roll) packages Hawaiian buns, or as needed

Direction

- In a slow cooker, mix ranch dressing, hot sauce, and chicken. Then cook for 6 hours on medium. And shred the chicken then serve on top of buns.

Nutrition Information

- Calories: 456 calories;
- Total Fat: 3.6
- Sodium: 1638
- Total Carbohydrate: 44.5
- Cholesterol: 128
- Protein: 47.3

945.   Slow Cooker Texas Pulled Pork

Serving: 8 | Prep: 15mins | Cook: 5hours | Ready in:

Ingredients

- 1 teaspoon vegetable oil
- 1 (4 pound) pork shoulder roast
- 1 cup barbeque sauce
- 1/2 cup apple cider vinegar
- 1/2 cup chicken broth

- 1/4 cup light brown sugar
- 1 tablespoon prepared yellow mustard
- 1 tablespoon Worcestershire sauce
- 1 tablespoon chili powder
- 1 extra large onion, chopped
- 2 large cloves garlic, crushed
- 1 1/2 teaspoons dried thyme
- 8 hamburger buns, split
- 2 tablespoons butter, or as needed

Direction

- In the bottom of a slow cooker, add the vegetable oil. Put the pork roast into the slow cooker; add chicken broth, apple cider vinegar and the barbecue sauce. Mix in thyme, garlic, onion, chili powder, Worcestershire sauce, yellow mustard and the brown sugar. Cover up and cook on high for 5 to 6 hours, until the roast shreds easily with a fork.
- Take the roast out of the slow cooker, and use two forks to shred the meat. Put back the shredded pork to the slow cooker, and mix the meat into the juices.
- Spread the butter on the inside of both halves of hamburger buns. Toast the buns in a skillet over medium heat with butter side down, until golden brown. Spoon the pork into the toasted buns.

Nutrition Information

- Calories: 527 calories;
- Total Fat: 23.1
- Sodium: 730
- Total Carbohydrate: 45.5
- Cholesterol: 98
- Protein: 31.9

946.   Slow Cooker Venison Sloppy Joes

Serving: 4 | Prep: 5mins | Cook: 8hours | Ready in:

Ingredients

- 1/4 pound bacon
- 2 pounds venison stew meat
- 1 large yellow onion, chopped
- 1/2 cup brown sugar
- 1/4 cup wine vinegar
- 1 tablespoon ground cumin
- 1 teaspoon chili powder
- 2 tablespoons minced garlic
- 1 tablespoon prepared Dijon-style mustard
- 1 cup ketchup
- salt and pepper to taste

Direction

- Cook bacon in big deep skillet on medium high heat till browned evenly. Take out of skillet; crumble. Put aside. In bacon grease, brown stew meat for flavor.
- Mix pepper, salt, ketchup, garlic, mustard, chili powder, cumin, vinegar, sugar and onion in slow cooker well. Add venison and bacon; mix together.
- Cook on low setting for at least 8 hours. Separate meat with a fork to sloppy joe-style and thick barbecue.

Nutrition Information

- Calories: 538 calories;
- Protein: 51.8
- Total Fat: 18.4
- Sodium: 1071
- Total Carbohydrate: 41.1
- Cholesterol: 191

---

947.   Smoked Salmon Sliders With Garlic Aioli

Serving: 12 | Prep: 15mins | Cook: 1hours30mins | Ready in:

Ingredients

- Brine:
- water as needed
- 1/2 cup salt
- 1 tablespoon dried tarragon
- 1 1/2 pounds salmon fillets
- Aioli:
- 1 cup mayonnaise
- 3 tablespoons fresh lemon juice
- 3 cloves garlic, minced
- 1 1/2 teaspoons ground black pepper
- 1/2 teaspoon lemon zest, or to taste
- salt, or to taste
- 1/2 cup apple wood chips, or as needed
- 12 slider-size burger buns

Direction

- Fill the large baking dish with enough water, about half of the dish. Mix in 1/2 cup of salt until it dissolves completely. Add the tarragon. Position the salmon in the brine, pouring in more water if necessary until the salmon is well covered. Use a plastic wrap to cover the dish. Refrigerate it for 2-12 hours until the brine is completely soaked into the salmon.
- In a bowl, combine a pinch of salt, garlic, mayonnaise, lemon zest, pepper, and lemon juice until the aioli turns smooth. Refrigerate the mixture for 30 minutes until chilled.
- Transfer the salmon from the brine onto the wire rack and let it dry for 30 minutes. Discard the brine.
- Arrange some applewood whips into the smoker. Position the salmon in the smoker. Follow the manufacturer's guides to smoke the salmon on low heat for 1 1/2-2 hours. The salmon should be flaked easily using the fork after smoking.
- Divide the salmon among the 12 buns to assemble the sliders. Put a spoonful of aioli on top of the salmon. Top the aioli layer with a bun to create a sandwich.

Nutrition Information

- Calories: 320 calories;

- Total Fat: 22.3
- Sodium: 141
- Total Carbohydrate: 159.5
- Cholesterol: 40
- Protein: 13.6

948. Sourdough Chipotle Chicken Panini

Serving: 1 | Prep: 10mins | Cook: 5mins | Ready in:

Ingredients

- 2 slices sourdough bread
- 1/4 cup Caesar salad dressing
- 1 cooked chicken breast, diced
- 1/2 cup shredded Cheddar cheese
- 1 tablespoon bacon bits
- 1 1/2 teaspoons chipotle chile powder, or to taste
- 2 tablespoons softened butter

Direction

- Preheat the panini press for medium-high heat.
- Scatter Caesar dressing on each side of every bread piece. Put the chicken over the bottom slice, scatter chipotle chili powder, bacon bits and Cheddar cheese on top. Onto the sandwich, put top piece of the bread, and with softened butter, butter the outside parts.
- On the prepped grill, let cook for 5 minutes till bread is golden brown and crispy, and the inner of sandwich is hot.

Nutrition Information

- Calories: 1243 calories;
- Total Fat: 83.9
- Sodium: 1813
- Total Carbohydrate: 31.9
- Cholesterol: 312
- Protein: 85.7

949. Spicy Buffalo Chicken And Blue Cheese Panini

Serving: 2 | Prep: | Cook: 19mins | Ready in:

Ingredients

- 2 tablespoons olive oil, divided
- 1/2 Spanish onion, sliced into rings
- 2 skinless, boneless chicken breast halves
- 1/4 cup light garlic cream cheese
- 1/4 cup hot pepper sauce (such as Frank's RedHot®)
- 2 tablespoons white vinegar
- 1 teaspoon garlic powder
- salt and ground black pepper to taste
- 2 tablespoons light garlic cream cheese, divided
- 4 slices focaccia bread
- 2 slices sharp Cheddar cheese
- 2 tablespoons blue cheese salad dressing
- 1/2 jalapeno pepper, cut into rings

Direction

- Heat 1 tbsp. of the olive oil on medium low heat in the small-sized skillet. Put in the onion; cook and whisk for roughly 5 minutes or till becoming tender and brown. Take out of the heat.
- Heat the rest 1 tbsp. of the olive oil on medium heat in the big skillet. Put in the chicken; cook for roughly 6 minutes on each side or till not pink in middle anymore and juices come out clear. Take out of the heat and shred with 2 forks.
- Stir the pepper, salt, garlic powder, vinegar, hot sauce and a quarter cup of the cream cheese to shredded chicken.
- Spread 1 tbsp. of the cream cheese on 2 slices of the focaccia; lay the Cheddar cheese over the top. Put heaping spoonfuls of the shredded chicken mixture in. Drizzle the blue cheese dressing over the top. Use the jalapeno rings

and onion to cover. Add the rest of slices of focaccia on top.

- Preheat the Panini press following the directions of the manufacturers. Cook the sandwiches for roughly 2 minutes till the Cheddar cheese melts.

Nutrition Information

- Calories: 864 calories;
- Total Fat: 44.4
- Sodium: 2157
- Total Carbohydrate: 70.1
- Cholesterol: 116
- Protein: 46.4

| 950. | Spicy Turkey Sloppy Joes |

Serving: 12 | Prep: 20mins | Cook: 30mins | Ready in:

Ingredients

- 2 pounds ground turkey
- 2 onions, chopped
- 1/2 cup chopped green bell pepper
- 1/2 cup chopped red bell pepper
- 1 serrano chile pepper, minced
- 1 fresh chile pepper, minced
- 2 cloves garlic, minced
- 2 cups ketchup
- 1 cup barbeque sauce
- 1/4 cup cider vinegar
- 1/4 cup packed brown sugar
- 2 tablespoons prepared mustard
- 1 tablespoon Worcestershire sauce
- 1 teaspoon Italian seasoning
- 1 teaspoon onion powder
- 1/2 teaspoon ground black pepper
- hamburger buns, split

Direction

- Place a large skillet on medium heat; cook while stirring in garlic, fresh chile pepper,

serrano chile pepper, red bell pepper, green bell pepper, onions and ground turkey for around 10 minutes, till the turkey is not pink anymore. Drain fat from the turkey mixture.

- Mix black pepper, onion powder, Italian seasoning, Worcestershire sauce, mustard, brown sugar, cider vinegar, barbeque sauce and ketchup together into the turkey mixture. Boil; turn the heat down to medium-low; simmer for around 20 minutes, till the vegetables becomes completely softened.
- Serve on split hamburger buns.

Nutrition Information

- Calories: 347 calories;
- Total Carbohydrate: 49.2
- Cholesterol: 56
- Protein: 20.1
- Total Fat: 8.3
- Sodium: 1009

| 951. | Spring Lamb Sliders |

Serving: 4 | Prep: 15mins | Cook: 3hours10mins | Ready in:

Ingredients

- 1 (3 1/2) pound bone-in lamb shoulder roast
- Kosher salt and freshly ground black pepper
- 1 tablespoon vegetable oil
- 1 onion, cut in large dice
- 4 cloves garlic, minced
- 1 cup chicken broth
- 1/2 cup cider vinegar
- 1/4 cup honey
- 1/4 teaspoon red pepper flakes
- 2 tablespoons fresh sliced mint
- 12 slider buns

Direction

- Set oven to 165° C (325° F) and start preheating. Season pepper and salt on all sides of roast.
- In a Dutch oven, heat oil on high heat. Beginning with the meat side down, brown all sides of roast; cook for 4-5 minutes or until browned well. Flip over and cook for 4-5 minutes, or until the bone side has been browned. When second side browns, arrange garlic and chopped onions around the roast. Onion will start to be translucent once roast browns. Add red pepper flakes, honey, cider vinegar and chicken broth and mix together, tossing to coat all sides of the roast.
- For the meat side up, put a cover on the pot and put into the center rack of preheated oven. Roast for 3 hours, or till meat is fork tender.
- Use a spoon to remove excess fat then break up the meat into small strips; arrange in a pot. Get rid of bones. Strain broth into the pot of picked meat. Cook on medium heat until simmering. Mix in chopped fresh mint.
- Arrange on toasted slider rolls to serve.

Nutrition Information

- Calories: 959 calories;
- Total Fat: 49
- Sodium: 474
- Total Carbohydrate: 498.4
- Cholesterol: 204
- Protein: 58.3

---

952.   Springtime Asparagus And Parmesan Sandwich

Serving: 6 | Prep: 15mins | Cook: 1mins | Ready in:

Ingredients

- 1 bunch asparagus spears, trimmed and cut in half
- 1/3 cup water
- 12 slices French bread

- 1/4 cup butter
- 1/3 cup mayonnaise
- 1/3 cup shaved Parmesan cheese
- 12 Bibb lettuce leaves
- freshly ground black pepper to taste

Direction

- In a microwaveable bowl, combine asparagus and 1/3 cup water. Set on high, microwave about 1 minute until tender. Wash tender asparagus with cold water and use paper towels to dry.
- On 6 slices of bread spread 1 side of each with 1/4 teaspoon butter and 1 tablespoon mayonnaise. Place asparagus on top to make a layer and drizzle with Parmesan cheese. Put lettuce on top of the asparagus then sprinkle with pepper and top the remaining 6 bread slices to make 6 sandwiches. Cut diagonally and serve.

Nutrition Information

- Calories: 343 calories;
- Sodium: 537
- Total Carbohydrate: 32.6
- Cholesterol: 30
- Protein: 10.3
- Total Fat: 20

---

953.   Stars And Flowers

Serving: 1 | Prep: 15mins | Cook: | Ready in:

Ingredients

- 2 (7 inch) whole wheat tortillas
- 2 slices Cheddar cheese, or to taste
- 2 thin slices ham, or to taste
- 2 tablespoons pimento cheese spread, or to taste
- 4 celery sticks, or to taste
- 4 baby carrots, or to taste

- 5 small black olives
- 2 tablespoons mixed nuts with sweetened cranberries (such as Craisins®)

Direction

- Slice Cheddar cheese and tortillas into flower and star shapes with cookie cutters. Put ham in between the cheese and tortilla shapes to make the sandwiches.
- Pour pimento cheese on top of celery sticks and slice into tiny pieces.
- Create bento box with celery pieces, baby carrots, black olives, mixed nuts and sandwiches.

Nutrition Information

- Calories: 644 calories;
- Total Carbohydrate: 64.4
- Cholesterol: 91
- Protein: 29.7
- Total Fat: 35.9
- Sodium: 1440

954.   Strawberry Spinach Salad Breakfast Wrap

Serving: 2 | Prep: 10mins | Cook: 5mins | Ready in:

Ingredients

- 1/4 cup walnut pieces
- 1/4 (16 ounce) package hulled and sliced strawberries
- 1 teaspoon coconut sugar
- 2 tablespoons nonfat Greek yogurt
- 1 teaspoon fresh lime juice
- 1/2 teaspoon honey
- 1 sheet lavash bread
- 3/4 cup fresh spinach
- 2 slices turkey bacon, cooked and crumbled
- 2 teaspoons chia seeds

Direction

- Turn oven to 350°F (175°C) to preheat. Distribute walnuts over a baking sheet and bring to toast for 5 to 8 minutes until fragrant, stirring a few times to make sure they are evenly browned.
- In a small bowl, combine coconut sugar and strawberry slices. Set aside, stirring occasionally, for 5 minutes.
- To make dressing, whisk together honey, lime juice, and yogurt
- Distribute dressing over the lavash bread. Add chia seeds, walnuts, bacon, strawberries, and spinach on top. Roll up the lavash bread with the filling and then cut in half to serve.

Nutrition Information

- Calories: 369 calories;
- Total Carbohydrate: 42
- Cholesterol: 25
- Protein: 14.9
- Total Fat: 17.5
- Sodium: 591

955.   Stroganoff Sandwich

Serving: 8 | Prep: 40mins | Cook: 5mins | Ready in:

Ingredients

- 1 (1 pound) loaf French or Italian-style bread
- 1/4 cup chopped green onions
- 1 tablespoon milk
- 1/8 teaspoon garlic powder
- 1 green bell pepper, sliced in rings
- 1 pound ground beef
- 1 cup sour cream
- 1 teaspoon Worcestershire sauce
- 3/4 teaspoon salt
- 2 tablespoons butter, softened
- 2 tomatoes, sliced
- 1 cup shredded Cheddar cheese

Direction

- Halve the loaf and use foil to wrap, then heat in a preheated 190°C or 375°F oven about 10-15 minutes.
- Cook green onions and beef in a big skillet on moderately high heat until beef is cooked through, then drain. Stir in pepper and salt to taste, Worcestershire sauce, sour cream, garlic powder and milk, then heat the mixture without boiling.
- Coat the cut surface of bread with butter. Spread each half with 1/2 of the meat mixture and top with green bell pepper and tomatoes, alternately, then use cheese to sprinkle over top.
- Put bread on baking sheet and bake at 175°C or 350°F until heated through totally, about 5 minutes.

Nutrition Information

- Calories: 493 calories;
- Total Fat: 29.8
- Sodium: 754
- Total Carbohydrate: 35.4
- Cholesterol: 84
- Protein: 21

956. Stuffy

Serving: 4 | Prep: 5mins | Cook: 15mins | Ready in:

Ingredients

- 1/4 cup mayonnaise, or to taste
- 4 hoagie rolls, split lengthwise
- 1 cup leftover roast turkey meat, shredded
- 1 cup prepared stuffing
- 1/2 cup leftover turkey gravy
- 1/2 cup cranberry sauce

Direction

- Turn on an oven to 350°F (175°C) to preheat.

- On each half of the split hoagie rolls, spread out mayonnaise. Layer 1/4 cup of turkey, 1/4 cup of stuffing, 2 tablespoons of gravy, and 2 tablespoons of cranberry sauce on each of 4 hoagie halves. Add the remaining 4 pieces of bread on top of each sandwich. Use aluminum foil to wrap each sandwich and put into the oven until heated through, 15 minutes.

Nutrition Information

- Calories: 536 calories;
- Sodium: 953
- Total Carbohydrate: 64.2
- Cholesterol: 32
- Protein: 19
- Total Fat: 22

957. Supa Dupa Egg Sandwich

Serving: 1 | Prep: 5mins | Cook: 10mins | Ready in:

Ingredients

- 1/4 pound extra lean ground beef
- 2 (1 ounce) slices bread
- ketchup
- mayonnaise
- 1 egg
- 2 slices mozzarella cheese
- 2 slices ham
- 1 slice fresh tomato

Direction

- Position a frying pan on medium heat. Shape the ground beef into a patty and cook till it reaches the preferred doneness. Fry egg in a slightly oiled small-sized pan on medium heat. Turn the egg over and cover using cheese. Cook till cheese melts and the yolk hardens.
- Spread mayonnaise and ketchup on the slices of bread. Add the egg onto one of the bread

slices. Heat the ham in the pan, and add over the egg. Add slices of tomato and hamburger on top. Position the other slice of bread on top, and then halve it.

Nutrition Information

- Calories: 643 calories;
- Sodium: 1120
- Total Carbohydrate: 35.9
- Cholesterol: 301
- Protein: 50
- Total Fat: 32.6

---

958. Super Easy Pulled Pork Sandwiches

Serving: 20 | Prep: 15mins | Cook: 9hours | Ready in:

Ingredients

- 3 tablespoons brown sugar
- 3 tablespoons paprika
- 1 1/2 tablespoons garlic powder (such as McCormick® California Style)
- 1 1/2 tablespoons ground black pepper
- 1 1/2 teaspoons salt
- 1/2 cup Dijon mustard (such as Hellmann's®)
- 8 pounds pork shoulder roast (butt roast), rind removed
- 1/2 cup barbeque sauce, or to taste
- 18 large hamburger buns, split

Direction

- Turn the oven to 250°F (120°C) to preheat.
- In a bowl, combine salt, black pepper, garlic powder, paprika and brown sugar. Spread over pork roast with the mustard and sprinkle the brown sugar mixture over, using the whole amount. Use aluminum foil to line a shallow baking dish. In the prepared baking dish, put a rack and put the pork roast on the rack.

- Put in the preheated oven and bake for 9-11 hours until the very soft. Allow the pork to cool, and then shred into bite-sized pieces. Moisten the pork by mixing barbeque sauce into it, enjoy with hamburger buns.

Nutrition Information

- Calories: 414 calories;
- Sodium: 866
- Total Carbohydrate: 44.9
- Cholesterol: 68
- Protein: 30
- Total Fat: 11.7

---

959. Sweet Breakfast Sandwich

Serving: 2 | Prep: 10mins | Cook: | Ready in:

Ingredients

- 2 tablespoons chocolate-hazelnut spread (such as Nutella®)
- 2 English muffins, split and toasted
- 1 banana, sliced
- 2 tablespoons marshmallow cream

Direction

- Spread on a half of each English muffin with one tbsp. of chocolate-hazelnut spread, then put on top with banana slices. Spread on the other half with one tbsp. of marshmallow cream, then press both halves together to make a sandwich.

Nutrition Information

- Calories: 282 calories;
- Total Fat: 5.7
- Sodium: 214
- Total Carbohydrate: 53.5
- Cholesterol: 0

- Protein: 6.2

- Cholesterol: < 1
- Protein: 3.1
- Total Fat: 2.5
- Sodium: 223

960. Sweet Potato Toast

Serving: 10 | Prep: 15mins | Cook: 28mins | Ready in:

Ingredients

- 1 large sweet potato
- 1 tablespoon olive oil
- 1 cup diced onion
- 1/4 cup chicken broth
- 1 tablespoon jarred minced garlic
- 1/4 cup whole milk
- 1 teaspoon dried parsley
- 1 teaspoon dried basil
- 1 teaspoon onion powder
- 1/4 teaspoon ground cumin
- 1/4 teaspoon ground cinnamon
- 10 slices bread

Direction

- Boil water in a big pot. Put in sweet potato, cook for 15-20 minutes until fork-tender. Strain and cool for 5-10 minutes until easy to work with. Peel the skin of the potato and use a fork to mash.
- In a big frying pan, heat oil over medium heat. Add onion, cook while stirring for 5 minutes until turning brown. Mix in garlic and broth, cook for 3 minutes until the onion is completely soft, tossing sometimes.
- In a blender, mix together cinnamon, cumin, onion powder, basil, parsley, milk, onion mixture, and mashed potato; puree until smooth.
- Toast bread slices, spread over the top with the potato mixture.

Nutrition Information

- Calories: 131 calories;
- Total Carbohydrate: 24.2

961. Sweet And Savory Slow Cooker Pulled Pork

Serving: 10 | Prep: 20mins | Cook: 6hours15mins | Ready in:

Ingredients

- 1 (4.5 pound) bone-in pork shoulder roast
- 1 cup root beer
- 2 1/2 tablespoons light brown sugar
- 2 teaspoons kosher salt
- 1/2 teaspoon ground black pepper
- 1 1/2 teaspoons ground paprika
- 1/2 teaspoon dry mustard
- 1/2 teaspoon onion powder
- 1/4 teaspoon garlic salt
- 1/4 teaspoon celery salt
- 1/4 teaspoon ground cinnamon
- 1/4 teaspoon ground ginger
- 1/4 teaspoon ground nutmeg
- 1/3 cup balsamic vinegar
- 1 1/2 cups root beer
- 1 1/2 fluid ounces whiskey
- 1/4 cup brown sugar
- 1 tablespoon olive oil
- 3/4 cup prepared barbecue sauce
- 10 hamburger buns, split

Direction

- In a large plastic bag, put the pork shoulder roast, then drizzle the meat with 1 cup of root beer; squeeze all the air out of the bag. Seal the bag, then refrigerate for 6 hours till overnight.
- On the following day, in a bowl, stir the nutmeg, ginger, cinnamon, celery salt, garlic salt, dry mustard, onion powder, paprika, black pepper, kosher salt, and light brown sugar together.

- Take the meat out of the marinade, shake off the excess. Rub spice mixture all over the meat, use plastic wrap to wrap, then refrigerate for half an hour to 2 hours.
- In a bowl, mix the brown sugar, whiskey, 1 1/2 cups of root beer, and balsamic vinegar together; stir until the sugar dissolves.
- In a frying pan, heat the olive oil over medium-high heat, then sear all sides of the meat for around 3 minutes each side until the meat forms a brown crust. Add the seared meat to a slow cooker. Drizzle the meat with the balsamic vinegar-root beer mixture, adjust the slow cooker to High, then cook for 6 - 8 hours.
- Take the roast out of the slow cooker, use 2 forks to shred the meat. Debone and discard all except for 1 cup of liquid in the slow cooker. Move the shredded meat back to the cooker, stir in the barbecue sauce, then allow to sit on Low until ready to serve. Serve piled on buns.

Nutrition Information

- Calories: 485 calories;
- Total Fat: 19.1
- Sodium: 985
- Total Carbohydrate: 45.5
- Cholesterol: 81
- Protein: 28.5

---

962. Sweet And Spicy Turkey Sandwich

Serving: 1 | Prep: 5mins | Cook: 10mins | Ready in:

Ingredients

- 2 slices (1/2 inch thick) hearty country bread
- 4 slices roasted turkey breast
- 1 slice pepperjack cheese
- 2 teaspoons butter
- 4 teaspoons strawberry preserves

Direction

- Set a small skillet on medium heat. Use a teaspoon of butter to coat one side of each of the bread slices. In the skillet, arrange one slice with the butter side down. Add cheese slices and turkey on top. Top with the second slice of bread with the butter side up.
- Flip and brown the other side of the sandwich once the first side turns golden brown until the cheese starts to melt, or for 3-5 minutes on each side.
- Transfer the sandwich onto a plate and arrange the strawberry preserves on top or serve preserves on the side.

Nutrition Information

- Calories: 434 calories;
- Total Fat: 16.3
- Sodium: 1817
- Total Carbohydrate: 47.1
- Cholesterol: 83
- Protein: 25.5

---

963. Tangy Turmeric Chicken Wraps

Serving: 4 | Prep: 15mins | Cook: 15mins | Ready in:

Ingredients

- 1 cup plain yogurt
- 1/2 onion, chopped
- 2 tablespoons lemon juice
- 1 tablespoon ground turmeric
- 1/4 teaspoon ground cumin
- 1/2 teaspoon paprika
- 1/2 teaspoon salt
- 1/8 teaspoon ground ginger
- 1/8 teaspoon cayenne pepper
- ground black pepper to taste
- 2 skinless, boneless chicken breast halves - cut into strips

- 1/4 cup water
- 1 teaspoon vegetable oil
- 4 pita breads
- 1 medium cucumber, diced
- 1 bunch fresh parsley, finely chopped

Direction

- In a big ceramic or glass bowl, combine black pepper, cayenne pepper, ginger, salt, paprika, cumin, turmeric, lemon juice, onion, and yogurt. Add chicken and stir until evenly coated. Cover the bowl with plastic wrap, and allow to marinate for at least 1 hour in the fridge.
- Turn an outdoor grill to high heat to preheat, and lightly grease the grate. Take chicken out of the marinade, and shake to remove excess.
- Grill chicken on the preheated grill for 5 to 7 minutes until chicken turns brown well and the center is no longer pink. Chop cooked chicken into bite-sized pieces; put to one side.
- Put remaining marinade, oil and water in a small saucepan and bring the mixture to a boil over high heat. Turn the heat to medium-low, and simmer for about 10 minutes until thickened and bubbling. Mix in the chicken.
- Serve chicken over pita breads. Add parsley and cucumber on top

Nutrition Information

- Calories: 307 calories;
- Protein: 22.1
- Total Fat: 4.7
- Sodium: 696
- Total Carbohydrate: 44
- Cholesterol: 37

964.   Teriyaki Chicken Wraps

Serving: 4 | Prep: 10mins | Cook: | Ready in:

Ingredients

- 1 cup shredded purple cabbage*
- 1/2 cup shredded carrots*
- 2 squares Land O'Lakes® Teriyaki Saute Express®
- 1 pound boneless, skinless chicken breasts, cut into strips
- 1/2 cup cashews
- 3 green onions, diagonally cut into 1-inch pieces
- 4 (8 inch) flour tortillas, warmed

Direction

- In a bowl, mix together carrots and cabbage; put aside.
- In a 12-in. nonstick frying pan, melt Sauté Express® squares over medium-low heat until start forming bubbles.
- Put in chicken. Cook until the middle of the chicken is not pink anymore, tossing sometimes, about 5-7 minutes. Add green onions and cashews, mix. Keep cooking until fully heated, about 1-2 minutes.
- Put onto each tortilla with 1/4 chicken mixture, put 1/4 cabbage mixture on top. Fold over the filling with the 2 opposite sides of the tortilla. To enclose the filling, roll up tightly beginning at the open end.

Nutrition Information

- Calories: 495 calories;
- Cholesterol: 84
- Protein: 32.9
- Total Fat: 22.2
- Sodium: 774
- Total Carbohydrate: 40.7

965.   Teriyaki Wraps

Serving: 4 | Prep: 10mins | Cook: 15mins | Ready in:

Ingredients

- 1 cup uncooked long grain white rice
- 2 cups water
- 2 tablespoons olive oil
- 1 onion, chopped
- 1 red bell pepper, chopped
- 1 small zucchini, chopped
- 1 small yellow squash, chopped
- 1 1/4 cups teriyaki sauce
- 3 tablespoons soy sauce
- 2 teaspoons garlic powder
- 1/2 teaspoon salt
- 1 teaspoon ground black pepper
- 4 (10 inch) whole wheat tortillas

Direction

- Bring 2 cups of water in a saucepan to a boil and put in rice. Lower heat and simmer with a cover about 20 minutes.
- In a big skillet, heat olive oil over moderate heat. Sauté together yellow squash, zucchini, bell pepper and onion until onions are soft then stir in teriyaki sauce. Once vegetables are softened, stir in pepper, salt, garlic powder, soy sauce and cooked rice, then simmer the mixture about 3-5 minutes.
- In each tortilla, put a quarter of rice and vegetables, then roll it up.

Nutrition Information

- Calories: 540 calories;
- Sodium: 4426
- Total Carbohydrate: 100.6
- Cholesterol: 0
- Protein: 15
- Total Fat: 7.8

966.   The Best BLT Sandwich

Serving: 1 | Prep: 5mins | Cook: 6mins | Ready in:

Ingredients

- 2 slices bacon, cut in half
- 1 teaspoon mustard powder
- 1 teaspoon curry powder
- 1 teaspoon red pepper flakes
- 2 slices bread, toasted
- 2 lettuce leaves
- 3 slices tomato

Direction

- In a skillet, cook bacon on medium heat. Combine red pepper flakes, curry powder and mustard powder. Once you flip bacon over, scatter the spice mixture onto the cooked side of bacon.
- Arrange tomato and lettuce on a toasted bread slice, then place seasoned cooked bacon on top. Add another slice of toasted bread on top to complete.

Nutrition Information

- Calories: 284 calories;
- Cholesterol: 20
- Protein: 13.2
- Total Fat: 11.5
- Sodium: 776
- Total Carbohydrate: 33.1

967.   The Legendary Egg Dog

Serving: 1 | Prep: 10mins | Cook: 5mins | Ready in:

Ingredients

- 1/4 teaspoon butter
- 1 egg, beaten
- 1 hot dog bun
- 1 dash hot sauce, or to taste

Direction

- In a nonstick skillet, melt butter on medium-high heat. Put egg into the melted butter and cook for a minute, until egg begins to bubble.

Turn egg and cook for 2-3 more minutes longer, until it is set. Roll egg and put in the hot dog bun, drizzle hot sauce on top.

Nutrition Information

- Calories: 201 calories;
- Sodium: 310
- Total Carbohydrate: 21.7
- Cholesterol: 189
- Protein: 10.4
- Total Fat: 7.8

968. The Real Reuben

Serving: 1 | Prep: 5mins | Cook: 3mins | Ready in:

Ingredients

- 2 slices dark rye bread
- 1/4 pound thinly sliced corned beef
- 3 ounces sauerkraut, drained
- 2 slices Swiss cheese
- 1/4 cup thousand island dressing

Direction

- On a broiling pan or baking sheet, arrange bread. Top each of bread slices with layer of corned beef, sauerkraut and cheese.
- Broil until the cheese melts on high heat, about 3-4 minutes. Add Thousand Island dressing to serve when it is still hot.

Nutrition Information

- Calories: 874 calories;
- Total Fat: 58.7
- Sodium: 2716
- Total Carbohydrate: 52.8
- Cholesterol: 152
- Protein: 36

969. Tomato Avocado Sandwich

Serving: 1 | Prep: 10mins | Cook: | Ready in:

Ingredients

- 1/2 avocado - peeled, pitted, and mashed
- 1 teaspoon garlic salt
- 1 slice ciabatta bread
- 3 slices tomato
- 1 pinch ground black pepper to taste

Direction

- In a bowl, combine garlic salt and mashed avocado and spread over the ciabatta bread. Spread the tomatoes on top of avocado and sprinkle black pepper.

Nutrition Information

- Calories: 335 calories;
- Sodium: 2157
- Total Carbohydrate: 41.5
- Cholesterol: 0
- Protein: 8
- Total Fat: 16.9

970. Tongue And Mustard Sandwiches

Serving: 12 | Prep: 5mins | Cook: 2hours30mins | Ready in:

Ingredients

- 3 pounds beef tongue, whole
- 1 tablespoon salt
- 1 onion, chopped
- 1 (1 pound) loaf rye bread
- 1 cup coarse grained prepared mustard
- 1 onion, thinly sliced

Direction

- Clean the beef tongue and set in a big pot. Add water to cover, then add the chopped onion and salt. Set to a boil, lower heat, then simmer for 2 - 4 hours or till tongue becomes tender.
- Take the tongue away from cooking liquid, then leave aside till cool enough to handle. Slice through tough outer skin, then peel it off. Trim any gristle or fat from the bottom of tongue. Cut tongue crosswise into a quarter-inch thick slices.
- Halve loaf of rye bread lengthwise. Scoop out a little amount of the soft interior. Pour the mustard over each half. Position tongue slices and onion over the bottom half of bread, then put other half on top and slice into single sandwiches.

Nutrition Information

- Calories: 391 calories;
- Total Fat: 19.7
- Sodium: 1224
- Total Carbohydrate: 28.1
- Cholesterol: 99
- Protein: 22

---

971. Tonya's Terrific Sloppy Joes

Serving: 8 | Prep: 10mins | Cook: 30mins | Ready in:

Ingredients

- 2 pounds ground beef
- 1/2 cup chopped onion
- 1/4 cup chopped celery
- 7 ounces ketchup
- 1 tablespoon brown sugar
- 1 1/2 teaspoons Worcestershire sauce
- 1 teaspoon vinegar
- 1/4 teaspoon dry mustard powder

- 1/8 teaspoon lemon juice
- 8 white or wheat hamburger buns

Direction

- Put a big skillet on medium-high heat. Crumble the ground beef in the skillet. Put celery and onion. Stir and cook the beef mixture for 7-10 minutes until beef is browned completely.
- Mix Worcestershire sauce, brown sugar, mustard, vinegar, lemon juice, and ketchup through the beef mixture. Lower the heat to medium-low. Cook the mixture at a simmer for around 20 minutes until the mixture gets hot and the sauce thickens.

Nutrition Information

- Calories: 362 calories;
- Total Fat: 15.3
- Sodium: 573
- Total Carbohydrate: 31.2
- Cholesterol: 71
- Protein: 23.7

---

972. Toronto Chicken Shawarma

Serving: 4 | Prep: 20mins | Cook: 20mins | Ready in:

Ingredients

- 1 tablespoon ground coriander
- 1 tablespoon ground cumin
- 1 tablespoon ground cardamom
- 1 tablespoon chili powder
- 1 tablespoon grill seasoning (such as Montreal Steak Seasoning®)
- 1 teaspoon smoked paprika
- 1/2 teaspoon ground turmeric
- 1 lemon, juiced, divided
- 1 large clove garlic, minced
- 5 tablespoons extra-virgin olive oil, divided

- 4 (6 ounce) skinless, boneless chicken breast halves
- 1 large onion, sliced
- 1 red bell pepper, sliced
- 1 yellow bell pepper, sliced
- salt and ground black pepper to taste
- 1 1/2 cups Greek yogurt
- 1/4 cup tahini
- 1 teaspoon extra-virgin olive oil
- 4 pita bread rounds

Direction

- Start preheating an outdoor or indoor frill to high heat and grease grill grate with a thin layer of oil.
- In a bowl, combine turmeric, paprika, grill seasoning, chili powder, cardamom, cumin and coriander; stir in 3 tablespoons of olive oil, garlic and juice of half a lemon to make a paste. Whisk together the coriander, cumin, cardamom, chili powder, grill seasoning, paprika, and turmeric in a bowl; whisk in juice of 1/2 lemon, garlic, and 3 tablespoons olive oil to form a paste. Brush spice paste all over the chicken breasts.
- Grill chicken breasts, about 6 minutes on each side, on prepared grill until no pink meat remains in the middle and the juices run clear. Move chicken into a plate and chill for 1-2 minutes; cut into thin slices.
- In a large skillet, bring 2 tablespoons of olive oil to medium-high heat. Blend in yellow pepper, red pepper and onion; add pepper and salt to season. Cook and stir often for about 5 minutes until vegetables are softened.
- In a bowl, combine the rest 1 teaspoon of olive oil, juice of half a lemon remaining, tahini and Greek yogurt until smoothened; add salt to season.
- Grill pitas for about 60 seconds on each side until toasted and charred a little on the outside. Layer some chicken slices, pepper mixture and a good dollop of yogurt tahini sauce onto each pita to put together a sandwich.

Nutrition Information

- Calories: 737 calories;
- Sodium: 1133
- Total Carbohydrate: 46.4
- Cholesterol: 114
- Protein: 49.1
- Total Fat: 39.6

973.   Traditional Gyro Meat

Serving: 10 | Prep: 15mins | Cook: 45mins | Ready in:

Ingredients

- 1/2 onion, cut into chunks
- 1 pound ground lamb
- 1 pound ground beef
- 1 tablespoon minced garlic
- 1 teaspoon dried oregano
- 1 teaspoon ground cumin
- 1 teaspoon dried marjoram
- 1 teaspoon ground dried rosemary
- 1 teaspoon ground dried thyme
- 1 teaspoon ground black pepper
- 1/4 teaspoon sea salt

Direction

- In a food processor, add onion and process until chopped finely. Scoop into the center of a towel with onions then bring up the ends of the towel and squeeze out liquid from onions. Put into a mixing bowl with onions together with beef and lamb. Use salt, black pepper, thyme, rosemary, marjoram, cumin, oregano and garlic to season. Use your hands to mix the mixture until well-blended. Cover and chill for about 1-2 hours to let flavors combine.
- Set the oven to 165°C or 325°F to preheat.
- Put into the food processor with the meat mixture and process for about 1 minute until the mixture feels tacky and chopped finely. Pack into a 4"x7" loaf pan with the meat mixture, being sure there are no air pockets.

Use a wet kitchen towel to line a roasting pan. Place on the towel with the loaf pan inside the roasting pan and put into the preheated oven. Fill boiling water into roasting pan until reaching halfway up the sides of loaf pan.

- Bake the gyro meat for 45-60 minutes, until it is not pink in the center anymore and its internal temperature reaches 75°C or 165°F measured by a meat thermometer. Drain any accumulated fat and let the meat cool a bit prior to slicing thinly and serving.

Nutrition Information

- Calories: 179 calories;
- Total Fat: 11.7
- Sodium: 97
- Total Carbohydrate: 1.9
- Cholesterol: 59
- Protein: 15.7

974.   Traditional Gyros

Serving: 12 | Prep: 15mins | Cook: 45mins | Ready in:

Ingredients

- 1 small onion, cut into chunks
- 1 pound ground lamb
- 1 pound ground beef
- 1 tablespoon minced garlic
- 1 teaspoon dried oregano
- 1 teaspoon ground cumin
- 1 teaspoon dried marjoram
- 1 teaspoon dried thyme
- 1 teaspoon dried rosemary
- 1 teaspoon freshly ground black pepper
- 1/4 teaspoon sea salt
- boiling water as needed
- 12 tablespoons hummus
- 12 pita bread rounds
- 1 small head lettuce, shredded
- 1 large tomato, sliced
- 1 large red onion, sliced

- 6 ounces crumbled feta cheese
- 24 tablespoons tzatziki sauce

Direction

- In food processor, put onion; blend until chopped finely. Place onion onto a piece of cheese cloth; then squeeze liquid out. Put onion into a large bowl.
- Using hands, mix onion with salt, black pepper, rosemary, thyme, marjoram, cumin, oregano, garlic, beef and lamb until mixed well. Wrap the bowl in plastic wrap. Place in the refrigerator for 120 minutes until the flavors blend.
- Start preheating the oven to 325°F (165°C).
- In food processor, put meat mixture; pulse for one minute, until they are tacky and chopped finely. Pack the meat mixture into a loaf pan (about 7x4 inches), making sure there have no air pockets. Position loaf pan into the roasting pan. Pour around loaf pan with enough of boiling water to reach halfway up sides.
- Bake in prepared oven for 45-60 minutes until middle is no longer pink. The instant-read thermometer should register at least 165°F (74°C) when inserted into middle. Pour off all the accumulated fat. Let cool slightly.
- Slice gyro meat mixture thinly.
- Spread on every pita bread with one tablespoon of the hummus; add tzatziki sauce, feta cheese, red onion, tomato, lettuce and gyro meat mixture over top of each.

Nutrition Information

- Calories: 425 calories;
- Total Carbohydrate: 42.8
- Cholesterol: 61
- Protein: 22.4
- Total Fat: 40.8
- Sodium: 620

975. Triple Decker Grilled Shrimp BLT With Avocado And Chipotle Mayo

Serving: 2 | Prep: 20mins | Cook: 20mins | Ready in:

Ingredients

- 1 cup mayonnaise
- 1 chipotle pepper in adobo sauce
- 1/2 lime, juiced
- 1 pinch salt
- 1 pinch ground black pepper
- 4 slices bacon
- 8 extra-large shrimp - peeled, deveined, and tails removed
- 1 tablespoon olive oil
- salt and ground black pepper to taste
- 1 avocado, peeled, pitted and sliced
- 2 leaves romaine lettuce
- 4 slices ripe red tomato
- 6 slices sourdough bread, toasted

Direction

- In a bowl, mix mayonnaise, lime juice, pepper, a dash of salt and chipotle pepper. Then puree with a stick blender until smooth. You can also puree the ingredients with a food processor if you don't have a blender. Cover the ingredients and then chill until when you are ready to prepare the sandwiches.
- Over medium-high heat, cook bacon in a deep skillet while turning frequently for about 10 minutes until browned evenly. Use a plate lined with paper towel to drain the slices of bacon.
- Medium-high heat, preheat the outdoor grill and then coat the grate lightly with oil. Toss shrimp in a bowl of olive oil, pepper and salt to taste.
- Let the shrimp to cook on the grill preheated for about 3 minutes per side until the center of the meat is no longer transparent and the outside is bright pink.
- To prepare the sandwiches: Onto one slice of bread, generously spread the mayonnaise

dressing prepared. Spread avocado slices and half of the shrimp at the top. On top of the avocado, put another slice of bread and then spread a layer of the dressing. Add on top two slices of tomato and a lettuce leaf and lastly a third slice of bread. To make the second sandwich, repeat this step with the remaining ingredients.

Nutrition Information

- Calories: 1433 calories;
- Total Fat: 119
- Sodium: 1769
- Total Carbohydrate: 59.6
- Cholesterol: 234
- Protein: 37.8

976. Tuna Egg Sandwich

Serving: 2 | Prep: 5mins | Cook: 10mins | Ready in:

Ingredients

- 1 (5 ounce) can tuna, drained
- 3 hard-cooked eggs, peeled and chopped
- 1 cup chopped celery
- 1 tablespoon mayonnaise
- salt and pepper to taste
- 4 slices whole wheat bread

Direction

- Combine mayonnaise, tuna, celery, and eggs in a medium bowl; sprinkle pepper and salt. Spread 1/2 of mixture on a slice of bread, spread the other half on a separate slice. Add the remaining bread slices on top. Serve.

Nutrition Information

- Calories: 389 calories;
- Total Fat: 16
- Sodium: 559

- Total Carbohydrate: 26.4
- Cholesterol: 340
- Protein: 33.3

977.　　Tuna Melts

Serving: 8 | Prep: 15mins | Cook: 10mins | Ready in:

Ingredients

- 1 (1 pound) loaf French bread
- 1 small sweet onion, peeled and diced
- 1 (12 ounce) can tuna, drained
- 2 cups mozzarella cheese, shredded
- 1 cup mayonnaise

Direction

- Set the oven at 350°F (175°C) and start preheating.
- Combine mayonnaise, mozzarella, drained tuna and sweet onion in a mixing bowl. Combine thoroughly.
- To make a sandwich, spread the tuna mixture on slices of French bread. Arrange the sandwiches on a cookie sheet.
- Bake for 10 minutes in the preheated oven.

Nutrition Information

- Calories: 483 calories;
- Protein: 24.5
- Total Fat: 27.7
- Sodium: 716
- Total Carbohydrate: 34.1
- Cholesterol: 41

978.　　Tuna Pita Melt

Serving: 1 | Prep: 10mins | Cook: 5mins | Ready in:

Ingredients

- 1/2 pita bread round
- 1/4 cup tuna, drained
- 1/2 dill pickle spear, diced
- 1 1/2 teaspoons mayonnaise
- 1 1/2 teaspoons olive oil
- 1/2 teaspoon garlic powder
- 1 pinch dried rosemary
- 1 slice Swiss cheese

Direction

- Toast pita bread slightly.
- In a bowl, break the tuna chunks into small pieces; mix in rosemary, garlic powder, olive oil, mayonnaise and pickle till evenly blended.
- In the pocket of the toasted pita bread, put Swiss cheese and spoon in the tuna mixture.
- Heat the pita sandwich on a microwave-safe dish in a microwave for 15-20 seconds, or till the cheese is melted.

Nutrition Information

- Calories: 394 calories;
- Cholesterol: 49
- Protein: 28.4
- Total Fat: 21.6
- Sodium: 482
- Total Carbohydrate: 20.7

979.　　Tuna Pita Melts

Serving: 6 | Prep: 10mins | Cook: 10mins | Ready in:

Ingredients

- 6 (6-inch) pitas
- 2 (5 ounce) cans tuna, drained
- 2 tablespoons mayonnaise
- 2 tablespoons dill pickle relish
- 1/2 teaspoon dried dill
- 1/4 teaspoon salt
- 1 large tomato, sliced into thin wedges
- 1 cup shredded Cheddar cheese

Direction

- Set the oven at 400°F (200°C) and start preheating. Arrange whole pita bread on a baking sheet, in a single layer. Bake till lightly toasted, 5 minutes.
- Combine salt, dill, relish, mayonnaise and tuna in a medium bowl. On each of the pita breads, spread an equal amount of the tuna mixture. Spread tomato wedges on top of the tuna; sprinkle shredded Cheddar cheese over tomato layer.
- Bake in the preheated oven for 5 minutes; or till the cheese is melted.

Nutrition Information

- Calories: 346 calories;
- Total Fat: 12.4
- Sodium: 654
- Total Carbohydrate: 35.2
- Cholesterol: 38
- Protein: 22.2

980.   Tuna Pockets

Serving: 8 | Prep: 15mins | Cook: 15mins |Ready in:

Ingredients

- 2 (5 ounce) cans chunk light tuna, drained and flaked
- 1 tablespoon finely chopped onion (optional)
- 1 tablespoon finely chopped celery (optional)
- 2 tablespoons shredded Cheddar cheese
- 1 teaspoon dried dill weed
- 2 tablespoons mayonnaise
- 2 (8 count) cans refrigerated biscuit dough

Direction

- Set the oven to 175°C to 350°F to preheat.
- Stir gently mayonnaise, dill, shredded Cheddar cheese, celery, onion and tuna together until well-blended.

- Flatten the biscuit dough to the thickness of about 1/4 inch and arrange on an ungreased baking sheet with 8 flattened biscuits. Put on top of each biscuit with 3 tbsp. of the tuna mixture and place another flattened biscuit on top of each. Seal in the filling by pinching the edges.
- In the preheated oven, bake for 15 minutes, until pockets are browned slightly and filling is hot. Chill the leftovers.

Nutrition Information

- Calories: 436 calories;
- Total Fat: 19.2
- Sodium: 1183
- Total Carbohydrate: 49.5
- Cholesterol: 14
- Protein: 16.2

981.   Turkey BBQ Sandwiches

Serving: 6 | Prep: 20mins | Cook: 8hours |Ready in:

Ingredients

- 2 turkey legs without skin
- 1/2 cup firmly packed brown sugar
- 1/4 cup prepared yellow mustard
- 1 tablespoon liquid smoke flavoring
- 2 tablespoons ketchup
- 2 tablespoons apple cider vinegar
- 2 tablespoons hot pepper sauce
- 1 teaspoon salt
- 1 teaspoon coarse ground black pepper
- 1 teaspoon crushed red pepper flakes

Direction

- Use nonstick cooking spray to spray inside the slow cooker, then put in the turkey legs. Mix together red pepper flakes, black pepper, salt, hot pepper sauce, cider vinegar, ketchup, smoke flavoring, yellow mustard, and brown sugar in a bowl until the sugar dissolves, then pour mixture over the turkey legs.

- Cook, covered, in the cooker that is set on a low setting for 8-10 hours. Take out the turkey legs and separate the meat from the tendons and bones, then shred the meat. Place the meat back into the sauce to serve.

Nutrition Information

- Calories: 279 calories;
- Sodium: 779
- Total Carbohydrate: 20.3
- Cholesterol: 131
- Protein: 32.7
- Total Fat: 6.9

---

982.   Turkey Sloppy Joes

Serving: 8 | Prep: 15mins | Cook: 15mins | Ready in:

Ingredients

- 2 1/2 pounds ground turkey
- 1/2 cup chopped onion
- 1/2 cup chopped green bell pepper
- 1/2 cup chopped tomato
- 1 cup no-salt-added ketchup
- 7 tablespoons barbeque sauce
- 2 tablespoons prepared yellow mustard
- 1 tablespoon vinegar
- 1/2 teaspoon celery seed
- 1/2 teaspoon ground black pepper
- 1/2 teaspoon red pepper flakes, or to taste
- 8 hamburger bun, split and toasted

Direction

- Over medium heat, heat a nonstick skillet and then cook while stirring tomato, bell pepper, onion and turkey for about 5 minutes until the turkey is no longer pink and it is crumbly. Mix in red pepper flakes, black pepper, celery seed, vinegar, mustard, barbeque sauce and

ketchup. Decrease the heat to low and let it simmer while stirring from time to time for 10 minutes. Serve the turkey mixture over the toasted hamburger buns.

Nutrition Information

- Calories: 393 calories;
- Cholesterol: 105
- Protein: 32.8
- Total Fat: 13.3
- Sodium: 525
- Total Carbohydrate: 36.4

---

983.   Turkey Wraps

Serving: 6 | Prep: 20mins | Cook: | Ready in:

Ingredients

- 1 (8 ounce) package cream cheese with chives
- 2 tablespoons Dijon mustard
- 6 (8 inch) whole wheat tortillas
- 1 1/2 cups finely shredded iceberg lettuce
- 12 slices thinly sliced deli turkey
- 3/4 cup shredded Swiss cheese
- 1 large tomato, seeded and diced
- 1 large avocado, sliced
- 6 slices bacon, cooked and crumbled

Direction

- Whisk together the Dijon mustard and cream cheese until smooth. Pour two tbsp. of cream cheese mixture on each tortilla, spread until it is one-fourth inch from the ends.
- Place about one-fourth cup of grated lettuce on each tortilla, and force the lettuce down into the cream cheese mixture. Put two turkey pieces on each tortilla over lettuce, and drizzle with two tbsp. of grated Swiss cheese. Garnish each tortilla evenly with avocado and tomato slices and bacon crumbles.

- Snugly roll up each tortilla, and slice diagonally in half across the middle.

Nutrition Information

- Calories: 457 calories;
- Total Carbohydrate: 37.1
- Cholesterol: 78
- Protein: 24.2
- Total Fat: 28
- Sodium: 1438

---

984. Turkey And Sun Dried Tomato Panini

Serving: 1 | Prep: 10mins | Cook: 5mins | Ready in:

Ingredients

- 1 tablespoon butter, or more if needed
- 2 slices ciabatta bread
- 6 slices deli-style sliced turkey breast
- 2 slices provolone cheese
- 3 sun-dried tomatoes packed in oil, drained and chopped
- 1/2 teaspoon Italian seasoning

Direction

- Follow the manufacturer's instructions to preheat a Panini press for medium heat.
- Spread the butter on one side of each piece of bread. Lay 1 bread slice on the preheated Panini press with the butter side down, layer with the sun-dried tomatoes, provolone cheese, and the turkey. Scatter with Italian seasoning. Place the second bread slice on top.
- Press the Panini maker down and cook for about 5 minutes, until the bread is toasted and the provolone cheese melts. Slice in half and serve while warm.

Nutrition Information

- Calories: 792 calories;
- Sodium: 3267
- Total Carbohydrate: 66.7
- Cholesterol: 138
- Protein: 53
- Total Fat: 34.9

---

985. Turkish Kebabs

Serving: 6 | Prep: 40mins | Cook: 10mins | Ready in:

Ingredients

- Marinade:
- 2 large onions, chopped
- 2 garlic cloves, crushed
- 1/2 cup olive oil
- 2 tablespoons lemon juice
- 1 teaspoon dried oregano
- 1 teaspoon ground black pepper
- 1/2 teaspoon ground turmeric
- 1 pinch curry powder
- 1 teaspoon salt
- 1 pound beef flank steak, thinly sliced
- Tzatziki Sauce:
- 8 ounces sour cream
- 2 tablespoons olive oil
- 1 tablespoon lemon juice
- 1/2 teaspoon salt
- 1/2 teaspoon ground black pepper
- 1 tablespoon chopped fresh dill
- 1 clove garlic, crushed
- 6 pita bread rounds

Direction

- In a large ceramic bowl toss in the chopped onions, crushing them with the bottom of a glass until onions become translucent and all the onion juices are squeezed out. Stir in 1/2 cup of olive oil, 2 crushed garlic cloves, 2 tablespoons of lemon juice, 1 teaspoon of black pepper, oregano, curry powder, turmeric, and 1 teaspoon of salt. Combine well and toss in the sliced beef, stirring the mixture to coat the meat. Place the bowl covered with the plastic wrap in the refrigerator and marinate overnight.

- In separate bowl mix 2 tablespoons of olive oil, 1 tablespoon of lemon juice, 1/2 teaspoon of black pepper, 1 crushed clove of garlic, dill, 1/2 teaspoon of salt and sour cream. Combine well all the ingredients; refrigerate overnight covered with plastic wrap.
- Set the oven rack about 6 inches from the heater and preheat the oven.
- Take the meat from the marinade, removing any extra onion chunks. Place all meat slices on a baking sheet and make sure they're not overlapping. Season with salt to taste. Broil until the meat chunks are brown and crispy for about 3 minutes per side, turning halfway through cooking.
- Spread the cooked meat on the pita breads and serve with drizzled tzatziki on top.

Nutrition Information

- Calories: 512 calories;
- Protein: 15.7
- Total Fat: 34.3
- Sodium: 891
- Total Carbohydrate: 36
- Cholesterol: 33

986.   Twice Baked Corn Dogs

Serving: 6 | Prep: 10mins | Cook: 20mins | Ready in:

Ingredients

- 6 corn dogs
- 1/2 cup leftover mashed potatoes
- 1/4 cup shredded Cheddar cheese

Direction

- Start preheating oven to 400°F (200°C). Bake corn dogs following the package instructions.

- Discard sticks once the corn dogs are cool enough to handle, then split in 1/2 lengthwise. Take out hot dog part, keeping cornbread shell intact. Dice hot dogs into small pieces. Put into medium bowl. Mix in mashed potatoes. Equally stuff potato mixture into each corn shell. Top with cheese.
- Put back to oven. Bake for 5 mins or until cheese melts.

Nutrition Information

- Calories: 291 calories;
- Sodium: 1042
- Total Carbohydrate: 26.5
- Cholesterol: 27
- Protein: 7.9
- Total Fat: 16.2

987.   Two Handed Crispy Fried Chicken Sandwiches

Serving: 4 | Prep: 20mins | Cook: 10mins | Ready in:

Ingredients

- 4 thinly sliced chicken breasts, halved
- salt and ground black pepper to taste
- 1 cup Italian-style panko bread crumbs
- 3 tablespoons peanut oil
- 2 green onions, thinly sliced
- 4 slices Cheddar cheese
- 4 hamburger rolls, split
- 1/4 cup mayonnaise

Direction

- In shallow bowl, add pepper and salt to season the chicken. Coat with panko breadcrumbs generously, pressing the crumbs into the chicken.
- In large skillet, heat the peanut oil over medium-high heat. Then fry the chicken for 4-5 mins or until crispy and browned at the

bottom. Turn each chicken piece over. Place the green onions and one slice of Cheddar cheese on top of 4 pieces. Fry the chicken for 4-5 mins or until the middle is no longer pink, and golden brown at bottom.

- Coat mayonnaise over hamburger rolls on both sides. On bottom of one roll, put one cheese-cover chicken piece and one plain chicken piece; arrange roll top over chicken.

Nutrition Information

- Calories: 673 calories;
- Sodium: 982
- Total Carbohydrate: 41
- Cholesterol: 100
- Protein: 36.6
- Total Fat: 39.9

988. Ukrainian Sandwiches

Serving: 25 | Prep: 15mins | Cook: | Ready in:

Ingredients

- 1 (8 ounce) package cream cheese, softened
- 1/2 cup butter, softened
- 1 tablespoon minced garlic
- 2 loaves French bread, sliced
- 1 pound sliced sausage of your choice
- 1 cucumber, sliced
- 3 medium tomatoes, sliced
- 1 hard-cooked egg, chopped

Direction

- In a small bowl, stir garlic, butter and cream cheese together. Spread some onto each bread slice; then put in tomato, cucumber and a slice of sausage, then top with some chopped egg. Serve open-faced.

Nutrition Information

- Calories: 233 calories;
- Cholesterol: 39
- Protein: 7.7
- Total Fat: 12.9
- Sodium: 470
- Total Carbohydrate: 21.9

989. Ultimate Jersey Ripper

Serving: 8 | Prep: 15mins | Cook: 8mins | Ready in:

Ingredients

- vegetable oil for frying
- 8 all-beef hot dogs
- 8 slices bacon
- 16 toothpicks
- 1 (16 ounce) jar pushcart-style onions in sauce
- 8 hot dog rolls
- 1 (8 ounce) package corn chips, crushed

Direction

- Heat oil to 175°C/350°F in big saucepan/deep fryer.
- Use bacon slice to wrap each hotdog; secure ends using toothpicks. Fry hotdogs in hot oil, 2 each time, for 3-4 minutes till they float to the surface; drain on paper towels.
- Put onions in small pot on low heat; mix for 5 minutes till heated through.
- In rolls, put fried hotdogs; garnish with crushed corn chips and onions.

Nutrition Information

- Calories: 513 calories;
- Total Fat: 29.9
- Sodium: 1417
- Total Carbohydrate: 46.8
- Cholesterol: 34
- Protein: 15.1

990.　Ultimate Roast Beef Blues Sandwich

Serving: 4 | Prep: 15mins | Cook: | Ready in:

Ingredients

- 4 whole wheat sub rolls, lightly toasted
- 1/3 cup light mayonnaise
- 16 fresh basil leaves
- 1 pound thinly sliced cooked deli roast beef
- 3/4 cup crumbled blue cheese
- 1/2 cup toasted walnuts

Direction

- Unwrap the rolls and lather 1-2 tablespoons of mayonnaise onto each side of the rolls. Set 4 basil leaves onto 4 of the rolls. Stack on the same 4 rolls with roast beef, 1-2 tablespoons of blue cheese and a few walnuts. Cover each with another half rolls.

Nutrition Information

- Calories: 583 calories;
- Cholesterol: 80
- Protein: 37.8
- Total Fat: 31.6
- Sodium: 2000
- Total Carbohydrate: 37.9

991.　Ultimate Steak Sandwich

Serving: 4 | Prep: 15mins | Cook: 15mins | Ready in:

Ingredients

- 4 hard rolls, split
- 1/2 cup mayonnaise
- 3 cloves garlic, minced
- 1 tablespoon Parmesan cheese
- 3 tablespoons olive oil
- 2 pounds round steak, thinly sliced
- 1 large onion, sliced and quartered
- 1 pinch coarse sea salt
- 1/2 teaspoon Worcestershire sauce
- 1/8 teaspoon liquid smoke
- 8 (1 ounce) slices provolone cheese
- 1/2 teaspoon Italian seasoning

Direction

- Set the oven to 500 degrees Fahrenheit (260 degrees C). Split open the rolls and toast them on a baking sheet as the oven preheats. Mix Parmesan cheese, garlic, and mayonnaise in a small bowl, then refrigerate until about to use. Take out the rolls from the oven once toasted to your liking.
- Heat up a big skillet with olive oil set on a medium-high heat. Place the steak slices and onions carefully into the pan and season with liquid smoke, Worcestershire sauce, and sea salt. Cook while stirring until the steak is brown and onions become tender, roughly 10 minutes.
- Spread the garlic-Parmesan mayonnaise generously onto both the toasted roll halves. Evenly divide the onion and steak mixture between the 2 bottom roll halves, piling them high. Top each one with 2 provolone cheese slices and sprinkle with Italian seasoning. Place the tops onto the sandwiches.
- Bake sandwiches on a baking sheet in the oven until the cheese melts, roughly 5 minutes.

Nutrition Information

- Calories: 949 calories;
- Total Fat: 62.9
- Sodium: 1039
- Total Carbohydrate: 27.7
- Cholesterol: 171
- Protein: 65.9

992. Uncle Bo's Hot Sandwiches

Serving: 32 | Prep: 25mins | Cook: 35mins | Ready in:

Ingredients

- 20 slices bacon
- 3 pounds chipped chopped ham, shredded
- 2 onions, chopped
- 1/2 cup barbecue sauce (such as Heinz® Original BBQ Sauce)
- 1/2 cup bottled sweet chili sauce (such as Heinz® Premium Chili Sauce)
- 1/2 cup sweet pickle relish (such as Heinz® Sweet Relish)
- 1/2 cup chopped sweet pickle slices (bread-and-butter type)
- 32 slices Cheddar cheese*
- 32 hamburger buns, split

Direction

- Set an oven to preheat at 175°C (350°F).
- In a deep, big pan, put the bacon and cook on medium-high heat for about 10 minutes, flipping once in a while, until it browns evenly. On a plate lined with paper towel, drain the bacon slices. Let the bacon cool then chop.
- In the bacon grease left in the pan, cook and stir the onion for about 10 minutes, until the onion becomes translucent. Stir in the chili sauce, barbecue sauce, chopped ham and bacon until the mixture is combined well. IN a big bowl, move the ham and mix in the chopped pickle and pickle relish.
- On a bun, put about 1/4 cup of ham mixture, then put a Cheddar cheese slice on top. Close the sandwiches and wrap in foil. Bake in the oven for15-20 minutes until the cheese melts and hot. Serve hot.

Nutrition Information

- Calories: 377 calories;
- Sodium: 1167

- Total Carbohydrate: 28.2
- Cholesterol: 55
- Protein: 19.6
- Total Fat: 20.6

993. Uptown Red Beans And Rice

Serving: 5 | Prep: 5mins | Cook: 30mins | Ready in:

Ingredients

- 2 tablespoons vegetable oil
- 1 pound smoked turkey sausage, sliced
- 1 (8 ounce) package ZATARAIN'S® Red Beans and Rice Mix
- 3 1/4 cups water
- Chopped green onions (optional)

Direction

- In a medium saucepan, warm the oil over medium-high heat. Cook sausage until all sides are browned.
- Add water and rice mix and bring it to boil. Adjust the heat to low and simmer it for 20-25 minutes, covered, until the rice is tender. Be sure to stir it occasionally during cooking time.
- Remove it from heat before stirring in green onions. Allow it to cool for 5 minutes before serving.

Nutrition Information

- Calories: 348 calories;
- Sodium: 1704
- Total Carbohydrate: 31.9
- Cholesterol: 68
- Protein: 23.3
- Total Fat: 14.5

994. Vegan TLT Sandwich (BLT Substitute)

Serving: 4 | Prep: 15mins | Cook: 10mins | Ready in:

Ingredients

- 1 (12 ounce) container firm tofu
- 2 tablespoons steak seasoning (such as Penzeys Mitchell Street Steak Seasoning), divided
- 2 tablespoons vegetable oil, or more as needed
- 4 tablespoons vegan mayonnaise, or to taste
- 8 slices bread, toasted
- 2 large ripe tomatoes, sliced
- 4 leaves lettuce

Direction

- Use paper towels to pat tofu dry gently. Cut into 1/8-in.-thick slices right onto the dry paper towels. Use 1 tablespoon of steak seasoning to season one side generously.
- Place a nonstick skillet on medium heat; heat oil. Using a small spatula, slip the tofu carefully into the pan, seasoned-side down. Use the remaining steak seasoning to season the top side.
- Cook the tofu for 4-5 minutes per side, till lightly browned and dried. Strain on paper towels.
- Spread mayonnaise over each slice of bread. Distribute lettuce, tomatoes and the tofu over 4 slices; use the tops to cover.

Nutrition Information

- Calories: 345 calories;
- Sodium: 1782
- Total Carbohydrate: 34.3
- Cholesterol: 0
- Protein: 11.7
- Total Fat: 19

995. Veggeroni

Serving: 12 | Prep: 20mins | Cook: 1hours | Ready in:

Ingredients

- 2 cups wheat gluten
- 1/2 cup isolated protein powder
- 1 tablespoon agar-agar powder
- 1 1/2 tablespoons paprika
- 1 teaspoon ground black pepper
- 1/2 teaspoon red pepper flakes
- 1/2 teaspoon cayenne pepper
- 1 tablespoon fennel seed
- 2 teaspoons garlic powder
- 1 envelope dry onion soup mix
- 1 envelope dry tomato soup mix
- 1 1/2 cups water
- 1 tablespoon vegetable oil
- 1 teaspoon liquid smoke flavoring

Direction

- Preheat an oven to 165°C/325°F.
- Grind tomato soup mix, onion soup mix, garlic powder, fennel seed, cayenne pepper, red pepper flakes, black pepper, paprika, agar-agar, protein powder and gluten for 2-3 minutes in blender into powder; put in a big mixing bowl.
- Mix liquid smoke flavoring, oil and water into powdered mixture till moist; knead dough for 3-5 minutes. Form dough into a 2-3-in. log; tightly wrap with aluminum foil. Put on a baking sheet.
- In preheated oven, bake vegeroni for 1 hour; before slicing, fully cool.

Nutrition Information

- Calories: 144 calories;
- Total Fat: 2.1
- Sodium: 376
- Total Carbohydrate: 13.1
- Cholesterol: < 1
- Protein: 17.1

996.   Vietnamese Sandwich

Serving: 4 | Prep: 10mins | Cook: 5mins | Ready in:

Ingredients

- 4 boneless pork loin chops, cut 1/4 inch thick
- 4 (7 inch) French bread baguettes, split lengthwise
- 4 teaspoons mayonnaise, or to taste
- 1 ounce chile sauce with garlic
- 1/4 cup fresh lime juice
- 1 small red onion, sliced into rings
- 1 medium cucumber, peeled and sliced lengthwise
- 2 tablespoons chopped fresh cilantro
- salt and pepper to taste

Direction

- Set the oven's broiler for preheating. Put the pork chops on a broiling pan and place under the broiler. Cook for about 5 minutes, flipping once, or until it turns brown per side.
- Open the French rolls and spread mayonnaise inside. Arrange a piece of a cooked pork chop into each roll. Scatter the chile sauce straight on the meat. Sprinkle with a bit of lime juice and top it off with slices of onion, cilantro, cucumber, pepper and salt. Finish with one more quick drizzle of lime juice.

Nutrition Information

- Calories: 627 calories;
- Total Carbohydrate: 72.1
- Cholesterol: 124
- Protein: 55.3
- Total Fat: 12.1
- Sodium: 908

997.   Waffle Sandwich

Serving: 1 | Prep: 5mins | Cook: 5mins | Ready in:

Ingredients

- 2 links pork sausage links
- 1 slice Cheddar cheese
- 2 frozen waffles, toasted
- 1/4 Red Delicious apple, sliced very thin
- 1/2 teaspoon cinnamon-sugar

Direction

- On medium heat, heat a small frying pan. Let the sausages cook in the hot frying pan for about 5 minutes, flipping from time to time, until no visible pink color in the middle. An instant-read thermometer inserted in the middle should register 70?°C (160°F).
- On top of one toasted waffle, put the Cheddar cheese, then layout apple slices on top of the cheese. Over the apple slices, sprinkle the cinnamon-sugar. Put the sausage links on top of the apples and finish the sandwich with the leftover waffle. Halve the sandwich.

Nutrition Information

- Calories: 469 calories;
- Total Fat: 26.6
- Sodium: 907
- Total Carbohydrate: 37.3
- Cholesterol: 80
- Protein: 20

998.   Warm Goat Cheese Sandwiches

Serving: 4 | Prep: 20mins | Cook: 5mins | Ready in:

Ingredients

- 1 (5 ounce) goat cheese, softened
- 1/2 cup basil pesto

- 3/4 cup sun-dried tomatoes, softened and chopped
- 2 pita breads, cut in half

Direction

- Preheat the oven to 350°F (175°C).
- Open the halves of pita bread into pockets. Spread one side of the inside of each pita pocket with goat cheese. Spread a pesto layer over the goat cheese. Decorate with sun-dried tomatoes. Place half of the pita on a baking sheet.
- In the preheated oven, bake just until the bread is lightly toasted and the filling is warm for 3 to 5 minutes.

Nutrition Information

- Calories: 393 calories;
- Total Fat: 25.5
- Sodium: 794
- Total Carbohydrate: 25.3
- Cholesterol: 38
- Protein: 17.4

999. Warm Tuna Buns

Serving: 6 | Prep: 15mins | Cook: 15mins | Ready in:

Ingredients

- 3 eggs
- 2 (3 ounce) cans tuna, drained
- 7 tablespoons mayonnaise
- 1/4 cup shredded processed cheese food (such as Velveeta®)
- 2 tablespoons sweet pickle relish
- 2 tablespoons minced onion
- 3 tablespoons chopped pimiento-stuffed olives
- 6 hamburger buns

Direction

- In saucepan, put the eggs and submerge in water. Boil, take off from heat, and rest eggs for 15 minutes in hot water. Take eggs out of hot water, cool in running cold water. Remove eggs shell and chop.
- Preheat the oven to 175 ° C or 350 ° F.
- In mixing bowl, mix chopped eggs with olives, onion, relish, processed cheese, mayonnaise and tuna. Distribute tuna mixture between bun bottoms, then put bun tops back.
- Wrap every sandwich separately with aluminum foil and put on baking sheet.
- In the prepped oven, bake for 10 to 15 minutes till cheese melts and tuna salad has heated completely.

Nutrition Information

- Calories: 345 calories;
- Sodium: 635
- Total Carbohydrate: 25
- Cholesterol: 113
- Protein: 15.7
- Total Fat: 20.2

1000. Wiener Winks

Serving: 8 | Prep: 15mins | Cook: 30mins | Ready in:

Ingredients

- 1 (16 ounce) package beef frankfurters
- 8 slices processed American cheese
- 8 slices bread
- 8 teaspoons butter

Direction

- Set oven to 175° C (350° F) and start preheating.
- Spread a teaspoon of butter on one side of a slice of bread. Turn bread over and put on a slice of cheese. Diagonally put a frankfurter on the cheese. Fold the bread corner to corner

around the frankfurter. Hold them together by inserting a toothpick. Follow the same manners for the rest of frankfurters.

- Put into the preheated oven and bake until golden brown, about 20-30 minutes.

Nutrition Information

- Calories: 393 calories;
- Total Fat: 30.3
- Sodium: 1260
- Total Carbohydrate: 15.4
- Cholesterol: 67
- Protein: 14.5

1001. Zucchini Wrapped In Tortillas

Serving: 4 | Prep: 20mins | Cook: 20mins | Ready in:

Ingredients

- 1 tablespoon vegetable oil
- 1 teaspoon mustard seed (optional)
- 1 teaspoon cumin seeds
- 1 small red onion, thinly sliced
- 1 tablespoon grated fresh ginger
- 4 cups grated zucchini
- 1/2 teaspoon chili powder
- 1/4 teaspoon ground black pepper
- 1/4 teaspoon ground cloves
- 1/4 teaspoon ground cinnamon
- salt to taste
- 4 (10 inch) flour tortillas
- 4 fresh chives
- 1/2 cup sour cream (optional)

Direction

- Heat the oil in a medium size sauté pan or wok on medium-high heat, then add cumin seeds and mustard. Once they start to pop, reduce the heat and add the ginger and onion.

Sauté until the onions turn light pink in color and tender.

- Add the shredded zucchini, then turn up the heat a bit. Mix often for about 5 to 10 minutes, until the zucchini is well cooked and soft. Stir in the salt, cinnamon, clove, pepper and chili powder.
- Warm the tortillas and put on a flat surface. In the center of each tortilla, put 1/4 of the zucchini filling. Roll up each tortilla and use chive to tie it closed. You may serve the wrap with a dollop of sour cream alongside to make a well-rounded wrap.

Nutrition Information

- Calories: 361 calories;
- Total Fat: 10.2
- Sodium: 376
- Total Carbohydrate: 48
- Cholesterol: 13
- Protein: 9.2

Index

A

Ale 7,201

Almond 6,131

Apple 3,4,5,6,7,8,10,11,13,14,16,22,31,81,103,134,202,209,213,224,318,343,344,345,353,410,450,462,472

Apricot 3,4,35,85

Artichoke 3,9,11,14,36,250,274,327,442

Asparagus 3,7,9,11,13,14,17,187,246,346,418,477

Avocado 3,4,5,6,7,9,10,11,13,15,16,23,36,38,74,77,85,87,113,139,204,281,293,318,319,332,348,349,350,355,416,431,438,485,489

B

Bacon 3,4,6,7,8,9,10,11,12,13,16,17,19,24,38,84,93,135,136,155,202,204,225,243,255,281,294,315,318,328,335,344,351,353,373,374,405,410,424

Bagel 3,4,6,8,9,38,65,142,233,272

Baguette 3,11,18,280,356

Banana 4,11,13,62,325,330,414

Basil 3,4,8,9,10,13,18,19,48,80,213,265,280,319,416

Beans 11,15,353,382,497

Beef 3,4,6,9,10,11,12,13,14,15,38,40,42,44,46,67,143,252,268,276,291,308,320,332,342,357,358,359,375,385,386,395,396,397,427,447,471,496

Beer 12,201,360

Berry 3,39

Biscuits 8,229

Boar 8,229,230

Bran 205

Bread 7,11,12,14,31,154,196,206,351,387,410,450,466

Brie 3,7,8,9,11,20,21,22,31,33,61,124,206,209,224,225,235,268,269,353,412

Broccoli 7,8,205,233

Buns 5,12,15,101,262,286,383,500

Burger 3,10,12,13,14,21,306,314,364,368,391,412,420,455,458

Butter 4,5,8,10,13,14,62,89,124,208,210,212,215,221,222,223,232,237,287,289,353,387,413,414,415,418,448,449,450,457,459

C

Cabbage 3,11,12,42,325,368

Cake 12,14,372,461

Camembert 8,210

Caramel 3,9,10,11,18,238,291,343

Carrot 12,372

Cashew 5,6,91,138

Catfish 9,248

Cauliflower 11,12,349,372

Champ 3,40,76

Cheddar 3,5,8,11,16,17,20,29,37,93,168,183,201,202,203,205,206,207,209,211,212,213,215,216,219,220,222,224,225,226,229,230,234,235,236,242,245,272,273,282,295,300,306,318,319,321,324,329,333,335,337,338,344,351,355,369,372,373,374,375,381,386,399,403,406,418,421,423,424,425,427,430,433,435,436,440,457,467,468,475,476,477,478,490,491,494,495,497,499

Cheese 3,4,5,6,7,8,9,10,11,12,13,14,15,16,17,18,23,24,25,26,27,28,29,30,33,34,52,84,88,89,93,140,183,191,201,202,203,204,2

G

H

I

J

K

L

Conclusion

Thank you again for downloading this book!

I hope you enjoyed reading about my book!

If you enjoyed this book, please take the time to share your thoughts and post a review on Amazon. It'd be greatly appreciated!

Write me an honest review about the book – I truly value your opinion and thoughts and I will incorporate them into my next book, which is already underway.

Thank you!

If you have any questions, **feel free to contact at:** _author@persimmonrecipes.com_

Mary Thompson

persimmonrecipes.com

Made in the USA
Las Vegas, NV
01 November 2023